The OXFORD HISTORY of the
BRITISH ARMY

Dr David Chandler (General Editor) is a distinguished military historian with many successful books to his credit and a former head of the Department of War Studies at the Royal Military Academy, Sandhurst. He is President Emeritus of the British Commission for Military History, and a former Vice-President of the Commission Internationale d'Histoire Militaire.

Dr Ian Beckett (Associate Editor), a former Senior Lecturer at Sandhurst, is currently Professor of Modern History at the University of Luton. He is secretary of the Army Records Society.

The OXFORD HISTORY of the
BRITISH ARMY

GENERAL EDITOR
David Chandler

ASSOCIATE EDITOR
Ian Beckett

Oxford   New York

OXFORD UNIVERSITY PRESS

1996

Oxford University Press, Walton Street, Oxford OX2 6DP

Oxford New York
Athens Auckland Bangkok Bogota Bombay
Buenos Aires Calcutta Cape Town Dar es Salaam
Delhi Florence Hong Kong Istanbul
Karachi Kuala Lumpur Madras Madrid
Melbourne Mexico City Nairobi Paris
Singapore Taipei Tokyo Toronto
and associated companies in
Berlin Ibadan

Oxford is a trade mark of Oxford University Press

The text of this edition first published 1994 in The Oxford Illustrated History of the British Army
This edition first issued as an Oxford University Press paperback 1996

It should be noted that nothing in this volume necessarily reflects the view of the
Ministry of Defence (Army) or of the RMA Sandhurst

British Library Cataloguing in Publication Data
Data available

Library of Congress Cataloging in Publication Data
The Oxford history of the British Army / general editor, David
    Chandler; associate editor, Ian Beckett.
    Includes bibliographical references and index.
    1. Great Britain. Army—History.   2. Great Britain—History, Military.
I. Chandler, David G.   II. Beckett, I. F. W. (Ian Frederick William)
DA50.093   1996   355'.00941—dc20   96-13051
    ISBN 0-19-285333-3

10 9 8 7 6 5 4 3 2 1

Typeset by Best-set Typesetter Ltd., Hong Kong
Printed in Great Britain by
Mackays of Chatham,
Chatham, Kent

Preface

This book is an examination of the development of the British Army as an institution. Thus, while discussing the campaigns in which it has been involved, this account is far more wide-ranging than the traditional war-by war approach of the army's history in the manner of Sir John Fortescue's celebrated, but now outdated, *History of the British Army* published in thirteen volumes between 1899 and 1930. Inevitably, the space is more limited in order to fit the confines of a single volume. Yet the range is altogether wider, as befits the enormous amount of modern research on the army that has been undertaken since the last such scholarly single-volume treatment of the army's history appeared almost twenty-five years ago.

Each chapter can be read as a self-contained piece. The contributors have been encouraged to retain their individual styles of writing. Special subjects throughout are treated in a total of forty-two box features, the subjects for which were agreed between the editors and the individual contributors. Some deal with weaponry, others with organizations, key individuals, or specific battles or sieges.

The Chronology at the end of the book provides a clear and concise reference to the significant dates in the army's history. The Bibliography has been organized by chapter to give guidance to readers wishing to explore a period or subject in more detail.

D.G.C.
I.F.W.B.

Contents

List of Maps

List of Contributors

The contributors are all distinguished authorities in their respective fields. They are (in alphabetical order):

Dr Ian Beckett (Associate Editor) is Professor of Modern History, University of Luton, secretary of the Army Records Society, and editor of the Manchester University Press 'War, Armed Forces, and Society' series. His books include *Riflemen Form: A Study of the Rifle Volunteer Movement* (1982) and *The Amateur Military Tradition* (1991). In 1992-3 he held a visiting chair in the Department of Strategy, US Naval War College.

Brian Bond is Professor of Military History at King's College London, and President of the British Commission for Military History. His books include *British Military Policy between the Two World Wars* (1980) and *Liddell Hart: A Study of his Military Thought* (1977), and as editor, *The First World War and British Military History* (1980). In 1992–3 he was Visiting Fellow at Brasenose College, Oxford.

Dr Peter Burroughs was Professor of History, Dalhousie University, Canada, and is now joint editor of the *Journal of Imperial and Commonwealth History*. He has written books on Anglo-Australian and Anglo-Canadian relations, and recently completed a biography of the third Earl Grey. He has published articles on various aspects of the early Victorian army.

Dr David Chandler (General Editor) was Head of the Department of War Studies at the Royal Military Academy Sandhurst from 1980 to 1994. He is President Emeritus of the British Commission for Military History and an International Vice-President of the Commission Internationale d'Histoire Militaire. His twenty-four books include *The Campaigns of Napoleon* (1966; 1994), *Marlborough as Military Commander* (1973; 1994), and *The Art of War in the Age of Marlborough* (1975; 1994).

Dr John Childs is Professor of Military History at the University of Leeds. He has published a trilogy on the social and political history of the British army, 1660–1702, and his latest book is *The Nine Years' War and the British Army: The Operations in the Low Countries* (1991). He is currently writing a biography of the Duke of Marlborough.

Dr Alex Danchev is Professor of International Relations at the University of Keele. A former officer in the Royal Army Education Corps, he has held fellowships in the Department of War Studies, King's College London, the Woodrow

Wilson Center in Washington, DC, and St Antony's College, Oxford. He has written or edited two studies of Anglo-American relations during the Second World War, collected essays on the Falklands conflict, and a biography of Oliver Franks.

Lieutenant-Colonel Carlo D'Este holds an honorary doctorate from Norwich University, USA. From 1958 to 1978 he served in the US army. His books include *Decision in Normany* (1983), *Bitter Victory: The Battle for Sicily, 1943* (1988), *World War Two in the Mediterranean* (1990), and *Fatal Decision: Anzio and the Battle for Rome* (1991). He is completing *A Genius for War: The Life of General George S. Patton, Jr.*

General Sir Anthony Farrar-Hockley joined the British army under age in 1939 and served until 1982. His many post-war campaigns included Korea, Aden, and Borneo, and his last post was as Commander in Chief, Allied Forces Northern Europe. He received an M.Phil. from Oxford in 1970, and holds many decorations. His books include *Edge of the Sword* (1954), *Death of an Army* (1968), and *The British Part in the Korean War*, 2 vols. (1991 and 1993).

Dr David Gates is the Ministry of Defence Lecturer in Defence Studies at Aberdeen University. He was previously a research fellow at the German Military Archives and Albert Ludwigs University, Freiburg. His books include *The Spanish Ulcer: A History of the Peninsular War* (1986), *The British Light Infantry Arm, c. 1790–1815* (1987), and *Non-Offensive Defence: An Alternative Strategy for Nato* (1991).

Dr Alan J. Guy is Assistant Director and Head of Collections at the National Army Museum, Chelsea. His books include *Oeconomy and Discipline: Officership and Administration in the British Standing Army, 1714–1763* (1985), an edition of the Bagshawe Papers for the Army Records Society, *Colonel Samuel Bagshawe and the Army of George II* (1990), and as editor, *The Road to Waterloo* (1990).

Dr Tony Hayter is a former Senior Lecturer at Buckingham University. His publications include *The Army and the Crowd in Mid-Georgian England* (1978), the co-edited *The Europa Biographical Dictionary of British Women* (1985), and *An Eighteenth Century Secretary at War: The Papers of William Viscount Barrington* (1988). He has published a state-of-the-art review of eighteenth-century military literature in the *Journal of the Society for Army Historical Research*, 63/253 (1985).

Dr Tony Heathcote is Curator of the Royal Military Academy Sandhurst, Collection. He received his doctorate for a thesis on British policy in Baluchistan, and from 1963 to 1970 was a member of staff at the National Army Museum in charge of the Indian Army exhibition areas. His publications include *The Indian Army, 1822–1922* (1973) and *The Afghan Wars, 1839–1919* (1980).

Dr Michael Prestwich is Professor of History at the University of Durham and Pro-Vice-Chancellor. His work has led to a major reconsideration of the forms and impact of warfare in his chosen period. His publications include *War, Politics and Finance under Edward I* (1972), *The Three Edwards* (1980), and *Edward I* (1988).

Dr Ian Roy was Senior Lecturer in History at King's College London, where he taught for over thirty years. He published articles and edited texts on the English Civil War, the French Wars of Religion, the profession of arms, and English seventeenth-century urban history. Literary Director of the Royal Historical Society, he co-edited the Society's standard work of reference, the *Handbook of British Chronology* (1986).

Peter Simkins was for a period from early 1962 archivist and research assistant to the late Captain Sir Basil Liddell Hart. In September 1963 he joined the staff of the Imperial War Museum, and has held the post of Historian there since 1976. He is on the Board of War Studies of the University of London. His book *Kitchener's Army* (1988) was awarded the Templer Medal by the Society for Army Historical Research.

Dr Edward Spiers is a Professor of Strategic Studies in the School of History at Leeds University, and also serves on numerous committees including the Army Examining Board. His books include *Haldane: An Army Reformer* (1980), *Radical General: Sir George de Lacy Evans* (1983), *The Army and Society, 1815–1914* (1986), *Chemical Warfare* (1986), *Chemical Weaponry: A Continuing Challenge* (1989), and *The Late Victorian Army, 1868–1902* (1992).

Dr Hew Strachan is Professor of Modern History at Glasgow University and a Fellow of Corpus Christi College, Cambridge. His books include *European Armies and the Conduct of War* (1983), *Wellington's Legacy: The Reform of the British Army, 1815–1854* (1985), and *From Waterloo to Balaclava: Tactics, Technology, and the British Army, 1815–1854* (1985), which was awarded the Templer Medal. He is currently working on a history of the First World War.

Major-General John Strawson served in the 4th Hussars (Winston Churchill's first regiment) in the Middle East and Italy during the Second World War. He later took part in several internal security campaigns, including Malaya and Borneo, where he commanded his regiment, by then the Queen's Royal Irish Hussars. He has written a number of books on military history, including *Gentlemen in Khaki* (1989).

Dr Tim Travers is Professor and former Chairman of the Department of History, University of Calgary, Canada. He has written widely on British military history, and has published *The Killing Ground: The British Army, the Western Front and the Emergence of Modern Warfare, 1900–1918* (1987) and *How the War was Won: Command and Technology in the British Army on the Western Front, 1917–1918* (1992).

Michael Yardley has twice served in the British army, and since resigning his commission in a cavalry regiment in 1981 has devoted himself to journalism, broadcasting, and writing on mainly defence issues. His books include *Poland: A Tragedy* (1981), *Backing into the Limelight: A Biography of T. E. Lawrence* (1984), *Sandhurst: A Documentary* (1986), and (with Dennis Sewell) *A New Model Army* (1987).

Introduction

It is generally accepted that the regular standing army in Britain was officially created—in the sense of being fully accommodated within parliamentary control—in 1689, although it is, strictly speaking, only correct to
refer to the British army from the Act of Union with Scotland in 1707. It
is appropriate, therefore, that this illustrated history should mark approximately 300 years of the army's existence at a time when its immediate
future is uncertain at least in terms of its present size and functions.

That such a situation is not unfamiliar will be readily apparent to those
who read this volume for, in fact, there are remarkable continuities not
only over the past 300 years of British military history but also in terms of
those armies and military forces of the Crown and country whose existence long pre-dated the actual sanction of a standing army. Indeed, it
might be said that the underlying theme of this volume is continuity.

One such enduring theme of continuity is perhaps the anti-militarist
tradition of the British reflected as much in complaints of the Elizabethan
Council about popular pastimes such as bowls preventing regular archery
practice as in the relative lack of interest in defence issues in the late twentieth century. There was always a fear of the threat which might be posed
to civil liberties by a standing military force, seen equally in the political
controversies of the late seventeenth century and the near-hysterical reaction in some quarters in 1971 to the publication of Brigadier (later General
Sir) Frank Kitson's *Low Intensity Operations* coinciding with the heightened visibility of troops through deployment on the streets of Ulster. It
must be said, of course, that the long-standing role in aid of the civil power
also contributed to such fears. The Army substituted for a constabulary
until the mid-nineteenth century and was still likely to be employed on
occasions even thereafter, as at Featherstone in 1893 or in South Wales in
1911. Indeed, the last civilian killed by a soldier on the mainland of Britain
in support of the civil power died as recently as 1919 (apart from those terrorists killed in the siege of the Iranian Embassy in 1980). It may even be
said that the tradition is continued through the army's role in industrial
disputes since 1945.

There has also always been friction between soldiers and civilians despite the army's relative small size and frequent overseas postings. It has

tended to occur over such issues as billeting, which continued long after the Billeting Act of 1679, and despite the increasing construction of barrack accommodation in the late eighteenth century. However, the unrepresentative nature of the army's social composition under a system of mostly voluntary enlistment also distanced the army from society. Conscription was only introduced in 1916 and lasted, with the exception of its suspension during the inter-war period, only until 1963 with the result that there was never any well-developed sense of a commitment to national military service.

Soldiers were inevitably recruited from the dregs of society, Wellington's remark about his army being the 'scum of the earth' appearing little different from Field Marshal Lord Nicholson's observation in 1906 that the army depended upon the 'compulsion of destitution'. The unattractive features of service life which persisted until the very end of the nineteenth century were not conducive to recruiting the more respectable elements of society. Curiously, even the introduction of conscription in two World Wars did not materially make the army more representative as a whole due to the selective way in which it was applied, while the army's officers were just as broadly unrepresentative of society as a whole under the system of purchase that pertained prior to 1871 as they remained through the influence of the public schools until late into the twentieth century.

In a sense, of course, the narrow recruitment pattern of the army, which has persisted over time irrespective of the existence of what might be termed ethnic regiments, marks another continuity in the relationship between army and society in Britain, namely the interdependence which exists side by side with popular indifference to the military. The presence of soldiers inevitably meant trade for local businesses but the army also provided spectacle and often considerable inspiration for the purveyors of popular culture, be it in the form of literature, art, or song; in certain circumstances, such as major defeats, for instance Isandhlwana in 1879 or Dunkirk in 1940, or major invasion scares, or popular wars including the Great War or the Falklands campaign of 1982, soldiers suddenly found themselves extremely popular, if only temporarily.

Compared with other armies, the British army has been largely apolitical—no officer has been dismissed for his political views since 1764—but the army has played a political role. There was the initial tension over control of a standing army which Parliament wrested from the Crown in 1689 although the Crown continued to be active in seeking to exert influence over certain aspects of army administration until at least the end of the nineteenth century. That administration itself has frequently illustrated the conflict of soldiers and civilians during the development of the bureaucratic system, from a profusion of administrative agencies in the seventeenth and eighteenth centuries, to the emergence of a duality of Secretary of State for War and Commander-in-Chief in 1855, to the centralization of military advice through twentieth-century creations such as the Chiefs of Staff Committee and the Ministry of Defence.

Financial control and the pressure for economies has been another continuing feature of the army's existence and little in essence separates the conclusion of the Stephen Commission in 1887, that the system was one of 'extravagance controlled by stinginess'; from the Ten Year Rule of 1919 or the implications of *Options for Change* in the 1990s. Parliamentary control of the army's discipline, from the Mutiny Act of 1689, through the Army (Annual) Act of 1881, to the present Army Acts, is a further constant. Yet there have still been politically charged episodes between soldiers and politicians in peacetime such as the Curragh incident of March 1914 and the Chanak crisis of 1922.

There have been surprisingly few authoritative official statements as to what purposes the army exists to fulfil. There was the phrasing of the preamble of the Mutiny Act of 1689 concerning the maintenance of the balance of power in Europe but that was abandoned in 1868. Thereafter, until the modern practice of the annual defence policy statement became established after the Second World War, there was really only the Stanhope Memorandum of 1888 and the Inskip/Hore-Belisha policy of 1937. Clearly, however, the army always had a role to play in aid of the civil power and in defence of a Britain faced with possible invasion by the Spanish in the sixteenth century, the Dutch in the seventeenth, the French in the eighteenth and nineteenth, or the Germans in the twentieth. In passing, of course, it can be noted that, since the principal defence against invasion was always the Royal Navy, this contributed to the army being perceived as a small professional long-service body serving mostly overseas, out of sight and out of mind. In many respects, however, the real choice of priority has lain between the defence of a global empire and the question of involvement in Europe. The notion of the army being a projectile fired by the Royal Navy has been an attractive one over the centuries but the pull of European conflict has always effectively proved too great to avoid and a commitment to European defence has been central to the army's role since the Paris agreements of 1954.

In being compelled by historical circumstance to meet the challenge of sustaining such widely contrasting roles with often limited resources, the army's performance has sometimes also reflected the limitations imposed by tradition. In the past there have often been difficulties arising from prevailing attitudes towards professional education within the army while the effects of regimental tradition have worked both for and against it on the battlefield. None the less, the army has been remarkably successful and, over the course of its official existence, Britain has lost only one major war, namely that for American Independence between 1775 and 1783. Indeed, it might be argued that Britain has largely possessed a better army than she has sometimes deserved.

Readers will become aware of such recurring themes in this volume, which represents the interpretations of its distinguished contributors in the light of the most recent research. There are, inevitably, differences of emphasis and of perspective since each contributor has been free to develop his ideas within the overall parameters set by the editors. Indeed, there are reflected in the volume both the traditional concerns of the military historian with the study of campaigns, battles, and leaders and also the attempt to place this study within the wider context of the social, economic, and political environment in which armies exist and fight. It is offered to the reader in the hope that it recounts the story of the British army in a fresh way that will both entertain and educate.

D.G.C.
I.F.W.B.

1 THE ENGLISH MEDIEVAL ARMY TO 1485

MICHAEL PRESTWICH

A contemporary poet described the great host which Edward I led north from Carlisle in 1300. The army was divided into four main cavalry divisions, one composed almost exclusively of the king's own household troops. The sight was splendid:

'There were many rich caparisons embroidered on silks and satins; many a beautiful pennon fixed to a lance, many a banner displayed. The neighing of horses was heard from afar; the mountains and valleys were covered with packhorses and waggons with provisions, tents and pavilions.'

In this romantic picture, the foot soldiers scarcely obtained a mention, nor did the poet think to explain how it was that the king was able to recruit an army which totalled over 10,000 men.

The explanation would not have been easy, for on this occasion most of the normal medieval methods of recruitment were employed. The army was commanded by the king himself, and some of the cavalry were paid regular members of the royal household. Others were present because landowners had been requested to provide military service under the terms by which they held their land. Yet others served voluntarily at their own expense. Many knights and men-at-arms had entered into contracts to serve a magnate as part of his retinue. There were even a few foreign mercenaries. The infantry were mostly there unwillingly, recruited by royal commissioners. They were paid for their service, but their columns were diminished daily by desertion.

Edward I led this army of 1300 in person. Throughout the medieval period, if the king or a close royal relative took the field, he would naturally be in authority. This might cause problems. King Stephen lacked the voice to address his troops before the battle of Lincoln in 1141, while in 1314 at Bannockburn Edward II demonstrated complete military incompetence. More often kings proved to be highly competent as generals and, in the cases of Richard I, Edward III, and Henry V, they were much more than that. In the absence of a member of the royal family, command normally went to a great noble, for a man who lacked social position might not find it easy to win the respect of his men. The earls who held the offices of Marshal and Constable had a hereditary right to a high place in the military command structure. Knights of the royal household usually had extensive experience, and such men were often appointed to the command, if not of whole armies, of at least substantial forces. Odo Borleng, a knight of Henry I's household, was responsible for the victory of Bourgthéroulde in 1124 over Norman rebels. In the Hundred Years War the talents for command of experienced soldiers such as Robert Knollys or John Chandos were not ignored by the Crown.

The cavalry formed the élite of the army. The highest rank was that of banneret. Its holders were entitled to a square banner, and would command a substantial troop. Then there were the knights, men who had achieved this rank through birth or merit. Knighthood could be bestowed on the battlefield, but more commonly there was an elaborate initiation ritual with a significant religious element. Not all the cavalry were knights; in the course of the medieval period the status or rank of knighthood became increasingly exclusive. Below the knights were sergeants and squires, often termed simply men-at-arms. All the cavalry would have been similarly equipped with arms and armour to fight in the same way, with lance and sword. The horses were vital; specially bred stallions trained for war fetched a high price. Nor was one horse per man sufficient. Mid-thirteenth-century evidence suggests that there were on average two horses for every man, but by the fourteenth century a knight was expected to have four horses, and a squire three.

In the field, the cavalry were normally organized into troops of perhaps ten or fifteen men, each commanded by a banneret. Surprisingly little is known about the techniques of mounted warfare, though great individual skill was required to master the use of lance, sword, and shield. At Hastings in 1066, the Norman cavalry succeeded in executing the difficult manœuvre of a feigned retreat, while the force of their charge is vividly illustrated in the Bayeux Tapestry. In other battles of the Norman period, and in the later triumphs of the Hundred Years War, the cavalrymen often dismounted to fight, and used their horses only in the final rout. When a mounted attack took place, it must be doubted whether the cavalry were often capable of the disciplined co-ordination required for a knee-to-knee charge. When Prince Edward and his horsemen routed the Londoners in the baronial army at Lewes in 1264, it proved impossible to hold the force together, and to wheel them back into the fight. Battles were, however, rare in medieval warfare. Cavalry had immense value in swift raids into enemy territory, when villages were burned and crops destroyed. In the relatively static conditions of siege warfare, however, the mounted man had no advantage. In the siege of Caerlaverock in 1300, assaults by the cavalry forces served to display bravery, but achieved no more than buckled shields.

The core of the cavalry in English medieval armies was provided by the royal household. It is often pointed out that there was no standing army in this period, but the household came close to filling this role. In pre-Conquest times, although they did not fight on horseback, the king's *gesiths*, then his thegns, and finally his housecarls, provided much more than a bodyguard: they were the king's personal élite followers. For the Norman kings, the household, or *familia*, was essential in their military operations. Household knights organized the army that won the battle of Tinchebray for Henry I in 1106, and at Brémule in 1119 they formed one of the three divisions of the army. The chronicler Orderic Vitalis credited the household of Henry I with a capability of providing detachments of knights numbering 200 or 300, high figures when set against his total of 500 knights fighting for Henry at Brémule. According to later evidence, these knights received an annual fee of at least £5, and wages of up to 1s. a day while on duty. Their background was diverse. Some were members of great families, others from families which aspired to become great through household service. Some were foreigners, some important feudal tenants of the king. Some came from families with a tradition of loyal service, others from families of defeated rebels, anxious to regain favour.

Similar patterns can be traced in the households of later medieval monarchs. The size of the king's military household varied: reliable figures are available only from the thirteenth century onwards, and range from about thirty knights in time of peace to over a hundred in wartime. In addition there were the squires, more numerous than the knights. Numbers were increased further by the followers that the household men would bring with them on campaign. Edward I sailed for Flanders in 1297 with some 700 cavalry, virtually all household members. In his reign household knights and squires normally received robes and fees twice a year, and wages when on active service. In the fourteenth century Edward III maintained a large military household: there were some fifty bannerets and knights retained in his household in 1359–60. Just as in the Norman period William fitz Osbern, William de Warenne, Robert de Beaumont, and Ranulf le Meschin, all household knights, were granted earldoms, so Edward III made the four leading members of his household earls in 1337, with the titles of Northampton, Suffolk, Salisbury, and Huntingdon.

The household continued to provide the core of English armies in the fifteenth century. Henry IV's household was larger than Edward III's had been in the 1360s. Under Henry V the household played a prominent part in the campaigns in France, providing cavalry forces, some archers, and many of the technical experts such as gunners. The military element was less evident in the household of the unwarlike Henry VI, but under Edward IV it was once again at the centre of military affairs.

The Crown needed much larger armies than the royal household alone could provide. A complex system of military obligation existed in the Anglo-Saxon period, whereby every five hides of land owed one soldier for a sixty-day period. One estimate is that this could have produced an army of 14,000. These were not mounted knights, however, and after the Norman Conquest the Crown made use of a different form of obligation, which flowed from the feudal relationship between lord and tenant. The act of performing homage for land entailed acceptance of an obligation to perform knight service. Historians have long debated the origins of this system, for although there survives a superb record of it as it existed in 1166, there is remarkably little evidence as to how and when it was introduced. Was it brought in at one moment, or was there a steady evolution? It seems most likely that those who received land from William the Conqueror individually agreed the level of military assistance they would provide. In most cases quotas of service were set in decimal units of five and ten. This reflected the reality of organization in the field, though the probable limit of forty days did not mirror campaigning practice. A tenant-in-chief owing service to the Crown could grant out some of his land to knights, who would perform his service for him when required. Alternatively, he could rely on knights from his own household, or hire men. In theory, roughly 5,000 knights were owed under this system, a very substantial force if it was ever successfully mobilized in full. In practice, it is likely, even in the early days of the system, that the Crown would have demanded money, known as scutage, in lieu of service from some tenants-in-chief. By Henry II's reign, there were difficulties in obtaining the full level of service; in 1157 the king demanded one-third of the total. Two years later he preferred to take scutage from the bulk of his tenants, and hire soldiers with the money, rather than demand service in person. Levels of service were radically reduced in the early thirteenth century. For the Irish expedition of 1210 Geoffrey fitz Peter provided ten knights, rather than the ninety-eight and one-third he actually owed. In the Poitou expedition of 1214 the Earl of Devon served with twenty knights, not the eighty-nine of his formal obligation. By the time of Henry III's Welsh expedition of 1245, the new lowered quotas were firmly established. Even with the reductions, the forces yielded by a request for feudal service were far from insignificant. The first full record of a muster is that for the Welsh campaign of 1277, when Edward I obtained the service of 228 knights and 294 sergeants (two of the latter counting as equivalent to one knight). Despite such oddities as the man who in 1282 claimed that his tenure obliged him to appear with a side of bacon, and to depart once it was eaten, feudal service continued to be requested fairly regularly under Edward and his son. Numbers held up: in 1322 there were about 500 men performing service in Edward II's strikingly unsuccessful invasion of Scotland. These summonses were regarded seriously by the Crown: in 1316 those who did not comply were threatened with confiscation of their lands. Yet the system was in its final days; the last true feudal summons took place in 1327. A revival of feudal service in 1385 was no more than a means of raising money through fines and scutage.

The survival of feudal service for so long is surprising. The Crown was certainly not anxious to perpetuate an increasingly obsolete system. Feudal summonses were not issued for all Edward I's armies: he tried to recruit a fully paid army for Wales in 1282, and non-feudal summonses were used for Flanders in 1297 and for Scotland in 1298 and 1301. Pressure for the continued issue of feudal summonses probably came from the magnates, as they could gain financially by imposing scutages on their tenants when the king summoned the feudal host. They may also have feared the precedents that might be set by newer methods of recruitment: there was certainly widespread alarm in 1297 when Edward I used what was seen as a novel form of writ to try to recruit men for his Flanders campaign.

Men could be persuaded to fight by appealing to the fealty and affection they owed to the king, rather than by stressing the obligation resulting from feudal homage. Under Edward I a considerable proportion, up to three-quarters, of the cavalry forces served at their own expense in response to such pleas. Some magnates were reluctant to accept the degree of subordination that was a consequence of taking royal pay. The pride of a great earl might not permit him to take the king's wages, but he was ready to serve voluntarily with many more troops than he was formally obliged to provide. The earls' resistance to accepting pay began to fade under Edward II, when the majority of the earls, though not those of Cornwall, Gloucester, or Lancaster, accepted royal wages. Under Edward III, there were no remaining compunctions. Magnates had never had the same reluctance to take pay when fighting in France as in Britain, and in these circumstances pay was universally accepted, and only very rarely not offered. In 1370 pay was promised to Robert Knollys and his men on a *chevauchée*, or mounted raid, for the first thirteen weeks only; after that plunder was to make the force self-financing.

There were obvious dangers in relying too heavily on voluntary service by the magnates. In the thirteenth and fourteenth centuries the Crown tried to develop reliable forms of military obligation which would yield more substantial numbers of troops than the feudal quotas of the day. There was an obligation on all free men to bear arms in defence of their country, which can be traced back to Anglo-Saxon times. In 1181 Henry II introduced the Assize of Arms, which defined the military equipment men of different degrees of wealth should possess. A knight, or man of equivalent wealth, should have a coat of mail, helmet, shield, and lance. There was a tacit assumption that those who possessed military equipment would be expected to use it. In 1213 King John, threatened by foreign invasion, summoned all who were capable of bearing arms to muster at Dover for the defence of the land. This was not a summons of the feudal host, but demonstrated that it was possible to recruit forces by means of an appeal to a general obligation.

In Henry III's reign the practice of compelling, or distraining, men of appropriate wealth to become knights was adopted. The usual qualification was set at possession of land worth £20 a year. In 1242 the Assize of Arms was revised, with the highest level of equipment being a coat of mail, iron helmet, sword, dagger, and horse, and the wealth qualification for this was put at £15 worth of land. The military obligation was still to defend the land; it would not apply to offensive expeditions. This was not a substitute for feudal military service. The situation changed under Edward I. In 1282 he summoned all who possessed £20 worth of land, whether they were knights or not, to meetings at York and Northampton, where they were persuaded to grant subsidies as an alternative to service in the field. There was a clear implication that the king considered that they had an obligation to fight in his Welsh war. In 1295 inquiries were ordered into the number of men who held at least £40 worth of land: such men were to be ready to set out on campaign at royal wages, properly equipped, at three weeks notice. The scheme was enforced in 1296. In the next year, the wealth qualification was halved to £20, new lists were ordered to be drawn up, and the king summoned all such men to a muster at London. This was in preparation for a campaign in Flanders, and there was widespread opposition to the king's move. Of 713 men named in the surviving returns made by the sheriffs, only seventy-six can be shown to have gone on the expedition when it eventually sailed in August.

This failure did not deter the government. A similar method of recruitment was attempted again in 1316, when service was demanded from all men holding £50 worth of land. No mention was made of pay, and the measure was justified in terms of the common obligation to defend the realm, which was under threat from the Scots. Once again, the measure aroused hostility. It was one of the reasons for the Earl of Lancaster's effective resignation from government. The years after the royalist triumph over Lancaster at Boroughbridge in 1322 saw determined attempts to extend military obligation. The government was anxious to establish the principle that all knights and men-at-arms were obliged to serve when required. In 1324 lists were drawn up by the sheriffs, and commissioners were employed to array knights, squires, and men-at-arms for service in Gascony. The campaign never took place, and with the collapse of the regime in 1326 the experiments in extending military obligation were temporarily abandoned.

In the mid-1330s Edward III revived these methods, with orders for all men-at-arms to serve at his wages in Scotland, under threat of forfeiture of their lands. Land was assessed to provide given numbers of men: a man with £40 worth of land was obliged to provide two men-at-arms. This was developed further in the 1340s, with a complex scheme of military service in proportion to wealth setting out a scale from £5 to £1,000 worth of land. The measure was extremely unpopular and, had 1346 not seen such astounding successes in war as the battles of Crécy and Neville's Cross, Edward III would undoubtedly have faced a major political crisis at home. In 1352 the king conceded a statute, which stated that no one was under obligation to provide men-at-arms, hobelars, or archers save when a specific grant was made in parliament. The Crown had failed to transform the nature of military obligation.

The attempt to develop the general obligation to bear arms in defence of the country into a more specific form of military obligation which

The Longbow

The most effective weapons are not always the most sophisticated ones. In the hands of skilled men, the longbow proved to be astonishingly devastating. In the fourteenth century, English forces equipped with the longbow demonstrated their mastery of the battlefield first in Scotland and then in France. The more complex crossbow proved no match for the longbow: heavily armed cavalry forces faltered and were routed by the hail of arrows with their sharp barbs and goosefeather flights.

The origins of the longbow are obscure. One popular theory is that while the normal bow, which could only be drawn back to the chest, was well known in England, the longbow, which was drawn to the ear, was a Welsh weapon, whose full potential was first realized by Edward I. The evidence for this, however, is flimsy. Long bows, up to 6 feet in length, were almost certainly known to the Anglo-Saxon invaders of England. While it is true that the infantry in Edward I's initial campaign in Wales were mostly spearmen, and the footsoldiers of his later Scottish campaigns largely archers, there is no evidence that the Crown took any active steps to supply, or promote, the use of any particular type of bow. Nor is there any evidence to suggest that contemporaries made a significant distinction between longbows and short bows. Rather, the distinction was between longbows and crossbows. It is likely that bows did become longer between the eleventh and thirteenth centuries, but there was no sudden revolution marked by the discovery of the longbow. Contemporary illustrations suggest one change in the first half of the fourteenth century. The bow of 1300 was characterized by projecting lumps on the outer face, perhaps carved, perhaps natural. Fifty years later bows all appear to have been smooth, almost certainly with a D-shaped cross-section. Whether this change of style meant greater efficiency is a matter for guesswork.

The longbow was a massive weapon. A legal record of 1298 described a bow of yew approaching 6 feet in length, and 6 inches in circumference, with a hemp bowstring. Yew, sometimes imported from Spain, was the best wood, providing the most elasticity and power, but bows of elm are also mentioned. The wood had to be seasoned for a long time, and the staves then shaped into a D section, tapering towards the tips, which had 'nocks' cut into them to take the string. The effective range of the longbow, shooting a steel-headed arrow, was probably between 150 and 200 yards. An experienced archer could fire some ten flights a minute, far faster than was possible with a crossbow. The sound and sight of incoming flights were terrifying and bewildering both to horses and men.

Archery was very significant in the warfare of the Norman period. The death of King Harold, an arrow in his eye, demonstrates the role of the archers at Hastings in 1066. At Bourgthéroulde in 1124 archers devastated rebel forces, bringing down the horses in the same way that English longbowmen were to do during the Hundred Years War. Later in the twelfth century, however, it was not the longbow but the crossbow which was regarded as a particularly deadly weapon. Its use was prohibited in vain by the papacy, and there was an irony in the fact that Richard I, who made much use of crossbows in his campaigns, himself died from the wound caused by a crossbow bolt. There is surprisingly little evidence for the use of longbows in war until the late thirteenth century: accounts of the battles of Lewes (1264) and Evesham (1265) place no emphasis on archery. However, the late twelfth-century writer Gerald of Wales had emphasized the skill of the south Welsh in archery, and a century after he wrote recruitment of archers from south Wales took place on a very substantial scale under Edward I. Archers (not crossbowmen as one chronicler has it) proved their worth in the closing stages of Edward's Welsh wars, at Maes Moydog in 1295. At Falkirk in 1298 they ran out of ammunition, but nevertheless played a vital role in the English victory. It was, however, not until the 1330s that their full value began to be recognized, with the victories of Dupplin Moor (1332) and Halidon Hill (1333). The English began to mount their archers, so that they could keep pace with the cavalry on rapid marches and raids. The scene was set for the triumphs of the longbow in the French wars, at Crécy (1346), Poitiers (1356), and Agincourt (1415). By the mid-fourteenth century the Crown was taking trouble to ensure that armies were properly equipped with weapons, and orders were issued for the collection of large quantities of bows and arrows. In 1359 some 3,300 bows and 7,000 sheaves of arrows were ordered from various English counties.

There has been much argument about the way in which the archers were disposed on the battlefield. An ambiguous phrase in Froissart, that they were organized *en herse*, can bear various interpretations. It probably means in a harrow formation; but harrows varied in shape, some being triangular, others rectangular. The archers were normally placed on the flanks, from where they could devastate an advancing enemy, and were probably formed up in wedge formation. At Agincourt they employed stakes, hammered into the ground, to provide protection should enemy cavalry reach their position.

To be effective, archers must have been trained. Yet there is remarkably little evidence for this. In 1363 Edward III complained that his subjects were playing football and other vain games instead of learning the art of archery. All were to practise with bows and arrows, or crossbows, on all feast days and holidays. A celebrated illustration from the Luttrell Psalter shows archery practice taking place, but it must be suspected that most men learned their skill either as poachers, or when actually on campaign.

Archery continued to be important in warfare to the end of the medieval period and beyond. An archery exchange began the battle of Bosworth in 1485, and it was not until the second half of the sixteenth century that the longbow's dominance of the battlefield had clearly come to an end.

---

could be used to recruit men for overseas expeditions was not in the end successful, and had proved politically dangerous. In place of compulsion and unpaid voluntary service, the most effective technique was to offer men pay, and above all to enter into contracts for the provision of troops.

Paid troops were important in English armies as early as the eleventh and twelfth centuries. The employment of mercenaries, hardened professionals mostly drawn from the Low Countries, was a notable feature of the period. Such men formed a high proportion of the paid element in English armies. In 1101 Henry I contracted with the Count of Flanders for the supply of 1,000 knights in return for an annual subsidy. The skill of mercenaries is well attested in the chronicles, and in some circumstances, notably those of civil war, they might prove more loyal than English troops, provided they received their rewards. In the great rebellion of 1173–4, Henry II relied extensively on Brabançon mercenaries, to considerable effect. King John depended greatly upon his Flemish hired troops, and the loss at sea of troops provided by Hugh de Boves was regarded by him as a major set back. These men were, however, extremely unpopular. They were condemned by the pope in the third Lateran council of 1179, and their expulsion from the realm was demanded in Magna Carta in 1215. Little use was made of mercenaries in England in the rest of the thirteenth century. Edward I employed a few foreign knights in his household, and although he made effective use of a troop of Gascons in his second Welsh campaign, that of 1282–3, they can hardly be regarded as true mercenaries, for he was Duke of Gascony, and they were his subjects. Under Edward III some notable foreigners served in English armies, men such as Eustace d'Aubrichecourt and Walter Mauny. The Hundred Years War also saw England begin to be a provider of mercenaries as well as an employer of them. Men such as Sir John Hawkwood, Sir Robert Knollys, and Sir

Hugh Calveley made names for themselves as soldiers of fortune in France, Spain, and Italy.

It was not only foreigners who might be paid for their service. The troops of the royal household were usually paid, as were those temporarily hired to bolster the household's numbers. In John's reign cash advances were even made to those performing feudal service, though these could be reclaimed later by the exchequer. An important development in the late thirteenth century was the use of contracts, in which magnates agreed to provide specified numbers of troops for campaigns. Edward I used this system when sending forces to fight in Gascony, and for winter service in Scotland. When a great royal army was recruited for a summer campaign, there was little need for contracts, as the household administrative staff were present to work out numbers and pay wages on a regular basis. When this was not the case, if the king was not present on a particular campaign, it made sense to enter into a contractual arrangement. The first army re-cruited entirely by means of contract was that sent to Scotland in 1337, and there was a scheme in 1341, which was not put into effect, to send a con tract army to France. Contract became the standard method of recruit-ment. In 1346 Thomas Dagworth agreed to go to Brittany with a force of 300 men-at-arms and 600 mounted archers in return for 2,500 marks. Wages were at the usual rates, and Dagworth was entitled to all the profits due to the king in Brittany. There is a multitude of examples from later in the Hundred Years War. In 1372, for instance, the Earl of Salisbury agreed to provide 120 men-at-arms, twenty of them knights, and 200 archers. There might be tough negotiations about the terms of contracts. John of Gaunt succeeded in negotiating a 50 per cent increase in pay rates in 1369, and in the following year obtained a promise of double wages. In 1443 the Duke of Somerset negotiated with the council, and it was agreed that the duke should go to France with 'as many as he may gete unto the nombre or undre of four barons, eight banncrets and thirty knights'. Initial pro-posals that there should be 1,000 men-at-arms were whittled down to 800. As captain of the expedition, Somerset was to have full rights to dispose of conquered territory, and the king gave up his right to one-third of the pro-ceeds of plunder and ransoms. A system under which men could negoti-ate the terms of their service was clearly more attractive than one under which they had no say in their conditions.

One obvious problem with a system of contract was that it could be abused, by magnates bringing less men in their contingents than had been agreed. In Edward III's reign numbers were carefully accounted for. Under

Henry V a system of regular musters was established for the English troops serving under contract in Normandy. Garrison forces were usually mustered on a quarterly basis, and field armies monthly. Care was taken to ensure not merely that numbers were properly maintained, but also that the men had the appropriate equipment. The contract system, originally so simple, became more and more bureaucratic.

Contract did not take over completely as a method of recruitment in the later Middle Ages. It was not used for the major royal campaign of 1359, when the troops were directly paid by the clerks of the royal household. In the period of the Wars of the Roses, the Crown used contracts and indentures for such purposes as the keeping of the northern marches, but in the difficult situation of civil war reliance was placed more on simple requests for military assistance from the magnates, and on offers of wages. Hope of the political gains that would come with victory were often a powerful inducement to men to serve in those difficult days.

The contract system depended on the ability of lords to recruit their own retinues. Great men had always brought their own followers with them on campaigns; for reasons of prestige no noble could go to war without a respectable troop at his command. Magnates could call on their own tenants to serve under them in war, but by the late twelfth century this element was becoming less important. The relationship between landlord and tenant turned from one of personal loyalty into one of legal formality. Charters have been used to identify the knights who formed the core of the entourage of William the Marshal, Earl of Pembroke, who died in 1219: eighteen are shown to have been associated with him for substantial periods. A majority of these were not his tenants. The bonds that linked these knights to their lord were not those of landholding: as was the case with the royal household knights, grants of fees and wages and hope of reward were central to the relationship. Lists survive for the household of Roger Bigod, another holder of the office of Marshal. In 1297 he had five bannerets and nine knights, along with about twenty squires and sergeants, named as members of his household. They were the core of his military resources, but this could be expanded. In the autumn of the same year Bigod contracted to provide no less than 150 heavily armed cavalry to fight in Scotland. In the Hundred Years War retinues were larger still. John of Gaunt's personal following when he led a disastrous expedition to France in 1373 consisted of 780 men-at-arms and 800 mounted archers.

The rates of pay that the Crown offered were not such as to bring men flooding to the royal banners. Knightly pay rose in the twelfth century from a level of 6*d.* or 8*d.* a day to 2*s.* a day by John's reign, but changed little thereafter. For a very brief period at the start of the Hundred Years War Edward III offered his troops double wages, but financial exigencies meant that this could not be maintained. Even the massive dislocation of the labour market caused by the Black Death in the mid-fourteenth century did not affect the general level of military wages: a knight serving Henry V at Agincourt was paid at the same rates that his predecessors had received under Edward III and Edward I, though he might expect to receive in addition a bonus, or 'regard'. Service as a Member of Parliament, although far safer and more comfortable than campaigning, was rewarded at double the rate of military pay.

There were other inducements that the Crown could offer as well as pay. Cavalry were offered some protection against the major financial loss involved should horses be killed. It was customary for those who accepted royal wages to have their horses formally valued at the start of an expedition. If the animal was killed, the owner would be recompensed. Those who campaigned for the king customarily received assurances that their lands were under royal protection, free from any threats of legal action.

If a campaign of conquest was successful, grants of land might follow. The completion of the conquest of Wales in 1284 was followed by a distribution of estates. The failure of Edward I to take similar action in the aftermath of the battle of Falkirk in 1298 led the Earl of Norfolk and others to abandon the campaign, and in his later campaigns the king was, by necessity, more generous. Henry V's conquest of Normandy was accompanied by a deliberate policy of granting to his followers lands and titles that came into his hands.

Expectations of winning booty, or making a fortune by obtaining a rich ransom from some high-born captive, varied. Campaigns in Wales and Scotland did not offer much, but there were lucrative pickings in the Hundred Years War. As early as 1340 Sir Walter Mauny made £8,000 by selling prisoners to Edward III. In 1347 Sir Thomas Holland made £13,333 from the Count of Eu, whom he sold to the king. At a lower level, John Jodrell from Cheshire made £8 from a silver salt-cellar belonging to the French king which he looted at Poitiers in 1356. In any calculations, however, the danger of losing equipment, and of being captured, had to be set against any possible gains. By 1376 Jodrell was penniless, unable to meet a request for 1,000 francs for his own ransom. There can be no doubt, however, that hope of profit was very important in persuading men to fight.

Threats as well as promises might be used to persuade men to go on campaign. Those who were reluctant to fight for Richard I in France were fined, and some lands were seized. Magnates who resisted King John's summonses, especially that to Poitou in 1214, found themselves subjected to a potent mixture of menaces and concessions from the king. The fact that many magnates owed large sums of money to the Crown was a significant element in compelling them to obey requests. In one well-known incident, Edward I forced the Earl of Arundel and a group of magnates to go to fight in Gascony, by threatening that if they did not do so, exchequer officials would levy long-standing debts, which in the earl's case totalled over £5,000. By the time of the Hundred Years War, however, such methods of persuasion were less necessary; the reasons for fighting outweighed those for staying at home.

There were intangible factors that led men to war: there was honour and glory to be won, and, no doubt, there was dishonour in remaining at home. The example of Sir William Marmion, instructed by his lady love to make his helmet known in the most perilous place in Britain, who went off to fight at the siege of Norham castle in Edward II's reign, is an extreme case of romantic chivalry in action. Edward I made a great occasion of the knighting of his son in 1306, holding a great Feast of the Swans at which those present swore oaths to pursue the war in Scotland. In the early days of the Hundred Years War Edward III's Feast of the Heron provided a similar opportunity to reinforce commitment to the English cause. The military ethos was a powerful one: a knight had to win renown, if he could, by performing feats of arms. There was an undeniable glamour involved in warfare at the knightly level. This is not to deny the horrors that war might bring, with the burning and pillaging of lands on a systematic basis, or even the discomforts of riding for days in soaking clothes, with little if anything to eat. One of Henry V's soldiers wrote 'Pray for us that we may come soon out of this unlusty soldier's life into the life of England'.

The changing patterns in the way in which the cavalry forces were recruited were complex. Some elements were always present, notably those of the royal household. Pay was significant throughout the medieval period, though it was not until the fourteenth century that armies were almost wholly composed of men in receipt of wages. Compulsion became less important, either in the form of the traditional feudal knight service, or of newer systems based on an assessment of wealth. Wars were not invariably popular. Throughout the thirteenth century it had been very difficult to recruit for overseas expeditions, but with the Hundred Years

War, attitudes changed. The chronicler Jean le Bel was most impressed by the love of the English magnates and knights for their king, and their consequent willingness to fight for him abroad.

The cavalry were the cream of medieval armies, the élite whose deployment was expected to bring victory, whose conduct was determined by the expectations of chivalric society. No pride of place was accorded to the infantry. In practice, however, they were often responsible for success in war. In the Norman period, at such battles as Tinchebray or Brémule, many of the knights fought on foot, with invaluable support provided by common footsoldiers armed with bows or pikes. The thirteenth century saw the heyday of the cavalry, but at Stirling Bridge in 1297 the English horsemen were cut down by Scottish footmen. At Falkirk in the following year the infantry, by now mostly equipped with the devastating longbow, played a decisive part in breaking the powerful Scottish circular defensive formations, the schiltrons. In 1314, at Bannockburn, the English cavalry were again shown to be incapable of dealing with an imaginative enemy reliant on a strong defensive infantry formation. In the 1330s English commanders rediscovered the use of archers combined with dismounted cavalry. At Dupplin Moor in 1332, and at Halidon Hill in 1333, such a formation proved devastatingly effective. An important step was to provide the archers with horses, so that they could keep up with cavalry on the march. They and the bulk of the cavalry would dismount so as to fight in effective combination in battle. In this way the English developed the forces that were to achieve such astounding successess in the Hundred Years War as those at Crécy, Poitiers, and Agincourt.

There was no obligation on the ordinary people of England to serve in war which could compare with the feudal duty borne by their social superiors. There was, certainly, a general obligation on all free men to bear arms in defence of the country, which dated back to Anglo-Saxon days. The *fyrd*, the Anglo-Saxon host, was based on a personal obligation, and also on a basis of landed wealth: one man, according to the Domesday inquest for Berkshire, was to be sent from every five hides. Failure to perform *fyrd* service was a serious offence, punishable by a fine. There has been much debate about the nature of the *fyrd*: was there on the one hand a royal, select *fyrd* with service due on the five-hide basis, and on the other a more general obligation to provide defence forces for shire and borough? The evidence is not as clear as might be hoped, but in the Anglo-Saxon systems of military obligation there were precedents for the recruitment of

Armour

Developments in the technology of defence are usually a response to developments in offensive weapons. The medieval period saw developments both in weaponry and in armour, but it was the latter that underwent the greatest transformation, while the main weapons of attack, lance, sword, mace, and arrow changed relatively little. Changing styles of armour were dictated in part by straightforward factors—the effectiveness and cost of different types—but style and fashion played a part. There was no perfect solution to the problem of providing individual protection for soldiers: equipment which resisted blows best limited mobility unduly, and was hot and uncomfortable.

Sophisticated armour of many different types, including mail and plate, was widely used in the ancient world. A superb Anglo-Saxon helmet from the seventh century survives, preserved in the Sutton Hoo burial. The military equipment of the eleventh century is splendidly illustrated in the Bayeux Tapestry. Helmets were conical, with a simple nose piece (the nasal) providing limited facial protection. The body was protected by a single mail garment, a hauberk, extending from a hood, or coif, for the head, down to knee-level. Wide sleeves allowed for maximum movement. The illustrations in the Tapestry suggest mail trousers, which would have done little for the wearer's virility. Much more plausible are other sources which suggest that the hauberk was formed into a split skirt.

By the mid-twelfth century the helmet began to change in style. Round topped helmets without nasals began to appear, followed by cylindrical ones with an almost flat top. Full face-guards, pierced to provide vision and ventilation, gave a high degree of protection. The full-armed knight of the late twelfth century looked very different from his predecessor of the Bayeux Tapestry, for a flowing surcoat covered most of his body. The mail hauberk, however, was little changed. It was not till the late thirteenth century that the revolution in armour began, with the introduction of solid metal plates to reinforce the mail. A brass of Roger de Trumpington, who died in 1298, shows him in a full suit of mail, reinforced by plate or leather *poleyns* over his knees. His head rests on a massive conical helmet. The brass of Sir John de Creke, dating from about 1325, shows his mail armour substantially reinforced with plate. He has a skull-cap, or *bascinet*, on his head, *brassarts* on his upper arms, and gauntlets protecting his hands and wrists. On his legs he has *poleyns*, while greaves protect his shins, and jointed *sabatons* cover his feet. The flowing surcoat makes it hard to distinguish the body armour clearly, but he may even have worn a 'coat of plates', formed of iron plates riveted to leather or cloth, between the surcoat and the hauberk. The triangular shield is small and manœuvrable, a great contrast to the long, kite-shaped shield of the Norman period.

By the fourteenth century, the great helm, often featuring an elaborate crest, had become a piece of specialized tournament armour. For battle, the lighter *bascinet* was far more practical. One characteristic form was fitted with a projecting snout-like visor, which could be easily raised. Breastplates may have developed first for tournaments, but were soon incorporated into battle armour. The appearance of the knight was transformed when the tight-fitting *jupon* replaced the old-style surcoat.

In the fifteenth century plate armour was fully developed. It became fashionable to wear 'white' armour, displaying the bare metal without any *jupon* or surcoat, though the tabard, featuring the wearer's coat of arms, was also worn. The mail *aventail* which had protected the neck was replaced by the plate *gorget*, and elaborate fan-shaped guards protected vulnerable joints at the elbow. A popular type of helmet was the *sallet*, rounded in shape and reaching down to the shoulders, with a visor covering the face-opening. The manufacture of this full plate armour was very skilled; the market was dominated by Milanese and German armourers.

Horses as well as their riders might be fitted with armour. The late thirteenth-century paintings in the Painted Chamber at Westminster show not only horses caprisoned with full cloth trappings, but also two apparently bearing a full mail covering, or trapper. The *chanfron* protecting the head was the most common piece of horse armour, but by the fifteenth century a full covering of plate was occasionally in use.

Illustrations often show all those involved in battle fully armoured in up-to-date fashion. The reality was very different. Many men would have been protected by quilted jackets, *gambesons* or *aketons*, with hardened leather, *cuir bouilli*, serving in many cases where steel would have been better. Pieces of armour might well have been acquired at different times and might not match. While the mail coats of the eleventh century were certainly expensive, treasured items, pieces of armour might not be very costly by the fourteenth century. In 1324 John de Swinnerton possessed a *habergeon*, with *aventail* and other pieces, three *bascinets*, and plates for thighs and shins, with *poleyns* for his knees, worth in total less than £10.

It is difficult to know how effective armour was, but the transformation from the flexible mail of the early Middle Ages to the elaborate jointed plate of the fifteenth century does not seem to have had the effect that might be expected on casualty rates. At the battle of Brémule in 1119 it is said that only three knights out of 900 were killed. Evesham in 1265 was a vicious battle, ending a civil war; yet only eighteen sword belts 'of enemies of the king killed in battle' were delivered into the royal wardrobe. In the Hundred Years War, on the other hand, casualties might be very high. It is estimated that 40 per cent of the French cavalry were killed at Poitiers. The skill of the armourer was more than matched by that of the archer.

---

footsoldiers which could be developed. The *fyrd* itself did not long survive the Conquest. On one celebrated occasion it was summoned by William Rufus, only for his officials to take from the men the money they had been given for their subsistence. This was so that more effective mercenary troops could be hired.

The evidence for the recruitment of infantry troops before the reign of Edward I is scanty. Footsoldiers were undoubtedly used in substantial numbers in Henry II's Welsh expeditions. English as well as Flemish infantry were involved in the rebellion of 1173–4. The Assize of Arms of 1181 laid down that men who possessed at least 10 marks worth of rents or chattels must be equipped with a quilted hauberk, iron helmet, and spear. There are occasional references to infantry receiving wages: in 1193 500 foot at Bristol were paid for seven weeks, and a further 500 at Windsor for forty days. Under Henry III, the principles of the Assize of Arms were used to recruit men: in 1231 one-third of those men sworn to arms in the border counties were asked to serve in Wales, bringing with them sufficient food for forty days. In the civil war conditions of the 1260s, orders were issued for the selection of appropriately armed infantry from the counties: four, six, or eight men from each vill, provided with expenses for forty days.

Wales was a major recruiting-ground. The Earl of Chester appeared with 'a dreadful and unendurable mass of Welsh' at the battle of Lincoln in 1141. Henry II recruited extensively in Wales, notably for campaigns in France, and in 1196 Richard mobilized 2,100 Welshmen to serve in Normandy. In 1213 King John had 1,200 Welsh foot in pay. Much later in the thirteenth century Edward I recruited extensively in Wales. Many of the infantry in the armies which conquered Wales were themselves Welsh, as were half the footsoldiers in the 1298 Scottish campaign.

A transformation of the quantity, if not of the quality, of infantry forces took place under Edward I. Over 30,000 were mustered to deal with the

Welsh rebellion of 1294–5, and some 24,000 were recruited for the Falkirk campaign of 1298. Sheriffs were used to collect men for the first Welsh war, in 1277, but in 1282 special commissioners of array were appointed, usually men of military experience. The actual task of selection seems usually to have been left to the local communities, with the commissioners then carrying out an inspection. In 1295 Hugh Cressingham and William Mortimer came to Norfolk, and assembled a large number of men at Newmarket. Their equipment, consisting of white tunics, knives, and swords, was provided by their home villages, at considerable expense. Those not up to standard were sent home at once. It was usual for the local communities to bear the costs of the operation until the county muster was held; from that point, the Crown took over. In the field the various county contingents were held together, subdivided into companies of a hundred men, and platoons of twenty.

Desertion was a major problem, notably in the Scottish wars. As the obligation to serve was ill defined, the only offence that deserters could be charged with was that of misappropriating their wages. Since in many cases wages were either not paid, or paid substantially in arrears, there was little that could be done to prevent the constant haemorrhaging that took place. When armies were fighting in France, desertion was less of a problem as it was less easy to return home.

Under Edward II, attempts were made to improve the quality of the infantry. Heavily armed infantry were demanded from the towns; the Crown was taking a much greater interest than in the past in ensuring that the footsoldiers were properly equipped. Another innovation was the use of requests to great nobles to provide infantry as well as cavalry. In 1319 the earls and a number of other magnates were asked to provide cavalry and as many foot as they could muster for the relief of Norham castle. Another idea was to obtain a grant of footsoldiers, one from every vill in the land. This was first put forward in 1311, and was suggested again in 1316 when the local communities were asked to pay the men for sixty days in the field. The levy was cancelled at a late stage, but in 1322 the scheme was revived and carried through, with the sixty days of 1316 reduced to forty. As many as 7,000 men were recruited in this way.

Yet the English military enterprises of Edward II's reign were conspicuously unsuccessful, and many of the experiments in recruiting footsoldiers were not repeated. A vital advance came in the 1330s with the appearance of the mounted archer. Such men had been used in the twelfth century, but their use had subsequently been abandoned. Now, these men were increasingly recruited alongside the heavily armed cavalry; by the late fourteenth century contracts commonly required the provision of knights, men-at-arms, and horse archers. Commissions of array continued to be used, however, both for campaigns against the Scots and for expeditions to France. The practice was unpopular, not only because men were impressed against their will for service, but more importantly because the counties had to bear the cost of equipping them and paying them until they reached the muster point. In 1355 archers from Gloucestershire 'contemptuously refused to come' when required to set out for Scotland.

Armies in the Hundred Years War were, with the exception of that recruited for the Crécy–Calais campaign of 1346–7 with over 30,000 men, generally much smaller than those of Edward I's day. This reduced the burden on the English shires. The fact that an increasing proportion of the archers were found by magnates, rather than being recruited by commissioners of array, further eased the situation. Obligation was becoming less important for the infantry just as it was for the cavalry.

Commissions of array were not abandoned, however. They continued to be used during the Wars of the Roses. One muster roll, for Bridport in Dorset in 1457, survives. Over 180 men were listed. Of these, about seventy can be described as well equipped. Bows and arrows were common, as were swords, helmets, and bucklers. Towns in the fifteenth century produced substantial, well-armed contingents. In 1455 Coventry paid for a splendid new banner, a multi-coloured uniform for the captain of its contingent, and red and green sashes for 100 men.

For the infantry, the glamour of war and the promise of fame and fortune were less convincing reasons for fighting than they were for the nobles. They faced a dismal prospect of discomfort and exhaustion, dysentery and sickness. If they were captured, they were not worth ransoming, and so were far more likely to be killed in battle than the knights and nobles. There was no calculus of rewards and menaces to explain why they fought: the only group which received significant favour from the Crown in exchange for fighting were criminals. From 1294 a standard recruiting technique was to promise pardons to criminals in return for service: the country's gaols were emptied every time that there was a major recruiting drive.

The Crown made surprisingly little effort before the fourteenth century to ensure that ordinary footsoldiers were adequately supplied with weapons, though crossbowmen were certainly properly provided for under Richard I and John. Under Edward I nothing was done to provide an archer with more ammunition once he had fired off the two dozen arrows in the quiver he brought with him. Matters changed with Edward III, and great efforts were made to ensure that there were adequate supplies of arms and ammunition. Between 1353 and 1360 William de Rothwell, royal artiller, added no less than 15,365 bows, 4,000 bowstaves, 23,643 sheaves of arrows, and 341 gross of bowstrings to the stock of supplies in the Tower of London, which was all provided for the use of the great 1359–60 expedition to France.

The infantry often wore uniform of a sort, perhaps as much as a means of identifying deserters as a method of recognition in battle. In Edward I's Welsh wars, armbands with the red cross of St George were employed, while the white coats of the Norfolk men recruited in 1296 made them easy to spot. Welsh infantry at the start of the Hundred Years War were all clothed in the same manner. Cheshire archers in the fourteenth century wore coats and hats in green and white, and it is likely that some other units were as easily recognizable.

A vital element in many campaigns was provided by the engineers with the siege machines and, from the fourteenth century, guns, that they brought with them. At the siege of Caerlaverock in 1300 it was the engineers with their stone-throwing trebuchets who forced the surrender of the castle, rather than the knights or infantrymen. Such men had long been important. In the Norman period Robert de Bellême employed a skilled engineer, experienced in Crusade warfare. Under John, Master Urric was making siege engines at Chinon in 1202, and in Ireland in 1210 he headed a team of nine carpenters. Castle-builders also served as castle destroyers. The great master mason James of St George was the senior of the engineers at the siege of Stirling in 1304, when thirteen great engines were directed against the castle. While guns were of relatively little use in the field of battle, their role in siege warfare was central from the late fourteenth century. Between 1382 and 1388 the Crown bought eighty-seven cannon at a cost of almost £1,800. The men who managed these weapons were an essential element in any major army.

The recruitment of troops was only one element in organizing a successful expedition. The logistical problems involved in feeding large numbers of men and horses were immense. Small-scale plundering expeditions could live off the land, but a complex supply network was needed for major expeditions, particularly if they were campaigning in hostile terrain in Wales or Scotland, or engaged in lengthy sieges. Henry II made extensive arrangements for his Irish campaign of 1171, and King John's plans for a war in Wales in 1212, which never took place, show that he was well aware of the need to provide sufficient supplies. By the late thirteenth century the system was well established. The Crown used a traditional right, that of prise, to collect very large quantities of foodstuffs. This right of compulsory purchase had originally been intended purely for the supply of the royal household, but it was now extended to the whole army. Sheriffs were ordered to collect huge quantities of grain, salt meat, and fish; payment was promised but all too often not made to those whose foodstuffs were taken from them. The goods were then sent by water, to the victualling centres for the campaigns. Chester served this purpose for wars in Wales, while major royal supply bases were set up for the Scottish wars at Berwick in the east, and Skinburness near Carlisle in the west. The system was remarkably successful, and highly unpopular.

In the Hundred Years War the problems of supply were less acute. Armies were, for the most part, smaller than they had been under Edward I, and they could realistically hope to live off the land in France. It was indeed often a deliberate strategy that they should do so, plundering and ravaging as they went. The Crown turned to contracts with merchants in preference to the politically unpopular use of prise. In the Wars of the Roses, problems of supply were a determining factor on several occasions. It was not easy in a civil war to make adequate preparations in advance, and armies often had to rely on foraging.

There was much work to be done to organize the transport of men, horses, and supplies. The Bayeux Tapestry gives a vivid picture of the equipment and foodstuffs being loaded on to the ships of the Conqueror's invasion fleet. Naval transport proved essential during the English wars in Wales and Scotland: on occasion supplies were brought all the way by sea from the Isle of Wight to the Firth of Forth. The transport of armies to fight on the Continent was a major enterprise. Figures show that it was quite normal for there to be one sailor to every two soldiers, and for a large army the call on the country's shipping was very considerable. Edward I's small expedition to Flanders in 1297 was transported across the Channel in no less than 273 ships, and about 750 were needed in 1346–7 for the campaign which achieved the victory at Crécy and the capture of Calais. The only obligatory naval service was that of fifty-seven ships for two weeks due from the Cinque Ports in the south-east. For the bulk of its naval transport requirements, the Crown had to rely on an unpopular process of impressment.

War was the most complex enterprise in which the medieval English state was involved. Though the size of armies appears small in comparison to the forces mobilized in more recent times, the scale of the effort that went into such operations as Edward I's Scottish campaigns, or the 1346 expedition to France, should not be under-estimated. The efforts to recruit men, both cavalry and infantry, to provide them with the supplies they needed, and to finance the campaigns, involved the marshalling of the country's resources on a massive scale. There was great professionalism on the part of many commanders as well as occasional chivalric bravado. The major successes, the campaigns of conquest, the great battles, and the major sieges, were the product of careful organization and staff-work quite as much as were the victories of more modern periods.

2 TOWARDS THE STANDING ARMY 1485–1660

IAN ROY

At the end of the fifteenth century England was no longer a great military power. The Angevin kings had ruled both England and much of France; the Lancastrian Henry V had renewed that claim after Agincourt. But in the years that followed the nation lost her French possessions, with the exception of Calais, and her kings, although in the long run capable of quelling their 'overmighty subjects' and preserving the authority of central government in spite of widespread disorder and rival claims, had not begun to build a standing army, and the semi-permanent military administration to maintain it, of the kind being developed on the Continent. Nor had the internal wars—the Wars of the Roses—been sufficiently severe and continuous to change the long-term, generally peaceful development of the country, which had no need to build new castles to match those of the past, improve existing fortifications, or even repair the ancient walls which most towns still possessed. Country houses were increasingly built for comfort and not for their capacity to withstand attack. The nation sheltered behind the 20 miles of water which protected her from foreign invasion, and for which a small navy seemed the most useful and inexpensive form of defence.

Contemporary foreigners observed that, although the English still enjoyed a high reputation as 'strong and courageous' soldiers, they were ignorant of continental methods of warfare. The nation was backward and insular in military terms. In the age of gunpowder she remained attached, for sentimental reasons, to the traditional longbow. English noble families played an important role in the Wars of the Roses, but on a diminishing scale as the wars dragged on. The decisive battle of Bosworth, which placed the house of Tudor on the throne, was won by a small army mainly recruited abroad.

The military system of the early Tudors therefore was bound to recognize these limitations, and the dangers in too great a dependence on the armed followers of leading noblemen. It lacked imposing defensive works guarding the frontiers or protecting the major centres of population. Englishmen were unfamiliar with the latest weapons and tactics developed in the wars in Italy, where in former times an Essex man, Sir John Hawkwood, had won a brilliant military reputation as the leader of mercenaries. As the founder of a new dynasty attempting to gain recognition from the great powers of Europe, Henry VII proceeded cautiously. He was content to threaten his neighbours with military action and allow himself to be bought off—as he was when he appeared before Boulogne in 1492—rather than suffer the great expense of going to war. He secured the future of his line with diplomacy and subsidy, and the minimum of direct military action.

The nucleus of a larger force did exist, however. His Yorkist predecessors had formed a 200-strong company of archers as a palace guard, no doubt in imitation of the Scottish archers who protected the King of France, but it was Henry who instituted the Yeomen of the Guard, similarly armed, for the same purpose. To them were added, in the next reign, the Gentlemen Pensioners, a smaller body of mounted men, armed with poleaxes, and well placed, as 'the nearest guard' to the sovereign, to attract the aristocratic and the aspiring. Varying in size, depending upon the current state of government finance, the Pensioners could be used as a cadre of young officers when the need for an army arose. Henry VII also maintained the Calais garrison at its old level, having purged it of dissident elements. It was easier for him to do so, for the troops there were self-financing; Calais was the staple for the marketing of England's main export, raw wool, and the customs duties on that paid for the garrison. It was of strategic importance, threatening France at a point close to Paris, and opening a bridge to the wealth, industry, and culture of the Netherlands towns, which were passing, as part of the old Burgundian inheritance, into the hands of the rulers of the Empire.

Like the medieval castles of England and Wales, which remained as a reminder of past wars and conquests, the many old bulwarks on the coast were largely useless and unmanned; only Dover, and the castles at Berwick and Carlisle which guarded the Scottish border, had small garrisons. In all there were no more than 2,000–3,000 men in arms at the accession of Henry VIII in 1509. How could the nation raise forces as needed, given these limitations? As we have seen, one solution was for the Crown to contract with loyal noblemen and prominent courtiers to bring their retinues to the colours. Of increasing importance, however, was the age-old military obligation of all men between the ages of 16 and 60 to serve in arms for the defence of the realm, as their sovereign ordered. But custom, and political and legal constraints, limited the period of such service to forty days, and to within the borders of the county of the men raised. Henry IV had given statutory basis to the commissions of array by which such troops were mustered in each shire. The fifteenth-century wars had been fought in part by forces raised in the counties by such royal commissions, and the following century would see this obligation modernized and increasingly made the backbone of the nation's defences on land.

Henry VII may have been reluctant to go to war, but his court was imbued with the cult of chivalry, partly imported from abroad, which found its highest expression in the tournament. His son, Henry VIII, imbibed this martial atmosphere and starred in his father's jousts: perhaps the most popular of the items on display at the Royal Armouries today is his magnificent suit of plate armour for the tilt. Now that the Tudor dynasty was well established Henry aspired to play an active part on the European stage. He revived the interest in military pursuits of the old nobility, and the new men he favoured were those, like the Duke of Suffolk, who acquitted themselves best in the tilt (Suffolk, however, taking care to lose to the king), and who sought military glory. Henry saw himself as the heir of Henry V, and strove to imitate his triumphs in France: he spent a quarter of his reign at war with England's traditional enemy.

He was also a Renaissance prince, and saw it as his duty and delight to promote the arts and artefacts of war. He sought out the rich (i.e. expensively and artistically decorated) arms and armour produced by the leading centres in north Italy and south Germany. Not content with this he imported the best foreign craftsmen, such as the 'almain armourers' who made the fine armours for the tilt close to the tournament yards at Greenwich. More practically, he rapidly expanded his artillery train, buying the celebrated 'twelve apostles', the great bronze cannon, from the foundries at Malines, near Antwerp, and over a hundred others. His taste for war over a long reign ensured that the beginnings of the cannon-founding industry in England would develop rapidly, and by the 1540s native craftsmen, as well as those from abroad, were able to produce bronze as well as cast-iron pieces. The Tower of London, housing the Office of Ordnance, controlled the output of cannon, and the arsenal there supplied the newly enlarged fleet, the new forts on the coast, and the armies Henry sent to France.

The Crown could not remedy overnight the shortage of portable firearms, and of English soldiers skilled in their use. The gunsmiths' company of London was not incorporated until Charles I's reign, and the prohibition of private ownership of firearms was not relaxed. Henry had to import handguns, and employ foreign mercenaries or auxiliaries supplied by his imperial ally, to achieve a balance of arms in his own forces. Of the large number of English troops, mostly bill- and bowmen, assembled for the campaign of 1544, only 10 per cent was 'shot'.

The changing face of warfare meant that he needed a variety of skills: on foot, pikemen, such as German *Landsknechts*, with their 18-foot long weapon, were highly prized, but, by mid-century, their companies were at least a quarter arquebusiers; on horseback, the heavy cavalry which England lacked, and mounted arquebusiers, with their short calivers, or the new weapon, pistols. The mixture was truly international, an exotic addition being stradiots (a form of light skirmishing horsemen, comparable to hussars) from the Balkans. Altogether foreign troops constituted about a quarter of the 44,000 the king had in the field. This was the largest army ever seen under English command on the Continent until the late seventeenth century.

A Welsh soldier deplored this motley and extravagant crew:

So many depraved, brutish soldiers from all nations under the sun—Welsh, English, Cornish, Irish, Manx, Scots, Spaniards, Gascons, Portingals [Portuguese], Italians, Albanians, Greeks, Turks, Tartars, Almains, Germans, Burgundians, Flemings, who had come there . . . to have a good time under the king of England, who by nature was too hospitable to foreigners.

Fortunately for him this Welsh critic of the king took the precaution of recording his views in his native language.

Entering as a principal into the European conflict was hazardous and expensive. Henry had not only to build up the English munitions industries and furnish a large expeditionary force, but guard his own shores against invasion. His council undertook surveys and listings of those liable for home defence. In 1545 the local levies were sufficient to beat off a small French landing party on the Isle of Wight. It was on this occasion that, in full view of the king and his assembled forces, his flagship, the *Mary Rose*, keeled over and sank, without any assistance from the approaching French. In 1539–40, having lost the support of the Emperor Charles V in

Early Firearms

Gunpowder was probably Chinese in origin and brought to the West by Arab scholars. Given its black magical properties, errant monks or alchemists, in league with the Devil, were commonly and mistakenly credited with its invention. Nevertheless by the end of the thirteenth century devices were being developed to make use of the new explosive mixture. The earliest representation of a gun dates from 1326, and shows a vase or pot firing what appears to be an arrow. This was the usual case of an innovation following the form or appearance of the thing it replaces.

These early devices can hardly have been very effective or portable. In the course of the fourteenth century, however, great strides were made, especially in cannon of the largest size: enormous bombards, such as Mons Meg in Edinburgh castle, have few equals in later history in terms of size and weight. 'Artillery' originally meant any form of missile-throwing device, large or small, using gunpowder or not. Slowly, however, the division arose between the cannon, for the field or the siege, and the smaller hand-held firearm.

The latter differed from the former only in size. At its most primitive it consisted of an iron tube, tightly bound to a wooden pole or stock, which could be placed on the shoulder or tucked under the arm. Ignition was by means of a slow match, normally a piece of thin, hempen rope soaked in soluble nitrates, applied to the touchhole in the breech. Such a device was clumsy and difficult to aim, and to steady the gun and limit its fierce recoil several early examples were fitted with a hook protruding from beneath the lock or barrel, which could be placed in a cavity in the wall or barricade. Such a hole can still be seen in the window sills at Elcho castle in Scotland. Guns of this type were known as hookguns in several languages: *hagenbuch, harquebus, hagbut a croc.* As the latter, found frequently in Tudor English, literally means 'hookgun with hook' it can be seen that the original meaning of *hagbut* has been lost, and a variant, arquebus, became the most common term for handgun, long after the hook had disappeared; the soldier who carried such a weapon was known as an arquebusier.

Improvements in design, to make it more effective and accurate and easier to use, were continuous throughout this period. To allow the gunner to hold and aim the piece with both hands, a stock which fitted the shoulder was developed. Most ingenuity was applied to the lock, the metal plate which secured the stock to the breech, and to which the firing mechanism was attached. The basic matchlock was simply an S-shaped lever, or serpentine, pivoted at its centre: moving one end brought the other, the cock, which held the burning match, down on the touchhole. But to the art of the locksmith was soon added that of the clockmaker; and more complicated spring-operated mechanisms were introduced which connected the cock to a trigger. Pressing the trigger released a catch which allowed the match to fall sharply on the pan of priming powder which in turn fired the charge in the breech.

Carrying a match, continuously alight, made the arquebusier prone to accidents and in the course of the sixteenth century notable minds pioneered alternative methods of firing the gun. One was the wheel-lock, an experimental blueprint for which, by Leonardo himself, survives. A steel disk or wheel with a serrated rim was attached to a powerful spring, and wound up by a form of spanner. When released, and rapidly rotating, it struck sparks from a piece of iron pyrites, held in the jaws of the cock. Another was the flintlock, in which the sparks were obtained by striking a flint against a steel plate, positioned above the pan; this was the principle of the later tinder box.

In the course of the century all these forms of lock were to be seen, though usually later in the British Isles than elsewhere, and many different types of gun were developed. The pistol, and the calivor or carbine, both lighter, with smaller bore and shorter barrels, than the 4-foot long musket barrel, were suitable for men on horseback, the first for cavalry the second for dragoons. They made their appearance in the middle of the century. Henry VIII's bodyguards possessed a remarkable form of pierced shield, which concealed a matchlock pistol; they can still be viewed at the Royal Armouries. Pistols allowed cavalry to answer fire with fire, and the wheel-lock became the most common form carried on horseback. Perhaps it was also appropriate for officers on shipboard; Frobisher shows his in the portrait of the 1570s. Cavalrymen in the Civil War period were commonly armed with a brace of wheel-locks.

By the time of the Civil War English infantry observed the ratio of two musketeers to every pikeman, and the former were almost uniformly armed with the heavy matchlock musket, firing twelve bullets to the pound. Weighing 20 pounds it was heavy enough to require a rest. Several of standard issue survive from the Cromwellian period at Littlecote House in Wiltshire. The flintlock was confined to more specialist uses, such as in sporting guns ('fowling pieces'), or issued to élite troops, such as the commander's lifeguard, or those protecting powder stores.

All these guns were muzzle loaders. The charge of powder, finely calculated, the leaden ball, the wad to keep it in place, had to be carefully loaded from the muzzle and rammed home. Woe betide the gunner who, in the heat of battle, did this incorrectly, or left the ramrod in.

In the century which followed the Civil War the matchlock, cheap and uncomplicated, was slowly replaced by a form of flintlock, and the musket became lighter, more reliable, and easier to handle. The rest could be dispensed with. As the 'brown bess' this was the weapon which was carried by redcoats all over the world and remained standard in the British army until the next round of scientific advances transformed firearms in the nineteenth century.

---

his continuing war with Francis I of France, and been excommunicated by the pope, he ordered the construction of the largest and most comprehensive system of coastal defences since the forts of the Saxon shore had been built in late Roman days. The wealth of the abbeys, and even in some cases materials from their dismantled buildings, was used to construct a series of bulwarks and castles, from Hull in the north-east to Milford Haven in west Wales. They incorporated some of the modern ideas of meeting cannon fire with fire, arranging tiers of guns in rounded bastions placed in concentric circles. Deal, one of the 'three castles that keep the Downs', the chief naval anchorage off the east coast of Kent, remains a good example. They did not adopt the fashionable angled bastion, developed in Italy, but may have borrowed from the designs current in northern Europe.

While a prominent Moravian engineer was employed, the scale of the works, the length of the wars, and the possibility of more continuous employment encouraged the development of native talents. The first English professional military engineers emerged in the building of these coastal works and those constructed at Calais and, from 1544 to 1550, Boulogne. In the same way Henry's massively expanded military and naval establishment could begin to provide a career structure for professional soldiers, although one interrupted by periods of peace, and far from straightforward.

To engage in war with France often brought in its train, for the English Crown, hostile action by the Scots: the Auld Alliance was still in place, though other forces were working in Scottish politics to promote the English cause, and the Tudors and Stuarts were now linked by marriage.

Henry's brother-in-law, James IV, was also a Renaissance prince with strong military/artistic interests, who imported fine arms and armour, as well as heavy artillery and other munitions, from France. Undeterred by the memory of his grandfather's death (James II had been killed by an exploding cannon), he set up a cannon-founding industry. The Scottish bodyguard at the court of the Valois kings was of long standing, and other Scots units were often to be found in French service; equally, at moments of danger, French mercenaries aided the Scots.

Scotland's military strength lay in the many hardy footsoldiers the greatest supporters of the Crown could bring into the field, both Lowlanders and Highlanders. If the Swiss could decide battles by the tactical use of massed pikes the Scots should have been equally successful, with their half pikes, long spears, and Lochaber axes. And if, to leaven the pikes, the Spanish introduced sword and buckler men, on the Roman model—attractive to Renaissance soldiers fascinated by the discovery of the classical past—the Scots already possessed men simply equipped with basket-hilted swords and round targes. With the development of more effective firearms body armour was going out, and their enemies remarked on the Scots' lack of expensive protection. On the other hand the Scots' weakness in firearms, and in heavy cavalry, counted against them.

The Scottish campaigns, linked to the French wars fought in 1513, 1522–3, 1543–50, and 1558–60, were in the main decisive victories for the English forces sent north. Their commanders used shire levies from the four northern counties, with the important addition of Italian men-at-arms (heavy cavalry) hired for the purpose, and ruthlessly employed scorched earth policies, destroying the great Border abbeys and burning and looting from Edinburgh to the Tweed. Scotland suffered, it was said, 'plague, war, sword and fire all at once'. James IV and much of his nobility were destroyed at Flodden; at Solway Moss an army three times greater than their English opponents was scattered, and many drowned; James V died shortly afterwards. More crushingly still, at Pinkie, outside Edinburgh, in 1547, the Scots threw away a strong position at the urging of their clergy, for whom this war was one to defend Holy Church against the heretics, and their casualties were great. The victors left behind a string of garrisons the better to control the Lowlands. Part of the explanation for these disasters was that the leading families were, for much of the time, divided among themselves, from the king, and into pro-French and pro-

Soldiers of Fortune

With the increasing complexity of warfare and specialization in the use of tactics and arms, there was a growing demand in early modern Europe for a variety of military skills. These were marketable. Princes whose subjects did not possess the right mix of skills were forced to hire foreign experts; others might fear to arm their own populace (in many states the private possession of the new firearms was forbidden), who in any case might prefer to pay professionals to fight their battles for them.

The great Italian city states of the fourteenth and fifteenth centuries provided a model. They were rich enough, and their politics turbulent enough, for their rulers to wish to hire, as and when required, the protection they needed, and relieve their citizens of an unpopular duty. Just as certain towns, when danger threatened, might buy arms and armour from a centre of manufacture, so they agreed with professional contractors to supply the soldiers skilled in their use, or hired the best engineers to improve their defences. One of the most famous and successful mercenaries was the Essex man, Sir John Hawkwood, who led the famous White Company of free-lances in the service of Florence; his portrait, on the wall of the cathedral, survives to this day. Similarly, although in a very different setting, the gallowglass employed in their wars by the old Irish chieftains were in origin Highland mercenaries.

We have seen that in the sixteenth century, Henry VIII, when going to war with France, was handicapped by the shortage of firearm specialists other countries possessed. He was forced to employ mercenaries of all kinds— heavy cavalry, light skirmishing horse, crossbowmen, arquebusiers, and artillery and fortification experts from many nations. But as well as these units there were individual soldiers with the same career in mind. The soldier of fortune, as he became known in the mid-seventeenth century, was a representative figure in the warfare of the time. The 'iron century' saw conflict on a scale and duration that promised almost continuous employment for those who sought adventure, excitement, and the spoils of war, and who had little prospect of advancement at home. Regions naturally poor were often the richest in such men: in the British Isles the Welsh, prominent in Elizabeth's wars, the Scots, often in the service of the French Crown, and the Irish, the 'Wild Geese' usually fighting for Spain or other wealthy Catholic powers.

The enviable security of England, behind her wooden walls, her tiny military establishment, and long years of peaceful coexistence with her neighbours, forced many dedicated to a military career to follow in the footsteps of Sir John Hawkwood and seek their fortunes abroad. Sir John Wallop, the leading captain of Henry VIII's reign, was at various times a soldier of fortune and a pirate. With the reduction in the armies after the loss of Calais and the end of the French and Scottish wars, men like Sir John Norris, one of five famous military brothers, fought in the French religious wars, while others offered their swords to those fighting the Turk in Hungary. The famous Welsh soldier, Sir Roger Williams, fought for the Spanish as well as the Dutch in the Low Countries' wars of Elizabeth's reign.

As well as soldiers of fortune, military professionals, there were gentlemen volunteers, young men, often of high birth, who wanted a short spell of active service in foreign campaigning. It was easy enough to obtain, for military activity, like that at sea, was often a mixture of state and private enterprise, and those who had made a financial investment in an 'adventure' could join it in person; several expeditions, which involved captains-at-land as well as sailors, wore mobbed by enthusiastic gentlemen volunteers. It might be said that an early version of the later grand tour was a summer's campaigning In the Low Countries, when a gentleman might 'trail a pike' as a volunteer in one of the English or Scottish regiments in Dutch pay, or in one of the Irish units serving the Crown of Spain.

British and foreign soldiers of fortune played an important role in the conduct of the Civil War. Both sides valued the skills acquired in the Thirty Years War, and many veterans rose to high command. Fairfax had gained his experience in the Dutch Wars; the commander of the Scottish Covenanting forces, Lord Leven, in Swedish service in Germany. The king's own nephews, the Princes Rupert and Maurice, brought not only other military experts with them to England but the codes of conduct familiar enough on the Continent but till then largely unknown in England. Two Parliamentarian generals, Philip Skippon and Edward Massey, both of whom had served in the Netherlands in lowly posts, were accused by their enemies of being mercenaries who had made their names and fortunes out of the misfortunes of their fellow countrymen. At his worst the soldier of fortune could be ruthless and unprincipled. The remarkable Croatian soldier, Carlo Fantom, boasted: 'I care not for your cause: I come to fight for your half-crown and your handsome women'. He joined Parliament's forces, trained their horse, became a notable ravisher, changed sides, and was hanged—for ravishing. If the Civil War turned England into a war-torn Germany, as some have argued, these men were in part responsible.

English factions. The defeat of the French at Leith, in 1560, confirmed the supremacy of the latter, and moved Scotland thereafter into the English camp.

The Scottish borders remained turbulent throughout Elizabeth's reign. In the Highlands and Islands the Scottish Crown, like the English Crown outside the Dublin Pale, had only limited real authority over a society with its own language and customs, ruled by often warring chieftains. The lordship of the Isles was suppressed by James VI, but the ancient Gaelic institutions survived. The failure of the reformed religion, after 1560, to reach most of the Highlands, further separated them from the Lowlands. The Western Isles looked not to Edinburgh but south to Ulster, whither since medieval times the Highlanders had emigrated and where many had acted as mercenary soldiers in the incessant wars between the feuding lordships. The Gaelic term for foreign soldier was *galloglaith*, and the 'gallowglass' would become familiar to Elizabeth's soldiers fighting in Ireland later in the century.

Henry VIII's enormous ambition, and matching expenditure—from 1538 until his death in 1547 he spent over £2.5 million, equivalent to twelve times the annual revenue of his father—had achieved some success. He had secured his frontiers with the subjugation of Scotland and the creation of new coastal defences, assessed the strength and readiness of the militia, fostered native munitions industries, and given an impressive display of armed might on the borders of France. Much had been done by the hiring of foreign mercenaries, for the permanent military establishment remained small. But his conquests proved fragile. Just as the seizure and fortifying of the town of Tournai, early in his reign, was soon shown to be costly and futile, so the acquisition of Boulogne, in 1544, was only temporary. It was unfortunate for the nation's strength and reputation in arms that his death was followed by the short reigns of a minor and a woman, and the succession of another: in the eyes of the world none was fitted for leadership in war. By 1550 Boulogne and the major garrisons in Scotland were lost; German *Landsknechts* had been needed to suppress popular risings at home; and, the crowning humiliation, Calais itself fell to the French in 1558, in the closing months of Mary's reign. In England her Spanish husband was widely blamed for this disaster. With the succession of another daughter of the old king, Elizabeth, it seemed to many foreign observers that any gains made by Henry would be permanently lost, and England was in a most vulnerable position. A Spanish envoy, who had been favourably impressed by 'the Lady Elizabeth' before she ascended the throne, but who was no doubt now displeased that, unlike her sister, she seemed to be embarking on an independent line, commented sourly that the queen had 'no friends, no council, no finances, no noblemen of conduct, no captains, no soldiers, and no reputation in the world'.

Had Elizabeth died of the smallpox she caught in 1562 the nation might indeed have slid into civil disorder and religious conflict, with the strongest Catholic powers—the long Habsburg–Valois struggle having ended in 1559—deciding to take advantage of the northern heretic nation's weakness and division. Instead the queen took emergency action to secure her position, in an—as it turned out—uncharacteristic display of willingness to hazard troops, ships, and money to support her external policies. She helped the English party to power at Edinburgh and neutralized the threat from Scotland thereafter; the new fortifications of Berwick acted as a guarantee of the good behaviour of James VI, who, in spite of the execution of his mother, Mary, Queen of Scots, remained on good terms with the Government of England, in the hope, eventually realized, of his own succession to the English Crown. Having thrown the French out of Scotland she tried to wipe out the disgrace of the loss of Calais by exploiting the growing religious divisions in France to gain a presence there; but in this she was wholly unsuccessful.

It may have been this failure which persuaded her of the expense and unpredictability of warfare, and the nation's lack of adequate preparation for it. Elizabeth may have boasted that she was her father's daughter, and, standing by his portrait, invite comparisons from her courtiers, but she did not, like Henry VIII, love war and soldiering, even if her sex had permitted it. In the complexities and uncertainties which the unfolding international situation posed for the nation, many of the queen's counsellors, courtiers, and commanders, however much they differed on what action to take, were agreed on the excruciatingly dilatory, cautious, and penny-pinching approach of their sovereign, who, as Ralegh said, 'did everything by halves'. But given the flamboyance, quarrelsomeness, and extravagance of most of those who executed her commands their criticisms have not always been echoed by historians.

Elizabeth's father had been forced to rely, for the troops required for his French campaigns, on the retinues of his greatest supporters, and, given the deficiencies in English recruiting methods and soldierly skills, on expensive foreign mercenaries of all kinds. In the 1570s the Privy Council, with only the residue of the huge windfall gains made by Henry when he dissolved the monasteries, began to make better and more cost-effective use of the nation's own resources by delegating, to the most prominent and loyal individuals in every county, the power to carry out their orders for home defence, and confining the general obligation of Englishmen to serve in time of war to a selected, much smaller number of men. The new Lords Lieutenant, and their deputies, took charge of the mustering, arming, and training of these—soon to be called the trained bands—together with all the other measures necessary, such as the maintenance of beacons, the raising of the military rate, the finding of recruits for overseas expeditions, and the like. At their best, when the national mood, in time of invasion threat, was co-operative, units of the militia were regularly trained, sometimes by professional officers, and could be introduced to the new weapons, pike and musket, with some hope in due course of their being mastered. A typical county in the front line of the war from the 1580s, such as Kent or Essex, might muster 4,000 trained men. In the north a poorer region, such as Lancashire, whose defence and contribution to forces sent to Ireland were no less vital, could produce 500 trained and armed, and a further 4,000 in so-called freehold bands, a second line of defence.

Elizabeth's state was being organized for war. Her first minister, Lord Burghley, and her secretary, Sir Francis Walsingham, were the key figures in the administration, which included a network of spies. With the aid of the new county maps, themselves an important military asset, and the other pieces of information which came to him, Burghley knew where the working gentry—deputies to the Lords Lieutenant, or trained band captains—resided in each locality; how many horse and foot were available in an emergency; where the county's arms were stored; and how much the military rate could raise. The maps were the key to strategically sensitive areas, such as the Isle of Wight; the Kent and Sussex coast, and the line of beacons which constituted the Elizabethan early warning system; Ireland, always of great concern in security matters; and the Scottish borders. However efficient, in contemporary terms, the system was it depended ultimately on the willing co-operation of the unpaid office-holders, the country gentry; if the government lost that the war could not be carried on.

With home defence better ordered, when the revolt of the Netherlands forced a reluctant queen to authorize hostilities, which had been at first informal and unofficial, against Spain rather than the traditional enemy, France, the opportunities offered to Englishmen for profitable, exciting—and dangerous—active service against the common enemy were legion. Now that the Atlantic was not the outer edge of the world but the gateway to new trade routes, fisheries, colonies, and—it seemed— boundless commercial opportunities, England occupied a central position in European affairs, and her wars would be fought at sea as much as by land. As a result the exploits of the great sailors, and the defeat of the Spanish Armada, are much better known than the military successes of such 'great captains' as the Veres, the Norris brothers, and Lord Mountjoy in the Netherlands and Ireland. The latter, however, were a vital contribution to the defence of the realm. It is also worth recalling that the great expeditions, of Drake to the Caribbean, or the Earl of Essex to Cadiz, carried with them thousands of soldiers, for an assaulting and occupying force was an essential part of the operation. The earlier success in Scotland had been the result of close co-operation between both arms; it proved supremely difficult to achieve similar success on the Iberian peninsula and the Spanish main, but this was not for want of trying. The loss of life among the crowded soldiery and crew on these sea voyages was horrendous. In the Low Countries and the Caribbean English soldiers and sailors combined self-interest, Protestant zeal, and a sturdy patriotism. They also acquired an excellent training in arms, alongside the foremost warriors of the age.

Nor was the nation any longer at a severe disadvantage in the matter of arms and equipment. It was discovered that the growing iron industry of Sussex and Kent—there were fifty or so furnaces and associated works in the Weald by 1570—could produce the best quality iron ordnance in Europe. With the need to arm fleets with large numbers of guns carried broadside, and the development of both field artillery and specialist pieces for siege warfare, in which, as we have seen in the case of Henry's coastal forts, the defenders needed adequate fire-power as much as the attackers, English cast-iron cannon was highly sought after and fetched high prices abroad. For England it became a battle-winning commodity. At the same time, also in the south-eastern corner of the country, gunpowder-making was first developed as a native industry. By the time England did embark on full-scale war with the greatest power in Europe she was better equipped to sustain her war effort by land and sea.

In the course of the last two decades of the reign the nation poured out blood and treasure on an unprecedented scale. Over 200 ships voyaged to the Caribbean in search of trade and plunder during these years. When Spain launched the famous 'Invincible' Armada of 1588, the assembly of the trained bands in London and the southern counties, gathered to resist invasion, was impressive, however unrealistic their confidence, if ever they had faced Parma's veterans of the army of Flanders, might appear to historians. It has been calculated that over 100,000 men were raised for service overseas in these years, some 15 per cent of all able-bodied males in a population of less than 5 million. Some were drawn from the trained bands, the usual objections having been, in the national emergency, over-ruled. Larger numbers were pressed by the Lords Lieutenant, each region contributing to the nearest war zone: the southern counties to the Low Countries, the north-west to Ireland, the four northern counties to the defence of the Scottish border. In 1585, the major commitment, the Earl of Leicester led 6,000 men to aid the Dutch; some 500 of these were his own tenants, an echo of the now discarded reliance on baronial retinues in the new age of warfare. While their earliest exploits were almost uniformly disastrous, they grew into a formidable fighting force which was to play an important role—for example, in 1588–9 helping to preserve the key fron-tier stronghold of Bergen-op-Zoom in Zeeland—in the defence of the United Provinces, as the independent Netherlands became. The regi-ments of the Anglo-Dutch Brigade provided thereafter, even when Eng-land was at peace, experience of modern warfare for generations of English gentlemen.

The long continuance of the war ensured, for the first time for the Eng-lish, that the nation's military institutions as well as her arms production were eventually brought up to the standard of those on the Continent. The reading public was avid for news of the Low Countries, of the English contribution there, as of the tales of exploration and adventure popular-ized by Hakluyt. Almost 200 titles of war-related works were published, from military manuals to generals' memoirs. That late Renaissance influences were still at work can be gauged from the respect accorded, by public and soldiers alike, to the classical past, and the belief that those aspiring to command should be skilled in mathematics and foreign lan-guages. The polyglot and cosmopolitan nature of military art meant that the terms adopted in England for most things martial in the period were of foreign origin, from colonel to corporal, culverin (French for snake) to musket (Italian for sparrow-hawk). Translations of military works, ancient and modern, such as those of Machiavelli, were made available; but many gentlemen's libraries were furnished also with the lat-est texts in Spanish or Italian. Shakespeare's plays are full of military imagery; *Henry V* has a topical reference to the queen's favourite, Essex, going to Ireland in 1599. Long campaigns also allowed talent to rise to the top and careers to develop. Some, like Leicester, failed. Others, like Sir Francis Vere in a new key post, became the very model of a sergeant-major-general, and acquired a European reputation.

The war, already global, would extend to Ireland before the end of Elizabeth's reign. A series of ruthless and bloody guerrilla campaigns broke out into open warfare with the rebellion in 1598 of the chief of the O'Neills, the Earl of Tyrone, and the armed intervention of Spain. Elizabeth was forced to mount a major expedition, leadership of which she gave to the Earl of Essex, anxious to win the fame and fortune which had eluded him elsewhere. The first forays into this last Gaelic stronghold were disastrous. Tyrone's men had exchanged their ancient weapons for the musket, Ulster's terrain was impenetrable, and the people hostile and elusive, for even their villages were transportable. It was not until Essex was replaced by competent professional soldiers—as in the Low Countries—that success was assured. It was Lord Mountjoy who eventually achieved the renown which Vere and others had won on the Continent, defeating the rebels and their Spanish reinforcements at Kinsale in 1601.

The great cost of Elizabeth's wars was not only in money and men—the Irish war alone cost each year as much as the Crown's annual income had been before 1570—but in a growing war weariness even before her death. In the last parliament of her reign, 1601, Secretary Cecil asked for better provision for the many maimed and diseased soldiers streaming back to England from service abroad: 'War is a curse to all people, and especially the poor creatures that come from the wars poor, friendless and unhappy'. The calamities of war included, for those in authority at home, high taxation, billeting of troops, and the enforced recruitment every year of their fellow countrymen. When these coincided with harvest failure and general hardship, MPs, JPs, and local communities alike became less co-operative towards the demands of government. James VI and I, Elizabeth's successor, capitalizing on the public mood, and the fact that Spain had been exhausted by the long war as much as England had, was able and willing to make peace. The conquest of Ulster permitted the planting of English and Scots there, and a reduction in the number of government troops. The union of the Crowns meant that the garrisons of Berwick and Carlisle could be disbanded.

The run-down of the Elizabethan war machine in the years of peace and government parsimony which followed was compounded by social and political changes. The Lieutenancy and the trained bands shared in this general decay and neglect. The failure to pass a Militia Act, which

The Military Revolution

The term 'military revolution' has gained currency among some historians, to describe the changes which took place in military organization, tactics, and weaponry during this period. In one interpretation, that of Professor Michael Roberts, the historian of seventeenth-century Sweden, the important developments were those between 1560 and 1660. Armies grew much bigger and came increasingly under absolute state control, which was both a cause and a consequence of their increased size and efficiency. They became the instruments of state-building. There was a resultant loss of individuality, with the need for better organization, good training—especially in drill—and strict discipline; other tactical improvements, introduced by the great Swedish king, Gustavus Adolphus, in the Thirty Years War, capitalized on these changes.

More recently these views have been supplemented rather than challenged by Professor Geoffrey Parker, the historian of Spain. He sees the revolution taking place over a wider time span, 1550–1720, and, while accepting the thesis that increased army size is crucial to other developments, has drawn attention to another constraint removed in the period—that of finance. Parker argues that fiscal thresholds, which in the past had limited the capacity of rulers to make war, were crossed, with the development of more sophisticated credit machinery in most European states. Much more could be spent on the sport of kings—war. Parker has gone on to argue that, in a wider context, European arms developed in a manner which ensured their world supremacy when overseas expansion brought their exponents into contact with the rest of the world in the seventeenth and eighteenth centuries.

There is much that is attractive in these views, and they have proved popular, helping to simplify and make sense of complex and—to the layman—rather specialized and technical changes. But it may be doubted whether the term 'revolution' should be used of developments in the military field which take a century or two to mature. The starting-points of the revolutions each historian has suggested might be questioned, for, after the invention of gunpowder and its application to military uses in the fourteenth century, the improvement in the effectiveness of artillery and portable firearms and the matching sophistication of defensive systems (for example, Henry VIII's new coastal forts) were rapid and continuous over the whole period. The balance between offence and defence was constantly changing in the early modern world as in the modern one. No one doubts that the face of warfare in 1500 had undergone profound alteration by 1700, but by no means always in the same direction or at the same pace. Years of peace saw reductions in the size of armies, rather than a general increase; particular changes in certain countries or regions were not adopted Europe wide, so that the conduct of war remained a patchwork quilt, so to speak, rather than a uniform. And if calculations of size and expense in military matters are considered of crucial importance—which of course they are—then the big increase in Europe's population and the price of most goods during the sixteenth century will need to be fully taken into account. Measured by the standards of the fifteenth century, the number of men in arms and their cost to the government during this later period may not be so impressive. From some later perspectives, indeed, it could be argued that what most European nations experienced, in spite of the Thirty Years War and its attendant horrors, and, with overseas exploration, the prospect of widening conflicts, was a weakening of the military ethic among the ruling élite, a diminution of participation rates for the general populace, and a reduction of the proportion of national budgets devoted to the armed forces. Civilian life would in the end prove a robust competitor to the attractions of, and the need for, the military.

would update and clarify the military obligations of the subject, throughout the early Stuart period, was symptomatic of a wider malaise. Musters became less frequent, the interest in matters military declined, and the essential local positions, the backbone of the militia, were either avoided by the working gentry or suffered from being the prey of local political rivalries. The Lieutenancies became hereditary in certain aristocratic families. Official positions in the tiny military establishment, such as in the Henrician coastal forts or the palace guards, became sinecures for the socially ambitious rather than active military commands. English and Scottish soldiers seeking experience had to serve foreign masters abroad, or obtain commands in the Anglo-Dutch Brigade. Ralegh lost his head when he tried to renew the old conflicts.

The outbreak of the Thirty Years War on the Continent and the accession of Charles I, reliant on the great Duke of Buckingham, much altered the immediate circumstances, but not the underlying trends. The nation's attempts to influence the outcome of the wars were largely fruitless. The third Earl of Essex had even less success at Cadiz in 1625 than his father had had thirty years before, and even the Duke of Buckingham failed to relieve the besieged Huguenots of La Rochelle in 1627. The loss of life in these expeditions was very great: Members of Parliament were shocked by the sight of discharged sailors and soldiers dying in the streets of west country ports. Parliament made plain its discontent in the Petition of Right of 1628, which placed severe restraints on the demands which the Crown could make on the subject in time of war.

The king's attempts to reform the militia in the years when, having brought the wars to a close, he ruled without parliament, met the same opposition. Forced to recall parliament when he failed to subdue his Scottish subjects—for once united, in a National Covenant, against his Church policies—the king found that he could not accept all the demands of the 'popular party'; these included the Militia Bill, which would have given the power of the sword to the Long Parliament. Revolt in Ulster by the native Irish, and the invasion of Whitehall by London crowds—when the opprobrious terms 'Cavalier' and 'Roundhead' were first heard—led to heightened political excitement in the capital. The king withdrew to the north, and the shooting war began.

After a long period of peace the Civil War was a rude shock to most Englishmen. It was a transforming event. From a low base—a puny military establishment and a part-time militia—the leaders of both sides had to create war machines comparable to those now laying waste whole areas of the Continent. In this task Parliament had a great advantage, for in abandoning London Charles had left behind the government of the realm. John Pym, the leader of the 'popular party' in the Commons, had reformed the fiscal system just before the war, and was able to introduce the legislation needed to pay for a long war. Crucial to his success was the aid of the City of London, and the size (a third of a million population) and wealth of the capital generally. The ports, the navy, the existing stores of arms in the Tower, and the munitions industry of the south-east which it controlled, fell to the opponents of the king. Control of the sea gave them access to the arms markets of Europe and kept any major foreign intervention on behalf of the king at bay. The blockade was not complete, however, and royalist gun-runners brought arms and men, and methods, from the Continent; as a result the Civil War was fought on lines not dissimilar to the wars abroad. Harsh measures were adopted by both sides, including conscription, requisitioning ('plunder'), the seizure or destruction of enemy property, and the widespread use of fire and sword on the civilian population. This was the sense in which, it was said, 'England turned Germany' in the course of the 1640s.

Parliament's first armies were led by the Earl of Essex, the hero of the 1625 Cadiz expedition, whose family had a long history of opposition to the court. He rallied many professional soldiers to the cause. The king, however, had the support of the majority of the soldiers of fortune who flocked home from the European conflict. He appointed as the general of his cavalry—the strongest arm of the Cavaliers throughout the war—his nephew, Prince Rupert of the Rhine. If in the end the war would be won by the Roundheads' superior resources, in the first two years the king's men fought gallantly and well. In 1643 Rupert took Bristol, the second port of the realm, and in the following year Charles himself dispersed Essex's army in Cornwall. The one major victory of Parliament was in the north, the result of the alliance with the Scottish Covenanters and the emergence of a powerful cavalry under a Huntingdonshire squire, Oliver Cromwell, 'old Ironsides'; Marston Moor (July 1644) was a crushing defeat for the prince and led to the loss to the king of most of the north.

It was this military stalemate, after more than two years of intensive struggle, that prompted Parliament to reform its forces from top to bottom. Out went the old commanders, including the Earl of Essex, and all others who were MPs or peers, whose high office owed more to political influence and social rank than military merit. A 'new model' army was created from the remains of the old, with a new set of commanders, most of whom had proved themselves in the war. Sir Thomas Fairfax was made Commander-in-Chief, and Cromwell, exempted from the general purge, given command of the horse. Promotion was on merit, the best units of previous forces—like Cromwell's famous double regiment of cavalry—were preserved, and, after the City had made further loans of money, the whole army was well equipped and (for a time) well paid. The New Model Army was wholly under the control of Parliament rather than the many competing local interests which had impeded the rational deployment of the forces in the field before, and the MPs wisely decided to leave the running of the first campaign, in 1645, to the men on the spot. When this army faced that of the king at Naseby, in Northamptonshire, in June 1645, it was fully equal to its opponents in most departments (including morale) and was much superior in size. The royalists had also made the fatal mistake of underestimating the results of the sweeping reforms Parliament had accomplished. The Cavaliers' main army was destroyed; and after the New Model Army had defeated the other forces of the king in the west at Langport in the following month there remained little more to do than mop up the remaining royalist garrisons. The war was won for Parliament by 1646.

The unprecedented nature of the Civil War itself was matched by the revolutionary events which followed. Cromwell had chosen officers and men who were imbued with the same fervour as himself, radicals, often humbly born, who, as he put it, 'knew what they fought for and loved what they knew'. With the failure of the more conservative elements on the winning side to reach agreement with the king for a lasting political settlement, the New Model Army, its officers combining with representatives of the rank and file, began to make demands, at first for the payment of their arrears (good pay had not lasted long), then for some say in any projected agreement about the future. Radicals like the London Levellers and members of the Puritan sects began to exercise some influence. It was part of the astonishing novelty of the situation that ideas of religious toleration, adult male suffrage, and soldiers' rights could be fiercely debated in an army council that included ordinary soldiers. A new civil war had to erupt and a further invasion by the Scots—this time to aid Charles—had to be defeated before Cromwell and other generals, with radical support, took the final step of executing the king in January 1649.

The British Isles, which had resisted attempts to bring it into the European conflict, was now as war torn as many others; it had acquired a large standing army and was soon to increase its navy. The new republican regime was ringed by enemies abroad because of the decision to execute the king, and there was resistance in Ireland and Scotland. The first task of Cromwell, now the foremost general upholding the civilian government of the Rump (the purged House of Commons), was to quell opposition there. In three years' campaigning, from 1649 to 1651, he overcame the regime's enemies, and, with the enormous prestige he had acquired, he seized power for himself and his political and military allies in 1653. The Protectorate of Oliver Cromwell was, in origin, a military regime, in which his comrades-in-arms had clearly an important role, no more so than when, to put down royalist risings and enforce better order, he parcelled up the country into major-generalships, each with its active and inquisitive military 'dictator'. But superficial impressions are misleading. Cromwell, throughout his rule until his death in 1658, sought to gain the consent of the governed, reconcile the gentry to his leadership, reach agreement with the parliaments he persisted in calling, even when each failed his expectations, and establish a due measure of religious and political liberty. His court came to embody the most moderate elements of those who had opposed the king; his government even made use of ex-royalists. The army had been reduced to no more than half its strength, and its role was greatest, not in keeping order at home, but in seizing

Jamaica and Dunkirk from Spain in a renewal of the old conflicts of Elizabethan days.

Oliver failed, however, to reconcile the existence of a standing army,
written into the constitution on which the Protectorate had been
founded, with the low taxation that the gentry had been used to before
the Civil War. In that sense the war had never gone away, and none of the
regimes which briefly followed his death—including those in which the
old generals recaptured the power they had once enjoyed—could resolve
this dilemma. It was an independently financed regional force, under
George Monck, which, from its secure (and well-paid) base in Scotland
and purged of dangerous radicals like the Quakers, marched south to
establish law and order. Its warm reception, especially in London, encouraged its commander to recall the exiled son of the old king, and proclaim
him Charles II, to general approval, in 1660.

It is often said that the lesson of the Civil War and the Cromwellian
Interregnum is that large standing armies, the high taxes which are needed
to pay for them, military government, and ambitious generals who intervene in politics, are anathema to the British and foreign to the British
State. It was certainly the case that the monarchy of Charles II avoided,
wherever possible, the example of its predecessor, reducing the armed
forces to the smallest possible extent. Only the powerful navy of the
republic, which constituted little threat to the State, and a small residue of
the great army, to protect the royal palace (that lesson had been learned)
and England's first overseas colonies, remained. But the other side of the
coin is that, because it was seen by its neighbours to lack legitimacy and
faced great opposition within the borders of the British Isles, the republican government of England, capitalizing on the transformation of the
nation which had taken place in the Civil War, was forced to enter into a
cycle of war and conquest, whether it willed it or not. In the process, it
united the British Isles, acquired colonies and a bridgehead in Europe, and
a big military reputation. The policies of the Interregnum laid the foundations for great power status. A standing army would remain for many
years a matter of political controversy, but it proved a necessity in the
modern world, for good or ill, and there is a certain finality about the tortuous process, over 175 years, by which the nation arrived at this solution.

3 THE RESTORATION ARMY 1660–1702

JOHN CHILDS

On the return of Charles II to England in May 1660, four British armies existed. The core of the New Model Army under General George Monck was quartered in and around London; Sir William Lockhart commanded a brigade of the New Model Army in Dunkirk and Mardyke; Charles II's army of exiled Irish and royalists was also billeted in Dunkirk; and there remained the Cromwellian garrison in Ireland. Charles and his lord chancellor, the Earl of Clarendon, viewed the New Model Army in all its guises as a potential threat to the restored monarchy and set about its demolition. Between September and Christmas 1660, the New Model Army was disbanded at a cost of £835,819. 8s. 10d. leaving intact just the horse and foot regiments of Monck, now elevated to the dukedom of Albemarle. In Dunkirk and Mardyke, Lockhart's brigade of the New Model Army and the army of exiled royalists were merged into an unhappy garrison of 6,600 men; the old royalists were formed into a regiment of foot guards under Lord Wentworth and the small number of cavalrymen were amalgamated into the Duke of York's troop of Life Guards. In October 1662, Charles II sold Dunkirk to Louis XIV of France for 5 million *livres*. Wentworth's Guards returned to England to join the 1st Foot Guards, York's Horse went into the French army as a mercenary formation, and the regiments from the New Model Army were sent to fight in Tangier and Portugal.

Charles favoured the foundation of a new army under royal control and was working towards an 'intended establishment' as early as August 1660. He realized that one of the causes of his father's political weakness in 1641 and 1642 had been his lack of a reliable coercive force. In addition, the restored regime was unstable and, in some quarters, deeply unpopular. A large army was out of the question as Charles had insufficient money but a military royal household of 'guards and garrisons' to protect the royal person and the key points of the kingdom was both feasible and realistic. The obvious model was the Maison du Roi of Louis XIV although on a much smaller scale. On 23 November 1660, Colonel John Russell formed the 1st Foot Guards, later known as the Grenadier Guards, consisting of twelve companies each of 100 men. In the aftermath of Samuel Venner's Fifth Monarchist rising in London in January 1661, Monck's regiment of foot was re-engaged in the royal service as the 2nd Foot, or Coldstream, Guards. Some cavalry was required to complement the infantry. Charles had enjoyed the services of a Life Guard of eighty men during his exile and this had been augmented to 600 on his return to England. After attending the king at his coronation, 200 were 'retired' and the remaining 400 sent to Dunkirk. Venner's insurrection caused this force to be withdrawn into England, expanded to 500 men, and formed into three troops of Life Guards.

Cromwell's old Life Guard of Horse was reformed as the cadre for the Royal Horse Guards, the Blues. These four regiments and a smattering of garrison companies cost the king £122,407. 15s. 10d. per annum, roughly 10 per cent of the king's annual income which had been awarded by parliament.

From these modest beginnings, the peacetime Restoration army steadily grew in size. By the end of Charles's reign in February 1685 there were 7,472 men in marching regiments and 1,393 permanently stationed in the garrisons. The Duke of Monmouth's rebellion in 1685 allowed James II to augment his standing forces to 19,778. The emergency created by William III of Orange's invasion in November 1688 saw the army grow to a paper strength of 34,320 soldiers. Naturally, during the time of Charles II the peacetime establishment had been greatly enlarged on a number of occasions to deal with wars and threats of wars. The army increased to over 20,000 during the Second and Third Anglo-Dutch Wars (1665–7 and 1672–4) and to around 37,000 in 1678 when England participated in the closing stage of the Franco-Dutch War (1672–8). In May 1689, England declared war on France and joined the Grand Alliance. Immediately, to deal with war in Ireland, Scotland, and the Low Countries, the army was expanded to 73,692 rising to 93,635 in 1694. After the Peace of Rijswijk (Ryswick) in 1697, parliament hacked the army down to a cadre of 7,000 men.

Scotland and Ireland enjoyed separate military establishments after the Restoration although they became unofficially merged with the English

Tangier

Tangier had been a Portuguese colony since 1471. It came into the hands of Charles II, along with Bombay, in 1661 as part of the dowry of Catherine of Braganza and it soon became evident that Alfonso VI had not been generous. Although superficially attractive as a base for the Levant trade, Tangier lay to the west of the Pillars of Hercules on the stormy Atlantic coast rather than within the sheltered Mediterranean. To make it an operational harbour, an artificial mole had to be constructed but, despite twenty years of effort, it was never finished, the engineers encountering insuperable problems. Worse, Tangier was surrounded by high land, a spur of the foothills of the Atlas Mountains, enabling the warring Moorish factions who controlled Morocco to overlook the town. Fortunately, when the 3,000-strong British garrison arrived on 29 January 1662 under the command of Henry Mordaunt, second Earl of Peterborough, the local Moorish leader, Abd Allah Ghailan, was involved in a war with the 'Saint of Sallee', the ruler of the pirate den at Salé.

Ghailan, who regarded Tangier as part of his own territories, soon attacked the interlopers. The rugged ground aided the Moorish ambushes and surprise attacks where cold steel was more effective than firearms. On numerous occasions their tactics unnerved the newcomers; the Portuguese had usually been able to deal with their primitive opponents but only because they had made few attempts to extend their authority beyond the town walls. The poor fighting performance of the British was partly explained by the internal tensions resulting from the explosive mixture of old soldiers from the New Model Army, ex-royalists from the Dunkirk garrison, and Irish Catholics. There were never enough commissioned officers and discipline rapidly deteriorated. The health of the troops was poor, the death-rate high, and morale permanently low. As there was no system of reliefs, the men regarded a posting to Tangier as a death sentence. The diet of the troops was appalling, all food having to come from England. Pay was often nine months in arrears and there was such a shortage of men during the 1670s that the entire garrison had to be placed on double duty in order to build the mole, unload ships, police the town, and man the defences. Mutinies occurred throughout the occupation and many soldiers were so desperate that they deserted to the Moors where certain slavery awaited them. The only means of lightening the gloom was alcohol, 'liberally taken by all sorts as an antidote to drive away sorrow'. Drunkenness was the scourge of Tangier.

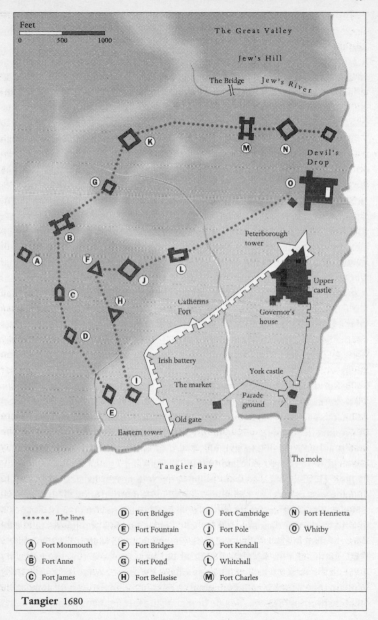

The Restoration Army 1660–1702

Feet
0   500   1000

The Great Valley

Jew's Hill

The Bridge   Jew's River

K

M   N   Devil's Drop

G   O

B

A   F

C   J   L   Peterborough tower

H   Upper castle

Catherina Fort   Governor's house

Irish battery

I   York castle

E   The market   Parade ground

Old gate

Eastern tower   The mole

Tangier Bay

•••••• The lines   (D) Fort Bridges   (I) Fort Cambridge   (N) Fort Henrietta

(E) Fort Fountain   (J) Fort Pole   (O) Whitby

(A) Fort Monmouth   (F) Fort Bridges   (K) Fort Kendall

(B) Fort Anne   (G) Fort Pond   (L) Whitchall

(C) Fort James   (H) Fort Bellasise   (M) Fort Charles

Tangier 1680

The size of the garrison diminished rapidly. This was due to the difficulty in finding recruits and by the need for the government to economize. In 1672, the paper establishment was reduced to 1,630 although the garrison mustered only 1,215 men. When fraud, casualties, and sickness are taken into account, throughout the later 1670s the garrison actually numbered no more than 700 effective men. In response to the serious Moorish attacks of 1679 and 1680, the garrison was reinforced to 3,221 in 1681 but this had fallen to 2,299 by the evacuation in 1684.

When Andrew Rutherford, Earl of Teviot, assumed the governorship, he immediately improved the defences. He realized that the key to Tangier lay in controlling the overlooking heights. During his governorship (1663–4) he built five forts and redoubts beyond the city walls, covered by the main artillery along the curtain. Subsequent governors—Sir Tobias Bridge (1664), John Fitzgerald (1664–5), John, Lord Bellasise (1665–7), and Henry Norwood (1667–9)—extended the fortifications to form two rings, the forts and blockhouses connected by trenches, breastworks, and palisades, known as the 'lines'. The largest of the works, Fort Charles, had four bastions and could accommodate a garrison of 300 men; the smallest, Devil's Drop, was a crude earthwork housing a dozen soldiers. These 'insignificant' fortifications, the work of Sir Bernard de Gomme, the surveyor-general and engineer-general of the English ordnance office, were poorly designed. In 1683, a commission recommended that a sum of £4,798,561. 16s. 6d. was required to make Tangier defensible. This was enough to persuade Charles II to abandon the town.

A series of reverses were suffered during the occupation. Under Peterborough's pusillanimous command (1662–4) the garrison allowed itself to be locked within the town following the defeat of Major Nathaniel Fiennes. A dynamic leadership was required and this was provided by Teviot until he overreached himself and was killed in 1664 when his reconnaissance party was cut off on Jew's Hill. Intermittent skirmishing continued throughout the 'peace' (1666–9) but thereafter a constant state of war existed, although the fighting was generally small-scale. By 1677, the internal state of Morocco had stabilized sufficiently for the emperor in Marrakesh to turn against Tangier. A night attack on 7 January 1678 wrecked Forts Kendall and Henrietta but the Moors failed to exploit their success. However, on 25 March 1680, an army of 7,000 men under the Alcaide of Alcazar began systematic attacks against the forts on the western side of the lines where the defences lacked depth. Using modern techniques taught by an English deserter who had served at the siege of Maastricht in 1673, the Alcaide breached the fortifications within one month but a sortie by the entire garrison on 27 October 1680 drove back the Moors and led to a 'lasting peace' on 29 March 1681. But the old lines and forts had been lost, the mole was unfinished, and Tangier drained the royal revenues to no obvious purpose. Early in 1684, it was evacuated. Although no one mourned Tangier's passing, the potential mercantile and military benefits of a naval base near the mouth of the Mediterranean were not forgotten. Gibraltar was captured in 1704 and retained at the Peace of Utrecht in 1714.

army during the Nine Years War (1688–97). The Cromwellian garrison of Ireland declared its allegiance to Charles II in 1660 but it was too large for peacetime purposes and partially disbanded. The Restoration army in Ireland was mainly officered by ex-Cromwellians and loosely organized; it was not even regimented until 1672. During Charles II's reign, its establishment averaged 7,500 rising to 8,644 in 1685. During the reign of James II, the Duke of Tyrconnell, in his capacity as Lord Lieutenant and Lieutenant-General of the Irish army, removed most of the Protestant officers and men and replaced them with Catholics as part of a general policy to Catholicize the government and institutions of Ireland. When William of Orange invaded England in 1688, Tyrconnell led the Irish army in a rebellion against the government of the English in Dublin which, initially, was hugely successful in reducing the Protestant forces to the garrisons of Enniskillen and Londonderry. James II joined Tyrconnell in Ireland in March 1689. The Jacobite Irish army had an establishment strength of 36,000 in 1689, 45,000 in 1690, and 30,500 in 1691 but the effective strengths were probably not much more than half of these totals. The Treaty of Limerick, which ended the Jacobite War in September 1691, disbanded the Jacobite army sending 12,000 of its members to France to form a private army for the exiled James II. The remainder of the Jacobite troops were transferred to Williamite allegiance and then disbanded. Thereafter, the Irish army resumed its Protestant hue and returned to its role as the English army of occupation. In 1697 it was fixed at a peacetime strength of 12,000 men. The Scottish army was minute. Even during the campaign against the Covenanters in 1678–9 it only numbered 2,754 and its strength in 1685 was 2,199. During the reign of William III, it became increasingly combined with the English establishment.

As well as the armies in England, Ireland, and Scotland, Charles II employed numerous corps on foreign service. A British brigade fought with the Portuguese army in their war for independence from Spain between 1662 and 1668 and a corps fought in the French army from 1672 to 1674. Some of these troops remained in French service until the end of the Franco-Dutch War in 1678. A mixed Scottish and English force had served in the Dutch army since 1585. Following its re-formation in 1674, the three English and three Scottish regiments of the Anglo-Dutch Brigade recruited in Great Britain until their amalgamation with the English army in 1688 and 1689. Technically, the Anglo-Dutch Brigade was a part of the British army on permanent loan to the Stadtholder of the United Provinces. Individuals and formed units, especially from Ireland, fought as mercenaries in the French army, the Spanish army, the Imperial armies, and the Swedish and Russian services. Small bodies of British troops garrisoned the colonies of the West Indies and North America as well as Bombay until it was sold to the East India Company in 1668. However, the major overseas station was Tangier.

The army belonged to the king. In peacetime, a standing army was unknown to English statute law and the army was not knowingly recognized by parliament. The army was commanded by the king and ranked as a department of the royal household. It was accordingly directed by the king's ministers and nominees. Until his death in 1670, the day-to-day affairs of the army were run by Albemarle in his rank of Lord General but, thereafter, no individual was to achieve such prominence in the army until Marlborough during the reign of Queen Anne. Charles's bastard son, the Duke of Monmouth, was appointed Captain-General of the expedition against France in 1678 but he then dabbled with the cause of Exclusion and was dismissed. After 1670, the civilian secretaries of state administered the army and exercised political control on behalf of the sovereign; in peacetime, these two politicians effectively commanded the army. A lower tier of civilian officials and staff officers managed the various departments of which the most important was the secretaryship at war. Sir William Clarke and Mathew Locke were merely clerks to the Commander-in-Chief, when such existed, their principal task being to issue marching orders. William Blathwayt extended the functions of the office to cover virtually all aspects of routine administration excluding those relating to finance—the issue of marching orders, the registration of commissions, billeting instructions, regimental precedence, and standing orders. Blathwayt created the first War Office although he remained a relatively junior subordinate of the secretaries of state. Army pay was the concern of the paymaster-general, a lucrative office from the profits of which

Sir Stephen Fox built Holland House in London and Richard Jones, first Earl of Ranelagh, amassed huge sums by naked fraud. The commissary-general of the musters worked closely with the paymaster-general to make sure that pay was only issued to effective soldiers. The medical service was administered by a surgeon-general, a physician-general and an apothecary-general. The task of the judge-advocate-general was more complex.

As the army was not recognized within the law, its own code of internal discipline, the Articles of War, first issued in 1663, had no legal power before the courts. The Articles could only function as the rules of a private club. This meant that specifically military offences, such as disobedience or desertion, had to be represented as felonies if they were to be punished according to English law. This was extremely difficult to achieve. What tended to happen was that purely military offences within the army were adjudged before courts-martial according to the Articles, but offenders could only be punished by stoppages from pay, suspension, or dismissal. If a civilian was involved then the case could usually be brought before a law court and legal punishments exacted. Only if martial law had been declared through the use of the royal suspending power could the army properly try and punish its own personnel. This state of affairs was most unsatisfactory, especially during James II's reign when it proved awkward to punish the considerable number of desertions which occurred after 1685. The legal affairs of the army were not put on a regular footing until the passing of the Mutiny Act. This recognized the legal existence of both the standing army and its court-martial, permitting the latter to extend punishments to the taking of life and limb for certain offences according to the Articles of War. However, the importance of the Mutiny Act should not be overstated. It was passed in 1689 during a time of national emergency when the loyalty of the armed forces was split between the new regime and the old. The Mutiny Act did not give permanent parliamentary sanction to the existence of a standing army in peacetime nor did it specifically make the Articles of War into a recognized legal code. When the Mutiny Act lapsed between 1698 and 1701 it did not adversely affect military discipline. However, the Mutiny Act gained importance during William III's reign as parliament found it a convenient device for annually regulating the affairs and abuses of the army. When on service overseas the British army was disciplined by the full rigour of martial law as described in the Articles of War.

England's new standing army emerged at an important point in European political development. Across Europe, the century of religious wars

(*c.*1567–1648) had encouraged the growth of the nation-state characterized by a strong, centralized, monarchical government allied closely to the
nobility and the Church. One of the hallmarks of this absolutism was the
emergence of the national standing army. France, Sweden, Denmark,
Russia, Spain, Savoy, Austria, and a host of small Germanic states within
the Holy Roman Empire adopted regular armed forces in peacetime after
1648 and used them to assist in the process of unifying and subjugating
their territories. The upkeep of the new armies necessitated sharp increases in taxation which, simultaneously, led to the maturation of bureaucratic methods of government capable of exacting and administering
the augmented revenues. Armies became the principal concern of many
governments consuming the majority of state revenues. England was not
foreign to these trends. Her own Civil Wars (1642–6 and 1648) had resulted in regicide and a succession of unpopular governments, all of which
rested heavily upon the support and co-operation of the New Model
Army. Indeed, most of the political, religious, and financial events between 1646 and 1660 had occurred because of the difficulties in providing
pay for the New Model Army. After 1660, Charles II clearly saw a standing army as an instrument capable of enhancing the battered edifice of
monarchical rule. However, Charles's condition differed from that of his
European cousins.

In the first place, he had very little money and the English constitution
insisted that the Crown could only raise additional revenue through parliament. Armies were very expensive. Secondly, the whole experience of
the Civil Wars and the Interregnum had left both the English political
élite and much of the public with a profound distaste for armies and a
sharp nose for any whiff of military involvement in civil government.
These sensitivities were exacerbated by Francophobia and concerns over
religion. Roman Catholicism was perceived as a threat to the social, political, and economic position of the Anglican aristocracy and gentry and
they were perpetually on their guard against the infiltration of popery into
government. Charles II was suspected of being a closet papist and his
brother and heir, James, Duke of York, was publicly revealed as a Catholic
in 1673. Much of this anti-Catholicism was closely related to a fear of
France. Louis XIV was absolutist, aggressive, and Catholic. After the over-
ture of the War of Devolution (1667–8), French armies invaded the Dutch
Republic in 1672 and overran five of the seven provinces within six weeks.
Charles II's known predilection for France and suspected Catholicism
made parliament increasingly wary after 1672. The country majority in

the Lords and Commons suspected Charles of attempting to subvert parliament and govern England through a Catholic absolutism bolstered by a strong standing army. At the termination of the Anglo-Dutch Wars in 1667 and 1674 there were deep concerns that Charles would not disband his additional troops but would retain them in order to suppress parliament and rule by the sword. In 1678, Charles actually diverted the money voted by parliament to disband the wartime levies at the end of the Franco-Dutch War to keep his extra forces on foot. Although this was probably a reaction to the uncertain diplomatic conditions on the Continent, this was not fully explained to the Commons. However, with the onset of the Popish Plot and the Exclusion crisis, Charles had to retreat and a second Disbandment Act provided funds to remove the military danger. Whether Charles ever really intended to govern with his army remains equivocal but he gave this impression on several occasions. Parliament was also aware that the garrison of Tangier, the Anglo-Dutch Brigade, and the corps in France between 1672 and 1678 constituted a substantial overseas reserve which Charles could call upon to reinforce his troops in England. The enigmatic and secretive royal policies towards religion and France also heightened suspicion.

Although this fear of the new army revolved mainly around the polarities of France and Catholicism, it was assisted by the role of the army in everyday society. Restricted to revenues from pre-industrial economies, governments in western Europe were unable to afford both armies and large bands of civilian employees to assess and gather taxes and maintain law and order. Given the choice, nearly all governments adopted armies as they were capable of executing both military and civilian functions. The British army acted as a national and local police force. Cavalry patrolled the highways to apprehend highwaymen and footpads, footsoldiers escorted mercantile convoys along the main roads, soldiers protected the royal theatres, whilst horsemen uprooted illegal tobacco crops in the West Country. Soldiers also fought fires, repaired roads and bridges, guarded prisoners, and controlled both urban and rural riots. The army was also the major component in the coercive power of the monarchy—it enforced the Conventicle Acts, suppressed religious dissent in Scotland, and protected the Crown during the Exclusion crisis. If the political aims of the Crown were suspect then the army was automatically guilty by association. The army also harboured a number of Catholics, mostly old royalists commissioned at the Restoration. Although many were removed by the Test Act of 1673, numbers lurked in Tangier and foreign stations.

Parliament's ghosts became realities under James II. He wanted religious toleration for his Catholic subjects but in order to do this he had to overcome the national antipathy towards his own religion. The only enduring method of achieving this was through the parliamentary repeal of the Test Acts and the Elizabethan Penal Laws, a procedure which required James to trample on the political, social, and religious privileges of the Anglican gentry and aristocracy to such an extent that when William of Orange invaded in 1688 support for the legitimate monarch was slow to materialize. James also wanted to strengthen the central government by reducing the power and independence of the counties and the major towns, a continuation of his brother's policies. In reaching for both these ends, James employed his army extensively. The unsuccessful insurrection by the Duke of Monmouth in 1685 gave James the excuse to increase the army to nearly 20,000 men whilst the poor performance of the shire militias presented him with the justification for using the army more widely in the maintenance of local law and order. James also altered the complexion of the officer corps. During his brother's reign, the peacetime army had been officered by the sons of gentlemen and aristocrats, those who had a stake in the political and religious welfare of the kingdom. Career, professional soldiers mostly served abroad on foreign service stations, particularly Tangier, France, and in the Anglo-Dutch Brigade, returning to take up temporary commissions when the home forces were expanded for war. On the conclusion of peace, they departed overseas. In order to officer his expanded army, James brought a considerable number of these professionals, some of them Catholic and many of them Irish, on to the English peacetime establishment.

Simultaneously, many of the aristocratic and gentry officers were either dismissed from the service or resigned in protest at James's religious attitudes. The resultant army was more plebeian, commanded by officers who had few interests in the country and who depended utterly upon the king for career and advancement. James created an ideal instrument to use in his search for increasing governmental authority and extending religious toleration. The army was employed to persuade towns to surrender their charters, to assist at elections, and to support the work of the Commission for Ecclesiastical Causes. Dragoons were quartered on the 'factious' Lancashire towns of Lancaster, Liverpool, Preston, Warrington, and Ormskirk in 1685 whilst the 'honest town of Wigan' was spared. St Albans, Gloucester, Bristol, Hull, Huntingdon, Warwick, Carlisle, and the City of London all suffered the heavy hand of deliberate quartering to enforce political requests. It began to resemble the *dragonades* of Louis XIV against the Huguenots.

The Glorious Revolution abruptly terminated these developments. William III and Mary were Protestant and the former was far more interested in using British resources to prosecute his war with France than in attempting to extend royal authority in England. Indeed, by the winter of 1693–4 he was so desperate for more British troops, ships, and money that he was prepared to secure them by selling some of his prerogatives. The Statute of Rights declared that a standing army in peacetime was only legal with the consent of parliament. That single clause removed the standing army from the royal household and placed it firmly under the control of parliament making it a national institution. In 1690, parliament began a process which, by 1697, had emasculated the fiscal independence of the monarchy. Both constitutionally and financially, the Crown could no longer employ the army as its own political tool; the British army was now destined to be the servant of parliament. However, it would be inaccurate artificially to contract the pace of this development. Anti-militarism, arising from the Civil Wars, Cromwell, France, and James II, was exceptionally strong and well developed and coloured English civil–military relations until the appearance of mass conscript armies in the twentieth century. When the Peace of Rijswijk brought the Nine Years' War to a close in 1697, parliament whittled the wartime army down to 10,000 men and then 7,000 (although a further 17,000 were allowed for Ireland and elsewhere overseas), and allowed the Mutiny Act to lapse, still fearful of the political possibilities presented by a peacetime standing army. However, in reality the danger was over. If it had not been for William of Orange's intervention in English affairs in November 1688, an intervention which was motivated by European rather than English concerns, it is quite conceivable that James II and his army might have wrought a marked change in the direction of English political and religious development. Whatever the political and social arguments for discounting the importance of the Glorious Revolution, 1688 brought a profound and lasting alteration in the relations between the Crown, parliament, and the army.

Two additional aspects of military life further encouraged popular anti-militarism. Soldiers were very poorly paid. A line infantryman received 8 *d.* per day and a foot guardsman was given 10 *d.* In Ireland, the equivalent rates were 6 *d.* and 8 *d.* From this miserable sum, his captain deducted daily 'off reckonings' of 2 *d.* to meet the costs of his uniform, accoutrements,

The Army and The Glorious Revolution

To bring the Duke of Monmouth's rebellion crashing to defeat on Sedgemoor (5–6 July 1685), James II augmented the English army from 8,865 men to 15,710. By 31 December 1685, it had increased to 19,778. In contravention of the Test Acts, James commissioned a number of Catholics because, he said, insufficient qualified Protestants were available. For the remainder of James's reign (1685–8), roughly 10 per cent of the English officer corps were Roman Catholics. Perhaps 1,000 soldiers followed the same faith. As James ruefully remarked to his Dutch guards before his final flight to France on 22 December 1688, 'in his whole army of eighteen thousand men he believed that he had not a thousand Roman Catholics, "and your army, much inferior, hath two-thirds of my religion so cried out against" '.

The desertion of elements of the British army to the Dutch invaders in 1688 cannot be blamed upon the mass employment of Catholics. However, religion did play some part in determining the army's behaviour. Generally, officers who demonstrated overt dislike of James's religious policies were dismissed or obliged to resign. Some, like Thomas Talmash, took service in the Dutch Republic.

Commissions were the vital element in explaining the army's conduct. Commissions were property. They represented a marketable financial investment in a military career. Any threat to the ownership of a commission was an attack on the property of the individual. Unfortunately for James, most of the policies designed to further religious toleration infringed the rights of property in the Anglican Church, the universities, the militia, local government, and the army. As James recruited his English forces, he commissioned numbers of professional officers, many of whom had previously worked as mercenaries on foreign service. Men such as Charles Trelawney, Percy Kirke, Sir John Lanier, and Thomas Langston relied upon their military salaries, the perquisites of command and investment in commissions; their careers depended upon royal patronage. For them, dismissal usually meant a return to the uncertainties of mercenary service abroad. As a consequence, James's army, unlike that of his brother, had a far more plebeian officer corps. In Ireland, between 1685 and 1688, Richard Talbot, the Earl of Tyrconnell, removed virtually all the Protestant officers and men from the army and replaced them with Catholics. Rumours spread around the Hounslow training camp in the summer of 1688, that a similar purge was about to occur in the English army, caused a number of worried commission-holders to band together into the Association of Protestant Officers.

The army suffered from other ailments. As dissatisfaction with James's religious policies spread, Lieutenant-Colonel John Beaumont and five colleagues, the 'Portsmouth Captains', protested about the forcible inclusion of Irish soldiers in the ranks of the Duke of Berwick's foot. When news of the acquittal of the Seven Bishops reached Hounslow Camp it was greeted with shouts and cheers. 'It is nothing,' said the Earl of Feversham, James's Commander-in-Chief, 'only the soldiers rejoicing at the acquittal of the bishops.' 'Nothing', said James, 'you call that nothing?', and left the camp in a foul temper muttering, 'Tant pis pour eux, tant pis pour eux'. In fact, the naïve loyalty which tied the soldiers to the Anglican bishops was not a danger to James; that same naïve loyalty would turn against the Dutch invader in 1688 but amongst the more politically sophisticated officers it was a different matter.

Through the invitation of the 'Immortal Seven' and information from his own agents, William III, Prince of Orange, knew about, and was determined to exploit, the condition of the English officer corps in order to assist his intervention in English politics. If he could foment desertion in the army then James would be left helpless and William would be able to achieve the ideal of a bloodless invasion in which he could represent himself as a deliverer of England from popery to camouflage the reality that he was simply an armed invader. Through the Association of Protestant Officers, contacts in the Anglo-Dutch Brigade, and the Treason Club which met at the Rose Tavern in Covent Garden, William entwined an army conspiracy with plots in the north of England, the navy, and the household of the Princess Anne of Denmark. John and Sarah Churchill, Earl and Countess of Marlborough after 1689, were key figures in linking the various clandestine strands. Sums of money were also involved. The scheme called for certain officers to load their commands over to William as soon as he landed in England. In the event, although Lord Cornbury, John Beaumont, and Thomas Langston succeeded in deserting, they took few of their soldiers. However, such was James's irresolution that these few desertions were sufficient to make him lose confidence in his army and decide not to stand on Salisbury Plain. If James had determined to fight, the majority of his army would have cheerfully and loyally obeyed. The conspiracy might have failed to realize all its expectations, yet it achieved enough to shatter James and ensure that William was effectively unopposed as he marched eastwards. Once James had decided to withdraw to London, numerous officers hastened to join the invader. As the royal army straggled back along the Thames Valley, desertions escalated until only 4,000 out of the

original 30,000 troops who had concentrated at Salisbury trickled into the can-
tonment between Windsor and Uxbridge. There, on the orders of King James,
they were disbanded by the Earl of Feversham. In order to make use of the English army for his projected war with France, Prince William had to initiate a
complete reorganization.

---

and sword. This left subsistence money, which was supposed to be inviolate, from which the soldier found his food and lodging. By William III's
reign, the subsistence money was eaten into by the poundage payable to
the paymaster-general who took one shilling from every pound of army
pay as a perquisite; one day's full pay for the upkeep of Chelsea Hospital;
a fee to the clerk of the pells; 1s. 5d. a year to the regimental agent; 6d. a year
to the commissary-general of the musters; and further deductions for
drummers' coats, drums, the drum-major, escorting recruits, offerings to
the judge-advocate-general, and exchange rate commission. By the 1690s,
the soldier was lucky if he had 4d. a day in subsistence money. No one
could live on such a pittance, especially as the state only furnished accommodation and food on campaign overseas when bread was provided; even
then, 1¼d. was deducted from the subsistence pay as 'bread money'.
Dragoons and cavalrymen were better paid as they were usually drawn
from higher social categories but, from their daily wages of 1s. 6d. and 2s.
6d. respectively, they had to care for their mounts as well as themselves and
they were also subject to the racket of 'off-reckonings'. With little or no
money in their pockets, soldiers reacted in two ways. Many were unruly,
refused to pay for quarters, and behaved like armed thugs. Their officers,
knowing well both the origin and insolubility of the problem, were often
less than severe in imposing discipline. Indeed, during James II's reign indiscipline was encouraged to render the *dragonades* more effective. The
second and more common reaction was for the soldiers to take on paid
work in their spare time. In towns and cities, soldiers worked at their
trades or as labourers, whilst in the countryside they helped with the harvest and other seasonal agricultural employment. Some ran taverns and
alehouses. In this way, soldiers managed to supplement their income to
produce a better standard of living. On active service overseas, especially
in the Low Countries during the Nine Years War, the soldiers continued
with their moonlighting particularly during winter quarters, the British
troops usually wintering in the large towns of Flanders—Bruges, Ghent,
Ostend, and Nieuport. There was also a substructure of additional pay-

ments to troops in the field which are not recorded in the official establishments and pay returns. Substantial bribes were given to volunteers who worked in the trenches during sieges; grenadiers and 'forlorn hopes' who led attacks were heavily remunerated (and liberally dosed with drink); soldiers who worked on the building of fortifications, roads, and bridges were paid additional wages; officers employed many of their men as servants or to run errands; and recruiting parties received extra pay plus expenses.

The acquisition of civilian employment was made easier by the final cause of anti-militarism—billeting. There were some barracks in England, mostly in fortresses—Berwick, Portsmouth, Dover, Plymouth, Hull—but there were never enough for the steadily rising military establishment. During Charles's reign, the majority of the infantry were stationed in the garrisons whilst the cavalry were housed in small towns and villages mostly in the Home Counties and East Anglia. However, the expansion of the army between 1685 and 1694 meant that both the foot and the horse had to be billeted across the length and breadth of England. In 1686 William Blathwayt compiled a list of all available public beds and stables in England and Wales to act as a guide for quartermasters. The Petition of Right of 1628 declared it illegal to quarter soldiers on civilians without their consent, a sentiment which was reinforced by the Disbanding Act of 1679. Technically, soldiers had to be lodged in public houses but, in practice, this was often impossible. Blathwayt's list suggested 20,000 public beds, grossly inadequate when the army expanded for war, whilst many were situated in strategically unsuitable locations. The only solution was to billet soldiers on private householders after gaining their consent. This was frequently no more than a formality resulting in a further souring of civil–military relations. Even worse, it was often impossible for householders to oblige the impoverished soldiers to pay for their quarters. Barracks were more plentiful in Ireland and Scotland but here they served as military control posts in occupied countries.

Through their billeting arrangements, the majority of regiments and battalions were broken up into packets of four or five men to each billet. Battalions and companies could be spread between a number of villages making control, discipline, and unit cohesion difficult to maintain. Much responsibility rested on the non-commissioned officers rather than on their commissioned colleagues. However, such an arrangement greatly assisted the soldiers in finding part-time work. In 1697 the government showed some interest in a scheme to build a network of barracks across

England and Wales for the peacetime guards and garrisons to reduce the military burden on civilian society but it collapsed on the grounds of expense. This was the crux of the problem. The State wanted the services and flexibility of a standing army whilst it lacked the resources and administrative machinery for its support. As a result, soldiers worked and lived as civilians whilst their officers were entrusted with the task of running the army for the State in return for a host of semi-legal frauds and perquisites. Effectively, the army was rented to its officers who undertook to recruit, clothe, train, and pay their men on behalf of the State. The *quid pro quo* was that the State interfered as little as possible in the army's internal financial affairs allowing the officers to turn the army into a profitable business. There was supposed to be a British standing army in this period; *de facto* it was a territorial force.

The enormous increase in military expenditure after 1689 made no other solution possible. The English army and the Tangier garrison cost Charles II £257,796. 8s. 4d. in 1661 and although that basic figure fluctuated annually Charles was still spending only £283,775. 6s. 10d. on all his military commitments in 1684. James II's augmented establishment in 1685 cost £620,322. 17s. 11d. and his engorged army in 1688 would have cost £900,252 had it been retained for a full twelve months. Between November 1688 and October 1691, the army alone cost £3,481,585. 6s. 7¼d. and from 1692 to 1697 its average annual cost was £2,600,000. Between 1689 and 1699, £10 million were raised for the army's pay and contingencies, £4 million for its clothing, and £3 million for its transportation. During the same period, the navy cost £33 million. These vast sums had to be found by increased taxation and a revolution in the machinery by which the State borrowed money and serviced its debts. Whereas Charles II had spent around 20 per cent of his revenues on the army and James II around 33 per cent, the total military expenditure by William III during the Nine Years War far exceeded the State's revenues and could only be financed by long-term borrowing.

Recruiting was relatively easy in the aftermath of the Restoration as many from the New Model Army and the old royalist armies sought re-engagement. Thereafter, until 1685, the demand for recruits was low except during the expansions for war. Between 1685 and 1697, greatly increased numbers of recruits were required and the army had grave difficulties in filling its rolls. All recruits were supposed to be volunteers, a stipulation that was generally respected in the cavalry and the dragoons. However, in the infantry the press-gang was not unknown and professional recruiters, or 'crimpers', kidnapped men from the streets and then sold them to recruiting parties. In Scotland in the winters of 1693–4 and 1696–7, the Scottish Privy Council gave each town, city, and shire a quota of recruits to be raised. The local justices of the peace were made responsible for collection and failure to produce sufficient men was fined at a rate of £24 (Scots) per man. In England, after 1695, minor criminals were sentenced to service in the army or offered enlistment in lieu of a more severe sentence, and serving prisoners were granted their freedom if they volunteered. Many of the 'volunteers' were so enthusiastic that they had to be locked in local goals or the Tower of London until they were shipped to Flanders. Troops destined for the West Indies were interned on the Isle of Wight before embarkation in order to reduce desertion. In 1693, the Attestation Procedure was introduced via the Mutiny Act in an attempt to ensure that only genuine volunteers found their way into the infantry. However, it did little to stop the illegal traffic in 'volunteers'. In peacetime, with generous enlistment bounties and opportunities for part-time work, the army presented a more attractive image and experienced few difficulties in filling its ranks. However, in wartime, faced with the prospect of service in Flanders or certain death from disease in the West Indies, there was always a dearth of recruits.

The officers acted as the agents between the Crown and its army. As the army was a business as well as a career it followed that commissions were bought and sold. Commissions in regiments raised in wartime and liable to disbandment on the conclusion of hostilities were relatively cheap, colonelcies costing £1,000–2,000. An ensign might buy a place for £200. However, in guards regiments and other formations likely to survive a disbandment, prices were much higher, £12,000 when the Earl of Albemarle bought the captaincy of the 1st Troop of the Life Guard in 1699. Purchase provided a career structure and a rudimentary pension system, although it did lead to promotion through the purse rather than on merit. Oddly enough, this was not a problem during this period. Charles's army was small but sufficient places were available in Tangier, the Anglo-Dutch Brigade, the corps in France and Portugal, and other foreign service stations to ensure that competent officers without substantial means could follow a successful military career. James expanded his army bringing these gentlemen on to the English and Irish establishments by the creation of new regiments in which commissions were cheap whilst reasonably priced commissions were readily available throughout the Nine Years' War. Battle casualties also improved the prospects of the impecunious officer. After the disbandment in 1698 and 1699, a half-pay system, which had existed partially since 1641, was more widely developed.

Drawn mainly from amongst the younger sons of the nobility and landed gentry, the Restoration officer corps proved adequate for the demands of peacetime soldiering. When William III took the country to war in 1689 he placed little trust in the majority of the senior British officers, preferring the proven abilities of Dutchmen and Germans. However, even during Charles's reign, senior commands had sometimes gone to foreigners. Herman von Schomberg commanded the British Brigade in Portugal and the British expeditionary corps for the attack on Walcheren in 1673. A Huguenot refugee, the Earl of Feversham, commanded James II's armies against Monmouth in 1685 and William of Orange in 1688. Gradually, during the Nine Years War, British officers—Marlborough, Thomas Talmash, Sir Henry Bellasise, George Ramsey—came to assume senior commands within the Confederate Army of the Grand Alliance but it was a slow process. The chief obstacle was the behaviour of the army towards James II during the campaign of 1688 which left William with the impression that the officers were untrustworthy caballers and political time-servers. Even the few with some military aptitude, like Marlborough, demonstrated alarming personal tendencies and extreme unreliability. The only British officers who prospered under William III were those who had served in the Anglo-Dutch Brigade. Until 1689, the British army was far more of a political army than an offensive and defensive force. In this respect, it followed very closely the precedent set by the New Model Army during the 1650s.

With England's entry into the Nine Years War in 1689 and the change in its political function and status emanating from the Glorious Revolution, the army began to assume a different role. It was still required to support the civil power in England and retained its occupation duties in Scotland and Ireland but it was moving towards an apolitical position. Simultaneously, the army commenced the continental commitment which was to dominate its role down to 1815 and re-emerge in the twentieth century. The France of Louis XIV was a land-based power with territorial ambitions towards the Rhine and the Spanish Netherlands. France, which was largely self-sufficient in economic necessities, could not be defeated at sea. Only by combating her massive armies in the Rhineland and the Low Countries could the Grand Alliance halt French aggression. The initial British commitment to the armies of the Grand Alliance was a modest 10,000 in 1689 as the majority of British forces had to be sent to

Ireland and Scotland to oppose the Jacobite rebellions. The Treaty of Limerick in 1691 released the troops to fight in the Low Countries and the British corps in that theatre grew to 40,000 in 1692 and 56,000 in 1697.

The British units in the Netherlands did not fight as a single formation but were dispersed amongst the Confederates in brigades, the largest semi-permanent tactical organization consisting of between three and five regiments or battalions. Administratively, each regiment and battalion was independent under the personal direction of the lieutenant-colonel. Infantry were armed with muskets and pikes. Each company consisted of two-thirds matchlock muskets and one-third pikes but when a battalion drilled or fought as a unit all the pikes were massed in the centre with the muskets, or 'shot', in two bodies on either flank. The battalion fought in line, the musketeers six ranks deep, and the pikemen five ranks deep. The tactics had altered little from the Swedish evolutions of Gustavus Adolphus. The musketeers fired in volleys by rank and the pikemen gave protection against cavalry. Most battalions possessed a grenadier company which stood independently to the right of the battalion line and was armed with muskets and grenades. Gradually, the matchlock musket was replaced by the flintlock. The Duke of York's Maritime Regiment of Foot, raised in 1664, was armed solely with flintlocks as were the Royal Fusiliers, founded in 1685. By 1697, the majority of British infantry were equipped with the new type of gun although some of the remote garrison companies still sported the ancient variety. The bayonet also made its appearance, ultimately leading to the total demise of the pike. The plug version was adopted by grenadier companies after 1678 only to be steadily replaced by the socket model during the 1690s. It also spread from the élite grenadiers into the line companies. By 1697, the proportion of pikes to muskets had been reduced from one to three to one to four with the majority of the musketeers carrying a socket bayonet. During the War of the Spanish Succession (1702–14) the pike disappeared from the British army and the line infantry possessed a standard equipment of flintlock muskets and socket bayonets; the pikeman and the musketeer had been combined to produce the all-purpose infantryman. Despite their lack of experience in large-scale warfare prior to 1689, the British army performed creditably during the Nine Years War earning the praise of William III and Field Marshal Georg von Waldeck. British infantry fought stubbornly in the vanguard action at Steenkirk in 1692 and were not disgraced during the defeat at Landen (Neerwinden) in 1693. Whilst their combat performances were not outstanding, the British were not markedly deficient when compared with the Dutch, Danish, and German contingents which composed the Confederate Army.

Cavalry and dragoon tactics are not easy to envisage from the drill manuals. Probably, they deployed in three ranks but charged at the trot in two ranks. The cavalry were armed with pistols and sabres whilst the dragoons also carried carbines. The artillery, both field and siege, was the responsibility of the Board of Ordnance as was the pontoon-bridging train and the engineering services. The commissariat was exceptionally small and the provision of bread to the troops and winter feed to the horses in Flanders and Ireland was entrusted to civilian contractors.

Between the Restoration and the death of William III in 1702, the army underwent profound changes. The new army of 1661 was the first peacetime standing army since the Roman occupation of Britain but as a consequence of its domestic employment by Charles and James the army became heavily politicized executing unpopular policies. Only the intervention of William of Orange in 1688 and the resultant Glorious Revolution turned the army into the servant of the public concerned with the defence of the kingdom and the execution of foreign policy overseas.

4 THE GREAT CAPTAIN-GENERAL 1702–1714

DAVID CHANDLER

Between the years 1702 and 1711 the army of Queen Anne—commanded in Flanders (and, in 1704, in the Danube valley) by its Captain-General, John Churchill, first Duke of Marlborough, earned a formidable reputation. The duke, enthused Captain Robert Parker 'never fought a battle which he did not gain nor laid siege to a town which he did not take'. Marlborough's four great battles, two actions, three passages of strong lines, and thirty sieges—all undertaken in the space of ten successive campaigns—brought English (and from 1707, British) arms a degree of martial success and international recognition that they had not known since the Middle Ages. Few commanders born in the British Isles have achieved as much as Marlborough. None has achieved more.

To this record should be added two successful amphibious operations—the seizures of Gibraltar in 1704 and of Minorca in 1708—the capture of Barcelona in 1705, the consolidation of the East India Company's small but significant possessions in Bengal (by 'John Company's' own raised and paid forces), and the making of considerable headway in North America against the French and Spanish, the highlight being the capture of Port Royal (renamed Annapolis Royal) in 1710.

There was also a reverse side to this impressive record of success. The Allied campaigning in Portugal and Spain between 1706 and 1714—in which Queen Anne's regiments took a large part—has been well dubbed 'the First Spanish Ulcer', for this difficult war front soon saw heavy casualties and led to ultimate failure. Against such successes as the capture of Barcelona in 1705 by the mercurial Charles Mordaunt, Earl of Peterborough, or the brave march by the Huguenot general, Henri de Massue de Ruvigny, Earl of Galway, to capture Madrid in 1706, must be placed the latter's disastrous defeat at Almanza (1707) by Marlborough's

Roman Catholic nephew, the Duke of Berwick, and Stanhope's capitulation at Brihuega in 1710. 'Queen Anne's War' in North America saw failure on the St Lawrence (1711), whilst in Flanders the reputation of even Marlborough's army was diminished after his fall from favour and replacement in command by Ormonde in early 1712 for the last and politically discreditable stages of the long War of the Spanish Succession (1701–14) which dominated the period covered by this chapter.

Nevertheless, over these years the British army earned the reputation of being the best in Europe, and its successes underlay the questionable procurement of the favourable terms of the Peace of Utrecht concluded by Great Britain, the United Provinces, Portugal, Savoy, and Brandenburg-Prussia with France, Bavaria, and Spain between April and July 1713 (which left only Austria at war with Louis XIV and Philip V until the Peace of Radstädt in 1714). The terms of Utrecht were advantageous to Great Britain. She received Gibraltar, Minorca, Newfoundland, Acadia (Nova Scotia), and territory around Hudson's Bay, besides trade concessions and recognition of the Protestant Succession, in return for leaving the war and accepting Philip V as King of Spain and the Indies. Thus were laid the foundations for the widespread expansion of the First British Empire during the following half-century.

The army itself was, of course, largely the creation of King William III as described in the last chapter. Under the sovereign's centralizing powers, there were first the 'subject troops'—men recruited from England (and Wales), Scotland, and Ireland. Each of the three constituent countries had in effect a separate army establishment with its own idiosyncracies of pay and other details, all costs being borne by the nation of origin until the Union with Scotland in 1707 simplified the situation, at least in part. On posting to European fronts, all formations were habitually transferred to the English establishment for the duration, while local recruiting made good the gaps so caused. Native troops, however, rarely accounted for as much as half the troops authorized by parliament. In the second place there were two categories of foreign mercenary troops: regiments 'in pay' comprising, for example, Danes, Hanoverians, and Hessians, officered by their own countrymen but organized and paid on English lines; and other formations of foreign 'subsidy troops' provided by friendly European countries in return for annual lump sum payments to their rulers. Lastly there was a minority of units made up of refugees (especially French Huguenots), turned prisoners-of-war, or deserters under British or their own officers but all subject to British establishments and British pay.

The size of the subject troops was determined in Queen Anne's reign under five main headings by parliament, the sole source of the necessary finance required each year. The 'Guards and Garrisons' were basically the minimum peacetime establishment deemed necessary to guard the monarch and maintain a number of manned fortresses such as, in the case of England, the Tower, Dover castle, Kingston-upon-Hull, Berwick, and Carlisle. Secondly, from 1702 there were 'the 40,000'—troops provided to fight overseas in Flanders, only 45 per cent of whom were to be subject troops—the balance being hired from continental sources. Thirdly, there was 'the Augmentation'— an additional 20,000 men, half to be paid for by Britain's Dutch allies, the balance to be provided by Great Britain, only 30 per cent to be 'subjects'. Fourthly, from 1702 to 1713 there was also separate provision made for the war in the Iberian peninsula, including subsidies paid to Portugal and the Archduke Charles, the Allied Pretender to the Spanish throne. In 1707, there were almost 29,000 subject troops in Spain and Portugal. In 1711, under this head, to include land forces in Gibraltar and Minorca, the provision required had fallen to 18,377 subject troops and perhaps 25,000 others in pay of one sort or another. And lastly there was the annual Ordnance vote—providing for the Board of Ordnance's artillerymen, engineers, and their civilian assistants (all still kept apart from the authority of the Captain-General in times of both peace and war—in the latter circumstance including the costly provisions of trains of artillery for service abroad). It was in many ways an inadequate system, yet it worked.

Thus in 1702 the subject troops element amounted to 31,254 men, almost double the peacetime establishment approved the previous year; this number rose to some 50,000 by 1706 (the *annus mirabilis* of the Second Grand Alliance which saw both Marlborough's great victory at Ramillies and Prince Eugene's complementary triumph at Turin); and peaked at 75,000 men five years later for Marlborough's last campaign, which included his passage of the lines of Non Plus Ultra and the ultra-difficult yet successful siege of Bouchain. Thereafter, however, following Marlborough's fall from favour and command in late 1711, the number rapidly declined to only some 23,500 by 1713. But when all other categories of wholly and partly paid troops are also taken into account for the highest year, the total forces of Queen Anne amounted to 150,000 in the field

The Battle of Ramillies

Following the great success at Blenheim-Höchstadt in 1704, the year 1705 had proved disappointing. Marlborough's first plan for 1706—a bold march from the Netherlands to Italy to support Eugene—was aborted by an unexpected French offensive on the middle Rhine. Restricted to another campaign in Flanders, a despondent Marlborough decided to trail his coat in the vicinity of Liège and the lines of Brabant in an attempt to lure Marshal Villeroi into battle. He was not, however, very sanguine. Unbeknown to the duke, however, Louis XIV was persistently goading an unwilling Villeroi into avenging the humiliations suffered by French arms in 1704. Accordingly, the Marshal set off from Louvain at the head of seventy battalions, 132 squadrons, and some seventy cannon—comprising an overall force of 60,000 men—and provocatively marched towards Léau.

Learning that the enemy had thus obligingly crossed the Dyle on 19 May, an incredulous Marlborough ordered his troops to concentrate at Corswaren. The Anglo-Dutch-German army, with the Danes nearby, numbered some 62,000 troops (74 battalions and 123 squadrons, with 120 pieces of ordnance). Expecting to encounter Villeroi on 24 May, Marlborough sent off Cadogan at 1 a.m. on 23 May to reconnoitre the next night's camp site on the plateau of St André near the village of Ramillies. This position set amidst the Rivers Gheete, Little Gheete, and Mehaigne, was a well-known camping area and, by coincidence, Villeroi had also decided to camp there. So it was that Cadogan, emerging from a thick morning fog, discovered the massed tents of the Franco-Bavarian army.

Riding ahead of his four columns, the duke joined Cadogan by 10 a.m. Before them, in a 4-mile concave arc, stretched Villeroi's army. Its position atop a low ridge appeared strong. Villeroi's left—infantry supported by fifty squadrons of horse—was placed near Autre Église behind the marshy Little Gheete. His centre, anchored upon Ramillies and Offus, comprised mainly infantry and guns. His right wing, similarly protected from any outflanking move by the Mehaigne, was further protected by the outlying villages of Franquenée and Taviers, garrisoned by five battalions. To the south of Ramillies stretched 2,000 yards of unrestricted plain, ideal for cavalry action, and eighty-two squadrons of French cavalry supported by three brigades of Bavarian foot were drawn up there. Two large batteries were placed on each side of Ramillies.

However, to hold the whole ridge Villeroi had overextended his army. His concave position would make it difficult to transfer troops from one flank to the other. The cavalry near Autre Église was also placed uselessly behind the marshes. So Marlborough determined to concentrate his approaching army along a 3-mile front between the horns of the French position, and use the advantage of interior lines to swing troops from one wing to the other as need or opportunity arose.

Shortly after 1 p.m. the battle opened. To the south, Dutch guards battalions, supported by two large guns and six Danish squadrons, fell upon first Franquenée and then Taviers, and by 3.15 p.m. both villages were in Allied hands. A riposte by two battalions of Swiss and fourteen squadrons of dragoons was routed, and Villeroi ordered the Bavarians to intervene. After a fierce fight, these troops were isolated amidst the marshes—and Villeroi's right wing was deprived of all its foot.

Meanwhile, on the opposite flank, Orkney was advancing against Autre Église over waterlogged ground, his twelve British battalions supported by thirty-nine squadrons. The infantry made their way over the Little Gheete with difficulty, to find themselves counter-attacked in strength, Villeroi, newly joined by the Elector of Bavaria, drawing much infantry from his centre to reinforce the area. Thus by 4 p.m. both French flanks were heavily engaged, and one isolated.

Attention shifted to the south, where the Allied centre was advancing on Ramillies and Offus, supported by Overkirk's sixty-nine squadrons. The sixty-eight French squadrons of the right wing charged and, aided by its remaining infantry, eventually gained the advantage. Ordering a disgruntled Orkney to transfer eighteen squadrons and then a further twenty-one from the right wing to the left, Marlborough personally led his staff in two charges to check the French. Some 25,000 horsemen were now engaged, and soon the Allied cavalry intervention from the far right and a Danish twenty-one-squadron envelopment from the Mehaigne flank defeated the flower of the French cavalry. Deprived of sufficient infantry support by earlier detachments, the whole French right wing gave way and swung back north-westwards, until it was at right-angles to Ramillies and the French centre.

Marlborough realized the supreme moment had come. Bringing half of Orkney's disengaged battalions southwards—less their colour-parties left behind the protective ridge to fool the French—he built up a commanding superiority opposite Ramillies and launched Schulenburg forward in decisive attack. A third of Villeroi's army stood mesmerized by Orkney's colour-poles

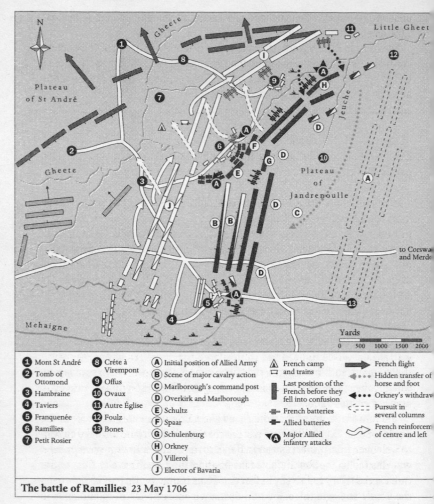

The battle of Ramillies 23 May 1706

while a large Allied battery smashed the defences of Ramillies. The French centre collapsed under this remorseless pressure, and by 7 p.m. Villeroi and the Elector were swept away amidst their army's flight, narrowly avoiding capture as Orkney swept forward through Autre Église. The pursuit continued all night.

The French left 13,000 casualties on the field and a further 6,000 were taken prisoner, besides all their cannon and camp. By comparison, the Allies lost 1,066 killed and 2,560 wounded.

The fruits of victory were astounding. The whole of the Spanish Netherlands lay at the mercy of the Allied army; the surrender of Ath on 6 October followed that of Louvain, Brussels, Antwerp, Ghent, Bruges, Ostend, and Menin. Marlborough had achieved his greatest success.

---

in the year of Malplaquet (1709), 69,000 being subject troops. It should, however, be noticed that these figures are all based on numbers voted by parliament rather than numbers actually in the field, which were often considerably less.

Inevitably, the cost of finding, equipping, clothing, paying, feeding, moving, and generally maintaining the army at home and overseas was immense, and steadily grew over most of the period of the war. The vagaries and inconsistencies of early eighteenth-century accountancy make it difficult to gain an accurate impression. For example, scholarly estimates of the total cost to England of the War of the Spanish Succession vary from a low of somewhat over £59.3 million to a high approaching £94.7 million—the latter figure being the more probable. Nevertheless, some generalized conclusions may be cautiously entertained. In round terms, war expenditure appears to have averaged out over the eleven years of active warfare at over £8 million per annum, ranging from £3.3 million in 1702, through £5.7 million in 1706/7, and peaking at £12.6 million in 1711. Small wonder there was a growing clamour for peace from 1709 onwards on economic grounds alone.

The amount allocated in the Army and Ordnance votes taken together rise from over £1.2 million (37 per cent of the whole) in the first year of war to well over £5.1 million (41 per cent) in 1711. A generally lower percentage was allotted to the Royal Navy (although in 1702 and 1711 naval expenditure exceeded that of the land forces). Thus it may be suggested that over the whole struggle the army and ordnance accounted for 50 per cent of war expenditure to the navy's 35 per cent. The balance was expended over many associated headings, of which subsidies to a dozen allies, headed by Denmark, Prussia, and Portugal, took up £500,000 a year. Relations with the United Provinces became strained periodically over accusations of non-fulfilment of variously shared subsidy and treaty obligations.

It is instructive to summarize the allocation of battalions and squadrons to war fronts. Inevitably, Flanders took the larger share (58 per cent overall) with between sixteen (1702) and twenty-seven battalions (in 1709/10), and a steady seventeen regiments of horse (rising to nineteen in 1711 only) deployed. The Iberian theatre between 1704 and 1711 absorbed a minimum five battalions and seven regiments of horse in 1705 rising to twenty-three battalions in 1707 and eight mounted formations in 1709— but there were wild fluctuations in various years. Gibraltar required a garrison of four battalions in the year of its capture from Spain (1704) and for the siege that followed, before settling down from late 1705 to a steady two.

For the rest there were requirements for a steady six battalions for service as marines on board the fleet, varying numbers for sundry expeditions, the garrisoning of Ireland (six to fourteen battalions and ten to fourteen regiments of horse), and varying numbers for home defence according to the requirements of the changing strategic situation. Thus in early 1708 the French invasion scare required the temporary switch of the 'ten eldest regiments of foot' from Flanders to England for a month between mid-March and mid-April—but once Admiral Byng could report that Forbin's fleet was in full sail for France the troops were returned to their former stations. The garrison of Great Britain moved between 7,300 (1702) and 19,000 troops (in 1712, as troops began to be withdrawn from Flanders), while the West Indian colonies needed between 600 and 2,750 men (the figures for 1702 and 1712 respectively).

As peace approached there were wholesale disbandments. Of sixty-nine new regiments raised since 1702, only thirty-four remained by late 1712. In 1707 there had been in all thirty-eight regiments of horse and dragoons, four of them on the Scots and six on the Irish establishments. By late 1713, there remained only sixteen (including one in Scotland and two in Ireland). Of eighty-five regiments of foot (three Scots and nineteen Irish as before), only forty-two survived (including one Scots and five Irish). All retained regiments were reduced to peace establishments. By 1714 there perhaps remained 26,000 in pay.

For parliament to vote establishment increases from 1702 was one thing; actually to find the necessary soldiery quite another. The initial problem at the outbreak of war was not too difficult: there were plenty of unemployed veterans from the Nine Years War disbanded in 1697 only too willing to re-enlist—and the same was true of half-pay officers. The immediate increases in the army in 1702/3 were carried through by doubling the peacetime establishments of existing regiments and by raising new ones. Thereafter, however, as replacements for the growing toll of casualties caused by action and sickness, which were rarely allowed for in the parliamentary votes of manpower—12,000 in 1708 alone to make good the losses of 1707, and all of 18,685 in 1709 after the very active campaign of 1708 to cite two examples—had to be added to the requirements of an expanding war effort, the problem steadily grew. It reached a critical peak after the bloodletting of Malplaquet in 1709: 8,000 of the 24,000 Allied casualties sustained on 11 September out of 110,000 allies originally engaged were British subject troops.

Recruitment measures employed included all those utilized in the previous reign, both legal and illegal. Recruiting parties made full use of the glamour of Marlborough's name from 1704 to attract volunteers—one recruiting song included the refrain, sung to the tune of the later *Waltzing Matilda*, 'who'll come a-soldiering with Marlborough and me?' But the tricks and machinations of Captain Plume and Sergeant Kite in George Farquhar's popular contemporary play, *The Recruiting Officer* (1704), doubtless reflected reality. Even these would not suffice to fill the quotas, so the size of monetary bounties and rewards inevitably soared—from £2 a head in 1703 to £5 in 1708. Still the ranks remained unfilled, and parliament had recourse to no less than nine Recruiting Statutes during the twelve-year struggle, attempting to solve the unsolvable.

The criminal classes continued to be unloaded into the regiments: to the customary biannual jail deliveries were added the recruitment of insolvent debtors (the subject of two special statutes as early as 1702 and 1703), and then the forcible enlistment of vagrants, 'such able-bodied men' as were without lawful calling. The military life remained unpopular with society at large. As Daniel Defoe noted in descending order of preference: 'In winter, the poor starve, thieve or turn soldier.' Conditions of army life were hardly enticing. Pay (rarely paid without long delays) was, at an unchanging 8*d.* a day before deductions, lower than the agricultural wage which rose from 10*d.* to 12½*d.* during the reign. Inadequate quarters (barracks—apart from London's notorious Savoy recruit reception centre or dank, unhealthy fortress casemates—were still nonexistent), brutal discipline ('flog, hang, or shoot' was the slogan), and widespread social scorn and disapproval for the profession of arms, were other disincentives to genuine volunteering. As a result, criminal practices inevitably proliferated. A whole class of bounty-jumpers grew up: men who enlisted into a regiment, collected their bounty-money, and then absconded (risking the direst legal penalties if apprehended) to repeat the process elsewhere. Hard-pressed recruiting officers would sign on

The Logistics of the March to the Danube, 1704

The Duke of Marlborough's transfer of his army from the Spanish Netherlands to the Danube front between 19 May (the date he left Bedburg near Ruremonde) and 22 June 1704 (the date his force linked up with its Austrian allies at Launsheim) has long been acclaimed as a major military achievement. The purpose of this bold manœuvre—carried out mainly through friendly territory (but with large enemy forces nearby in a position to intercept or sever the line of march)—was to regain the initiative in the Spanish Succession War (1701–14) for the Grand Alliance. By forestalling the impending Franco-Bavarian onslaught on Vienna, he hoped to prevent its fall—an event that might prove fatal to the confederacy. Only the timely reinforcement of the Austrians could hope to achieve this, as the armies of Louis XIV were strongly placed.

The 350-mile length of the march was daunting in terms of early eighteenth-century concepts of waging war for several reasons. The wear and tear to be expected from such an enterprise—given the poor roads of the period—and the appalling wet weather which dogged it almost from first to last, might well have caused a major diminution in fighting power. As it was, the duke only lost 900 sick and stragglers by the wayside out of a force that started out about 21,000 strong but arrived at the rendezvous with the Margrave of Baden's forces with 40,000 men, having picked up sundry Allied detachments at Koblenz and Mainz *en route*. That it arrived in good order is indicated by Prince Eugene's encomium on the fine fettle of the cavalry at Gross Heppach on 12 June, and above all by the force's ability to take a major part in the storming of the heights above Donauwörth on 2 July. The vital and successful fooling of both unwilling allies and advantageously placed opponents as to his ultimate intentions add further lustre to Marlborough's achievement, although due credit must also go to his key subordinates on the staff: Cadogan, Cardonnel, and Davenant. The march's speed—averaging a little over 10 miles a day—was not so remarkable as its sustained nature over five weeks. But above all it is the logistical and administrative skills displayed by 'the Old Corporal', which alone made the feat possible, that repay study.

As he would be crossing Allied territory, it was not feasible for Marlborough to sweep the countryside clear of all food and fodder so as to feed what were eventually 40,000 men—an estimated 60,000 if accompanying horses, gun, and waggon teams are included. Instead he had to rely on a prearranged supply organization and on winning local co-operation. The contractors Solomon and Moses Medina—operating from the army's financial base at Frankfurt—were entrusted with arranging food supply through subcontractors, paying in gold supplied from England to ensure local co-operation. Each regiment had its own civilian sutlers to complement and supplement the contractorial system.

In 1704, therefore, the 'scarlet caterpillar', for a ten-day phase of marching over a distance of 100 miles, foraging to a distance of 5 miles on each side of its line of march, required a foraging area of 1,000 square miles. Such a relatively prosperous area of central Europe at that time could support 45,000 inhabitants. In late spring the remaining corn and flour from the last harvest could be calculated as amounting to five-months' supply. The army would, all told, require 60,000 bread rations each day, and, as it marched remorselessly onwards, would consume some 10 per cent of local reserves—and the same proportion of wine, beer, and meat. Finding fodder for the horses was the biggest single challenge, but the problem was supportable providing the local town authorities and population were co operative—although all prices would inevitably rise. To find Marlborough's needs, the Medinas needed to order sufficient supplies two weeks ahead, and the regimental sutlers their requirements on a basis of two days in advance. Every fourth day the army halted, established its ovens, and baked bread. Spare shoes and saddlery were prepositioned at Heidelberg. Sufficient powder and shot (100 rounds per cannon) either accompanied the army, or was passed forward from the Netherlands in guarded convoys. Special light two-wheel waggons were provided, and the larger guns deliberately left behind.

The march routine was carefully controlled. Captain Parker recalled:

We frequently marched three, sometimes four days, successively, and halted a day. We generally began our march about three in the morning . . . and reached our ground about nine. As we marched through the countries of our allies, commissaries were appointed to furnish us with all manner of necessaries for man and horse; these were brought to the ground before we arrived, and the soldiers had nothing to do, but to pitch their tents, boil their kettles, and lie down to rest. Surely never was such a march carried on with more order and regularity, and with less fatigue both to man and horse . . .

At first Marlborough's lines of communication ran parallel to his line of march up the Rhine, but as there was no covering force between Koblenz and Philippsburg and the French corps of de Coignies might, and indeed did, attempt to sever them, after passing Mainz on 3 June the duke switched his communications to run up the River Main into safe Hessian territory and thence south through Nuremberg to a forward base and hospital established at Nordlingen, north-west of Dönauwörth.

By these means Marlborough transformed the campaign—and the war.

---

suspected deserters without asking awkward questions, and magistrates often turned a blind eye to bare-faced abuses including kidnapping. Strangely enough the legalized naval press-gang was never made available to the army—although steps were taken to ensure that sailors were not recruited into the army. Despite all these measures every formation remained seriously under-recruited. The pervading morale of the regiments was initially low, as was reflected in the near-contemporary adage: 'The army passed over into Flanders, and swore horribly.'

Fortunately for the reputation of the army, such unsatisfactory human material could respond to the inspiration and appeal of a Marlborough, and every regiment contained an element of genuine recruits and professional soldiers who proved to be the leavening in the loaf.

Regimental officers varied almost as much as their men. As earlier, purchasing of commissions remained the universal practice, and officer absenteeism, wholesale exchanging from unit to unit, quarrelling, and duelling remained prevalent. A colonel empowered to raise a new regiment received a lump sum from the government for initial setting-up and an issue of cross-belts, swords, and muskets (and eventually socket bayonets as well) from the Tower of London or other royal arsenal, but thereafter he was usually left to his own devices. To make a profit out of his unit a colonel often had recourse to appointing a regimental agent. Some were honest men, but abuses and even bare-faced fraud were frequently resorted to over uniforming, feeding, and, when necessary, re-equipping the men—and also in the issuing of commissions. Patronage and greed led to some strange anomalies. In 1705 Queen Anne found it necessary to restrict the practice of commissioning children to only two aged under 16 per regiment. Many officers regarded their commissions as little more than investments to be handled as they saw fit. Marlborough himself had once to write to a Major Cookman of Brigadier-General Joseph Sabine's Regiment of Foot (later the 23rd, the Royal Welch Fusiliers), absent 'for so many years past', recovering from wounds, requiring his presence forthwith as 'the regiment must be utterly ruined unless there be more officers to do the duty'.

The standard of officer varied considerably. In a period when promotion was determined as much by purchase or influence as by proven merit, it is remarkable how good a great many were. On the other hand, there were also patent disgraces. Brigadier-General Richard Kane 'was once at a review, when the commanding General of the troops was reviewing a Regiment of Foot, where were present the Colonel, Lt. Colonel, Major and most of all the Captains, and yet not one of them capable of going thro' the discipline of the Regiment, of which the General very justly took publick notice'. The same author was even more outspoken about certain officers 'who instead of treating their men with GOOD NATURE, use them with CONTEMPT and CRUELTY; by which those gentlemen often meet their FATE in the day of battle from their own men'. What a later generation of Americans would term 'fragging' indubitably happened on occasion: one instance occurred immediately after Blenheim, when an unpopular major—who had cravenly promised his men that he would mend his ways if he survived the battle—fell riddled with friendly bullets as, vastly relieved to be still alive, he turned to address them. These were clearly in many ways parlous times, but somehow the army muddled through as often as not to achieve success.

Fortunately for posterity, there were a number of soldier eye-witnesses to the Marlburian age whose letters, journals, and chronicles—however incomplete—give us the image of the time, warts and all. They include General (later the first Field Marshal) George Hamilton, Lord Orkney, Brigadier-Generals Richard Stearne and Richard Kane, both of the later 18th Foot (the Royal Regiment of Ireland); Colonels Cranstoune and St Pierre, the lugubrious Lieutenant-Colonel Blackadder of the Cameronians, Captains Robert Parker (again of the 18th), the changecoat Peter Drake, and Andrew Bonwell of the Train of Artillery; not to overlook Lieutenant Pope of Schomberg's Horse or James Gordon of Craichlaw; or, again, Dr Hare (Marlborough's chaplain) and Chaplain Noyes. Even rarer are voices from the NCOs and rank and file, the humble 'hatmen'. The few available include Sergeants John Millner and John Wilson, 'the old Flanderkin serjeant', of the prolific 18th and 15th Foot (later the East Yorkshire Regiment) respectively, Corporal Matthew Bishop of the 8th Foot (later the King's Liverpool Regiment). Sentinel John Marshall Deane of the 1st Foot Guards, and an anonymous Royal Dragoon of Lord Raby's Regiment in Spain bring up the rear of this precious list of soldier narrators and historians of these campaigns.

Many of the deficiencies displayed by, and problems inflicted upon, the officers and men of Queen Anne's army are attributable to inadequate, slow-working administrative machinery—and stem from the ever-present chronic economic constraints of the day. With one exception, the system was inherited practically intact from King William III, and therefore requires no elaboration here. The exception is the creation in February 1706 of the Board of General Officers. An *ad hoc* predecessor existed in 1705 presided over by Lieutenant-General Charles Churchill, Marlborough's brother, to look into and redress 'Great Abuses and Disorders committed by Severall Officers and Souldiers of Our Army', including disputes between officers, recruiting irregularities, and complaints from civilian sources in general. From 1706 seven generals were the required quorum. The Board could itself impose punishments, or refer cases to courts-martial. Few records of its precise activities have survived, and although it was revivified in 1711, and empowered to set up 'inferior boards' or subcommittees as needed, it would seem that the Board rapidly became bogged down in bureaucratic detail concerning all 'Misbehaviour of any Officer or Souldier in our Service' over such irksome matters as pay, clothing, charitable and seniority disputes, and irregularities. The Board at first met about eight times a year, but as peace approached its meetings proliferated to as many as fourteen in July 1712 alone. Small wonder that in 1717 attendance on the Board would be described as 'this troublesome service' by the Secretary at War of the day.

The pair of Secretaries of State (for the Northern and Southern Departments respectively) remained the key ministerial appointments for military affairs. The Secretary at War—originally simply the salaried secretary to the Commander-in-Chief—became increasingly the effective link between the queen's ministry and the army on the one hand, and parliament on the other over certain financial and establishment matters—sharing with the paymaster-general the key duty of presenting the annual estimates to the House of Commons. William Blathwayt, who held the Secretaryship at War from 1683 until April 1704, regarded himself as a royal servant, albeit an increasingly important one, but stage by stage the post became increasingly politicized under his successors, particularly Henry St John and Robert Walpole. St John went on (as Viscount Bolingbroke) to become a Secretary of State from 1710 to 1713, while Walpole was destined to become the nation's first Prime Minister in the early Hanoverian period. The Lord Treasurer—for many years Marlborough's friend Sidney Godolphin—was Queen Anne's most influential minister.

Mention must also be made of the so-called 'Secret Committee'—an unofficial grouping of Secretary of State Lord Nottingham, Marlborough (when available), Godolphin, Blathwayt, four naval commissioners, and other key advisers which met frequently as a kind of War Cabinet to consider matters of grand strategic and alliance policy, and to co-ordinate military and naval activities. As Marlborough's influence waned from 1709, so this committee became rather less significant, but it was of the greatest importance from 1703 to 1708 and represented the Captain-General's main means of influencing decision and home politics.

Passing on to consider the organization, equipment, training, and exercise of the army, we find more anomalies. Although the horse, dragoons, and foot came directly under the authority of the commanding general in the field, the train of artillery (comprising the guns and engineer services) did not—being the responsibility of the Board of Ordnance, whose Master-General was a separate high officer of state. In the early eighteenth century, it was indeed a fortunate coincidence for the operational efficiency of the army that Marlborough combined in his person the positions of Captain-General and MGO. In 1716, following his restoration to his former posts (but not to his former all-pervading influence) by George I two years earlier, it was at Marlborough's request—his last great service to the army—that the immediate predecessor of the Royal Regiment of Artillery was created, and the guns brought into the main army organization (although it would be some decades more before the Corps of Royal Engineers was brought into existence).

The organization of the army in the field remained based upon the individual constituent regiments. Although the old *tercios* of the mid-seventeenth century and earlier had been replaced by the brigade of three or more battalions, these formations remained essentially *ad hoc* organizations, rarely surviving unchanged in composition for more than a campaign. The senior colonel present—or more often the senior officer commanding, for in the age of colonels-proprietor the majority of such officers would also hold higher rank in the army and have other duties to perform—would be appointed the temporary brigade commander. Thus at Malplaquet (1709), the Royal Regiment of Foot of Ireland (later the 18th Foot) was in fact commanded by its major—brevet Lieutenant-Colonel Kane—although its colonel was Lieutenant-General Richard Ingoldsby (serving in Ireland as Commander-in-Chief at the time) whilst the regiment's second-in-command, brevet Colonel Robert Stearne, was also absent. Command therefore devolved upon the next senior officer present—the major.

Although there were no divisional or army corps organizations in existence in Marlborough's day, there was a rough allocation of duties on the battlefield in the organization of lines or orders of battle. Positions in the first (or front) line were regarded as more important than those in the second; and both were more significant than those in the third (or reserve) line, when one existed. Command of the formations comprising the right wing in the front line was generally considered the post of greatest honour. While there were appointments as generals and lieutenant-generals of horse and foot, considerations of seniority were the most significant in determining the allocation of command posts on days of battle.

It was therefore standard practice for the Captain-General to send messages to brigade or regimental commanders directly. Although no more than a very rudimentary staff organization existed, Marlborough, as William III before him, was assisted by a personal staff. His skill in selecting first-rate assistants was a vital factor in making possible the high level of success achieved. As Quartermaster-General (and unofficial chief of staff), he was fortunate to employ the loyal services of William Cadogan. As Military Secretary, Adam Cardonnel proved no less vital—tackling much of the crippling load of diplomatic and political correspondence that dogged his master in and out of campaign. In 1704, the financial skills of Henry Davenant largely underwrote the daring march from Bedburg to Blenheim. The duke's choice of heads of services proved equally inspired. Colonel Holcroft Blood (son of the would-be thief of the Crown Jewels in Charles II's reign) was an invaluable commander of the artillery train in 1704 and again in 1706, while Colonel John Armstrong proved an invaluable senior aide-de-camp and engineer officer—earning himself no less than three recognizable portraits in the series of Blenheim Tapestries woven to commemorate Marlborough's achievements in the field. Lieutenant-Colonel James Bingham was a much valued equerry to the duke, until his head was taken off by a cannon-ball as he assisted his chief to mount a horse at Ramillies—the fatal missile allegedly passing between Marlborough's leg and the saddle as he swung his leg over.

Adequate command, communication, and control arrangements were as vital prerequisites of battlefield success at this period as in any other. Less recognizable than the senior staff officers but no less important were the anonymous 'running footmen'—young officers and NCOs handpicked by Marlborough to carry his messages and bring him reports on days of battle. Equipped with gold-, silver-, and bronze-tipped staffs to indicate their status, these two dozen or so young men permitted their commander to keep a sensitive finger on the pulse of battle on the more smoke-obscured and distant sectors of the battlefield. Marlborough preferred their services to those of mounted aides because he deemed them less likely to become casualties. Wearing their jockey-caps, these vital assistants figure on several of the Blenheim Tapestries.

On a number of grave occasions Marlborough convened councils of war comprising all general officers and senior staff in the army. He used these events sparingly, and he is only rarely known to have accepted their collective advice when this ran contrary to his own instincts. An occasion when he did so—and lived to regret it—was during his first campaign of the Spanish Succession War, in early August 1702, when he heeded the objections of the attached Dutch deputies and for political rather than military reasons called off a very promising attack against Marshal Boufflers near Lille Saint-Hubert. On another occasion—during his tenth and last campaign in August 1711—he called another council of war to consider the feasibility of attacking the seemingly impregnable Wavrechin outwork during the siege of Bouchain. All save Cadogan and Armstrong were strongly against it—but Marlborough backed the minority view, and ultimately the operation succeeded.

Good strategic and field intelligence was another notable aspect of Marlburian campaigning. The duke—usually so parsimonious—appears to have spent guineas freely to gain valuable information. For many years he remained in touch with his nephew, Marshal Berwick (the secret 'oo' correspondence), and appears to have had an invaluable contact on Louis XIV's Conseil d'en Haut whose identity has never been revealed. Much of this shadowy activity was co-ordinated by Cadogan, and conducted through Mr Craggs. Allies as well as opponents were watched, with good reason. In the field successful deception was often resorted to. In the early stages of the march towards the Danube in 1704, for example, Marlborough openly spoke of marching up the Moselle to confound the spies, and the night before Blenheim 'deserters' were sent into the enemy camp to fool Marshal Tallard into thinking that the Allied activity dimly perceived towards Dönauwörth presaged a march to the north towards Nordlingen, and never an intention to attack his strong position the next morning. Most obligingly he snapped up the bait. Before his skilled passage of the lines of Non Plus Ultra in 1711 under the very nose of the able Marshal Villars, Marlborough conducted an ostentatious reconnaissance of an in fact irrelevant sector of the French defences, once again fooling his adversary before a critical move. The Captain-General was without a doubt a master of guile and deception.

The individual regiments of horse, dragoons, and foot, together with the trains of artillery, formed the backbone of Queen Anne's army as of its predecessors. In basic organization they differed little from William III's army. Mounted troops accounted for possibly 27 per cent of the army. Regiments of Horse had varying establishments, but averaged out at about 300 men organized into six troops; dragoon formations—which fought mounted or on foot—were larger, perhaps 480 men in eight troops. Three or four of these sub-units were often brigaded to form squadrons on days of battle. Marlborough encouraged his cavalry to operate as a shock force, using twin-squadron charges delivered at a fast trot after the Swedish fashion. He reduced their pistol ammunition accordingly, and withdrew their iron back-plates. Massed cavalry was reserved for the *coup de grâce* in three of his great battles, but what his horsemen could achieve was graphically demonstrated early in the day at Blenheim when five squadrons under Lieutenant-Colonel Palmes routed eight of the élite Gendarmerie to the dismay of Marshal Tallard. At the climax of the same battle the massing in Marlborough's centre of eighty Allied squadrons, properly supported by twenty-three battalions of foot and some guns, in due course overwhelmed the sixty available French squadrons and nine battalions, opening the way to victory. Other examples of the correct use of massed cavalry to clinch success were Ramillies and Malplaquet.

In the case of the infantry, the key development was not so much the final transition from the pike and matchlock combination to the socket-bayonet and flintlock musket (completed by 1703), but rather the tactical improvements this made possible. Battalions now drew up only three ranks deep. The line was then subdivided into up to twenty-four platoons organized into three firings, groups of eight platoons apiece distributed equally along the front. Each firing discharged in turn before reloading, and the whole evolution could be repeated twice a minute. This achieved better continuity, fire-control, and hence accuracy, whilst one-third of a battalion was reloaded at any particular moment. There were several variants of this fire-tactic, and it proved markedly superior to line or company volleys as practised by the French until after 1709. A test-case action took place that year at Malplaquet in a woodland clearing, where two rival battalions fought it out according to the rival systems: Captain Parker noted that the routed Irish Regiment in the French service lost forty casualties to the British Royal Regiment of Foot's ten, concluding that 'this is undoubtedly the best method that has yet been discovered for fighting a battalion'. The psychological pressure this exerted, backed by aggressive bayonet charges and close fire-support provided by a pair of light guns attached to each regiment, gained the tactical edge in many individual actions, and so impressed Louis XIV that he specifically ordered Marshal Villeroi in 1706 to 'pay special heed to that part of the line that shall sustain the first shock of the English troops'—an instruction which in fact led in no small measure to the loss of the battle of Ramillies.

Similarly it was the more imaginative use of artillery on the battlefield rather than any great difference in types or capabilities that underlay the British superiority in the Marlburian period. All guns were heavy, slow-moving pieces which placed a drag on the conduct of war, but the Captain-General's cannon moved as well as fired on the field of battle. Thus at Blenheim Colonel Blood contrived to drag eight guns over the Nebel and its marshes at the height of the battle to help contain the garrison of Oberglau village and then to support the Allied cavalry onslaught. Similarly at Ramillies it was the aggressive forward deployment of two large guns that enabled the Dutch Guards to take the fortified villages on the French right flank.

Evidently it was the correctly co-ordinated employment of horse, foot, and guns that was one secret of Marlborough's success as a battlefield commander. Brigadier-General Lord Orkney's intervention in the centre at Blenheim makes the point admirably. 'I marched with my battalions to sustain the Horse, and found them repulsed, and crying out for Foot . . . , I went to the head of several squadrons and got 'em to rally on my right and left, and brought up four pieces of cannon and then charged.' Combined action led to the repulse of the French cavalry, who, blown by their attack, were then incapable of withstanding Marlborough's second cavalry attack with fresh squadrons, properly supported. Small wonder that the Duke's native forces gained such a repute for invincibility.

Another attribute that underlay the success of the armies under Marlborough's personal command (and one that was not shared with British forces serving in Spain or elsewhere) was the relative success of his field administration. Ammunition supply was the responsibility of the Ordnance, but food and fodder was drawn from a number of sources. On campaign when conditions permitted, carefully organized grand forages were used to sweep enemy countryside bare—as in Bavaria during July 1704 when several hundred villages were also burnt. Most supplies, however, had to be drawn from pre-stocked depots and supplied to the army by waggon-trains. These depots were filled by contractors, who included

The Complexities of Siege Warfare: Lille, 1708

In the early eighteenth century the capture and defence of major fortresses and cities absorbed a great deal of both the time and the resources available for most campaigning seasons, especially in the 'Cockpit of Europe'. Fortified towns represented rich prizes by which the ebb and flow of a war could be judged. They could also act as magnets attracting the attentions of relieving forces and these operations could (albeit rarely) lead to a major engagement between main armies. Captured towns were also valuable pawns in peace negotiations. However, sieges could be very expensive in terms of casualties, disease in the trenches and encampments and within the walls being a major hazard, and posed great logistical problems for the besieger if at all protracted.

Marlborough—for all his reputation as a battle-seeking general—undertook at least thirty sieges. That of Lille—12 August to 10 December 1708—well illustrates the complexity and types of operations associated with a major siege, extending as it did well into the winter season.

Regarded as one of Vauban's masterpieces of defensive engineering, and as the most important fortress on France's north-eastern frontiers, Lille was defended by a garrison of 16,000 men under Marshal Boufflers. To undertake the siege, and provide a sufficiently strong covering force, required Marlborough and Eugene to deploy 100,000 men. After their victory at Oudenarde on 11 July 1708, Marlborough had hoped to mount a large advance into France along the Channel coast, drawing rations from the fleet and thus bypassing the fortress zone. Such a bold concept did not receive Eugene's support, however, so the capture of Lille was selected instead.

Preliminary operations began on 22 July with the movement of the first large convoy from Brussels to the Scheldt. Successfully completed, the second, or 'great convoy', comprising eighty siege guns and 3,000 waggons, marched on 6 August for Menin under Cadogan's command, covered by Eugene with 50,000 men near Ath and Marlborough with 40,000 more from near Oudenarde. No French interception was attempted, and on 12 August the complicated move was completed.

The blockade of Lille began that day, and by 21 August the circum- and contra-vallation trench lines completely encircled the city. Directed by Eugene with fifty battalions, the approaches and parallels were next started on 22 August against the north-eastern sector of Lille's defences. On 27 August eighty-eight guns opened long-range fire.

On Louis XIV's order, the French massed 110,000 men at Grammont, crossed the Scheldt at Tournai, and marched on Mons-en-Pevelle. But Marlborough, with the covering force, moved to block this challenge, calling up Eugene with 30,000 men from the siege lines to make 70,000. From 4 September to 17 September the two armies faced each other, but despite their superiority and Boufflers's attempted sortie on 5 September, the French dared not attack the duke's prepared positions, and fell back. Eugene had meanwhile returned to the siege, where he stormed part of Lille's counterscarp on 7 September for 3,000 casualties. In a new assault on 21 September, another 1,000 men were lost for scant gains—and Eugene himself was wounded. Marlborough accordingly took over both siege and covering role. He found everything behindhand and a critical shortage of munitions—whereas on 28 September a desperate French operation had at heavy cost managed to pass some gunpowder into Lille.

As the siege slowly progressed, the French next attempted to sever the Allied supply lines from Brussels and Antwerp by seizing the Scheldt. In this they succeeded by mid-September; but when they tried to cut off the new supply-point of Ostend by flooding, General Lamotte's 22,000 men intercepted General Webb's convoy escort of 11,000 at Wynendael on 28 September, only to be soundly beaten. The convoy safely reached the siege lines on 30 September. Furious, Vendôme challenged action near Oudenburg, but, when Marlborough marched up with 45,000 men, he fell back to Bruges. The link from Ostend to the lines before Lille remained tenuous as the flooding spread, but flotillas of boats and galleys kept supplies moving.

By mid-October the Allied breaching batteries were in position, and soon several large breaches had been made. Very short of supplies, on 23 October Boufflers offered to surrender the city in return for a three-day truce to allow the free withdrawal of his men into the citadel and the evacuation of his sick and wounded to Douai. These terms were agreed and the Allies prepared to attack the citadel by opening new trenches on the Esplanade. A French surprise attack captured Leffinghe near Ostend on 24 October, so the supply battle remained critical.

On 3 November the French—now commanded by the Elector of Bavaria—decided on one last large attempt to save Boufflers. By marching against Brussels it was hoped that Marlborough would attempt to save the city. The French duly bombarded Brussels into ruins from 22 November to 29 November—but suddenly found themselves in danger. For on 26 November four strong Allied columns pounced on crossing places over the Scheldt. The French barrier along the Scheldt was shattered, and the Elector's communications placed in

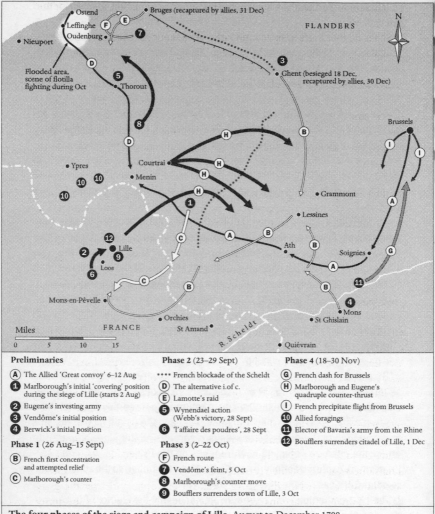

The four phases of the siege and campaign of Lille August to December 1708

Preliminaries

(A) The Allied 'Great convoy' 6–12 Aug
(1) Marlborough's initial 'covering' position during the siege of Lille (starts 2 Aug)
(2) Eugene's investing army
(3) Vendôme's initial position
(4) Berwick's initial position

Phase 1 (26 Aug–15 Sept)

(B) French first concentration and attempted relief
(C) Marlborough's counter

Phase 2 (23–29 Sept)

•••• French blockade of the Scheldt
(D) The alternative i.of c.
(E) Lamotte's raid
(5) Wynendael action (Webb's victory, 28 Sept)
(6) 'l'affaire des poudres', 28 Sept

Phase 3 (2–22 Oct)

(F) French route
(7) Vendôme's feint, 5 Oct
(8) Marlborough's counter move
(9) Boufflers surrenders town of Lille, 3 Oct

Phase 4 (18–30 Nov)

(G) French dash for Brussels
(H) Marlborough and Eugene's quadruple counter-thrust
(I) French precipitate flight from Brussels
(10) Allied foragings
(11) Elector of Bavaria's army from the Rhine
(12) Boufflers surrenders citadel of Lille, 1 Dec

deadly danger. Forthwith he abandoned his guns and wounded, and fled for the safety of Mons.

Realizing that there was now no hope of succour reaching him, Boufflers capitulated on 10 December. To capture Lille had cost the Allies some 15,000 casualties—and taken all of 120 days.

---

the reliable brothers Solomon and Moses Medina, Hecop, and the less satisfactory Machado and Vanderkaa. There were scandals and misappropriations, but although Marlborough's political foes tried to implicate him in these it remained his proud boast that 'our army in Flanders has been regularly supplied with bread during the war, and has received it with an exactness that will hardly be thought consistent with the secrecy and suddenness of some of the moves'. To assist these, the employment, on Marlborough's insistence, of large numbers of light two-wheeled waggons drawn by two horses was an important contributory factor. But many waggons and horses still had to be hired locally. At regimental level reliance was placed on enterprising civilian sutlers.

The Captain-General's army was also provided with a sufficiency of gold with which to pay its way through friendly or neutral territory—a considerable innovation. Prices invariably rose, but willing suppliers were far more co-operative than sullen, ex-appropriated peasantry. But what could be achieved logistically in fertile regions such as Flanders, France, or Germany could not be copied in largely barren Spain or the North American wilderness. In those theatres supply was sporadic at best.

The nickname, 'the Old Corporal', was not lightly bestowed on Marlborough by the British soldiers. It reflected his general care for his men whom he did not wish to see unnecessarily wasted. He never revolutionized the supply or administrative systems of his day, but he somehow made them work to their limited capacity by fair but strict supervision. The same was true of the crude medical services of the time. Hospitals were established at Nordlingen in 1704, for example, and after the gory day of Malplaquet waggons were supplied for the transport of the enemy wounded back to the French lines. As Corporal Bishop observed in 1708, 'The Duke of Marlborough's attention and care was over all of us.' His minute eye for detail—for instance the provision of hand-mills for every regiment in 1705—was widely remarked, and from attention to such small things came disproportionate advantages. His troops willingly gave of their best whether in battle or on the seemingly interminable marches.

Although the Duke of Marlborough remains an enigmatic figure, whose character has attracted as much criticism as praise, there can be no doubt about his formidable military impact upon his own generation and upon the British army he did so much to inspire. Some have claimed that he owed much to his 'twin-captain', the brilliant Prince Eugene of Savoy, who shared in three of the four major battles. That they were a well-matched pair of closely co-operating and mutually supportive senior commanders—despite a thirteen-year disparity in age and many contrasting characteristics of race and breeding—there is no denying. Their mutual trust and respect for one another was total and unshakeable, as was widely remarked by their contemporaries. Eugene earned military fame at Zenta in 1697, achieved a great double success at the siege and battle of Turin in 1706, and would go on to an even greater achievement at Belgrade in 1717. But he also had his failures—at Staffarda (1690), Toulon (1707), and Denain (1712). As for Marlborough, he never faced a major defeat, his skill at siegecraft was unparalleled, and his overall grasp of strategic realities and possibilities was unmatched. His rule-defying march to the Danube in 1704 remains a military masterpiece, as does his conduct of the entire campaign of 1706 from 23 May to 6 October; and Ramillies—fought without the assistance of Eugene—was arguably his greatest battle in that same *annus mirabilis*.

Some have claimed that he faced only indifferent opponents—and that had he fought Condé, Turenne, or Luxembourg, rather than Tallard, Villeroi, or Vendôme, the outcome would have been different. This overlooks the facts that Turenne taught him much of his martial trade as a young officer attached to his army in 1674–5, and that Vendôme proved very successful in Spain after Oudenarde and Lille. More significantly, Marlborough proved 'more than a match for all the generals of that nation [France]' as Captain Parker noted—not excluding the great Marshal Villars, whom he bettered (albeit narrowly) at Malplaquet in 1709, dominated throughout 1710, and completely outmanœuvred and all but humiliated in 1711 at the passage of the lines of Non Plus Ultra and the subsequent capture of Bouchain, achieved under the Marshal's very nose after the most difficult siege operations the duke ever undertook. Yet Villars would become one of only four Marshal-Generals of France.

The Captain-General's martial impact and revealed abilities are irrefutable. Doubtless he was a born intriguer, insatiably ambitious for honours such as the Captain-Generalcy-for-Life (which eluded him), ever grasping after money to add to his immense fortune (even, it is claimed, asking one million *louis d'or* from the Sun King as the price for securing him a reasonable peace)—and yet bearing the reputation of being the meanest of men alive. Much of this is true. But if he was parsimonious with his guineas he was equally careful of his soldiers' lives—save on great days of unavoidable battle—as they indeed appreciated. Their grief at his removal from command was genuine: as witness Corporal Bishop: 'Oh!' said I, 'must we part from such a man whose fame has spread throughout all the world?'

That fame was indeed widespread. Peter the Great's navy included a large warship called the *Marlburrow*. His foes were only slightly less euphoric in according him his due. Vendôme noted with disquiet the extent of Marlborough's charisma at Valenciennes in 1706, reporting to Louis XIV that 'everybody here is only too ready to raise their hats at the mention of Marlborough's name'. Evidently there was 'something inexpressible' about John Churchill, as the Prince of Vaudemont had percipiently noted in a letter to William III as early as 1691. At the head of the army William had done so much to create, the future duke surely laid the foundations of the British army's future achievements.

5 THE ARMY OF THE GEORGES 1714–1783

ALAN J. GUY

The butcher's bill of Malplaquet in 1709, the vaulting ambitions of the over-mighty subject John Churchill, and the ostentatious post-war life-style of his associates—especially his former quartermaster-general William, Earl Cadogan—whose attempts to bribe the electors of Reading in 1714 were greeted with derisory calls of 'No Hanover, no Cadogan'—did nothing to lessen the proverbial antipathy of Englishmen to a standing army. Nor did the relentless growth of Marlborough's military machine during the late war and the opportunities this seemed to give one English political faction, the Whigs, to subvert traditional values and social relationships by the gift of army commissions or lucrative supply contracts.

Worse, and this perhaps is what the Reading electors most resented about Cadogan, the new and alien dynasty relied on armed force—first during the Jacobite rebellion of 1715, when government margins of victory on the battle-field were perilously narrow—and later in the 1720s and 1730s, when genuine fears of Jacobitism were linked by Sir Robert Walpole, the deeply loathed 'prime' minister, with elements of fantasy and political calculation to make Whig government backed by military power seem indispensable. The paranoid belief in October 1715 that the Jacobite scholars of Oxford were about to declare for the Pretender resulted in the city being first blockaded by Major-General Pepper's regiment of dragoons and then occupied by Brigadier Handasyde's regiment of foot. (The principal 'conspirator' escaped over Magdalen wall in his nightgown.) The unravelling of the Atterbury Plot of 1723 was followed by a government show of strength, with thousands of troops marching through London to leaguer in Hyde Park. Almost any civil tumult, and there were many in early-Georgian England, was scrutinized for Jacobite influence, while the notorious Sussex smugglers gleefully retaliated by assuming the sobriquet of 'the English Rebels' (1745).

The candour with which Walpole, one eye on the unstable European diplomatic scene and the other on the security of the new dynasty at home, stated that force was necessary for the support of government (*his* government) appealed neither to the Tory Opposition, who resented their post-1714 exclusion from local and national administration, nor to cross-bench 'country' ideologues, intrinsically hostile to the growth of the fiscal–military complex. As John, Lord Hervey, told George II 'there was nothing so odious to men of all ranks and classes in this country as troops; that people who had not sense enough to count up to twenty, or to articulate ten words together on other subjects had their lessons so well to heart that they could talk like Ciceros on this topic and never to an audience that did not chime in with their arguments.'

The annual parliamentary debate on the Mutiny Bill (originally an instrument to validate punishment for the military crimes of mutiny and desertion, but transformed in 1713 into a rudimentary Army Act, authorizing the number of troops to be maintained each year) gave Opposition MPs the chance to browbeat ministers on the themes of Cromwellian despotism and the suppression of European liberties by standing armies. Government responded by approaching the session with exquisite care: army estimates, already pared to the uttermost farthing, were presented in a way which cloaked the real cost of the military establishment, so perpetuating a network of customary arrangements that shifted much of the responsibility for maintaining the army on to the shoulders of military proprietors—the officers of company and field rank who had invested in their commands by purchasing commissions, from which they expected to receive a steady return, not unlike an investment in stocks.

This was the same system of military management encountered by William III on his arrival in England in 1688. Even then it had offended against European best practice, but it functioned adequately enough and as William had a European war on his hands he left it alone. Devices and dodges in the system had been not uncongenial to Marlborough who, rather than assuming the mantle of a military reformer, concentrated on winning the century's most devastating victory at Blenheim in 1704. The fact that the British military machine, however 'gothick' it appeared to a candid observer, worked in practice—at least until 1780, when looming disaster in America was attributed to degenerate administrative

Rank and File

In the era of proprietary command, the common soldiers of King George's army were commodities—human resources to be recruited (often at considerable expense), drilled and exercised, managed as an investment, discharged when they were worn out, or drafted from one regiment into another ordered on active service. Such a regime, in which units were often chronically under strength, suffering from too high a turnover of men, yet with too great a proportion of recruits under arms to be classed as 'fit for service', was not calculated to encourage the idea of the regiment as a brotherhood of men. It is not until the 1770s that we find occasions like Minden Day, celebrating the overthrow of the pride of the French cavalry by nine battalions of British and Hanoverian infantry at the battle of Minden on 1 August 1759, being used to invoke the corporate spirit of a regiment. Also new was the attitude of an officer like Lieutenant Stephen Payne Adye, Deputy Judge Advocate in America during the War of Independence who, when he argued that 'every soldier is a human creature, susceptible of the same feelings and passions with other men', echoed the Enlightenment thinking of Montesquieu and Beccaria. Majority opinion remained that only those officers who treated their men with severity were likely to be well served by them, and it was typical of a paternal, hierarchical society that savage punishments, publicly inflicted, were juxtaposed with equally dramatic reprieves and rehabilitation. Ultimately, British officers had ambivalent feelings about the men under their command; on the one hand viewing them as incorrigible, yet, as citizens living under a free constitution, inherently nobler and more courageous than their German allies, and they often expressed great pride in their humane and honourable conduct.

The task of recruiting was devolved to the regimental officers, assisted in wartime by the civil power in the localities, who under the aegis of temporary recruiting acts implemented a limited conscription of the able-bodied poor. Ideally, it was intended at all times to fill the ranks with volunteers. Until 1771, when regiments were first allowed to recruit Roman Catholics in Ireland, recruits were to be known Protestants only; other criteria governing age and height were set by the War Office. Field officers commanding regiments guided their recruiting parties as to how these should be applied in practice: instructions issued for the 93rd Foot in 1760 warned that all recruits were to be 'able Bodied, Sound in their Limbs, free from Ruptures, Scald [sic] heads, Ulcerous Sores or any remarkable deformity . . . No Strolers [sic], Vagabonds, Tinkers,

Chimney Sweepers, Colliers or Saylors to be Inlisted, but such men only as were born in the Neighbourhood of the place they are inlisted in, & of whom you can get and give a good Account'.

It is safe to assume that the motive underlying many enlistments was economic; partly a consequence of the decline or collapse of traditional forms of employment but also a by-product of the chronic seasonal underemployment affecting labouring men. Conversely, the coming of harvest saw regiments hit by outbreaks of short-term desertion which, given the army's reputation of being over-ready to resort to the lash, were often treated with remarkable tolerance. Other influences were also at work on recruiting, for the pool of the nation's unemployed was invariably greater than the number of vacancies in the ranks, yet the regiments were rarely up to establishment. As always, perhaps, the notion of 'going for a soldier' appealed most of all to men who wished to liberate themselves from humdrum daily existence or domestic entanglements. Whatever lured them away from home it could scarcely have been the pay which, until a modest increase was granted in 1792, had remained substantially unaltered since the reign of Charles II. As it was, many soldiers had to supplement their income by taking off-duty civilian jobs, or doing tailoring or cobbling for the regiment itself.

Rapid wartime expansion made recruiting highly competitive as parties bid against each other in a dwindling market. Even the Highlands of Scotland, an abundant recruiting-ground during the Seven Years War, was becoming starved of men by the late 1770s. It was in these inaccessible parts of Britain that forced enlistments were sometimes attempted, drawing upon the anachronistic authority of clan chieftains. An alternative response to the shrinking pool of manpower was to lower the standard of recruit—with consequences which are shocking to modern sensibilities. The 93rd Foot, mentioned earlier, which was by no means a badly run regiment, succeeded in recruiting a consumptive, several men suffering from blindness, lameness and scorbutic ulcers, worms, epilepsy, and ruptures, and even poor 50 year-old John Knowlan who suffered from 'Piles of many years standing'. Another contingent of unlikely heroes, fortunately intercepted on their way to the front in Portugal in 1762, included men with fingers, arms, and ankles out of joint.

As yet, all too little is known about 'army women', as they were called in eighteenth-century parlance, but they must not be overlooked. Often functioning under a discipline as strict as that applied to their menfolk, they served as laundresses, nurses, cooks in garrison (on campaign the soldiers catered for themselves), or as sutlers, selling merchandise, liquor, and victuals. An object of irritation to the officers, who tended to classify them indiscriminately as 'strumpets', it would appear that contrary to popular belief many were legally married, while most of the remainder lived in fairly stable common-law relationships. A mere six women per company were permitted to accompany their husbands on active service, and a grim fate awaited those left behind. 'There is no part of the Expedition I so much dread', wrote one officer whose regiment was posted to India in 1754, 'as the parting of the Soldiers from their Wives and Children, nor is there any thing more discouraging to the Men than their Cries and Lamentations [for] the greatest part of them have it not in their Power to subsist otherwise than from Hand to Mouth.'

---

practices—meant that criticism by such penetrating minds as Philip Francis, First Clerk at the War Office, 1762–72, could be disregarded.

Simply expressed, a military proprietor's income was obtained from his pay, plus any legitimate surpluses from the public money he was given to provide his soldiers with their subsistence, clothing, and equipment. For its protection, the State relied on manpower audits by civilian commissaries independent of the uniformed hierarchy, in conjunction with inspections by senior officers and the quality control of items supplied by the proprietor. This system originated in the late Middle Ages and worked tolerably well as long as the troops did not change location too frequently. Just as it was understood that at times there would be paroxysms of profit-taking (implying that the narrow line between legitimate perquisite and embezzlement would be crossed and recrossed many times) it was cynically assumed that on other occasions the officers would have to dip into their own pockets to recruit, feed, and clothe their men.

Opportunities for the misappropriation of public money were increased by the fact that the eighteenth century was a time of 'small government'. The early Georgian War Office was a minuscule organization, staffed by a dozen or so clerks—in peacetime it had long been a refuge for gouty, superannuated cronies of Sir Robert Walpole. Much of the small detail of administration was entrusted to regimental agents, civilian servants of the colonels, who acted as clerks, money-brokers, and link-men between their patrons and the government offices. As for the civilian commissaries, who were supposed to muster regiments in their country quarters, there were only six of these for the whole of England and Wales and one for 'North Britain' (Scotland), all of them part-time administrators who combined their appointments with other genteel pursuits. Commissaries appointed to garrisons abroad were frequently absent from their posts, and their attendance on troops on active service was even less punctual, although one commissary, Thomas Pitcher, secured his place in history by holding up the fortification of the doomed post of Oswego while he mustered its garrison in 1756.

In a country almost without conscription (other than for the militia, itself moribund until mid-century), where every soldier was supposed to be a volunteer, the proprietary regiment was the ideal mechanism for raising troops. It was an administrative rather than a tactical formation; many European regiments were multi-battalion units with a significantly smaller cadre of officers than in Britain, where the 1,000-man 'battalion' of foot and the 'regiment' were for the most part synonymous. In Britain it was the lure of preferment and the proliferation of office that motivated aspiring commanders to enlist men at inflated bounties, or seek out fresh supplies of manpower in the Highland glens or the mountain fastnesses of Wales.

Ultimately, however, every man raised by this network of private enterprise was at the State's disposal. Recruits became effective fighting men much more quickly in seasoned units, so active service regiments were completed to war establishment by taking drafts from those left behind. The result was that although many of today's most famous regiments trace their ancestry back to Britain's eighteenth-century wars, and bear their proudest laurels from Quebec or Minden, regimental history as we know it was created by a small number of long-suffering officers, rather than by the human traffic directed so quickly and so ruthlessly through the ranks.

What is so striking in the period before the rationalized phase of Empire which began in 1763 is how little like an army in the modern sense some parts of the Georgian armed forces actually were. The independent companies of foot in historic imperial garrisons like Jamaica or New York were virtually ignored by the home government, with the result that they merged year by year with their host communities and were frequently dependent upon them for basic necessities. (Ironically, the disbandment of these companies in 1764 after their undistinguished performance in the Seven Years War, by depriving upwardly mobile colonial gentlemen of their chance to wear the king's red coat became a minor contributory factor in the American rebellion.)

The situation of entire battalions sent overseas could be equally dismal. That of the 38th Foot, sent to the Leeward Islands in 1707 and recalled in 1764, was by common consent the worst. In 1752, its new colonel, Alexander Duroure, arriving in Antigua on a tour of inspection, discovered that the regiment was stricken by disease and that most of the survivors had taken up private work, subsidizing comrades to stand guard for them. Officers who lacked friends or family in the islands were also doing civilian jobs—a shocking abandonment of status. This was the *second time* in three decades in which this unfortunate unit had more or less disintegrated.

Prior to 1780, when the Commissioners of Public Accounts began to sift the debris of the military effort in America in the name of 'economical reform', the House of Commons, though watchful of military expenditure, did not concern itself with the betterment of the army. In 1745, after setbacks in Flanders and mainland Britain, where a Jacobite army had roamed unchecked for a time, parliament's attention briefly focused on the state of the land forces, but it is likely that the only members of the Commons Committee who understood what they were told by expert witnesses were army-officers—government stalwarts to a man. Victory over the Jacobites at Culloden in April 1746 put a stop to this tedious and perplexing inquiry.

In fact, for most of our period the only reforming initiatives came from the Crown. Despite being figureheads of a dominant faction (the Whigs) which somewhat undermined their personal popularity and effectiveness, the first two Georges were soldier-kings in the German tradition. Both had commanded troops with gallantry and some distinction in Europe, and were much more suitable heads of the armed forces than poor moribund Queen Anne. The only other claimant to supreme military authority, the Duke of Marlborough, was rehabilitated by George I in 1714, but effectively relegated to honourable and swiftly encroaching dotage (he died in 1722). His refulgent title 'Captain-General' was not bestowed upon another soldier until it was awarded to William Augustus, Duke of Cumberland, a prince of the blood, in 1745.

King George II was the last British monarch to lead his troops into action, at Dettingen on 27 June 1743. His self-satisfaction radiates from John Wootton's painting of the event. Like his martinet cousin, King Frederick William I of Prussia, George identified himself closely with his officers. He wore a brown coat for civil business and his red coat for the military and he kept a book close by for making notes on his officers' characters and attainments (a relatively easy thing to do early in the century when there were only a couple of thousand of them). He jealously guarded promotions to senior ranks and struggled with tolerable success to keep politicians out of the arena of military patronage. A passionate man, who was capable of vindictively ruining an officer's career, he was also too fond of the well-ordered soldiers of his Hanoverian Electorate. This latter tendency, although not unreasonable, given the English forces' occasional sloppiness and want of discipline, went down about as well with George's officers as William III's fondness for his Dutch guards had done a generation or so earlier, but the king's impact on the army, like that of his father, was overwhelmingly beneficial.

Features of royal intervention included the regulation of the purchase and sale of commissions (1720, 1722, 1768) which had the effect of stabilizing prices and, in the longer term, excluding the all-important colonelcies of regiments from the market-place. A royal warrant of 1751 ended the custom of designating regiments by the name of their current colonel, introducing instead numbered titles which (typically) took some time to catch on. The colonels were also prohibited from placing their personal coats of arms on regimental colours (1751), and the appearance and quality of the uniforms they provided for their men were subjected to progressively stricter controls (1729, 1736, 1751). Of equal, possibly greater, importance was the accumulation of financial regulations which circumscribed junior proprietors' ability to profit from their captaincies of troops (of cavalry) and companies (of foot). These included the banning of fictitious names, 'dead pays', from muster-rolls (1716, 1747); the regulation of stoppages from soldiers' pay, a constant source of discontent and desertion (1717, 1721, 1732, 1749); and restrictions on the dividends to which captains were entitled from surpluses in the regimental accounts (1749, 1761, 1766). Associated with these initiatives was the increasing use of the Board of General Officers from November 1714 to advise the king on military administration and devise army-wide regulations and, from 1716, the delegation of royal power to inspecting generals given the task of reviewing regiments each spring—a vital element in creating an atmosphere of gentlemanly competition between individual units. From 1747 this activity was linked to a reinvigorated and more effective machinery for mustering regiments in the field.

Direct royal intervention also took place in the area of the army's weapons drill and tactics. The Duke of Marlborough's *New Exercise of Firelocks and Bayonets* (1708), itself upgraded by Field Marshal Lord Orkney in Flanders in 1711, was reaffirmed by royal command in 1716 and specifically extended to Ireland in 1723. The influential *Regulations* of 1728, substantially unaltered until 1748, were a direct consequence of George II noticing that 'the Regiments do not use One and the same

Exercise, and that every Colonel alters or Amends as he thinks fit'. The *Regulations* of 1748 were set in train by the king's son and Captain-General, William Augustus, Duke of Cumberland, and the *Standing Orders* issued under his authority in May 1753, which dealt with the myriad duties of units on campaign, in camp, and on the march, were extracted from general orders he had issued as commander of the forces in the Low Countries from 1745 to 1748.

On the debit side, notwithstanding the weight of royal authority behind them (literally in Cumberland's case—increasing corpulence and a nagging leg wound from Dettingen threatened to render him immobile) these warrants and regulations were diluted by the friction of distance, administrative obstacles, and personal factors. Close to home the military prerogatives of the Lord Lieutenant of Ireland partially excluded Cumberland from control of an administratively discrete peacetime establishment of 12,000 officers and men, enlarged to 15,325 in 1769. The Lord Lieutenant at that time, Lieutenant-General George, Viscount Townshend, noted with alarm the same discrepancies and dissimilarities between regiments that had offended George II nearly fifty years previously. Moreover, invasive regal power still left many of the colonels' perquisites intact, notably their right to handle clothing contracts, worth £500 or more to them per annum. But, most importantly, when the colonels were senior enough to become members of the Board of General Officers or reviewing generals themselves, they became judges in their own cause. Sharing power with their royal master, their allegiance was conditional and incomplete—a way of thinking and acting which, extended as it was to the officer corps as a whole, had wider implications for the mentality of King George's army.

Other than in the so-called 'Scientific Corps' of Artillery and Engineers, separately administered by the Board of Ordnance, there was no requirement for a young man wishing to enter the army to obtain a formal military education or qualifications. This was at variance with trends in the other great professions—the law, medicine, and the ministry—but perhaps this did not matter a great deal. The principal weapons system in use, the flintlock land pattern musket and bayonet, was simple to operate; drill and tactics were straightforward at the level most regimental officers were expected to carry them out; military accounting could be learned on the job, and as the financial reforms initiated by the first two Georges began to bite into proprietary incomes, it tended to be dumped on the non-commissioned officers. Most importantly, as long as officers could be assumed to be gentlemen, there was no need to study leadership in the abstract. British officers learned their profession 'by going on as other people did', and while editions of ancient and modern military textbooks attracted long lists of subscribers, theirs was at bottom a practical, non-theoretical, training regimen.

The utility of this service mentality was enhanced by a tradition of long regimental service which, once understood, completely overturns the stereotype of an army led by languid incompetents. It has been calculated that at the end of the long peace in 1740 captains of foot had served for an average of nineteen years before obtaining their companies, and that even in 1759, at the height of a world war, the average length of service was still ten years. Appointments to the senior regimental grades of major, lieutenant-colonel, and colonel, which came under royal scrutiny, were reserved for men of merit and service to the partial exclusion of market forces. Of 290 colonels appointed between 1714 and 1763, over twenty had served for more than forty-five years before obtaining their regiments; over sixty had served between thirty-five and forty-five years, ninety for more than fifteen years, and most of the rest for over a decade. In 1740, lieutenant-colonels of foot had served an average of twenty-seven years before reaching that rank and majors twenty-six years. In 1759 these averages were still thirteen and seventeen years respectively and in 1786, three years after the end of the American War, twenty-one years six months and eighteen years. A succession of campaigns, augmentations, and imperial expansion had combined to make the army significantly younger than it had been in 1740, when an embarrassing number of officers had been too decrepit for their units to go on active service, but not so young as to imply ignorance or lack of experience.

Long-distance regimental service, it must be said, does not automatically equate with military competence. Neither for that matter does deep reading. After his death in action in 1758, Major-General Alexander Dury's extensive library was disposed of at a special sale complete with printed catalogue, but in terms of generalship he was reckoned to be a dunderhead. Taken as a group, however, the officers of the Georgian army accumulated a wide operational repertoire. In England and Wales they wore themselves out in petty warfare against smugglers and riotous assemblies (there was no civil police force) and in doing so they attained a high level of expertise in the Georgian equivalent of low intensity operations. Ireland and Scotland could both be regarded as territories under military occupation; Ireland to a lesser extent, for the country was docile under the rule of law until the outbreak of the Whiteboy disturbances in the early 1760s, but not so Scotland where, in the wake of the brutal Culloden campaign and well into the 1750s, the Highlands fretted under military control; punitive counter-insurgency campaigning alternating with tedious garrison duty and road-making details, where scurvy was a greater threat than rebel bullets.

Further afield, officers acquired knowledge of major siege operations, either as defenders, successful and otherwise at Gibraltar (1727, 1778–83) and Minorca (1756, 1781–2) or as part of major amphibious expeditions; Louisbourg (1758), Quebec (1759), Havana (1762), and Charleston (1780). These concentrations of artillery fire-power at the culminating point of a lengthy chain of logistics had much in common with American wilderness warfare, for this too depended upon the movement of quantities of men, guns, and warlike stores across trackless hostile terrain. Even the conventional combat of infantry and cavalry in Europe (1743–8, 1758–63), the most glamorous theatre of operations and source of most of the familiar imagery of eighteenth-century warfare, had on its fringes, where light infantry, riflemen, and light cavalry grappled in the incessant war of outposts categorized as *la petite guerre*, linkages to the savage warfare of America or Scotland. And, on the far side of the world, from 1754 onwards a growing number of the king's troops campaigned in support of the Honourable East India Company, against the huge armies of oriental potentates, struggling with logistical complications previously alien to the Western experience of warfare.

In a different mental world these varied, yet often subtly linked, experiences, which owed much to the British army being the spearhead of a paramount naval power, might have been encompassed by a corpus of doctrine, but, with the periodic return of peace, the disbandment of many regiments, and the drastic reduction of the remainder, attention reverted to basic arms drills that could be performed by detachments in isolated quarters or colonial outposts. Soldiers considered themselves fortunate to muster in battalion strength once a year for the spring review, let alone be brigaded in multi-regiment formations to act as an army ought. Advanced training of this sort was almost always a wartime luxury.

A minority of privileged officers—Peers of the Realm, Members of Parliament, and their close connections—clustered thickly in the upper reaches of the hierarchy as generals, governors of the larger garrisons, and colonels of regiments. Their grip on the high command was viewed with satisfaction by statesmen who understood that rather than the standing

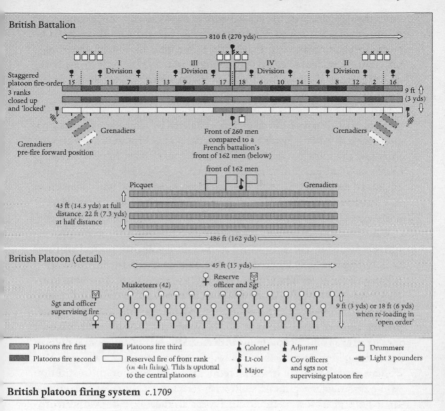

British platoon firing system *c.*1709

army threatening to militarize the State as Opposition spokesmen claimed, the army was itself effectively civilianized and tamed by its symbiotic relationship with property and aristocracy. 'Has it not always been with good reason urged', declared Henry Pelham in 1744, 'that our liberties are in no danger from our standing army because it is commanded by men of the best families and fortunes?'

Most officers, lacking this group's superior patronage leverage, expected to end their careers as captains, majors, or lieutenant-colonels at best. They included members of the middling and lesser gentry: men from gentry families that had earlier branched out into trade and commerce, sons of the clergy, and a contingent of Huguenot refugees and their descendants. Field Marshal Jean Louis, Lord Ligonier, the army's

Commander-in-Chief, 1757–66, was the most famous representative of this group. By the 1770s, the penetration of the British officer corps by Irish Protestant gentlemen that began at the time of William III's reconquest of Ireland had resulted in as many as one-third of the officers being of Irish origin; the fact that military commissions were included in the Lord Lieutenant's patronage armoury meant that the longer a regiment stayed in the sister kingdom the more Irish it became. After 1745, the growing Britishness of the army was enhanced by an influx of Scotsmen, some with distinctly Jacobite antecedents and others with very modest fortunes; the most notable was Colonel Simon Fraser, Master of Lovat, once a militant Jacobite who, after his return from exile in 1750, raised a Highland regiment (the 78th Foot) in 1756–7 and served with distinction in Canada and Portugal. By the mid-1760s Scotland was providing the army with somewhere between one-fifth and one-third of its officers.

These incomers participated in the major expansion of career opportunities provided by the three world wars of the eighteenth century: the war against Spain which merged into the War of the Austrian Succession (1739–48), the Seven Years War (1756–63), and the War of American Independence (1775–83). Average annual army personnel in this triad of conflicts escalated from 62,373 to 92,676 to 108,484: in individual years a still greater number served. In 1762, for example, the military establishment totalled 111,583 officers and men, with an additional 24,000 maintained in Ireland.

This growth pattern, it will be recalled, was based upon the institution of the proprietary regiment, each with its quota of thirty or so commissioned officers. Most of the 'young corps' as they were known were disbanded at the end of a war, while the 'old corps' were reduced in numbers, yet the number of regiments retained in peacetime rose inexorably as the century progressed. From 1763, an innovative commitment to imperial strategic planning also resulted in the retention of a higher ratio of officers to men than previously.

For most officers, their investment of life and limb was matched at least once in their careers by cash payment for a commission. George I restricted the free market by his 1720 tariff, and from then on an officer wishing to sell was usually obliged to offer his commission at a regulated price to the man with the most regimental seniority in the rank beneath him. If that man was unable to buy, the commission was offered to the next most senior, and so on. The purchaser got the rank, but not the seniority of his predecessor, becoming the most junior captain, lieutenant, or ensign for the time being. When a captain sold his commission, a chain reaction began which might stretch down to the 'youngest' ensign in the regiment and out into civilian life, where young gentlemen queued to join the army.

These frequent, protracted, and often frustrating negotiations could be a source of friction and instability, but the fact that as many as one-third of vacancies were filled *without* purchase provided the all-important safety-valve. The gift of a commission was usually the result of a death vacancy, which could occur in peacetime but much more frequently on active service, when regimental seniority came into play, subject to the approval of the theatre commander. Many subaltern commissions also were bestowed without purchase, on the condition (honoured more often in the breach than the observance) that what had been given could not later be sold. It was an unlucky officer who could not at some time in his career save or borrow enough money to buy at least one of his commissions, and this reconciled men to the situation where the greatest prizes were reserved for those of the highest social status.

To mid-century and perhaps beyond the workaday profile of the army, the relative ease of advancing through its hierarchy to the respectable and moderately rewarding grades of captain, field officer, the lieutenant-governorship of an important garrison, or the command of some humble fort, meant that peers and commoners rubbed shoulders in the mess without the friction or snobbery of later decades. Lieutenant-Colonel Charles Russell of the Foot Guards looked down his nose at the officers of the Royal Welch Fusiliers (one of George II's favourite corps) whom he dismissed as 'a good sort of people, very well in their way, but low enough', but the concept of a 'crack regiment' only began to emerge among the cavalry in the aftermath of the Seven Years War. For the time being, if a man was not already a member of polite society, his commission gave him entry, and the contemporary definition of the title of gentleman, 'commonly given in England to all that distinguish themselves from the common sort of people by a good garb, genteel air or good education, wealth or learning' suggests ample latitude in the way in which social acceptability could be achieved.

To counterbalance this relative ease of entry, the prevailing *culture* of the officer corps was predominantly aristocratic in tone, based as it was upon a pre-Enlightenment honour code with quasi-medieval trimmings, seen at their most extraordinary in the Philadelphia *Mischianza* of 18 May 1778 which celebrated the imminent departure of Lieutenant-General Sir

Contrasts in Tactics

At about 10 o'clock on the morning of 13 September 1759, General Louis Joseph, Marquis de Montcalm gave the fateful order for his little army of regular French battalions and Canadian militia (about 4,500 men) to advance from Quebec across the Plains of Abraham. Facing him was an equally small British army led by Major-General James Wolfe, which had taken up position there the night before. But Wolfe had seven battalions of regular infantry in his line of battle, with four more on his left flank and in reserve—4,441 men, according to the official return.

The French came on with a cheer, but much too fast; almost at a run, said eye-witnesses. Approximately 130 yards from the British they commenced a ragged fire. The redcoats, drawn up two deep, waited impassively—each musket loaded with an additional ball. When the enemy came within a hundred yards, they marched steadily up to them, giving a well-directed fire. As the range closed to 20 or 30 yards they let fly with a general volley—the simultaneous explosion of their musketry was said by French officers to have resembled a cannon-shot. It was, declares Sir John Fortescue, the army's historian, the 'most perfect volley ever fired on a battlefield'. Within minutes the French were fleeing towards the city.

British infantry had been renowned for the killing-power of their musketry since the days of Marlborough. For the first half of the century they used the technique known as 'platoon fire': the men were drawn up in platoons, distinct from the companies in which they normally served, and then told-off into three firings, which were posted along a three-deep line of musketeers in chequer formation. Shooting in strict numbered sequence, the firings generated a rolling spread of musketry along the entire frontage of the battalion, although this fire was unaimed other than in the general direction of the enemy. From the mid-1750s, platoon fire was simplified by utilizing the men's companies as the actual fire units.

For most people, this methodical, even stately way of fighting sums up the warfare of the eighteenth century. And, in truth, if a regiment succeeded in delivering one or two well-synchronized volleys in battle—each firelock well charged and the ball rammed home—it had gone a long way towards fulfilling its purpose, for the execution could be devastating. The opening British volley at Fontenoy on 11 May 1745 killed and wounded 700 officers and men in the front ranks of the French army.

After these initial exchanges, however, firing tended to degenerate into a random fusillade, each man blasting off just as soon as he could reload. Ranks and files became intermingled, deaf to the hoarse shouts of their officers or the beat of drum until, at last, the whole mass shambled into motion forwards or backwards. Over several hours, this intense form of combat probably resulted in levels of traumatic stress equal to, if not greater than, those experienced in twentieth-century wars and was mitigated only by the relative infrequency of pitched battles.

As the century progressed, the British army, in common with its European counterparts, experimented with novel tactical arrangements and new varieties of troops. In North America from 1755 soldiers adapted to the 'ranging and wood service' by lightening their gear, docking their full-skirted uniform coats, cropping their hair, and relinquishing their swords in favour of hatchets or tomahawks. They were taught to load and fire from a prone position; to take cover in the forest—'tree all!' was the word of command for doing this—and to aim and fire independently. From 1757, rifles made their tentative appearance in the army, most likely for shooting game for the pot rather than Indians or Frenchmen. In December 1757, a light infantry battalion, armed with shorter and lighter firelocks, was formed under officers and NCOs skilled in ranger duties. From the 1758 campaign onwards, one company per battalion was detached as light infantry, an innovation which lapsed at the end of the war until its reinstatement on an army-wide basis in 1771.

In 1759, the Commander in-Chief in America, Major-General Jeffery Amherst, authorized the use of a two-deep line, as in his view the paucity of French regulars made the third rank unnecessary. A two-deep line in open order was the norm for the army in America during the War of Independence when, as Sergeant Roger Lamb recalled, the essence of infantry fighting lay in priming, loading, firing, and pushing ahead with the bayonet as quickly as possible.

But to veterans who had fought in Germany after 1758, alongside the forces of Frederick the Great of Prussia, these tactics seemed very careless. Light troops had played a prominent part in that conflict too; so much so that their further development was Eurocentric to the virtual exclusion of colonial influences. The British light dragoons and Highlanders had distinguished themselves in night-time raids, skirmishing, and reconnaissance in Germany, and Captain William Phillips of the Royal Artillery was the first to bring guns into action at the gallop in support of the cavalry during the battle of Warburg on 30 July 1760. Yet the German War was chiefly characterized by daring outflanking movements and the imaginative co-ordination of infantry, cavalry, and artillery, backed up by meticulous staff-work, which made Sir William Howe's frontal assault on the American entrenchments at Bunker Hill on 17 June 1775 look amateurish by comparison. 'A *German* would have taken the *Bull* by the *ribs* and *nose* not by the *Horns*', complained William Phillips as he contemplated the gruesome casualty list. As difficulties accumulated in America, the 'Germans' began to view the 'Americans' with something akin to contempt, although, as usual in the British army, their differences had as much to do with personal friction as with any deep reasoning.

William Howe for England. Under the guidance of Captain John André (later hanged by the Americans as a spy) 'Knights of the Blended Rose' rode in the lists against the 'Knights of the Burning Mountain' in honour of two English and two American 'Queens of Beauty', each of whom was attended by Turkish-clad damsels. As one officer observer commented, 'The "Knights of the Burning Mountain" are tom-fools, and the "Knights of the Blended Rose" are damned fools! I know of no other distinction between them', but the extravaganza was an outward and visible sign of an élite culture under extreme pressure from events—Sir William was an inglorious commander and the evacuation of Philadelphia only a few weeks away. As the doomed war lurched towards its humiliating conclusion at Yorktown (1781) and the ruling class found its privileged position in the State called into question, the 'fire and sword men' in America, including Lieutenant-Colonel Banastre Tarleton, a leading light in the *Mischianza*, took up the challenge by waging war on the assumption that 'war was hell' long before Sherman coined the phrase. This ruthlessness not only survived the American War, but was typical of the sprigs of nobility and the new hard men from the Celtic peripheries who re-established British military power in insurgent Ireland (1798) or conquered India from the 1790s. It is probably no coincidence that Lieutenant-General Gerard, Lord Lake, scourge of the rebel Irish (1798) and the Marathas (1803–5), first saw service as a young officer at Yorktown, or that the efficient, predatory campaigning of Lieutenant-General Charles 'No Flint' Grey in the West Indies during 1794 was founded on the unforgiving methods he had applied to the Americans.

The era of the Victorian public schools, which succeeded in ironing out regional and social distinctions to produce a recognizably standard and interchangeable version of the English officer and gentleman had not yet arrived, and this sometimes left officers floundering when they tried to reconcile an aristocratic honour code with the need for military subordination and the demands of polite society. The result was that army life sometimes resembled an endlessly prolonged rite of initiation. Its worst feature, the duel, may even have been on the increase as the army absorbed a throng of young Irish gentlemen from what was still, in some ways, a colonial society. At another level, officers who convinced themselves that they had been passed over for promotion, denied a lucrative posting, or that their behaviour in some public place or on the battlefield had been called into question, hounded their comrades, senior officers, and even the king's ministers for public acknowledgement of their pretensions that would reaffirm their status in the narrow world of the Georgian military. Such basic uncertainties alternated with strident self-assertiveness that more than once tumbled into eccentricity—a characteristic believed to be peculiarly British, deriving from the effects of a free constitution. Civilians, officers of the Royal Navy, colonial Americans, and the 'Meer Merchants' of the East India Company were victims of this insufferable attitude. In one extreme case, Captain Philip Thicknesse, Lieutenant-Governor of Landguard Fort in Suffolk (1753–66) hounded Colonel Francis Vernon of the Suffolk militia with scurrilous verses, the 'gift' of a piece of driftwood as a battalion gun, and legal action which led to Thicknesse being clapped into the King's Bench prison for three months, fined £100, and bound over to keep the peace for a period of seven years. (Thicknesse, who was more than somewhat deranged, claimed that sleepy little Landguard was a 'frontier garrison of importance', a statement best appraised in the light of the fact that until the mid-nineteenth century there was no road leading from the fort in any direction.)

The monarch himself was not immune from such breakings-out of 'the stubborn English Spirit'. Guards officers who thought that their exploits at Dettingen had attracted insufficient praise from George II ridiculed him for his attachment to his Hanoverian soldiery, while two prominent generals resigned—one, Charles, third Duke of Marlborough, because he had not received a coveted promotion to major-general and the other, the veteran John, Earl of Stair, commander of the British contingent, because George had ignored his strategic ideas before the battle and his tactical advice during it. Stair followed up his resignation with an impertinent justification, clearly intended for public consumption.

The most damaging of these squabbles for the army at large involved the protracted vilification of the Duke of Cumberland. After 1748, Cumberland's unmilitary elder brother, Frederick, Prince of Wales, and his political allies did their best to discredit him as a militarist and a threat to the constitution. When Frederick died prematurely in 1751 it was even suggested that 'the Duke', as he was known, stood in the same relationship to the adolescent Prince George as 'Crookback Richard' once had to the princes in the Tower. Cumberland was also disliked in some sections of the army, partly on account of his all too well publicized proposal in 1748 to disband one of the 'old corps' out of sequence, an injudicious attack on the property rights of its officers from which he was at length dissuaded by his father's ministers. The main cause of irritation, however, was his well-merited reputation as a martinet, which did not sit well with the convention that strict rules of conduct and peremptory orders should be 'softened by gentle persuasive arguments by which gentlemen, particularly those of a British constitution, must be governed'. This vocal undercurrent of resentment was given a substantial boost in 1750 by the defection of Lieutenant-Colonel the Hon. George Townshend, one of the Duke's own aides-de-camp, a mercurial young man who turned his merciless gift for caricature against his old chief and espoused the cause of a revived militia as a counterpoise to the regular army, a country platform with which, as he well knew, Cumberland disagreed. Though Cumberland did not lack his own cadre of loyal supporters in the army (one of them, Lieutenant-General William Strode, commissioned a posthumous equestrian statue of him; unveiled in 1770, it was London's first out door statue of a soldier), there are clear signs that he was wearying of his self-imposed task to regenerate the army long before his defeat and disgrace after the battle of Hastenbeck in 1757. Cumberland's fall opened the way for Townshend's return to the army and a brigadier's command in the Quebec campaign of 1759, when, as might have been expected, his volatile personality jarred repeatedly with that of his commander, Major-General James Wolfe, another notable disciplinarian and eccentric. Ironically, in later years, as Lord Lieutenant of Ireland, George, Viscount Townshend (as he became on the death of his father in 1764) was forced to emulate Cumberland in a not unsuccessful attempt to tackle the disorganization and indiscipline of the Irish army between 1767 and 1772.

Fortunately these theatrical displays of mutual antagonism so typical of the Georgian officer corps were neutralized by a change in the public's appreciation of the army which can first be detected as our period draws to its close. The triumphant latter years of the Seven Years War first rescued the army from the position of low esteem it had occupied since the days of Cromwell and the major-generals, a trend which proved strong enough to

survive the shock of defeat in America. Military subjects made their tentative appearance on the printed ceramics manufactured for Britain's burgeoning consumer market. The shiny bald head of Lieutenant-General
John, Marquess of Granby, the gallant cavalry commander of the German
War, adorned jugs and teapots (and a multitude of inn-signs); likewise the
craggy features of Lieutenant-General George Augustus Eliott, defender
of Gibraltar. The intrepid Major-General Charles, Earl Cornwallis, was
similarly commemorated, more likely on account of his achievements at
Brandywine in 1777 and Camden in 1780 than for the surrender at Yorktown. Bloodthirsty Colonel Tarleton was depicted on a jug in a transfer-
print version of his famous portrait painted by Sir Joshua Reynolds.
Meanwhile, the print version of Benjamin West's *The Death of General
Wolfe* (1770–1), one of an innovatory group of canvases which broke new
ground in history painting by depicting heroic contemporaries in their
military uniforms rather than Roman togas, became one of the most com-
mercially successful engravings ever published, and was also reproduced
for the mass market on Wedgwood pottery. Thus, even before the dawn of
the age of Wellington and Moore, the British army and its leaders were
poised on the brink of becoming heroes in their own epic.

6 THE ARMY AND THE FIRST BRITISH EMPIRE 1714–1783

TONY HAYTER

The response of the British army in the eighteenth century to overseas campaigning was at first slow and uncertain. The operations in North America in the 1740s showed not much advance in technique from the isolated operations there in Queen Anne's reign, and in the Caribbean little seems to have been learned since Elizabethan times. A certain confidence in planning and execution can be observed in the Seven Years War, but up until 1783 the experience of troops abroad was harsh and bitter, and the hazards, particularly of tropical disease, were appalling.

In the years after the great reduction of the army after the Treaty of Utrecht no more than nine regiments of foot were stationed overseas. Of these four served in Minorca, three in Gibraltar, one in North America, and one in the West Indies. The Gibraltar garrison was from time to time reinforced above this figure if danger threatened from Spain. During these years the troops endured all the difficulties of long garrison duty: acute boredom relieved by alcohol and punctuated by the spectacle of savage military punishment, an inadequate monotonous diet, and ever-present danger, not from His Majesty's enemies but from lethal epidemics. The regiments on Gibraltar were losing men through disease at the rate of 17 per cent a year during the 1740s. No system of relief, whereby regiments could be brought home from abroad and others sent out, was instituted until 1749. The oft-quoted case of the 38th Foot, which remained in the Leeward Islands for sixty years, is only the worst of a number of bad examples.

Few Englishmen wasted a thought on troops overseas in conditions of dreary squalor and boredom. In spite of this indifference everyone knew that service abroad was dangerous, and it was wise for recruiting parties to be non-committal about the destination of the regiment when they were trying to get men for it. Recruits for the West Indies were often ticket-of-leave criminals with whom a bargain had been made with the authorities to commute a sentence of death or transportation, or, in years when the land press was in force, paupers and vagabonds unable to avoid being taken up. When, later in the century, a military presence was set up in Senegal the garrison was a penal battalion. There is evidence that some convicted criminals, who had no doubt learned about the conditions on the West Africa station, preferred to abide by their original sentence than commute for service there. Existing regiments on learning that they were to be sent to a tropical area often became disaffected and liable to desert or resort to mutiny.

After 1739 the world began to change a good deal. Under Walpole foreign policy had been peaceable and mainly concerned with the balance of power in Europe, a factor specifically mentioned in the preamble of the annual Mutiny Acts. This period of Augustan tranquillity gave way to a more ambitious and adventurous foreign policy under pressure from British merchants, which generated first in 1739 a war of probing and learning, and, after 1754, a more directly and energetically prosecuted war to get colonies.

The army made a bad start in 1741 with the famous fiasco at Cartagena in central America, and its subsequent performance in other theatres was not impressive. For this it was much blamed at the time. But the years of peace and official neglect after Utrecht had taken their toll. Military matters had not been high on Walpole's agenda, except as a source of patronage for his followers. No one in power enquired what sort of an army was needed by Great Britain. Its main role at home in ordinary circumstances was to be a police force to suppress riots and uprisings, and in unusual circumstances to protect the country should invaders give the Royal Navy the slip and appear on English soil. In fact there was a vigorous political debate for years about the merits of a continental policy or a blue-water maritime policy free from European commitments. But the implications of this argument for the army were not discussed. Such training as took place was designed to produce tightly controlled disciplined regimental firing machines advancing across a battlefield towards an opponent presumably doing the same thing.

However, a much greater degree of flexibility was needed for colonial wars and the British army was forced to acquire it. Indeed, colonial wars could not have been fought without making some bold adaptations. By 1763 Britain had not only a very large army by her standards, she had also

The Cartagena Expedition

The British attack on Cartagena in 1741 was an unmitigated disaster for the British army. Later in the century Britain came to be the experts in the field of amphibious warfare. But the school of experience in which they learned the lessons was a harsh and bitter one, and Cartagena was the worst episode.

Soon after the beginning of the War of Jenkin's Ear the British government, aware of the clamour from the merchant community, and no doubt with an exaggerated idea of the wealth of the Spanish Main, determined on a bold stroke. For the subsequent failure Walpole and the commander on the spot were until recently censured by historians. The modern view is that less blame attaches to them than to Vernon, the admiral commanding, and that in any case many of the problems were not capable of being solved at that date.

The king was unwilling to let seasoned troops out of the country in case the French joined the Spaniards and threatened an invasion of Britain. Two weak regiments on the Irish establishment, the 15th and 24th Foot, were built up by drafts from other regiments. To these were added six newly raised regiments of marines, and the raising of a new corps in the colonies, the American Regiment, was also resolved upon. This force, with the addition of 750 men of Dalzell's 38th Foot in garrison in the Leeward Isles and 815 men drafted from the independent companies in Jamaica, made up one of the largest British expeditions ever sent into the Caribbean.

The voyage out was probably no worse than such voyages usually were, but it was a bad start. Some attempt was made to adhere to elementary health rules, but the transports were too crowded and disease was soon rife. When the fleet arrived at Port Royal in Jamaica in December 1740, 1,288 men on board were sick, and 484 had died on the voyage, including the commander, Lord Cathcart. The command therefore devolved upon Brigadier Wentworth, a man of limited experience and conscious of his own shortcomings and of the poor state of his command even before operations had commenced. This made him the more ready to defer to the experience of Admiral Vernon. The lack of trust between the two men did a good deal to contribute to the failure of the enterprise.

The enfeebled survivors of the troops, knowing nothing of the quarrels of their leaders, crept out of the noisome verminous transports, in no condition to withstand the next danger, the yellow fever or *vomito negro*.

Yellow fever was the most feared of the tropical diseases. Over a long period of time it is probable that malaria killed more people, because it repeatedly attacks victims. But yellow fever was more dramatic and terrifying in its effects: of those infected 85 per cent would die. One classic requirement for an epidemic was the arrival of a supply of non-immune subjects from a temperate part of the world. Therefore the appearance in the Caribbean of a large force of English and American redcoats was sure to be followed in a week or so by an appalling epidemic.

The Spanish empire in the Caribbean and central America was thus very effectively defended by the local disease pattern. The other and complementary factor was the fortress. Expensive fortresses of great strength and sophistication in the tropics were not necessary: a fort had served its purpose if it merely held up the attacking force for a few days, thus allowing the microscopic allies of the Spaniards to do their work. From the attackers' point of view a war of observation and posts was therefore dangerous. Only a lightning *coup de main* would do.

Wentworth was afterwards depicted by Vernon as a fool, unaware of the problems of tropical warfare. In fact Wentworth was as aware as anyone of the need for haste. But it took some time to force the entrance to the lagoon and for the gun platforms on the central island of Tierra Bomba to be neutralized. The landing of troops near the fortified town was not effected until 5 April 1741. The road into the place now appeared open. But neither Wentworth nor Vernon thought it practicable to rush the fortress. They consulted their engineers and invested the fortifications in due form as if they had been in Flanders or Westphalia. Meanwhile the death-rate from yellow fever mounted. The dreary routine of men collapsing and dying had a demoralizing effect on the survivors. An attempt to take the outlying fort of St Lazar was bungled, mainly because the scaling ladders were too short. In all, 200 men were killed and 377 wounded, after which morale withered away. More inter-service recrimination followed. There was, however, unanimity on one point—that the expedition should withdraw. Subsequent attempts to succeed elsewhere, at Santiago on Cuba, or at Panama, were abortive. The arrival of a reinforcement of 3,000 men only served to enlarge the target of host subjects for the yellow fever virus. Lieutenant-Colonel Durrand wrote: 'We are in a Mesirable condition for want of fresh provisions, our meet is salt as brine, our bread as it lays on the table swarms with Maggots, & the water here fluxes us all'. Of the 10,000 British soldiers of the expedition only 2,600 were still alive in October 1742. A little over 600 had died in action; disease had killed the rest. Of the 4,163 Americans only 1,463 survived.

learned important lessons. Those lessons had been acquired in the two previous wars. In the first there were enormous losses in central America. The operations in North America were inconclusive and only set the stage for a far bigger conflict in the future. The only successful action was the capture in 1746 of Louisbourg, a powerful Vauban-style fortress dominating the mouth of the St Laurence river, by a force of provincials from New England protected by British seapower. This success curiously did not make British officers change their views about American military prowess, of which they were contemptuous.

The Treaty of Aix-la-Chapelle in 1748 was only a breathing space. The rivalry of Britain and France in North America was approaching a climax, and the Caribbean continued to beckon, its wealth seen increasingly not as Spanish silver, but in terms of sugar islands from which the French had to be evicted. The British expeditions sent into the Caribbean in the Seven Years War show signs of improved technique, and were successful because of a more unequivocal command of the sea by Britain than in either the 1739 or the 1775 war. But no one in the eighteenth century could solve the problem of tropical disease. At least there was after 1756 a more recent body of experience upon which to draw. The theory, beloved of Corbett and Richmond and other imperial historians at the beginning of the twentieth century, that the elder Pitt's role in co-ordinating and planning was crucial, is less favourably regarded by modern historians. The credit at least has to be shared with others, particularly Anson at the Admiralty. The written instructions given to commanders of expeditions in the Seven Years War followed word for word Cathcart's brief for the Cartegena enterprise. Experience and the ability of commanders on the spot explain the difference.

The appearance of Molyneux's book *Conjunct Expeditions* in 1759 marks a new level of sophistication in enquiring into the principles of amphibious warfare. A large part of his book was taken up with a historical survey of former expeditions over the centuries. He pointed out that from the days of Sir Walter Raleigh there had been sixty-eight British expeditions overseas: of these thirty had succeeded, seven of them great expeditions (i.e. involving more than 4,000 men) and twenty-three small. Thirty-eight had failed. The second part of this remarkable book contained a long constructive survey of suggestions for avoiding confusion and streamlining the logistical arrangements of expeditions.

For the common soldier his diet, his clothing, and his daily routine were all sufficiently inconvenient and burdensome when he was stationed in a temperate area of the world. In the fever-ridden plains and swamps of central America and the islands every daily circumstance was horribly affected by the local conditions. The Caribbean in the eighteenth century did not provide for the British soldiers' food and a great deal had to be imported. The diet was repetitious and boring. Beef was allowed at the rate of 7 lb. per man per week. Pork was thought to be more nutritious and 4 lb. a week was reckoned to be the equivalent of 7 lb. of beef. Biscuit, or flour to make bread, was also rationed at 7 lb. a week. These made up the staple of the diet, varied by dried peas, rice, dried raisins, and butter when available. Often the provisions were unsafe, condemnable, but not condemned. Meat in barrels could only be preserved by steeping it copiously in brine; the authorities did not worry their heads too much about the palatability, or indeed the long-term danger to health of such a regime. This dreary diet was much more inadequate and unsuitable in temperatures in excess of one hundred degrees. The salt meat caused agonies of thirst, and scurvy was not the least of the difficulties faced by forces overseas. Spruce beer, a fermented drink made in the North American colonies, containing the toppings from the spruce tree, was found to have an anti-scorbutic effect in the Caribbean, and officers tried to secure supplies of fresh fruit and vegetables to maintain the health of the troops. Alcohol, mainly rum, was not surprisingly relied upon a great deal. Doctors criticized its use in vain, alleging that it was a major contributor to tropical disease. It was an age where drinking to excess was treated tolerantly. Also officers realized that drink for men posted in the tropics and doomed to be decimated by disease was a means of keeping at bay the horror of their situation. There developed on these campaigns a tacit system of complicity between officers and men, a realization that both were victims of a strange and terrible predicament. And although officers recognized that drink undermined discipline, in the exceptional circumstances of the Caribbean depriving men of liquor could be worse.

In North America the beginning of the Seven Years War was not auspicious, with the virtual destruction of General Braddock's force by French and Indians in the ravines and forests by the Monongahela river on 8 July 1755. The episode has given rise to a good deal of stereotyping by earlier historians, who depicted Braddock as a pig-headed leader trying to fight a parade-ground battle on the European model. In fact, Braddock was aware of the dangers, and of the manner in which he might be attacked. He had spent some time in trying to train his men to deal with the unusual threats of wilderness war. But he had not time enough to do this fully, and his scratch force mainly consisted of two regiments taken from the Irish establishment and hastily made up to numbers by drafting elements from no less than six other regiments. Braddock's men plodded wearily through thickly wooded country making a military road as they went. They had almost reached Fort Duquesne, their objective, when they were set upon by the enemy. With swarming but frequently invisible foes on all sides the redcoats fired largely ineffectual volleys in the general direction of their tormentors for about two hours. This was their main tactical technique and it did not work. Eventually confusion set in and the survivors broke and fled.

Clearly new combat techniques were called for. The Austrians had pointed the way with their light troops in the 1740s. In America during the Seven Years War light companies began to be added to existing regiments, composed of men capable of showing individual initiative in scouting, skirmishing, and protecting the flanks of a marching force. Eventually entire battalions of light troops were formed, such as the 80th, 85th, and 90th Regiments. The 60th Royal Americans, a giant of four battalions, was raised not long after the Monongahela disaster, and showed a number of new techniques in its training, although it was not at that time a true light infantry regiment. Its commander, Colonel Henry Bouquet, trained his men in the conditions of broken forested country, making them run individually and in formations and even swim, and to load and fire with great rapidity and accuracy while using available cover. He also trained them in self-sufficiency in the wilderness, which involved finding food, making shelter, and building bridges. The men's uniform was made more convenient, and the best marksmen in each battalion were given rifles. When Lord George Howe brought his regiment—the 55th Foot— to America, he immediately fell in with the new ideas, and consulted experienced Americans, such as Robert Rogers, who commanded an irregular unit of rangers. The rangers must have seemed to many British officers of the formal conservative type to embody all that was worst in American soldiery: drunk, undisciplined, at times mutinous, and, as mercenaries, expensive. But until the British could train some units of their own in woodcraft, individual initiative, and intelligence-gathering, they would have to rely on rangers or Indians, otherwise they ran the risk of being blind and deaf in the forests of North America. In showing a willingness to take lessons from American leaders such as Rogers, George Howe was unusual, and his death at Ticonderoga in July 1758 was a serious loss.

In North American warfare, logistics was as important a matter as tactics. A European army operating in that theatre needed men whose talents were for organizing as well as fighting. More engineers, makers of roads, and contrivers of transport were needed. Supplies in America were put on a better footing as early as the spring of 1756, when the London firm of Baker, Kilby, and Baker contracted to supply the army with all necessaries, including the subsistence of each man at the rate of 6 *d.* per day. In the next two years the firm supplied 5 million rations and were paid over £120,000. Transporting these rations as well as all warlike stores required a good many vehicles. Lord Loudoun, whose reputation does not stand high in the history books, should at least be remembered for having created a good system of supply and transport, both by land and water. Water transport also benefited from Loudoun's efforts in standardizing the boats on lakes and rivers. But when all improvements had been made, transport into the interior of the continent remained a ponderous and fatiguing process. Wagons pulled by horses and in some cases oxen made their painfully slow way along woodland tracks until a river was reached, when the supplies were transferred to the new *bateaux.* The danger of ambush by French and Indians was always present in the minds of the soldiers. But with each campaign a little more had been learned, and the British columns gradually closed in on the French-held posts. Success had consisted mainly in sound strategy, planning, and supplying.

After the Treaty of Paris the army was drastically reduced and some of the new knowledge and technique of wilderness fighting probably declined in the twelve years of peace. For one thing, the reduction in 1763 axed the tenth company of the marching regiments of foot, and it was the light companies that were disbanded. New regulations for drilling troops were published by the authority of the Crown in 1764, partly influenced by the great prestige of the Prussian example. The platoon exercise reduced the number of evolutions required in loading and firing; this exercise was in use for the next thirty years. By 1768 the new drilling had been taught to British soldiers almost everywhere at home and abroad. Peacetime manœuvres were organized on the model of the classic European battle, and most officers seem to have taken little interest in new ideas. But all was not lost. Light companies appeared again in 1770 at the time of the Falkland Islands war scare. Several books were written by English officers, indicating that not all the officer corps were indifferent to innovation in tactics. The most interesting were Robert Rogers's *Journals* (1765), Robert Stevenson's *Instructions for Officers Detached* (1770), and Major Robert

The Capture of Quebec

The Quebec campaign of 1759 seemed to be an imperialist romance of the sort cherished by Victorian writers—the impregnable lair of the enemy crowning the heights, the lonely leader, mortally ill and misunderstood by his colleagues, the stealthy approach to the cliffs under cover of darkness, the magical appearance of the lines of redcoats on the Heights of Abraham, and the death of both commanders in battle. But epics still need explaining in material terms, and much hard work and organization was necessary. Sea power made the expedition up the St Lawrence river feasible. The two naval commanders, Saunders and Holmes, brought the troops into the area and remained in the tideway to give assistance. The French on the other hand could receive little help from the mother country.

During the last days of June 1759 Wolfe's force occupied the Isle of Orleans. He had with him the 15th Foot (Amherst's), the 28th (Braggs's), the 35th (Otway's), the 43rd Highlanders (Kennedy's), the 48th (Webb's), and the 58th (Anstruther's), the 78th Highlanders (Fraser's), and two battalions of the Royal American Regiment. The grenadiers of the regiments were formed into a separate force, the Louisbourg Grenadiers. There was also some light infantry.

A few days later they crossed to Point Levis on the south bank. The French became uneasy as the blockade grew tighter and the nearby countryside was ravaged by the enemy. But to the British the view across the river was not encouraging, and a certain despondency settled upon the officers. They had indeed cut off Montcalm and his men, but there seemed no way of dislodging them from such a place of strength. The French had only to keep the game alive until the onset of the terrible Canadian winter.

By September Wolfe was at his wits' end. He invited his brigadiers to consult and produce their own plan. It was an odd request, but Wolfe's illness had deprived him of much of his fiery enthusiasm. In fact the plan they suggested—to approach Quebec on the side upstream—had been one of the options in Wolfe's mind from the beginning. Here there was a high cliff wall, upon which Montcalm rested his confidence, although he prudently placed a small detachment at the summit. The weak point was a small diagonal path in the cliff-face.

On the night of 12 September 1759 Admiral Saunders stood into the north shore downstream of Quebec, where a large part of the French forces were encamped. The bluff was effective: the ships fired their broadsides and boats were lowered to give the impression of an imminent landing at that point. Meanwhile the bulk of Wolfe's force was being ferried across to the Anse de Foulon, the little cove where the obscure cliff-path began. By good fortune the sentries on the beach had been told to look out for a French provision convoy from upstream. The convoy had been cancelled but the guards at that point had not been informed. A Scottish officer and former Jacobite, Captain McDonald, answered a sentry's challenge in French, and no resistance was made as the force disembarked. The path was just possible to climb, and the lackadaisical group of guards at the top was fired upon and chased away.

By daybreak on 13 September 1759 Wolfe's entire force of ten battalions was drawn up on the Heights of Abraham. Montcalm at first refused to believe the report and rode out himself. 'I see them where they have no business to be' was

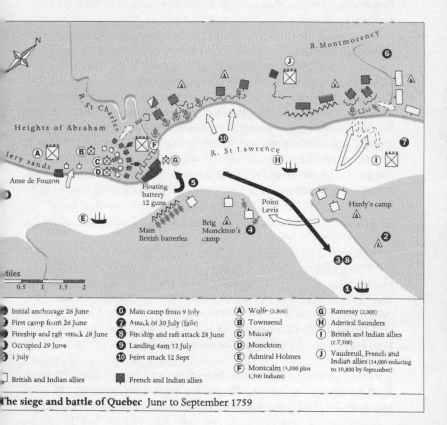

Initial anchorage 26 June	**6** Main camp from 9 July
First camp from 26 June	**7** Attack of 30 July (fails)
Fireship and raft attack 28 June	**8** Fireship and raft attack 28 June
Occupied 29 June	**9** Landing 4am 12 July
1 July	**10** Feint attack 12 Sept
British and Indian allies	French and Indian allies

(A) Wolfe (3,800)
(B) Townsend
(C) Murray
(D) Monckton
(E) Admiral Holmes
(F) Montcalm (3,500 plus 1,300 Indians)
(G) Ramesay (2,000)
(H) Admiral Saunders
(I) British and Indian allies (c.7,500)
(J) Vaudreuil, French and Indian allies (14,000 reducing to 10,800 by September)

The siege and battle of Quebec June to September 1759

his terse comment. He hastily assembled his men and moved out to meet his opponent. His force numbered roughly the same as Wolfe's, but a large part of them were local levies of Canadian and Indians, upon which he placed little reliance.

What followed was a small-scale example, rare in warfare in America, of a battle of the European type. The French attacked in three six-deep columns, the British forming a two-deep line with 40-yard gaps between the battalions. This formation had only been introduced since January 1759 at Amherst's order. Amherst reasoned that two ranks would be sufficient to drive off Canadians and Indians; however, the formation was found to answer well against regular troops. The men had also been taught the new method of alternate fire, instead of platoon fire. This meant that the men fired by companies either from one wing to the other, or from the centre outwards, or from the flanks inwards.

In the event the effectiveness of the British musketry ensured that the battle did not last very long. Wolfe had issued strict instructions to his men not to throw away their fire by taking pot shots at extreme range. The order to fire was given when the heads of the French columns were only 40 yards away. The first devastating volley brought the French attack to a halt. The fire of Kennedy's 43rd Foot was particularly destructive. A second volley followed, then the British line, unaware that their leader had received a fatal wound, charged and scattered the French. While attempting to stem the torrent of retreat, Montcalm was also gravely wounded. He was carried into the fortress and died the following day. The French Governor-General, the Marquis de Vaudreuil, fled to Montreal with a rabble of fugitives, abandoning Quebec to its fate. The troops left behind in the fortress surrendered a few days later.

Donkin's *Military Collections and Remarks* (1777), all three of which had something to say about *petite guerre* operations. In 1774 General William Howe (the brother of Lord Howe killed in 1758), who was also an enthusiast for light tactics, supervised the new training of light companies at a camp outside Salisbury.

By contrast, in the overseas possessions of the Crown much less was achieved in training, and boredom and sickness succeeded the drama of wartime. At least a system of rotation had been set up in 1749 whereby regiments in Gibraltar and Minorca could be brought home. In 1765 Welbore Ellis the Secretary at War began a new system of relief for regiments, which had a partial success. He proposed replacing five regiments in North America in 1765, five in 1766, and three in 1768. But the system never worked as well as Cumberland's before the Seven Years War, and some regiments remained in overseas garrisons for many years. The 8th Foot, for example, remained in Canada from 1768 to 1785, and the 16th, dispatched from Ireland to America in 1767, stayed there until 1782. For such regiments recruiting parties would have to be sent home to make up numbers, which was expensive. Discipline was sometimes relaxed because officers feared that the men might desert or mutiny, and when relieved the regiment would come home in a shattered condition, its ranks much thinned with disease. The surviving soldiers might also be rather elderly. It would then take a year or two to rebuild it so as to make it fit for the searching eye of the reviewing general.

The British government was not indifferent to the welfare of soldiers. Aside from humane considerations, each soldier was a financial investment. The government knew that mortality on voyages or within a very short time of arrival in a foreign station was unacceptably high, even by the standards of the age. In 1767 the Secretary at War called upon the governors of overseas territories 'to transmit a Report of the most Eligible Season for landing Troops in each of their respective Districts, so as to avoid as much as possible the Inconveniencys of the Climate.' Grenada, Jamaica, and Antigua, and other Caribbean stations, for example, reported that July to mid-October should be avoided, adding ominously 'Certain Destruction to Troops who arrive at that time.'

One of the worst examples of sickness and death at this period was recorded at Pensacola (West Florida), acquired by Britain from Spain in 1763. The 31st Regiment, sent to relieve the 35th in 1767, arrived on 25 July, the worst possible time to bring in troops unaccustomed to the climate. Their colonel, Major-General Oughton—who was not with his regiment; colonels in the eighteenth century seldom were—reported to the War Office that the regiment was in good heart on arrival, but:

being encamped on a loose burning Sand, the weather being intensely hot and not having a vegetable Diet to refresh them, nor any sustenance but Salt Provisions and Water, the Calenture with fluxes, Yellow Fevers, Black Vomits and Coups de Soleil raged in a few days with the impetuosity of a Plague by which every Officer was infected but two, that the Regt. tho' landed compleat, could furnish but a Corporal and four Men for Guard; that in less than Six Weeks a Captain, Lieutenant, Surgeon, two Volunteers, five Officers Wives out of six, ninety five Men, and above forty Women and Children were swept away.

None of the surviving officers seems to have suggested that the regiment might quit this plague-spot; their chief concern was to have a scheme of succession in the regiment approved by the king, whereby they would all get promotion to the rank of their dead colleagues. The other suggestions made by their colonel to the War Office—more fresh meat and vegetables, spruce beer, proper shelter—were eventually attended to after the leisurely fashion of eighteenth-century bureaucracy.

It is tempting to write off the doctors of this period as ineffective and probably drunken bunglers. It is true that many of their treatments derived from ideas of the medieval or even the ancient world. Sick soldiers were harassed with bleeding, cupping, purging, and with ineffective and sometimes harmful drugs. Recent research, however, indicates that although guided by an admittedly faulty theoretical framework, the doctors did their best and were not entirely ineffective. Even more surprising is to find that some doctors in remote foreign stations busied themselves with compiling statistics in order to throw light upon the local patterns of disease and mortality. These men, often Edinburgh trained, reduced what had been mere impressions and anecdotes about the sickness-rate into hard facts about the time of year, the weather, and the geographical location of troops. But they had little success in persuading government to follow up their ideas. In the Seven Years War the number of men who died from disease was eight times the total killed in action.

The Seven Years War was Britain's most successful war of the century. But overseas possessions, particularly American, involved the expenditure of far greater sums of money. Between 1750 and 1754 (the last real year of peace) the annual cost of the army, navy, and ordnance had averaged £2.5 million. Schemes were discussed and tried after 1763 for reducing the postwar expenditure back to the pre-1754 level but in vain. The average expenditure under the same heads between 1764 and 1775 was over £4 million a year. Fifteen regiments were now needed to police America. In 1774 it had risen to seventeen, in 1775 to twenty-six, and in 1776 with the war in full swing, it amounted to forty-four regiments of foot and two of cavalry, involving great financial outlays for paying and supplying. Even so, once the war had started these numbers were found to be insufficient in such a vast country. It has been truly said that the British could subdue Americans but not America. And the nature of the war was quite different from previous conflicts. In the Seven Years War the British had to deal with small European forces much like their own. The difficulties of geography and terrain were the same for one side as for the other. Britain had the edge on her opponent largely because her sea power defended the Atlantic supply-lines. In the American War the colonists fought on their own ground while the British had to transport men and all needful things across the Atlantic. Moreover, at a critical juncture, Britain lost command of the sea.

In 1775 the British began the American War with a certain degree of confidence. Britain was a great power: arguably she also had the best army in the world. The spirit of the soldiers was excellent. One British officer wrote, 'I never saw better stuff, and they are as keen for action as ever men were.' Certain European powers kept greater numbers of men under arms, but in terms of martial qualities, particularly dogged persistence in attack and defence, and the ability to improvise and to develop new tactics, the British army was second to none. Their greatest mistake was to be contemptuous of American fighting abilities. Colonials, judging from previous wars, when they had been unreliable allies, were regarded as amateurs, small in numbers, and difficult to discipline, and the officers were certainly not gentlemen. Lord Percy continued to call them ragamuffins even after the battle of Bunker Hill. Politicians in London at first looked upon the outbreak of hostilities as a great riot rather than as a war. Riots, though annoying, were short lived and only needed a firm hand.

Not everyone on the British side was so sanguine. Lord Barrington, the Secretary at War, believed that outright war on land in North America was unwise. If it were to succeed the price would be too great, 'more than we can ever gain by our success'. The Adjutant-General Edward Harvey was of the same mind. Barrington had already in 1766 recommended withdrawing the army from its vulnerable and scattered posts in the Thirteen Colonies so that they could be concentrated in Canada, Nova Scotia, and Florida. Long experience of supervising the army in Britain had taught him that the presence of redcoats was itself provocative when the populace was in a volatile state. Now he renewed his suggestions, and urged a naval blockade, which would quickly hurt the colonists' trading activities. But the government in London paid little heed to these ideas. It overestimated the number of loyalists in America, and continued to do so until a late stage in the war. Ministers regarded Thomas Gage, the Commander-in-Chief in North America, as being unnecessarily alarmist when he asked for massive reinforcements.

The opening moves in the game were ominous for Britain. Gage sent a force of twenty-one companies of foot (about 800 men) to destroy a stock of arms that disaffected colonists had made at Concord, some 18 miles from Boston. The British column collided with a small detachment at Lexington Green, and the first shots were fired. The Americans, about seventy in number, were brushed aside with a few casualties, and the British pressed on to Concord, where they destroyed the warlike stores there. By now the whole countryside was alive with armed men, who harassed the British all their way back to Boston. Gage's report sent to London three days later recorded that the column had been 'attacked from all quarters where any cover was to be found'. The withdrawal became a retreat and almost a rout. Avoiding direct contact, the colonists, some of them armed with rifles, caused severe losses. A relief column under Lord Percy came out from Boston and arrived opportunely to assist the baffled and exhausted men back to their base. Some officers thought that without Percy's aid they would not have got back at all. This episode, in which seventy-three British soldiers were killed and over 200 wounded, was a grim foretaste of what was to come in this conflict.

As a result of the early actions of the war both sides to some extent modified their methods. At the commencement the major British tactic was the disciplined advance under orders in line abreast and two deep and the discharge of massed musketry in controlled volleys. This was the classic manœuvre of the European battlefield. Whenever they could get a chance to do this in the American War it was usually successful. On the American side the colonists did not exploit sufficiently the irregular style with which they began. Washington and most of his generals seem to have had a rather conventional view of tactical forms. Consequently both armies in a sense moved towards each other in their method, with the Americans learning regular tactics, while the British sought to relearn the more flexible mode used in the Seven Years War. Washington's success was to consist largely in keeping his army in being rather than in winning great set-piece battles.

Generalship on the British side was not remarkable. William Howe was capable and worked to improve open-order tactics. But he proved to be lacking in creative ideas, and oddly wary about following up success. No doubt he was uneasy about casualties and the difficulty of replacing them; however, a commander who constantly thinks thus will seldom achieve much. Certainly pessimism took hold of him as the war went on. Clinton was similarly cautious. Burgoyne was a more colourful character, keen on promotion and military glory, a Member of Parliament with excellent connections, and in private life a playwright and friend of David Garrick. Even before his historic disaster some observers detected his swaggering and unreliable side. Horace Walpole wrote damningly of him, 'A vain, very ambitious man, with a half-understanding which was worse than none.' No Wolfe or Clive emerged on the British side: if they had it is hard to see how they could have succeeded. America was found to be a theatre in which victories did not bring the fruits one could reasonably have expected if they had occurred in Europe.

The Lexington–Concord débâcle encouraged the Americans to close in upon Boston, and within a short time the British there found their authority virtually confined to the town itself. By the end of May 1775 Gage had been reinforced with several battalions from England, and had begun to feel a little more confident. On 17 June British troops were ferried across the water from Boston to the Breed's Hill peninsula, which was occupied by rebel forces. What followed was an alarming example of a new American attribute, their stubbornness in defence and ingenuity in field fortification. A determined attack eventually forced the colonists to withdraw, and the British therefore claimed the victory at the battle of Bunker Hill. However, the cost was immense: 226 dead and 828 wounded. As Clinton observed soberly: 'It was a dear fought victory, another such would have ruined us.' There was no pursuit, and indeed very little activity on the part of the British for a year after this Pyrrhic victory.

It was clear that the war would be long and hard, in which matters of supply and geography would become crucial. Both sides had great difficulties in keeping their armies in the field. Washington was often at his wits' end, pleading with men at the end of their term of service to re-enlist. On the British side camp-followers and refugees with the army increased the problem of rations. Nearly all the food had to come across the Atlantic, and the estimated consumption of the British forces rose to 300 tons a month. Bad weather and American privateers prevented many supply-ships from getting through, and by the time the British were evacuated from Boston in May 1776 they were half-starved.

In the summer of that year the army opened a campaign in the area of New York and soon turned the Americans out. But these operations showed no sign of bringing the rebels to their knees, and the action at Princeton at the end of the year showed that Americans could stand firmly to a fire-fight like veterans. The battle of Trenton a few days earlier had demonstrated their inventiveness at mounting a surprise attack. The two battles cost the British some 1,250 casualties and demonstrated to the colonists their own quality.

The British were determined to make 1777 the decisive year. The plan was for General John Burgoyne to invade southwards from Canada by way of Ticonderoga and Lake Champlain to Albany. It was envisaged that his force and the army of General Howe should eventually meet and co-operate. It was the sort of plan that looks better on paper than on the ground. No specific order was given to Howe to move northwards to meet Burgoyne, although some wiseacres after the event claimed to have suggested it. In fact the Secretary of State Lord Germain permitted Howe to move in another direction, towards Philadelphia, which he was ambitious to capture.

Burgoyne began well enough. He recaptured Ticonderoga without difficulty, but thereafter his progress was slow. He was encumbered with an immense train of baggage, fifty-two cannons, some of which were heavy 24-pounders, and a number of camp-followers, including women and children. His Canadian auxiliaries, of whom he had all too few, had to construct a roadway through wild country, and to build over forty bridges. The enemy had made things as difficult as possible for him by felling trees and even diverting and damming streams. Sharpshooters, frequently invisible, continually caused casualties, a high proportion being officers. In three weeks he only managed to advance for 20 miles. Burgoyne had been forced to leave men behind to garrison Ticonderoga, and his force was further reduced by battle at Bennington and Freeman's Farm. Eventually Burgoyne's force was halted, indeed deadlocked. His only hope was a diversion on the part of his brother generals. But Howe was miles away with his mind on Philadelphia. Clinton at New York, lacking reinforcements, made an attempt to send some troops northward in the direction of the Highland Forts. On 15 October they reached Kingston, 45 miles to the south of Albany. By then Burgoyne's fate was sealed. On 7 October he had made a last attempt to cut his way out of the trap. At the battle of Bemis Heights he was defeated with heavy loss. The 62nd Regiment was said to have only ten men in each company surviving. The mortality of officers was again noticeably high, attributed to the marksmanship of David Morgan's riflemen. The American forces were now nearly double the British. With no hope of help from the south Burgoyne asked for terms. On 17 October 1777 the general who had once confidently claimed that there were 'no men of military science' on the American side capitulated with 5,900 British and Hessian troops.

It ought to have become clearer to British leaders after the example of Saratoga that they were playing a losing game. The cutting-off of 5,000 or 6,000 men in a European war would not have raised much interest; in America it was crucial, and the intervention of France would soon follow. In Europe a general, if successful in battle, would expect to capture and hold enemy territory. In America the enemy would close in behind the advancing force: any district more than two days from a British force was vulnerable. An army resembled a swimmer cleaving the water, which would close in behind again.

But Britain continued to fight, convinced that many areas of America were swarming with loyalists, who only required British protection to rise and declare themselves. In fact as the war went on the British were clearly losing the battle for hearts and minds. The passions and hatreds that arose in this war more resembled those in Europe after the French Revolution. Historians have customarily described *ancien régime* warfare before 1792 as being limited in aims and methods. The sort of atrocities that had characterized the Thirty Years War in Europe, they alleged, disappeared in the eighteenth century. This theory of limited war where voluntary restraints were observed, works fairly well for western and central European wars, but less well for eastern Europe, for example the wars of Russia and Turkey. It also breaks down in wars of rebellion, as in the suppression of the Jacobite rebellion in Scotland in 1746, and in the American rebellion. Courtesy and honour is for equals, which is not how rebels were regarded. Accusations of atrocities began immediately in the war: after Lexington a patriot was accused of scalping a British soldier. One British officer, thinking nothing too severe for rebellious subjects, advocated shooting them with arrows dipped in a tincture of smallpox. Americans were convinced that British soldiers killed the prostrate wounded with bayonets after a battle. And the longer the war lasted the more persistent became the actual as well as the rumoured breaches in the laws of war. The frequency with which official orders were given out to forbid soldiers to steal from, or offer insult to, the populace indicates the extent of the problem. The courts-martial records tell a dreary tale of military–civilian crime in America. The very nature of the war, with sentries and stragglers being picked off by invisible partisans with long-range weapons created a mounting exasperation and desire for retribution. Officers who might have restrained these crimes increasingly condoned them through indifference, or even in some cases approved them as a well-merited policy to terrorize a people beneath contempt.

The intervention of France and later of Spain multiplied the strategic problems for the British. They continued to mount fresh attacks, mainly in the southern colonies, to disclose possible sources of loyalism, always hoping that one more campaign would do the business. After the news of the disastrous battle of Cowpens reached London, Horace Walpole wrote mockingly: 'America is once more not quite ready to be conquered, although every now and then we fancy it is.' After the capture of Charleston an optimist, as late as 1780, could feel that the war was still on the hinge. And the battles at Camden and Guildford Court House showed that even at this late stage of a hopeless war British troops could still inflict mortifying defeat on Americans. It also demonstrated the extent to which the army had adapted intelligently to conditions.

In the summer of 1780 Congress sent General Horatio Gates, the victor of Saratoga, with an army to turn the British out of the Carolinas. On 16 August Gates with 4,100 men faced General Lord Cornwallis with 1,500 redcoats. Cornwallis also had with him the British Legion, a mobile mounted force commanded by Lieutenant-Colonel Banastre Tarleton. Loyalists to the number of 500 increased his total, but he was still outnumbered by Gates's force. However, this disadvantage was partly reduced by his excellent position astride the road to Camden, with both flanks protected by gum swamps. The action began soon after dawn. The British were drawn up in three 'divisions'. On the right wing the light infantry and the companies of the 23rd and 33rd Regiments were commanded by Lieutenant-Colonel Webster. Placed thus they were opposed by the militia of Virginia and North Carolina on the American left. The demeanour of the militia on that day would seem to have borne out Washington's low opinion of them. The British regulars attacked in open order using cover as they fired. One disgusted American wrote afterwards, 'The impetuosity with which they [the British right] advanced, firing and huzzaing, threw the whole body of the militia into such a panic, that they generally threw down their *loaded* arms and fled in the utmost consternation. The unworthy example of the Virginians was almost instantly followed by the North Carolinians.' This was no orderly retreat, rather a *sauve qui peut* rabble, which stripped away a great section of the American line and left exposed the flank of those who stood their ground. Cornwallis intervened and forbade pursuit of the fugitives, instead turning his wing on to the continental troops in the centre. The men of the 1st Maryland Brigade resisted bravely, but Cornwallis committed his reserve, the Highlanders. It was enough: the Americans broke, and Cornwallis released his cavalry under Tarleton. Tarleton's men harried the fugitives for over 20 miles.

Cornwallis deserved his victory. He had made a good disposition beforehand but showed he was capable of thinking on his feet and improvising according to the changing events of battle. But as so often in the American War his success was of little use to him. His army was exhausted, his 300 casualties, though much less than the loss on the other side, were difficult to replace. He reported to Lord George Germain in London: 'the Corps with me being totally destitute of Military Stores, Cloathing, Rum, Salt and other articles necessary for troops in the operations in the field, and provisions of all kinds being deficient, almost approaching to a famine in North Carolina, it was impossible for me to penetrate into that province before the harvest.' Not for the first time the cold reality of logistics rendered all the British efforts null.

The final disaster at Yorktown in October 1781 largely came about because for a short but critical window of time Britain lost her naval supremacy in the Chesapeake area, and the army of Cornwallis was hemmed in by sea and by land. The position of the army under bombardment became untenable and surrender was inevitable. The government at home was living out its last days as the news of Yorktown reached London. The conflict had become a world-wide war and it was necessary for Britain to extricate herself with as little damage as possible. To the end the British soldiers had done what was required of them. They had performed in regular operations of battle and siege. There were even a few cavalry charges. But they had also shown an ability to break away from European methods and to learn irregular tactics in a different and difficult terrain. This had influenced the way they would fight in the future. In 1785 Cornwallis observed with disapproval the inflexible movements of the Prussian army on manœuvre. Their evolutions, he wrote derisively, 'were such as the worst General in England would be hooted at for practising—two long lines coming up within six yards of one another and firing until they had no ammunition left; nothing could be more ridiculous.'

The British army, excellent as it was, had fought a war which in eighteenth-century conditions was not winnable. As Lord Chatham had warned in his last speech: 'You cannot conquer America.'

7 THE TRANSFORMATION OF THE ARMY 1783–1815

DAVID GATES

In the decade that elapsed between the end of the struggle for the American colonies in 1783 and the outbreak of war with republican France, the British army sank into dereliction. Defeated and demoralized, 'Our army was lax in its discipline, entirely without system, and very weak in numbers', recalled one contemporary soldier. 'Each colonel of a regiment managed it according to his own notions, or neglected it altogether. There was no uniformity of drill or movement. Professional pride was rare; professional knowledge still more so.' Yet, only a few years later, Britain's land forces were the envy of Europe; they had emerged with scarcely a battle lost during the long, bitter contest with Napoleon and had crowned their many victories with the triumph of Waterloo. How had this remarkable transformation been effected?

At the commencement of the war with France in 1793, there were several main problems to be surmounted. First was the question of how the army could find the requisite manpower to meet its burgeoning commitments. The regular army expanded in the course of the French Revolutionary and Napoleonic Wars from some 40,000 in 1793 to a peak of over 250,000 personnel in 1813. An average of between 3 and 4 per cent of the population was thus active in the service during the conflict with France. Whilst this was a very high proportion, the calculation excludes the Royal Navy's requirements. At the end of the American War, for instance, the navy totalled some 110,000 seamen and marines. During the 1790s, its strength was usually nearer 120,000, climbing to over 140,000 personnel and 1,000 vessels as the struggle with Napoleon unfolded. Even then, the Admiralty regularly complained the fleet needed another 16,000–20,000 mariners to bring its crews up to strength.

Mobilization on this scale was unavoidable in the pandemic warfare heralded by the French Revolution. The *levée en masse* (23 August 1793) had put scores of thousands of conscripts at the French government's disposal, and forces of unprecedented dimensions were threatening Britain's interests and security. Although most of her continental allies had at least crude mechanisms for calling much of the population to arms in times of emergency, Britain lacked both the necessary bureaucracy and the legal framework for doing so. Mindful of the events of the English Civil War and the monarchy's attempts in 1688 to use the military to restore its full powers, parliament had an atavistic dislike for large, standing armies, whilst any attempted move—real or perceived—towards a universal draft was certain to encounter resolute popular resistance: Pitt, for example, tried unsuccessfully to man the navy through the Quota Acts of 1795–6; there was intermittent, widespread disorder because of the fear that the government was seeking to impose a *levée en masse* via the militia's enlistment system; and the provisions of the Permanent Additional Force Act of 1804, which imposed substantial fines on parishes that failed to fulfil their recruitment quotas, ran into extensive opposition, with many parishes electing to pay the penalties rather than furnish the troops.

Indeed, until around 1808, service in the regular army was broadly seen as disadvantageous when compared with alternative occupations, including a stint in the volunteers or militia. The last of these made up, on average, some 20 per cent of the country's land forces. Recruits were selected by ballot and had to serve for five years. The force was restricted solely to home defence operations and there were various other inducements, such as parish relief for dependants left at home, which regular troops did not enjoy. Volunteers, too, were only compelled to do limited service and underwent two or three weeks' training per year. Around 400,000 enlisted by the end of 1803 and, two years later, there were still in excess of 300,000 volunteers. When, in 1808, Lord Castlereagh restructured the militia into 'regular' and 'local' bodies, however, many of these men elected to join the latter, sending the strength of the volunteers into decline. Lastly, there was the Army of the Reserve. Again, this was raised by ballot and was intended for the protection of Great Britain alone. Hopes of mustering 50,000 troops were not fulfilled, but a sizeable proportion of those who were recruited subsequently transferred to the regular forces.

This process proved a valuable infusion for the professional army, for many militiamen were also persuaded to go on to enlist for unlimited service, especially following the fading of the invasion scare in 1805 and the introduction of Castlereagh's reforms in 1808. Indeed, around 74,000

Amphibious Warfare

For the British, maritime power and the ability to intervene abroad through amphibious operations were crucial. Whilst her insular nature made Britain difficult to invade, it also rendered the task of attacking any enemy that much more tortuous, particularly at a time when, as during the Napoleonic Wars, sufficient resources had to be retained for the defence of the homeland base, the colonies, and sea lanes. Once dispatched, fleets were difficult to recall or redirect if circumstances changed, and so mounting large-scale, lengthy campaigns was eschewed as far as possible; the emphasis was on sudden coups against vulnerable targets not too far from friendly waters. Options were further limited by the problems involved in keeping soldiers and horses at sea for prolonged periods, and by the amount of shipping required to transport troops and heavy equipment. It was estimated, for instance, that 20,000 infantry would call for 30,000 tons of shipping, whereas deploying just 2,000 horsemen or 1,500 artillery personnel and their guns would take 16,000 and 10,000 tons respectively.

Rarely could the Royal Navy spare vessels in these quantities; and, when it could, actually embarking or disembarking the troops and their equipment was a time-consuming and hazardous business. Even a ship of the line only had enough boats to ferry some 230 soldiers at a time; most frigates could land just 100. At Mondego Bay in 1808, for example, the disembarking of 9,000 troops, with horses for just 200 cavalry and eighteen artillery pieces, took five days. Admittedly, this particular undertaking was hampered by a heavy swell which overturned at least one craft, claiming sixty lives. But this type of occurrence was the rule; for, besides facing enemy action, amphibious forces constantly risked disruption and destruction by the elements. The Royal Navy lost 317 ships between 1803 and 1815, 223 of which either foundered or were wrecked. Many took precious troops and equipment to the bottom with them. Storms, an adverse, or no, wind frequently delayed movements or scattered convoys, while sea-sickness rendered whole battalions temporarily unfit for duty. Often, those forces that could be mustered on time proved fatally feeble in numbers and lacking in artillery and cavalry support. Securing and sustaining logistical lifelines for units ashore was also problematic, as was the gathering of intelligence; much depended on winning the support of friendly locals.

There are few better examples of amphibious warfare than the campaigns conducted by the British against America between 1812 and 1815. These

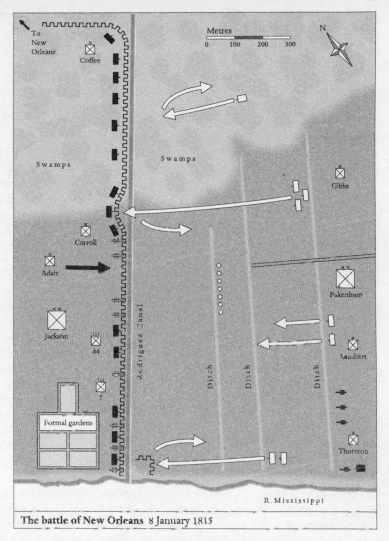

The battle of New Orleans 8 January 1815

events took place against the backcloth of the ongoing struggle with Napoleon; and Britain's need to devote the bulk of her resources to that life-or-death confrontation largely determined the scale and nature of her operations along America's eastern seaboard and the Canadian frontier. That said, expectations and objectives fluctuated according to the mood prevailing within the Cabinet in London. When fortune seemed to smile on their efforts, there were hopes of avenging the humiliations of the American War, and even of restoring some of the territories lost in that conflict to British dominion. At other times, ambitions were more modest: only minimal and indispensable goals were to be pursued, and those at a cost which an over-taxed and war-weary public would pay. As Lord Liverpool revealingly observed to Wellington in September 1814, although the amphibious operations were 'creating the greatest degree of alarm and rendering the [American] government very unpopular, ... I wish we were well out of it'.

This encapsulated the Cabinet's dominant attitude. The overarching concern was to bring the war with America to a speedy conclusion; and military success, even if it did not secure better peace terms, might achieve that. Thus, we find Lord Bathurst asking Wellington what blow might give rise to the conflict's swift and 'honourable termination'. Wellington replied he could imagine no operation 'which would be so injurious to the Americans as to force them to sue for peace, which is what one would wish'. Yet, others argued, the war was not universally popular within the states and, given this perceived lack of unity, American cohesion might be undermined. Clearly, the theatre of operations was too distant to give detailed strategic prescriptions. But supported, it was anticipated, by negro slaves in the South, the Indians around the Gulf of Mexico, the Creole and Hispanic inhabitants of Louisiana, and, perhaps, some disenchanted New Englanders, a handful of enterprising naval squadrons—acting largely on their own initiative, and with their reach and punch enhanced by a few thousand troops—might drub the American 'Spaniel' into good behaviour.

This was not mere wishful thinking. The vast American littoral was dreadfully vulnerable to prowling warships mounting opportunistic attacks: the Royal Navy had blockaded the coast, bottling up enemy vessels and forming a nigh impenetrable screen behind which their own flotillas could, weather permitting, move with virtual impunity and unpredictability; there were few fortifications with heavy ordnance; and the dearth of good roads limited the Americans' ability to respond to *coups de main* or to move reinforcements rapidly to endangered areas. In any case, whenever a serious threat did materialize, the raiders' ships spirited them out of harm's way, landing them further along the coast to wreak fresh havoc. This 'species of milito-nautico-guerilla-plundering warfare', as Sir Harry Smith termed it, caused appreciable panic and damage in Maine and the Chesapeake Bay region especially, and highlighted the efficacy of skilfully co-ordinated land–sea operations.

Indeed, their relative mobility was the principal explanation for the considerable success enjoyed by the British amphibious forces; and where that was effectively countered, as at New Orleans, the results proved devastating—the British, though often better trained and disciplined than their opponents, lacked the fire-power, numbers, and sustainability to take strong defensive positions with head-on assaults. Although ostensibly these failures cancelled out triumphs elsewhere, amphibious operations did prove a cost-effective way of prosecuting the war within the criteria set by the Cabinet. The true extent of their potency is perhaps best revealed by the fact that, in later Anglo-American crises, a repetition of such attacks was as much feared by Washington as it was earnestly contemplated by London.

---

men migrated from the militia to regular units between 1807 and 1812. Nor was this achieved to the detriment of the strength of the militia, since most of these recruits had already discharged their five-year obligation. A substantial pool of manpower, which had undergone at least rudimentary military training, was thus released for unrestricted duties.

This reversed the earlier trend of competition for manpower between, first, the army and the Royal Navy and, secondly, limited-service units, such as the volunteers, and the professional land forces. In 1804, for example, the Duke of York, Commander-in-Chief of the army, protested that, whilst enlistment in irregular, home defence bodies was proceeding apace, placing some 615,000 troops at the government's disposal, the regular forces were 30,000 men under strength. Competition for recruits with civilian occupations remained intense, too, soldiering being a hard way to earn a living even in peacetime; a private was paid 7s. 6d. per week in 1806, compared with the 28s. a labourer in His Majesty's dockyards took home. On top of this was the disparity in the bounty payments given to men who joined, on the one hand, the regular forces and, on the other, the militia: substitute recruits to the latter received £25, whereas those enlisting in the former collected less than a third of this amount. Their dependants, moreover, disqualified from receiving parish relief unlike the needy relatives of militiamen, often followed their menfolk on campaign as there was no system for forwarding the soldier's pay to his family home. In addition to these pecuniary considerations, regular troops effectively enlisted for life, which too frequently proved brutal and short. Besides the perils of the battlefield, they were confronted by the army's savage penal codes and the likelihood of service abroad. A posting to the Caribbean in the 1790s, for instance, was not to be seen so much as an exotic sojourn as a death sentence; thousands of men perished or were invalided for life by disease.

Certainly, given its very limited manpower reserves, the British regular army suffered a worrying attrition rate during the French Revolutionary Wars. In 1794, 18,596 soldiers died on active service, while, over the next two years, 40,639 men were discharged 'on account of wounds or infirmity' alone. These trends persisted throughout the Napoleonic Wars, 16,000–24,000 casualties being incurred every year. Direct recruiting and the influx of former militiamen helped fill the gaps in the ranks, but substantial numbers of foreign soldiers also had to be incorporated into Britain's land forces. Drawn from the colonies and from among Europeans hostile to Napoleon's empire, they included French royalists, Germans, Greeks, Corsicans, and Negroes. By 1813, one-fifth of the entire army, 52,000 men, was composed of such recruits.

Yet despite all these efforts to tap the available manpower, the British army, though bloated in comparison to its normal peacetime size, remained chronically short of personnel. For whilst the colonies and the motherland furnished thousands of recruits, most of these were consumed in the defence of Britain and her possessions around the globe; comparatively few could be spared for offensive action. In 1811, for instance, aside from Wellington's Peninsular Army, related garrisons on Mediterranean islands, and the garrison in Canada, there were 76,000 regular troops scattered in outposts extending from Africa through the Orient to Australia. A further 56,000 stiffened home defence forces. Among these were the 17,000 troops necessary to guard Ireland against enemy attacks, as had nearly occurred in 1796, and to prevent any repetition of the events of 1795–8, when, again encouraged by France, rebellion had erupted against British rule. Indeed, in the absence of any police force, innumerable, tiny detachments of soldiers were drawn into the day-to-day maintenance of law and order, the collection of taxes and duties, and combating smuggling.

Besides the grave repercussions this had for training units, both as a whole and in combination with others, for preserving an *esprit de corps* and for giving officers experience in the handling of substantial bodies of troops, it meant that assembling a force of appreciable size and committing it to a campaign outside the British Isles was a difficult and, sometimes, dangerous enterprise. Thus we find George Canning warning Sir John Moore in 1808 that the 32,000-strong corps 'appropriated by His Majesty to the defence of Spain and Portugal is not merely a considerable part of the disposable force of this country. It is, in fact, the British army.' Nor, as late as 1813, when the army totalled over 250,000 troops, could much over a third of this figure be spared for Wellington in the Iberian peninsula; his 60,000 British had to be supplemented with Portuguese brigades especially. Indeed, so restricting were the demands of colonial and home defence that on only one occasion during this era could two distinct armies of significant dimensions be simultaneously deployed on the European mainland; in the summer of 1809, there were roughly 44,000 troops participating in the Walcheren expedition, while a similar number was in Spain.

The strategic constraints imposed by the scarcity of manpower did not end at this, however. Whilst their continental colleagues had little option other than to prosecute what was frequently a war of attrition against France, with tens of thousands of troops regularly falling on each side in individual battles, British commanders had to be far more parsimonious. A single bloodbath on the scale of, say, Wagram would have effectively obliterated Britain's disposable land forces. Napoleonic period infantry and cavalry required exhaustive training if they were to be effective, and many officers were unwilling to countenance heavy losses of seasoned troops unless they could be certain of securing a decisive advantage. This attitude had characterized warfare in the eighteenth century: pitched battles were, wherever possible, shunned in favour of sustained campaigns in which the opposition was methodically worn out through marches and sieges; avoiding defeat was judged as important as seeking victory; and, in the wake of any clash, pursuit was invariably a somewhat circumscribed affair. Indeed, the whole approach was to conduct hostilities with essentially limited means and ends. Napoleon, by contrast, exploiting the material resources and ideological energy unleashed by the French Revolution, waged war with unprecedented dynamism and strategic breadth. For him, the crushing, in a decisive engagement, of an adversary's means and will to resist was the goal of military operations, and he was quite prepared to cross continents and dismember whole countries in furtherance of his wider, political aspirations. His innovative style of warfare was one which many opponents schooled in the campaigns of the eighteenth century found as arcane as it was apocalyptic; and those states which survived did so either by adopting his own methods or, as in the case of Britain, fighting only on terms which suited them. For the British, this meant using their financial wealth to subsidize a series of coalitions dedicated to defeating or at least containing Napoleon's expansionism; employing their maritime power to inflict economic hardship on France and her allies; and fielding a high-quality if small army on the fringes of the European land mass where, supported by a powerful navy, it could take advantage of the enemy's weaknesses while avoiding exposure to his strengths.

But even though it was thus to be spared the horrendous casualties its allied counterparts regularly sustained, the British army encountered difficulties enough in trying to preserve the quality of its forces. For instance, whereas most European armies had frequent camps for rehearsing tactics and manœuvres on a grand scale, Britain's, for the most part, neither did nor could. Scattered in scores of little entities from the plains of India to the forests of Canada, many units were denied opportunities for exercising as a body. It took up to two years of intensive instruction to prepare recruits for all the elaborate drills and evolutions expected of them, and the standardization of procedures was clearly crucial if forces were to act in concert when brought together. Yet, until 1792, the army, administered by a remote, divided, and frail bureaucracy, lacked even a comprehensive drill manual. The official with ultimate responsibility for the upholding of general discipline, the regulation and inspection of the training of the cavalry and infantry, and the appointment and promotion of officers was the Commander-in-Chief. This post, however, was only filled in wartime. Consequently, between the conclusion of the American War and the outbreak of the conflict with republican France ten years later, the office remained vacant; the duties of the Commander-in-Chief devolved partly on the Adjutant-General and partly on the Secretaries at and for War. Even when Lord Amherst dutifully assumed the position in 1793, he did so in name alone. The wretched man, enfeebled by poor health, was older than his 76 years and was quite content to leave his burdensome responsibilities to his ministerial colleagues; and, as one of them, Henry Dundas, later lamented, 'Amherst was a worthy and respectable old man, . . . but the mischief he did in a few years will not be repaired but by the unremitting attention of many'.

Blame for the army's malaise cannot, however, be laid solely at Amherst's door. Defeat in the struggle for the American colonies had tarnished the service's image and morale, while, generally neglected in the inter-war period, it had failed to keep abreast of military innovations in Europe. This remissness was particularly damaging, since many of the tactical lessons drawn from the battlefields of America were inapplicable to the European theatre. The relatively tiny forces engaged in the conflict with Britain's erstwhile dependencies, coupled with the dearth of cavalry and artillery, had encouraged dispersal and the use of mercurial, *petite guerre* operations. Such tactics, critics argued, would have but limited relevance were Britain to become embroiled in a confrontation with another European state; an adversary's cannon, heavy cavalry, and infantry would speedily overwhelm British troops seeking to fight the next war on the principles of the last. Solidarity, uniformity, and 'steadiness' had to be imposed.

But by whom? In the absence of a Commander-in-Chief, William Fawcett, the Adjutant-General, turned to the king himself and, 'By His Majesty's Command', an official manual was issued in 1786. These regulations were a small-scale work, derived from the *Elements of Tactiks* by Saldern, the Prussian army's Inspector-General. The book's aims were restricted to establishing basic principles which would serve as a substructure for more elaborate procedures. In fact, the work which ultimately shaped the manœuvres of British land forces until beyond the end of the Napoleonic War was David Dundas's *Principles of Military Movements*. Inspired, like Saldern's *Elements*, by the tactics of Frederick the Great, this first appeared in 1788 and, with its eighteen manœuvres, was the sort of sophisticated manual Fawcett had been searching for to supersede the 1786 *Regulations*. Supported by the king, York, and other notables, Dundas's drill was tested, slightly amended, and issued as the 1792 *Regulations*, becoming, with an updated platoon exercise, the backbone of the infantry's tactical system. Dundas also produced a companion volume for the cavalry.

However, devising official procedures was one thing; introducing and enforcing them throughout an army dispersed around the world was another. Until the 1792 *Regulations* were issued, commanding officers enjoyed almost total discretion when deciding what *modus operandi* their troops would follow. Predictably, measures seeking to impose uniformity encountered both wilful and inadvertent opposition. Lord Lynedoch, for example, noted the 'reluctance with which the study of this new system was undertaken by those who considered themselves too old and too wise to go to school', while another eyewitness lamented how the 1792 manual was 'ill written and led the large class of stupid officers into strange blunders'. Moreover, the standardization of tactical drills was but one of several cardinal objectives, the fulfilment of which ultimately rested with the officer corps. As the body that was to lead and inspire the rank and file both on and off the battlefield, the professionalism and general calibre of its members were of crucial importance to the army's effectiveness. Indeed, in endeavouring to develop an efficient officer cadre, the army's administration faced some of its most testing challenges.

Given the need for, roughly speaking, one commissioned or non-commissioned officer for every eight privates, the abrupt and massive enlargement of the service following the commencement of hostilities in 1793 created a recruitment problem which was as gargantuan as it was unprecedented. Like all other European armies, the British had traditionally drawn most of its officers from the politically dominant strata of society. Whereas in Prussia, for instance, the indispensable qualification for obtaining a command in the forces was noble birth, in Britain, wealth, notably in the form of property, on which enfranchisement was also dependent, formed the corner-stone of one's candidacy. Consequently, the majority of officers customarily came from landed gentry backgrounds. So great was the army's reflection of the socio-economic order of the eighteenth century, however, that a change in one was bound to provoke transition in the other. The pandemic, mass warfare triggered by the execution of Louis XVI was waged by armies which, in both their composition and cognizance, became increasingly nationalistic. In Britain, an institution that had once been the preserve of a few propertied families was compelled to open its doors to a far broader swathe of society. Affluence, if only on a comparatively modest scale, remained a prerequisite, but the landed gentry could not preserve its dominance of the army's hierarchy; men from other sectors of society, foremost among them the prosperous middle classes who had emerged in the aftermath of the agricultural and industrial revolutions, accounted for a growing proportion of the officer corps.

Wealth, regrettably, did not always go hand in hand with talent. Commissions had traditionally been bought and sold like property and, as the costs of the war escalated, devouring up to 90 per cent of government revenue each year, the purchasing scheme provided a handy source of income. Similarly, until York—who succeeded Amherst as Commander-in-Chief in 1795—introduced measures curtailing the worst excesses, promotion to a higher rank was not on merit but commonly secured either directly through payment or indirectly by the procurement of recruits through a 'crimp'. Political patronage and other dubious means were also exploited by those whose ambition outweighed their purse or principles. Although the system did facilitate the rapid rise of some able, young officers who coincidentally happened to have the requisite wealth—Arthur Wellesley, later Duke of Wellington, being the prime illustration—it did allow many unsuitable and less gifted men to acquire senior positions. This had repercussions which were as lamentable as they were ineluctable. 'The officers wish to be advanced, to get more pay and have less duty,' grumbled Colonel—subsequently General Sir—John Moore in 1796. 'Little can be expected from men formed and led by such officers,' he continued. 'They neither look up to them as officers, nor do they respect them as gentlemen.' Six years later, as commander of the forces in the Southern District of England, Moore advised York that 'To have a tolerable army, it will be necessary to take some strong measures.' Colonels whose units were found in a poor state should, he urged, be retired from the service and replaced not by majors 'who may be equally incapable, but . . . [by] officers of approved talents. One or two measures of this sort generally known would excite an exertion which at present is much wanted.'

Certainly, York did his utmost to Improve the quality of the officer corps but, at a time when the army's size was growing by leaps and bounds, raising standards proved problematic. The need to replace key personnel lost through retirement and, more pressingly, to disease and in action, compounded demand, while professional soldiering held few attractions for many citizens who might have been expected to make good officers. As the Peninsular War gathered momentum, the prestige of Wellington's victories enhanced the army's image, giving a boost to the number of men seeking to enrol. In a lot of cases, those doing so were quality volunteers. However, the bulk of the rank and file continued to be trawled from among the dregs of society—the destitute, the drunkards, the desperate. 'The principal motive for our soldiers to enlist is the propensity of the class from which we take them to drink,' Wellington once opined. Such ruffians, many officers reasoned, could only be animated and controlled by the threat of the lash and the gallows. Even then, alcohol too often proved the solvent of order. Any other considerations aside, exposure to the dangers, deprivations, barbarism, and other rigours of active service could fray the nerves of the toughest veterans, and periodic bouts of indiscipline were only to be anticipated. The capture of French strongholds in the Iberian peninsula, for instance, was regularly marred by British troops—many of them intoxicated—running amok and looting, raping, and pillaging their way through the town they had just stormed. This did little to endear them to the numerous Portuguese and Spanish civilians who, paradoxically, fell victim to the very soldiers supposed to be delivering them from French oppression. On the other hand, good civil–military relations were none too common even when the troops were not serving abroad. Units billeted in British towns for lengthy periods often got bored and quarrelled with the inhabitants, while the military's role in tax-collection and assisting local magistrates ineluctably brought soldiers into confrontation with civilians.

Some officers endeavoured to ameliorate their charges' gruelling and often thankless life-style by adopting a more paternalistic, benevolent approach to their training and discipline. Humanitarians, notably Sir John Moore, argued, in keeping with the intellectual spirit of the Enlightenment, that soldiers, if accorded dignity, kindness, and education, would be far better motivated than those whipped into obedience. Other commanders, however, favoured the draconian ways of the authoritarian system; troops should be mere automatons, conditioned to fear their own officers more than the enemy and his fire.

The clash between these two opposing schools of thought was symptomatic of a wider political struggle. Encouraging men from the lower classes to think for themselves was, in the view of the martinets, dangerous heresy; it smacked of the seditious creeds emanating from republican France. Yet the exploitation of meritocracy and patriotic fervour had helped bring the leaders of the Revolution and their successor, Napoleon, military success. The servile armies of the *ancien régime* had been defeated by the enthusiastic defenders of *La Patrie*. The large numbers of free-thinking, free-moving, free-firing skirmishers employed on the battlefield by the French were the very embodiment of Rousseau's concept of the 'natural man'; and, to overcome such troops, reformers like Moore in Britain and Scharnhorst in Prussia contended, it would be necessary to have at least some regiments equipped, both psychologically and doctrinally, to fight without the constraints of the orthodox, close-order formations which were to be found in the 1792 *Regulations* and other drill manuals stemming from the Frederickian period.

Thus arose the British army's first permanent, regular light infantry regiments. Trained by Moore and a group of like-minded colleagues, they became model units both on and off the battlefield. However, Moore's untimely death at Corunna (16 January 1809) robbed the humanitarian movement within the service of its most influential and distinguished advocate. Wellington—who not only superseded him as Britain's premier general but did so with such superlative success that his opinions outweighed all others for decades to come—was of a different persuasion. Although he always put order before justice, he could not fairly be described as an unreasoning martinet. Yet he had little sympathy for liberalism either, once testifying to a royal commission that he had 'no idea of any great effect being produced on British soldiers by anything but the fear of immediate corporal punishment'. For him, the key to upholding discipline lay in satisfying the troops' basic needs, such as clothing, shelter, adequate medical care, and regular pay and rations, and he sought to engender obedience, loyalty, passivity, and a lack of inquisitiveness among the rank and file. Dismissing schemes for the moral welfare and education of ordinary soldiers as subversive, he placed his faith in uncompromising disciplinary codes and the army's reflection of Britain's social hierarchy: the rank and file were the tenants of a feudalistic community; the officers its squires. The latter group were, by upbringing and temperament, destined and duty bound to furnish the former with leadership. Indeed, to this arch-conservative, the words 'officer' and 'gentleman' were synonymous, even though he acknowledged that many gentry were devoid of martial skill. But if he was critical of some elements of the officer corps, he was still less charitable in his estimation of the army as a whole. It was, he averred, 'composed of the scum of the earth, . . . fellows who have enlisted for drink—that is the plain fact'.

The organization of the various branches of the army barely altered between 1783 and 1815. Besides the more traditional foot batteries, horse artillery—in which the crews rode on the gun-limbers rather than march alongside them—had become universally fashionable in European armies by the late eighteenth century. British batteries were normally termed 'companies' and had six pieces; five 6-pounder or 9-pounder cannon and a howitzer was the common configuration. Whereas French artillery was invariably deployed *en masse*, British batteries were usually modest units judiciously sited to enhance the fire-power of the infantry. (The once widespread practice of permanently allotting a few light cannon to each infantry battalion was discontinued after 1801.) Indeed, if possible, foot companies would adopt a 'hull down' position, while the horse artillery would manoeuvre in support of movements by the infantry and cavalry. In 1803, to the long-established projectiles of round-shot, bagged

The Duke of York

Frederick Augustus, Duke of York and Albany from 1784, was born in 1763 and was the second son of George III. Although, through his Hanoverian lineage, he was elected Lay Bishop of Osnabruck—a post he retained until 1803—his career was principally that of a soldier and army administrator. Early service with the British and Hanoverian armies took him to Germany for a considerable period, and he married the eldest daughter of Frederick William II of Prussia in 1791.

His real rise to prominence commenced shortly after. On the outbreak of war with revolutionary France in 1793, he was appointed to lead a British expeditionary corps to Flanders. He invested Dunkirk and, on 6 September, fought a battle just to the east of that port at Hondschoote. His British and Hanoverian troops performed well against the French army of General Jean Houchard but, outnumbered by more than three to one, were pressed back. York had to forsake his siege guns and withdraw. Several months of minor actions and inconsequential marches ensued—giving birth to the nursery jingle *The Grand Old Duke of York*—during which the situation of the Allies in Flanders deteriorated sharply. In July 1794 the French occupied both Brussels and Antwerp, and the British corps was evacuated.

Then, in February 1795, Lord Amherst, the elderly and ailing Commander-in-Chief of the British army, retired. York, now a Field Marshal, superseded him. The office of Commander-in-Chief was only filled in wartime and, whilst its holder was the principal military adviser to the Crown, it did not confer the total control over the service which the title implies; the Commander-in-Chief shared responsibility for the army with a number of officials, including the Master-General of the Ordnance, the Adjutant-General, and the Secretary at War. This devolution and sharing of accountability—largely a result of a suspicious parliament's historical attempts to control the power of the military—clearly complicated any effort to overhaul the army and its constituent branches. Throughout the period 1793–1815 the engineers and artillery, for instance, remained answerable not to York, Wellington, or any other field commander, but to the Master-General of the Ordnance. Yet, if the army was to cope with the challenges posed by the era of mass warfare ushered in by the French Revolution, reform was imperative.

Combining extensive military experience with a flair for administration, York, who also had youthful energy on his side, was an ideal candidate for the enormous task in hand and, over the next few years, was to introduce a series of innovations that helped transform the British army. Through bad management and neglect, the service had degenerated into a deplorable condition which, in many regards, had been exacerbated by the army's abrupt and appreciable expansion on the outbreak of war in 1793; thirty new regiments had been created, together with a number of odd battalions and companies. Finding sufficient, suitable officers for all of these new units was just one of the problems confronting the duke. Recruiting them solely from the aristocracy and landed gentry, the traditional sources, was clearly impossible; more officers had to be drawn from the middle classes, which had thrived on the prosperity generated by the agricultural and industrial revolutions of the eighteenth century. The British government, however, desperate for funds, simply sold commissions and promotion to wealthy individuals, irrespective of their suitability for military service or command. Indeed, as one colonel observed, 'An officer who had money could purchase up to the rank of lieutenant-colonel in three weeks or a month.'

This had led to a 'palpable deterioration of the profession', which York did much to reverse. He stamped out the worst excesses of the purchase system by increasing the number of free commissions and by decreeing that a minimum of two years' service was required for promotion to captain; six years' experience was necessary to obtain a higher rank. Furthermore, although, as a wealthy and senior member of the royal family, the duke was probably less tempted to indulge in venality or nepotism than others might have been, he sought to reduce the scope for such practices by appointing a Military Secretary, who was to be the sole channel of approach to the Commander-in-Chief. York also established a Military College and a school for cadets, the latter evolving into the modern Royal Military Academy Sandhurst. Other reforms he initiated included improvements in rations, health care and barrack accommodation, some amelioration of the army's brutal penal codes, the standardization of tactical drills and manœuvres, and the creation of permanent, regular light infantry regiments. Through the medium of these new units especially, he was able to promote some of Sir John Moore's innovations which formed the roots of a new approach to discipline and welfare within the army.

York made a brief return to the battlefield, sharing command of the Russo-British corps in the ill-fated Helder campaign of 1799. For the most part, however, his duties as Commander-in-Chief kept him at the Horse Guards in Whitehall until 1809, when he resigned over a scandal involving his mistress,

Mary Anne Clarke. Reinstated shortly after, he sustained his policy of cautious, incremental reform for the remainder of the Napoleonic Wars, receiving parliament's acclaim for his services in 1815. In the opinion of Sir John Fortescue, the distinguished British military historian, York had done 'more for the Army than any one man has done for it in the whole of its history'.

---

grape, and canister, the British added shrapnel, a hollow sphere packed with shot around an explosive core. Some use was also made of crude rockets, though, except as incendiary devices, these glorified firecrackers proved of doubtful worth.

Engineering support, which until the 1760s had also been provided by the artillery, was furnished by the Royal Engineers and the Royal Corps of Artificers. Given the scale of Britain's commitments, the number of engineers was far too small; the conduct of most of the siege operations in the Peninsular War, for instance, suffered as a result of inadequate supervision by trained specialists. Similarly, the building of the lines of Torres Vedras, one of the Napoleonic era's greatest construction projects, had to be overseen by a handful of qualified technicians. The Royal Waggon Train, to which responsibility for the movement of supplies fell, was neglected, too, despite the entreaties of field commanders like Wellington who well understood how vital sufficient logistical support was for military success. To a Cabinet beset by financial problems, however, the retention of numerous draught animals and transport vehicles often seemed an expensive luxury. Ministers, swayed by the belief or hope that the army could always satisfy its needs with local resources, instigated repeated, savage cuts in the size of the Waggon Train. In the Peninsula, Wellington was compelled to depend primarily on unreliable, Spanish civilian muleteers, though a Commissariat Car Train was established in 1811 to supplement the few waggons available.

Cavalry continued to be divided into 'heavy' regiments—such as dragoons, the Life Guards, and Dragoon Guards—and 'light' ones. The latter were predominantly dragoons, though a handful of regiments were restyled as hussars in the course of this period. (The British army shunned the creation of lancer regiments until after the Napoleonic Wars.) Heavy cavalry, normally large men mounted on big horses, were intended for shock action, whereas light regiments rode smaller mounts and were primarily designed for missions like screening, reconnaissance, and pursuit. British cavalry usually had high-quality horses and, normally fielded in brigades of two or three regiments, typically giving between 700 and 1,000 sabres, could be formidable opponents. Their Achilles' heel seems to have been a lack of self-restraint which, as Wellington once complained, often sent them 'galloping at every thing, and . . . galloping back as fast'.

Turning to the army's foot troops, the majority of soldiers served in line regiments, which retained the basic structure that had evolved as early as the 1770s. Each battalion comprised ten companies, namely eight centre and two flank. A battalion had a theoretical complement of 950 officers and men. The flank companies, one each of grenadiers and light infantry, were somewhat bigger than the others, mustering 112 personnel as opposed to a centre company's eighty-six. Whereas light infantry platoons consisted of nimble, veteran soldiers trained, to some extent at least, in sniping and open-order tactics, the grenadiers were the most powerfully built and experienced soldiers in the battalion. Together with the light company, they frequently acted as an independent reserve of élite troops, tasked with fulfilling particularly demanding missions. The rest of the battalion were made up of soldiers ranging from seasoned veterans to new recruits; and, when circumstances permitted or required it, the more experienced among them would be transferred to fill gaps in the flank companies.

The technology employed by Napoleonic period foot troops scarcely differed from that of Marlborough's day. The standard small arm was the smooth-bore, flintlock musket. These muzzle-loading weapons fired a lead ball which weighed about an ounce and was propelled by black powder. Owing to the amount of windage in the barrel, accuracy left much to be desired and the effective range was less than 100 yards. Indeed, to render their weapons as efficacious as possible, infantry normally fired in volleys under the rigid supervision of their officers and, since they permitted the maximization of firepower, linear formations—usually with the men arrayed shoulder to shoulder and three deep—were predominant.

Throughout the eighteenth century, however, the progressive enclosure, afforestation, and urbanization of much of the European countryside imposed ever more constraints on infantry deployed in this fashion. The French were among the first to notice and exploit this topographical transformation, fielding an unprecedented number of both élite light infantry and, especially in the early stages of the Revolutionary Wars, agile, enterprising draftees who, whilst lacking the thoroughgoing training necessary for close-order manœuvres, made admirable skirmishers. Deployed in swarms and making use of any available cover, these *tirailleurs*—released both doctrinally and physically from the restraints of Frederickian tactics—employed aimed, independent fire to morally and materially weaken any opposing battle line. The controlled volleys delivered by infantry in serried ranks had little impact on such dispersed targets, whereas their own musketry, especially if directed against key personnel like officers, NCOs, and gunners, could inflict tremendous damage. Meanwhile, behind the *tirailleur* screen, the French heavy infantry, supported by an intense artillery barrage, would move forward in flexible, columnar formations, ready to consolidate and exploit any breakthrough. Once one had been achieved, the destruction of the enemy would be rounded off by the cavalry. Again, because of their superior motivation, the French horsemen were less inclined to abscond than their counterparts in the *ancien régime* armies; and this permitted victorious French generals, above all Napoleon, to unleash crushing, prolonged pursuits, uninhibited by the fear of mass desertion which had so circumscribed the operations of Frederick the Great and his contemporaries.

Containing the *tirailleur* attacks was gradually identified by the Allied powers as a crucial requirement for battlefield success. York and most British theorists, pointing to the experience of the Flanders and Helder campaigns of 1793 and 1799 respectively, argued that the best way to do this was by matching the enemy's skirmishers with light troops of equal proficiency. Accordingly, during the initial quinquennium of the nineteenth century, determined efforts were made to increase substantially both the quality and quantity of the army's light infantry. Several line regiments were converted and given special equipment and training, while a number of new units—notably the 95th Regiment, which was armed with Baker rifles and schooled in the art of sharpshooting—was formed. More attention was paid to the instruction of the line battalions' flank companies, too, and the light infantry skills of an assortment of foreign regiments in British pay were also drawn upon.

An additional spur to these endeavours was furnished by the invasion scare of 1803–5, when Napoleon massed a 160,000-strong 'Army of England' along the Channel coast. With transport flotillas assembling in Boulogne and other ports, it seemed to the British high command that a landing in Kent or Essex was imminent. Once infiltrated by the French, these counties, criss-crossed with the enclosed farms, fields, hop-yards, and market gardens which had flourished in the wake of the agricultural revolution, would offer an ideal environment for the operations of their light forces especially; sufficient British soldiers of similar training and quality had to be on hand to cope with such a threatening eventuality. Accordingly, substantial bodies of troops were concentrated along the southern and eastern coasts and kept there for a prolonged period. This not only enabled camps, above all that at Shorncliffe, Kent, to be established for the schooling of light infantry battalions, but also provided several British commanders with an almost unprecedented opportunity to practise manœuvring entire brigades and other large formations.

Further defensive measures, such as the construction of the Royal Military Canal in Kent and more than one hundred Martello towers to protect strategically salient points, were also taken in hand. As it happened, however, they proved unnecessary. By the summer of 1805, London's indefatigable exertions to combat French expansionism had yielded the creation of yet another coalition, the Third. Subsidized by Britain, Austria, Russia, and Sweden agreed to field forces, and there were high hopes that Prussia, too, would lend support. That August, Napoleon, unable to get his troops across the Channel in the face of British naval might, wheeled them into Germany to confront the advancing Austrians and Russians. Covering hundreds of miles in a few weeks, the *Grande Armée* descended on its largely unsuspecting opponents like a huge scythe. The Austrian main force, hemmed in at Ulm, surrendered before the Russians could arrive and, while Prussia prevaricated, Vienna fell. Meanwhile, with northern Europe temporarily denuded of French troops, Britain, anxious to recapture Hanover, George III's electorate, and liberate the strategically important Dutch littoral, had started ferrying the whole of her disposable army to the Elbe estuary. Plagued by atrocious weather, the operations slipped behind schedule; 2,000 men and several ships were lost in storms and it was 17 November before the vanguard arrived. By late January 1806, 25,000 troops had been assembled. By this time, however, the plan had been overtaken by events. Just as Nelson's victory at Trafalgar in October confirmed Britain's mastery of the seas and effectively ended—for the time being at least—any hopes Napoleon might have retained for an invasion of England, the emperor's triumph over the Austro-Russian army at Austerlitz on 2 December dismembered the Third Coalition and established France as Europe's ascendant land power. The Prussians, suitably cowed, postponed fighting until October 1806, while the British, bereft of continental allies and fearing a resurgent threat to their own shores, hastily evacuated Hanover.

Just as the need to safeguard the home base and colonies against attack absorbed disproportionate amounts of both the army and Royal Navy's resources, Britain's insular nature and her reliance on overseas trade and allies also dictated many elements of the strategy followed by those forces she could spare for offensive action. As her security and ability to project power ultimately rested on her fleet, the needs of Britain's navy were accorded crucial importance. Among these, timber, iron, pitch, tar, and hemp were necessities which were predominantly acquired in Scandinavia. Any direct or indirect threat to that region had, therefore, to be dealt with. For example, intermittently Britain feared that the Swedish, Russian, and Danish navies might, if only as a result of French duress, interfere with her shipping in the Baltic. As a result, she maintained a powerful naval presence in that sea and, in 1801 when confronted with the Armed Neutrality, used it to eliminate the Danish fleet at Copenhagen. In the aftermath of the Peace of Tilsit six years later, anxious that Denmark's warships should not fall into Napoleon's hands, London again took drastic action, despatching 18,000 troops and twenty ships of the line to capture or destroy them. Without any declaration of war, the British amphibious forces besieged Copenhagen until the Danish fleet was surrendered.

Indeed, because of Britain's geostrategic position, naval supremacy was a *sine qua non*. Achieving and then maintaining it, however, was far from easy. Whilst impressive victories at sea, like Cape St Vincent and Trafalgar, helped establish British dominance, such clashes were comparatively rare and their impact short lived; there was the nagging concern that the French, drawing on the combined resources of their allies and vassals, might muster a new armada of overwhelming size. Britain was thus obliged, first, to seal off the great dockyards of the Continent on a round-the-clock basis and, secondly, hamper, whenever possible, the construction of shipping within those ports. The irksome and often perilous work of blockading harbours was especially difficult at times of bad weather. It required, moreover, a handy network of logistical nodes to keep the patrolling squadrons at sea. In the Mediterranean, for example, Sicily replenished Malta and Gibraltar which, in turn, acted as pivotal bases for the fleet. Such depots had to be furnished with sufficient troops not only to protect them but also to enable them to reinforce other outposts or mount limited offensives as required. Sicily's garrison, for instance, regularly provided aid for operations in Portugal and Spain and, in 1806, struck at Calabria. This attack on mainland Italy was primarily intended to ward off an impending French invasion of Sicily. It culminated in the victory at Maida; and, thereafter, the Sicilian garrison was a thorn in Napoleon's side. Nevertheless, it did absorb an appreciable number of British troops, as did Cape Town. This was seized in 1806 on the grounds that, if it were to fall to a hostile power, it would give them a convenient base for severing the sea lanes to and from the Indian Ocean. Likewise, the need to cultivate and protect trade outlets, help preserve the Royal Navy's freedom of movement, and deny the enemy's maritime forces control of key sea areas compelled the army permanently to occupy various strategic islands, coastlines, and choke-points around the globe, irrespective of whether there was a discernible threat to their security. In fact, so dramatic was this expansion that, as H. A. L. Fisher commented in the *Cambridge Modern History* in 1934, 'Some writers have regarded the augmentation of the British Empire as the most important result of Napoleon's career.'

Endeavours to destroy enemy dockyards were other missions in which the army often had a hand. Particularly when the invasion scare was at its zenith, amphibious assaults on ports such as Dieppe, Calais, and Boulogne were tempting propositions. The Royal Navy intermittently tried bombarding these harbours during this period and, in 1804, there was an abortive scheme to block the egress of Boulogne by sinking hulks laden with stone in it. Had it been possible to land troops to support these undertakings, more significant and lasting damage might have been effected. However, in the face of unfavourable tide patterns and strong French defences, combined land–sea operations were rejected as too risky. The ports of the Scheldt, Maas, and Rhine estuaries, by contrast, appeared more vulnerable and, as they granted the French access to the expansive North Sea and the easily assailable Essex coast, very threatening; Napoleon himself described them as 'a pistol pointed at the heart of England'. Little wonder that naval preparations in the Scheldt repeatedly provoked the British into contemplating raids on Antwerp and Flushing until, in 1809, 44,000 troops and 235 armed vessels—including fifty-eight men-of-war and frigates—were committed in a massive amphibious assault which, it was hoped, would simultaneously serve as a diversion for a fresh Austrian offensive on the Danube. Bedevilled by bad weather, insufficient planning, and inept leadership, what had been intended as an ephemeral *coup de main* degenerated into a long, hard slog amid the insanitary dykes and polders of Walcheren. Disease, notably a type of malaria which was to recur among surviving veterans for years to come, killed some 4,000 soldiers and put a further 11,000 on the sick-list before the expeditionary corps could be extricated.

The Waterloo Campaign

The culmination of this campaign, the clash between Napoleon and the Allied armies under Wellington and Blücher at Waterloo, is perhaps the most famous battle of modern history. After his dramatic escape from Elba in February 1815 and the resultant collapse of the restored Bourbon monarchy in France, Napoleon, faced with an uncompromising coalition with immense manpower at its disposal, sought to deal a sudden blow which would shatter his adversaries' morale before they could fully mobilize their resources. Accordingly, while the bulk of the Austrian and Russian forces were still massing on France's eastern frontiers, Napoleon, with some 125,000 men, struck northwards.

His targets were an Anglo-Dutch army, 96,000 strong and commanded by Wellington, and a Prussian force under Marshal Blücher. They were cantoned across southern Belgium, with Wellington's troops in the west and Blücher's to the east. The former's communications stretched back through Brussels to Antwerp and Ostend; the latter's ran eastwards via Liège. Napoleon's bold plan was to cross the Sambre and seize a central position between these two opposing armies, preventing them from uniting. While holding one in check, he would crush the other, manœuvring on interior lines to achieve local superiority. With luck, both Blücher's Prussians and Wellington's heterogeneous army would be annihilated and the Low Countries recovered. The war would open with a stunning French success which would both rally French public opinion behind the emperor and end all Allied hopes of a rapid victory. Indeed, Britain, the coalition's paymaster, would be *hors de combat* for months; the government might even fall and be superseded by one more inclined to make peace. Similarly, the other allies, once disheartened, might sue for terms; and, if they did not, Napoleon, having secured his northern flank, would be free to wheel into the Rhineland with the majority of his forces, falling on his enemies much as he had in 1805.

It was not to be. Early on 15 June, the French, having concentrated in great secrecy, thrust through Charleroi. The Allies, though not entirely taken by surprise, were caught on the hop. Wellington, fearful for his links with the Channel, initially moved the epicentre of his army further west. Napoleon, meanwhile, having gained a twenty-four-hour start, consolidated his central position from where he could move 'with equal facility' against the Prussians or the Anglo-Dutch army.

Indeed, the next day could have decided the outcome of the campaign and,

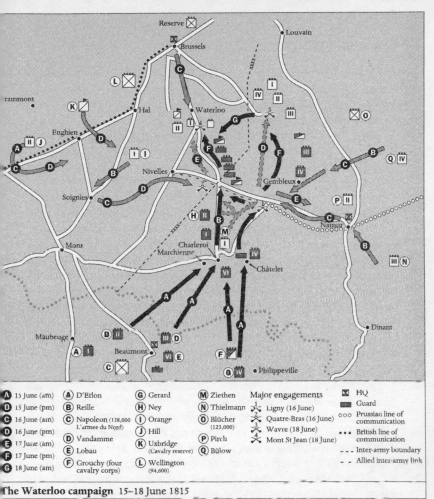

The Waterloo campaign 15–18 June 1815

Legend:

			Major engagements		HQ
A 15 June (am)	**A** D'Erlon	**G** Gerard	**M** Ziethen		Guard
D 15 June (pm)	**B** Reille	**H** Ney	**N** Thielmann	Ligny (16 June)	ooo Prussian line of communication
C 16 June (am)	**C** Napoleon (128,000 L'armee du Nord)	**I** Orange	**O** Blücher (123,000)	Quatre-Bras (16 June)	••• British line of communication
D 16 June (pm)	**D** Vandamme	**J** Hill	**P** Pirch	Wavre (18 June)	--- Inter-army boundary
E 17 June (am)	**E** Lobau	**K** Uxbridge (Cavalry reserve)	**Q** Bülow	Mont St Jean (18 June)	-- Allied inter-army link
F 17 June (pm)	**F** Grouchy (four cavalry corps)	**L** Wellington (94,600)			
G 18 June (am)					

perhaps, the war. Blücher, having amassed 84,000 troops at Ligny, unsuccessfully tried conclusions with Napoleon himself while, south of Brussels, Wellington's army, arriving in dribs and drabs, struggled to secure Quatre Bras, which was being menaced by the French left under Marshal Ney. 'Friction', however, mostly in the form of faulty staff-work, was already eroding Napoleon's advantage: an entire army corps spent the day marching between the two battlefields without interfering on either; and this, coupled with nightfall and deteriorating weather, enabled the Prussians especially to evade complete disaster. Nevertheless, Blücher was 'damnably mauled' and driven eastwards, leaving Napoleon at liberty to turn on Wellington's isolated forces and consummate his victory.

This he strove to do. While a third of the French army, under Marshal Grouchy, set out after Blücher, who was thought to be retreating on Liège, the emperor shifted the balance of his available troops to join Ney. He was aghast to discover that Ney, instead of pinning it down, had allowed the Anglo-Dutch army to retire unmolested. A frantic chase ensued, but Napoleon could not overtake Wellington, who, by nightfall, had safely ensconced his forces behind an irregular ridge just south of Waterloo.

Much of this pursuit was hampered by torrential rain and, throughout the night, sodden French columns arrived from Quatre Bras and squelched into position. Although the storm had finally abated by 8 a.m. on 18 June, the ground had been churned to a quagmire. Besides hindering manœuvre, this, Napoleon realized, would enervate the efficacy of artillery fire; so he postponed his planned attack until 11.30 a.m. to give the earth time to dry. Grouchy, meanwhile, had mishandled the hunt for Blücher, whose main body, leaving a rearguard at Wavre, was toiling westward to join Wellington. Instead of intercepting this movement, Grouchy merely followed the Prussians, becoming embroiled with the Wavre garrison. The majority of Blücher's army, some 72,000 men, thus descended unimpeded on the Waterloo battlefield; indeed, by 1.30 p.m. they were already molesting Napoleon's exposed right flank.

This effectively sealed the fate of the 72,000 French confronting Wellington's polyglot force of 68,000 men. As the day progressed and Blücher's hordes crowded into action, enveloping the French right and rear, Napoleon had to divert the bulk of his reserves to stave off this new threat. Meanwhile, Ney, fighting more like a trooper than a marshal, led the dwindling balance of the French forces in a succession of unco-ordinated assaults on Wellington's ridge: a feint attack on the Allied right backfired, sucking in more French than enemy troops; a hammer-blow assault by four infantry divisions in dense columns failed to overthrow Wellington's left; and then unsupported cavalry assailed his centre in a series of reckless charges. Finally, across the debris of these earlier attacks, came elements of the Imperial Guard which, after a brief but bitter struggle, were likewise repulsed. Simultaneously, Napoleon's right wing sagged under Blücher's onslaught and, with Wellington's forces everywhere assuming the offensive, the French army, heroically covered by the remnants of the Guard, fled the field, pursued by the Prussian cavalry. On hearing of the calamity, Grouchy, victorious at Wavre, executed an exemplary with-drawal to France.

The very thing Napoleon had sought to avoid had occurred: the Allied armies had united, squashing his main force between them. This defeat dashed his hopes of clinging to the French throne and, within days, he was to abdicate for the second time. Yet for all the misfortunes and errors of the French, the battle, as Wellington conceded, had been 'a close run thing'. His defence in depth had held, but at a terrible price: the duke's army had suffered well over 15,000 casu-alties and Blücher's another 7,000; some 25,000 French were slain or wounded. Wellington, sickened by the bloodshed, remarked: 'I hope to God that I have fought my last battle.' He had.

The historian J. F. C. Fuller once observed that: 'Without Trafalgar there could have been no Peninsular War, and without the Peninsular War it is hard to believe there would ever have been a Waterloo.' Spectacularly victorious against Prussia and Russia in his campaigns of 1806–7, Napoleon set the seal on France's hegemony over mainland Europe with the Berlin and Milan Decrees and the Tilsit Treaty. This was something of a concession to London's virtual immunity from direct, military pressure; for the Berlin and Milan edicts established and consolidated the Conti-nental System, which sought to deny Britain outlets for her trade. How-ever, if, because of the Royal Navy's supremacy, the British Isles were invulnerable to invasion, Britain's geographic seclusion and the defeat of her continental allies left her facing impotency on the strategic level, too; she might pluck at the outer threads of Napoleon's imperial tapestry but, single-handedly, could not hope to unravel it. Indeed, this stalemate was effectively acknowledged when, in the autumn of 1807, London also re-sorted to economic instruments of warfare, imposing sanctions on France and her allies through Orders in Council enforced by the navy.

Fortunately, Napoleon's embargo was applied neither long nor consis-tently enough to succeed. Although it did intermittently cause acute eco-nomic hardship as markets for manufactured goods and colonial produce disappeared, gaps repeatedly opened up, allowing British merchants in. This was intolerable for Napoleon, since even small chinks in the block-ade would enable London to continue raising revenue and prolong the war. Certainly, the need to preserve its integrity significantly contributed to his decision to invade Portugal and Spain during 1807–8 and, more fatefully still, Russia in 1812.

Both of these events were to have enormous repercussions. The war in the Iberian peninsula, however, allowed the British to break the strategic deadlock that had evolved. Indeed, aiding the Spanish and Portuguese had much to recommend it: Britain secured fresh allies and a foothold on the European mainland; Napoleon was denied control of not only Portugal and Spain but also of their colonies in the New World, with whom Britain needed to trade; the Royal Navy gained use of the peninsula's valuable ports, whereas the French fleet lost it; and, by absorbing so many of Napoleon's disposable forces, the conflict virtually ended the threat of a major French blow against either Britain herself or some important possession overseas. Furthermore, the geography of the peninsula was ideally suited to Britain's military strengths. Bounded on three sides by the sea, it was an environment where maritime power could exert tremendous influence while, exploiting the mountainous and barren terrain to compensate for its relative weakness in numbers, artillery, and cavalry, a small but redoubtable British army—supplemented with Portuguese divisions and acting in conjunction with Spanish regular and irregular forces which tied down masses of French troops—made damaging forays into the interior. As well as giving British generals a dominant role—Wellington even became the Spanish army's Commander-in-Chief—this war, moreover, furnished British diplomats with a convenient excuse for avoiding military entanglements elsewhere. The conflict in central Europe was left to Austria, Prussia, and Russia, though, after 1812, London genuinely regretted not having more troops available for the unsought war with the United States of America and for occupying key strategic areas like Holland.

The Peninsular War had two distinct parts. The opening phase was essentially defensive, with the British seeking to establish a toe-hold on the Continent. This was quickly achieved with the victory at Vimiero; the French evacuated Portugal and London's attention moved to liberating Spain. An army under Moore duly ventured towards Madrid but, confronted by a massive counter-stroke directed by Napoleon himself, fled to Corunna, where it was to be extricated by the Royal Navy. In the battle fought with the vanguard of the pursuing French, Moore was mortally wounded. His redcoats, however, drove off their assailants and the embarkation went ahead unhindered. Nevertheless, the relinquishing of Spain and the loss of Moore and some 7,000 other ranks scarcely made the expedition appear a success. Was Britain's intervention in the peninsula going to prove any more efficacious than previous endeavours to molest the periphery of Napoleon's empire? Should Portugal, too, be abandoned?

A report compiled by Moore in November 1808 had concluded that Portugal was 'not defensible against a superior force . . . If the French succeed in Spain it will be vain to attempt to resist them in Portugal.' On assuming command of the British corps in April 1809, however, Wellington took a contrasting view: given Napoleon's commitments, the French would not have sufficient troops to seize Portugal in time to prevent the British, supported by the Portuguese units they were training, entrenching themselves. This opinion prevailed within the Cabinet and was vindicated by subsequent events.

After first securing his operational base by evicting the French from northern Portugal, Wellington advanced on Madrid in concert with two Spanish armies. Although victorious at Talavera, he prudently withdrew before superior enemy forces. This retreat, however, coincided with the Walcheren disaster and the defeat of Britain's ally, Austria, at Wagram; and Wellington, fearing that Portugal might soon be invaded by irresistible forces, ordered the secret construction of the lines of Torres Vedras—a network of formidable, concentric defences around Lisbon. When, ten months later, the French finally mustered sufficient strength to attack Portugal again, their advance was, first, checked at Bussaco by Wellington's army and then brought to a standstill by the lines. Eventually starved into retreat, they sustained a further defeat in the battle of Fuentes de Oñoro. Similarly, their forces in southern Spain failed to make headway.

His army now battle hardened and substantial, Wellington promptly took the initiative. Boldly seizing Ciudad Rodrigo and Badajoz, by early 1812 he enjoyed control of both the northern and southern corridors into Spain. Thrusting forward, he shattered the French army at Salamanca, captured Madrid, and besieged Burgos. After retiring once again, he opened a fresh offensive in June 1813 which climaxed with Vitoria. This effectively ended French control of Spain, though more bitter fighting ensued as the enemy was cleared from the Pyrenees and various beleaguered strongholds. Meanwhile, Napoleon, ousted from Russia, was also losing his grip on Germany. Indeed, as Wellington's forces crossed onto French soil and threatened Bayonne, the emperor finally succumbed to overwhelming odds at Leipzig. Followed into France, he fought a brilliant campaign but, with Wellington now before Toulouse and the Austrians, Prussians, and Russians menacing Paris, further resistance was futile. He abdicated on 6 April.

This was not quite the end, however. Within a year, he was back, having escaped from exile. In the ensuing Waterloo campaign, British troops again played a key role in his downfall. As had so often happened in the peninsula, Wellington's stratagems effectively neutralized those which had brought the French innumerable victories. Skilfully deployed on the reverse slopes of a ridge to screen them from observation and artillery fire, and sheathed by a protective cordon of light infantry which kept the enemy's *tirailleurs* at bay, Wellington's line battalions, usually deployed only two men deep to maximize their frontage and firepower, repeatedly surprised, overlapped, and overwhelmed attacking French columns before they could redeploy for a fire-fight.

Such tactics demanded unfaltering obedience and steadiness on the part of the individual soldier; and their successful application is indicative of the superb training, discipline, and skill with which, by 1815, the British army had been imbued.

8 AN UNREFORMED ARMY?
1815–1868

PETER BURROUGHS

In 1815 Britain emerged victorious from the French and Napoleonic Wars. The circumstances created by this triumph, as well as the memories of military success, profoundly affected the development of the British army, both positively and negatively, for much of the nineteenth century. With its supremacy as a world power unchallenged by foreign rivals, Britain enjoyed almost four decades of peace in Europe, and this in itself sapped the army's preparedness to fight a large-scale land war. Until 1854 military intervention to uphold a balance of power on the Continent was not contemplated, even by the meddling Lord Palmerston, as an adjunct to diplomatic action. Unlike the navy, the army had no role to play as an instrument of foreign policy. Both in official strategy and in popular perceptions, its position appeared secondary to that of the Senior Service as the front line of national defence, the foundation of Britain's power and status, and the guarantor of trading routes throughout the world so vital to a commercial nation. These circumstances weakened the army's capacity to command public attention and scarce resources. Home defence reinforced the tendency. Foreign invasion seemed a remote possibility after 1815, despite popular 'panics' in 1846–7, 1852–3, and 1859 that a French attack was imminent. Except in Ireland, where substantial numbers of troops were required to maintain law and order, home stations were kept small and scattered, and the Englishman's traditional aversion to a standing army could be indulged in an island kingdom shielded by the navy.

Faced with public indifference and parliamentary preoccupation with retrenchment, the army was to a large extent run by the military high command without interference. Here the collective memory of victory over the French exerted a detrimental influence, since it strengthened and legitimized the forces of habit and torpor so ingrained in the operations and ethos of an authoritarian, hierarchical institution. Until the Crimean War traditionalism and complacency were not subjected to the test of battle; in the many colonial engagements of the period British numbers, discipline, and fire-power were usually sufficient to secure comforting victories. In the Duke of Wellington, too, the army had a formidable commander and spokesman whose conservative leanings were seldom successfully challenged by civilian administrators and politicians.

The problems that confronted senior military officers and successive British governments between 1815 and the outbreak of the Crimean War arose from the interaction of three decisive factors—commitments, expenditure, and manpower. At home the army fulfilled a policing role at times of civil disturbance, an unpopular duty that had to be executed with inadequate numbers, and with troops dispersed in small units and kept constantly on the move. In 1819 some 64,000 officers and men were stationed in Britain; by 1825 the number had fallen to 44,000. Some augmentation occurred in the early 1840s to meet the challenge of Chartism.

The demands of domestic security took second place to those of colonial defence, the overriding determinant of the British army's operations and organization after 1815. Since the Seven Years War (1756–63), permanent military garrisons had been stationed in the colonies, a strategy routinely pursued in an empire that continued to grow in all quarters of the globe. These imperial responsibilities fell into three, sometimes overlapping, categories: preventing external aggression by a foreign power, subduing unstable or lawless frontier regions, and maintaining internal security. Fear of territorial aggrandizement by the United States, manifest in the war of 1812, prompted ministers to retain at least 5,000 troops in British North America and spend money there on military canals and fortifications. Despite the generally harmonious course of Anglo-American relations, periodic frontier disputes, as over the Maine–New Brunswick border in 1841–2 and the Oregon border in 1845–6, and instability caused by the Canadian rebellions, 1837–8, and later by the American Civil War, 1861–5, meant that a respectable military presence had to be preserved. India was the other theatre where fears of external attack came to loom large in the minds of some Britons who imagined Russian hordes swarming over the North-West Frontier.

Besides posing persistent military problems, turbulent border regions also afforded sufficient opportunities for profit, promotion, or fame to encourage local commanders to employ their forces for the personal gain or glory that might stem from conquest and annexation, whatever the policies or preferences of their political superiors at home. This was especially true in Asia where a tradition established by Robert Clive and continued by Lord Wellesley was revived by Lords Ellenborough and Dalhousie in the ill-fated Afghan adventure of 1839–42, the conquest of Sind in 1843, the acquisition of the Punjab after two Sikh wars, 1845–9, the second Burmese war of 1852 to avenge an 'insult offered to the British flag at the mouth of the Ganges', and the annexation of Oudh in 1856. Lord Elgin led punitive expeditions against Canton and the mainland Chinese between 1857 and 1860. Meanwhile in South Africa frontier skirmishes between Boers and Bantu were exacerbated by repeated annexation of territory, often brought about by masterful military men on the spot like the flamboyant Sir Harry Smith. Periods of warfare raged on the eastern frontier of the Cape colony in 1834–5, 1846–7, and 1850–3.

A constant commitment of British garrisons overseas, especially in colonies at first without civilian police, was guarding against internal subversion and quelling disturbances, as on the gold-fields of Victoria at the Eureka stockade in 1854 and in Montreal during rioting in 1832, 1849, and 1853. This was a demanding role because many new colonies contained alien Europeans and/or indigenous peoples who might suddenly challenge British rule. The major confrontations of the rebellions in the Canadas and the Indian mutiny had minor echoes in Demerara in 1823, Mauritius in 1832, Ceylon in 1848, Cephalonia in 1849, and Jamaica in 1865. The obligations of colonial defence were extended by the rise of British humanitarian sentiment in the early nineteenth century. The disruptive process of abolishing colonial slavery seemed to require the presence of more soldiers throughout the Caribbean to guard against revolts, such as that in Jamaica in 1831, whether by blacks or by whites. Fears of the slaughter of Europeans or the extermination of the Maori later led to the involvement in New Zealand of thousands of British soldiers (18,000 at one point) in what became an intermittent war of conquest on behalf of white settlers in the years 1845 to 1872.

If commitments remained substantial and unpredictable, military administrators were constrained in their responses by the dictates of retrenchment. In the decades after 1815 a passion for economy raged in parliament; it affected all areas of government spending and the policies of all ministries. The army budget declined from £43 million in 1815 to £10.7 million in 1820, and to under £8 million in 1836. During the 1840s, with Chartist troubles and invasion scares, the army vote rose to some £9.5 million a year, still a far cry from the costly fighting in the mid-1850s in the

Crimea and India. The fixation with economy adversely affected military reform, because the prevailing supposition was that improvements in the conditions of army life and terms of service must necessarily entail additional expense.

One of the most prominent items of military expenditure was the army establishment, whose numbers came under annual parliamentary scrutiny. With a temporary easing of domestic tensions in the 1820s and the absence of crises abroad, successive ministries gradually reduced the strength of the army, which fell from 233,952 men in 1815 to 102,539 in 1828, and 87,993 ten years later. The trend was then reversed as additional duties overseas and concern about discontent at home produced a steady rise in effective strength from 91,388 in 1839 to 116,434 in 1846. Slight reductions in the late 1840s and early 1850s represented a brief respite before the Crimean War and the Indian mutiny; by 1861 Britain had 217,922 men under arms. Although critics denounced such a force as excessive for a maritime nation generally at peace, military manpower was constantly overstretched as it struggled to meet a multiplicity of commitments.

Part of the reason for this lay in the composition of the army. Imperial garrisons were almost wholly supplied by infantry regiments of the line. Guards battalions seldom went on foreign service and most cavalry regiments remained in Britain, though some served in India. As specialist corps, engineers and artillery were ordered to colonies in small detachments as the need arose. Of the 103 infantry regiments in the 1820s and 1830s, as many as seventy-nine might at any given time be stationed abroad or in transit, the remaining twenty-four at home preparing to embark when their regular turn came. In 1846, with 112 infantry battalions and 100,600 men, the respective distribution of troops and regiments was 23,000 (23) in India, 32,620 (54) elsewhere in the Empire, and 44,980 (35) in Britain.

Not only were more than two-thirds of the infantry committed overseas but colonial service represented a more onerous and costly operation than home defence. This was reflected in the intractable size of the pension list: more ex-soldiers drew pensions in the 1830s than in 1815 despite strenuous efforts at reduction. The army estimates in 1836 included the sizeable sum of £1.3 million for 84,960 out-pensioners (those not attached to Chelsea Hospital), about the same number as the current army establishment. Moreover, especially before mid-century, infantrymen posted abroad could calculate on an absence of ten or twelve years, and closer to twenty years if destined for India. Such long spells of duty exacted a heavy toll in human life and health, particularly at tropical stations. Successive Secretaries at War therefore had every incentive to diminish the disproportionate costs of colonial service by reducing the wastage of manpower resulting from death, disease, invaliding, and desertion.

Statistical data compiled from medical officers' reports at the War Office in the late 1830s starkly revealed for the first time the ravages of mortality and sickness among British troops. Deaths among soldiers in Britain averaged 15.3 per thousand of the mean annual strength in the period 1815–39 and 17.5 per thousand 1839–53. With 929 admissions per thousand, sick soldiers at home were hospitalized every thirteen months. At overseas garrisons, in the years 1825–36, mortality per thousand ranged from 668 on the Gold Coast to 130 in Jamaica, 69 in India (18 among sepoy troops), 22 at Gibraltar, 19 in Canada, and 15 at the Cape. Hospital admissions per thousand ranged from 1,812 in Jamaica to 1,678 in Ceylon, 1,142 in Malta, 991 at the Cape, and 900 in North America. Between 1839 and 1853 the British army, home and abroad, amassed 58,139 deaths, producing annual rates per thousand averaging 33 for NCOs and men and 16.7 for officers. Not until the 1860s did the health of the army noticeably improve, and even then a force of 70,000 Europeans in India lost 4,830 men a year by death, or nearly five regiments, and had 5,880 hospital beds constantly occupied by the sick.

A further serious wastage of manpower occurred at some garrisons because of desertion. Especially in British North America, Australasia, and to some extent the Cape, this haemorrhage constantly, though erratically, sapped the strength of regiments. Close proximity to the safe sanctuary of the American republic along an extended frontier and the powerful attractions of high wages, accessible land, and the prospect of comfortable independence induced several hundred soldiers a year in the Canadian provinces to desert. The same allurements and facilities operated in Australia and New Zealand where desertions averaged 4 per cent during the 1850s. The compelling forces of discontent and hatred of army life also played their part in encouraging desertion. The soulless drudgery of unvarying military routine, with its harsh discipline and endless drills, dispirited morale. Within the British Isles, several thousand men absconded each year, partly because the lure of home beckoned, but also because the system of enlistment was repellent.

The army's problems relating to manpower were compounded by its perennial failure, through a system of voluntary service, to attract sufficient recruits to meet its needs, let alone improve the quality by greater

Colonial Corps

In addition to the sepoy troops employed by the East India Company, the British government raised local corps in several parts of the Empire in an attempt to relieve the pressures of colonial defence on regiments of the line and the financial strain on the Treasury. This policy represented the cheapest form of defence, since pensions were not paid to these troops and in tropical colonies indigenous soldiers had far lower rates of mortality and sickness than Europeans. Army administrators like Lord Howick also thought that such troops might be employed for policing and detached duties, leaving scaled-down imperial garrisons, concentrated at key points and easily reinforced, to guard against external attack and internal revolt. Lord Hill as Commander-in-Chief did not share this enthusiasm for colonial corps. The British army ought to be constituted of forces available for duty in any part of the world where they were needed, and Hill doubted the efficiency of local battalions as trained, professional soldiers.

This difference of opinion was sharply reflected in the Caribbean when in the 1830s Howick urged an augmentation of the two West India regiments, formed of negroes, including those taken off slave ships captured by Royal Navy patrols. Hill opposed the extended use of negro forces in colonies where they might refuse to suppress mass violence by ex-slaves. In 1836 the establishment of the West India regiments was raised to 1,500, thus facilitating a reduction in the serving companies of two British regiments and the withdrawal of a whole battalion from Guiana. Similarly in West Africa, the authorities tried to overcome the high mortality among Europeans by raising the Royal African Colonial Corps, but discipline, training, and efficiency fell far below that of negro troops in the Caribbean. White officers and NCOs sent to command the force were laid low by disease and were mainly intent on surviving their one-year stint of duty. In 1840 the corps was amalgamated with the West India regiments which thereafter covered Sierra Leone as well as the Caribbean. This relocation, the authorities hoped, might beneficially sever the African soldiers' local connections and bring them into contact with better trained negro troops and a more advanced state of society.

Meanwhile in South Africa British regiments were assisted by corps composed of 2,000 Khoikhoi or 'Hottentots' between 1819 and 1827 and later by three companies of Cape Mounted Rifles. The men were skilled in patrolling the bush, a task which British troops ill performed and the authorities did not want to call on the Dutch farmers to provide. Because the force of 200 'native' police could not adequately cover an extended frontier, the governor doubled its size in 1833, and, when fighting subsequently broke out in these districts, Howick increased the unit to 860 in the hope that several British battalions might eventually be withdrawn from the Cape, an ambition blighted by further warfare in 1846–7 and 1850–3. Other problems were posed by irregularities among the 'Hottentots' and a shortage of recruits from among an apparently dwindling population. Low morale and indiscipline led to a mutiny in 1838, and a reorganized force of six mounted companies of eighty men each again mutinied in 1851.

More effectively than at the Cape, responsibility for internal security in Ceylon rested with a local regiment of sixteen companies: ten Malay companies recruited in Ceylon and Java, three sepoy companies raised in India, and three negro companies drawn from Goa, Mauritius, and Mozambique. One dilemma facing the government in the 1830s was to decide whether the Ceylon Regiment, then well under strength, should continue to comprise three ethnically diverse groups or be made an exclusively Malay force. The latter were favoured as being the most efficient soldiers, as well as the healthiest, and the companies had their own subalterns, a practice which attracted high-caste recruits. Although the Horse Guards feared that a wholly Malay corps might combine for mischief if it was the only non-European force in Ceylon, the Colonial and War Offices worked towards the creation of a Malay regiment.

A related stratagem for local defence involved veteran battalions. Even after the disbandment in 1828 of the Royal Veteran Companies in New South Wales and Van Diemen's Land, Newfoundland continued from 1824 to be garrisoned by three companies of veterans, drawn from Londoners on the out-pension list and volunteers from regiments returning from India. Despite high rates of mortality and invaliding, Howick supported retention of the Newfoundland force. Developing this expedient, he proposed in 1836 a special élite corps for Canadian service and their settlement in military communities at strategic locations adjacent to the American frontier. They would themselves be discouraged from deserting by being given higher rates of pay, a pension after ten years' further service, and separate cottages with plots of land to cultivate. The scheme was conceived, not as a bait to lazy, improvident veterans, but as a reward to seasoned, well-conducted men with fourteen-years' service. Despite opposition from the Commander-in-Chief who thought the project impractical and detrimental to regimental efficiency, the Royal Canadian Rifle Regiment was eventually established in 1840, but subsequent requests from lieutenant-governors to have the scheme extended to New Brunswick and Prince Edward Island were rejected.

In 1846 Grey envisaged the enrolment of pensioners, not serving soldiers, settled with their families in the colonies as a reserve force ready to be called out in an emergency to reinforce the regular troops. The initial field for Grey's experiment with soldier settlers was New Zealand, though the plan encountered practical difficulties and the first 500 men located at Auckland proved to be idle, intemperate recruits with little taste for farming. Grey also formed three military villages in South Africa but these pensioners were massacred by Bantu in a surprise raid while eating Christmas dinner in 1850. As these various expedients suggested, greater reliance on colonial corps did little to relieve the regular British army of its arduous, world-wide commitments, except in India and potentially in colonies of settlement.

selectivity. While some might have fancied army life or dreamed of adventure, the vast majority of rank and file found themselves in the army unwillingly through pressure of economic necessity. Yet a simple correlation often made by contemporaries between unemployment and enlistment failed to reflect regional variations, changing terms of service, and the mixed motives of individuals. Moreover, large numbers of unemployed men of military age remained immune to the army's blandishments. Soldiering was not considered a popular or honourable occupation among the labouring classes despite the guarantee of food and shelter, pay and pension, which must have attracted some idle characters as well as the indigent. For the army offered an escape from domestic troubles and a refuge for a variety of inadequates, misfits, and rascals: drunkards, bigamists, adulterers, debtors, criminals, and those who had quarrelled with family, friends, or employers.

In the view of contemporaries, prevailing methods of enlistment, in which liquor and deception played a prominent part, adversely affected the numbers and the quality of recruits. Though the regular resort to 'seduction, debauchery, and fraud' was persistently criticized, the traditional methods of inveigling 'the foolish, the drunken, the ungodly, and the despairing' into the army were not abandoned until after 1867. Never able to raise sufficient numbers, the military authorities were not concerned about respectability and sobriety. Virtually the only requirements were a minimal degree of physical fitness and a certain minimum height which, though constantly changed as the demand for men rose or fell, never yielded the numbers needed. One estimate made in the 1840s suggested that a long-service force, in which soldiers served in practice about twenty-one years in the infantry and twenty-four in the cavalry, required some 11,000–12,000 recruits a year to replace the annual wastage, let alone increase the size of the establishment.

During the century the army was unable to broaden its appeal or its social composition. It remained principally dependent on the unskilled, casual labourer, though demographic changes in Britain meant that it drew increasingly on recruits from populous urban areas rather than the countryside. The urbanization of the Victorian army was accompanied by changes in national composition. In 1830 42,897 NCOs and men (42.2 per cent) were Irish, the vast majority Roman Catholic; in 1840 the percentage stood at 37.2; by 1871 it was 24.5 per cent. The smaller proportion of Scots, principally Presbyterians, among NCOs and men was better sustained: 13,800 (13.6 per cent) in 1830 and 17,011 (9.3 per cent) in 1868. But recruitment, even in Scottish regiments with local attachments, came to rely more and more on English and Welsh, whose numbers grew from 44,329 (43.7 per cent) in 1830 to 106,810 (58.4 per cent) in 1868.

Senior army administrators therefore faced the perennial question of how better to adjust scarce manpower and tight budgets to meet heavy, unpredictable commitments. Those not content with habit and complacency sought to make more effective use of available resources, and two avenues in particular were explored. One approach, actively taken up in the 1830s, was to apply the criteria of efficiency and cut wastage by improving the health of valuable personnel and by rendering army life more attractive to serving soldiers and future recruits. The other, more ambitious, and longer-term design, first set out in a Cabinet paper in 1846, envisaged a new strategy of defence for the age of steam navigation and colonial self-government, involving the redeployment of British troops and greater reliance on self-defence in settlement colonies. Both these developments had made some headway before the Crimean War intervened.

In an age of reform when currents of change were coursing through civilian society in Britain, the military could not be wholly immune to the climate of the day. Nevertheless, in the unique institution of the Wellingtonian army, major obstacles stood in the way of initiatives and movements for reform. Individual regiments had their martinets and stern disciplinarians, and some officers were indifferent to the concerns of their men. A wide, unbridgeable gap of social standing and human sympathy existed between officers and other ranks. Very few rankers sought or received commissions; aspirants were actively discouraged as unsuitable material and uncongenial companions. Officers continued to be drawn from a narrow segment of society, principally from the landed aristocracy and gentry, often from families with a military tradition. Such restricted recruitment and social homogeneity enabled officers to perpetuate the values and pretensions of the officer gentleman, with accepted standards of behaviour and an acute sense of honour and duty, as well as of regimental *esprit de corps*.

Nevertheless, many officers did display a paternalist concern for their men. Lieutenant-colonels such as Henry Oglander and Armine Mountain of the 26th Foot, and general officers like Sir John Moore and Sir Charles Napier, took a benevolent interest in the material and spiritual welfare of the ordinary soldier; they adopted more lenient regimes that relied on 'moral influence', subscribed to funds for widows, and formed libraries and savings banks. The problem was that these remained individual initiatives confined to particular regiments, often discountenanced by the higher authorities, not a widely articulated and co-ordinated programme for change. Military reformers tried to educate a broader public concerning the ills of army life and conditions of service, and to generate demands for remedial action, through the pages of specialist journals such as the *United Service Magazine* and the *Naval and Military Gazette*. But to create an effective movement for reform and secure practical changes required support from senior military administrators or outside civilian opinion. In both respects reformers encountered further obstacles in the shape of army bureaucracy and public indifference.

Conservatism was bound to be well entrenched in an authoritarian and largely self-contained institution dominated by a closely knit group of senior officers, personified by the Horse Guards, who evinced an unyielding traditionalism and unquestioning adherence to Wellingtonian practices. The traditionalists' power was decisively reinforced by a cumbersome, hydra-headed system of military administration, whereby responsibility for army affairs was divided among six major departments: the War Office, Colonial Office, Home Office, Treasury, Horse Guards, and Ordnance. Such a structure produced rivalries, procrastination, and inertia. It also afforded military leaders sufficient independent authority to thwart or delay proposals and policies they disliked. Periodically, plans of bureaucratic reform were discussed by ministers and in 1836 by a royal commission headed by the reforming Secretary at War, Lord Howick. But objections were raised to the creation either of an all-powerful war minister or of a board like that of the Ordnance or that introduced at the Admiralty in 1831–2, and successive Cabinets were too timid to override the implacable hostility of Wellington and senior officers to any administrative change that would diminish the authority and independence of the Commander-in-Chief or subject the army to greater political control. The duke advanced hoary constitutional arguments against such a development and appealed with fatal success to superior professional expertise in order to fend off meddling politicians whom he denounced for indifference to the army's true welfare.

Failure to reconstruct the bureaucracy precluded a wide-ranging programme of military reform in the years before the Crimean War. Neither from within the army nor from civilian society were countervailing pressures generated of sufficient force to overcome the combined resistance of tradition, routine, and apathy. This was illustrated by the frustrated endeavours of several reform-minded Secretaries at War, especially the Tory soldier Sir Henry Hardinge and the Whig politician Lord Howick, to ameliorate the lot of the ordinary soldier. Nor did civilian campaigners come to their aid by launching the kind of pressure groups that accomplished so much in British society for the causes of philanthropic, sanitary, and administrative reform. Parliament, for its part, regularly criticized the scale of military expenditure but otherwise showed a conspicuous neglect of the soldier, except over corporal punishment.

At the heart of the debate over military reform in the pre-Crimean period lay two contrasting sets of arguments and assumptions. One turned on whether a particular proposal was necessary, advisable, and safe. Traditionalists took the view that what had served the army and the nation well in the past was the surest guarantee of continuing success amid the uncertainties of future warfare, and no practices or arrangements should be lightly overturned lest this adversely affected discipline, efficiency, or regimental pride. Reformers found that in peacetime arguments deriving from practical necessity, from the difficulties of matching scarce resources with expanding commitments overseas, or from imperative considerations of humanity carried little weight against the military expertise claimed by senior officers. On another level, the value and feasibility of changes to enhance army life revealed rival views of the character of the common soldier. Traditionalists disparaged the rank and file as incorrigibly idle, dissolute, vicious reprobates who required stern discipline to restrain their animal instincts. Any misguided attempt to improve their

Barrack life

Barracks at home and abroad varied considerably in size, design, and construction, embracing castles and forts at Edinburgh, the Tower of London, Gibraltar, and Halifax; the grand buildings of the Knights of St John in Malta and a former Jesuit monastery in Quebec; wooden cabins raised on piles at Honduras; wattle and mud huts with thatched roofs in Jamaica. Often forming three or four sides of a barrack square, buildings might comprise from one to four storeys, some surrounded by verandahs, colonnades, or galeries, according to the climate or local architectural style. Whatever their construction, most barracks were severely overcrowded. The sleeping space allotted to infantrymen in the West Indies was until 1827 only 23 inches in breadth; when beds replaced hammocks that year each man gained 39 inches. In St Mary's casemates, Chatham, in a space suitable for 600 men, the regulations stipulated 1,128 and the actual number in 1861 was 1,410. Barrack rooms and hospital wards seldom provided sufficient air for healthy respiration. Often soldiers had to make do with 200–300 cubic feet of air per man, when 600 was considered the minimum essential in British prisons. Even in 1861 the sanitary commission reported that in 162 barracks inspected in Britain, 5,339 rooms accommodated 75,801 men but 21,995 of them still enjoyed less than the standard of 600 cubic feet.

Conditions within such barrack rooms were unwholesome and squalid. Daily ablution might be performed at standpipes or watertanks in the yard but frequently soldiers washed indoors, the overnight urine tub being used for this purpose, until the sanitary commission in 1857 advocated ablution rooms and baths. It also espoused improved ventilation, though the men might deliberately block up any vents of fresh air to avoid draughts and cold weather. The fetid atmosphere of barrack rooms was sometimes exacerbated by noxious surroundings outdoors. At the Tower of London guardsmen were accommodated close to a wet ditch used for sewage; one barrack at Gibraltar was situated directly over the town's main sewer.

At least until the mid-century, soldiers spent much of their time in these crowded, noisome, and cheerless barrack rooms, with limited allowances of firewood and candles in winter. The same rooms were used for eating as well as sleeping and lounging. The standard diet consisted of a daily ration of one pound of bread, eaten at breakfast with coffee, and three-quarters of a pound of meat boiled for midday dinner in large coppers in cookhouses. Until more varied cooking facilities were introduced in the 1860s, men were unable to roast, bake, or fry meat and had to endure a monotonous diet of boiled beef or mutton, sometimes thickened into a broth by flour, rice, or yams, as available, accompanied by potatoes in Britain and any vegetables the men bought out of their own pay. A deduction of 6*d.* a day (4½*d.* from 1854) was made for the meagre rations from the soldier's basic pay of 1s. a day (1*s.* 3*d.* for cavalrymen). Further 'stoppages' were made for laundry, hair-cutting, cleaning materials, replacement of clothing and equipment lost, damaged, or worn out prematurely, medical treatment in hospital (9*d.* a day), and barrack damages when troops departed. Army regulations specified that soldiers must receive at least 1d. a day after deductions; many would be fortunate to be left with a few coppers to spend on beer, tobacco, or groceries.

Living in the same barrack rooms as the majority of bachelors were the wives and children of soldiers who had married with the permission of their commanding officers. Only wives on the official role were provided with accommodation and half-rations by the State, and these were limited to six per 100 infantrymen, chosen by lot when regiments went abroad. Wives may sometimes have stowed aboard ship or evaded the regulations but those left behind received nothing but their fare to a stated destination in Britain and what their husbands could transmit from savings of pay. In return for free food and lodging, and children enrolled in regimental schools, wives 'on the strength' might earn a pittance by doing soldiers' laundry; they might serve as auxiliary cooks or as nurses to the sick. For married couples there was no privacy beyond a blanket curtain and not always much decency as women lived, gave birth, fell ill, and died in communal barrack rooms. Married quarters were not generally provided until the 1850s, and the sanitary commission found in 1857 that only twenty of 251 stations in Britain offered separate quarters. Even so, the plight of wives 'off the strength' was more insecure and heart-breaking, since no provision or official acknowledgement was vouchsafed them.

The army authorities positively discouraged marriage among the rank and file, pleading the lack of married quarters, the discomforts of communal habitation, and the expense of transporting families between stations. Senior officers also regarded such marriages as an inconvenient distraction from military service and regimental life. Beyond this attitude lay preconceptions about the army as a male preserve and about masculinity. The authorities accepted that soldiers' natural instincts would lead them to brothels and beer houses and that 'diseases incent to lust' were a corollary of keeping the rank and file unmarried. In the 1860s official concern about misspent leisure and an apparent upsurge in venereal diseases led to the passage of contagious diseases acts. Seeking to regulate the supply rather than the demand, the legislation of 1864 stipulated that any woman accused by a policeman before a magistrate in closed court of acting as a prostitute within certain 'protected areas' around fourteen large military and naval bases in Britain was liable to compulsory hospitalization. Under an 1869 act such women were to receive five days' incarceration before being physically examined, and were thus denied the right of habeas corpus. A large body of vocal opinion opposed the legislation on moral, libertarian, or practical grounds, securing its eventual repeal in 1886, but this did little to alter the prejudices and proclivities preserved in a male institution where women were unwelcome intruders.

---

minds, morals, or conditions of service would be utterly futile and would undermine discipline by fostering dissatisfaction and insubordination. Paternalists and reformers, in contrast, evinced a more benevolent view of human nature and potentialities. They emphasized the environmental factors that influenced soldiers' conduct: the severe disciplinary code, the monotonous routine, the insanitary living conditions, the inducements to drunkenness and trouble-making. They believed that the State had a duty to promote the well-being of the ordinary soldier through material and moral improvements in army life.

These contrasting attitudes were most sharply demonstrated in the controversy over the causes and punishment of crime in the army, which centred round the question of flogging. This was a significant issue, in part because it aroused active parliamentary and public concern. For once critics capitalized on the more humane spirit of the times as well as reformist penal practices in civil society. Moreover, ministers and military defenders of the lash calculated that removal of the blatant excesses of corporal punishment might be the surest way of preserving it in the face of mounting public condemnation. To this end they put pressure on the army authorities to acquiesce in a gradual reduction in the scope of flogging. Before 1829 the three grades of courts-martial—general, district or garrison, and regimental—had almost unlimited powers, but that year the two former were restricted to 500 lashes and regimental courts to 300, figures reduced in 1833 to 300 and 200 respectively. In 1836 the maximum sentences of the three courts were further cut to 200, 150, and 100 strokes, but traditionalists remained keen to retain flogging for major crimes— mutiny, desertion, insubordination and violence, disgraceful conduct, and stealing army property—especially at a time when transportation to Australia no longer seemed a deterrent. Imprisonment increasingly became an alternative penalty, and in the mid-1840s military prisons with strict regimes were built at home and abroad. In 1846 the lash was reduced to 50 strokes maximum, the tally of soldiers flogged falling to 652, a number that steadily declined until the Crimean War and the Indian mutiny. Restricted to mutiny and violence to superiors in 1867, and the following year to troops on active service, corporal punishment was finally abolished in 1881.

The controversy over flogging became directly linked with the wider question of army reform through the inquiries of a royal commission appointed in 1834 to investigate military punishments. A report of 1836 defended corporal punishment for serious offences but addressed the prevention of crime by advocating the introduction of good conduct pay and badges, better regulated canteens, fines for drunkenness, libraries and reading rooms, regimental schools, and improved sporting facilities. What rendered the commission's report so influential was that it coincided with Howick's recent appointment to the War Office. Son of the former Prime Minister Earl Grey (and himself the third earl in 1845), Howick was an energetic, if at times impulsive, young man full of reformist zeal and impatience with military lethargy. Fighting battles of attrition with rival departments, especially the Horse Guards and the Treasury, both as Secretary at War, 1835–9, and later as Colonial Secretary, 1846–52, Howick accomplished a variety of valuable though modest measures, demonstrating the possibilities and the limitations of what an individual administrator could achieve for the pre-Crimean army. In the late 1830s he instituted a scheme of good conduct pay and badges; he authorized regimental savings banks in which soldiers might deposit spare cash, for the use of wives and families or the augmentation of pensions, instead of squandering it on drink; he created permanent libraries at the principal barrack stations, though he did little to tackle illiteracy until regimental schools for the men were begun in 1846; and he urged the provision of facilities in barrack yards and adjacent open spaces for games and healthy exercise.

The other major stimulus to Howick's exertions in the late 1830s came from the statistical investigations into military mortality and sickness conducted at the War Office by Henry Marshall and Alexander Tulloch. Having exposed the scale of human suffering and wasted manpower, Tulloch recommended a range of sanitary reforms which Howick at once sought to implement. Given the direct link indicated between army rations and ill health, he took steps, despite Treasury aversion, to introduce a more wholesome diet by reducing consumption of salt meat, eaten at many stations several days a week, and to encourage provision of a third hot meal at suppertime. He tried to restrict consumption of liquor by abolishing the free spirit ration issued to troops overseas and by regulating canteens more closely. Howick also took up Tulloch's call for improved barrack accommodation, especially at garrisons abroad where cheap materials and shoddy workmanship or a lack of proper maintenance by distant, neglectful authorities produced squalid death-traps, but his persevering efforts were hamstrung by divided departmental responsibilities. In addition to Treasury parsimony, the Ordnance, which was primarily charged with the erection and upkeep of military buildings, was notoriously slow moving and tardy in pursuing the tortuous procedures and interdepartmental communications involved in the design, costing, contracts, and construction of new buildings and in the appraisal and funding of repairs to existing structures. Despite repeated remonstrances from medical officers, governors, and the War Office, it took eleven years to repair condemned barracks at Orange Grove, Trinidad, seven to renovate the hospital at Fort Wiltshire on the Cape frontier, and twenty to erect a new barrack at Fort Charlotte in the Bahamas.

To ease the burdens of infantrymen overseas, Howick sought to reorganize the pattern of foreign service so that battalions would undertake shorter spells of duty and not be stationed the whole time in one location, whether unhealthy or salubrious. He planned a regular rotation of regiments, initially in the western hemisphere, by which troops would become acclimatized in the Mediterranean to a hot, dry climate before experiencing the deadlier heat and humidity of the West Indies, and completing their stint in the cooler, healthier environment of North America. Howick foresaw the scheme later being extended to the eastern hemisphere, where India was already relieved in part by regiments stationed first in Australia, by linking these locations with Ceylon, Mauritius, or the Cape in a regular tour of duty. While such measures helped to reduce the time spent at insalubrious stations, shorter postings abroad ultimately depended on Britain possessing fewer colonies, or raising more troops, or redeploying existing forces.

With this in mind, Grey in 1846, now Colonial Secretary, undertook a wide-ranging review of Britain's military strategy and the state of the army. Faced with a French invasion scare, the urgent need to strengthen home defence, and a tight military budget, he advocated a concentration of troops in Britain rather than dispersal across the globe. Despite a slight redistribution in recent years in favour of the British Isles, four-sevenths of infantry regiments were still tied up in colonial defence. Most colonies, Grey reasoned, now had nothing to fear from internal disturbances or sudden external attack, and in the age of steam their security could safely depend on naval power, prompt responses to threats of foreign aggression, and greater reliance on local corps and provisions for military protection. This transfer of responsibilities applied with particular force to colonies of European settlement, which were then in the process of obtaining self-government and ought therefore to assume the burdens and expense of defending themselves. Recognizing that such a policy would be unpopular with colonists, Grey and his successors in office showed caution and flexibility in working towards the goal of withdrawing British battalions from settler colonies as circumstances permitted.

In 1851 Grey transferred to the Australian authorities responsibility for military buildings and works required by diminishing garrisons. He proceeded more circumspectly in British North America, where commercial difficulties in the late 1840s and talk of annexation delayed the full rigours of self-defence. The uncertain course of Britain's relations with the United States, and later the emergency of the American Civil War, meant that it was not until 1870 that British troops withdrew from Canada, except for token units at Halifax and Esquimault. Meanwhile in New Zealand sporadic outbreaks of fighting prolonged the commitment of British regiments until ministers decided in the 1860s on disengagement, a process completed in 1868. Periodic conflict in South Africa precluded total withdrawal, and the security of India placed heavy demands on British military resources, so that the shift in strategy announced by Grey, pursued by Newcastle and Carnarvon, and realized by Granville and Cardwell, secured only modest reductions in overseas commitments and limited redeployment.

It was in the context of creating more flexible reserves of manpower to facilitate his new strategy that Grey proposed in 1847 a scheme of short-term enlistment, which he also hoped would make military service more popular and ease problems of recruitment. Soldiers would engage for ten years and then have the right to join reserve companies, organized along the lines of pensioner battalions but paid an annual gratuity and a pension at the age of 55 or 60. Wellington, however, objected to shortening the engagements of any serving soldiers, even if each regiment were restricted to twenty-five men a year, as Grey's modified plan envisaged. This would disrupt the rhythm of army life, bleed battalions of their best men, and excite discontent among those eligible for discharge but excluded by the limitation on numbers. The duke wanted the hazardous experiment confined to new recruits, a fatal restriction to which ministers agreed. It took over another twenty years before politicians were prepared to override military objections to short-term enlistment, and Grey was unduly optimistic in seeing his scheme as a major contribution to 'raising the character of the Army, and improving the condition of the soldier'.

By the early 1850s, therefore, the cause of army reform had achieved only limited, piecemeal success. With Wellington's death in 1852 Hardinge showed himself to be a more open-minded Commander-in-Chief, sympathetic to pragmatic change. In the brief period before the Crimean War broke out he was induced by renewed fears of a French invasion to adopt a variety of useful reforms. He ensured the introduction of an efficient rifle and established the Hythe School of Musketry to promote its effective use. He fostered schemes for the professional education of junior officers and for staff training. He arranged a camp at Chobham for exercises by massed bodies of troops and initiated the purchase of land at Aldershot for a permanent camp of instruction. Nevertheless, neither Hardinge, nor his contemporaries in the decades between 1815 and 1854, seriously considered what seemed the remote contingency of troops being called to fight a large-scale land war against a European enemy. In structure and size the British army remained geared to the dual purposes of home and colonial defence. Organized in small units around the single battalion, little thought was given to concerted action by brigades or divisions, let alone staff-work and administrative co-ordination, in the event of a major campaign. The authorities had also failed to generate the manpower to meet a serious, sustained emergency with their inconclusive discussions of schemes to reshape the depot system, integrate the militia with the line, or create a trained reserve. In 1854, therefore, the British army was required by the politicians to embark on a war for which it was unprepared and lacked sustainable human resources.

The reasons why Britain went to war in the Crimea stemmed from Russian territorial designs on Turkey, with their implications for the balance of power in Europe, and the surge in Russian naval strength in the Black Sea which, unless checked, threatened British maritime supremacy in the eastern Mediterranean and potentially further afield. After Turkey's declaration of war against Russia in October 1853 and the destruction of the Turkish fleet at Sinope, a bellicose mood among Britons preceded hesitant British intervention, in uneasy partnership with the French, in March 1854. Ministers disagreed, however, whether to conduct a limited war to dislodge the Russians from the Danubian principalities or launch an offensive against Russian power in all theatres, the Baltic as well as the Crimea. Even when an attack on Sebastopol emerged as the focus of the government's operations, argument arose over the respective merits of a sea-borne strike and a landward siege by an army controlling the Crimean peninsula. Military opinion doubted the wisdom and feasibility of sending such an expeditionary force, urged by naval enthusiasts led by Sir James Graham at the Admiralty, and attempting to capture Sebastopol without sound intelligence on the state of the fortifications and garrison. As the bold assault on the symbolic base turned into a battle of attrition, the pressures on meagre manpower soon became apparent. The initial force of some 26,000 men comprised three guards battalions, sixteen cavalry squadrons, and twenty-five infantry regiments, hastily completed with raw recruits and devoid of the ready means of renewal. Casualties sustained in bloody but inconclusive battles in the autumn of 1854—on the River Alma, at Balaclava, with the dashing charges of the Heavy Brigade and the Light Brigade, and on the heights of Inkerman—the ravages of cholera and other diseases, and the severe climate, all took a heavy toll and placed intolerable burdens on the besiegers of Sebastopol. The arrangements for supply and transport were also at first woefully defective, with acute shortages of food, clothing, and shelter. When supplies did arrive by sea at Balaclava, their rapid distribution was hampered by the lack of pack-horses and waggons and by chaos in the commissariat, staffed by civilian clerks unfamiliar with field service and hidebound by red tape. Treatment of the sick and wounded was impeded by scarcities of doctors, auxiliary personnel, and medical supplies, by insanitary, overcrowded hospitals, and by divided responsibilities within the ill-prepared army medical department. Similar rivalries and disunion paralysed the activities of Lord Raglan as Commander-in-Chief and other senior officers.

Human suffering and bureaucratic muddle on this scale could not long be kept secret and within months an angry public outcry erupted in Britain. Late in 1854 critical editorials began to appear in *The Times*, based on graphic despatches from its war correspondent, William Howard Russell, portraying the deprivations and squalor being endured by heroic troops, the shortages of supplies, the administrative bungling, and the neglect evinced by the high command. Descriptions of deplorable conditions in the hospitals at Scutari caught the public imagination and led to Florence Nightingale going out to head a government nursing service. Private letters from soldiers confirmed the veracity of *The Times*'s reports. By January 1855 other newspapers joined in the denunciations and the demands for sweeping reforms.

The Charge of the Light Brigade at Balaclava

To prosecute the capture of Sebastopol after an indecisive encounter on the River Alma on 21 September 1854, the British forces under Lord Raglan took up their chosen position, to the south of the Russian base, on the heights a few miles above the small harbour of Balaclava. Thus placed on the eastern sector of the besieging forces, the British were in the direct line of any attack on the Allied armies by the Russian field army. Such a counter-offensive might have been expected but Raglan made inadequate and tardy preparations to fortify his position against a possible assault. An inner line of defence around Balaclava on high ground was formed by marines manning heavy naval guns. An outer line lay along the spine of Causeway Heights, associated with several redoubts hastily constructed and weakly garrisoned by Turkish soldiers. Beyond this ridge lay the north valley flanked by Fedukhine Heights. Overlooking the south valley, guarding the approach to Balaclava, were the 93rd Highlanders under Sir Colin Campbell and the cavalry commanded by Lord Lucan, comprising the Heavy Brigade under Sir James Scarlett and the Light Brigade under Lord Cardigan.

On 25 October General Liprandi began a surprise advance on Balaclava with a Russian force of 25,000 infantry, thirty-four squadrons of cavalry, and seventy-eight guns. After the Turkish outposts had fallen, a major assault by Russian cavalry was directed against the Highlanders, 550 men drawn up two deep, a 'thin red streak tipped with a line of steel'. Volleys at long range failed to check the Russian charge, but at 250 yards, as the cavalry wheeled to the left to perform an outflanking movement, a further volley put them to flight. By steadfastness and nerve, the 93rd had repulsed a Russian attack without much bloodshed on either side. Another Russian cavalry advance over Causeway Heights was beaten off by the Heavy Brigade whose six squadrons Scarlett swiftly launched without knowing enemy numbers and, by 'sheer steel and sheer courage', 800 British cavalry put 3,000 Russians to flight. This might have become a complete rout had British commanders acted decisively to exploit the advantage, but Cardigan, with his brigade of 673 men, watched the Russian retreat without making a move, and Raglan had little control over operations from his distant vantage-point.

The Heavy Brigade's signal triumph was overshadowed by the more celebrated though militarily less significant charge of the Light Brigade, which

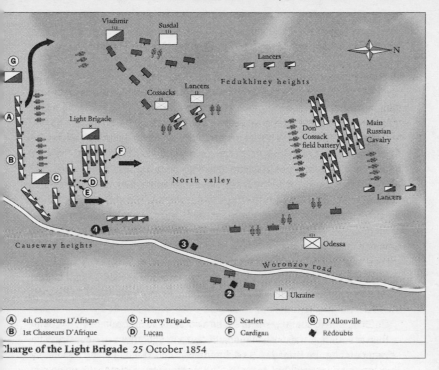

Ⓐ 4th Chasseurs D'Afrique	Ⓒ Heavy Brigade	Ⓔ Scarlett	Ⓖ D'Allonville
Ⓑ 1st Chasseurs D'Afrique	Ⓓ Lucan	Ⓕ Cardigan	◆ Redoubts

Charge of the Light Brigade 25 October 1854

originated in indistinct and misinterpreted orders. Annoyed by the loss of initiative after the Russian retreat, Raglan sent a verbal message to Lucan requesting him to occupy the ground the Russians were vacating. Without infantry to assist in this operation, the imperious Lucan declined to regard the message as an order. The Russians took advantage of the respite from harassment to remove the guns from the redoubts they had earlier overrun. To deny them these prizes, Raglan now sent his ADC Captain Lewis Nolan, 15th Hussars, with a written message to Lucan ordering the cavalry 'to advance rapidly to the front' and 'to prevent the enemy carrying away the guns'. From a lower position Lucan could not see the guns in question and assumed these must be Russian guns further down the valley which, he realized, it would be reckless and futile to assail. A bad-tempered exchange ensued between an irate Lucan and an insolent Nolan, with the latter pointing vaguely into the distance without clarifying the ambiguous message. Reluctantly taking it as an order, Lucan instructed Cardigan, his haughty, headstrong brother-in-law, to advance, which he did after having acknowledged that it would be suicidal without the customary support of cavalry on the flanks and infantry close at hand.

Cardigan's brigade consisted of the 13th Light Dragoons and the 17th Lancers, followed by the 4th and 11th Hussars, and the 8th Hussars in the third line. As they set out at a steady trot, Nolan tried to divert their fatal progress by galloping across the front and pointing frantically with his sword but he was killed before he could avert the catastrophe. Raked and thinned by enemy fire from the hills and then from thirty cannon ahead, the cavalry, 'in all the pride and splendour of war', rode with quickening pace across the one and a half miles of plain into 'the arms of death'. They reached the guns, cut down the gunners, and dashed on to confront Russian cavalry massed at the end of the valley, from whence the only escape was to turn and ride back again, running the same gauntlet of deadly fire. The incident lasted only twenty minutes: 113 of the 673 men failed to return and 134 were wounded; most of the horses were killed or had to be destroyed. Imperturbably Cardigan rode back to his yacht moored in the harbour and sought solace in a bath and a bottle of champagne.

The heroism of this futile action was graphically portrayed in W. H. Russell's account for *The Times*. Readers at home were gripped by his embellished reports of British valour, soon to be thrown into sharper relief by the coincidence of suffering and mismanagement. But what contrived to immortalize the charge of the Light Brigade was Alfred Tennyson's reading of the newspaper report which inspired him to dash off a poem, whose metrical pattern was apparently copied from a celebration of 'Agincourt' by Michael Drayton, an Elizabethan poet with a patriotic bent. Although Tennyson identified imaginatively with the triumphs and toils of soldiers in the Crimea, he agonized over whether to retain the phrase 'Someone had blundered' before sending the poem to John Forster for publication in the *Examiner* on 9 December. Several of Tennyson's friends and critics disliked the glorification of a disastrous display of military valour, but it caught the popular mood of the moment and soldiers in the Crimea read it with enthusiasm. The chaplain at the hospital in Scutari requested copies for distribution and 2,000 sheets were sent. This might not have secured for the charge of the Light Brigade a permanent place in the collective memory of the British public had not Tennyson become so popular and honoured a writer in Victorian England. Even more important, several succeeding generations of schoolchildren, required to learn poetry by heart, found that Tennyson's poem, with its stirring narrative and singsong rhythm, was ideally suited to memorization, along with Coleridge's *The Rime of the Ancient*

Mariner and Longfellow's *Hiawatha*. It was this concatenation of fortuitous occurrences which guaranteed for a minor, uninfluential action during the battle of Balaclava immortalization as a supreme example of fruitless heroic sacrifice.

The Crimean débâcle was taken up in parliament and J. A. Roebuck, a pugnacious radical MP, secured a select committee to investigate the conditions of the army before Sebastopol and the conduct of the departments responsible for military administration, after Aberdeen's Government had been defeated and replaced by a Palmerston Ministry. Criticisms in parliament and the press of military mismanagement became more wide ranging, with strictures on aristocratic monopoly of power and patronage in all areas of British government. The Roebuck committee's report in June 1855 criticized arrangements for transport, provisioning, and hospital care and condemned ministers for having sanctioned an expedition without sufficient military intelligence and preparedness for a protracted war. By that time, however, feelings of indignation and revenge had cooled and Roebuck's motion of censure came to nothing. With the capture of Sebastopol that September, diplomatic replaced military activity as the French dragged Britain towards peace. The final surge of parliamentary interest in Crimean mismanagement came in January 1856 with the report of the commission, headed by Sir John McNeill and Alexander Tulloch, and appointed a year earlier to inquire into the working of the commissariat. Their pointed criticisms of five senior officials provoked heated exchanges in the Commons, but, when an ensuing commission of inquiry exonerated all concerned, the campaign to expose military bungling quietly expired.

During the brief interlude of war, army affairs commanded unprecedented public and parliamentary interest. Tested by a major engagement the Wellingtonian army had been found wanting. And yet it survived the popular clamour largely unchanged and unscathed; after the flurry of agitation subsided, progress of military reform resumed its former unhurried pace along the grooves of gradual amelioration and piecemeal replacement. One reason for this relapse was that the outcry had reflected emotional outrage, not a secure basis for prolonged, constructive pressure; unfocused denunciations of the way the army was run produced no coherent, detailed programme of change. The highly personalized, vindictive search for scapegoats was also bound in time to rouse a backlash of sympathy and a closing of ranks between senior officers and harassed ministers. Admittedly, in response to events, some administrative changes were made in 1854–5: the military duties of the Colonial Secretary were transferred to the War Office, which also took over the commissariat from the Treasury; the Board of Ordnance was abolished, its responsibilities shared between the new Secretary for War and the Commander-in-Chief. These adjustments simplified the bureaucratic structure but they left untouched the fatal political–military divide.

Any explanation of the traditionalists' reasserted control over the course of army reform must recognize the decisive impact, within a year, of the Indian mutiny. Trouble began in May 1857 among Indian troops at Meerut near Delhi who mutinied in support of sepoys who had been publicly disgraced and imprisoned for refusing to use cartridges greased with beef and pork fat. The revolt spread quickly but unevenly to other sepoy troops disaffected by recent violations of their religious sensibilities and military privileges. Of the seventy-four infantry regiments in the Bengal army, forty-five mutinied and twenty-four others were disbanded or disarmed, though only two Indian regiments were affected in the Bombay command in the west and none in Madras in the south-east. The military revolt was accompanied by rebellion among the civilian population of recently annexed provinces in northern India alienated by the disruptive effects of modernizing policies on traditional society. Over a vast area the British temporarily lost control and for a few months many contemporaries feared that the uprising might succeed, especially since only 45,000 of the 277,000 regular British forces and East India Company troops were Europeans, and reinforcements had far to travel.

British authority was restored only after fourteen months of fierce fighting which assumed, on both sides, the horrors of a war of races marked by mindless slaughter and bloodthirsty reprisals. Public opinion at home was shocked and outraged at the challenge to Britain's civilizing mission and lurid accounts in newspapers of atrocities perpetrated on European women and children stirred up fears, fantasies, and racial animosities. Vengeance and retribution were demanded of the army, and subsequent victories were reported by a jubilant press which overlooked the indiscriminate killing, burning, and looting committed by British soldiers, the vital contribution of loyal sepoy troops, and the defects of supply and medical services (8,987 of the 11,021 British casualties died from sickness or sunstroke). Unenlightened by critical reporters on the spot, British newspapers drew exaggerated comparisons between the army's exploits in India and the Crimea, and unstinting praise was now lavished on the generals, none more so than Sir Henry Havelock, hailed as a Christian martyr after his death in the siege of Lucknow. Ordinary soldiers, too, were portrayed as accomplishing feats of heroism, impressions which heightened the popular image and reputation of the army at home and associated it directly, for the first time, with an Indian empire that had captured the public imagination.

The commitment to India necessarily entailed additional military burdens if British control was to be secured and the threat of further rebellion minimized. With the proportion of Indian to European troops prudentially reduced, at least 60,000 British regulars were thereafter stationed in India, compared with some 120,000 sepoys. More controversial was the future role of locally recruited regiments when ministers decided to transfer the government of India from the Company to the Crown in 1858. The dispute was effectively resolved by mutinous protests among Company troops who were eventually permitted to obtain their discharge. When 10,116 of the 15,000 men chose this option, the ministry was obliged to disband the separate army in 1860.

Military success in India and the waning of public disquiet over army affairs adversely affected the cause of reform in the ensuing decade. Campaigners could no longer look to urgent practical necessity. The French invasion scare of 1859 excited a flicker of popular concern about national defence; distant rumbles of the American Civil War and Prussia's military rise aroused some unease; but a rash of imperial wars and skirmishes hardly seemed to strain British capabilities. The press lost interest in a subject that had disappeared from the national agenda, and parliament, once more preoccupied with economy, displayed only sporadic attention to the soldier. Reformers also encountered on many issues a resuscitated complacency and conservatism at the Horse Guards under the Duke of Cambridge and sometimes at the War Office after Sidney Herbert left in 1861.

Sanitary reform sustained the greatest impetus, chiefly because of the unremitting energies of Nightingale and her acolytes who kept up a vigorous campaign of publicity and private pestering to improve the health and living conditions of soldiers. A damning report of the sanitary commission in 1857 attributed military mortality in Britain, double the rate among civilians, to overcrowded, ill-ventilated accommodation with deficient water supplies and sewage disposal. A major programme of barrack construction and improvement was launched, costing £726,841 in 1859–60, but reformers underestimated the massive task and ministers shrank from the sustained high spending needed.

Money was not the only constraint, as the slow progress of army education showed. In the post-Crimean period the civil and military authorities displayed much interest in better officer training in order to enhance staff-work and inculcate more professional attitudes. But disagreement arose over the role of particular colleges as well as the content of courses taught, and the proposed amalgamation of Sandhurst and Woolwich was defeated in the House of Commons in 1858, though both institutions were remodelled. Many officers continued to scorn specialized military education and regard the study of war and the acquisition of professional qualifications as less valuable than qualities of character and gentlemanly breeding. Controversy also centered on whether all officers should be obliged to undertake a course of professional study and pass a general examination as a prerequisite for obtaining commissions and promotion. The education of the rank and file was less contentious, except whether schooling should be voluntary or compulsory, given the low rates of attendance. Many officers doubted the necessity or even the wisdom of teaching soldiers to read and write, but in 1861 an army certificate with three levels of attainment was linked with promotion in the ranks.

Other aspects of the soldier's life and conditions were equally slow to change. The authorities tried to tackle drunkenness by transferring canteens from private contractors to regimental management in 1863. Middle-class campaigners encouraged temperance societies within the army and individual activists and churches established soldiers' homes with recreational facilities and spiritual uplift. In 1868 a system of fines for drunkenness was instituted and the summary powers of commanding officers increased. Serious military offences appeared to be rising in the 1860s, a peak for the whole century being reached in 1868 with 13.7 per cent of soldiers court-martialled, or 25,612 convictions among a force of 186,508 men. Despite the enhanced image and reputation of soldiers in middle-class society, soldiering did not become more popular among the labouring classes and the army failed to attract sufficient numbers. In 1860 a royal commission investigated recruitment and reflected on ways of strengthening the army's appeal. Its members expressed much genuine bafflement but produced no wide-ranging programme of measures. Government and parliament, on their part, displayed a lack of concern and political will in an age of peace, despite ominous developments on the Continent. In 1868, as in 1815, the same basic problems of squaring commitments, manpower, and expenditure remained unresolved, and army reform required a new initiative and a fresh approach.

9 THE LATE VICTORIAN ARMY 1868–1914

EDWARD SPIERS

During the late Victorian and Edwardian years, the army had to meet steadily expanding commitments at home and in the defence of the Empire within the constraints of voluntary enlistment and tight budgetary limits. It had to adapt to the demands of small colonial warfare, the challenges of new weaponry, and the organizational requirements of dispatching expeditionary forces overseas at short notice. In garrisoning and expanding the Empire, and in ultimately preparing for service on the Continent, the army depended upon personal qualities of courage and resolution, a highly disciplined organization, and an innovative leadership, both military and civilian.

During his period as Secretary of State for War (1868–74), Edward Cardwell undertook the comprehensive reform of the administration and organization of the late Victorian army. He established a statutory division of duties within the War Office, allocating military, supply, and financial matters to the Commander-in-Chief, the Surveyor-General of the Ordnance, and the Financial Secretary respectively. He also affirmed his authority over the Duke of Cambridge (Commander-in-Chief, 1856–95), by removing the latter from the Horse Guards to the War Office in Pall Mall. By these measures Cardwell largely consolidated and developed the departmental reconstruction begun by Sidney Herbert after the Crimean War.

In seeking to make the army more economical and more efficient, he began by sustaining his predecessor's policy of colonial withdrawal. The reduction of garrisons in Australia, Canada, and New Zealand not only saved money but it also fostered a degree of colonial self-reliance, concentrated forces at home, and reduced the prospect of protracted periods of overseas service for new recruits. Above all, it facilitated the introduction of short-service enlistments—a reform which had often been advocated as a palliative to enhance the appeal of service life and improve recruitment. Short service, which only applied to the infantry of the line initially, was gradually extended to the other arms with varying terms of enlistment. The infantry had an initial engagement of six, later seven, years serving with the Colours and the remainder in the reserve. Although soldiers could still extend their period of service with the Colours to twenty-one years, it was expected that the vast majority would pass out of the army at the end of the minimum period. Cardwell hoped thereby to reduce the pension list, form a reserve (which numbered some 80,000 by the end of the century), ensure that the army contained men in the prime of life, and induce a better class of man to enlist.

As another economy, he proposed abolishing the ranks of ensign and cornet, thereby modifying the extent of the purchase system. Although this measure had been promoted by Sir John Pakington, his Conservative predecessor and a known defender of the purchase system, it was vehemently opposed by many army officers and Members of Parliament, who were concerned about the failure to recognize claims for over-regulation payments. Cardwell promptly withdrew his proposal and consulted the Cabinet, which was unwilling to give official sanction to an illegal practice. He had the issue investigated by a royal commission, which confirmed that the practice of over-regulation payments, though illegal, had become customary within the army and could not be prevented under existing statutes. Unwilling to connive in an illegal practice, or to abandon his plans to link the purchase officers of the regular army with the non-purchase officers of the reserve forces, he resolved to abolish the purchase system.

In this bold approach, he had the useful advice of some individual officers (Sir William Mansfield, Major George Colley, and Lieutenant Evelyn Baring) and the support of Gladstone and the Liberal chief whip. This proved invaluable as he encountered resolute parliamentary opposition from the vested interests in favour of purchase. Although he managed to overcome the filibustering of 'the Colonels' in the Commons in July 1871, he failed to secure the passage of the Bill through the Lords. The government quickly resolved the impasse by announcing the abolition of purchase by Royal Warrant from 1 November 1871. Thereafter Cardwell was able to proceed with the fusion of the regular, auxiliary, and reserve forces. By the Localization Bill of 1872, he divided the country into sixty-six territorial districts and based two line battalions, two militia infantry battalions, and a quota of volunteers in each district with a depot to receive new recruits. The scheme was designed to foster local connections (and thereby attract more and better recruits), to improve the efficiency of the auxiliary forces, and to induce men from the militia to enter the line. One of the two regular battalions was to be based at home while the other served abroad, and the home-based battalion was to train recruits and to supply drafts and reliefs for the battalion overseas. The system, in effect, depended upon a balance between the battalions at home and abroad (in 1872, there were seventy battalions at home and seventy-one overseas, with the Queen's Own Cameron Highlanders not being linked until 1897).

However impressive in theory, the Cardwell system hardly transformed the army. Cardwell had neither anticipated the persistence of recruiting difficulties nor the strains which the home army would experience from the recurrence of overseas campaigns. Almost immediately the balance of battalions was upset, albeit modestly by the Ashanti War (1873–4), but, by the Zulu War, in 1879, there were only fifty-nine battalions at home supporting eighty-two abroad. The economies of successive governments and their tendency to make policy decisions 'by crises', involving the periodic dispatch and sometimes the retention of battalions overseas, ensured that the correct balance was never restored during the remainder of the century. The home battalions languished as 'squeezed lemons', supplying drafts and reliefs for a larger number of battalions abroad. Depleted in strength, the home battalions rarely served as entities without volunteers from other units or later reservists to replace the young or the unfit soldiers. Although the Stanley Committee of 1876 and the Airey Committee of 1878–9 revealed many of the strains upon the home-based forces, they were ignored. Indeed in 1881 Hugh Childers sought to complete the Cardwell scheme by permanently linking the regular battalions and by locating the auxiliary forces battalions of the regular regiments, within specific geographical areas.

Childers had hoped that local recruiting would flourish and so remedy the deficiencies in the quality and quantity of recruits which had bedevilled the Cardwell system. These hopes foundered because successive governments never substantially increased the pay of soldiers, which remained uncompetitive throughout this period, and because they only marginally improved the conditions of service. Admittedly they eased the harshness of military discipline, abolishing branding in 1871 and flogging in 1881, introduced more wholesome rations, and instituted a large barrack building programme in the 1890s (after the revelation of the fever-ridden conditions in the Royal Hospital Barracks, Dublin). But they still discouraged marriage, provided little scope for learning a trade, and disdained any responsibility for finding employment for reservists or pensioners in civilian life. One-quarter of the soldiers who left the Edwardian army became unemployed or unemployable vagrants. Governments also made scant provision for recreation, and so left the task of trying to wean soldiers from the temptations of the demon drink to temperance officers like Lord Roberts or religious activists, like Mrs Louisa Daniell and Elsie Sandes, who established soldiers' homes in many garrisons. In effect, the image of military service never significantly improved; soldiers, despite the popularizing of their imperial role, remained objects of discrimination in theatres, restaurants, and on omnibuses, and many families regarded it as an utter disgrace if any of their members enlisted.

Recruiting, as a consequence, rarely met its annual targets. Although the army nearly doubled the intakes of the late 1860s (and attracted even larger numbers during emergencies like the Second Boer War), it frequently failed to offset the much larger wastage of trained men caused by the short-service enlistments. Nor did the army broaden its appeal; unable to compete with urban rates of pay, and handicapped by the contraction of its traditional sources of supply—the rural population generally and the Irish in particular—it depended heavily upon the urban unemployed. Even so, the recruiting service had to employ additional expedients, lowering age and more often physical standards, and making 'special enlistments', namely under-age or under-sized adolescents who seemed likely to become fit soldiers in about four months with regular food and exercise. As governments were normally more interested in cutting the estimates than in enhancing the appeal of service life, and as they deplored the alternative of conscription, voluntary recruiting remained an insoluble problem.

The social composition of the officer corps proved resistant to change, too. Abolishing purchase had little effect, as the low rates of pay, the high cost of living, and the expensive uniforms and regimental traditions ensured that officers came from broadly the same classes in 1914 as they had done in 1870. Many were the products of the public schools, and most possessed a private income which, in 1902, amounted to £100 to £150 per annum for an infantry officer and £600 to £700 per annum for a cavalry officer. As the public schools did not teach military subjects, the army required about half of their officers to pass through Sandhurst (for the infantry, cavalry, and the guards) and Woolwich (for the artillery and engineers), with the bulk of the remainder coming from the militia and a much smaller number from the universities and the other ranks. Opportunities for further study were fairly restricted other than in the technical arms; by the end of the century the Staff College was producing only thirty-two graduates per annum.

Some officers advanced their careers without either money or Staff College credentials. Garnet, later Viscount, Wolseley gained promotions by distinguished service in Burma, the Crimea, India, and China. He wrote a highly acclaimed field service manual, *The Soldier's Pocket Book* (1869), commanded successful expeditionary forces to Red River in Canada (1870) and in the Ashanti War (1873–4), and undertook administrative service in Cyprus and South Africa. Popularly known as 'Our Only General', he belatedly received command of the forces in the Zulu War and then achieved his greatest triumph in the annexation of Egypt after the decisive victory at Tel-el-Kebir (13 September 1882). He was also appointed to command the force which was tardily sent to relieve Major-General Charles 'Chinese' Gordon, who had exceeded his orders and remained in Khartoum. As the relief columns failed to reach the city before the Mahdists broke through its defences and killed Gordon (26 January 1885), Wolseley's active service career ended in tragedy.

He remained prominent within the War Office, none the less. Having served as quartermaster-general and adjutant-general, he commanded the forces in Ireland before eventually replacing the Duke of Cambridge as Commander-in-Chief (1895–1900). A staunch supporter of the Cardwell system, he was favoured by successive administrations as a military reformer and as a modern counterpoise to the reactionary influence of the Duke of Cambridge. The latter, who had served as Commander-in-Chief without any limitation of tenure (until pressed to resign in October 1895), feared lest reform would undermine the prestige of the army and impair regimental traditions. He regarded the efficiency of the army as proven by its wartime successes and by the turn-outs at the endless round of field days and parades which he personally inspected. So long as he remained in office, bolstered by his royal connections (he was a cousin of the queen), many officers hoped that he could arrest the pace of reform and thwart the ambitions of Wolseley and his small clique of supporters.

The more astute Secretaries of State tried to exploit the divisions between these men, who heartily disliked each other and held profoundly different views on the value of short service, the reserve, and regimental

Viscount Wolseley

By the mid-1870s, Sir Garnet Joseph (later Viscount) Wolseley had earned the confidence of Liberal and Conservative governments and widespread popular acclaim. The phrase 'all Sir Garnet' had become a synonym for efficiency—a remarkable tribute for an officer who was barely in his forties. As a subaltern he had displayed conspicuous gallantry, cool judgement, and competent staff-work in four highly different campaigns (the Second Burma War, the Crimean War, the Indian mutiny, and the China War). Severely wounded on two occasions (losing the sight of one eye in the Crimea) and repeatedly mentioned in dispatches, he had gained a brevet lieutenant-colonelcy after only eight years' service. He had also written about the China War and the American Civil War, and had produced a well-received manual, *The Soldier's Pocket Book* (1869) which stressed the importance of preparing for war in time of peace. Finally, he had revealed his talents as a field commander in the Red River expedition, displaying a mastery of logistical preparations, and in the Ashanti War (1873–4), where, despite thick bush and a debilitating climate, he had rapidly defeated the enemy at Amoafu and occupied their capital, Kumasi.

Wolseley gained a reputation as an army reformer. Although he did not secure a War Office appointment until May 1871 (and so was not closely involved in the conception of the Cardwell reforms), he firmly promoted the virtues of short service, the army reserve, territorial localization, and the amalgamation of the regular army and auxiliary forces. In publicizing these views, he earned the lasting enmity of the Duke of Cambridge and the many officers who feared that Cardwell's reforms and their extension by Childers had damaged regimental *esprit de corps*. Wolseley, though not denying the importance of *esprit de corps*, did not believe that it could only be found within the confines of long-service regiments. In raising his expeditionary forces, he sought to rely upon élite formations, properly prepared and practically equipped for war. He offset any shortages in the home-based units by creaming volunteers from other units and, in assembling his staffs, relied primarily upon a 'ring' of officers, first formed in the Ashanti expedition and composed of Red River veterans, officers who had distinguished themselves in battle, and others who had shown promise at home, particularly Staff College graduates. The ring included Lieutenant-Colonels John McNeill, and Evelyn Wood, Majors George Colley and Robert Home, and Captains Redvers Buller and Henry Brackenbury among others.

The Wolseley ring aroused bitter controversy. By appointing so many talented officers for the Ashanti and subsequent campaigns, Wolseley established some continuity and cohesion among his staff and enabled these officers to gain war experience, public recognition, and rapid promotion. Yet this ring, like the ring formed by Lord Roberts in India, accentuated the divisions and rivalries within the service. Moreover, it neither replaced the need for a general staff (which Wolseley opposed) nor for systematic staff arrangements. Indeed Wolseley had a distinctly limited view of staff duties. He depended largely upon his own judgement in the planning of campaigns and in the preparation of operations, and looked to his staff for administrative support, information from local intelligence and reconnaissance, and the supervision of communications and supply. He never encouraged initiative in a chief of staff, and in his most celebrated victory at Tel-el-Kebir was effectively his own chief of staff.

The ring proved a pragmatic adaptation to the demands of small colonial warfare, especially in the period 1873–82. However, the apparent exclusiveness of the ring hardly endeared it to outsiders. The Duke of Cambridge reasonably claimed that Wolseley, by relying upon the ring, had depressed morale elsewhere and had failed to bring on new men, especially in his appointments for the Gordon relief expedition. The latter charge was somewhat exaggerated, as the ring was neither a compact nor totally exclusive group. Wolseley periodically had to rearrange his staff as some men were unavailable for active service, and others had died (Home) or been killed in action (Colley), but he undoubtedly relied on veterans of the ring and struggled to accommodate many senior officers in the Sudanese expedition. Several proved strong-willed and self-opinionated; they disdained local or outside opinion in their logistical preparations and fell out amongst themselves as the campaign foundered.

Wolseley's career as a field commander ended with the failure to relieve Gordon, but he continued to serve in the War Office. As Adjutant-General (1882–90), he modernized the infantry drill book, established mounted infantry schools, and advocated improvements in the diet and clothing of soldiers (including the move away from the wearing of conspicuous scarlet tunics and white helmets on active service). He supported Brackenbury in seeking an expansion of the intelligence branch and in preparing plans for mobilization, and backed the Duke of Cambridge in demanding more resources from successive governments and in sounding the tocsin over home defence.

After commanding the army in Ireland, Wolseley returned as Commander-in-Chief in 1895, deeply aggrieved by the reforms which had curtailed his new responsibilities. He did not prove a particularly effective Commander-in-Chief, disliking Lord Lansdowne intensely and succumbing to a serious illness in 1897 from which he never fully recovered. Nevertheless, he found support from several parliamentarians, newspaper commentators, and Lord Lansdowne for his protests over underfunding, and gained parliamentary approval for a significant increase of men, batteries, battalions, and horses in 1898, the creation of a special reserve of 5,000 men, and the acquisition of 41,000 acres for manœuvres on Salisbury Plain. He also felt vindicated by the speed and efficiency with which an army corps was mobilized and dispatched with all its equipment to South Africa, but this achievement was soon overshadowed by the failings of generalship, staff-work, and tactics displayed in the Black Week of December 1899. Wolseley's administrative career, in effect, ended in anticlimax; he had in many respects laid the foundations for army reform, but the army still had much to learn in South Africa and required considerable direction thereafter to become a more professional body.

---

esprit de corps. In seeking the support of military reformers, ministers were trying to compensate for their own lack of knowledge or experience in military matters (only one of Cardwell's fourteen successors, Colonel F. A. Stanley, had had any regular military service). They also held office with a limited and uncertain tenure; there were six Secretaries of State during the 1880s, and, over the whole period to 1914, only three ministers emulated Cardwell's feat of serving for more than five years in office (Edward Stanhope, Lord Lansdowne, and Richard Haldane).

The military, though, were not hopelessly divided. The duke and Wolseley both resented any interference by civilians in professional and technical matters. They wished to wrest control of the supply services from the civilians, and claimed that recurrent cuts in military spending had left the army undermanned, ill equipped, and poorly quartered. They never accepted that their advice had to be related to the party political and economic pressures in the Cabinet. Indeed, they saw themselves as first and foremost servants of the Crown (even if Wolseley often felt himself ill used by the royal family). The royal connection pervaded the army; it found reflection in ceremonials, in medals (the much coveted Victoria Cross), and in the military service of members of the royal family. The queen not only had a 'special' feeling for the army, derived from the involvement of the late Prince Albert, but also hoped that her son, the Duke of Connaught, would eventually succeed her cousin as Commander-in-Chief.

Neither the Duke of Cambridge nor Wolseley challenged the authority of the responsible ministers. What they resented was the way in which that authority was exercised, particularly in the control over matters of finance. Keenly aware of Treasury attitudes, the military regularly demanded too much in order to compensate for the expected reductions. As a royal commission concluded, 'extravagance controlled by stinginess is not likely to result either in economy or efficiency'. This tension came to a head in the late 1880s after an invasion scare and the revival of fears for home defence, when neither the duke nor Wolseley would accept responsibility for the efficiency of the army. In 1888, the government made considerable concessions to the military by abolishing the post of surveyor-general, consolidating the authority of the Commander-in-Chief, and transferring supply and transport to the quartermaster-general. Financial control, none the less, remained with the civilians, especially the Financial Secretary.

This reorganization had not resolved the basic problem of providing professional advice for the Secretary of State, as the Commander-in-Chief was now even more overburdened with responsibilities and duties. A general staff on the continental pattern was an obvious alternative, and a nucleus existed in the Intelligence Branch, revived by Wolseley as a department in 1886 and directed by the ambitious Henry Brackenbury. A member of the royal commission chaired by the Marquess of Hartington which reported in 1891, Brackenbury was widely credited with its proposal that the post of Commander-in-Chief should be abolished (after the duke's retirement) and replaced by a War Office Council, with the principal military adviser being a 'Chief of the Staff', heading a General Staff. Opposed by the queen and duke, and denounced by leading Liberals who deplored the concept of a military planning department, the proposal was dropped, although a War Office Council (and later an Army Board) were established. These reforms hardly transformed the War Office but they broadened the basis of professional advice for the Secretary of State. They evoked complaints from Wolseley that his authority as Commander-in-Chief had been diminished, and that he had become a 'fifth wheel to a coach'. In fact, he retained considerable administrative responsibilities and the planning remit of a chief of staff: any failure to exercise them almost certainly reflected his declining personal faculties and memory losses.

Nevertheless, the late Victorian army benefited from three crucial planning and procurement decisions. In 1886 Brackenbury undertook the first systematic analysis of the available forces of the home army, determining that two army corps, with appropriate supporting forces, should become the standard for mobilization. Stanhope not only accepted this proposal but he also responded to the recurrent requests of Wolseley that the army should have a definitive statement of the purposes for which it existed. In his memorandum of January 1888, Stanhope placed aid to the civil power as his first priority, the garrisoning of India and the colonies as his second and third, home defence as the fourth, and the 'improbable' employment of two army corps in a European war as a final task—a ranking which would later be criticized as anachronistic and irrelevant to the needs of imperial defence. The memorandum largely reflected current concerns about public order (not only in Ireland but also in Wales, the Western Isles, and in the Trafalgar Square riot of November 1887), and about home defence after the recent invasion scares (although the navy and not the army had tended to become the main beneficiary of these alarms). Even so, the memorandum confirmed a feasible goal for mobilization planning, one which produced the successful dispatch of the field force to South Africa in 1899.

The army profited, too, from an extensive rearmament during the last three decades of the nineteenth century. The introduction of breech-loading rifles (the Snider and Martini-Henry) increased the rates of fire and enabled soldiers to fire from a prone position. The addition of further refinements, including a bolt mechanism and magazine, smaller calibre ammunition, and smokeless propellants (in the Lee-Enfield rifle) enabled infantry to sustain rapid, aimed fire without powder obscuring the field of vision. The Royal Artillery also converted to breech-loading ordnance (after a brief reversion to muzzle-loading in the 1870s and early 1880s) and adopted a smokeless propellant in the 1890s. Finally, the army experimented with different machine-guns before adopting the relatively light and genuinely automatic Maxim machine-gun.

This weaponry was tested in numerous small wars and colonial campaigns. Every year, apart from 1883, the army saw active service in campaigns of conquest or annexation, in actions to suppress an insurrection or lawlessness and in punitive expeditions to avenge a wrong, wipe out an insult, or overthrow a dangerous enemy. Although it struggled periodically, suffering notable defeats at Isandhlwana (22 January 1879), Maiwand (27 July 1880), and Majuba Hill (27 February 1881), the army generally excelled in this form of warfare. Officers and men, argued Wolseley, benefited from 'the varied experience, and frequent practice in war' and from 'the sensation of being under fire'.

Improvisation was a prerequisite in colonial campaigning partly because the army lacked a general staff and partly because of the immense diversity of the foes, terrain, and tactics encountered. Over three decades, they met enemies like the Maoris, Ashanti, Afghans, Zulus, Boers, and Dervishes who differed greatly in their tactics, weaponry, and fighting qualities. At one extreme Colonel Arabi's Egyptian army, trained and armed by Europeans, resembled a regular army in organization. At the other extreme, the primitively armed Ashanti were able to lay ambushes and mount flank attacks, but lacked the discipline and cohesion to survive determined assaults. In between these extremes, the highly disciplined Zulu *impis* could manœuvre with speed and precision across the veld, but their primitive weaponry and commitment to the offensive proved disastrous at the battle of Ulundi (4 July 1879). Better armed but less mobile, the Maoris proved resourceful defensive fighters around their earthen strongholds known as *pas*. Whereas the Xhosa tribes rarely presented a target and usually withdrew before advancing forces, the Mahdists were religious fanatics, who were willing to charge the enemy in mass frontal assaults. The Boers presented even more problems. Fine marksmen and highly mobile, they were often well armed, resourcefully led, and capable of operating together in comparatively large bodies, even without a permanent military organization. British forces, in short, had to adapt to a variety of challenges posed by different foes, employing different weapons and tactics.

Compounding these difficulties were the problems of moving forces over immense distances across arduous terrain, and often in debilitating climates. As natural obstacles frequently posed the greatest threat to the health and manœuvrability of the expeditionary forces, the army sought to surmount them with the skills of the Royal Engineers and the labour of civilian auxiliaries. Engineers not only cut paths through forests, built fortified stations, and erected bridges, but they also provided telegraphic communications, aerial reconnaissance from balloons, and rail transportation in some operations. During the Egyptian campaign, Major W. A. J. Wallace, RE, commanded a railway company which delivered some 9,000 tons of stores to the front in less than a month. In the absence of railways or roads, navigable rivers sometimes facilitated movement; in the Red River expedition, Wolseley's force had to master the techniques of white water navigation and spent thirty-nine days traversing 1,370 kilometres of rocky, watery wilderness. Conversely, a shortage of water bedevilled several campaigns, particularly those in the Sudan and in Abyssinia, where Sir Robert Napier's expedition had to carry much of its own water as it moved across 400 miles of largely arid, mountainous terrain. Finally, many of these hazards had to be overcome within limited periods of time. Napier had to reach Magdala before the rains blocked the mountain passes; Wolseley had to defeat the Ashanti before rains thickened the tropical rain forest and decimated his troops with fever.

As these campaigns placed a premium upon careful logistical preparations, Victorian commanders and their staffs became adept at calculating their supply, transport, and support arrangements. They repeatedly had to cope with difficulties of transportation, especially the variable quality of animals procured and the poor standards of animal husbandry in the field. They often had to procure vast numbers of animals (in Zululand, Lord Chelmsford ultimately employed 27,000 oxen and 5,000 mules to haul over 2,500 vehicles), and had to adapt their transport to local circumstances. They employed bullock carts, elephants, and camels in India, waggons drawn by oxen and mules in southern Africa, bearers in west Africa, boats in Perak, and pack-animals in mountains and across roadless country. Commanders also improvised and adapted their transport arrangements in the field, compensating for the manpower shortages of the commissariat and transport staff. Indeed post-campaign reports upon the shortcomings of the support services (not only supply and transport but also the hospital services in Egypt), and the support needs revealed by Brackenbury's mobilization planning, prompted the reform of these services. The Army Service Corps was formed in December 1888, with specialized training, improved pay, and career opportunities for incoming officers. Medical pay was improved, the nursing service expanded (with female nursing given a greater, if still limited, role), and the whole service consolidated with a royal prefix as the Royal Army Medical Corps in 1898.

In colonial campaigns, commanders normally paid close attention to the collection and assessment of intelligence from local sources. They also depended upon the creation of secure base camps and lines of communication, permitting the forward movement of supplies, ammunition, reinforcements, and information, the return of the sick and wounded to the rear, and the provision of a line of retreat if necessary. Only in exceptional circumstances did field forces cut themselves loose from their lines of communications (in March 1880 Sir Donald Stewart led his men over 260 miles from Kandahar to Haider Kel, and, some months later, Roberts led the more notable march from Kabul through extremes of climate, duststorms, and enemy action to relieve the beleaguered garrison at Kandahar).

Enemy forces normally required less food and ammunition than their British counterparts. They neither required a fixed system of supply nor a line of communications, and, in many cases, made little provision for the care of their wounded. They frequently held the initiative; they could assemble quickly, transfer forces from one part of the theatre to another, and disperse after defeat, so hindering attempts to follow up victory in the field. In these circumstances where strategy and terrain favoured the enemy, commanders generally sought to fight and not manœuvre, thereby maximizing their advantages of fire-power, tactical flexibility, and disciplined manpower. Although British forces were always ready to engage in hand-to-hand combat, and made a notable bayonet charge at Tel-el-Kebir, they relied primarily upon fire-power. Breech-loaders, machine-guns, and later magazine rifles, firing small-calibre ammunition, enabled British forces to fight at longer range and to sustain rapid bursts of fire. This fire power, none the less, had to be employed effectively. British forces sometimes fought in the traditional line formation (at Isandhlwana and Omdurman), but they frequently fought in squares. Less rigid than implied by their name, these formations simply showed a fighting front in all directions. They could be employed offensively or defensively, whether as an order of battle or on the line of march, and at the halt when resting for the night. They could be compact in form (when facing a fanatical attack), or much more loose during bush or hill warfare. Although squares were now obsolete in continental warfare, they still appealed to small field forces which had to protect their supplies and wounded and had to counter enveloping forces in Zululand or shock charges in the Sudan. Volley-firing remained equally useful as a means of maintaining fire-control against determined assaults. It also helped to conserve ammunition and maintain discipline, particularly among small hard-pressed forces facing overwhelming odds (as at Rorke's Drift, 22–3 January 1879).

If the infantry was the main arm of colonial warfare, it relied upon support from other arms, the Royal Navy, and civilian auxiliaries. The artillery rarely served in mass formations (other than in Egypt), but proffered additional fire-power from small mobile detachments. These were often dispersed in different parts of squares (sometimes reinforcing the vulnerable corners), and, in Wolseley's opinion, their effects were more moral than material. Mobile patrols by cavalry and mounted infantry supported field forces (other than in thick bush or in mountainous terrain). They undertook reconnaissance missions, protected the flanks and rear of mobile square formations, and provided additional fire support. The cavalry also seized opportunities to charge with the *arme blanche*, routing the Zulus after Ulundi and the Egyptian forces at Kassassin (28 August 1882). Civilian auxiliaries accompanied most expeditions; they served not only as labourers and bearers, but also as guides, scouts, and in some campaigns as mounted riflemen. Finally, the Royal Navy proved invaluable in many campaigns, providing safe passage, coastal bombardment, and protection for bridgeheads ashore. Naval forces directly supported riverine operations and sent detachments with guns, rockets, and machine-guns in support of land-based operations. Despite this localized co-operation, though, inter-service co-operation never developed at a higher level.

These wars, however, were essentially limited in scale and scope, and the army's record of successes, culminating at Omdurman (2 September 1898), hardly prepared it for the challenges posed by the Second South African War (1899–1902). Facing the formidable Boers, British forces experienced for the first time the difficulties of crossing battlefields swept by smokeless, magazine rifles. Having invaded Natal and Cape Colony, the Boers invested Kimberley and Mafeking, and, after reverses at Talana Hill (20 October 1899) and Elandslaagte (21 October 1899), defeated the British forces at Nicholson's Nek (30 October 1899), driving the remainder under Sir George White back into Ladysmith. The relief forces dispatched by the newly arrived Commander-in-Chief, Sir Redvers Buller, suffered humiliating defeats at Stormberg, Magersfontein, and Colenso —the infamous Black Week of 10–15 December 1899. Lord Roberts replaced Buller as Commander-in-Chief, with Lord Kitchener as his chief of staff. He issued new tactical guidelines, insisting upon careful reconnaissance before an attack, the avoidance of frontal attacks in mass formations, more use of cover by the infantry and artillery, the use of continuous rather than sporadic bombardments, and better horsemastership by the cavalry.

Although Buller's forces in Natal suffered further defeats at Spion Kop (26 January 1900) and Vaal Krantz (5–7 February 1900), they eventually broke through the Boer positions to relieve Ladysmith on 28 February 1900. Roberts meanwhile concentrated upon the relief of Kimberley and a flank march to Bloemfontein, during which he surrounded General Cronje's forces at Paardeberg and forced them to surrender (27 February 1900). After capturing Bloemfontein on 13 March 1900, he halted for six weeks to reorganize before pressing north to capture Pretoria on 5 June

1900 and to sever the Boer's last link with the outside world by advancing to Koomati Poort on the border with Portuguese East Africa.

Confident of victory, Roberts returned home to replace Wolseley as Commander-in-Chief, but the war had merely entered its third stage as the Boers, under resourceful leaders such as Christiaan de Wet, Jan Smuts, and Louis Botha, embarked on a protracted guerrilla struggle. Kitchener sought to undermine the Boer resolve by burning their farms, seizing livestock, and detaining the families of commandos in concentration camps—highly controversial tactics which were described as 'methods of barbarism' by the Liberal leader, Sir Henry Campbell-Bannerman. Kitchener also sought to counter the Boers' mobility by constructing blockhouses across the veld linked by barbed wire, and by repeatedly sending columns of mounted infantry in drives across the blockhouse sections in search of the enemy. Although these tactics failed to produce any decisive successes, they eventually undermined the Boer will to resist and a peace was signed at the Treaty of Vereeniging on 30 May 1902.

The scale of the war had exceeded all expectations. It had required the services of 448,435 British and colonial troops and had cost the British taxpayer some £201 million. In all, 5,774 men had been killed in action and another 16,168 had died of disease or wounds. A further 22,829 had been wounded, and another 75,430 had left South Africa as sick or wounded. The war, which many had expected to be over by Christmas 1899, had become increasingly unpopular and had fuelled demands for the wholesale reform of the War Office and the army.

William St John Brodrick, the Secretary of State for War, and Lord Roberts struggled to meet these expectations. While Roberts pressed ahead with the preparation of new drill books and reforms of training in light of the South African experience, the introduction of the short Lee Enfield rifle, loaded on a clip system for the infantry and cavalry, and the rearmament of the horse and field artillery with quick-firing guns, Brodrick sought the radical reform of the home army. He proposed the creation of six army corps at home, based upon a vast increase in enlistments and military expenditure, bringing the estimates to 50 per cent above their pre-war total. He sought to attract more recruits by altering the terms of enlistment to three years initially, with improved rates of pay, especially for those who chose to extend their initial periods of service. Blocked by his Cabinet colleagues from resorting to compulsory service, he had gambled upon the post-war levels of recruiting and the deployment of battalions after the war. As most of his assumptions proved erroneous, the expensive army corps scheme remained a theoretical concept and incurred increasing criticism from the press and parliament. After further demands for reform were occasioned by the report of the Royal Commission on the South African War in the autumn of 1903, and coincided with a political crisis over tariff reform, Arthur Balfour, the Prime Minister, reshuffled his Cabinet. He replaced Brodrick with Hugh Arnold-Forster, a renowned critic of the Cardwell system, and appointed a small committee, headed by Lord Esher, a confidant of the king and a former member of the Royal Commission on the South African War, to report upon the reform of the War Office.

In a series of reports, the Esher Committee recommended the strengthening of the interdepartmental Committee of Imperial Defence, with the addition of a permanent secretariat, the creation of an Army Council, and the replacement of the Commander-in-Chief by an Inspector-General of the Forces. It also favoured the creation of a General Staff, headed by a Chief of the General Staff with a seat on the Army Council. Balfour accepted these proposals and the recommendation that the reforms should be preceded by a 'clean sweep' of the War Office, removing Lord Roberts and the heads of the four military departments. Thereafter Balfour left the details on the formation of a General Staff to his officials, while he concentrated on questions of imperial strategy in the Committee of Imperial Defence (pronouncing firmly in favour of the maritime view on home defence).

Arnold-Forster, meanwhile, had hastily submitted new proposals on army reform. Determined to implement his own ideas on entering office, he had to find the substantial economies expected by the Treasury and the House of Commons and offset a major recruiting crisis (as the vast majority of the three-year infantrymen had chosen to enter the reserve). He sought to do so by abandoning the army corps scheme of his predecessor and the Cardwellian system of linked battalions. He proposed to create an army with concomitant long and short terms of service—men enlisted for nine years to garrison foreign stations and provide a striking force, and three-year men, retained at home, who would feed the reserve. A firm believer in the ability of the navy to defend the country against the invasion, he saw little need for large auxiliary forces, charged with defending the homeland. Consequently he sought substantial economies by reducing the volunteers, disbanding half of the militia, and absorbing the remainder into the home army.

Tactless and self-opinionated, Arnold-Forster encountered fierce opposition from within the Cabinet, from supporters of the militia in the Lords, and from MPs in the Commons who were themselves volunteers. Forced to modify his proposals on the auxiliary forces, he eventually had to abandon them altogether. The feasibility of his 'New Army Scheme' was challenged by three of the four members of the Army Council, by Brodrick and Lord Lansdowne, former War Ministers sitting in the Cabinet, and by Esher and Sir George Clarke, the permanent secretary of the Committee of Imperial Defence. Although Arnold-Forster persevered and eventually gained Cabinet approval for long-service enlistments in October 1904, and an experiment in short-service recruiting in June 1905, his victory was essentially Pyrrhic. The scheme had too little time to take effect as the government fell from office in the following December; it also lacked credibility as it had failed to carry informed opinion or to meet the political desire for substantial savings in military expenditure.

As the new Liberal Secretary of State for War, Richard Burdon Haldane entered office without any preconceived ideas on army reform. He resolved from the outset to pare down the draft estimates of £29,813,000 bequeathed by Arnold-Forster, and determined that any reorganized army had to conform to the limits of an arbitrary, but politically acceptable, ceiling of £28 million. Assisted by his military secretary, Colonel Gerald Ellison, he envisaged the creation of a two-line army—a striking force of three army corps, supported by elements from the militia and yeomanry, and a Territorial Force, created from the volunteers and the residual elements from the militia and yeomanry, which could support and expand the striking force in the later stages of a protracted war. He aimed thereby to free the forces from home defence (apart from guarding against coastal raids), and to administer the Territorial Force on a decentralized local basis by county associations, so establishing a British version of a nation in arms based on voluntary service.

Haldane subsequently claimed that a meeting with Sir Edward Grey, the Foreign Secretary, on 8 January 1906, had alerted him to the possibility of a German attack upon France and had given a continental purpose to his military planning. If prudently concealed so as not to alarm his parliamentary colleagues, a continental perspective may have been useful in setting standards for mobilization, especially the advance preparation of all ancillary and support services. Yet Haldane could never reform the army purely to meet the demands of a possible war in Europe. He had, above all, to meet more immediate requirements, namely the annual provision of drafts for the battalions overseas and cuts in military expenditure. Hence he restored the Cardwellian system by reverting to the old terms of service (seven or eight years' service in the Colours, followed by five or four years' in the reserve), and rectified the imbalance between the seventy-one battalions at home and eighty-five abroad, withdrawing or disbanding some of the overseas units to leave a balance of seventy-four battalions at home and abroad. In effect, his Expeditionary Force of six large divisions, comprising sixty-six line battalions and six guards battalions, supported by a cavalry division, was simply the largest force which could be raised from the peacetime army. A continental strategy may ultimately have provided a purpose for the Expeditionary Force, but it neither determined its size nor its composition.

Unlike Arnold-Forster, Haldane ensured that he had the support of the Army Council and the Cabinet before he presented his proposals before parliament. He found little difficulty in reducing the regular forces as the vehement Conservative opposition merely rallied the support of parliamentary Liberals behind him. He also constituted the General Staff, deftly amending the Army Order to meet Esher's concerns over the role of the Chief of the General Staff in making staff appointments. He encountered more opposition to the proposed Territorial Force and made a series of concessions before and during the passage of the Territorial and Reserve Forces Bill (1907). In deference to the yeomanry commanders and volunteer colonels, who recoiled at the thought of being administered by county associations, he abandoned the elective basis of the associations, and later extended the control of the Army Council over them. He agreed to appease the Unionist leadership in the Lords by excluding the militia cadres from the Territorial Force. He thereby left former militiamen with the option of enlisting in a special reserve (with six months' training as a support for the Expeditionary Force) but reduced the likelihood of the Territorials ever reaching their target of 312,300 men. He tried to mollify Radical and Labour fears by switching the purpose of the force from overseas service to home defence, and by preventing the county associations from financially supporting their local cadet corps from funds voted by parliament. By these concessions, Haldane had effectively emasculated the nation in arms concept, but he secured the passage of his Bill, which received the Royal Assent on 2 August 1907.

Thereafter Haldane embarked upon the task of establishing the county associations for which the formal ceremonial endorsement by Edward VII proved vital. It legitimized the Territorial Force, disarmed some critics, at least temporarily, and ensured that the county élites would become involved in the associations (by November 1909, 115 Members of the House of Lords were serving in the county associations). Having launched the force, Haldane toured the country proselytizing on behalf of the Territorials and opening branches of the Officers' Training Corps at various schools and universities. Although recruiting was brisk at first, possibly fuelled by another invasion scare in 1909, neither the Territorials nor the special reserve nor the OTC ever met their full establishments. By March 1914, the special reserve languished some 18 per cent short of its establishment. It was particularly short of subalterns, and, by May 1912, had received only 283 officers from the OTC (and not the 800 per annum forecast by Haldane). The Territorials had only 236,389 men by 30 September 1913, with a mere 1,090 officers and 17,788 non-commissioned officers and men prepared to volunteer in advance for overseas service in the event of mobilization. Part-time soldiering, in sum, had a distinctly limited appeal; and, as the expected numbers failed to materialize, the Territorials incurred increasing criticism, especially from those in the National Service League who promoted the cause of compulsory service.

Haldane's achievement was none the less real. Compulsory service was never politically feasible in peacetime, and the Territorial Force, though wedded to home defence, was more organized and more complete in its arms and equipment than the old volunteers. It had field artillery, companies of engineers, medical, veterinary, and supply services: it could have taken the field after the requisite period of training as a mobile field force. Haldane had provided the machinery or framework of a reserve which could have been used in war (although in fact it never was as Kitchener, who knew little of the home army when he became Secretary of State for War in August 1914, chose to dispense with the Territorial organization).

While Haldane concentrated upon the raising of the Territorial Force, he relied upon officers who broadly sympathized with his own objectives to implement the details of reform within the army and to sustain the evolution of tactics and training. Major-General Douglas Haig was particularly helpful; as Director of Military Training, he sought to inculcate the precepts of uniformity, efficiency, and preparedness by organizing staff tours, formulating mobilization plans, devising training schemes, and testing embarkation and disembarkation procedures. As Director of Staff Duties (1907–9), he supervised the preparation and testing of the *Field Service Regulations, Part II*, the first manual of its kind which covered the organization of the army in the field. Equally important, though, was the

The Battle of Omdurman

The battle of Omdurman on 2 September 1898 proved not only the decisive engagement of the Second Sudan War but also the high-water mark of British imperialism. Lord Salisbury's Government had authorized the intervention in, and later the reconquest of, the Sudan to thwart the French (lest they move upon the Upper Nile) and relieve pressure on the beleaguered garrison at Kassala after the Italian defeat at Adowa on 1 March 1896. A decade had elapsed since the death of Gordon in Khartoum (26 January 1885), but Britain could now return, employing both a reorganized Egyptian army and the finances of Egypt restored after a decade of British control.

The Sirdar of the Egyptian army, Major-General Horatio Herbert Kitchener, under orders from Lord Cromer in Cairo, assumed command of the Anglo-Egyptian army. Urged repeatedly by Cromer to economize, and armed with excellent intelligence gathered by Reginald Wingate and his spies, Kitchener resolved to avoid the costly mistakes of the Gordon relief expedition. In authorizing the laborious construction of the Sudan Military Railway, which reached Atbara some 385 miles from Wadi Halfa in July 1898, he was able to bring brigade-sized forces, fully supplied and equipped, to within striking range of the Khalifa's fortress of Omdurman. Kitchener led some 8,200 British and 17,600 Egyptian and Sudanese troops, and had at his disposal 44 guns and 20 machine-guns on land, another 36 guns and 24 machine-guns on gunboats, 2,469 horses, 896 mules, 3,524 camels, and 229 donkeys. Some of these officers and men, like Brigadier-General 'Andy' Wauchope, were veterans of previous Egyptian and Sudanese campaigns, many others had recently crushed the Dervishes at the battle of Atbara on 8 April 1898.

By the end of August, Kitchener had brought these forces to the vicinity of Omdurman. Seeking to minimize his own casualties by avoiding hand-to-hand combat within the fortified city, he ordered gunboats and the 37th Field Battery Royal Artillery with six 5-inch howitzers firing 50-lb. lyddite shells, to bombard the Mahdi's tomb and the gun positions in Omdurman. He also sent forth mounted patrols and promptly recalled them when the Khalifa's army, possibly numbering some 52,000 men, emerged from the city. By the evening of 1 September, Kitchener had deployed five of his six brigades in an arc some 2,000 yards from end to end, with their backs to the River Nile, facing west (and with the reserve brigade, cavalry, camel corps, auxiliary services, and baggage bivouacked between the perimeter and the river). Fearful of a night attack (lest

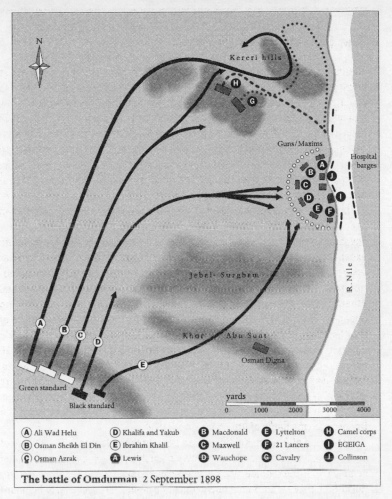

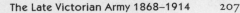

(A) Ali Wad Helu	(D) Khalifa and Yakub	(B) Macdonald
(B) Osman Sheikh El Din	(E) Ibrahim Khalil	(C) Maxwell
(C) Osman Azrak	(A) Lewis	(D) Wauchope
(E) Lyttelton	(H) Camel corps	
(F) 21 Lancers	(I) EGEIGA	
(G) Cavalry	(J) Collinson	

The battle of Omdurman 2 September 1898

it neutralize his fire-power), he kept his whole force at arms all night, posted pickets, dispatched strong patrols, and swept the ground in front of the *zariba* (the thorn hedge erected in front of the perimeter) with searchlights from the gunboats.

The Khalifa waited fatally, with his massed forces installed on heights to the south-west of the Anglo-Egyptian position. At dawn he set the bulk of his forces in motion, moving across the Anglo-Egyptian front from left to right. As they encountered a devastating broadside from the Sirdar's artillery, the left flank moved towards high ground in the north while the centre and right flank wheeled to launch a mass frontal assault across open ground upon the centre and left of the perimeter. Faced with colossal fire-power from the guns, Maxims, and infantry, firing magazine rifles and expanding ammunition, only a few Mahdists got within 300 yards of the Anglo-Egyptian positions.

By 8 a.m. the first phase of the battle was over and the 21st Lancers under Colonel R. H. Martin were duly ordered to harass the remnants from the attack and prevent them from reaching Omdurman. Martin, though, was lured into a trap and launched his lancers into a charge against a thin line of Dervishes only to find the remainder concealed in a dry watercourse. Within a few minutes of ferocious hand-to-hand fighting, the British sustained 40 per cent of all their casualties as five officers, sixty-five men, and 119 horses out of less than 400 were killed or wounded. Although the press extolled the courage of the lancers, and three Victoria Crosses were rightly awarded, this spectacular charge was quite unnecessary.

At about 9 a.m. Kitchener, who acted as his own chief of staff rushing from place to place throughout the battle, ordered his brigades to begin the 7-mile advance towards Omdurman. The echelon moved unevenly and soon left considerable gaps in the line, but the two Mahdist counter-attacks failed utterly. Indeed, Brigadier-General Hector MacDonald, having faced an assault from the south, was able to realign his Sudanese and Egyptian brigade, three batteries (18 guns), and eight Maxims through 90 degrees to face an attack from the north. Aided by the Lincolns sent by Wauchope to support his right, MacDonald was able to destroy this attack and so enable Kitchener to complete the rout of the enemy and enter Omdurman in triumph.

Although the press lauded the victory and the avenging of Gordon, the battle ended in controversy. Ernest Bennett of the *Westminister Gazette* deprecated the bayoneting of the wounded (a practice defended as common prudence by most of the press corps). The queen was appalled by the desecration of the Mahdi's tomb (intended to prevent it from becoming a focus for political resistance) and the Sirdar's suggestion that the Mahdi's skull should be sent to the College of Surgeons in London (the skull was promptly buried). Nevertheless, Kitchener consolidated the victory by pressing up the White Nile and thwarting French ambitions at Fashoda. He was duly rewarded with a peerage and £30,000, while Wingate completed the reconquest of the Sudan by hunting down and killing the elusive Khalifa at the battle of Um Dibaykarat on 24 November 1899. If the railway had laid the basis for the triumph, Anglo-Egyptian fire-power had proved decisive in battle: whereas Kitchener's forces suffered some forty-eight fatalities, nearly 11,000 Mahdists died at Omdurman. Winston Churchill aptly claimed that this battle was 'the most signal triumph ever gained by the arms of science over barbarism'.

contribution of Major-General Henry Wilson as Director of Military Operations (1910–14). If less supportive of Haldane, he was a fastidious planner who was appalled by the lack of any mobilization schedule in 1910, the dearth of rail, naval, and horse supply arrangements, and the want of staff arrangements at the ports. He badgered Haldane and his Chief of the General Staff, Sir William Nicholson, to focus upon these issues and to permit him to negotiate with the railway departments, the Admiralty, other departments in the War Office, and even with his counterparts in the French General Staff. Although some of the details were resolved before Haldane left office in April 1912, Wilson had to persevere over the next two years to ensure the preparation of railway time tables, shipping arrangements, and matters such as the provision of horse stall fittings and gangways at the French ports. The alacrity with which the British Expeditionary Force (BEF) was mobilized and transported to France in August 1914 owed much to the initiative and tenacity of Wilson.

The impressive performance of the BEF in the field reflected the improvements in military training during the Edwardian period. By frequent practice on the rifle range, rates of fire were developed (fifteen rounds per minute at 300 yards) which greatly exceeded equivalent rates in conscript armies. The rates of fire enabled the army to compensate for cuts in the ammunition allowance and for the refusal to concede more than two machine-guns per battalion. Using squads or sections attacking each other in company training, the principles of fire and movement in attack and of regulated fire from defensive positions were regularly practised. Seizing the offensive remained the essence of peacetime training, with fire support remaining secondary to the movement of troops. The aim was to maximize the moral advantages of the assailant—his initiative, freedom of action, and power of manoeuvre—and so overcome the fire effect of modern weapons from defensive positions. If some obsolete tactics were preserved, particularly the cavalry's preference for the *arme blanche* (even restoring the lance as an active service weapon), all arms were much better trained. They benefited from the rivalry of regimental competition, the regularity of large-scale manœuvres, and the frequent practice of mobilization.

Although the army lacked any opportunity to display its professional skills until August 1914, it was periodically employed in its traditional policing role within the United Kingdom. It drew appropriate lessons from the Featherstone colliery riot (7 September 1893) in which two by-standers had been killed by stray shots. Henceforth when soldiers were dispatched in aid of the civil power during industrial disturbances, they were normally deployed in strength, with the minimum of friction, and without recourse to firearms. Military discretion, though, was less evident in Ireland where many Ulster Protestants had become fiercely opposed to the prospect of Irish Home Rule. When the government wished to move more troops into Ulster to protect ammunition depots in March 1914, some officers suspected that the aim was to coerce Ulster. After indicating that sixty officers of the 3rd Cavalry Brigade at the Curragh would prefer dismissal to being ordered north, Brigadier-General Hubert Gough received a written assurance from the Cabinet, amended in more precise language by Sir John French, the Chief of the Imperial General Staff. When the government promptly repudiated any notion of a private bargain with a few officers, the signatories of the document—French, Sir J. S. Ewart, the Adjutant-General, and J. E. B. Seely, the Secretary of State for War, proffered their resignations. More of an 'incident' than a mutiny (no orders were actually disobeyed), the Curragh affair damaged personal relationships within the army and bequeathed a legacy of suspicion between the military and political leaders.

Nevertheless, the British Expeditionary Force remained well prepared for war. Its social composition had not changed significantly since the late Victorian period but it had improved professionally. It had profited from the South African experience and from the post-war reforms, particularly the creation of a General Staff. It had developed tactical skills which were relevant to the new conditions of warfare and had trained systematically at section, company, and divisional level. It had acquired, above all, a new organizational framework and a sense of purpose from the Haldane reforms. As the official historian of the First World War recalled, it was 'incomparably the best trained, best organized, and best equipped British Army which ever went forth to war'.

10 THE ARMY AND THE CHALLENGE OF WAR 1914–1918

TIM TRAVERS

At the start of the First World War, Britain did not have an army capable of fighting a major war on the Continent. Hence, on 4 August 1914, the regular British army, not including reservists, consisted of only 247,432 officers and men, about one-third of whom were in India. In contrast, after four and a half years of war, on 1 November 1918, British troops in France, not including colonial troops, amounted to 1,497,198 officers and men, while the British army everywhere at the same date totalled 2,075,275, again not including colonial troops. To this should be added another 1,383,311 British officers and men stationed at home in November 1918, for a total of 3,458,586. Thus the British army had multiplied in size fourteen times over during the period of the war, and so the history of the British army in the First World War is a history of tremendous change and adaptation.

The original British Expeditionary Force (BEF) that crossed to France in August 1914 consisted of just four infantry divisions and five brigades of cavalry. It is of interest that the Indian Army was called upon to supplement this tiny BEF, so that by December 1914, of 9,610 British officers in France, 20 per cent were from the Indian Army, and of 76,450 other ranks, 16 per cent were from the Indian Army. But perhaps the sense of change from 1914 to 1918 can best be illustrated by noting that the total number of British forces in France in December 1914 (229,782) was actually three times smaller than the eventual number of British officers and men killed during the war (702,410).

But the British army that started the war was also not the same *type* of army that ended the war. Hence, although the original BEF's mix of arms

Table 10.1 *Percentage Changes within British Expeditionary Force, 1914–1918*

	Sept. 1914	Sept. 1915	Sept. 1916	Sept. 1917	March 1918	July 1918
CAVALRY	9.28	3.88	3.02	2.77	1.65	1.65
INFANTRY	64.64	69.89	61.74	58.69	53.71	51.25
RFA/RHA	18.27	14.32	15.48	13.56	16.67	18.30
RGA	1.31	2.73	4.24	6.21	7.90	8.68
RE	5.91	7.96	10.89	12.28	10.11	11.24
TANK CORPS			0.04	0.50	1.05	1.20
RFC	0.59	0.44	1.16	1.90	3.24	—

[*RFA/RHA = Royal Field Artillery; *RGA = Royal Garrison Artillery; *RE = Royal Engineers; *RFC = Royal Flying Corps]

was reasonably well suited to the mobile conditions of 1914, it was not so well adapted to the trench warfare of 1915 to 1917, or to the set-piece tactics of 1918. Therefore, some significant comparative shifts occurred within the BEF, as might be expected. Table 10.1 shows the percentage changes that can be discerned when the numbers of British other ranks in selected arms are compared to the total combatant and non-combatant BEF strength over time. From this, it is clear that the cavalry had the largest percentage decline, while the more technical arms, the engineers, tank corps, and flying corps, had the largest percentage increases. In addition, the garrison artillery, with its heavy-calibre guns, from 5 inches up to 15 inches, were much more useful in static and set-piece warfare, and so also made a considerable percentage increase. The fact that the infantry more or less maintained its ranking suggests that for all of the new technology, the BEF in France remained essentially a manpower army, with the infantry as the centre-piece of war, supported by other arms.

These considerations prompt two central questions: what particular problems did the British army face in 1914? And did the British army significantly improve its performance, both on the Western Front and abroad, as the conditions of the battlefield evolved from 1914 to 1918?

In regard to the first question, it is useful to look briefly at the areas of doctrine and command. Doctrinally, the British army before 1914 was poorly prepared, as its major experience of war since the Crimea had been colonial wars, of which the latest was in South Africa (1899–1902). As a result of this war, the infantry improved their field-craft and shooting skills, but no doctrine emerged. The Russo-Japanese conflict (1904–5) provided some clear indications of the incredible impact of fire-power, but since the aggressive Japanese had defeated the defensive-minded Russians through costly attacks with the bayonet, the wrong lessons were drawn.

In fact the British army developed no particular doctrine before 1914 except that of the offensive under almost all circumstances. Senior staff anticipated heavy casualties, but expected to overcome the enemy's fire-power through mobility in the attack, the offensive spirit, and moral force. Indeed there was no institution through which the army could engage in serious thinking about war before 1914, and army manuals were often written by poorly prepared staff—thus one officer before 1914 found himself writing three manuals at once: one on infantry training, the song-book of the British army, and the handbook of the 4.5-inch gun! Moreover, the traditional rivalries of cavalry, infantry, and artillery would have made an integrated doctrine very difficult to achieve even if new ideas had been adopted. In any case, it was assumed that the war would be short, lasting perhaps only six months, so that simplicity of tactics in the offensive, supported by discipline, morale, and good leadership, were really all that was required. But was good leadership available?

Leadership at the regimental level was generally reliable, but staff officers and the higher commanders were not adequate to the task. Some older or incompetent regimental officers could not stand the strain in 1914 and had to be replaced; for example, two battalion commanders in 4 Division, who officially surrendered the town of St Quentin in late August 1914. But most performed well and often heroically in the long retreat of August and September 1914. Even so, many older and less efficient officers continued to serve, so that when the future Field Marshal, Montgomery, was appointed Brigade Major to 104th Brigade in 1916, he remembered his Brigadier 'was an old retired officer . . . a very nice person but quite useless and it would be true to say that I really ran the Brigade, and they all knew it'. But these inefficient officers were a minority, and were slowly weeded out in the first years of the war, the slow pace of their retirement occurring partly because there was no reserve of officers in 1914 to draw upon.

On the other hand, divisional and corps commanders, the staff at GHQ, and the Commander-in-Chief of the BEF, Sir John French, had little practice at their respective levels of command, and did not do as well in 1914. Officers were trained to command divisions, but not above that level. For corps commanders there was equally little experience, and it is significant that at the annual army manoeuvres in 1913 Sir John French's two corps mistakenly diverged, a problem that repeated itself in 1914. Another concern was health and physical fitness—probably the best corps

Sir Douglas Haig and the First World War

Douglas Haig was very much a product of the late Victorian and Edwardian army in two ways. First, he was a beneficiary of the patronage system of promotion, and, secondly, he inherited late nineteenth-century ways of thinking about warfare and command. Turning first to the question of promotion, Haig found that connections to the royal family through his sister, and the influence of powerful patrons such as Sir John French, Sir Evelyn Wood, and Lord Esher, smoothed his way towards the top. Haig also progressed upward by virtue of being ambitious, working hard, and taking his profession seriously, which were not common virtues in the British army of the time. A spell at Oxford (1880–3) gave an educated slant to Haig's prospects, and later attendance at Staff College (1896–7) produced valuable connections. Haig was assisted, too, by the fact that he was a cavalryman, and promotion at the highest levels in the army appeared to come more easily to cavalry officers. Thus, after leaving Sandhurst, Haig's promotion was initially normal, but then fairly rapid. Soon after the Boer War, Haig became Inspector-General of Cavalry in India in 1903, Director of Military Training at the War Office in 1906, Director of Staff Duties in 1907, Chief of the General Staff, India, in 1909, and Commander-in-Chief, Aldershot Command, in 1912. At the outbreak of war in 1914, Haig was selected to command I Corps under his mentor, Sir John French. However, French obviously did not anticipate that Haig would assist in his removal and replace him as Commander-in-Chief of the British Expeditionary Force (BEF), which occurred on 19 December 1915.

At this point Haig's nineteenth-century style of thinking about war becomes important. Apart from his cavalry inclinations and background, which he never rejected, Haig inherited from the nineteenth century, and from lectures at the Staff College, the idea that war was mobile, structured, and decisive. Battle was the decisive act of war, and the Commander-in-Chief should aim at the defeat of the main enemy army. Battles were inevitably fought in three stages: preparation and the wearing out of enemy reserves; a rapid, decisive offensive; and cavalry exploitation. All of this would take place quickly, perhaps in one day, and since both sides were technically much the same, the decisive elements were morale, determination, and the will of the commander. Essentially Haig did not change his ideas about all this throughout the war, and his long drawn out campaigns at the Somme and Passchendaele were lengthy, partly because he had learned at Staff College that the commander who hung on longest would win, and partly because of his desire to use up enemy reserves before launching the decisive offensive, which in the context of the huge armies on the Western Front, and the availability of railroads, was bound to take some time.

Haig also learned that the role of the Commander-in-Chief was simply to set strategy and then stand aside and let army and corps commanders get on with the job with minimal interference. However, this hands-off style of command led Haig to focus on strategy and he largely forgot about tactics, at the very moment on the Western Front when tactics were actually more important than strategy. This detached attitude was compounded by the fact that Haig was by training and experience primarily a staff officer, again just at a time in warfare when GHQ was located many miles behind the front, and so Haig became distant from battlefield events both physically and mentally. Furthermore, Haig was personally stern and unapproachable, so that few people, let alone his staff or army commanders, dared confront him, or even approach him for open discussion on critical matters. And his liaison officers, who did visit the battlefields, were insecure enough to tell him what he wanted to hear. Moreover, Haig's own fixed mind-set, his structured life-style, and his obsession with social hierarchy and etiquette, all gave him little chance to change his ideas throughout the war. Not surprisingly, this set of factors led to problems such as command vacuums before critical offensives such as the Somme and Passchendaele, when army commanders felt they could not sit down with Haig to iron out differences. Another result of this command style was that offensive plans were themselves rigid and centralized, and a top–down system of command developed which made innovation at GHQ or in the army difficult.

As an example of Haig's command style, it is relevant to look at the planning of the Passchendaele offensive of 31 July 1917. Here Haig chose a poor battlefield since his artillery was overlooked by the enemy and the German defensive system on the ridge was extremely strong. But Haig was more interested in the strategy of reaching the Flanders coastal ports than in the tactical difficulties of the offensive, and he was content to attack the strength of the main enemy army. Haig also chose a particularly obtuse commander, Gough, to direct the attack, and he confused Gough by failing to make clear whether the offensive was to be a breakthrough attempt or a limited-objective advance. Haig's instructions were certainly vague—'wear out the enemy but have an objective'—and Gough simply assumed that Haig wanted a breakthrough. Gough also recognized specific problems on the right flank, where the entire ridge was not included in the attack, before the offensive started, but he was too apprehensive to approach Haig with his concerns, and predictably the offensive was held up on the right. It is not surprising that the offensive stalled on the Passchendaele ridge, despite the replacement of Gough by Plumer a month later. The Passchendaele offensive continued until November, ostensibly to protect the mutinous French army, but really because Haig expected to wear out the German army's reserves before the end of 1917, and thus provide an opportunity for the decisive offensive.

In early 1918, Haig survived an attempt by Lloyd George to replace him, partly because there was not anyone sufficiently better to justify the uproar that would undoubtedly follow, and partly because several changes, such as a new Chief of the Imperial General Staff, new staff at GHQ, a Supreme War Council at Versailles, and Foch as Commander-in-Chief of the Allied armies, had modified Haig's power. In fact, as Allied forces survived the German spring offensives and moved towards victory later in 1918, Haig's power continued to erode. Army commanders took over the running of BEF offensives and an increasingly mobile style of warfare dictated a decentralized command structure until the Armistice.

Haig commanded the BEF in nineteenth-century style and he never changed his mind about the structured offensive, so that the period from 1916 to 1918 was really a lengthy application of the wearing-out process, in effect an attrition policy waiting for the right moment for the decisive offensive. Haig's defence is that his policy eventually worked, while the criticism is that more flexible ideas and a more open command style would have prosecuted the war more effectively and might have saved casualties.

---

commander, Sir John Grierson, though fluent in French and German, and well read, was overweight, and used to say with a laugh that his greatest battles had been fought with a knife and fork. Grierson collapsed and died in the train on his way to command II Corps in 1914. Similarly, Lieutenant-General Sir Archibald Murray, chief of staff to Sir John French, suffered a number of partial collapses, and finally collapsed at GHQ at the end of August 1914.

Nor can it be said that the Staff College had prepared senior commanders very well for modern war since there was a great deal of emphasis on detail, facts, standardized learning, and social correctness. There was little stress on independence of mind, and the result was a strictly hierarchical army headed by largely unimaginative leaders, as the future tank theorist and Staff College student, J. F. C. Fuller, remarked: 'At present we are controlled . . . by a hierarchy which, though autocratic, is sterile. It fears initiative, it is terrified of originality and it suppresses criticism.' While this is severe, Sir Douglas Haig, Commander-in-Chief of the BEF from 1915 to 1919, was certainly a man of detail, a stickler for social and military etiquette, and possessed of no great imagination. However, Sir John French, also a cavalry general, tended to operate more by intuition and impetuosity than by rational calculation, and was ill suited to command in 1914. It was said, unkindly, that French had tried to read Hamley's *Operations of War* but could not digest the material, and never borrowed another book. And yet something must have stuck, for when Sir John French thought of retiring into the fortress complex of Maubeuge on 24 August 1914, an act which would have doomed the BEF, he did not, he says, because he remembered Hamley's criticism of the ill-fated decision of Marshal Bazaine in 1870 to retire into the similar fortress of Metz. Yet at the end of August 1914 Sir John French also wanted to retire to one of the west coast Channel ports and evacuate the BEF, or simply remove and refit the BEF in a quiet area west of Paris for ten days, both of which alternatives would have had very serious results. It seems that Sir John French had lost confidence in the French army and in the BEF at this point.

Therefore, in regard to the leadership qualities of the higher command in the BEF, this was obviously an army in the very difficult process of transition from a colonial army into a continental army. The old army was bred from narrow regimental and army loyalties, it was trained for imperial duties, it was socially comfortable and intellectually undemanding, and it was as much interested in sport as in soldiering. Thus it is hardly surprising that senior officers were not well adapted to the tremendous stresses of 1914, even if regimental officers and men doggedly stuck to their tasks and frequently saved their superiors' reputations.

Turning therefore to the large second question, how the British army performed from 1914 to 1918, this chapter will look chronologically at the Western Front, and other campaigns such as Gallipoli and the Middle East, before coming to a general summation of the achievements of the British army in the First World War.

During August 1914, the BEF engaged in a series of hard-fought stands and retirements in the sweltering heat of the French summer before the counter-attack at the Marne in early September. At Mons on 23 August, the BEF's II Corps faced the German 1st Army as it attempted its encirclement manoeuvre around the left wing of the Anglo-French force. At this point Sir John French's GHQ appeared to lose control of the battle, while the commander of II Corps, General Smith-Dorrien (replacing

Grierson) stepped in to fill the command vacuum. Sir John French did not issue any written orders between late 21 August and the evening of 24 August, and indeed motored off on the day of the battle to Valenciennes, and did not return to his headquarters until the afternoon. In fact, GHQ essentially left the BEF's two corps to their own devices. However, II Corps did defend the line of the canal, and checked the mass German attacks with accurate rifle fire.

The retreat continued, but now Haig's I Corps and Smith-Dorrien's II Corps diverged, one each side of the forest of Mormal. I Corps failed to notice that there were roads through the forest which could be used by the enemy, and so were surprised at Landrecies. Thereafter the two corps diverged even further, some 8 miles apart, with Smith-Dorrien's II Corps left to face the enemy alone. Independently of GHQ, Smith-Dorrien decided his corps could not retreat any more, and so stood and fought at Le Cateau on 26 August. Apart from the loss of thirty-eight guns, II Corps succeeded in stopping three German corps and again demonstrated the quality of the British infantry. But the main problems had been lack of co-ordination so that I Corps failed to deliver a flanking attack; and the absence of control by GHQ, which on the day of Le Cateau moved back from St Quentin to Noyon without leaving cable communications or notification of their change of address.

For the next few days, Sir John French and GHQ were in a state of pessimism, while the front-line soldiers were much more cheerful, even if dog tired. II Corps had sustained most of the fighting, while I Corps had been relatively untouched, and continued to retreat away from II Corps, producing a gap of 15 miles by 28 August. One explanation for this was that Haig was seriously worried, sending a message to GHQ that day that read 'Situation very critical.' In fact Haig had overreacted, but the result was a distinct lack of co-operation between the two corps. GHQ also displayed its nerves by rapidly leaving their new HQ at Dammartin, leaving an unsuspecting adjutant-general behind, and with Sir Henry Wilson reportedly urging his chauffeur to 'Drive like hell for Paris.' Then news of Sir John French's plans to withdraw the BEF from the line for rest brought Kitchener to Paris, where he steadied the BEF's commander, and on 5 September Sir John French agreed to join the French counter-attack at the battle of the Marne. The BEF turned and fought on 6 September, but it was still noticeable that Haig's I Corps lagged behind II Corps and the newly formed III Corps. Nevertheless, the counter-attack succeeded and forced the German army back toward the Aisne, where the line stabilized, despite some anxious moments at the first battle of Ypres in October and November.

The achievement of the British army in 1914 was that it had fought larger German forces to a standstill, and that it had survived. As expected, casualties had been heavy: approximately one-third of the original force were dead, and more were wounded or missing. By the end of the year, the BEF, now amounting to seven infantry divisions, had suffered about 90,000 casualties, larger than the entire force that had landed in August. Still, the most serious problems had been at the high command level—Sir John French and his GHQ had maintained only tenuous contact and control over the BEF at critical points such as Mons, Le Cateau, and the Marne. At the first battle of Ypres, Sir John French at one point banged his fist on the table and shouted at his chief of intelligence, 'How the Hell do you expect me to carry out my plan of campaign if you keep bringing up these blasted [German] divisions?' Clearly, Sir John French's imperial service, his cavalry career, and his staff appointments, were inadequate to the demands of modern war. Of the corps commanders, Haig had shown a strange reluctance to assist II Corps, and had marched off in a divergent direction at Le Cateau. Co-operation in the BEF was obviously weak above divisional level.

Command problems were also important in a Franco-British attempt to outflank the Turkish empire in 1915, and this was the campaign at Gallipoli. After the original failure to force the Straits by naval attack, the War Office was compelled to engage in a land campaign which Kitchener could never quite decide whether to support fully or not. Sir Ian Hamilton was appointed Commander-in-Chief, and his four divisions prepared to make a landing on Gallipoli. But now the Turks knew that an attack was coming, although not the exact locations. At dawn on 25 April 1915, the landings commenced, and the underestimated Turks were discovered to be determined fighters, while the troops on the various assault beaches found that direction from their commanders was sometimes lacking, and that, once ashore, the forbidding geography of Gallipoli led to loss of direction and great confusion. Thus at Z beach, the Anzac landing was almost unopposed because an unexpected current had placed the troops ashore at the wrong place, but the mass of ravines and gullies soon disrupted their advance. Then at Y beach, the troops scrambled up steep cliffs, but once on top it was not clear who was in command, and Hunter-Weston, GOC 29 Division, could not or would not order an advance to capture key points, which were then unoccupied. An innovative attempt was made at V beach, where the collier ship *River Clyde* was run ashore with troops inside, but overwhelming Turkish fire prevented success.

However, the landings showed imagination, and might have succeeded except for the previously mentioned problems, plus the fact that the British army was too rigidly structured easily to attempt difficult amphibious operations. It is true that the whole Gallipoli expedition lacked men, supplies, artillery, ammunition, mortars, bombs, and grenades, but it was really the antiquated command structure that impeded progress. Time and again opportunities were thrown away because of ineffective leadership at critical points, and this was especially true of Hamilton himself, who took a hands-off attitude to operations and was barely in command. Finally, Hamilton did not grasp the reality of warfare on Gallipoli for some time—his mind-set favoured gallant bayonet charges rather than 'ghastly trench warfare'. Only in mid-summer did Hamilton wake up to reality: 'The old battle tactics have clean vanished. I have only quite lately realised the new conditions.'

Armed with this knowledge, Hamilton again devised an innovative series of landings in early August 1915, since land-based operations had gone nowhere. The landing was a surprise, but confusion ashore, lack of water, exhaustion, and, once more, poor leadership, halted the advance just when success was at hand and expected, because Stopford's IX Corps deployed 25,000 troops against only 1,500 defenders. Hamilton had much to contend with, not least some poor subordinate commanders and a tough Turkish defence, but this was a commander and a force with nineteenth-century ideas and structure involved in twentieth-century warfare.

Ironically, the most effective Gallipoli operation was the evacuation of the peninsula, which took place with very few casualties in December and January, after Kitchener and the government decided that the venture had failed. Gallipoli also pointed up the debate in the British army between Westerners and Easterners, the former favouring concentration on the Western Front, and the latter emphasizing defence of the Empire and campaigns conducted away from the bloodshed of the Western Front. In reality both schools of thought appreciated the objectives of each other, and differed mainly in regard to emphasis. But in 1915 the Western Front was still developing as the main theatre, and the BEF remained a junior partner to the French army. However, under pressure from the Allies the BEF engaged in relatively minor offensives at Neuve Chapelle, Aubers Ridge, Festubert, Givenchy, and Loos, while fighting a bitter defensive second battle at Ypres in April and May 1915.

By August 1915 there were twenty-eight BEF divisions on the Western Front, comprising some 900,000 men. However, not only were the men inexperienced, but so were their senior commanders. Forced into offensives for the first time, generals discovered that ordering an attack and obtaining their objectives were two very different things. Into their language crept phrases that became all too common, such as 'at all costs' and 'regardless of loss'—often leading to needless casualties. For example, Rawlinson's attack at Neuve Chapelle in March 1915 bogged down on the first day, but fruitless attacks continued for the next two days, and resulted in overall losses to his corps of 7,500. And at Loos in September, after the initial offensive by IV Corps had been halted, the follow-up attack the next day by two untried New Army divisions produced 8,200 casualties in just over one hour.

The problem in almost all these 1915 attacks was that the artillery preparation was not capable of properly cutting enemy wire or destroying enemy trenches; there were not enough heavy guns or shells; communications from front to rear were slow and unreliable, thus leading to false optimism and renewed but hopeless attacks; and army and corps commanders were naïve in their expectations of what could be achieved. Yet Rawlinson, now IV Corps commander, already had the clue to solving a crucial difficulty. In letters written after BEF attacks in 1915, Rawlinson actually recognized that artillery could not destroy deep dug-outs, and that, when the artillery lifted off enemy trenches, the German infantry had time to man the parapets before the attack arrived. If only Rawlinson had paid attention to his own lessons one year later at the Somme in 1916!

But before preparations began for the Somme offensive, there was a change of command in the BEF from Sir John French to Sir Douglas Haig at the end of 1915. French had been a poor but reasonably popular leader with the soldiers, yet his manner of dismissal revealed the personalized and often self-serving way in which the British army frequently managed promotions and dismissals. In this case Haig, Rawlinson, and others had trumped up a charge that French had held up the arrival of the reserves at Loos, whereas in fact Haig's own 1st Army had largely been responsible for their slow progress. However, French was sent home and Haig inherited his position. Nevertheless, French himself had earlier invented reasons to get rid of Smith-Dorrien, who had seriously annoyed him by being successful at Le Catcau in 1914!

In 1916 the British army began to take a major role on the Western Front, if only to help hold the main alliance of Britain, France, and Russia together. After various discussions as to where an attack might take place, the French and British agreed to make a major assault astride the Somme river in the summer of 1916, with Rawlinson's 4th Army undertaking the British part of the offensive. There now began an awkward planning process between Haig and Rawlinson, since each wanted a very different kind of attack. Haig wanted an offensive aimed at capturing deep objectives, while Rawlinson wanted a much more limited attack that would use a lengthy artillery bombardment to take the first line of German trenches, and then consolidate and destroy the inevitable German counter-attacks. This process would then be repeated—a 'bite and hold' system of assault.

Rawlinson and Haig sparred over their respective plans, but Rawlinson deferred to Haig in most matters. The final plan therefore was an unhappy mixture of the two original conceptions of the offensive: the objectives would be much deeper than Rawlinson wanted—to the second German line of trenches—but the offensive would be a deliberate affair with a long bombardment, which Haig had not desired. Later, the 4th Army's chief of staff acknowledged, 'I admit at once the objectives were too deep and too broad for the troops and guns available'. If this was so, why did Rawlinson not meet with Haig and work out a better plan? The answer is that Rawlinson was apprehensive of the austere and unapproachable Haig, and did not dare actually to confront Haig. And so, as happened again at Passchendaele, there was a command vacuum just before the commencement of the offensive with the greatest number of British casualties in the war.

This command problem and the mixed plan were not the only reasons for serious trouble on 1 July 1916. The most important cause of the disaster that followed was that the final Somme plan was essentially an artillery plan—and the BEF's artillery was called upon to achieve much more than it was capable of. In seven days of bombardment the artillery had to destroy German trench defences, cut wire, eliminate German artillery pieces, and finally provide a barrage on 1 July behind which the infantry were to advance and take the first and second line of German trenches. There were not enough heavy guns to destroy deep German dug-outs, just as Rawlinson had foreseen in his 1915 evaluation after Givenchy. Wire-cutting was not as successful as suspected, despite around 1 million shells being devoted to this task along the whole front. Counter-battery work (the destruction of enemy artillery) in the central and northern parts of the line did not achieve much in the days before 1 July because of technical deficiencies; because of the low priority given to this task; and because of bad weather during the seven days before 1 July, when RFC spotter aircraft could not always operate to report the fall of shell back to their batteries.

Most importantly, the artillery barrage that was supposed to take the infantry through to the German trenches failed because it moved too quickly for the infantry, and left the defenders with sufficient time to man the trenches before the attack arrived. This is what happened along much of the line at zero hour, 7.30 a.m. on 1 July, when fourteen BEF infantry divisions began their advance towards the first line of German trenches. British divisions were decimated either by machine-gun and rifle fire, or by artillery not destroyed by counter-battery work. Altogether the BEF experienced 57,470 casualties on 1 July, the greatest loss in one day in the history of the British army.

The Somme campaign actually marked a turning-point in the emergence of a more technically capable British army on the Western Front, but the change was gradual, and it may not have been apparent to the troops involved in the fighting during the second half of 1916. By the end of operations in November 1916, the Somme had gone on far too long under adverse weather conditions, and with no realistic objectives except attrition. Casualty figures have been controversial, but the BEF suffered some 420,000 casualties during the course of the Somme campaign, the French around 200,000, and the Germans about 500,000. Haig and GHQ did have reason to think that the German army was running out of men, and it is certain that the German army could less afford this casualty list than the British army and its allies, yet the cost was bitter and led to criticisms of the high command.

Meanwhile on another front, the British army found the Turks in the Middle East a tougher proposition than expected, while the mistakes of Gallipoli were repeated as objectives were set that were beyond the capacity of the army. This was especially the case in Mesopotamia, where the original objectives of defending oil supplies and impressing Arab opinion soon gave way to a more aggressive campaign aimed eventually at capturing Baghdad. There was confusion between command centres in India, the War Office, and Mesopotamia as to objectives, but in late 1915 Major-General Townshend, GOC 6 Indian Division, was ordered to advance on Baghdad. In fact, Townshend's division was simply not powerful enough to take the several lines of Turkish defences, and was brought to a halt by the Turks after losing half of its men. Not being able to advance further, and unable to remain where he was, Townshend was forced to retreat back into Kut under merciless attacks by the Turks. There he was besieged, and

The First Day of the Somme, 1 July 1916

At 7.30 a.m. on 1 July 1916, fourteen British divisions and two French divisions attacked north of the Somme river, while another three French divisions attacked two hours later, south of the Somme. By the end of the day, British Expeditionary Force casualties amounted to 57,470—the greatest loss that had ever befallen the British army in one day. In contrast, the French suffered many fewer losses, perhaps only some 2,250 on 1 July, an average of around 450 per division, while British casualties averaged more than 4,000 per division. Additionally, the French succeeded in obtaining their objectives all along the line, and actually went much further south of the Somme, while British divisions failed in the north and centre of the line, and only succeeded in the south. Obviously something had gone very wrong for the British, and very much better for the French.

The French and British agreed to attack astride the Somme, partly because it was there that the two armies adjoined, although GHQ also said it was 'a place that had not been tried before and was likely to be dry going'. Sir Douglas Haig, Commander-in-Chief of the BEF, asked the commander of the 4th Army, Lieutenant-General Sir Henry Rawlinson, to submit plans for the attack. However, the two men had very different ideas on how to attack, since Haig wanted a short hurricane bombardment to achieve surprise, and a rush through to the second line of German trenches and beyond, followed by cavalry pursuit, while Rawlinson wanted a cautious bite and hold plan. This would see a lengthy bombardment, then the capture of the first line of German trenches only, followed by an important phase of consolidation, and then finally the destruction of the inevitable German counter-attacks. This was the concept of attrition, which Rawlinson had learned from offensives in 1915; where the first line of German trenches could always be captured after a severe artillery bombardment, but the real problem was consolidation before the German counter-attacks. Haig, on the other hand, thought in strategic terms and wanted an optimistic break-through strategy, but did not focus sufficiently on the tactical difficulties of achieving this.

After sparring over the two concepts, Haig and Rawlinson eventually adopted a mixed plan. There would be a lengthy bombardment as Rawlinson wanted, but the optimistic aim was the capture of the entire second line of German trenches except in the south, followed by cavalry exploitation as Haig wanted. However, Rawlinson basically stuck to his bite and hold conception,

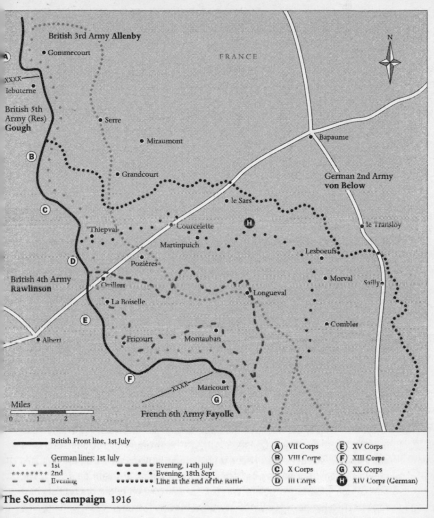

British 3rd Army **Allenby**

Gommecourt

FRANCE

N

XXXX
Iebuterne

British 5th
Army (Res)
Gough

Serre

Miraumont

Bapaume

German 2nd Army
von Below

Grandcourt

le Sars

le Transloy

Thiepval

Courcelette

H

Martinpuich

Lesboeufs

Pozières

British 4th Army
Rawlinson

Ovillers

Morval

Sailly

La Boiselle

Longueval

Combles

Albert

Fricourt

Montauban

Maricourt

XXXX

Miles

0   1   2   3

French 6th Army **Fayolle**

British Front line, 1st July	**(A)** VII Corps	**(E)** XV Corps
German lines: 1st July	**(B)** VIII Corps	**(F)** XIII Corps
1st — Evening, 14th July	**(C)** X Corps	**(G)** XX Corps
2nd — Evening, 18th Sept	**(D)** III Corps	**(H)** XIV Corps (German)
Evening — Line at the end of the Battle		

The Somme campaign 1916

despite the depth of the objectives, and loaded up his infantrymen with 70 pounds of shovels, sandbags, Mills bombs, and 200 rounds of ammunition, in anticipation of the consolidation and German counter-attack phase of the operation. Rawlinson did not anticipate his infantry rushing across no man's land, partly because of what his infantry were carrying, and partly because of his focus on consolidation rather than the capture of the first line of German trenches, since he felt the latter was the easier operation, as in 1915. However, he did allow his divisions freedom to decide how they would cross no man's land, and not all divisions attacked in slow, methodical waves. Yet because Rawlinson doubted the reliability of the new divisions, he did suggest that 'the attack must be made in waves with men at fairly close interval in order to give them confidence'. Finally, and most important, Rawlinson relied very heavily on the artillery bombardment to cut German wire, destroy enemy trenches and batteries, and, on the day of the offensive, carry the infantry through the German trenches.

However, Rawlinson knew from 1915 that it would be very hard to destroy deep German dug-outs, and that if the artillery lifted off the German trenches too soon as the assault went in the enemy would be able to man his parapets with machine-guns and cut down the attacking troops. Rawlinson considered the use of gas to sink into the deep dug-outs, but gas shells were not available; he also thought of smoke to shield the attack, but, where it was used, particularly at Gommecourt, it was too thin and blew away. As for the race to reach the German parapets before they could be manned, a problem which proved critical on 1 July 1916, Rawlinson either had not learned this lesson, or the preliminary bombardment over seven days of 1.7 million shells, fired by 2,200 guns, and the 1 July barrage of 600,000 shells, fired by 1,500 guns, was so overwhelming that he felt the artillery had solved the difficulty.

Yet the artillery did not have the accuracy, experience, survey methods, or heavy guns, to do the job. Consequently, wire was often not cut, deep dug-outs were largely untouched, and not enough enemy batteries were destroyed. This failure to eliminate enemy batteries was one major problem on 1 July. The other, more important problem, was that, at 7.30 a.m. on 1 July, the artillery barrage lifted in jumps of 100 yards at a time, leaving the infantry far behind, and, most vitally, lifted past the front-line German trenches some minutes before the British infantry could reach them. This was really the critical mistake, because if the artillery had not even attempted its preliminary lifts, but had simply fired on the German trenches until the last moment, then many British casualties would have been saved. But this did not happen, the race for the parapet was won by the German defenders, and the offensive was a disastrous failure in the north and centre of the line. Yet, in the south, the BEF's 18 and 30 Divisions, and all the French divisions, were particularly successful.

The difference was that German defences were weaker in the south, and there was some tactical surprise, particularly for the French; the distances to be covered were shorter; tactics were smarter, with swifter open order movement, and some British troops starting from no man's land; the French were aided by mist from the Somme river and marshes, and flatter ground to attack; and, above all, German defences and artillery were defeated before the assault began because of overwhelming artillery superiority. Thus, with the aid of French heavy artillery, 18 and 30 Divisions were able to destroy German dugouts and artillery, so that the German XIV Corps north of the river lost 109 guns, while Montauban was completely destroyed by a French heavy mortar. Below the Somme, the French had an incredible superiority in heavy batteries of eighty-five against eight German heavy batteries, German defences were much weaker, and the late start at 9.30 a.m. helped considerably.

These factors explain the success of the southern BEF divisions and of the French offensive generally. It is also notable that the Allies had air superiority, 386 planes against 104, and, without this, British casualties on 1 July would likely have been even greater. But, at the end of the first day on the Somme, the BEF had not managed a breakthrough, and had suffered enormous casualties. The only vindication for the first day of the Somme is that attrition would eventually favour the Allies and help pave the way for victory in 1918.

---

urgently requested assistance. However, the relief Tigris Corps was brought to a halt and actually lost 23,000 men in an effort to save the 12,500 men in Kut. By the end of April 1916, Townshend was forced to surrender Kut to the Turks—sending shock waves through the British army. Another disaster then occurred—the brutal treatment of the captured British and Indian troops as they were marched to Turkish prison camps and labour duties. Altogether 70 per cent of the British rank and file died in captivity, mostly as a result of rough treatment.

Later, in 1916 and 1917, reinforced British forces, increased artillery, new leadership, and much improved communications, transport, and administrative systems enabled the Mesopotamian expedition to recapture Kut, then Baghdad, and, after further severe fighting in 1918, to compel the surrender of the Turkish 6th Army. The British army had really muddled through in Mesopotamia, but it took the fall of Kut for the army to be fully supplied and rearmed, and it was this logistical substructure that made the final success possible.

A rather similar story occurred in the other major Middle East theatre, namely Palestine and the Hejaz, where initial success led to interim failures before reinforcements and proper preparation provided the base for future success. In 1916, the commander in the Middle East, Sir Archibald Murray, captured the Sinai, at the same time building a supporting railway and water pipeline across the desert. As in Mesopotamia, what was originally a largely defensive campaign now became more aggressive. The next target was Gaza, but the problem here was water, and wells had to be captured within twenty-four hours to supply the horses and men. The first attack on Gaza in March 1917 was successful, but a withdrawal was mistakenly ordered and carried out. Murray cabled London in over-optimistic terms and was ordered to repeat the attack and advance on Jerusalem. But, as in Gallipoli, the Turks were now forewarned, Gaza was reinforced, while Murray's force was under-gunned—one division had no artillery at all. Hence the second attack on Gaza was a disaster, Murray was recalled, and Allenby was sent out instead.

Just as in the Mesopotamian campaign, where a change of command occurred after Kut, and considerable reinforcements were then sent out, so Allenby received more troops, producing a superiority over the Turks of two to one in infantry, and eight to one in cavalry. Not only did Allenby receive more troops and artillery, but also enough aeroplanes to achieve air superiority—essential in Palestine and the desert. Murray was largely forgotten, but his railroad and water pipeline were critical. Allenby moved his headquarters out to the desert from Cairo, and did away with Murray's pernickity preoccupation with details and correct dress. But Allenby's aggressive outlook earned him the nickname of the 'Bull', so that when he departed from his GHQ a kindly signals officer broadcast the message 'BBA', standing for 'Bloody Bull's About.' Nevertheless, on balance, Allenby was a positive factor.

A new plan of attack called for a feint at Gaza, but with the real attack at Beersheba, and then a swing back to an attack on Gaza two days later. Considerable efforts at deception also helped the plan. Allenby accepted the idea, and with the aid of a night march by the Desert Mounted Corps and a charge by the Australian Light Horse, Beersheba was taken. Two days later Gaza fell, and Allenby pressed his troops hard to pursue the Turks, despite objections from commanders and staff. Under this kind of pressure, Jerusalem fell in December 1917. Meanwhile, in the Hejaz desert, acting Colonel T. E. Lawrence had created a legend for himself by fomenting the Arab revolt, and by a brilliant 800-mile ride through the desert to attack and capture Aqaba in July 1917. Other exploits by Lawrence were to follow, though Lawrence's military role, while important, was not critical to the Middle East campaign.

At the beginning of 1918, Allenby appealed for more troops if the new objective was to be the distant Aleppo, and he received another three divisions and a cavalry brigade—a very different result from Kitchener's rejection of Hamilton's timid requests for more men for Gallipoli. During the summer of 1918, Allenby failed in two risky attacks across the Jordan river, and then regrouped and went on the offensive in September 1918. Once more, there was great emphasis on deception, so that the offensive worked better than expected. As before, Allenby ruthlessly pushed the pursuit— Damascus fell at the very end of September and then, at the end of October, Turkey sued for peace. Allenby's success in 1918 owed much to staff planning and well-organized deception measures, but he was not a superman, he did make serious mistakes, and much of his success was because his troops heavily outnumbered the enemy. As in Mesopotamia, but unlike Gallipoli, ultimately the superiority in men and material were what made the difference.

Back on the Western Front, there was a striking success at Vimy ridge in April 1917 by the Canadian Corps, due to careful preparation and effective artillery work, plus German defensive errors. Then came the success of the limited-objective, mine-based attack at Messines in June, as a prelude to the major Passchendaele offensive of 31 July. The opening phase of this latter campaign showed that Haig and some members of GHQ had learned little from the lessons of 1916 and early 1917. Haig had chosen a battlefield at Passchendaele that put his army at a grave disadvantage in terms of artillery observation and strength of German defences. He also failed to recognize that strategy depended on tactics, and simply ignored the difficulty of taking the Passchendaele ridge, which he thought of as just an obstacle on the way to capturing the Flanders coastal ports.

There were many other problems with the offensive plan, while the basic tactics of the offensive on 31 July had not fundamentally changed since 1916—there was the same long bombardment for a fortnight before 31 July which cratered the ground with water-filled shell-holes and impeded the attackers' progress; and there were the same mass attacks in equal strength along the line as at the Somme, geared to a clockwork-style artillery timetable. But the new creeping barrage helped, and British counter-battery work, aided by a temporary air superiority, eliminated around 50 per cent of the German heavy guns. However, this was not enough, and the new German defence-in-depth scheme was quite sufficient to halt the attack on the right, limit it in the centre, and prevent a gain of more than 2 miles on the left. Then the rain came for a fortnight, and, after a series of costly pushes in August, Haig prudently turned over the offensive from Gough to the more cautious and reliable Plumer.

Essentially, Passchendaele then settled into a similar pattern to the Somme, and the strategic aims of the campaign similarly withered away. Now that the coast could not be reached, the continuation of Passchendaele was justified by Haig and GHQ by invoking the mutinies of the French, the disorder in Russia, the setbacks in Italy, the need for attrition, and, finally, the desire to capture Passchendaele village. The miserable, water-logged, mud-stained existence of the soldiers over the course of a campaign lasting three and a half months has often been described, and still evokes compassion and anger. In the end BEF casualties at Passchendaele of 271,000 could only be vindicated in the same way as at the Somme—sooner or later, the German army would run out of men.

Nevertheless, in late November 1917 occurred the battle of Cambrai, where some of the changes in the British army that had commenced at the Somme now came to fruition. The plans for Cambrai finally gave up on the inflexible, artillery-dominated mass offensives of 1916 and 1917. What were really needed were limited-objective, set-piece offensives that combined surprise and flexibility. Cambrai was such an attack, with predicted artillery fire (eliminating the previous registration of guns, which gave away the objectives), accurate maps of enemy targets (which, together with prediction and tanks to crush wire, avoided lengthy bombardments), and infantry trained to work with massed tanks, of which 324 were used on the first day. Tanks had first been used in small numbers during the Somme, and then throughout 1917, but they had not distinguished themselves due to mechanical problems, vulnerability to artillery, and unsuitable ground. Now the ground was suitable, there was artillery and infantry support, and surprise was to be applied for the first time since 1915.

On 20 November 1917, the initial Cambrai attack was very successful, and achieved a depth of 3 or more miles on most sectors of the front. However, after the initial surprise and considerable gains the cavalry failed to follow up and exploit (which they had been waiting to do for three years), and Haig made a dubious decision to continue the offensive after the second day, when further gains were unlikely. This stubborn continuation of the offensive followed the same pattern as at the Somme and Passchen-daele, but an unexpected German counter-attack sent some BEF divisions reeling back in panic. Haig and GHQ did not realize that this counter-attack actually followed new principles of infiltration and surprise which would be employed in 1918 against the British army on a much larger scale.

However, while military ideas were changing on the Western Front, in-novation could hardly help another British theatre of war—Salonika—where several Franco-British-Serb attacks between 1916 and 1918 found the mountainous terrain a very costly obstacle. The Salonika campaign eventually succeeded, but it penned up four to six British divisions for four years. Meanwhile, manpower problems were becoming significant in the British army in late 1917, and this was not helped by the departure of five BEF divisions for Italy to stabilize that front. BEF morale was also at a low level after the Flanders flounderings of 1917, questions were being asked in parliament about the competence of the British high command, and the replacement of Haig was contemplated. This unease was drasti-cally reinforced by the German March 1918 Michael offensive, which caught the BEF unprepared and sent the 5th and 3rd Armies hustling back into a 40-mile retreat. The reasons for this retreat, which almost split the British and French armies apart, and nearly sent the BEF back to the Channel ports in a prefiguring of 1940, are not hard to find. Haig and GHQ were supremely over-confident; the attack was expected further north; the new style of German attack was a surprise (though the German counter-attack at Cambrai might have warned GHQ); and, above all, the BEF had borrowed the German defence-in-depth system, but had not properly understood or applied it.

In the 5th and 3rd Armies, headquarters were retreating faster than their troops, and this in turn caused a knock-on effect, resulting in unnecessary withdrawals. The near disaster for the British army in the few days fol-lowing 21 March was partly caused by the new German offensive methods, yet the extent of the retreat was almost entirely due to British command errors. The troops themselves fought well when they had the chance—but they were often undermined by their headquarters. Eventu-ally the German advance was stopped, partly due to stiffening British ar-tillery and machine-gun defences, partly because of German errors, and partly because the offensive itself ran out of steam. Several other German offensives were then launched, but they all followed the same sequence of initial stunning advances and then gradual failure. Thus the German 'peace offensives' failed, and German morale and discipline sagged. The

BEF and the French began to prepare cautiously to go over to the offensive.

But at this point, certain important changes occurred in the BEF. First, the command style changed, both outwardly and inwardly. Outwardly, as a result of the March crisis, Haig and the BEF now became officially subordinate to Marshal Foch, as Allied Commander-in-Chief. Inwardly, the real leadership in the BEF was now shifting further down the command chain, so that Haig evolved into something of a figurehead, and real power was exercised by the army commanders. But they in turn relied ever more on lower-level corps and division leadership and staffs for expertise as the war became more mobile and technical. And even these middle-level commanders became something like administrators as their subordinates exercised local command, and told their superiors how best to fight. Secondly, the BEF was now much more liberally supplied with arms and ammunition, including newer weapons such as Mark V tanks, Whippet armoured cars, mustard gas shells, rifle grenades, mobile trench mortars, smoke, and improved types of aeroplanes. There were also vastly greater supplies of more traditional weapons and ammunition, such as artillery, Lewis guns, and machine-guns. Moreover, the artillery in 1918 developed into a very effective force due to many more guns, greater experience, and much improved survey methods. Thirdly, the previous question of how to save manpower became critical, for there were very few more men available to the British army in 1918. One solution was the use of mechanical warfare (meaning the liberal application of tanks, planes, machine-guns, and artillery) to save lives and win the war, although Haig, GHQ, and much of the army favoured the more traditional infantry-centred warfare.

At first, the battles of Hamel and Amiens in July and August 1918 respectively were fought in the new combined mode of tanks, artillery, air, infantry, and surprise, and scored impressive victories. Amiens in particular was a resounding success under the command of a temporary supporter of mechanical warfare, Rawlinson, and was spearheaded by the two most effective corps on the Western Front—the Australians and Canadians. The fire-power available, 2,000 guns, 450 tanks, and 1,900 planes, was simply overwhelming. German artillery was largely eliminated, tactical surprise was achieved, and German defences were not very strong, so that the offensive on the first day gained 8 miles, captured 400 guns and 12,000 prisoners, and caused another 15,000 casualties, while British casualties amounted to 8,000. Amiens really marked the beginning of the end on the Western Front, but curiously there were no more manpower-saving offensives, based on surprise, mass tank, artillery, and infantry attacks, as there had been at Amiens. Instead a series of offensives, aimed at breaking the various German defensive lines, were launched in August and September. The cost was high—BEF infantry and cavalry casualties from 21 August to 11 November 1918 amounted to 264,383, while there were only 33,382 casualties during the Amiens period of 7 to 20 August. There was no easy way to win the war, but the figures suggest that Amiens-type offensives might have been less costly in defeating the enemy.

Nevertheless, between late August and mid-October, the main German defensive lines were successfully broken by set-piece attacks, and the last month consisted mainly of chasing German units as they retreated. What was the immediate reason for the British army's victory in 1918? Essentially, the German army had been worn down by continuous Franco-British offensives. The key to this success was the application of very large amounts of semi-traditional technology, especially artillery. Thus a British signals officer noted in 1918, 'for every shell the enemy sent over he received 10 or 20 back', and the greatest British expenditure of ammunition over twenty-four hours in the whole war took place between 28 and 29 September 1918, when 945,052 shells were fired.

In larger terms, how were the German army and its allies defeated between 1914 and 1918? On the Western Front battlefields, the answer lies partly in the effects of attrition from 1914 to 1917 (which wore down the smaller resources of Germany faster than those of the British army and its allies), and partly through the use in 1918 of a great deal of semi-traditional technology applied in a series of offensives aimed at crumbling the German line rather than breaking through. This process was aided by German errors in their 1918 offensives. In other theatres, Turkey was the main enemy, and here, apart from Gallipoli, the process was one of initial over-confidence, then reverses, and finally the application of larger amounts of technology and manpower. Gallipoli was the one campaign abandoned, partly because Britain had greater interests in the other theatres.

In conclusion, and to answer the fundamental question posed earlier: did the British army significantly improve its performance between 1914 and 1918? Yes, it did, especially technically, and ultimately it played as large a part as any army in winning the war. Yet leadership problems at the high command level, in France as well as in Gallipoli and the early Middle East campaigns, plagued the British army throughout the war. In 1914 and 1915, the army still essentially operated in a pre-war mode of thinking and fighting, and changes were those of scale rather than substance. The turning-point came in 1916 despite massive losses during the Somme offensive, as the army began to learn lessons and improve technically. But, at higher levels, there was much less change—Haig, for example, never grasped that tactics had swallowed strategy—and the BEF in particular was still rigidly controlled in a centralized, hierarchical manner. This was reflected in the Passchendaele offensive, which reached the limits of the rigid, centralized, artillery-controlled type of attack. Then Cambrai in late 1917, the German spring offensives of 1918, and greater mobility in the battlefield, led to attempts to introduce similar flexibility in the British army. This produced a split in the BEF in 1918 in which the higher levels of Haig, GHQ, and, to some extent, the army commanders, became less relevant, while the rest of the army went its own way and was able to introduce less structured combined arms methods which were successful. At the same time, the mechanical warfare supporters were deflected and ultimately the British army on the Continent and abroad won the war in semi-traditional ways. This was to have considerable impact in the inter-war period, and ultimately influenced the structure of the next BEF in France in 1940.

11 THE FOUR ARMIES 1914–1918

PETER SIMKINS

Britain's army in the First World War was the largest in the nation's history. Between August 1914 and November 1918, 5,704,416 men passed through its ranks. Of the 4,970,902 who joined after the outbreak of war, 2,446,719 were volunteers. The overall total of those who served represented slightly over 22 per cent of the male population of the United Kingdom. The creation of the country's first ever mass citizen army was the product of a gigantic act of national improvisation which had considerable repercussions throughout British society. Increased government intervention in many aspects of daily life, the greater participation of women in industry, and the growing influence of organized labour were all given enormous impetus by the rapid expansion of the army and the parallel mobilization of manufacturing resources necessary to maintain it in the field.

By the end of 1915, Britain's military forces comprised three main elements or armies, each with its own formations and character. Two of these elements, the regular army and the Territorial Force, existed before the war. The third—Kitchener's New Armies—sprang from the Secretary of State for War's successive calls for volunteers from August 1914 onwards. With the introduction of compulsory military service in 1916 a fourth 'army' of conscripts was added. In the latter case, however, the men were recruited for general service and posted to units as required, not raised as a body of distinct formations. Together with the effects of battle losses and of industry's manpower demands upon army organization, the influx of conscripts therefore tended to remove or blur many—though not all—of the differences between the army's other main elements towards the end of the conflict.

When Britain declared war on Germany on 4 August 1914, the total strength of the British army, including the Special Reserve and Territorial

Force, was 733,514. The regular army's principal operational component, the British Expeditionary Force (BEF) of six infantry divisions and a cavalry division, was earmarked for France on mobilization. Despite improvements in terms and conditions of service the regular army in August 1914 still drew the biggest proportion of its recruits from the urban unemployed and unskilled. The officer corps too continued to rely upon traditional sources of supply such as the peerage, military families, the gentry, and, to a lesser extent, the clergy and the professions. Most young officers in 1914 had a public school education but comparatively few were from an industrial or commercial background. Having secured an average annual intake of only 29,626 recruits since 1908–9, the regular army was about 6 per cent below peacetime establishment in May 1914. The Special Reserve, fashioned by Haldane from the old militia to provide drafts for the expeditionary force, was also 13,699 short of its establishment of 74,166.

The part-time Territorial Force of 'Saturday afternoon soldiers', raised and administered by local County Associations, could furnish fourteen infantry divisions and fourteen mounted yeomanry brigades. It attracted middle-class recruits and skilled artisans into its ranks but, like the regulars and Special Reserve, leaned heavily on the working class for volunteers and was consistently below establishment in the years before the war, numbering 268,777 officers and men in July 1914. If Haldane had first envisaged the Territorial Force as a basis for expansion and as a possible reserve for the field, its primary role had come to be regarded, by 1914, as home defence. Territorials were invited, from 1910, to accept a liability to go overseas on mobilization yet less than 20,000 had undertaken this Imperial Service obligation before the outbreak of war. Thus, although the BEF was committed to fight in a continental conflict, the implications of that commitment had not been thoroughly explored and no detailed blueprint existed for the raising of a mass army or for a corresponding growth in munitions output. In short, there was a yawning chasm between Britain's chosen strategy and her actual military organization or long-term planning.

On 5 August 1914 Field Marshal Lord Kitchener was persuaded by Asquith, the Prime Minister, to accept the post of Secretary of State for War. Kitchener had spent most of his life abroad and admitted his ignorance of domestic affairs, entering the War Office with some reluctance. Even Asquith described the appointment as 'a hazardous experiment' although the public greeted it with enthusiasm and relief. Apart from Douglas Haig, Kitchener was virtually alone among Britain's military and political leaders in forecasting a long and costly war, lasting three years or more. In his opinion, Britain's full military might could not be deployed until 1917 but its weight was then likely to prove decisive. While his short-comings as a Cabinet minister, administrator, and strategist subsequently became all too apparent, Kitchener, in the opening weeks of the war, was widely seen as a symbol of national unity, standing above party or sectional interests. It was in convincing the government and people that they must brace themselves for a protracted struggle and mobilize their resources accordingly, that Kitchener made his most important contribution to the nation's war effort.

Correctly judging Britain's available forces as being totally inadequate for the conflict the country faced, Kitchener immediately set about the task of expanding the army. On 7 August, after obtaining parliamentary approval for an initial increase of 500,000 men, he published his first appeal for 100,000 recruits, aged between 19 and 30, who were to enlist for three years or the duration of the war. Kitchener bowed to the views of his Cabinet colleagues that conscription would be nationally divisive and decided to raise his new formations by means of the established voluntary system. He aimed to construct a series of New Armies, complete in all their branches, with each New Army duplicating the six infantry divisions of the BEF. This was to be done through the normal regular recruiting channels rather than through the Territorial Force County Associations. The scheme for the First New Army, or New Expeditionary Force as it was originally called, was announced on 12 August. Six of the eight regional commands—that is, all except Aldershot Command and the London District—were each to provide an infantry division by recruiting at least one Service battalion for every line regiment. Instead of a Southern Division, however, there would be a Light Division, formed by adding extra battalions to light infantry and rifle regiments.

Much criticism has been levelled at Kitchener for refusing to use the Territorial Force as the framework for his New Armies. There is some evidence that the course he adopted was conditioned by a genuine concern about invasion and the advisability of maintaining efficient home defence formations. With the invasion threat in mind, the problem, as Kitchener summarized it, was 'to produce a force independent of those forces which had formed a part of pre-war calculations'. Moreover, at the beginning of the war, Territorials had no statutory obligation to fight overseas. On 9 August the Army Council noted Kitchener's decision that if any Territorial units volunteered *en bloc* for foreign service their offer would be accepted. Two days later it was agreed that, if some members of a formation held back, units of those volunteering would be organized, 'the residues being re-formed into complete units for the Home Defence Force'. The initial response from the Territorials was, in fact, somewhat patchy. Married men or those with well-paid jobs wanted time to consider their options and, in some battalions, less than half the members volunteered in the first instance. Such hesitation was not universal. By 25 August seventy Territorial battalions had volunteered and even units which experienced early difficulties soon found the required numbers. Nevertheless, during the very period when Kitchener was trying to shape the New Armies, a few doubts remained concerning the extent to which Territorials would be prepared to undertake active service abroad.

These arguments notwithstanding, it is hard to avoid the conclusion that Kitchener's attitude to the Territorials stemmed mainly from ignorance and prejudice. His description of them as a 'Town Clerks' Army' was doubly ironic, since local government officers were to play a central role in the raising of his own New Armies. In the end, Kitchener permitted the Territorials to expand side by side with the New Armies, to finish their training where possible, and to volunteer for active service or relieve regular units in India or colonial garrisons, but it was a policy which led inevitably to competition and a dissipation of effort which harmed both organizations.

At this stage Kitchener was also unsure about the ultimate size of the army he was building. His 'rough-hewn' intention was simply that at 'the conclusive period of the war', when her allies were feeling the strain, Britain should have 'the maximum trained fighting army this country could produce'. On 25 August 1914 he predicted that the army might expand to thirty divisions 'continually maintained in the field'. This estimate rose by mid-September to fifty divisions, then to seventy by July 1915, although the figure was subsequently adjusted, in April 1916, to fifty-seven divisions overseas and ten at home. Given the deficiencies of pre-war planning, the uncertainty about objectives was not entirely Kitchener's fault, and the Cabinet's reluctance to countenance conscription in 1914 obliged him to accept recruits as and when they were ready to enlist whilst attempting to balance the needs of the BEF, home defence, and the new units. But the government's manpower policy in the autumn of 1914 remained haphazard, with the War Office often reacting belatedly to unforeseen developments instead of ensuring that army expansion proceeded along predetermined and manageable lines.

The enlistment returns for the opening weeks of the war show that recruiting got off to a moderately slow start, the number of recruits attested daily rising gradually to 7,020 on 11 August and 9,699 a week later. Even these relatively modest returns were enough to upset recruiting machinery geared to an annual pre-war intake of 30,000 men, yet, within the next fortnight, enlistment totals began to exceed 10,000 a day and climbed steeply until they reached 33,204 on 3 September, the highest number of recruits attested on a single day during the whole of the war. Some 761,000 joined the army in the first eight weeks but, by 30 September, the daily returns had fallen below 4,000.

Several factors conspired to cause the brief recruiting boom of late August and early September 1914. First, news of the retreat from Mons revealed the gravity of the situation in France and prompted an upsurge in patriotic response to a perceived crisis. Secondly, an appeal by Kitchener on 28 August for a further 100,000 volunteers, and the raising of the upper age limit to 35 for new recruits, also boosted enlistments. Thirdly, increased civilian participation in the recruiting process, especially at a local level, overcame many of the problems confronting overworked military personnel, not least by making municipal buildings available to house additional recruiting offices. A fourth and related factor was the raising of the Pals battalions, which harnessed local loyalties to national patriotism in a manner that proved irresistible to tens of thousands of potential recruits.

Uncomplicated patriotic ideals and an innate sense of obligation to King and Country unquestionably impelled large numbers of men to enlist in 1914–15. Public school codes of duty, self-sacrifice, and discipline which had permeated every level of society through the education system, youth movements, and Sunday schools, underpinned the patriotic response of many volunteers. But it would be utterly misleading to suggest that these were the only reasons for the huge recruiting totals. Motives for enlistment were, indeed, extremely diverse. For countless working-class or lower middle-class recruits, the chance to break free from an arduous or boring job and the lure of travel and excitement were far more powerful inducements to enlist than straightforward patriotism, particularly in the climate of industrial uncertainty, with its concomitant rise in unemployment and short-time working, at the beginning of the war. Others joined because of pressure from social superiors and employers or because all their friends were enlisting. Some even took the King's shilling as a means of avoiding arrest or imprisonment.

The Pals Battalions

There are few more potent symbols of Britain's military effort in the First World War than the Pals formations. These units, which initially were nearly all infantry battalions, were mainly raised, with War Office approval, by the mayors and corporations of large towns and cities, by Members of Parliament, or by self-appointed committees of industrialists or leading local citizens. The popular description of them as Pals battalions derived from the fact that the raisers of many such battalions deliberately encouraged men who lived in a particular city or district, or who shared a common social and occupational background, to enlist with their friends and workmates on the understanding that they would be allowed to train and fight together. Their emergence, in late August and early September 1914, quickly altered the pattern of enlistment, offering individual communities additional opportunities to express their patriotism in a specific way by raising units with a pronounced local identity. In some respects, the Pals battalions may be seen as among the last manifestations of late Victorian and Edwardian Liberalism and of a unique combination of political, social, economic, and military factors which disappeared in 1916 in the face of conscription and the unrelenting demands of modern war. Above all, they were the product of the British voluntary tradition and of that peculiar mixture of patriotism, parochialism, accelerating urbanization, and civic pride which characterized early twentieth-century Britain.

In its 1914 form the Pals concept appears to have germinated in the War Office. On 19 August, Major-General Sir Henry Rawlinson, then Director of Recruiting, proposed the raising in London of a battalion of City employees who might be willing to enlist 'if they were assured that they would serve with their friends'. By 27 August, the 10th (Service) Battalion of the Royal Fusiliers, popularly known as the 'Stockbrokers' Battalion', numbered 1,600. All the same, it was in the northern industrial cities that the idea truly came to fruition and some battalions were formed with astonishing speed. In Liverpool, where Lord Derby obtained Kitchener's consent for the raising of a battalion from among the city's business houses, sufficient men for three City battalions had volunteered by 4 September, only five days after recruiting had begun. Manchester raised four City battalions between 1 and 16 September. In Glasgow, where the municipal authorities decided, on 3 September, to try to raise at least two battalions, James Dalrymple, the manager of the Corporation Tramways Department, telephoned the tramcar depots at 5 p.m. that evening, asking for the names of employees who would be prepared to join a 'Tramways Battalion'. Next morning he received a list of 1,100 names. The unofficial titles of many of these units—such as the 'Accrington Pals' (11th East Lancashire Regiment), the 'Newcastle Commercials' (16th Northumberland Fusiliers), and the 'Miners' Battalion' (12th King's Own Yorkshire Light Infantry)—testified to their social, geographical, or occupational origins. By the end of September 1914, fifty locally raised or Pals battalions were complete or in course of formation.

Kitchener quickly appreciated that the Pals movement offered the War Office a practical means of relieving the strain on its own recruiting organization and of solving some of the short-term financial problems arising from the massive and sudden growth in the size of the army. By mid-September 1914 he had made it known that he would authorize local battalions only when their raising committees were willing to shoulder the initial costs and to assume responsibility for housing, feeding, and clothing their own recruits until the War Office was ready to take them over and refund such expenses. Men joining Pals units generally had a smoother introduction to army life than recruits in the first three New Armies for, in many cases, they were allowed to live at home and report daily whilst their first training camps were being built. In this respect too the raisers of Pals units enjoyed advantages over the orthodox military authorities, as they could exploit local government machinery and their knowledge of local contractors and conditions to ensure closer supervision of the building work.

In all, 145 Service and seventy reserve battalions were locally raised under this system. Thus, excluding new Territorial units formed during the period, nearly 40 per cent of the Service and reserve infantry battalions created between August 1914 and June 1916 were raised, in the first place, by bodies other than the War Office. In addition, similar local effort raised forty-eight companies of engineers, forty-two brigades of field artillery, twenty-eight garrison artillery batteries, and eleven divisional ammunition columns between January 1915 and January 1916. Exactly how far the recruiting pendulum swung towards civilian effort and local units can be gauged from the fact that, after 1 October 1914, only nineteen service battalions were raised by the War Office while eighty-four locally raised battalions were sanctioned.

The granting of commissions to potential officers, discharges of under-age or unfit recruits, transfers, desertions, and deaths from accidents or illness all altered the composition of many Pals battalions even before they reached the fighting fronts. In the 1st Birmingham Battalion (14th Royal Warwickshire Regiment), 302 other ranks were commissioned before the end of 1915. Of the 1,028 officers and men on the nominal roll of the Leeds Pals (15th West

Yorkshire Regiment) shortly before embarkation, only six officers and 534 men were original volunteers from September 1914. The huge losses suffered by the locally raised battalions on the Somme inevitably caused further changes, especially as, from the summer of 1916 onwards, casualty replacements no longer necessarily came from the unit's own recruiting areas. As an example, the Sheffield City Battalion (12th York and Lancaster Regiment), which incurred 495 casualties, including 248 dead, on 1 July 1916, had received drafts from the South Lancashire and Burton on Trent areas before the end of October that year. The terrible impact of these losses in such a concentrated form upon particular communities ensured that the Pals experiment was never repeated but, while it lasted, it did much to give the British army of the First World War its unique character.

The first six Kitchener divisions—the 9th (Scottish) to 14th (Light) Divisions—officially came into existence on 21 August. As the tide of volunteers continued to flow, surplus recruits were used, from 27 August, to bring Special Reserve battalions up to a strength of 2,000. On 29 August the Adjutant-General was asked to draw up proposals for the raising of another six divisions and the Army Council began to refer to the first six collectively as the First New Army or 'K1'. The recruiting surge in early September spurred Kitchener to authorize the formation of two more series of divisions, to bring the total of New Army divisions to twenty-four, irrespective of the locally raised Pals units for which no clear scheme of organization had yet been devised. The Second New Army, containing the 15th (Scottish) to 20th (Light) Divisions, was formally created on 11 September followed, two days later, by the Third New Army (21st to 26th Divisions). A Fourth New Army was to be formed in due course from the surplus recruits who, from 27 August, had been posted to Special Reserve battalions.

Meanwhile, the Territorial Force was also expanding. Orders issued in August and September gave County Associations authority to form a 'second-line' Territorial unit for every battalion accepted for foreign service. In November 1914 it was decreed that, when a Territorial unit went overseas and was replaced at home by a second-line formation, a reserve or 'third-line' battalion should be raised, so that even second-line units could be released for foreign service in time. By November 1918 the Territorial Force had embraced 692 battalions during the war, a total which compared favourably with the 267 regular or reserve battalions and the 557 Service and local reserve battalions raised for the New Armies.

Rapid expansion threw together volunteers from all occupations and classes, changing the army's social composition almost beyond recognition. Lawyers, engineers, and teachers drilled alongside labourers, miners, and shop assistants, especially in units of the first three New Armies, which were raised on a more random basis than later New Army formations, but, again, the overall patterns of enlistment were much more complex and uneven than they might superficially appear. Lancashire, Yorkshire, and Scotland together furnished over one-third of the 250 battalions in the first three New Armies, whereas Devon, Dorset, Cornwall, and Somerset produced only eleven Service battalions between them. Units from agricultural areas often had to be filled up from the main population centres. For example, when formed, the 9th Devons contained barely eighty Devonians, the majority of recruits coming from Birmingham and London. Similarly, the 6th Leinsters, in the 10th (Irish) Division, had to be strengthened, in September 1914, by 600 recruits from Bristol. Southern Ireland produced only eight battalions for the First New Army, seven for the Second, and none at all for the Third New Army. Less than 11 per cent of Irish males aged 15 to 49 enlisted up to December 1915 as against more than 26 per cent from Scotland and just over 24 per cent from England and Wales. As a result of these regional variations, the 'territorial' titles 'Northern', 'Irish', and so on were dropped for the divisions of the Third New Army. The recruiting returns also disclosed an inequality of response from an occupational standpoint. During the voluntary recruiting period, finance and commerce, the professions, and entertainment all contributed over 40 per cent of their pre-war work-force while the corresponding returns from manufacturing industry, transport, and agriculture were each under 30 per cent.

In expanding the army, Kitchener had to give immediate attention to the supply of officers. At the outbreak of war there were 28,060 officers available, including 12,738 regulars and 9,563 Territorials, but merely to cater for the new Service and Territorial infantry battalions raised during his term as Secretary of State for War, he had to find at least 30,000 more, even before taking into account the demands of other branches or the need to replace officer casualties. A partial solution to the problem of providing regular officer replacements for the BEF was achieved by shortening courses at Sandhurst and Woolwich and lifting the age limit for candidates to 25. For the new units, battalions of the BEF were each ordered to leave three officers at the depots on embarkation, while Indian Army officers home on leave and regular officers recovering from wounds were also held back. As these measures alone would not produce the requisite numbers, particularly of junior officers, it was decided to grant temporary rather than permanent commissions to suitable young men, a major source of applicants being the Officers' Training Corps. Between August 1914 and March 1915, 20,577 current or former members were commissioned from the OTC's Senior Division at the universities and Inns of Court or from the Junior Division at public and grammar schools. The OTC's contribution ensured there was no drastic change in the social composition of the officer corps in the first year of the war. Although the County Associations and raisers of Pals battalions were allowed a great deal of latitude in recommending candidates for commissions, and sons of local businessmen or prominent tradesmen began to appear more frequently as officers in Territorial and Pals units, a university, public school, or grammar school education remained a standard qualification for acceptance in 1914–15.

Some of the new divisional commands were filled by transferring brigadier-generals from the BEF, a notable example being Ivor Maxse, who left the 1st (Guards) Brigade in France to take over the 18th (Eastern) Division. Many of the battalion and company commands in the New Armies went to retired officers or 'dug-outs' of varying quality. As the earliest to be formed, First New Army battalions often had as many as seven regular or ex-regular officers from the outset but the supply was already dwindling when the Third New Army was created in September 1914. All the battalion commanders in the 21st Division had been in retirement on 4 August and only fourteen other officers possessed previous experience in the regular army. The rest, numbering over 4,000 officers, had all been commissioned since the war started and had little or no officer training.

For all the efforts of Kitchener and the War Office to keep pace with developments, their initial failure to impose a ceiling on enlistments, or regulate the flow, caused them to lose control of recruiting within six weeks and to depend increasingly upon civilian help. Overcrowding at depots and training centres and severe shortages of uniforms, personal equipment, bedding, and even rations provoked mounting criticism, forcing the War Office to apply a temporary brake to recruiting by introducing a scheme of deferred enlistment whereby volunteers, once sworn in, could stay at home or work until the army was in a position to handle them. On 11 September 1914 the minimum height requirement for recruits was temporarily lifted to 5 feet 6 inches. The following week the daily average of enlistments dropped to 6,382 but these steps had more damaging long-term effects than expected, as they seemed to signal that the army could pick and choose men as it wished and might therefore no longer require as many volunteers as previously thought.

Four Territorial divisions had sailed for Egypt and India by the end of December 1914 while individual Territorial battalions had been sent to Aden, Cyprus, Gibraltar, and Malta. An additional five regular infantry divisions were created from the troops thereby released from overseas garrisons, the total of regular divisions rising to twelve when the Guards Division was formed in France in August 1915. Twenty-three Territorial infantry battalions went to France and Belgium before the end of 1914 though it was not until early March 1915 that the first complete Territorial division, the 46th (North Midland), reached the Western Front.

The losses of the BEF had, by then, made it obvious that the New Armies too might well incur heavy casualties when they entered the fray and so would need their own draft-finding system. In December 1914 the locally raised battalions were instructed to organize depot companies which, the following summer, were grouped into local reserve battalions to supply drafts to their parent units. The original Fourth New Army, made up of the surplus recruits posted to Special Reserve battalions earlier in the war, was broken up in April 1915 to provide reserve battalions for the 9th to 26th Divisions of the first three New Armies. The eventual Fourth and Fifth New Armies (30th to 41st Divisions) were composed largely of the Pals and other local units raised by cities, towns, and private committees. The BEF's regular divisions continued to be fed by the Special Reserve battalions and third-line Territorial units performed the same function for their first and second-line battalions. In fact, many men who enlisted in 1914–15 went straight into a reserve formation and only joined a field unit or Service battalion at the front itself instead of training with it at home. The 3rd (Special Reserve) Battalion of the Lincolnshire Regiment, for example, furnished drafts totalling over 5,400 men for battalions on active service in 1914–15 and most reserve units provided replacements and reinforcements on a similar scale in the first seventeen months.

The basic structure of the expanded army was in place by mid-1915 but it took longer to overcome the problems arising from the absence, in August 1914, of a systematic plan for a major increase in munitions output. Minimal attention had been paid to possible demands other than the need to sustain the BEF in a campaign expected to last only a few months. At the start of the war barely 6,000 rifles a month were being produced and

Housing and Equipping the New Armies

One of the most urgent and daunting tasks confronting Kitchener and the War Office in the early autumn of 1914 was that of housing the multitude of volunteers then flocking to the recruiting offices. When war was declared, there was sufficient accommodation in barracks for 174,800 men. Even after married quarters had been occupied and the space allotted to each man reduced from 600 to 400 cubic feet, the maximum number of men that could be housed in existing facilities had only risen to 262,000. Regimental depots, intended to accommodate between 250 and 500 men at most, were rapidly swamped by the tide of recruits. By 12 September, six depots held over 2,000 recruits each and 3,052 were crammed into the Cheshire Regiment's depot at Chester. Instructions to depot commanders to process volunteers and dispatch them to their respective units as quickly as possible merely transferred the overcrowding to the training centres earmarked for the New Armies. At Aldershot in September, the 8th Black Watch and the 5th Cameron Highlanders, battalions of the 9th (Scottish) Division in the First New Army, were obliged to share quarters designed for a single battalion. For recruits in the Second and Third New Armies, early experiences of army life were even more discouraging. At Wareham, in Dorset, the camping ground chosen for the 7th Green Howards, of the 17th (Northern) Division, had scarcely half the necessary number of tents, compelling many of the men to seek shelter in the town at night.

Despite a massive hutting programme to provide accommodation for some 850,000 troops, shortages of skilled labour owing to unrestricted enlistment, as well as poor workmanship and the lack of seasoned timber, contributed to hold-ups in completion of the big new training camps. Until their hutments were finished, a large proportion of the New Armies had to remain in tented camps where conditions were tolerable while fine weather prevailed. However, in mid-October 1914 a period of almost incessant rain began. Sickness increased and 1,508 cases of pneumonia, including 301 deaths, were recorded by 31 January 1915. A wave of unrest swirled through the training camps of the first three New Armies in November 1914, with mass meetings and strikes taking place, notably among battalions of the 22nd Division at Seaford in Sussex and the 25th Division at Codford in Wiltshire. Some Territorial and Special Reserve battalions had been billeted in private houses and other buildings since August, but the rising level of discontent drove the War Office to extend this policy to the New Armies as 1914 drew to a close.

Approximately 800,000 troops were billeted in this way in the first winter of the war—a feat equivalent to that of rehousing the combined 1914 populations of Sheffield, Cardiff, and Sunderland. Not surprisingly, as the nation was brought face to face with its citizen army on an unprecedented and totally unexpected scale, a host of social problems arose, some of them the result of deeply ingrained pre-war attitudes and parochialism. The presence of High-land battalions in towns like Bedford was, for example, greeted with consider-able apprehension by local residents and traditional fears of the 'brutal and licentious soldiery' meant that the reception accorded to troops was some-times unfriendly. By the same token, civilians often had genuine grounds for complaint about drunkenness or petty theft, and the pessimistic predictions of anxious moralists seemed to be confirmed by an increase in the illegitimate birth-rate in 1916. Billeting hindered training, since valuable hours were wasted assembling and dispersing the men at each end of the day. Neverthe-less, as a solution to a short-term but immense accommodation crisis, the bil-leting system was remarkably successful. The situation greatly eased in 1915 as more hutted camps became fit for occupation and units of the first three New Armies began to proceed overseas.

Emergency measures also had to be taken in the absence of adequate sup-plies of khaki service dress, for the civilian clothes in which men enlisted were soon ruined during training. Like the munitions industry, clothing manufactur-ers needed time to adjust to the new demands and, in the interim, the War Office obtained 500,000 suits of blue serge uniform which became known as 'Kitchener blue'. These uniforms were not wholly popular with recruits, many of whom felt that they resembled postmen or tram drivers rather than soldiers, but 'Kitchener blue' reduced the immediate clothing problems of the New Armies and gave units at least a modicum of military appearance. Severe shortages of the standard 1908 Web Equipment were largely overcome by the adoption of a modified version—the 1914 Pattern Infantry Equipment—in which only the pack and haversack were made of webbing, the remainder con sisting of leather accoutrements. Devised and approved within a month of the outbreak of war, it was the 1914 equipment, and not the 1908 pattern, that was later issued to the majority of New Army and second-line Territorial battalions.

The most serious handicaps suffered by the New Armies in training were, of course, caused by shortages of weapons. Right up to the final weeks of their training period, comparatively few infantry battalions possessed a complete set of rifles of any type. The Sheffield City Battalion did not receive its full quota of Short Magazine Lee-Enfield service rifles until 30 November 1915, a week before it sailed for Egypt. Supplies of small arms ammunition were similarly restricted and delays in the production and delivery of Vickers and Lewis guns prevented many battalions from carrying out realistic machine-gun training for several months. New Army artillery units fared no better. The gunners of the 15th (Scottish) Division acquired proper sights only three weeks before crossing to France and the 176th Brigade, Royal Field Artillery—part of the 34th Division—was still waiting for its last 4.5-inch howitzers in November 1915, permitting only three days' training with complete equipment prior to embarkation. Through no fault of their own, the men of many New Army formations learned to handle their weapons the hard way, in the harsh and unforgiving school of battle.

---

the output of shells for the four main types of gun then used by the BEF was little more than 30,000 rounds per month. Matters were not helped by Kitchener's failure to find the right compromise between the manpower requirements of industry and the army. Indiscriminate recruiting in the autumn of 1914 had serious effects on industry, for the many skilled men who enlisted then were not easily replaced or retrieved from the army in succeeding years. Kitchener was also apparently unable to grasp that in a modern total war involving mass armies, questions of labour distribution and the mobilization of manufacturing resources went far beyond the normal bounds of War Office authority. While David Lloyd George, the Chancellor of the Exchequer, pressed for a more vigorous prosecution of the war effort, including tighter state control of manpower supply and manufacturing capacity, Kitchener's opposition to outside interference hampered early attempts to solve these broader problems and limited the ability of industry to respond fully to the new demands. In fairness to Kitchener and Major-General Sir Stanley von Donop, the Master-General of the Ordnance, the necessary restructuring of industry could not be accomplished overnight. Besides, the huge armaments programmes which *were* instituted by the War Office and the Cabinet Committee on Munitions in the opening months of the war undoubtedly laid the foundations for the spectacular achievements of later years and shared much of the credit for the initial expansion exemplified by the increase in shell production from 871,700 rounds in 1914 to 23,663,186 in 1915.

It can be argued, then, that the shortages of shells for the BEF in the spring of 1915 resulted from delays in production and delivery rather than lack of orders. However, when, in mid-May, *The Times* published a dispatch from its military correspondent linking the shortages to the recent setback at Aubers Ridge, the ensuing 'Shells Scandal'—coupled with the resignation of Admiral of the Fleet Lord Fisher, the First Sea Lord, over the conduct of the Dardanelles campaign—led directly to the formation of a coalition Cabinet on 25 May. Next day the public were told that a new Ministry of Munitions, under Lloyd George, was being created to take over the duties of supplying munitions to the Royal Navy and the army. Whatever the War Office had achieved to date, it was from this point that the real transformation of industry began, with Lloyd George ultimately exercising greater control over capital, machinery, raw materials, and labour than any previous Cabinet minister. The Munitions of War Act of July 1915 prohibited lock-outs and strikes and suspended restrictive practices in armaments factories; 'men of push and go' were appointed to key posts in the new Ministry; National Shell, Projectile (for heavy shells), and Filling Factories were established and multiplied; and, despite lingering trade union opposition, growing numbers of women and unskilled men were employed to swell the labour force and allow the skilled workers still available to be used to maximum effect. In July 1916, when Lloyd George left the Ministry, some 520,000 women were engaged in munitions work compared with 212,000 two years before. Thanks in no small measure to Lloyd George's own drive and foresight, shell deliveries rose from 5,380,102 between July and December 1915 to 35,407,193 in the second half of 1916. Of no less importance was the vital stimulus given to the development and manufacture of heavy artillery and of the Stokes mortar, the Mills bomb, and the Lewis gun during Lloyd George's time at the Ministry. The total number of trench mortars produced grew from twelve in 1914 to 5,554 in 1916 while grenade production increased from 2,164 to 34,867,966 and machine-gun output from 287 to 33,507 in the same period. The crushing weight of fire-power at the BEF's disposal in the final months of the war was the priceless legacy of the munitions organization shaped in 1915–16.

As the war went on, the supply of manpower to the expanded army proved a more intractable problem than the supply of munitions. In February 1915 the monthly enlistment total fell to 87,896, the first time the monthly returns had dropped below six figures since the outbreak of war. The decline in voluntary enlistments continued throughout the year even though the Parliamentary Recruiting Committee, using the extensive network of local political organizations, waged an intensive and increasingly strident recruiting campaign, arranging thousands of meetings and issuing millions of posters and leaflets. True, the lowering of the height standard back to 5 feet 3 inches on 5 November 1914 had temporarily reinvigorated enlistments but neither this nor the official encouragement given to the raising of 'Bantam' battalions—composed of men between 5 feet and 5 feet 3 inches in height—succeeded in reversing the overall trend. Persistent recruiting problems in southern Ireland, the growing protection from recruiting granted to workers in key industries, and the activities of pacifist-orientated groups such as the No Conscription Fellowship, all exacerbated the situation yet economic factors probably played the biggest part in precipitating the fall in enlistments. The labour shortages resulting from unrestricted recruiting in 1914 caused a reduction in unemployment and an improvement in wage rates, conditions which militated against enlistment, particularly in areas busy with new army contracts.

With recruiting totals of around 95,000 for June and July and a further drop to 71,617 in September, the possibility of compulsory military service became a dominant issue in the second half of 1915. The National Register, taken on 15 August to give the government a more accurate picture of Britain's manpower resources, revealed that 5,012,146 men of military age were still not in the forces. Of the 2,179,231 single men in this total, only 690,138 were in starred occupations such as munitions work, mining, or railways. In October, as the casualties at Loos became known, Kitchener estimated that 35,000 recruits a week were required even to keep existing units at strength, a target which, though exaggerated, was somewhat in excess of the actual weekly average. A last attempt to preserve voluntarism was made when Lord Derby was appointed Director-General of Recruiting in October 1915, his principal task being to administer a scheme under which all men between 18 and 41 were asked to attest their willingness to serve when called. The attested men were divided into various classes and would be summoned in strict order, starting with single men of 19 and ending with the oldest married men. Those in starred occupations would be exempt. When the returns from the Derby Scheme were analysed in mid-December it was found that nearly half the available single men, including 651,160 not in starred occupations, had failed to register. This helped to remove the final barriers to conscription. On 27 January 1916, the Military Service Act became law, introducing compulsory military service for single men between 18 and 41, exempting the unfit, approved conscientious objectors, sole supporters of dependants, and men engaged on essential war work. A system of local, intermediate, and central tribunals was instituted to consider claims for exemption. Partly because there was still no co-ordinated general manpower plan for industry as well as the army, partly because the army's own manpower demands were unrealistic after eighteen months of industrialized war, and also because the new tribunals were perhaps too liberal in granting exemptions, recruiting returns in the first months of 1916 remained insufficient to maintain the army at the agreed size or to replace the anticipated casualties from the forthcoming summer offensive. Following the call-up, in March 1916, of younger married men who had attested under the Derby Scheme, pressure grew for equality of sacrifice and universal conscription. On 25 May a second Military Service Act extended liability for military service to all men, single or married, aged 18 to 41. Voluntary recruiting was retained in Ireland, however, since it would have been hazardous indeed to impose compulsion there in the wake of the Easter Rising.

All the New Army divisions were deployed overseas before the Military Service Acts had taken full effect. The last to embark, the 40th Division, crossed to France in June 1916. By the end of that month, there were sixty-five British divisions on active or garrison service abroad. They included three regular cavalry and two Territorial mounted divisions, together with twelve regular, thirty New Army, and seventeen Territorial infantry divisions, the total being completed by the 63rd (Royal Naval) Division. Whereas the Territorial formations stayed largely exclusive in composition in 1916, regular and New Army units were interchanged, primarily as a means of stiffening inexperienced Kitchener divisions with more seasoned soldiers. During that year, six regular divisions contained four or more New Army battalions while six New Army divisions incorporated four or more Regular battalions. One New Army division, the 39th, contained four Territorial battalions and another, the 9th (Scottish), received a complete South African brigade. Consequently, when the war entered its third year, the three-tiered organizational structure of the expanded army as developed by Kitchener in 1914–15—with its regular, Territorial, and New Army formations—was already being modified and dismantled.

Though, for the time being, the Territorial formations remained relatively intact in an organizational sense, the essential character of the Territorial Force was eroded in other ways. Taking Pals and Territorial units together, 643 out of 994 new infantry battalions formed during Kitchener's period at the War Office were raised by local effort outside the standard War Office recruiting channels but, with the Derby Scheme and the passing of the Military Service Acts, direct recruiting into the Territorial Force ceased, pre-war Territorials were no longer able to seek their discharge at the end of their term of engagement, and transfers were permitted between Territorial and other units. Now that men were called up for general service and sent where they seemed to be most needed, the drafting of reinforcements and casualty replacements from a parent regiment to its own units at the front could not be guaranteed. Shortly after suffering heavy losses at Gommecourt on 1 July 1916, the 1/9th London Regiment (Queen Victoria's Rifles) received drafts totalling 494 men from nine different units, including the London Scottish and the Middlesex Regiment. At home, the demise of separate Territorial recruiting marked a significant stage in the progressive whittling away of the powers and responsibilities of the County Associations.

The continuing irregularity of enlistment patterns, the uneven casualty rates suffered by units at various times, and the difficulties of supplying replacements on each occasion from the parent regiment, hastened a major reorganization of the reserve and drafting system. On 1 September 1916, New Army reserve battalions were reclassified and renumbered as Training Reserve Battalions, losing their regimental designations. In May 1917, some Training Reserve Battalions were converted into Young Soldier Battalions, which took in recruits aged 18 and one month and, after giving them basic training, posted them to one of a series of Graduated Battalions, where they completed their preparation for overseas service. Later in the year, Graduated Battalions once again received regimental titles but these usually bore little relation to the original. For instance, from September 1916, the 12th (Reserve) Battalion of the Welsh Regiment was successively transformed into the 58th Training Reserve Battalion, the 230th (Graduated) Battalion, and, finally, the 51st (Graduated) Battalion of the South Wales Borderers. The cumulative effects of this drafting policy, and the drawing of replacements from a common pool of conscripts, made the impact of losses on particular communities less concentrated and dramatic, but also further diluted units at the front. By the summer of 1917 the 16th Highland Light Infantry—the Glasgow Boys' Brigade Battalion—contained men from Nottinghamshire, Derbyshire, and Yorkshire. Similarly, in the 1/6th Cheshires, a Territorial battalion, only 20 per cent of the men by 1918 came from the unit's original recruiting area around Stockport and barely half were from the county. As its distinctive, highly localized character of early 1916 evaporated, the army increasingly became a 'nationalized' force.

The officer corps was not immune to changes. In all, 229,316 combatant commissions were awarded during the war and the pressures arising from expansion and casualties produced a shift in the educational and social background both of regular officers holding permanent commissions and of the 'temporary gentlemen'. By 1917 there was a noticeable increase in lower middle-class entrants to Sandhurst and Woolwich. The same pressures prompted the War Office, in February 1916, to introduce a fresh and more uniform system for selecting and training junior officers by creating Officer Cadet Battalions. Henceforth, temporary commissions were granted only to those who had passed through a cadet unit, unless they had previously been an officer, and candidates for the four-month course had to have served in the ranks or in an OTC contingent. With the advent of conscription, the Officer Cadet Battalions supplanted the OTC as the principal route to a temporary commission, 107,929 being awarded under this system up to December 1918. But, according to a recent study, while the majority of these new officers may have come from a different background to the pre-war regular officer class, many of the distinctions between regular, Territorial, and temporary officers, especially in the technical arms, 'disappeared or seemed less important on active service'.

While the officer corps came to include a larger proportion of the commercial and clerical classes than hitherto, it would be wrong to assume that the army was more representative of society as a whole after conscription than it was from 1914 to 1916. The percentage of the labour force enlisted from the commercial sector went up from 41 to 63 per cent and, in the case of manufacturing industries, it increased from 30 to 45 per cent between 1916 and 1918, the earlier gap, in percentage terms, thus being maintained or even widened. Low fitness standards also meant that there was a high proportion of working-class recruits among more than a million men rejected by medical boards in the last year of the war. What did alter was the balance between different branches of the army. Infantry constituted nearly 54 per cent of the BEF on the Western Front in 1914 but under 32 per cent in 1918. During the same period there was an increase of nearly 20 per cent in the non-combatant branches in that theatre.

Conscription failed to provide a magic solution to the army's growing manpower problems which, admittedly, were not helped by the army's own tendency to regard its claims as paramount and its frequent misuse of men when it received them. Both Asquith and, for a time, Lloyd George—who succeeded him as Prime Minister in December 1916—were unable or unwilling to apply compulsion with sufficient vigour to ensure a more rational co-ordination of military and industrial demands. Legislation in April 1917 and February 1918 removed a variety of grounds for exemption but a scheme launched in 1917 by the newly created Department of National Service under Neville Chamberlain failed to give the government full powers to regulate the allocation of manpower because it still relied on voluntary enrolment for 'work of national importance' and lacked the bite of statutory obligation. The crucial step was not taken until August 1917 when Brigadier-General Auckland Geddes, formerly Director of Recruiting, took over from Chamberlain at the head of a department which was upgraded to ministerial status and given appropriate political authority. At long last, properly co-ordinated use of mobilized manpower began, a fact underlined by the transfer of the control of recruiting from the War Office to the new Ministry on 1 November. The outcome was not totally to the army's liking as, from this point, its manpower demands were generally accorded a lower priority than those of shipbuilding and tank and aircraft production. With a 'wastage' level of some 76,000 men a month in France and Flanders in the autumn of 1917—double the rate of enlistments—the army faced its worst manpower crisis since the start of the war. The Military Service (No. 2) Act of 1918, which became law in April that year, conscripted men aged 41 to 50 and allowed for a further raising of the upper age limit if necessary. It also provided for the extension of conscription to Ireland although, in the event, the government was never prepared to grasp that particular nettle. The enlistment totals climbed briefly to over 80,000 a month in May and June 1918, yet the army was now scraping the bottom of the manpower barrel and the temporary improvement came too late to prevent another upheaval in the army's organization. On the Western Front, the BEF was forced to reduce the number of infantry battalions from twelve to nine in forty-eight of its divisions during the first three months of 1918 and ten more divisions in France and elsewhere suffered the same fate later in the year. Of the six divisions which retained twelve battalions, four, in the Middle East, were 'Indianized', receiving eight or nine Indian battalions in place of purely British units. Ten divisions on the Western Front were either reconstituted or reduced to cadre, so losing much of their original composition and character.

Recent scholarship suggests that there was no true 'universality of experience' in the army during the First World War and that gulfs remained between, for example, officers and men, volunteers and conscripts, and front-line troops and rear echelons. However, one should also re-emphasize that, in the second half of the war, organizational changes and the intermingling of regulars, Territorials, New Army men, and conscripts in formations at the front blurred the outlines of the 'four armies' to a considerable extent. Whatever gulfs, or imbalances, in the social distribution of enlistments may still have existed, the army was closer to being a 'nation in arms' in those years than ever before in its history.

12 THE ARMY BETWEEN THE TWO WORLD WARS 1918–1939

BRIAN BOND

A graph of the British army's fortunes between 1918 and 1939, as indicated by annual budgets and strategic priorities, would suggest a story of political neglect after the unprecedented national effort during the First World War. The line would plunge steeply from the Armistice, when there was over 3.5 million troops on the British establishment, to the end of 1920 when there was only 370,000. Another sharp drop was effected in 1922 when the Geddes Axe drastically reduced both numbers and expenditure, and thereafter the army's annual budget fell steadily every year from just over £43.5 million in 1923 to just under £36 million in 1932. The renewed threats from Japan and Germany in the early 1930s scarcely affected the army for several years, and even the start of rearmament proper in 1935 brought only meagre increases in funding. Only in 1938, with a defence loan of nearly £36 million supplementing a budget of £87 million, can the army be truly said to have begun preparing for war.

At least by 1923 the worst of the inevitable post-war upheavals were over and the army, reduced to its pre-1914 establishment and dependent on voluntary enlistment, was settling down again to the humdrum routines of home security and imperial policing. Kipling's bitter lines about the public's indifference to 'Tommy Atkins' once a great war was over were more than ever appropriate in the disillusioned mood of the 1920s. Lacking either the traditional esteem of the Royal Navy or the novel appeal of the Royal Air Force, the army soon felt itself to be the 'Cinderella service'— criticized in the press, always short of men despite continuing high unemployment, and increasingly dependent on obsolescent weapons and equipment.

In the aftermath of the First World War the British Empire reached its maximum extent, with the enormous additional responsibilities of mandated territories in the Middle East, and occupation duties in the former Ottoman empire and the Rhineland. The largest commitment, India, required approximately 70,000 British troops, but there were also sizeable garrisons in Egypt, Iraq, and Northern Ireland. Despite being overstretched in terms of manpower, the War Office had a vested interest in the 1920s in maintaining the army's policing role in the Middle East and on the North-West Frontier against the RAF's claims to perform this function more effectively and more cheaply. As the limitations of policing dissident tribesmen from the air began to attract both operational and moral criticism, so the role of ground forces expanded. By the late 1930s, for example, the growing Arab rebellion in Palestine had drawn in the infantry component of almost two divisions; the North-West Frontier saw a series of costly punitive expeditions; and substantial mechanized forces were dispatched to Egypt to guard against the Italian threat from Libya. Greatly reduced reserve forces meant that the army was harder pressed to meet these commitments than before 1914.

It is not therefore surprising that, as the horrific experience of war receded, to be replaced by the onerous problems of peacetime soldiering, the feeling should grow that the unprecedented war effort of 1914–18 had been unique, even an aberration. No less an authority than the Chief of the Imperial General Staff (CIGS), Sir George Milne, endorsed this view in 1926 when he described the recent war as 'abnormal'. At present, he added, the army could not even mobilize a single corps; it was most unlikely ever again to be required to fight a European war. The phrase 'never again' was frequently used about such a nightmarish prospect; politicians implied scornfully that they would not send troops to 'the trenches', and even the use of the term 'Expeditionary Force' was deplored in government discussions and official reports.

In extenuation of official neglect of the army, it must be stressed that until the appearance of the threat from Nazi Germany it had no obvious European enemy—the United States and Japan as theoretical antagonists being almost entirely naval concerns. War with Britain's recent ally, France, was scarcely credible, and was in any case mainly a contingency for the RAF. Consequently in the later 1920s and early 1930s the army's wargaming was primarily concerned with a Soviet threat to India through Afghanistan. In these circumstances, and in view of acute domestic social and economic problems, the government's informal imposition of a

Fuller and Liddell Hart

Both John Frederick Charles ('Boney') Fuller and Basil Henry Liddell Hart were among the most interesting and widely read military critics and historians ever produced by Britain. If Liddell Hart is probably now better known, it is well to remember that Fuller was seventeen years older and a regular officer who had served in the South African War, published books, and attended Staff College before 1914, when Liddell Hart acquired a wartime commission from Cambridge. Furthermore, before they corresponded and met shortly after the war, Fuller had served as chief staff officer of the Tank Corps where he had conceived the visionary Plan 1919 which would have used tanks on a massive scale to achieve a breakthrough.

Consequently, for most of the 1920s Fuller was acknowledged by Liddell Hart as his senior partner and mentor. It was initially Fuller who was the out-and-out advocate of mechanization and a key role for tanks in the British army. As Chief Instructor at the Staff College (1922–6) and Military Assistant to the Chief of the Imperial General Staff (1926–7), he was excellently placed to promulgate his views, quite apart from the spate of provocative articles and books which he published. Though his intellectual interests were always remarkably wide, it was with tanks and mechanization that Fuller's early reputation was established and endured—particularly in Germany. His lectures, published as *Field Service Regulations, Part III* (1932) was one of the most imaginative, yet also objective, expositions of the future role of armoured forces.

In terms of original ideas Fuller has been described as 'a blazing comet', while Liddell Hart was 'a less brilliant but steadier star'. Unfortunately for the army and his own career, Fuller's impatience and arrogance resulted in intemperate criticisms of senior officers, the refusal of an appointment (in 1927) involving the command of experimental mechanized units, and taking retirement on half-pay in 1930. Soon afterwards he became an open supporter of Mosley and his Fascists and thereby virtually forfeited his opportunity to influence developments in the British army. For the remainder of his life he maintained a prodigious output of books, many of them avowedly polemical; but inclining later to serious studies of military history. Fuller was in short an eccentric genius with remarkable abilities but also flaws of character which unsuited him to a career in the British army—especially in peacetime.

Captain B. H. Liddell Hart was an outstanding military journalist, critic, and historian in the era of the two World Wars. His experience at Ypres and on the

Somme, where respectively he was wounded and gassed, made him a lifelong critic of war and generalship, though never a pacifist. He began to write on infantry tactics while still serving and, soon after being obliged to resign on health grounds, he became successively military correspondent for the *Daily Telegraph* (1925–35) and defence correspondent of *The Times* (1935–9). In these years he probably reached the peak of his military and political influence despite his comparative youth. He rapidly expanded his tactical ideas (the 'expanding torrent' of attack based on the German offensive of 1918) to the strategic sphere ('the strategy of indirect approach' culled from a wide reading of history), and, ultimately, to grand strategy and national policy (the 'British Way in Warfare' based on naval power and economic blockade, and 'limited liability' with regard to an army commitment in Europe). Above all, with Fuller, Liddell Hart became internationally famous as the proponent of mechanization and armoured warfare. His books and articles were widely read in progressive circles in the British army, where he fostered a remarkable number of influential contacts, and also in Germany though it is very doubtful if he was so influential there as he was to claim after 1945. He emphasized the importance of air support to tanks as well as the need for mechanized infantry, arguing that such forces would restore mobility and dooioiveness to warfare. Neville Chamberlain specifically urged Hore-Belisha to read his book *Europe in Arms* (1937), and in 1937–8 he reached the peak of his influence as Hore-Belisha's unofficial advisor.

This partnership between 'H.-B.' and 'L.-H.' proved to be a mixed blessing for the latter. With rearmament at last gathering momentum and war threatening it was a hectic and exciting time for the young journalist. He advised Hore-Belisha on virtually every aspect of military reform, including reduction of the establishment in India, changing the Cardwell system, anti-aircraft defences, and mechanization. On the debit side he was blamed for some of Hore-Belisha's shortcomings for which he had no responsibility.

Worse still, in the late 1930s his personal and professional lives were simultaneously in crisis. He was at odds with *The Times*' editorial line which supported appeasement further than he was prepared to go; while his fervent opposition to sending an army to the Continent seemed to clash with his earlier support of armoured warfare. In the summer of 1939 he suffered a collapse, and a few months later lost his post on *The Times* for advocating a negotiated peace with Hitler. Thus in the years 1939–45 Liddell Hart's reputation suffered a severe decline. With considerable moral courage he continued to oppose Churchill's policy of total war, particularly conscription, strategic bombing, and 'Unconditional Surrender'. In contrast to Fuller, however, Liddell Hart largely recovered his reputation after the Second World War. He was certainly influential for more than forty years in that his enormous output of books and articles was internationally read: he was at least equally important as a gadfly stinging the assumptions of soldiers and politicians in positions of authority even if they did not always agree with him. He was also a self-publicist with an insatiable craving for fame who was apt to overestimate his influence on individuals and events. This has inevitably led to attempts to debunk his reputation. Nevertheless, one can confidently predict that his name will always figure prominently in any account of the British army in the mid-twentieth century.

Ten-Year Rule from 1919 with regard to defence expenditure was eminently sensible. All three services were to plan on the assumption of no major war for the next ten years and the army was specifically advised that no expeditionary force would be required for such a purpose. However, in the mid-1920s the Rule was put on a moving basis and was not abandoned until 1932 on the urgent pleas of the Chiefs of Staff.

Therefore, in its early years especially, the Rule simply acknowledged the fact that no funding was available for military expansion and very little for technical innovation or training. While it may have contributed to the Army's introspection, social snobbery, and conservatism—later to be epitomized by David Low's caricature 'Colonel Blimp'—it certainly did not cause those negative features of peacetime soldiering. It did, however, give the Treasury the whip hand over expenditure and cause considerable irritation in numerous disputes over penny-pinching which Colonel J. F. C. Fuller and other satirists gleefully exposed. The much more serious faults of the Rule were that it was maintained for several years too long, allowed the domestic arms industry virtually to disappear, and rested on the dubious assumption that Britain would have the will-power, industrial capability, and, above all, time to rearm once an enemy (or as it turned out three potential enemies) had appeared.

The dispatch of the Shanghai Defence Force in 1927 made public what was already well known to the army's leaders; namely, the difficulties entailed in mobilizing even a division shorn of a considerable amount of its guns, vehicles, and heavy equipment. Only the previous year, during the General Strike, the CIGS had referred to the nightmare of an overseas crisis necessitating the dispatch of available regular infantry units coinciding with widespread industrial disorder at home. On more than one occasion he stated officially that the army was 'completely out of date' and was unfitted to respond to any contingency in Europe.

Soldiering in these unpropitious conditions could be dull and frustrating. Given also the slow promotion system and the tendency of senior officers to hang on as long as possible in service, it is not surprising that many imaginative, progressive-minded officers either left the service or lost some of their enthusiasm. Even later well-known generals like Wavell, Dill, and Ironside were affected by these adverse conditions. Field Marshal Chetwode's farewell address as Commander-in-Chief in India in 1934 was perhaps the most devastating indictment of the military profession in this era by an insider, including the reflection that: 'The longer I remain in the Service, the more wooden and the more regulation-bound do I find the British officer to be.' Liddell Hart, Fuller, and others made equally scathing criticisms of the army at home.

Against this gloomy background, however, it is possible to be favourably impressed by the progressive spirit and ideas displayed by a minority of zealous professional officers, especially in the 1920s, when reforms and innovations could be discussed fairly objectively without the need to focus on a particular enemy. Thus Fuller and Liddell Hart were only the most famous of a band of middle-ranking officers and ex-officers who established international reputations with a spate of publications critical of the conduct of the recent war and advocating a variety of reforms. Journals such as that of the Royal United Services Institute and the *Army Quarterly* suggested a ferment of proposals for reform, not least in the annual prize essay competitions setting a specific contemporary issue for discussion. At the Camberley Staff College, a dynamic Commandant such as Ironside recruited top-class instructors such as Dill and Fuller who were eager to disseminate the tactical lessons of the First World War.

Above all, it remains a matter of astonishment that the numerically declining and underfunded British army should have continued its pioneering efforts on tanks and mechanization generally from the First World War through to the early 1930s. In particular the trials and manœuvres between 1927 and 1931 of mixed and, eventually, wholly mechanized units communicating by radio set the standard which the larger European armies would not emulate for several years. In 1927, for example, the first experimental manœuvres were handicapped by the miscellaneous nature of the available tanks, armoured cars, and other vehicles and by the lack of radio communication between the tanks. Non-existent anti-tank guns were notoriously represented by flags. Nevertheless the manœuvres impressed observers with the potential mobility and striking power of armoured formations. Despite numerous technical problems and the deliberate handicapping of the mechanized forces to prevent demoralization of the traditional arms, considerable progress had been made by 1931 when Brigadier Charles Broad carried out a brilliant demonstration on Salisbury Plain by moving 180 tanks in dense fog with 'an almost inhuman precision' by radio control. This seemed to herald a new era of armoured and mechanized formations, including air co-operation, in which horsed cavalry and marching infantry would have no part. On the theoretical side, Broad had already, in 1929, published the official booklet *Mechanized and Armoured Formations* (better known from its cover colour as 'The Purple Primer'), and three years later Fuller would bring out the influential *Field Service Regulations, Part III*, which analysed the likely nature of combat between armoured forces. By the early 1930s, however, Milne and his successor as CIGS, Montgomery-Massingberd, had made it clear that they favoured the gradual mechanization and motorization of all arms, including the conversion of the cavalry to light tanks or armoured cars, rather than concentrating on the expansion of the small Royal Tank Corps (only four battalions in 1932) as the basis for larger armoured formations. There was undoubtedly a conservative and even reactionary aspect to this War Office policy which generally prevailed through the 1930s and it was bitterly criticized by Fuller, Liddell Hart, and other proponents of armoured warfare; see, for example, the latter's *Memoirs*, i (1965) for a detailed account of Britain's surrender of her lead in what was soon to be termed the blitzkrieg style of warfare.

Various explanations can be offered for what in retrospect was to seem an egregious error in rearmament policy. First, the War Office's financial resources for weapons development of all kinds remained meagre, and the facilities for tank-building almost non-existent. Successive CIGS's took the view that limited resources must be thinly spread across all the arms of the service rather than concentrated on tanks. More open to criticism was the weak design and development section of the General Staff concerned with tanks, and also the protracted uncertainty about which tank models to put into production and for what combat roles.

But by far the most important inhibiting factor, in this author's view, was the government's continuing hesitation about the continental role of the army until almost the eve of the Second World War. Tanks did not fit comfortably into the Cardwell system for garrisoning the Empire by the routine alternation of infantry and cavalry units, and they were bound to be given a very low priority so long as deterrence through air and sea power dominated the government's, and not least the Treasury's, defence policy. Anti-aircraft guns and air defence generally received a much higher priority than tanks. Only an earlier political undertaking to send an Expeditionary Force to the Continent would have opened the possibility of creating a more tank-orientated army, and even then it is difficult to envisage the appearance of panzer-style armoured divisions in the anti-war, disarmament-orientated Britain before the spring of 1939. In the defence review completed in December 1937, for example, the estimated savings on tanks would exceed all other army economies added together. In that year too the War Office actually underspent its allocation for warlike stores by nearly £6 million due to lack of industrial facilities and indecision over designs and long-term orders. Generals such as Ironside and Burnett-Stuart, or journalists like Liddell Hart, who opposed the continental commitment, should have perceived the close link between the army's projected role and the low priority given to the creation of armoured divisions.

A little more needs to be said about the place of the army in the National Government's conception of defence policy because this is crucial to an understanding of the service's slow development throughout the 1930s. In November 1933 the government set up the Defence Requirements Committee (DRC), composed of the Chiefs of Staff and representatives of the Treasury and the Foreign Office, to report on the three services' worst deficiencies with a programme to remedy them over the next five years. This was therefore emphatically not the first step in rearmament; indeed such a policy was expressly denied until 1935.

The General Staff proposed, and the DRC accepted, a total of £40 million for the army based on a calculation of what the War Office could actually spend, given the run-down of the arms industry, rather than on a realistic appraisal of needs. Colonel Pownall, then on the Secretariat of the Committee of Imperial Defence (CID), reckoned that to produce an Expeditionary Force of four regular divisions with an adequate reserve of Territorial divisions would need about £145 million over five years. In addition £30 million was required to implement the Defence of India Plan.

As the generals anticipated, it was the proposal to prepare a modest Expeditionary Force (smaller than that available before 1914) equipped to fight on the Continent which aroused ministerial opposition. The attack was led by the Chancellor of the Exchequer, Neville Chamberlain, behind whose ruthless logic it is possible to detect an emotional revulsion against the attritional nature and heavy casualties of the First World War, coupled with a fear that if the War Office's proposals were accepted they would lead to a repetition of the trench stalemate. Curiously, politicians who had fought in the war, including Churchill, Eden, Duff Cooper, and Macmillan, took a more robust view about the need to prepare an army for a possible European campaign than those who had not, such as Chamberlain, Hoare, and Simon.

The nub of the Chancellor's case was that the Maginot Line rendered the French frontier impregnable so the real problem was Belgium. If her ground defences were strong they would be overcome by German air-power; if not a British Expeditionary Force could not possibly prevent a German breakthrough. Since Britain could not afford to rearm all three services the Chancellor favoured concentrating on the navy and air force which, he believed (unlike the army) would exercise a deterrent effect; the army should be left to concentrate on its extra-European role, apart from its contribution to the air defence of Great Britain (ADGB).

Despite Pownall's sarcastic diary entry to the effect that the Chancellor's ideas on strategy 'would disgrace a board school', they generally prevailed, even though the Chiefs of Staff preserved at least a façade of unity in arguing consistently that an ability to put a small army on the Continent should be a vital component of Britain's defence policy. The army's allocation from the DRC was halved to £20 million; and although the continental commitment was never expressly ruled out, very little was done to provide the training, equipment, weapons, and, particularly, ammunition to enable even the first two divisions to take part in a European war. Worse still, as the fear of a knock-out blow from the air increasingly alarmed the electorate, the Territorial Army was largely diverted to the role of anti-aircraft defence. In this period (1934–5) the army probably reached the nadir of its fortunes in the inter-war years and, despite the valiant efforts of its minister Lord Hailsham, its demands were largely overruled just when the shortages resulting from the Ten-Year Rule needed to be tackled. As Hailsham remarked, the army had been cast as 'a Cinderella of the forces'.

As if the army's existing problems were not enough, two crises in the Mediterranean theatre in the mid-1930s added to the strain in terms of manpower and equipment, and strengthened the views of soldiers and politicians who believed that a military commitment in Europe should be renounced. First the Abyssinian crisis of 1935–6 raised the possibility of war with Italy in which the army's responsibilities would include the defence of Egypt and the Mediterranean bases. In September 1935 three battalions were dispatched from England to Malta and an extra brigade to Egypt. Later reinforcements to Egypt included a battalion of light tanks, a company of medium tanks, and a mechanized brigade of the Royal Artillery. These reinforcements helped to form the nucleus of the desert army which excelled against the Italians in 1940, and it is easy to understand how senior soldiers, such as General Ironside, could view their role as an alternative to that of a continental campaign against Germany.

The second crisis concerned the persistent, if sporadic, rebellion of the Palestinian Arabs from April 1936 onwards. The security of Palestine was regarded as hardly less important than that of Egypt for Britain's Middle Eastern and imperial strategy. It provided an essential staging post for Britain's air routes to India and the Far East; it was viewed as a buffer zone for the defences of the Suez Canal; and in Haifa lay the terminus of the pipeline for vital oil supplies from Persia and Iraq. After a year or so of comparative quiet, full-scale rebellion broke out again in the summer of 1938 and continued into the autumn, thereby creating a serious distraction and dispersion of trained battalions which could be ill spared. Colonel Pownall's diary entry for 29 August 1938 evokes the problem as viewed by the General Staff:

sending troops to Palestine is like pouring water onto the desert sands—they are immediately absorbed, the thirsty sand cries for more and one never gets a drop back. At the end of September they'll have 11 [infantry] battalions and a cavalry regiment . . . two of our colonial divisions in effect . . . God, what a mess we have made of this whole Palestine affair!

By this time the Cabinet appeared to have discounted any army contribution to a European ally at the outset of a war. In confirming the revised strategic priorities proposed by the Minister for the Co-ordination of Defence, Sir Thomas Inskip, in December 1937, the army's responsibilities were listed in the following order: the provision of anti aircraft defences at home; followed by the reinforcement of imperial garrisons; the dispatch of the field force to 'an Eastern theatre'; and, last of all, 'co-operation in defence of the territories of any allies Britain might have in war' though it was unlikely that much could be done under this last heading. Inskip at least showed awareness of the risk his proposals entailed. But as Michael Howard commented, 'What was generally termed a policy of "limited liability" in Continental warfare had now shrunk to one of no liability at all.'

Apart from the diehards on the General Staff, who understandably feared that, if war occurred and the ill-trained and underequipped field force was dispatched to a shambles, they would be held responsible, the army's European role had few supporters in the months before the Munich crisis. The Royal Navy's and the RAF's interest in a continental commitment had declined for different reasons; Sir Maurice Hankey had withdrawn his influential support, and with the replacement of Duff Cooper by Hore-Belisha in May 1937 even the War Minister ceased to fight the army's corner on this vital issue, the latter being a believer in the impregnability of French defences and therefore in the feasibility of 'limited liability' for the British army.

During Hore-Belisha's first year at the War Office he was preoccupied, above all other reforming projects, by Britain's pathetically inadequate ground defences against the *Luftwaffe*'s anticipated attempt to strike a knock-out blow. Duncan Sandys, MP, had made trouble for him on this issue, and the Munich crisis demonstrated that London was for all practical purposes defenceless. Nevertheless Hore-Belisha drew a different lesson from the crisis. For all the government's declarations to the contrary, he now believed that the field force *would* be dispatched to France in the event of war. He was appalled at the prospect. Quite apart from the lack of tanks, guns, and reserves of ammunition, the troops would have had no winter clothing in 1938. This was a state of neglect almost comparable with the condition in which the army had been sent to the Crimea. Almost immediately Hore-Belisha began a courageous and very unpopular campaign in the Cabinet, though he was soon to receive valuable support from the Foreign Secretary, Lord Halifax, to give the European commitment first priority so as to loosen the iron grip of the Treasury. To resurrect the programme refused two years previously would cost about £200 million—a seemingly impossible goal in view of the other services' existing programmes.

It is unnecessary here to cover in detail the complex process which led to the government's volte-face and reluctant acceptance of a continental commitment for the regular army divisions in February 1939 beyond stressing that Hore-Belisha played a leading part in it. This was acknowledged by his arch-critic (in the privacy of his diary), Major-General Henry Pownall, in 1938–9 Director of Military Operations and Intelligence at the War Office. On 20 February he recorded 'a great victory'; namely the launch of an adequately funded programme to equip the field force properly for a continental role, though this still only applied to the first four regular divisions and four Territorial divisions. Pownall saw a demonstration of new weapons at Aldershot and was 'much comforted'. 'The Army', he noted, 'really is coming to life again, no longer a "depressed class".' He envisaged the creation of a really high-class modern army—small but efficient and well equipped.

This ideal was not to be realized because it ran counter to Pownall's conflicting and prophetic insight that, unless Britain lost a short war, she would be forced to mobilize national resources and eventually to clothe, arm, and accommodate a national army on a large scale. Hore-Belisha began this movement in March 1939 when, partly as a publicity stunt to exploit the recent rush of volunteers to the Territorial Army, he raised the establishment to war strength (170,000) and, by a proverbial stroke of the pen, doubled it to the goal of 340,000. This alarmed some of Hore-Belisha's Cabinet colleagues as heralding a commitment to a new mass war in the trenches of France. But in the short term it created enormous administrative problems due to shortage of drill halls, equipment, uniforms, and, most seriously, instructors many of whom would have to be taken from regular units.

In the following month Hore-Belisha performed the bravest action of his political career in forcing Chamberlain to accept a measure of compulsory service in peacetime despite repeated pledges to the contrary. The War Minister was responding to French pressure for *un effort du sang* and to permit at least a portion of the anti-aircraft defences to be manned round the clock against a threat from the *Luftwaffe* which did not actually exist. But beyond these needs, Hore-Belisha wished to strengthen overseas garrisons and the field force—as the former Expeditionary Force was now termed.

Coming so soon after the nominal doubling of the Territorial Army, the arrival of 200,000 conscripts for six months' training created unimaginable chaos in the summer of 1939, what one War Office critic moderately described as 'a proper granny's knitting'. He also admitted that it was preferable to get the worst of this confusion over before war began. On the debit side, however, critics like Liddell Hart pointed out that the War Office had apparently abandoned any hope of creating a small, high-quality mechanized field force and seemed bent on conscripting a vast, immobile, and underequipped conscript army suited only to a static attritional war like that of 1914–18.

In the summer of 1939 strenuous efforts were made to foster close Anglo-French relations and to co-ordinate inter-Allied arrangements at

Leslie Hore-Belisha

When Leslie Hore-Belisha was unexpectedly made Secretary of State for War in May 1937 at the early age of 43, a glittering political future seemed assured; indeed he was tipped as a future Prime Minister. He was an outstanding parliamentary speaker and enjoyed good relations with the press. Although a National Liberal in a Tory-dominated government, he was well regarded by Neville Chamberlain who had given him his chance at the Ministry of Transport where he had done very well, particularly in reducing the number of traffic accidents. Hore-Belisha had attained the rank of major in the Royal Army Service Corps in the First World War, but in 1937 he lacked strong views on strategy. Consequently he was regarded by the Prime Minister as a safe appointment who would uphold the current policy of limited liability towards a continental commitment for the army, so that priority in rearmament could continue to be given to the Royal Air Force and the navy. But in internal army affairs, Hore-Belisha was undoubtedly seen as a new broom who would sweep away conservative cobwebs and anomalies.

Unofficially advised by *The Times*'s defence correspondent, Captain B. H. Liddell Hart, Hore-Belisha carried through a remarkable batch of reforms which went far to transform the army in the remaining months of peace. Having first obtained a more co-operative team of generals by purging the Army Council, including the Chief of the Imperial General Staff General Deverell, Hore-Belisha next tackled the recruiting problem by drastically improving the ordinary soldier's terms of service and living conditions. Before the outbreak of war he also doubled the Territorial Army and—displaying great political courage—forced a reluctant Chamberlain to introduce a form of compulsory service. This created chaos in the short term but greatly eased the way for more thoroughgoing conscription in wartime.

Hardly less significant were the reforms affecting the officers' career structure. Hore-Belisha abolished the half-pay system, introduced definite periods of tenure in command and staff appointments, speeded up and regularized the promotion system, and lowered the age limit at which senior officers must retire. Though widely applauded these reforms also made enemies among those passed over or summarily retired.

Hore-Belisha's greatest challenge was to prepare the small, badly organized and ill-equipped army for the war against Germany which seemed increasingly likely despite the government's policy of appeasement towards

Hitler. After the Munich crisis Hore-Belisha changed his strategic views and campaigned bravely in Whitehall for the necessary priority and funding to form and equip a field force which could be sent to fight on the Continent. He did so well in this political struggle that even his severest critic on the general staff, Major-General Henry Pownall, paid him grudging compliments in his diary. Only in February 1939 did the government make a definite commitment to prepare this field force for continental war. It was therefore greatly to the War Minister's credit that a field force of five divisions was wholly motorized (i.e. not dependent on horse transport) and ready to be sent to France soon after the outbreak of war.

Hore-Belisha's flamboyant manner and tactlessness had made him some powerful enemies both military and political. For example, he was scarcely on speaking terms with the CIGS, Lord Gort, and had alienated Churchill by a *contretemps* with the latter's son-in-law Duncan Sandys. So far from enhancing his authority, the advent of war weakened it: the army's comparative inactivity provided no useful publicity, and the War Minister failed to command the respect and loyalty of some of the senior soldiers, notably Ironside at the War Office and Lord Gort, commanding the field force in France. It was ironic that in an attempt to win publicity for himself and the army, he provided the hatchet which his enemies gleefully wielded against him. After a visit to France in November 1939 Hore-Belisha criticized the rate at which field fortifications ('pill-boxes') were being built. This so outraged the generals that they enlisted the support of the king and determined to oust him. Chamberlain attempted to mollify him with a lesser government appointment but this was refused and Hore-Belisha resigned, to the bewilderment of the popular press, in January 1940. During the war it seemed possible that his star would rise again but it did not, and he died disappointed, in 1957, having earlier accepted a peerage. He deserves to be remembered for his valiant efforts to reform the British army under the shadow of impending total war.

---

all levels so as to avoid the friction which so many British senior officers in 1939 could recall from the First World War. Amicable arrangements were made concerning the French ports to be made available to the field force, its assembly area to the north-west of Amiens, and its place in the line on the French left—all almost uncannily reminiscent of 1914. The two governments agreed on the composition and role of a Supreme War Council and on the British Commander-in-Chief's place in the French chain of command, but no permanent joint staff organization was ever achieved.

As a consequence of inter-service rivalry throughout the inter-war period, the field force would sail to France with only the meagre air support of the air component, consisting of two bomber reconnaissance squadrons, six army co-operation squadrons, four fighter squadrons, and two flights of a headquarters communications squadron. The two services were about equally to blame for the lack of an agreed tactical doctrine for close air–ground co-operation. The RAF's leaders were adamant that the bomber was not a battlefield weapon: it would be wasteful and inefficient to employ bombers in 'penny packets' under the orders of army commanders on tasks which could be more suitably carried out by artillery. This was probably the operational issue on which there had been least progress since 1918, and where recent practical experience—particularly on the North-West Frontier of India—had been completely neglected in Britain.

In view of the late acceptance of a continental commitment, followed by the enormous influx of untrained Territorials and conscripts, no amount of hard work and improvisation could equip and train the field force for a European campaign in less than eighteen months. A review of the regular infantry divisions of the field force in July 1939 revealed, for example, that there were available only 72 out of 240 heavy anti-aircraft guns and 144 out of 240 anti-tank guns. The field artillery requirements had not yet received any of the new 25-pounder guns. In August a War Office spokesman admitted that only sixty infantry support tanks were available against a requirement of 1,646. There had been no large-scale manœuvres for several years as part of the economy drive; hence even the regular divisions lacked basic tactical skills. The mobilization and movement to France of the first four regular divisions in September 1939 went off remarkably smoothly, but they were inadequately trained and short of every type of equipment, especially tanks, guns, and ammunition. The vast citizen army assembling in Britain lacked even the equipment for realistic training.

It is often claimed that the field force was the only national contingent to go to war in 1939 'fully mechanized'. True, the army no longer depended on horse transport, but a more accurate term would be 'motorized' and even then military vehicles had to be supplemented by large-scale requisitioning from civilian firms. In his *Memoirs*, Field Marshal Montgomery described, in September 1939, how the countryside of France was strewn with broken-down vans and lorries from his 3rd Division. He concluded a long list of deficiencies with the damning verdict that 'we sent our Army into that most modern war with weapons and equipment which were quite inadequate'.

By the end of September 1939 more than 160,000 soldiers and airmen with over 23,000 vehicles and a vast tonnage of stores and supplies had been safely landed in France. By mid-October I and II Corps (the first four divisions) had occupied the Franco-Belgian frontier defences on the allotted British sector between Maulde and Halluin. This was no mean achievement for an army which only a year previously had been assigned to an extra-European role against inferior oppositions. Unlike their predecessors in 1914, however, the soldiers in 1939 were not immediately swept into a costly encounter battle and were in fact to have more than six months to prepare themselves before the blow fell. Shattering though the experience of battle was to be in May 1940, it must be considered fortunate from the viewpoint of the British army that the blitzkrieg was not launched earlier. A high price had to be paid in this and subsequent campaigns for the political indecision of the 1930s. It makes no sense to criticize the character and ethos of the British army in the inter-war period without taking full account of the social and political environment in which it struggled to maintain its traditional professional standards.

13 THE ARMY AND THE CHALLENGE OF WAR 1939–1945

CARLO D'ESTE

When Britain declared war on Germany on 3 September 1939, her army was unprepared to fight an enemy equipped with modern weaponry and innovative new tactics. Its fighting formations were scattered in small garrisons around the country, training lacked purpose, and the government and military leadership could not even agree on the mission of Britain's armed forces in the event of war. Transportation, communications equipment, artillery, engineer, and logistical support units were in such short supply that it was often impossible to train or conduct exercises.

When Germany invaded Poland in September 1939 the German army had over a million men under arms and three and a half million more available for immediate activation. By contrast, the British Expeditionary Force that was ordered to France consisted of four infantry divisions, which by May 1940 had risen to only twelve.

The mounting and dispatch of an Expeditionary Force to France was organized in haste and carried out in an atmosphere of desperation. As Field Marshal Bernard Montgomery would later write, 'In September 1939 the British Army was totally unfit to fight a first class war on the continent of Europe. It must be said to our shame that we sent our Army into that most modern war with weapons and equipment which were quite inadequate, and we had only ourselves to blame for the disasters which early overtook us in the field when fighting began in 1940.'

In April 1940 the first shots of the Second World War between Britain and Germany were fired in Scandinavia when a small Anglo-French-Polish Expeditionary Force sent to occupy Norway was defeated by a larger German naval and land force with the same objective, the securing of ports of passage for vital Swedish iron. After nearly two months of fighting, much of it around the northern port of Narvik, which a small German force managed to defend stubbornly, the Allies abandoned Norway at the same time as the BEF was being lifted from Dunkirk. Despite heavy losses, the Royal Navy defeated the German navy, thus preventing any invasion of Britain in 1940. However, the ground campaign was a military disaster that resulted in the downfall of Neville Chamberlain's Government and the installation of Winston Churchill as the new Prime Minister.

Lord Gort's British Expeditionary Force was hastily deployed along the southern plains of Belgium on 10 May 1940 when the Germans launched their long-awaited offensive against France, Belgium, and Holland with a lightning blitzkrieg attack through the Ardennes forest. The French 9th Army on the right of the BEF bore the brunt of the German onslaught and soon collapsed. Within days the British were cut off from the main elements of the French army and forced to begin retreating towards the coastal city of Dunkirk where they were surrounded. Faced with either surrender or somehow escaping across the English Channel, General Sir Alan Brooke's II Corps fought a magnificent delaying action for the main body of the BEF, while the Royal Navy hastily organized an emergency evacuation of Dunkirk.

More than 339,000 British and French soldiers escaped the German trap at Dunkirk. This miraculous escape saved the British army from virtual destruction. Unlike its heroic portrayal by Churchill as 'a miracle of deliverance', Dunkirk was in reality the dreadful price paid for two decades of unpreparedness. Its only positive aspect was the saving of the senior officers and men who were the heart of the British army and who were the only professional soldiers capable of defending the United Kingdom against what was then thought to be certain invasion by Hitler. They would also form the core of a newly conscripted, trained, and equipped wartime army.

Dunkirk was the first of a long series of disastrous setbacks that were to beset the British in the early days of the Second World War. With all of continental Europe under Nazi occupation, the success of the RAF during the Battle of Britain in September and the saving of the BEF were virtually the only glimmers of hope in the fateful year of 1940.

Until Pearl Harbor brought the United States into the war against Germany in December 1941, Britain and her army fought alone against overwhelming German and Japanese strength in a global theatre of war unprecedented in the history of warfare. Stretching from Norway and Dunkirk in 1940, to Greece, North Africa, and Crete in the west in 1941 and Burma and Hong Kong in Asia, to Dieppe and Tobruk in 1942, the British army suffered one calamitous defeat after another. Everywhere the British were on the defensive, with no end in sight to the reversals. The challenge facing the British leadership was to create a modern army out of the chaos of Dunkirk that was capable of fighting the German and Japanese armies on equal terms.

The massive mobilization of the entire nation for war and the beginning of what would soon become a flow of arms and military hardware from the United States were all positive steps but, as the war coalition government of Winston Churchill quickly learned, the years of neglect of Britain's military machine could not be easily overcome. After Dunkirk the army could barely muster fifteen divisions, most of which were sparsely equipped and lacked mobility.

During the first two years of the war British resources were perilously strained. Military forces in the Far East were virtually on their own, half a world away, and in the Mediterranean Italy had declared war on Britain and France on 10 June 1940. Although the British army fought in far-flung corners of the Empire, early in the war Churchill's vision was to bring the United States into the war and launch a Second Front with a cross-Channel invasion of north-west France that would eventually lead to the occupation and defeat of Germany.

Both Churchill and the future Chief of the Imperial General Staff, General Sir Alan Brooke, and General Sir Bernard Paget, the commander of the British Home Forces, all understood that a Second Front was not even remotely possible without American aid and active participation in the war, as well as the creation of an entirely new British army. Under their tutelage the remnants of the BEF became the nucleus of a modern new force. New infantry, armour, engineer, artillery, and anti-aircraft regiments were activated, along with unconventional new organizations created solely to meet a variety of requirements, such as the Special Air Service for special operations; logistical formations to keep the implements of a modern army functioning; parachute and glider regiments to redress the need for airborne and glider operations, and the Combined Operations Headquarters under Mountbatten, to plan retaliation against German forces and develop new military equipment and the means to employ it. In the aftermath of Dunkirk an entirely new army was created and trained. From these humble beginnings in June 1940 it eventually expanded to more than 3 million men and 300,000 women.

Unable to attack the German armed forces directly, Churchill resorted to limited operations in North Africa against Mussolini's Italian army. General Sir Archibald Wavell's Western Desert Force became the nucleus for what later became the 8th Army. In early 1941 the British army won its first victory of the war when a mobile armoured force under the command of Lieutenant-General Sir Richard O'Connor outflanked and crushed the Italian 10th Army at Beda Fomm, in Cyrenaica. After advancing more than 500 miles in what has endured as a masterstroke of armoured manœuvre, O'Connor's force destroyed ten divisions, captured 130,000 prisoners and seriously threatened the Italian foothold in North Africa. For the next twenty months there was little else to sustain British morale as defeat piled upon defeat. In early 1941 Hitler sent a German expeditionary force under the command of General Erwin Rommel to North Africa to bolster the sagging fortunes of the Italians.

While Rommel prepared to advance against the British, a little known war was being fought in East Africa against the Italians in Eritrea, Ethiopia, Italian Somaliland, and Kenya by a combined Commonwealth force of British, South African, and Indian divisions. A two-pronged offensive began in January 1941 in Kenya and Italian Somaliland in the south and from the Sudan into Eritrea in the north, culminating in May 1941 with the surrender of all Italian forces in East Africa. Over 420,000 Italian and African troops were captured, Ethiopia was liberated, and Emperor Haile Selassie restored as ruler.

In early 1941, about the time Rommel began an aggressive series of forays with his German-Italian force against the British, Wavell's desert force was decimated by the transfer of a substantial portion of O'Connor's force to Greece and East Africa. In March 1941 Rommel attacked the British at El Agheila and boldly advanced into Cyrenaica towards Gazala and Tobruk, which was encircled and unsuccessfully attacked in late April and early May. For two months the two sides battled one another to a standstill. The Australian 9th Division gave Rommel a bloody nose at Tobruk but Wavell's counter-offensives at Sollum in mid May, and Operation Battleaxe, near Bardia, in mid-June both failed and the British withdrew behind the Egyptian border. Tobruk remained cut off and under siege, reinforced only by sea. On 5 July General Sir Claude Auchinleck replaced Wavell as Commander-in-Chief, Middle East.

During the remainder of 1941, Auchinleck reorganized the Western Desert Force for Operation Crusader, a counter-offensive aimed at relieving Tobruk and ejecting Rommel from Cyrenaica. Even though the British outnumbered Axis forces both on the ground and in the air,

Crusader was only partially successful, even though the offensive which began on 28 November caught Rommel flatfooted and obliged his Deutsches Afrika Korps (DAK) to retreat first to Gazala and, as 1941 ended, back to El Agheila. In mid-December the Western Desert Force was redesignated the 8th Army, under a new commander, Lieutenant-General Neil Ritchie, who replaced Lieutenant-General Alan Cunningham after the latter was sacked for mishandling Crusader. Rommel was resupplied in January 1942 and counter-attacked an over-extended 8th Army, forcing its retreat to the Gazala Line.

Elsewhere in 1941 the British army suffered defeat in Greece in one of the most ill-timed misadventures of the war. In March, Churchill ordered a British Expeditionary Force to Greece to reinforce the beleaguered Greeks. The decision not only stripped the Western Desert Force of vital troop units at a crucial moment of the desert war but quickly ended in heavy losses and yet another emergency evacuation, this time from the Peloponnese at the end of April.

In May 1941, German airborne forces suddenly invaded Crete. Although the Germans suffered heavy losses, the British garrison was compelled to evacuate the island whose capture seriously threatened British control of the eastern Mediterranean. Only in the Middle East was there a semblance of success in 1941 when, in June, a Commonwealth offensive to protect the vital oil pipelines from Iraq wrested control of Syria and Lebanon from Vichy French forces before the Germans could intervene.

At the end of May 1942, Rommel launched a fresh offensive against Tobruk by outflanking the heavily mined Gazala Line with his armour and attacking from the south. Unable to collapse the British defences, Rommel withdrew and literally circled his tanks in a western-style defence, fending off furious British attacks before finally smashing the Gazala Line at a defensive position called Knightsbridge. Rommel's audacity left him free to attack Tobruk, whose garrison surrendered on 21 June, resulting in huge losses in both men (30,000 captured) and *matériel* (3,000,000 rations and 500,000 gallons of precious petrol). Sensing imminent disaster if Rommel were permitted to retain the initiative, Auchinleck immediately relieved Ritchie and assumed direct control of the 8th Army which retreated in disarray 300 miles east into Egypt. It was the worst British defeat of the protracted desert war.

By late June, new defensive positions had been hastily established around El Alamein, as Rommel, now a field marshal, again attacked, this time in an attempt to finish off the 8th Army and break out into the Nile delta beyond. The first battle of Alamein raged for three weeks and when it ended on 3 July the 8th Army had held. In early August Churchill and Brooke visited the 8th Army and the Prime Minister decided the time had come for a change of command. Churchill relieved Auchinleck and replaced him with Lieutenant-General 'Strafer' Gott, who was killed *en route* to assume command and the little-known Montgomery was summoned from England to command the 8th Army.

Immediately after the surprise attack on Pearl Harbor on 7 December 1941, the Japanese began a series of offensives to capture strategically important locations in the Far East. The first to bear the brunt of Japanese aggression was Hong Kong on 8 December. The British-Canadian garrison consisted of only six battalions and twenty-eight artillery pieces. After holding out for five days from the New Territories to Kowloon, the remnants of the garrison withdrew to Hong Kong island which the Japanese invaded the night of 18–19 December, after a call for surrender was spurned by the British commander. Despite a gallant stand, the British and Canadian defenders were vastly outnumbered and could neither be reinforced nor escape. The survivors surrendered on Christmas night and those that managed to survive captivity were inhumanly treated by the Japanese.

On 8 December the Japanese landed unopposed in southern Siam and northern Malaya, quickly seized Bangkok, and began a drive into central Malaya which was defended by Lieutenant-General A. E. Percival's 10th Army, a mix of Australian, Indian, Malayan, and British troops. The insatiable world-wide demands for British and Commonwealth troops had left the 10th Army at only two-thirds of Percival's needs. In addition, his army was poorly trained and complacent, mistakenly believing they outmatched their Japanese opponent.

The British had no strategic plan for the defence of Malaya and had long gambled on defending Singapore and the strategically important British naval base against an attack from the sea. Thus, when the Japanese began a two-pronged ground offensive towards Singapore, Percival was unable both to defend against their advance and adequately prepare to defend the city. Even as the Japanese 25th Army began tightening the noose on Singapore, the 10th Army was attempting to defend the wrong approaches to the island. In seven days the Japanese overran Singapore and captured the bulk of the 10th Army on 15 February in what is widely regarded as the worst military disaster in the history of the British army and a terrible blow to Britain's war aims in the Far East. The capture of 130,000 British and Commonwealth troops was not only a humiliating defeat but also the latest in a series of military disasters that highlighted Britain's unpreparedness for global war. Churchill referred to the loss of Singapore as a 'grievous blow' and Brooke wrote in his diary: 'If the Army cannot fight better than it is doing at the present we shall deserve to lose our Empire.'

Japan's next target was Burma which was lightly defended and near the bottom of British military priorities in the Far East. With Siam safely under Japanese domination, Burma was invaded by elements of the 15th Army on 20 January 1942. Japanese spearheads succeeded in penetrating into central and northern Burma, and capturing the city of Lashio in late April. The main Japanese effort was aimed at Rangoon and, although four brigades of British and Commonwealth troops were rushed to Burma, they were only able to delay the fall of the Burmese capital until early March. Churchill sent General Sir Harold Alexander to Burma but he arrived in time only to preside over a mini-Dunkirk, the evacuation of Burma by sea.

In the West, a dramatic reversal of British fortunes in North Africa took place with the arrival of Montgomery and Alexander, the new Commander-in-Chief, Middle East. Montgomery galvanized the troops of the 8th Army by restoring their morale and fighting spirit. For the first time they became convinced that their new commanders would not let them down. Backed by Alexander, who ensured that the 8th Army's logistical needs were fully met, Montgomery readied his army to counter the long-awaited new offensive by Rommel. When it came on 31 August 1942 at Alam Halfa, the Axis offensive was aimed directly into the heart of Montgomery's well-planned defences, which were centred on Alam Halfa Ridge. By 7 September when Rommel's fuel and ammunition shortages led him to break off the attack, the 8th Army had won a defensive victory and bought the time Montgomery sought to permit preparations for a major British counter-offensive.

For nearly two months Montgomery continued to reorganize and train the 8th Army. New equipment included 300 Sherman tanks furnished by the United States, and air support was significantly enhanced by Montgomery's insistence that Air Marshal Arthur Coningham's RAF tactical air headquarters be co-located with the 8th Army. This became a model for air–ground co-operation on the modern battlefield. Montgomery's carefully prepared battle plan took full advantage of British superiority in troops, artillery, tanks, and aircraft. When it opened with one of the most thunderous artillery barrages of the war on 23 October 1942, the battle of El Alamein became the first time since 1940 that the British army was on the offensive.

The battle raged for twelve days. British artillery attacks were followed by a massive tank engagement in which both sides battered one another to an apparent bloody standstill. However, the 8th Army had more tanks and, in what became a battle of attrition, Rommel's tanks were steadily written off until a mere thirty-five of an original 500 remained operational. The long-sought breakthrough came near the coast at Kidney Hill on 3 November when the Axis minefields were finally breached. Despite heavy tank losses, which Montgomery could afford and Rommel could not sustain, the battle ended when Rommel broke contact and ordered the remnants of his panzer army to begin a fighting retreat into Libya. Alamein cost the 8th Army 13,500 casualties and 30,000 of Rommel's men were captured and 1,000 guns and 450 tanks lost.

El Alamein was the turning point of the war in the west, leading Churchill to proclaim: 'Before Alamein we never had a victory. After Alamein we never had a defeat.'

After regrouping, the 8th Army pursued Rommel's panzer army which fought a series of bloody rearguard actions with the British spearheads. Montgomery has been criticized for failing to trap and annihilate Rommel's army but bad weather, a rapidly lengthening supply line, the problem of administering a growing number of prisoners, and the fact that Rommel's rearguard remained capable of fighting effectively have all been cited as factors in his decision to take a more cautious approach. In mid-November, as Allied forces struggled to establish a fully operational front in western Tunisia, the 8th Army reached Tobruk, the scene of its severe defeat six months earlier.

Hitler reacted to the Allied Torch landings in French North Africa in November 1942 by ordering the immediate reinforcement of Tunisia and creating the 5th Panzer Army under Colonel-General Jürgen von Arnim. The first of some 100,000 additional German and Italian troops began arriving in Tunisia in early November.

The original aim of Allied operations in Tunisia was to secure the ports and lines of communication and then to trap and destroy Rommel's army in Tripolitania between the advancing 8th Army and the British 1st Army. By early February 1943, Rommel had retreated westward into the formidable Mareth Line. An attack by the 8th Army was certain but Rommel's major concern was an attack from the rear by Allied forces in Tunisia.

Field Marshal Bernard Montgomery

Bernard Law Montgomery was born in 1887, graduated from Sandhurst in 1908, and laboured for most of his long military career in the relative obscurity of the regular establishment, where he was known as an outspoken, if somewhat eccentric, officer whose only interest was in his profession.

During the First World War Montgomery served as an infantry officer and was severely wounded at the first battle of Ypres in 1914, won a DSO, and later became a divisional chief of staff, emerging from the war as a temporary lieutenant-colonel. The Great War left Montgomery appalled that battles such as the Somme, Arras, and Passchendaele produced tactics which turned men into cannon fodder and determined that no troops he led would ever be subjected to such 'colossal, murderous, mismanaged butchery'. The war also left him with a clear vision that 'the profession of arms was a life-study, and that few officers seemed to realise this fact'.

The neglect of the army during the inter-war years became proof of Montgomery's observation that the British were ill equipped, ill trained, badly led, and without adequate strategic and tactical doctrine to fight a modern war.

By the outbreak of the Second World War, he had risen to major-general and the command of the 3rd Division, which was in the vanguard of the British Expeditionary Force (BEF) in France in 1940. Montgomery fought brilliantly in France and was one of the last senior British officers to depart the beaches of Dunkirk. Despite the quaint British practice of magically turning military débâcles into glorious occasions, his assessment of the army had become a tragic reality at Dunkirk. Thereafter, he was given increasingly important assignments in the defence of England, first the command of the V and XII Corps, then, in November 1941, Eastern Command.

In early August 1942 Auchinleck was sacked by Churchill and Montgomery was summoned to North Africa to assume command of the 8th Army. Virtually overnight he became a hero throughout Britain for his exploits in besting Rommel, first at Alam Halfa and six weeks later at El Alamein. Henceforth, he became internationally known simply as 'Monty'.

Montgomery's meteoric leap from anonymity to national hero stirred the passions of friend and foe as no other Allied general of the Second World War has done. His hold upon the troops of the 8th Army was extraordinary. When Monty arrived in the desert he bluntly informed his officers and men that there would be no further withdrawal and no surrender. 'We will stand and fight here. If we can't stay here alive, then let us stay here dead.' His transformation of the 8th Army into the most successful fighting machine of the British army of the Second World War was one of the greatest leadership feats of that or any other war.

Monty's professionalism included an ability to select top-notch commanders and staff and leave them to perform their jobs. Those who failed to measure up were ruthlessly removed and replaced with 'Monty men', many of whom he had personally trained. He was an eminently practical soldier who exercised command with the loosest of reins, was notorious for rarely issuing written orders, and disdained uniform regulations. His own unauthorized uniform consisted of a plain grey sweater or a khaki shirt and either his famous black beret or an Australian bush hat festooned with the regimental badges of the units of the 8th Army.

Monty was never hesitant to state his views, no matter how blunt or outrageous, often causing even his staunchest mentors, such as Brooke, to despair over his lack of tact and his seemingly endless controversies with other senior Allied officers, particularly the Americans. British historian Shelford Bidwell has written of him: 'The trouble with Monty was that he was anything but a "nice chap", as Tedder said disparagingly of the desert generals who preceded him. He was cocky, boastful, exaggerated his successes and refused to admit to the slightest error, of which he made a number, as generals will, ran down his contemporaries and was in a very un-English way, unabashedly his own PR man.'

After Alamein he was promoted to full general and knighted but was criticized for his failure to destroy Rommel's German–Italian army during the pursuit from Alamein to Tunisia. In early 1943 the 8th Army fought for the first time as part of the new Anglo-American coalition led by General Dwight Eisenhower. Monty commanded British ground forces during the invasion of Sicily in July, and became embroiled in controversy with Patton over the capture of Messina.

Monty led the 8th Army in Italy until the end of 1943 when he was named to command the 21st Army Group for the long-awaited cross-Channel invasion of north-west France, Operation Overlord. As the acting Allied ground Commander-in-Chief, Monty revised the Overlord plan and commanded the highly successful Allied invasion on 6 June 1944.

When a stalemate seemed inevitable in July 1944 after the British 2nd Army was unable to capture Caen and the strategic Falaise plain, there were calls for his removal. Monty weathered these storms and was promoted to field marshal in September but generated further controversy over his handling of the

ill-fated airborne–ground operation, Market-Garden, intended to liberate Arnhem and obtain a bridgehead over the Rhine and a clear path to the Ruhr.

In December 1944, he took over the northern sector of the Allied front during
the Battle of the Bulge but so outraged Eisenhower by his repeated attempts to
gain control of all Allied ground forces that he was nearly relieved of command.
During the remaining months of the war, he led a large Anglo-American force
across the Rhine river and into the heartland of the crumbling Third Reich. In
May 1945 he accepted the surrender of German forces on the plains of
Lüneberg heath.

Complex, vain, irascible, opinionated and frequently controversial, Bernard
Montgomery was a superb trainer of troops, an inspirational leader, one of the
outstanding British generals of the Second World War, and one of a kind whose
like may never be seen again.

Rommel understood he had no prospect of defeating the 8th Army but by
defending the Mareth Line with minimum forces an opportunity existed
to attack and possibly defeat the inexperienced United States II Corps in
south-western Tunisia, which he and von Arnim nearly did at Kasserine
Pass and Sidi Bou Zid in mid-February.

The final battle between Montgomery and Rommel took place in early
March at Medenine, when Rommel launched an ill-conceived spoiling attack that was intended to disrupt the forthcoming 8th Army attack against
the Mareth Line. Montgomery had established powerful defensive positions between Medenine and Mareth, into which the unsuspecting Afrika
Korps plunged. By early April the 8th Army had cracked the Mareth Line,
and joined the Allied force in Tunisia.

For the first time in the war the British troops fought as part of an
Anglo-American coalition. This required a considerable adjustment for
Montgomery and his fiercely independent soldiers. No longer was the 8th
Army free to develop and implement its own operations; they were now
part of a larger Allied army group under Alexander, who reported to the
American Commander-in-Chief, General Dwight D. Eisenhower.
Throughout the remainder of the war there would be friction on both
sides over strategy on the battlefield.

Between December 1942 and May 1943 the newly created 1st British
Army fought its first battles in Tunisia where its inexperience often
showed. On 12 May 1943, von Arnim surrendered with the 250,000 sur-

vivors of Army Group Africa and the following day Alexander cabled Churchill to announce that the Tunisian campaign was over: 'All enemy resistance has ceased. We are masters of the North African shores.'

As would later happen in north-west Europe, British success in the North African and Tunisian campaigns was enhanced by Ultra intelligence derived from intercepts of the German Enigma cypher machine. Ultra intelligence was processed and disseminated by the clandestine government code-breaking facility at Bletchley Park and remained the best kept secret of the war until its revelation in 1974.

In January 1943, the Allies met at Casablanca to decide future strategy. The British declined to support the American desire for a cross-Channel invasion of north-west Europe in 1943. Churchill sought to buy time for its planning and preparation by nibbling away at what he termed 'the soft underbelly' of Germany. Only in the Mediterranean was there any immediate possibility of continuing the momentum of victory that had begun in North Africa. It was agreed that the Allies would invade the island of Sicily in the summer of 1943.

During the spring of 1943 the planning for Operation Husky, the invasion of Sicily, was frequently contentious when the Allied air, ground, and sea commanders could not agree on a plan for the assault landings. Finally, a compromise plan put forth by Montgomery was accepted.

The invasion of Sicily was spearheaded by the 8th Army and Lieutenant-General George S. Patton's US 7th Army. The 8th Army landings on the south-eastern coast between Syracuse and Cape Pássero were so successful that Montgomery ordered XXX Corps to push inland and XIII Corps to thrust up the coast towards Catania without delay. During the night of 13–14 July Montgomery launched a daring night airborne and glider operation to seize a key bridge on the northern edge of the plain of Catania by *coup de main*.

However, the airborne landings failed and, even when reinforced, XIII Corps failed to advance north of the bridge and capture Catania and the undefended coastal road to Messina north of the city. After a savage five-day battle Montgomery conceded failure and switched his main offensive effort to the north-west, where XXX Corps was ordered to break the German defences along the newly formed Etna Line and sweep around the northern edge of the Etna massif to the coast below Messina. But, by shifting his main effort to the west, Montgomery had split the 8th Army and unwittingly enabled the Germans to defend successfully against both the advance inland and along the coast. With Montgomery's blessing, Patton's 7th Army captured Messina in mid-August to end the Sicily campaign.

The Sicily campaign was the first example of Anglo-American discord and was so loosely controlled by Alexander that Montgomery and Patton were permitted to fight what amounted to two separate campaigns. The result was that the Germans were able to escape intact with most of their forces to the Italian mainland. Sicily also offered the first clear evidence that Montgomery's veteran army was showing distinct signs of having lost its edge after many months of unrelieved fighting in North Africa.

The Italian campaign opened on 3 September 1943 when Canadian and British infantry landed on the Italian side of the Strait of Messina only to discover that the Germans had withdrawn several days earlier and now oc-cupied positions in the rough mountainous terrain of central Calabria, at the neck of the Italian boot. During the first five days of the new campaign the 8th Army advanced with relative ease some 100 miles up the Italian boot and into southern Italy, while on the east and south-west coasts fur-ther landings were carried out by elements of the 8th Army.

Opposing the Allies in Italy was a German army group under the com-mand of Field Marshal Albert Kesselring, who skilfully manœuvred his forces during what became the longest and bloodiest campaign of the war fought by the Allies in the West.

On 9 September 1943 an Anglo-American task force of Lieutenant-General Mark Clark's US 5th Army made an amphibious assault landing below Naples, at Salerno. Code-named Avalanche, the Salerno landings were bitterly contested by the German 10th Army and for some days the outcome was in doubt as the Germans threatened to push the invaders back into the sea.

The Allied high command mistakenly believed that the German de-fence of Salerno presaged a full-scale retreat into northern Italy and a de-fence in the Apennines centred on Pisa and Rimini. The belief prevailed that Alexander's 15th Army Group would soon capture Rome, probably by the end of October 1943. Instead, the Germans began a fighting retreat to the north to the heavily defended Gustav Line, which was anchored at the town of Cassino.

Most of the Allied troops were exhausted after months of combat and in poor shape to sustain an offensive in the harsh weather and terrain of Italy. The most seriously impacted was the 8th Army, whose many veteran divisions were spent from endless combat that for most dated from El

Alamein the previous year. The battle ineffectiveness of the 8th Army was exacerbated by a growing manpower shortage throughout the British armed forces that seriously curtailed reinforcements for Italy, which was rated as a secondary theatre of war and given a very low priority.

A series of bloody battles lasting into mid-December failed to capture Cassino and turned the campaign into a stalemate. Allied strategy shifted towards finding a means of advancing into the Liri valley and thence to Rome. Alexander had concluded that he could not capture Rome unless the Allies initiated an amphibious end-run to draw away German troops manning the Gustav Line. An Anglo-American amphibious landing, code-named Shingle, was launched 80 miles to the north, at Anzio, by the US VI Corps on 22 January 1944.

The landings were virtually unopposed but by the end of D-Day the Germans had hastily moved 20,000 reinforcements to the vicinity of Anzio, and, in the days that followed, their build-up continued at a relentless pace. Unable to advance to Rome, the Allied force assumed a defensive posture. Hitler ordered a counter-offensive to 'lance the abscess south of Rome' by driving a wedge into the Allied left flank and destroying the beachhead. This commenced on 16 February and obliged the beachhead commander to commit every available resource to aid the beleaguered British and American defenders.

By 18 February the battle had reached the final Allied defensive line outside Anzio, where a valiant last-ditch stand successfully averted the collapse of the entire Allied left flank and the certain loss of the Anzio beachhead. This action was one of the finest examples of Anglo-American co-operation during a campaign that was otherwise marred by constant discord within the Allied command in Italy.

In December 1943, Montgomery was selected to command Allied ground forces for the cross-Channel invasion in 1944 and was succeeded by a protégé, Lieutenant-General Sir Oliver Leese, who lacked his predecessor's charisma and was unable to sustain the extraordinary pride and aura of invincibility that had so distinguished the 8th Army under Monty. Between December 1943 and March 1944 two attempts to capture Cassino and the ancient abbey on the heights above the town failed. In mid-March 1944 a third attempt was made when a thunderous artillery barrage from 900 guns and a massive aerial bombardment pulverized the town. However, the follow-up ground attacks on both ended in failure and heavy casualties.

On 11 May 1944 Alexander launched Operation Diadem, the fourth

D-Day, 6 June 1944

On the morning of 6 June 1944, Allied forces launched the greatest amphibious operation in the history of warfare; 155,000 Allied troops parachuted from the skies, landed by glider, and stormed the beaches of Normandy from Caen in the east to the Carentan peninsula in the west. Operation Overlord, the long-awaited cross-Channel invasion, was the result of planning, logistics, and execution on a scale never before attempted.

The invasion of Normandy began late on the night of 5 June and the early morning hours of 6 June when massive airborne landings took place near Caen and in the western sector in the Carentan peninsula. The British 6th Airborne Division assaulted both sides of the Orne river and the Orne canal sector north of the ancient city of Caen by parachute and glider landings. Their mission was to secure intact the vital Pegasus bridge, the only bridge over both the river and the canal between Caen and the sea, and to destroy German communications centres and strongpoints that menaced the nearby landings on Sword beach by the British 3rd Division. Major John Howard's glider-borne infantry of D Company, 2nd Oxfordshire and Buckinghamshire Light Infantry, captured and held Pegasus bridge against determined German attempts to retake it.

At dawn, Lord Lovat's élite 1st Commando Brigade landed on the extreme left flank of the British sector. Their mission was to knock out the German artillery batteries at Ouistreham, link up with the 6th Airborne Division, and hold the left flank of the beachhead until the British I Corps was established ashore.

At the same time the US 82nd and 101st Airborne Divisions were parachuted into the Carentan estuary to secure the terrain and support the landings on Utah beach by the US VII Corps. In the darkness the paratroopers landed over a wide area and were unable to link up with their units. Nevertheless, operating in small groups, they severely disrupted German attempts to interfere with the Utah landings on 6 June.

Before dawn over 1,000 British aircraft dumped more than 5,000 tons of bombs on the German coastal defences in the British landing sector. Then the guns of the Allied fleet opened fire across the Normandy front.

On D-Day Allied ground forces landed in three separate sectors. In the east, Lieutenant-General Miles Dempsey's 2nd British Army landed three divisions and three armoured brigades of the I Corps on Sword, Juno, and Gold beaches

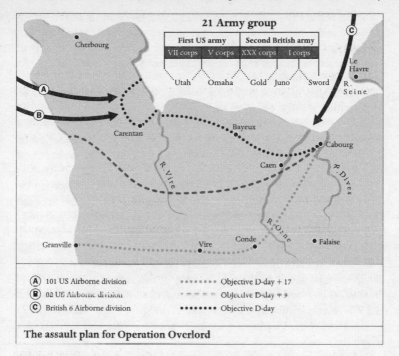

The assault plan for Operation Overlord

Legend:
- (A) 101 US Airborne division
- (B) 82 US Airborne division
- (C) British 6 Airborne division
- • • • • • • • Objective D-day + 17
- – – – – – Objective D-day + 9
- • • • • • • • Objective D-day

in the Caen sector. Their mission was to seize Caen and anchor the Allied left flank. Within two and a half hours 30,000 men, 300 guns, and 700 armoured vehicles came ashore. Although the Canadian 3rd Division took more than two hours to crush German resistance in the Juno sector and open exits so that they could begin moving inland, overall the British landings went exceptionally well.

In the US sector, the VII Corps landings on Utah beach by the 4th Infantry Division achieved total surprise, the least opposition, and the fewest casualties of any Allied assault unit. The landings on Omaha beach by the veteran 1st Infantry Division and a regiment of the 29th Infantry Division ran into heavy resistance from the German 325th Division which, despite Ultra, had managed to escape the attention of Allied intelligence when it moved into the Omaha sector three months earlier. From the steep bluffs overlooking Omaha beach the Germans poured artillery, mortar, and automatic weapons fire, inflicting heavy casualties on the confused and badly exposed troops.

For the first six hours the invaders held only a few yards of beach, which remained under intense enemy fire. It soon became evident to the American commanders that to remain where they were was suicidal and they rallied their men. American leadership and exceptional acts of gallantry by men of all ranks saved the Omaha beachhead.

Nevertheless, throughout 6 June the situation on Omaha remained so perilous that the US 1st Army commander, Lieutenant-General Omar N. Bradley, seriously considered evacuating the beachhead and switching the follow-up units to the British sector or to Utah beach. US casualties on D-Day in the Omaha sector alone numbered over 2,000 killed, wounded, or missing.

Despite often savage resistance, the Germans were unable to prevent the Allied invaders from establishing a firm beachhead in Normandy. Although Caen was not captured and the British later became stalled before the city, they had managed to fend off what were mostly weak and badly co-ordinated German counter-attacks.

On that momentous day over 130,000 Allied ground troops and 23,000 airborne were landed in Normandy. In spite of the unexpected setbacks at Omaha, the invasion was a stunning success. In all, 195,700 naval personnel in 6,939 vessels participated in one way or another in the D-Day landings: 1,213 combat ships, 4,126 landing craft, 736 ancillary ships, and 864 merchant ships.

On 5 and 6 June the Allied air forces flew 14,000 sorties in support of the landings. The Allies lost 12,000 officers and men killed and 2,000 aircraft in the period 1 April to 5 June in support of pre-D-Day operations over France.

Total Allied losses on D-Day have never been precisely established but appear to have exceeded 10,000, with American losses of 6,603 the highest: 1,465 killed, 3,184 wounded, and 1,928 missing in action. These figures include 2,499 killed, wounded, or missing in the two US airborne divisions. British and Canadian losses were approximately 3,000.

In April 1944 the German commander, Field Marshal Erwin Rommel, had predicted the importance of this day: 'The first 24-hours of the invasion will be decisive . . . the fate of Germany depends on the outcome . . . for the Allies, as well as Germany, it will be the longest day.'

Rommel was correct: 6 June 1944 was the most decisive day of the Second World War. It marked the beginning of the end of Hitler's Third Reich and, after 1,453 days of German occupation, the first step in the liberation of France.

attempt to break the Gustav Line. Allied preparations included the most massive build-up of artillery ever undertaken in the war. When the Polish II Corps succeeded in capturing the monastery of Monte Cassino on 17 May, the long-sought breakthrough was at last realized by British and Canadian troops. The collapse of the Gustav Line forced Kesselring to abandon the Cassino front and begin a full-scale retreat on 22 May.

The next day, after a siege that had lasted nearly four months, more than a thousand Allied guns signalled the opening of a similar Allied breakout offensive from the Anzio beachhead. The difficult and bitter final days of the Allied drive on Rome were characterized by the same bloodletting and painfully slow advances that were the hallmark of the entire Italian campaign.

The Allied capture of Rome on 5 June came at a terrible price. During the desperate months of the Anzio beachhead the Allies lost 7,000 killed and 36,000 more were wounded or reported missing in action. In addition, another 44,000 were hospitalized from various non-battle injuries and sickness. On 6 June 1944 the fall of Rome was all but forgotten as Operation Overlord, the long-delayed, long-debated cross-Channel invasion of Normandy commenced in France. The remnants of the German 10th and 14th Armies made good their northward retreat and between June 1944 and the end of the war in May 1945, the 8th Army remained in Italy and fought a long and bloody series of battles of attrition in northern Italy.

Dunkirk was avenged in June 1944 when the Allies launched Operation Overlord, the invasion of Normandy. The British element was Lieutenant-General Miles Dempsey's 2nd Army, an enormous force which eventually consisted of five corps, eight infantry, three armoured, and one airborne division, plus a large number of independent brigades.

Although the initial landing operations were a stunning success, the strategy devised by Montgomery for the 21st Army Group was thwarted by the fanatical resistance of German troops. Under the overall command of his long-time nemesis, Rommel, the German army in Normandy managed to hold the vital city of Caen and the strategically important Caen–Falaise plain to the south. An opportunity to have encircled Caen from the west shortly after D-Day was botched and repeated attempts to capture the city through frontal attacks produced not only heavy losses but mounting criticism that Montgomery had lost control of the campaign. By the end of June the two sides were locked in a protracted stalemate outside Caen.

The performance of the British army in Normandy was mixed. At

Montgomery's insistence, three veteran 8th Army divisions were in the vanguard of the invasion. But instead of providing the stability he had counted on, two were overcautious, fought poorly, and did not seem prepared to cope with the difficult *bocage* terrain of Normandy which the Germans used to great advantage. Too many months of combat, the loss of key NCOs and officers, and a growing belief that too much had been asked of them for too long led to the relief of several senior commanders of the 7th Armoured Division, the famous Desert Rats who had bested the Italians in 1940 and fought brilliantly at Alamein. In the 51st Highland Division there were similar sackings before performance eventually improved.

The heaviest casualties were in the infantry units where officers were being killed at an exceptionally high rate. Along with a steady wasting-away of the infantry in the Normandy *bocage*, there was a noticeable decline in the performance of junior leaders, mainly in the NCO ranks, where the best had either become casualties or been promoted to the officer ranks. This, in turn, resulted in company officers taking up the slack by accomplishing tasks normally performed by NCOs. By the end of June losses in company commanders had reached crisis proportions.

After many days of unrelieved combat, morale was often on the wane and in some units it was seriously deficient. British tactics contributed to the problem. It was not that the men of the infantry lacked courage, but a tendency to fight battles of attrition brought out a realism among their leaders which dictated that there were definite limits as to what they could expect from their men. Discipline, training, and morale were of the highest calibre in the airborne and commando units, but in the average British infantry formation problems all too often could be traced to generally inadequate battle indoctrination in England.

One of the deadliest battles took place in late June when the VIII Corps, aided by massive artillery support, launched Operation Epsom, an attempt to out-flank Caen from the west by a powerful right hook across the River Odon. Epsom became a desperate infantry struggle and one of the bloodiest battles fought in the Second World War by either side. The Germans turned a formidable obstacle called Hill 112 into a deathtrap and when German and British casualties became so high that it became dammed up with corpses, the usually placid river was dubbed the 'Bloody Odon'.

British problems were compounded by the steady drain of manpower which by early July was so critical that Montgomery and Dempsey were warned that the War Office could no longer keep pace with the growing number of reinforcements required in Normandy. By the end of July Montgomery was obliged to disband combat formations, including the entire 59th Division. The pressing need to avoid further heavy casualties also impacted the thinking of both Montgomery and Dempsey when planning their battles. One of the major operations of the Normandy campaign, Operation Goodwood, a massive British tank attack to break the German grip on Caen by employing heavy bombers to blast a path that three armoured divisions could exploit to gain access to the Caen–Falaise plain, was influenced by the need to reduce infantry losses at the expense of tank losses, which could be more easily replaced.

Although Goodwood failed, a similar American operation in the west, Operation Cobra, initiated by Lieutenant-General Omar Bradley, broke the stalemate and precipitated a break-out by Patton's 3rd Army at Avranches on 1 August. When German resistance collapsed east of the Caen–Falaise plain the Canadian 1st Army and Dempsey's 2nd British Army began a similar drive to the Seine.

After fierce battles Falaise fell to the Canadians on 16 August. Montgomery sent the Polish 1st Armoured Division and elements of a Canadian corps eastward in an attempt to block the mouth of the Falaise Gap. Three days later the gap was finally closed. Except for mopping-up operations the battle of Normandy was over.

In late August and early September British, Canadian, and American troops swept across France during the most fluid period of the Second World War in the western front. As the Canadian 1st Army began clearing the Pas de Calais and the heavily defended Scheldt estuary around Antwerp, spearheads of the 2nd Army slashed their way across the French border into southern Belgium.

The original Allied intent to pause and regroup at the Seine was hastily scrapped in favour of a pursuit designed to crush the German army before it had an opportunity to defend the borders of the Reich. This decision led to one of the greatest controversies of the war, the broad front versus the narrow front question that pitted Eisenhower and Montgomery against one another. Eisenhower's post-Normandy strategy called for a broad advance by the Allied armies into Germany. Montgomery's 21st Army Group would approach Germany through Belgium towards the Ruhr industrial complex, while Bradley's 12th Army Group advanced to the south, covering the British right flank. Eisenhower rejected Montgomery's plan for a single, full-blooded thrust towards the Ruhr with the two army groups abreast.

On 3 September Brussels was liberated by the British, as was Antwerp the following day. But, in what has widely been regarded as one of the great blunders of the war, neither Montgomery nor Dempsey ordered the capture of the vital Scheldt estuary which temporarily remained in German hands, thus delaying the opening of the port of Antwerp.

As the Allied armies advanced ever closer to Germany, plans went forward for the largest airborne operation of the war. In an attempt to keep alive his single thrust concept, Montgomery devised a daring plan to open the way to the heartland of the Ruhr by means of airborne and glider landings. The British 1st Airborne Division was to seize a bridgehead north of the Rhine river, at Arnhem, and this was to be followed by a ground thrust to relieve the airborne division by Dempsey's 2nd Army. The airborne part of the operation was code-named Market. Garden was the ground side in which XXX Corps was to link up at Arnhem by thrusting north along a narrow corridor opened by the US 82nd and 101st Airborne Divisions. Once in control of the vital Arnhem bridge, the 2nd Army was to turn the German flank and rapidly assault the Ruhr through the so-called back door to Germany, thus hastening the collapse of the Third Reich and likely ending the war in 1944.

On 17 September, the largest airborne and glider operation ever mounted took place. More than 5,000 aircraft participated but, though the landings initially went well, Allied intelligence had failed to heed reports from the Dutch underground that the German II SS Panzer Corps was bivouacked outside Arnhem. Lieutenant-Colonel John Frost's 2nd Parachute Battalion was the only unit to reach the bridge. The remainder of the division was soon pinned down in and around Arnhem.

The success of the operation hinged on the ability of XXX Corps rapidly to relieve the lightly armed airborne troops at each of the bridges along their route of march. Congestion and German resistance along the single narrow road to Nijmegen and Arnhem delayed the British ground advance. The attempt to relieve Arnhem failed even though Frost's gallant paratroopers held the northern end of Arnhem bridge against the 9th SS Panzer Division for four days before being overrun and captured.

By 25 September an attempt was made to save the remnants of the 1st Airborne Division but only 2,400 Polish and British paratroopers safely crossed to the south bank of the Rhine in small rubber boats. Of the

10,300 men who had landed at Arnhem, 1,300 had been killed and over 6,400 captured. The 1st Airborne ceased to exist as a fighting unit and was never reconstituted in the aftermath of the battle.

What had begun with high optimism had turned into a military disaster. Although the stand of Frost's battalion at Arnhem bridge is widely considered one of the most heroic episodes of the Second World War, Operation Market-Garden had failed to establish a bridgehead north of the Rhine in what has come to be popularly known as 'a bridge too far'.

The failure at Arnhem led to a stalemate during the autumn and early winter of 1944–5. Although Allied forces advanced to the borders of the Third Reich, a hasty defence by German units and the advent of bad weather left the Allies virtually immobilized in the mud, snow, and the harsh terrain of the outer Ruhr and in the Ardennes forest. During this period British forces fought a series of battles of attrition, gained little in the way of significant ground, but suffered greatly from combat losses and the winter weather.

Seeking to repeat the success of 1940, Hitler gambled on a last-ditch attempt to split the Allied armies by a sudden, lightning blitzkrieg thrust through the Ardennes to destroy all Allied forces north of a line running from Bastogne to Antwerp, naïvely believing his armies could drive clear to Antwerp and oblige the Allies to sue for peace.

The Battle of the Bulge began in heavy fog early on 16 December when two panzer armies attacked the most lightly defended sector of the US 1st Army. The Ardennes became bedlam as American units became entangled in a series of desperate battles around St. Vith, Elsenborn Ridge, Houffalize, and Bastogne. Although Montgomery took command of all Allied forces north of the German penetration, the Ardennes counter-offensive involved few British units. A crucial shortage of petrol and the gallantry of American troops fighting in the frozen forests of the Ardennes proved fatal to Hitler's ambition somehow to snatch, if not victory, at least a draw with the Allies and a voice in the terms of Germany's surrender.

By mid-January 1945 German attacks had run their course and the Allies had gone over to the offensive. German losses were estimated at over 100,000 and were irreplaceable. As the Allied leadership contemplated how to conduct the invasion of Germany the lingering arguments from the previous year resumed. Eisenhower insisted that his armies continue to advance across a broad front to the Rhine in the form of two major thrusts, one in the north under Montgomery, the other in the south under Bradley. Montgomery and the British Chiefs of Staff continued to

Field Marshal Sir William Slim

William Joseph Slim was born in London in August 1891, the son of a middle-class Bristol iron merchant. His ambition was always to become an army officer, and after being educated at St Philip's Catholic School and King Edward's School, Slim entered the army in 1914 through the Officer Training Corps with a commission in the Royal Warwickshire Regiment. He saw service during the First World War with the 9th Battalion, first in France and later at Gallipoli and Mesopotamia, where he was so severely wounded in 1915 that he was not expected ever to be reinstated to active duty. Even though not declared medically fit, Slim nevertheless returned to his unit in Mesopotamia and won a Military Cross, was again wounded, and was evacuated to India where he spent the remainder of the war.

In 1919 Slim transferred to the Indian Army and spent the inter-war years in a variety of command and staff assignments, gaining promotion and recognition as a quiet but brilliant officer of considerable promise. He returned to England to teach at the Staff College, Camberley, from 1934 to 1936 and to attend the Imperial Defence College in 1937. By 1939 Slim was a brigadier and, with the outbreak of the Second World War, he was sent to the Sudan in command of the 10th Brigade of the 5th Indian Division in late 1940, where he was wounded for the third time fighting the Italians.

Slim was promoted to major-general in 1941 and given command of the 10th Indian Division which fought in Syria, Iraq, and Persia, winning the DSO for his success against the Vichy French. He returned to India and in March 1942 was promoted to lieutenant-general and ordered by Wavell to organize and command the 1st Burma Corps. Slim's first duty was to oversee its retreat after Japanese invasion forces overran Rangoon and Burma was lost.

In the autumn of 1943 Slim became the commander of the new 14th Army and masterminded the creation and training of the first British force capable of beating the Japanese at their own game. He took advantage of the difficulty of operating offensively in the dense jungle and mountains of northern Burma and southern Assam by evolving a strategy of establishing heavily self-contained strong points around the vital towns of Kohima and Imphal that the Japanese must attack if their aim of annexing northern Burma was to succeed. Preliminary Japanese attacks in the Arakan in early 1944 were not only blunted but their offensive in the summer against Kohima and Imphal was shattered. Slim's strategy in Mandalay completely deceived the Japanese and enabled the 14th

Army to open an offensive that led to the recapture of Burma in the spring of 1945. In both defensive and offensive roles Slim proved himself a master strategist.

Throughout the Burma campaign Slim successfully contended with the command problems posed by Chiang Kai-shek and his Nationalist Chinese army and the independent-minded mavericks, Major-General Orde Wingate, the Chindit commander, and General 'Vinegar Joe' Stilwell, who was Chiang's chief of staff and the commander of all American forces in the China–Burma–India theatre.

In May 1945 the new commander of Allied Land Forces, South-East Asia, Lieutenant-General Sir Oliver Leese, capriciously dismissed Slim from his post as 14th Army commander. There was outrage and dismay in the 14th Army at what has come to be regarded as one of the most incomprehensible and ill-advised misjudgements by a British general during the war. At the instigation of the Chief of the Imperial General Staff, Field Marshal Sir Alan Brooke, Leese was himself relieved by Mountbatten and Slim was promoted to general and appointed to the post in August 1945.

Slim retired in 1947 but late the following year was recalled to active duty to become a field marshal and the Chief of the Imperial General Staff, succeeding Montgomery. He has been acclaimed as one of the most outstanding CIGS of the post-war era, a position he held until 1953. When he retired for the second time it was to become one of the most popular governor-generals (1953–60) of Australia ever to hold that post.

A commander of uncommon good sense, he was known familiarly and affec-tionately by his troops as 'Uncle Bill'. Slim was unpretentious and of modest temperament, yet the unwary soon learned that he was possessed of an iron will. To have succeeded in one of the most difficult theatres of war required both traits. One of the most successful British generals of the Second World War, Slim's post-war account of the Burma campaigns, *Defeat Into Victory*, has been hailed as one of the pre-eminent memoirs of the Second World War. Typ-ically, he gave the credit to the soldiers who fought under his command and thanked his sergeant-major during his cadet days for teaching him that there was only one successful principle of war: 'Hit the other fellow, as quick as you can, and as hard as you can, where it hurts him most, when he ain't lookin'!' Slim never forgot this counsel and in Burma was the architect who did indeed turn defeat into victory in the harshest terrain in which the British army of the Second World War fought.

The campaigns in the Far East never earned the fanfare of those in the West and Slim's quiet demeanour never brought him the publicity accorded other better-known commanders, such as Alexander and Montgomery. Yet, by the time he died in 1970, Slim's reputation as one of the great captains of the British army of the Second World War was secure. Lord Mountbatten has said that Slim was 'the finest general the Second World War produced' and his biographer, Ronald Lewin, has written of him: 'Few have surpassed William Joseph Slim in that gift which Liddell Hart attributed to Marlborough—"the power of commanding affection while communicating energy." His military distinction was founded on his humanity.'

support a powerful offensive in the north to breach the Rhine and capture the Ruhr. Eisenhower ceded priority of effort to the British and attached the US 9th Army to the 21st Army Group. In what constituted the largest military force ever assembled, nearly 4,000,000 US, British, and Canadian troops of three army groups, seven field armies, twenty-one corps, and seventy-three divisions were poised to launch the final offensive that would finish off Nazi Germany and end the war. By VE Day these numbers would grow to 4.5 million men and ninety-one divisions.

On 23 March 1945 Montgomery launched Operation Plunder, a massive offensive that included another large airborne and glider operation by two parachute divisions. The Rhine was breached at numerous points, while to the south Bradley's 12th Army Group also secured bridgeheads east of the river. By the end of March 300,000 enemy troops of Army Group B were trapped in the rapidly closing Ruhr pocket.

Throughout April the rampaging Allied armies began mopping up pockets of resistance from the central plains to the Alps, capturing tens of thousands of prisoners, and drawing the noose ever tighter. On 8 May 1945 the war in Europe formally ended when Germany surrendered unconditionally in Reims, France.

In December 1942, Wavell, now the Commander-in-Chief, India, took the first step towards liberating Burma when he ordered an offensive against the Japanese in the Arakan. However, it proved to be an ill-conceived venture, resulting in the virtual destruction of the 14th Indian Division in the spring of 1943.

Yet the tide began to turn in the Far East that spring with the appointment of Lieutenant-General Sir William Slim as commander of the newly created British 14th Army, which was mainly comprised of Indian Army formations. Operations were severely hampered by the immense jungle region that comprised the Burma theatre. The logistical considerations of building airfields (some behind enemy lines), roads, and the development of bases in India to support operations in Burma, necessitated that 95 per cent of resupply be carried out by air.

The British had better success when long-range forays deep behind Japanese lines by Major-General Orde Wingate's Chindit force harassed and distracted the Japanese and indirectly led to attacks by the 15th Army in the early spring of 1944 against British bases at Imphal and Kohima, in north-east India. The Japanese had previously elected for a defensive strategy in Burma but decided a limited offensive into north-east India would disrupt an expected British offensive into Burma later in 1944.

Imphal and Kohima were the decisive battles of the India–Burma campaign and when they ended in July 1944 had resulted in the loss of 30,000 killed and the virtual destruction of the Japanese 15th Army. Under Slim's steady hand the 14th Army began an offensive in late 1944 that drove the Japanese behind the Irrawaddy river and, by May 1945, out of Burma.

Although the British soldier of 1939–45 was better trained and equipped than his counterpart of the Great War, there was little to distinguish the two from one another. He fought well when properly led but lacked the soldierly instincts that characterized the German army. As General Sir David Fraser has written of the British army of the Second World War:

It was sometimes ponderous and lacking in élan. It rarely showed the 'handiness' in mobile battle which was the hallmark of the Afrika Korps. But it came to know its business. And, without histrionics, it did it. Providence, the extraordinary course of events, and the mistakes of the enemy provided time for the army to make good its mistakes, repair and restart the machine and drive it to ultimate triumph. They were, at the beginni ng, too often ineptly commanded and placed in situations where no soldier could win. They were, at the end, richly endowed with equipment, worthily led, confident, skilful and deservedly victorious.

14 THE ARMY AND THE HOME FRONT 1939–1945

ALEX DANCHEV

When this regiment was formed our country was doing pretty badly. Napoleon's armies were just across the Channel getting ready to invade us and a great many people thought we were finished. We weren't. But not because we were lucky. When the first battalion of this regiment marched it was against Napoleon. Talavera, 1809. That was the first battle they made their own. And they marched 42 miles in 24 hours of a Spanish summer. And every man jack of 'em carried a 60 lb pack. Talavera. Look at your cap badges, you'll see the name on it . . . and the other battles too: Barrosa, Sabugal. At Sabugal they defeated five times the number of Napoleon's troops. Salamanca, Orthez, Waterloo, Alma, Sebastopol, Tel-el-Kebir, Mons, Ypres, Somme . . . those are battle honours. You're allowed to wear that badge with those names on it to show that you belong to the regiment that won them and that when the time comes, you'll do as well as they did. Last year that badge was in France, this year in Libya. It hasn't been disgraced yet. And now *you're* wearing it . . .

Thus said Lieutenant Jim Perry of the fictitious DOGS (Duke of Glendon's Light Infantry) dressing down his platoon in the key sequence of *The Way Ahead* (1944), a somewhat belated attempt by the Ministry of Information to do for the army what *In Which We Serve* (1942) had done so successfully for the navy. The film-makers' declared aim was threefold: to make everyone who saw it say, 'There, that's what our Bert is doing. Isn't it wonderful?', or, 'See, we old-timers started something in the last lot', or, in the all-important American audience, 'The British Army is OK.' The project had been under discussion since 1942, sparked off by concern about the maintenance of morale, within the army and without, in the years after the Blitz and before Alamein—Elizabeth Bowen's lightless middle of the tunnel: 'Reverses, losses, deadlocks now almost unnoticed bred one another; every day the news hammered one more nail into a consciousness which no longer resounded. Everywhere hung the heaviness of the even worse you could not be told and could not desire to hear.' For 6027033 Private Ross J. (alias the dandy Julian Maclaren-Ross), languishing in the Infantry Training Camp at Blandford, Dorset, it was the Brown Period: ' "Browned-off" was the phrase one heard most often in X Company, the other recruits owing to difficulty in finding any skirt started jocosely to talk of having Bits of Brown [buggery], the RAF blokes stationed next door called us Brown Jobs, it was autumn and the leaves were brown, and everything was uniquely brown.' Propaganda films were not the only manifestation of official concern. The Army Bureau of Current Affairs (ABCA) was established precisely to combat barrack-room lassitude.

The Way Ahead derived from an original treatment by Major David Niven of the Rifle Brigade and Captain Carol Reed, Lieutenant Eric Ambler, and Private Peter Ustinov of the Army Kinematograph Service. Not surprisingly, given the galaxy of talent assembled, it is both more subtle and more revealing than a straightforward recapitulation of its aims might suggest. Perry, for example, is no chinless wonder. He is a garage mechanic who was in the Territorial Army before the war, commissioned after serving as a sergeant in France. He is energetic, capable, and humane. He is also working class. Improbably, he is played by Major Niven.

The film focuses on the officer, Perry, and seven newly conscripted men in his platoon: Davenport, a self-important store manager; Parsons, his fawning assistant; Brewer, a stoker at the House of Commons; Luke, a Scottish farmer; Lloyd, a pretentious rent collector; Stainer, an up-market car salesman; and Beck, a travel agency clerk. Symptomatically, the occasion for the dressing down is a military exercise in which the platoon, led by Lloyd and Stainer, deliberately allow themselves to be 'killed' in order to get back to barracks as early as possible, thereby letting down the whole battalion. One can imagine what Colonel Blimp would have said. 'Gad sir, the only way to teach people self-respect is to treat 'em like the curs they are.' Perry, it will be noted, does not fall for this. Instead he adopts a distinctly unblimpish approach. He plays on feelings of guilt. 'If you ever get near any real fighting—I don't suppose you'll ever be good enough, but *if* you do—you'll find that you're looking to other men not to let you down.' He is strong on tradition—the DOGS are clearly one of the better regiments—but is neither reactionary nor authoritarian. 'All right Sergeant,' he says in conclusion, 'they can have their tea.'

The principal characters in *The Way Ahead* are a roughly representative sample according to age, occupation, and social status of this latter-day new model army. Opinions differ on the effectiveness of the military melting pot. The poet Alun Lewis, a fiercely socialist subaltern in the South Wales Borderers, was shipped out to India on the *Athlone Castle* in October 1942. His report on the voyage raised a stir in the pages of the *New Statesman and Nation*.

The ship was monstrously overcrowded; a svelte luxury liner, it reflected precisely the social system that constructed it. The 500 officers had a pretty good time; all berthed in cabins, albeit overloaded; dining in a saloon as vulgarly sumptuous as any classy hotel with menus printed daily in bastard French and meals of impeccable quality and length; champagne at 7s. 6d. a bottle, spirits and liqueurs at 6d. The other ranks numbered upwards of 4,000. They lived in the rolling bowels of the ship, in tiered bunks that crammed the holds. Their quarters stank of sweat and vomit and oranges, of which there was a weekly free issue. As soon as we entered warmer zones the congestion was relieved by a rush to the open decks, where they slept like Arabs under the great tree of the stars. There was some resentment at the extreme difference between 'First' and 'Third', and one man was court-martialled for saying the officers were doing well for themselves. The truth of his statement was not the point at issue.

Nevertheless, he continued, morale was excellent. Life on the ocean wave had its compensations. There were ports of call in two continents, and many strange sights to be seen—whales and albatrosses, and even shipwrecked sailors.

And the ship itself we converted into something of a floating Utopia [Lewis himself was Entertainments Officer], with nightly concerts and daily Brains Trusts, Quiz contests and piano recitals, and public debates on the troop deck at a spot which was christened Hyde Park Corner. The audience at these meetings wore PT shorts, drank from beer and lemonade bottles and stood up and discussed Emigration, War, and Social Justice; a padre advocated Socialism, a Palestine Jew collective farming, a lieutenant-colonel a political Sermon on the Mount. *Pas mal!*

The National Service (Armed Forces) Act of 3 September 1939 made all men between the ages of 20 and 41 liable for conscription. Related acts extended the terms of service for all personnel, regulars and Territorials alike, to the conclusion of the present emergency; Territorials also became liable for overseas service. Initially the call-up proceeded at snail's pace.

The systematic registration of each age group reached those aged 27 in May 1940 and those aged 40 in June 1941. (Anyone who wished to hasten the process could volunteer; some 1.5 million did so during the course of the war.) The registrant had to give full details of his occupation and state a preference as between the three armed services. A schedule of reserved occupations with qualifying ages had been drawn up the previous year. If the man's occupation appeared on the schedule, he was 'reserved' from conscription provided that he had attained the relevant qualifying age (18 for lighthouse keepers, 21 for physicists, 30 for trade unionists). Alternatively, he could apply for deferment, or register his conscientious objection. Over the whole period more than 200,000 applications for deferment were accepted; a sizeable proportion of these were renewed. Conscientious objection fell sharply from twenty-two in every thousand called up in October 1939 to six in every thousand called up in July 1940. Forty years later the radical historian E. P. Thompson recalled the time when he was not an activist in the peace movement, but 'a soldier in what I supposed (and still suppose) to have been a necessary anti-fascist war'. Such was the prevailing sentiment. Hitler had to be squashed. There was no need for white feathers in the Second World War.

By mid-1941 the shortage of manpower had become acute. After much ministerial soul-searching, the National Service (No. 2) Act of 18 December 1941 required everyone between the ages of 18 and 60 to undertake some form of 'national service', and drastically extended the call-up: downwards and upwards to men of 18 and 51, and sideways to women— an unprecedented development, at first carefully circumscribed. Only un-married women between the ages of 20 and 30 were liable. They could choose between service in industry (usually in the munitions factories), civil defence, and the auxiliary services, of which the Auxiliary Territorial Service (ATS) was one. Those opting for the last were not given 'combat-ant duties' unless they volunteered for them. After a few months it became clear that only about 25 per cent would opt for the services. Further meas-ures had to be taken. Women born in 1920 and 1921 were withdrawn from their jobs and put into uniform, unless their work was deemed vital. In July 1943 it was announced that all women up to the age of 51 would be registered. The ATS reached its maximum strength (212,500) a few months later. War had compelled equality of a sort.

In total, these measures amounted to the most complete mobilization of any of the major powers, except perhaps the Soviet Union. At the be-ginning of the war the regular army consisted of some 259,000 men. The

Table 14.1 *Strengths of the Armed Services, 1945*

	Army	Navy	Air Force	Total	Ratio total: 20–5 male age group
UNITED KINGDOM	2,920,000	783,000	950,000	4,653,000	2.68
AUSTRALIA	366,000	34,000	170,000	570,000	1.84
CANADA	462,000	93,000	215,000	770,000	1.49
NEW ZEALAND	53,000	11,000	33,000	97,000	1.47
INDIA	1,730,000	30,000	29,000	1,789,000	0.11

[Figures for South Africa not available.]

Table 14.2 *Army Strength and Population*

	Army/strength June/July 1945	20–5 male age group	Ratio strength: age group
UNITED KINGDOM	2,920,000	1,737,000	1.68
AUSTRALIA	365,800 (473,800 max.)	309,500	1.18 (1.53)
CANADA	461,800 (479,000 max.)	518,000	0.89 (0.93)
NEW ZEALAND	53,000 (125,000 max.)	66,000	0.81 (1.89)
INDIA	1,730,000	16,315,000	0.11

[Figures for South Africa not available.]

total number of Territorials and reserves mobilized was 546,000. By 1943 the army numbered over 2,700,000 and the bottom of the barrel was in plain sight. So desperate was the shortage of infantrymen in 1944 that the RAF was forced to agree to the transfer of 26,500 airmen from the RAF Regiment to the army in the course of the year—a sharp reminder of the competing claims of a tri-service war. The eventual out-turn is summarized in Table 14.1.

'War is an option of difficulties', as Wolfe said. Scarce resources require careful allocation. But the strength of a nation's armed services is ultimately determined by the size of its population. More particularly it is determined by the availability of young men between the ages of 20 and 25, those best suited for battle. In time of peril, therefore, the conscription of that luckless cohort is only to be expected. The real measure of Britain's mobilization (or national sacrifice) in the Second World War is the extent to which it was found necessary to reach beyond the prime constituency of 20 to 25 year olds to the younger, the older, and the weaker, not necessarily to go over the top, but to support those who did. 'They also serve who only stand and wait.' Comparative figures for the armies of the British Empire are set out in Table 14.2. What these figures indicate is that, making allowance for the separate status of the Indian Army, the number of men in the army represented a considerable proportion of the number of men in the critical 20–5 age group. Indeed, when the Australian and New Zealand armies began significantly to exceed that number, the respective governments took steps to reduce their size. The exception to this pattern was the British army, which exceeded the imperial norm by an unrepentant 40 per cent.

What really counted was not aggregate totals of men, but the number of effective divisions they formed. 'How many divisions has the Pope?', Stalin is supposed to have enquired, scornfully. One might ask: how many divisions had the Prime Minister?

Throughout the war the British army formed forty-eight divisions: thirty-five infantry, eleven armoured, and two airborne. The constraints and contingencies of war often varied their constituent parts, making their operational condition (and even precise composition) difficult to specify. In terms of manpower, a full-strength division consisted of some 15,000–20,000 men. A 'divisional slice', the number of men required to keep one division in the field, was of the order of 60,000. The difference is what the Prime Minister called 'the fluff and flummery behind the fighting troops'. Of course, not all of these divisions were in being—still less in contact—at the same time. In his war memoirs Churchill boasted that only in July 1944 did the British Empire yield to the United States in the number of divisions engaging the enemy. His figures for that momentous month were thirty-eight and forty-two respectively. This was certainly an impressive statistic; but so presented as to mask certain important features. In the first place, the British and the American effort was dwarfed by the Soviets, who were then engaging about 70 per cent of all German divisions, something Churchill neglected entirely to mention. The perspective of 1944 conveniently foreshortened the middle of the tunnel, to say nothing of the disaster-strewn road which preceded it. The British Expeditionary Force which took the field in October 1939 consisted of just four divisions—to the French eighty—augmented over the next few months to a nominal fifteen, some of them sent to complete their training. They were not allowed that luxury. For two long years after the fall of France

ABCA

ABCA is dynamite. It ordains that, at least once a week, slap in the middle of working hours, platoons shall sit down and discuss Current Affairs. Once a week a soldier shall not only be entitled to ask, but encouraged to ask, 'Why Black Markets Are Allowed?' or 'Why America Isn't In Top Gear?', or 'Why Women Are Being Called Up?' No one pretends that they always get an answer or that they get the proper answer. The significant point is that they can ask. They can talk. They can unbosom themselves of doubt, ignorance and anger. It is a long way from Balaclava to ABCA—yet the jump has been made.

ABCA, the Army Bureau of Current Affairs, was born in June 1941. Its director was a civilian and a socialist, W. E. (Bill, later Sir Emrys) Williams, recruited from the world of Penguin Specials and the Workers' Educational Association (WEA). It was he who invented the felicitous acronym, and it was he who wrote the provocative passage quoted above. His service patron and confederate was the progressive Adjutant-General, Sir Ronald Adam, whose keen intelligence, pragmatic social conscience, and presumed political sympathies aroused grave suspicion among his traditionalist confrères. In October 1942 the Commander-in-Chief, Home Forces, wrote to the Secretary of State for War that 'the A-G is a serious menace to morale and discipline'. In January 1944 the Prime Minister wanted to expel him to Gibraltar. That fate was averted by his old friend the Chief of the Imperial General Staff (CIGS). In fact morale was one of Adam's central concerns. He was responsible for setting up the Army Council Morale Committee to monitor what was thought and felt in the ranks. He took ABCA seriously because he took morale seriously. The much abused concept of the citizen-soldier had real meaning for him. Army education, he wrote, aims 'to make the man a more enlightened individual, a more intelligent citizen, and therefore a better soldier. Those three aims are inextricably interwoven. Good morale is a resultant not of one only, but of all three. On all three aspects depends the production of a man who is alert, receptive, and fortified by a knowledge of the great issues for which he is fighting.' We catch the echo of Cromwell's plain russet-coated soldier, who knows what he fights for and loves what he knows: an ideal invoked mistily and often at the time.

The ABCA discussion group was usually led by regimental officers, not members of the Army Educational Corps. ABCA supplied weekly bulletins, in two series. *War* dealt with particular aspects of the military situation. *Current Affairs*, written for the purpose by the great and the good in their field, provided background material on the topic at hand: 'Our Ally Russia' (Sir Bernard Pares),

'The Yank in Britain' (Margaret Mead), most controversially, 'The Beveridge Report' (Sir William Beveridge). From November 1942, as the scheme expanded, these pamphlets were supplemented by another series, under the splendid rubric of *The British Way and Purpose* (*BWP*), examining various aspects of citizenship.

For many regimental officers the discussion was a daunting task. For some it was an unwelcome one. E. P. Thompson (the author of *The Making of the English Working Class*) remembered:

The Beveridge Plan came to me, in the form of an Army Bureau of Current Affairs pamphlet, three or four weeks before the final battle of Cassino. The squadron leader came out of his tent with it in his hand, spotted me, and said: 'Oh, Thompson! HQ insists that we get all the men together and run discussions on this. Do you mind taking it on? I'd do it myself, but it's rather difficult to argue *against* a thing when you don't know anything about it.'

The Beveridge Plan generated considerable interest among the troops. 'Every where across Italy,' Thompson has recorded, 'on wall newspapers, in bivvies round our tanks, in supply depots, the argument was going on. This curious half-chauvinist, half-anti-fascist, deeply anti-militarist and yet military competent army debated the principles out of which the National Health Service came.'

Thompson's was a positive, even romantic, vision of ABCA's reach. Others were less enthusiastic. As Anthony Burgess put it, 'unit officers were considered intelligent enough to take the facts of an ABCA pamphlet and process them into an enlightening discourse. This rarely happened. Most officers dutifully recited the pamphlets as if they were Army Council Instructions; the men did not understand and they were bored.' One of Mass Observation's correspondents sampled opinion in his unit after their first discussion, on 'War in the Desert'. A few were favourable. Most were not. 'Oh, it was comfortable, I had a nice sleep.' 'Not bad, it's a change from work. I don't mind.' 'All right but who wants to know about the bleeding Italians, they're done and finished with now.' 'No bloody good.'

Amongst politicians, however, ABCA always aroused strong feelings. Churchill's attempted suppression is well known. 'I hope you will wind up this business as quickly and as decently as possible,' he minuted the Secretary of State for War in October 1941, 'and set the persons concerned in it to useful work.' The minute was prudently buried by the Permanent Under Secretary, P. J. Grigg, and the squall passed. Again, in June 1943 Churchill instructed Sir John Anderson, Lord President of the Council, to conduct an investigation into ABCA's activities. Disappointingly, Anderson reported favourably. ABCA continued its work. The objection to that work is also well known. It is that ABCA politicized the troops—with politics of the wrong sort. On this argument the army (indeed, the forces as a whole) voted Labour in the 1945 General Election because of the insidious left-wing influence of the Army Bureau of Current Affairs. In the extreme, ABCA is supposed to have decided the outcome.

The argument is misconceived. It is true that the forces' vote was strongly Labour, more strongly than that of the country as a whole. But the young and the male were always more prone to support Labour. In numerical terms the forces' vote was insignificant (and their turn-out relatively low). Of the 25 million men and women who voted, only some 1.7 million were in the forces. Even on the unlikely assumption that service families were subject to the same malign influence, the total effect cannot possibly have been decisive across 640 constituencies. A few marginals may have been swung; but that is immaterial. Labour had a majority of 204. The whole country rejected the Conservatives in 1945—a groundswell of opinion detected by the Gallup Poll as early as 1942. ABCA's citizen-soldiers were merely part of the trend.

---

there were still only four British divisions in contact with the Germans, a total made slightly more respectable by the addition of ten more from the far-flung Empire.

Waging war on a shoestring is no easy task. One of Winston Churchill's supreme merits as warlord was his extreme intolerance of inactivity. For his generals, however, this characteristic was a sore trial. The misery of inquisition by Prime Minister was compounded by their bewilderment at the circumstances in which it was conducted, for the most remarkable feature of Churchill's war direction was its domestication. The circus surrounding the Prime Minister was a twenty-four hour event. Secretaries and shorthand writers were always on hand, as were members of his inner circle, various seers and satraps, and even a film projectionist. Business was conducted from bedroom and cabinet room alike. Meals were prolonged but also productive. Guests might be summoned at a moment's notice. Lieutenant-General Sir James Marshall-Cornwall, recently appointed commander of III Corps, received the call in July 1940.

I reached Chequers about six o'clock and was told that the PM was resting. Two hours later we sat down to dinner. It was indeed a memorable meal. I was placed on the PM's right, and on my right was Professor Frederick Lindemann ['The Prof'], Churchill's scientific adviser. The others around the oval table were Mrs Churchill, Duncan Sandys and his wife, 'Pug' Ismay (Military Secretary to the

War Cabinet), Jack Dill [the CIGS], Lord Beaverbrook, and one of the PM's private secretaries.

Churchill was bubbling over with enthusiasm and infectious gaiety. . . . As soon as the champagne was served he started to interrogate me about the condition of my Corps. I told him that when I had taken it over I had found all ranks obsessed with defensive tactical ideas, the main object of everyone being to get behind an anti-tank obstacle. I had issued orders that only offensive training exercises were to be practised, and that the III Corps motto was 'Hitting, not Sitting', which prefaced every operation order. This went down tremendously well with the PM, who chuckled and chortled: 'Splendid! That's the spirit I want to see.' He continued: 'I assume then that your Corps is now ready to take the field?' 'Very far from it, Sir,' I replied. 'Our re-equipment is not nearly complete, and when it is we shall require another month or two of intensive training.'

Churchill looked at me incredulously and drew a sheaf of papers from the pocket of his dinner-jacket. 'Which are your two divisions?' he demanded. 'The 53rd (Welsh) and the 2nd (London),' I replied. He pushed a podgy finger down the graph tables in front of him and said: 'There you are; 100 per cent complete in personnel, rifles and mortars; 50 per cent in field artillery, anti-tank rifles and machine-guns.' 'I beg your pardon, Sir,' I replied; 'that state may refer to the weapons which the ordnance depots are preparing to issue to my units, but they have not yet reached the troops in anything like those quantities.' The PM's brow contracted; almost speechless with rage, he hurled the graphs across the dinner-table to Dill, saying: 'CIGS, have those papers checked and returned to me tomorrow.'

An awkward silence followed; a diversion seemed called for. The PM leant across me and addressed my neighbour on the other side: 'Prof! What have *you* got to tell me today?' The other civilians present were wearing dinner-jackets, but Professor Lindemann was attired in a morning coat and striped trousers. He now slowly pushed his right hand into his tail-pocket and, like a conjuror, drew forth a Mills hand-grenade. An uneasy look appeared on the faces of his fellow-guests and the PM shouted: 'What's that you've got, Prof, what's that?' 'This, Prime Minister, is the inefficient Mills bomb, issued to the British infantry. It is made of twelve different components which have to be machined in separate processes. Now *I* have designed an improved grenade, which has fewer machined parts and contains a 50 per cent greater bursting charge.' 'Splendid! Splendid! That's what I like to hear. CIGS! Have the Mills bomb scrapped at once and replaced by the Lindemann grenade.'

The unfortunate Dill was completely taken aback; he tried to explain that contracts had been placed in England and America for millions of Mills bombs, and that it would be impracticable to alter the design now, but the PM would not listen. To change the subject he pointed a finger at Beaverbrook across the table; 'Max! What have *you* been up to?' Beaverbrook replied: 'Prime Minister! Give me five minutes and you will have the latest figures.' He rose and went to a telephone box at the far end of the room; after a very few minutes he rose and returned with a Puckish grin on his face. 'Prime Minister,' he said, 'in the last 48 hours we have increased our production of Hurricanes by 50 per cent.' . . .

The brandy and coffee had now circulated and the PM lit his cigar. 'I want the generals to come with me,' he said, and stumped off to an adjoining room, followed by Dill, Ismay and myself. On a large table was a rolled-up map, which the PM proceeded to spread out. It was a large-scale map of the Red Sea.

The PM placed his finger on the Italian port of Massawa. 'Now, Marshall-Cornwall,' he said, 'we have command of the sea and the air; it is essential for us to capture that port; how would you do it?' I was in no way prepared to answer a snap conundrum of this kind, and indeed had no qualifications for doing so. I saw Dill and Ismay watching me anxiously and felt that I was being drawn into some trap. I looked hard at the map for a minute and then answered: 'Well, Sir, I have never been to Massawa; I have only passed out of sight of it, going down the Red Sea. It is a defended port, protected by coast defence and anti-aircraft batteries. It must be a good 500 miles from Aden, and therefore beyond cover of our fighters. The harbour has a very narrow entrance channel, protected by coral reefs, and is certain to be mined, making an opposed landing impracticable. I should prefer to wait until General Wavell's offensive against Eritrea develops; he will capture it more easily from the land side.'

The PM gave me a withering look, rolled up the map and muttered peevishly: 'You soldiers are all alike: you have no imagination.' (James Marshall-Cornwall, *A Memoir: Wars and Rumours of War* (London, 1984), 186–170)

Such an encounter was for most generals a shock and a humiliation. Yet it was the common currency of Churchill's war direction. His first direct exposure to this highly personalized forensic approach left the imperturbable Wavell—in the Prime Minister's disparaging view 'a good average colonel'—sufficiently perturbed to tell Dill that 'the PM had asked him down to Chequers for the weekend but he would be damned if he would risk further treatment of the kind to which he had just been subjected'. Dill himself remembered another characteristic incident. 'The Prime Minister lost his temper with me. I could see the blood come up in his great neck and his eyes began to flash. He said: "What you need out there [the Middle East] is a court martial and a firing squad. Wavell has 300,000 men, etc., etc." I should have said, Whom do you want to shoot exactly? but I did not think of it till afterwards.' To come to terms with Winston Churchill's delinquent genius was an essential qualification for high command in the Second World War. For the Chief of the Imperial General Staff (CIGS) in particular it was *the* essential qualification.

Britain went to war on 3 September 1939. The very same day, as if to underline their resolve, Chamberlain's reconstituted War Cabinet decided to appoint a new CIGS. General Lord Gort, in post since 1937, became Commander-in-Chief of the British Expeditionary Force. He was succeeded by General Sir Edmund Ironside. Gort was relieved, Ironside astounded. The unsuitable had given place to the improbable.

'Tiny' Ironside was a mountain of a man—six foot four with a chest to match—of spartan tastes, dauntless courage, decided views, and severe limitations. His early exploits in South Africa, working for British intelligence disguised as an itinerant Boer trader, inspired John Buchan's war hero, Richard Hannay, of *The Thirty-Nine Steps*, *Greenmantle*, and other tales of derring-do. With good reason, Ironside prided himself on the breadth of his experience. He had a distinguished war record on the Western Front. He had been everywhere from Archangel to Cape Town. Extraordinarily, however, he had never served in the War Office. The culture of Whitehall and Westminster was utterly foreign to him, and rather distasteful. Neither temperamentally nor intellectually was he equipped to make the necessary adjustment. In committee he was a caged lion, angry and insensate. He wanted action, not interrogation. The politicians' ignorant talk drove him to distraction. He was an interpreter in seven languages. In this new environment he failed to master his own.

The blame was not all his. As Ironside himself acknowledged, he should never have been appointed. He was then put in an impossible position. Astonishingly, Gort was permitted to take with him the Director of Military Operations as his chief of staff. Thus at the outbreak of war the two men who knew most about the strategic situation departed the scene. From the beginning Ironside did not have the wholehearted support of the War Cabinet. His backers were Hore-Belisha, Secretary of State for War, and Churchill, then First Lord of the Admiralty. Hore-Belisha resigned (or was pushed) in January 1940. Churchill, a confirmed devotee in 1938–9, progressively lost faith during 1939–40. No doubt it is difficult to keep faith when nothing goes right. Ironside was an ardent sponsor of the ill-conceived Norwegian campaign—curiously, he called it 'a legitimate sideshow'—in the direction of which he clashed severely with the hyperactive First Lord. Churchill was lucky over Norway: this time the mud stuck to others. The unhappy CIGS was one. Strategically and politically, Ironside had failed. His supporters had had enough. On 25 May 1940, two weeks after becoming Prime Minister, Churchill forced his resignation.

The potential delicacy of this manœuvre was eased because a ready alternative lay to hand: General Sir John Dill, recently appointed to the new office of Vice-Chief of the Imperial General Staff. Dill was everything Ironside was not—gentle, undemonstrative, 'intellectual'; no fire-eater. He took over just as the evacuations from Dunkirk were getting under way. His accession was universally welcomed. The dominant perception was that the wrong done in 1939 (or 1937) had now been righted. This beneficent feeling could not last. Throughout 1940–1 Dill was the embodiment of professional caution. In the circumstances, this was a necessary function; but it did not endear him to the Prime Minister. Generalissimo Churchill was an impatient man. Dill's advice was like medicine: he knew he had to take it, but he found the taste revolting. Churchill railed against the constraint. Publicly he called Dill 'the dead hand of inanition'. Privately he was 'Dilly-Dally'. In the long run, without the palliative of victories in the field, such a relationship was unsustainable. By October 1941 the Prime Minister was actively seeking a replacement. The following month it was announced that on 25 December 1941, his sixtieth birthday, Dill would relinquish his post in favour of General Sir Alan Brooke. This was represented as the natural consequence of reaching the age of retirement. It did not escape comment that the Chief of the Naval Staff was already 64.

The new CIGS was a forbidding presence. The overpowering impact he made on others, 'his quite remarkable and palpable extension of personality . . . that curious electric awareness felt down to the tips of one's fingers of a given presence imparting a sense of stimulation . . . the consoling thought that someone of the sort was at the top', has been brilliantly captured by the novelist Anthony Powell. Brooke was an absolute master of his profession, and a formidable advocate. In debate his characteristic rejoinder was a bleak negative—'I flatly disagree'—accompanied by the snapping of a pencil. Churchill had finally found what he wanted. He craved disputation: here was the officer to provide it. Brooke lasted out the war. He is rightly regarded as the greatest CIGS the army has ever produced, but in one crucial respect he was fortunate in his inheritance. Unlike his predecessors, he had a framework on which to build. By 1941 the Chiefs of Staff committee was beginning to find its feet. Formalized in 1924, with an individual and collective responsibility to advise on defence policy as a whole, they had never before served with a Prime Minister and Minister of Defence, still less a Churchill, in war. In 1940 no one knew, and many doubted, whether such a combination could be made to work. Brooke's acceptability as Churchill's most intimate adviser-adversary in

1942–5 followed directly from Dill's purgatory in 1940–1. Dill had accustomed the Prime Minister to the trammelling of professional advice. 'I live a very hectic life,' he wrote. 'Most of it is spent trying to prevent stupid things being done rather than in doing clever things! However that is rather the normal life of a Chief of Staff.' Brooke said amen.

How did these men propose to win the war? Clearly, it would not be over by Christmas. This time they anticipated a long haul. In September 1939, assuming a three-year war, the Cabinet decided on forming and equipping fifty-five divisions (thirty-two British, the rest Indian and Dominion). This target, or something very like it, remained stubbornly in place as the war lengthened. By October 1940, when the danger of imminent invasion was known to have passed, there was growing confidence in the high command that they would not lose, but no clear conception of how they could win—other than with help from the United States, as yet imponderable. Everyone knew that it would take time for armies to collect and allies to coalesce. Meanwhile it was a question of attrition—the 'wearing out' of the first war translated into the 'wearing down' of the second—and blood, toil, tears, and sweat. Attrition in this war was to be accomplished, not by encounter battles on a static front, but by proxy: by bombing, blockade, and subversion. Given the predicament of 1940–1, a tendency to place excessive faith in each of these strategic expedients is readily understandable. It was, perhaps, consoling to forget that they were expedients. In the case of strategic bombing, faith assumed fanatic proportions. We now know that the fanatics were tragically misled.

As for committing the army, ideas (like landing-craft) were in distressingly short supply. Churchill's fertile imagination notwithstanding, the possible permutations seemed to be remarkably few. To meet the requirement for a major Anglo-American operation in the European theatre in 1942, for example, the invasion of North-West Africa (Torch) was eventually selected almost by default. The only alternatives seriously suggested were a lodgement in north-west France (Sledgehammer) or an operation of indeterminate character in northern Norway (Jupiter). The first of these, canvassed by the US army, was admittedly precarious and pitifully small-scale: perhaps six divisions at a time when there were some twenty-seven German divisions in the west, to say nothing of approximately 180 engaged by the Soviets in the east. Operation Sledgehammer was vetoed by the British Chiefs of Staff, who would have had to provide the majority of the troops. The second alternative was a cherished project of the Prime Minister's. 'Our whole power to help Russia in any effectual

Colonel Blimp

(Colonel) Blimp, a character invented by David Low (1891–1963), cartoonist and carica-
turist, pictured as a rotund pompous ex-officer voicing a rooted hatred of new ideas.
Hence blimp, a person of this type. Also blimpery, blimpishness, blimpism, behaviour or
speech characteristic of a blimp; blimpian, blimpish, typical of a blimp.

David Low met Horatio Blimp in a Turkish bath near Charing Cross in the early
1930s. The cartoonist had decided to invent a 'character' typifying the prevailing tendency towards what he called dogmatic doubleness. ('Look at those foreign agitators sapping the Constitution! We need a dictator like Mussolini.')
Ruminating on a name—Goodle? Boak? Snood? Glimmer?—he hit upon Blimp.
The associations were perfect. A blimp was a gas-bag with the fuselage of an
aeroplane slung experimentally underneath, and later, with equal felicity, a
barrage balloon. His name was settled. What of his occupation? There were a
number of inviting possibilities. Lord Blimp? Bishop Blimp? Dr Blimp? Turning
these over in his mind, Low overheard a conversation between 'two pink
sweating chaps of military bearing close by. They were telling one another that
what Japan did in the Pacific was no business of Britain.' Something clicked.
'In the newspapers that morning some colonel or other had written to protest
against the mechanization of cavalry, insisting that even if horses had to go, the
uniform and trappings must remain inviolate and troops must continue to wear
their spurs in their tanks. Ha! I thought. The attitude of mind! The perfect
chiaroscuro! *Colonel* Blimp, of course!'

Blimp was at once distinctive and ubiquitous. In appearance as in attitude,
he had the great advantage of being instantly recognizable to almost everyone.
His posture and physique—the ox-headed Saxon strain, as Robert Graves put
it—his wagging finger, his walrus moustache, his habitual bath towel: all this
was quintessential Blimp. His name somehow defined his expostulations, with
their invariable choleric preface. 'Gad, sir, Yeats-Brown is right. Wars are necessary—otherwise how can heroes defend their countries?' 'Gad, sir,
Churchill is right. The Govt. has evidently made an irrevocable decision to be
guided by circumstances with a firm hand.' 'Gad, sir, Lord Rothermere is right.
We must have a bigger Army to protect the Navy to protect the Army. Only then
can we fight the French and the Italians and the Abyssinians and keep the war
from spreading.' As his creator explained:

The need for defence of My Country is ever before Blimp. Let it not be imagined that 'My Country' carries any narrow proprietorial, or even territorial, implication; for it would be inadequate and unjust to picture Blimp defending to the death our Turkish bath merely, or limited to preventing with drawn sword enemies from diverting the course of the Thames. Neither take it that the people who inhabit the lands over which the flag of Blimp and me proudly floats are 'My Country'. The Colonel greatly admires, as we all do, an ideal British working-man whose most notable characteristics are Sturdy Independence coupled with Unquestioning Obedience; but in the world of reality the truth must be told that to Blimp the British working-man in bulk is an almost intolerable nuisance, with his ever-lasting grumbles about under-nourishment and his inconvenient yearnings for selfish improvement. Any display of Sturdy Independence in that quarter and Blimp calls the police.

Colonel Blimp will tell you that British-traditions-and-institutions are important elements in 'My Country', and this is so, if we push aside democracy and liberty and accept gold coaches, ceremonials involving large concourses of persons preferably armed and in coloured clothing, and high officials in strange hats reading things from parchments as representative British-traditions-and-institutions. More than anything else, however, 'My Country' is Britannia. Blimp would die for Britannia.

The prefix 'Colonel' naturally tended to identify Blimp with one particular brand of obscurantism. On the eve of war the egregious Hore-Belisha was rash enough to assure the House of Commons that he had buried Blimp long ago. A few months later the jubilant Colonel was toasting his dismissal. 'Gad, gentlemen, here's to our greatest victory of the war.' Gort and Ironside—that worthy pair—have been called blood-brothers of Blimp. It has even been suggested (wrongly) that the character was based on Lord Roberts. Low himself resisted such narrow interpretation. 'Never have I met a man with more numerous and powerful relations,' he wrote, mischievously, in 1938. 'A family tree that boasts of Mr Neville Blimp, the prime minister, Mr Herbert Blimp, the Labour leader, Sir John Blimp of the BBC, Mr Beverley Blimp, the writer on daffodils, Lord Blimp, the celebrated economist, Baron Blimp, the newspaper magnate, and George Blimp, the celebrated comedian, have no fear for the survival of its reputation.'

So the blimp class was born. It is a constant reference in the writings of George Orwell, who preferred the term blimpocracy and used it like a truncheon ('the huge blimpocracy which monopolizes official and military power and has an instinctive hatred of intelligence'). In 1940 it was a question of unblimping. Orwell wrote in his diary: 'Under the stress of emergency, we shall unblimp if we have time, but time is all.' Blimp himself achieved immortality of a kind in Michael Powell and Emeric Pressburger's complex masterpiece, *The Life and Death of Colonel Blimp* (1943). This extravaganza, dismissed by some as a sentimental travesty, roused the ire of the Prime Minister, who thought it disgraceful—a distinctly blimpish reaction—and did his utmost to prevent the film's release. In the event it was censored, in slightly mysterious circumstances, but not suppressed. The violence of Churchill's reaction is hard to understand, unless it is that Horatio Blimp and Winston Churchill were a little too close for Prime Ministerial comfort.

Colonel Blimp was officially declared dead by his creator in 1942. The news elicited an affectionate memorial from Robert Graves:

A word about the old man who has just died. He scraped through Sandhurst, where he learned drill and how to draw coloured maps, but nothing about geography or military history or field engineering. In the South African War he despised the Boers as much as his ancestor had despised the American revolutionaries, and won a DSO . . . In 1914 he returned as a dug-out to command a Kitchener battalion: in 1915, on his first night in the trenches near La Bassée, he went out with a flash-light to inspect the barbed wire and, fortunately for his men, was put out of action for the rest of the war by a German sentry. He was David Low's Colonel Blimp, whom we all know so well. His son—but his son is still alive and, I regret to say, still on the active list.

manner this year', he wrote in July 1942, 'depends upon our driving the enemy aircraft from the northern airfields of Norway': strategic dogma of breathtaking unreality. Operation Jupiter was an idea, but a poor one. Fortunately it was never taken seriously by the Chiefs of Staff of either nation. 'We'd better put an advert in the papers,' Churchill joked thinly a few days later.

After Operation Torch the logic of continued Mediterranean operations proved inescapable. As is well known, this 'indirect approach' was the one favoured by the British against the American fixation on a direct cross-Channel attack. His biographer has conceded that 'Brooke feared above all things a premature and unsuccessful return to the mainland of Europe'. He believed correctly that Fabian tactics in the Mediterranean were not merely complementary but indispensable to a successful cross-Channel attack; without closing and tightening the ring to its utmost, the final assault would certainly founder. The British were surely right to argue for a delayed Second Front. The CIGS and his colleagues were not completely averse to crossing the Channel. Brooke was too sound a strategist not to recognize that an amphibious operation in north-west Europe might ultimately be necessary and even desirable. At the same time he was content to postpone the day almost indefinitely—till the Greek kalends, as Michael Howard has said—in the fraying hope that a favourable decision might be achieved without it. To employ outmoded American terminology, he longed for a mop-up but acquiesced in a power-play.

In two respects at least the characteristic Fabianism of the British army paid off. In terms of casualties, Britain lost some 485,000 in the Second World War, historically a high figure, but by the standards of that gargantuan conflict proportionately and comparatively light. In terms of folk heroes, the army discovered in the messianic Montgomery of Alamein a people's general fit for a people's war—a general who beat the enemy and captured the imagination with equal relish. 'We have a new experience,' exulted Churchill in November 1942 after the battle which made Montgomery's name. 'We have victory. . . . Rommel's army has been defeated. It has been routed. It has been very largely destroyed as a fighting force.' Not only a British victory, then, but a British *army* victory, over a German opponent. The Desert Rats had run the lightless middle of the tunnel. The way ahead was clearer now.

15 THE POST-WAR ARMY 1945–1963

ANTHONY FARRAR-HOCKLEY

Looking back, years after the war, Lord Attlee remarked, 'You have to re-member that we could never be sure when the war was going to end. One day we were contemplating months of fighting for the Japanese islands, the next it was all over. Gearing to a war economy could not immediately be disengaged any more than war damage at home and abroad could im-mediately be mended.'

In the period 1945–7 the army lost the majority of its matured leaders and specialists just as new commitments were assumed. There was extra-ordinary promotion for those remaining to cope with the fresh national servicemen; in some cases corporals found themselves warrant officers overnight. To what end?

Burdened by huge international debts, Mr Attlee's Government had no intention of keeping the armed forces at their wartime peak of 5.1 million, but inescapable occupation and internal security duties in Europe, the Middle, and Far East could only be discharged by a large army. Still, with twenty divisions in the field and no major enemy in sight, some members of the parliamentary Labour Party believed that the army should be halved in 1946 and conscription abandoned as morally objectionable and abominated by the public. This latter view proved false. Families were so used to the process of the call-up that few queried its continuance. Con-scription of women ceased in 1945, and in that year, also, conscription of men for the mines came to an end; thereafter, all national service was un-dertaken in the armed forces. Yet when the young men were drafted to training units, they were taught during 1945–6 to fight an enemy frequently referred to inadvertently as 'Germans' or 'Japanese'. The im-ages on range targets manufactured in war validated these descriptions. Clearly this could not continue; but when non-commissioned officers asked how they should describe 'the enemy' in future to those in basic training, it was difficult to provide a close definition.

Threats to, or actual disruption of, peace and security took many forms. In the Mediterranean, the Yugoslavs were attempting to annex Venezia-Giulia, and the Communist EAM–ELAS to overthrow the Greek government. In Palestine, the Stern Gang and Irgun Z'vai Leumi sought to establish an independent Jewish state by terrorism. The Wafd or Moslem Brotherhood militated violently for full Egyptian sovereignty. In India, the potential for communal violence had heightened. In the Dutch East Indies, British troops were drawn into counter-insurgency with Indonesian nationalists. In Europe, where occupation duties were extensive, there were also indications that the Red Army of the Soviet Union might be turned upon its former allies.

As ever, the British soldier adjusted to the constraints of internal security operations—suppressing terrorism or maintaining order among local factions. Sometimes the demand for troops exceeded Britain's capacity. In 1947, the Viceroy of India warned that he needed a further seven imperial divisions to prevent communal violence if independence negotiations should fail. Precisely because none was available, political restructuring was accelerated. Separate states of Pakistan and India emerged, requiring the widespread resettlement of Muslim and Hindu communities with consequential massacres. British soldiers, often in isolated detachments under the command of a national service officer or non-commissioned officer, provided the only reliable force to protect refugees from fanatical mobs.

The reduction of army commitments was pursued vigorously over the years 1946–9 with some success. National service was reduced to twelve months. Troops engaged in the Dutch East Indies were withdrawn in 1946, and the British occupation forces in Japan in the following year. The evacuation of all imperial forces from India provided a substantial saving. Political settlement permitted the withdrawal of the garrison from Venezia-Giulia and Trieste in 1947 but not from Austria. The United States assumed the task of supporting and training the Greek army in its struggles against the EAM–ELAS guerrillas in 1948. Under American pressure, but by no means reluctantly, the British government abandoned its mandate in Palestine in the same year. As the Haganah, the Jewish underground army, surfaced to contest Arab claims on Palestinian territory, it was engaged by the forces of Jordan, advised, and in part commanded, by seconded British army officers.

By 1949, the army had been reduced in size to 700,000. Peacetime accounting had been introduced. Post-war reduction in ammunition expenditure and manufacture had relieved the defence budget, but otherwise it had not been easy to effect substantial economies. However, by 1949, 85 per cent of the estates and buildings taken into use during the war had been returned to their original owners or sold. A mass of hutted barracks remained. Plans were drawn for their replacement by permanent accommodation over a term of fifteen years—later extended to thirty years. The cost of maintaining the army, and the other two services, within a national economy strapped for cash and credit remained burdensome. Marshall Aid in 1948 mitigated pressures on the pound sterling but, almost at once, defence commitments increased.

In 1949, Britain was instrumental in the formation of the North Atlantic Treaty Alliance, and felt obliged to offer seven divisions to European defence, involving, *inter alia*, the modernization of the Territorial Army. At that time the Soviet Union threatened the oilfields in Iran, and the integrity of Austria and Yugoslavia, while, elsewhere, independence granted to Burma, India, and Pakistan, and the success of Sukarno in the Dutch East Indies, encouraged Chin Peng's Communist revolutionary group in Malaya. Chin himself was inspired by the success of Mao Tse-tung in China, which had brought the People's Liberation Army to a threatening posture on the borders of the New Territories of Hong Kong. Against these threats, national service was necessarily increased to eighteen months.

By the beginning of 1950, forces equating to two divisions were engaged in Malaya. An additional infantry brigade, the 27th, had been sent to Hong Kong to reinforce the garrison, a political gesture; the field forces there were outnumbered eight to one by the provincial Chinese Communist forces. One infantry brigade group, the 29th, remained in the United Kingdom as the imperial strategic reserve, together with a light force, the 16th Parachute Brigade.

Thus, when the Korean War began in June 1950, the British Chiefs of Staff advised the government against contributing troops to the United Nations force assembling under General MacArthur to assist the South Koreans. The Royal Air Force was similarly heavily committed and thus Britain's contribution was limited to the greater part of the Far East Fleet. But three United States divisions were unable to arrest the Communist advance in July. President Truman pressed the many states which had condemned North Korean aggression to send ground forces, and most urgently pressurized the British government, America's principal political ally. Mr Attlee and his Cabinet colleagues felt obliged to respond. The nearest British army element was in Hong Kong. The Foreign and Colonial Offices were in agreement that nothing should be removed from that garrison while the threat from Communist China persisted. Similarly, no troops could be spared from Malaya. The choice thus fell upon the 29th Independent Infantry Brigade Group. The brigade comprised fighting units low in numbers, scattered throughout the United Kingdom. Field Marshal Sir William Slim, Chief of the Imperial General Staff, informed the committee of service ministers on 31 July that it would be impracticable to send national servicemen to Korea while the term of service remained at eighteen months. Six months were required for training and drafting them, three months would be involved on the journey out and back, leaving only nine months in operations. He proposed that the term should be extended to two years. Meantime, he advised, 'to provide troops for Korea would mean; in addition to stopping the discharge of time-expired regulars, calling up no less than one fifth of the regular army reserve (including half the reserve of infantry) and thus greatly jeopardising the Army's mobilisation plans'.

The Prime Minister and Minister of Labour agreed that, if they had to find additional manpower for military service, it would be better to field young men, largely untrained for civil industry, than to recall the whole reserve, many of them skilled artisans. Due primarily to the needs of the army, therefore, a bill was hastened through parliament in September 1950, authorizing a conscription term of two years. But this was too late for the 29th Brigade, embarking in that month. Its ranks were filled out by reservists, and 500 national service officers and soldiers who volunteered for special engagements introduced for the war. With the aim of attracting more men to long service, pay and allowances were improved throughout the forces.

In Korea, the United Nations forces, American and South Korean, were in danger of defeat during August. The British ambassador in Washington put to London the case for the immediate dispatch of British troops. Attlee and Ernest Bevin, the Foreign Secretary, decided that, military vulnerability notwithstanding, Hong Kong must pass the 27th Brigade to Korea until the 29th arrived. This formation of two battalions, the 1st Battalions of the Middlesex Regiment and the Argyll and Sutherland Highlanders, lacking field artillery or engineers, was dispatched almost overnight in two warships and a merchantman, accompanied by one

Royal Artillery anti-tank troop. An Australian battalion followed them from occupation duties in Japan. New Zealand organized a field artillery regiment to join the force by the end of the year. On these grounds, Brigadier B. A. Coad changed the title of his command to 27th British Commonwealth Brigade.

Rarely in modern times has a British formation been sent into a theatre of war so ill equipped for a hard campaign. The army Commander-in-Chief in the Far East intervened to reinforce each battalion by cross-posting volunteers from other units in Hong Kong, and these increments permitted the manning of three, but not the established four, rifle companies organic to a battalion on war establishment. Even so, two-thirds of the junior ranks were national servicemen, some of whom had just arrived from recruit training. Middlesex and Argylls with less than eight months to serve were shed to the garrison.

The supply chain depended initially on a detachment of three soldiers in the Korean port of Pusan. Signals to the Singapore base were relayed through a busy American radio network via Japan. Although an under-strength ordnance field park and workshops followed the brigade, there was no second-line transport. Often, unit store trucks had to be used to lift the marching infantry when they moved long distances. The trucks had then to return to recover the stores. Despite these difficulties, the Middlesex and Argylls helped to stabilize the Naktong river defence line in September as MacArthur's strategy defeated the North Koreans. Reinforced by drafts from Britain and the Army of the Rhine at the end of the month, and by the 3rd Battalion, the Royal Australian Regiment, the brigade frequently led the United Nations advance into North Korea. At the end of October, within 40 miles of the Chinese frontier at Sinuiju, it was relieved to return to Hong Kong due to the arrival of the 29th Brigade.

At that point Communist China entered the war, committing 350,000 soldiers from the People's Liberation Army disguised as 'volunteers' rallying to the North Korean People's Army and nominally under its control, though actually armed, funded, and controlled by the Central Military Commission in Peking. At the beginning of November, as the winter began, the Chinese 13th Army Group fell upon the western and centre corps of the United Nations forces commanded by the United States 8th Army. Taken by surprise, the foremost American and South Korean divisions were routed. In this crisis, the 27th Brigade returned to active operations. Coincidentally, instructions arrived that local overseas allowance for service in the colony would be withdrawn, a severe decision for those officers and men who had families living there.

The British government, on the advice of the Chiefs of Staff, wanted the Americans to negotiate a cease-fire and to separate the two sides with a buffer zone. But General MacArthur believed he could still defeat the Communist forces. President Truman did not feel he could overrule the Commander-in-Chief and permitted resumption of the United Nations offensive on 24 November. This second advance was broken by massed Chinese forces reinforced by the 9th Army Group. The 27th Brigade became the rearguard to the United States IX Corps in the centre sector. At the end of the month, the British brigades met briefly. The 29th was rearguard to I Corps in the western sector. Its infantry and armour held the great bridges across the Taedong river at P'yongyang, where western and central withdrawal routes coincided. On the edge of the North Korean capital, the well-found 29th looked with wonder and respect as the ragged files of the 27th passed through them. When all had departed, the 29th Brigade field engineer squadron demolished the remaining bridges.

Between Christmas and the new year of 1951, the United Nations forces, which had successfully broken away in trucks and railway trains, reformed a line just south of the 38th Parallel. Delayed by lack of transport, the Chinese renewed the offensive on 1 January. In rearguard operations, the 1st Battalions of the Northumberland Fusiliers and the Royal Ulster Rifles, with armoured and Royal Artillery elements of the 29th Brigade, rebuffed Chinese forces attempting encirclement, though in breaking free the Ulster Rifles lost 157 killed or taken prisoner on 3/4 January 1951. The 27th and 29th Brigades withdrew into a winter defensive line south of the River Han in temperatures frequently below minus 30 degrees centigrade. Consulting frequently, the United States and United Kingdom governments believed that it might be necessary to evacuate Korea altogether. But the winter was more cruel to the Chinese than their foes. Poorly clothed and supplied, exhausted by marching and fighting, many thousands froze to death. Tens of thousands died of disease. Their difficulties were not immediately apparent to the United Nations command.

For several months, the ground forces command in Korea had been split. After the withdrawal to the 38th Parallel, all were subordinated to the 8th Army, itself under the command of General MacArthur, Commander-in-Chief of land, air, and local maritime forces engaged in the war. Lieutenant-General Matthew B. Ridgway was now appointed to command the 8th Army in Korea, and began to tour his force. He wrote later:

Every command post I visited gave me the same sense of lost confidence and lack of spirit. The leaders, from sergeant on up, seemed unresponsive, reluctant to answer my questions. . . . I could not help contrasting their attitudes to that of a young British subaltern [of the 8th Hussars] who had trotted off a knoll to greet me when he spotted the insignia on my jeep. . . . Knowing that the British [29th] Brigade had hardly more than a handful of men to cover a wide sector of the front line, with a new Chinese offensive expected almost hourly, I asked him how he found the situation.

'Quite all right, sir,' he replied quickly. Then he added with a pleasant smile, 'It *is* a bit draughty up here.'

The new 8th Army commander was encouraged by the spirit of the British and Commonwealth brigades, joined now by Canadians and an Indian field ambulance. Returning to the offensive, he restored the confidence of his American and South Korean soldiers by concerted use of fire-power on the ground and in the air, in which he had supremacy. By March, his international army had beaten the Chinese and North Koreans across the front. The Chinese Commander-in-Chief, P'eng Te-huai, withdrew north of the 38th Parallel behind outposts.

General Ridgway was ordered to remain in the area of the Parallel, but permitted to seize the road and rail communications in the central waist of Korea if opportunity offered. Anchoring his flanks, he advanced in the centre from mid-April. P'eng Te-huai's remit was quite different. It was to 'wipe out three divisions of the American Army, three brigades of British and Turkish troops, and two divisions of the Puppet [South Korean] Army . . .' Exploitation of strategic options arising from this offensive was left to him. Twenty-seven fresh divisions were among the forty under his orders.

On 12 April, General Ridgway was appointed Commander-in-Chief of the United Nations forces in place of General MacArthur. His successor in Korea was Lieutenant-General James Van Fleet. The first wave of the Chinese offensive was launched on 22 April, while the new army commander was making initial visits to his international force. In the west, the 29th Brigade held the sector on the Imjin river which P'eng intended to destroy prior to cutting in behind the American 3rd and 25th Divisions and the Turkish Brigade. In the centre, the 27th Brigade were in reserve behind a South Korean division, similarly marked for elimination to complete a pincer movement behind the American 25th and 24th Divisions. Heavy air attacks from ground and maritime air forces inhibited Chinese movement in daylight, but after nightfall the offensive swelled, carrying P'eng's assault forces into the United Nations defences with an advantage in numbers of about eight to one. On the Imjin river, the units of the 29th Brigade were rapidly engaged in an intensive battle involving three enemy divisions. They held their sector until ordered to withdraw but suffered considerable loss, including the greater part of the 1st Battalion of the Gloucestershire Regiment.

Above the Kap'yong river, the South Koreans in front of the 27th Brigade panicked as the Chinese attacked on the night of 22 April. Attempts to rally them were unsuccessful. In the process of relief by the 28th Brigade—the Argylls were out of the line, handing over their weapons and equipment to the 1st Battalion, the King's Own Scottish Borderers—the 27th had to occupy a blocking position a little to the north of Kap'yong town. The Australians, 2nd Battalion, Princess Patricia's Canadian Light Infantry, and the Middlesex, supported by the 16th New Zealand Field Artillery Regiment and a valiant American tank company, were assailed by first one then a second division of Chinese infantry from the night of 23/4 April to the morning of 25 April. By chance, the Chinese did not engage all units simultaneously. The Royal Australian Regiment, supported by the Middlesex, bore the first attacks, the Canadians the second. Despite some concession of ground, the brigade held firm. Having lost the greater part of its strength, the Chinese division drew off. After seven months in operations, the 27th Brigade withdrew to Hong Kong, passing their Commonwealth units to the 28th.

The United Nations actions during the fourth week of April 1951, in which the two British and Commonwealth formations played a vital part, were decisive in the Korean War. P'eng Te-huai failed to destroy the formations he had identified or to break open the opposing line. The 8th Army held together. Good use was made of its immense fire-power to inflict huge casualties on the Chinese and North Koreans. In May the 8th Army began to push their foes back to the 38th Parallel. Armistice negotiations began at Kaesong in June—moving later to Panmunjon on the Parallel. Political manoeuvring spun out these talks until the summer of 1953. The United Nations forces were disposed in a defensive line fully developed with strong points and obstacles. Its commanders were permitted to attack locally to gain ground of tactical value but otherwise were required to maintain a defensive strategy.

Battle of the Imjin River, 22 April to 25 April 1951

For our spring offensive, we have decided to make our objective the wiping out of three divisions (less one regiment) of the American Army, three brigades of British and Turkish troops, and two divisions of the Puppet [Republic of Korea] Army to the west of the northern Han river. First of all, we will mass our forces to wipe out the 6th Division of the Puppet Army, the British 27th Brigade, the American 3rd Division (less one regiment), the Turkish Brigade, the British 29th Brigade and the 1st Division of the Puppet Army . . . (Operational directive by P'eng Te-huai, Commander-in-Chief of the Chinese and North Korean Communist Forces in the field, 18 April 1951)

By the spring of 1951, the United Nations land forces in Korea had recovered the line of the 38th Parallel, the boundary between North and South Korea. Under Lieutenant-General Matthew B. Ridgway, South Korean and International troops, combined in the United States 8th Army, had recovered confidence in themselves, their weapons, and equipment.

Long marches and supply shortages had weakened P'eng's forces during the winter, but in March reinforcements were arriving, despite the United Nations' air supremacy. From mid-April he had twenty-seven divisions at full strength, supported by considerable artillery and an armoured element.

Prudently, General Ridgway anchored his flanks on the Parallel, while continuing a limited advance in the centre. Two formations held the western flank on the lower Imjin river: the 1st Republic of Korea (ROK) Division, and the British 29th Independent Infantry Brigade Group.

The mass of United Nations forces was concentrated, inevitably, on the central front of advance. The flanks, in particular the Imjin line, were attenuated. Brigadier Brodie's 29th Brigade had to hold 12 miles with his four battalions. Such a frontage obliged him to accept considerable gaps between his defended localities. On the left, at the end of a track through mountain gorges, he posted the 1st Battalion, the Gloucestershire Regiment (1 Glosters), under Lieutenant-Colonel J. P. Carne. This body, with its supporting 4.2-inch mortars in C Troop, 170 Battery, was separated from the remainder of the brigade by the towering mass of Kamak-san. The 1st Battalion, the Royal Northumberland Fusiliers (the 5th Fusiliers), under Lieutenant-Colonel K. O. N. Foster held the centre and right. Furthest right, across the river, the Belgian Battalion, under Lieutenant-Colonel A. Crahay, was sited to hold a hinge position between the defensive flank and central advance.

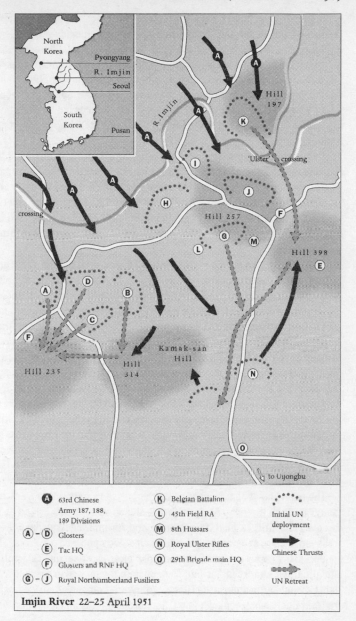

Imjin River 22–25 April 1951

North Korea
Pyongyang
R. Imjin
Seoul
South Korea
Pusan

R. Imjin

Hill 197

K

'Ulster' crossing

I

J

H

F

crossing

Hill 257

G

M

L

Hill 398

E

A

D

B

F

C

Hill 235

F

Hill 314

Kamak-san Hill

N

O

to Uyongbu

A 63rd Chinese Army 187, 188, 189 Divisions	**K** Belgian Battalion	.... Initial UN deployment
A – **D** Glosters	**L** 45th Field RA	
E Tac HQ	**M** 8th Hussars	➤ Chinese Thrusts
F Glosters and RNF HQ	**N** Royal Ulster Rifles	
G – **J** Royal Northumberland Fusiliers	**O** 29th Brigade main HQ	⟫⟫⟫ UN Retreat

During the first three weeks of April, the 29th Brigade patrolled extensively along and across the river. Several strong infantry columns, with the Centurion tanks of the 8th Hussars, challenged the half-starved Chinese rearguard screening P'eng's muster, skilfully concealed from ground and air observation. As a preliminary to attacking on the night of 22 April, he launched reconnaissance and infiltration groups on Saturday, 21 April. Some of these were exposed on the Sunday morning. Similarly, the initial assault parties and their artillery were discovered and attacked by United States aircraft and artillery that afternoon.

Forewarned that the expected offensive was about to open, the 8th Army commander, Lieutenant-General James Van Fleet, who had been in command for less than a fortnight, halted his broad advance. The flank forces increased their watchfulness as dusk fell on 22 April. In the 29th Brigade, the reserve battalion, the 1st Battalion, the Royal Ulster Rifles (1 RUR), commanded temporarily by Major Gerald Rickord, was put at two-hours notice to move to any part of the sector.

At 10.20 p.m., the Belgians were attacked, and at about the same time the Glosters ambushed a column of Chinese fording the Imjin. Shortly, after the foremost position of the 5th Fusiliers was also engaged. The 25-pounder guns of Lieutenant-Colonel M. T. Young's 45th Field Regiment and the heavy mortars of 170 Battery opened fire. A battle seemed to be stirring as the 8th Army had expected: a night of probing attacks on 22 April while the enemy closed up for a major assault on the night of 23 April. Actually, P'eng's leading divisions were already crossing the river. Three divisions of Yang Te-chih's 63rd Army were advancing in column against the 29th Brigade. One battalion closed upon the left forward Glosters' company; another, delayed by the river ambush, moved on to the right forward company. On the brigade's right flank, 1 RUR was ordered to secure the eastern bridges to the Belgian location but was pre-empted by the enemy. From midnight, the width and depth of the incursion became apparent: the Belgians were frequently assaulted, the 5th Fusiliers forced from several of their positions. The gun line was threatened.

The main line of communication on the brigade's right was a track running south through the hills. Anxious that it should not be cut, Brigadier Brodie ordered the RUR to hold its entrance and an intermediate pass, and was relieved to learn at dawn that the route remained open.

Chinese pressure abated temporarily after sunrise on 23 April, when American air attacks intensified. But, despite these, action persisted. On the left, Colonel Carne drew in the Glosters' forward companies. To the centre and right, Major H. Huth, commanding C Squadron, 8th Hussars, engaged his tanks in local counter-attacks. The 55 Field Engineer Squadron fought as infantry, recovering lost ground close to the gun line. Periodically attacked, the guns of 45th Field Regiment were sent to a rear location. As the 5th Fusiliers were driven from their remaining positions, visual contact with the Belgians across the eastern bridges was lost. An attack with an American battalion in the afternoon to recover the bridges failed.

However, the American intervention distracted the Chinese in this area. The Belgian vehicles, their British heavy mortar troop, and an American tank detachment shot their way across the river, escaping to the east. The infantry followed along the north bank. This was timely: the 3rd Division for whom the hinge had been secured had now returned to the main defensive line. The Philippine Battalion Group, which included tank and reconnaissance companies, and a light artillery battery, was sent from the 3rd Division to reinforce the 29th Brigade.

That night the Chinese 188th Division crossed the Imjin, and, with the 187th Division, attacked the RUR and Fusiliers holding the rearward track. The 189th Division was directed on the Glosters. The latter were surrounded during the night and by daylight on 24 April had concentrated on a feature overlooking its own supply track. Attempts by the Filipinos on 24 April to push through the gorges to reinforce them failed. The Glosters might have fought their way out that day, though casualties would have been heavy. Colonel Carne was ordered to hold fast.

On the right, pressure intensified through the day, though the track to the rear remained open. Chinese infiltrators were suppressed by Major Huth's tanks and the RUR. On the night 24/5 April, however, the hill positions on either side were repeatedly assailed. By the morning of 25 April, the 5th Fusiliers' sector was much reduced, though the RUR continued to hold both its features.

The 29th Brigade was by this time occupying a salient and held there because General Soule, commanding the United States 3rd Division and responsible for the sector, had orders from the corps commander to relieve the Glosters. But he dallied, then sent too little, too late. Surrounded, the Glosters were ordered to make their own way out. The medical officer, Captain R. P. Hickey, his staff, and Padre S. J. Davies gallantly remained with the wounded. Only two small groups of the battalion and artillery troop escaped. Running a gauntlet of fire, they fell in successfully with a rescue sortie made by American tanks and ROK infantry. The remainder were captured.

Withdrawal on the right involved a running battle, in which Colonel Foster was killed as he sought to co-ordinate events forward. The Chinese had cut the track at several points. The tanks, carrying some of the infantry, crashed the road-blocks but, raked by fire, lost vehicles and men *en route* to the exits held by the engineers. The RUR led the remainder over the hills into a newly formed United Nations' line.

The 29th Brigade had lost 1,091, about 20 per cent of its strength, half of them in the Glosters group. It had held the extended line for a crucial period against three Chinese divisions. Yet, after a night's rest, the whole formation was fit for further operations.

The 1st Commonwealth Division, formed in the summer of 1951 under Major-General A. J. H. Cassels, took a full part in this prolonged defence. Over thirty British units served within it, each on a tour of approximately one year. All gained considerable experience of defensive warfare. Although the line was never again in danger of being lost or breached after April 1951, several important local actions were fought, notably by the 1st Battalions of the King's Own Scottish Borderers, the Shropshire Light Infantry, and, later, the Black Watch and Duke of Wellington's Regiment, all in company with their Australian and Canadian comrades.

With few exceptions, operations were conducted with the weapons and equipment and using the tactical doctrine developed during the Second World War, chiefly in the mountains of Italy. The Canadians apart, rifles and machine-guns were of .303-inch calibre, and the Vickers medium machine-gun firing Mk VIIIZ ammunition was superior as a sustained fire weapon to all others—American and Russian—on the battlefield. Grenades were of British origin; the powerful No. 36 Mills pattern remained a favourite with the Commonwealth soldiers. The American 3.5-inch rocket launcher, developed post-war, was in common use throughout the theatre of war and, in the absence of numbers of enemy armoured vehicles, was employed chiefly to attack infantry bunkers. The capacity of the 2- and 3-inch mortars was limited by the manufacturing systems, particularly that of the cast bomb cases and tail assemblies of the latter, and compared poorly with the 60- and 81-mm. mortars of the United States in service with the Canadians.

The major new piece of equipment was the Centurion tank. Despite its weight and size, which some feared would deny its use in Korea with its indifferent roads, paddy fields, and narrow valleys, bold handling on the Imjin river disproved these apprehensions. The tank's function was, however, limited to direct fire support for the infantry. The predominantly mountainous country did not favour armoured battles but there were areas where these might have developed—for example, south of Seoul. The North Korean and Chinese armoured forces never gathered to fight in this way principally because of United Nations air superiority. In the subsequent defensive line, the 5th Dragoon Guards developed direct fire options among the infantry. The 17-pounder anti-tank gun, however, lacking armoured targets, was little used in Korea. The same was true for the Bofors cannons in their anti-aircraft role, though they gave direct fire support to infantry during the early mobile phase of the campaign. The prime equipment of the Royal Artillery, British and Commonwealth, was the 25-pounder gun, but included the 4.2-inch mortar. Control was perfected by the commander, Royal Artillery, and his staff to deliver graduated levels of fire to any target on the divisional or neighbouring fronts at very short notice.

The Royal Engineers divided their labours between work in and about the defensive positions—including mine-laying or lifting in no man's land—and maintaining routes forward across rivers and mountains in all weather. The latter involved replacement of bridges swept away by Imjin floods; and rigging cable-cars to remote mountain sites.

Light aircraft—Austers—supported the Commonwealth Division, which had no helicopters. The British army lagged in adoption of the latter, and thus depended throughout the war on the United States for their use, most frequently in the evacuation of those seriously wounded in forward positions. Behind the combat forces and their organic services, the Royal Army Service Corps, the Royal Army Medical Corps, the Royal Army Ordnance Corps, and the Royal Electrical and Mechanical Engineers, lay a comprehensive British Commonwealth line of communication in Korea with its base in Japan.

From September 1950 to July 1953, the Korean War tested to the full the British army's capability in fighting an infantry war with the benefits of supremacy at sea and in the air. Regulars, reservists, and national servicemen were not found wanting. Training methods in all arms proved to be sound. Weapons and equipment met their needs. Inadequacies in clothing for the winter of 1950–1 were remedied during 1952. In terms of expense, stocks remaining from the Second World War mitigated costs. The area of greatest difficulty was in manpower: NATO was just then evolving; and armed challenges continued in colonial territories. The most extensive of these, as already indicated, was in Malaya.

The Malayan Communist Party, predominantly Chinese in membership, had extended its power through the trade unions after 1945 as a means of seizing power. This was thwarted. The party took to a revolutionary war in the jungle as the Malayan People's Anti-British Army, later, the Malayan Races Liberation Army (MRLA), based on the suspended but by no means disbanded Malayan People's Anti-Japanese Army run by the Malayan Communist Party during the Second World War. These forces under Chin Peng, numbering about 4,000, expected to draw information and supplies from the Chinese subsistence farmers squatting on the fringes of the jungle. Terrorism would be the first step to insurgency, followed by revolution to supplant the colonial authorities by the Malayan Communist Party.

The British High Commissioner declared a state of emergency following a series of widespread attacks on plantations, utilities, and police posts in June 1948. Notwithstanding many other demands that summer, an additional brigade, and 500 British members of the disbanding Palestine police, reinforced Malaya. At the outset, the colonial government expected to suppress the MRLA by using the military to assist the police 'in aid to the civil power' as practised for many years in India and Burma. This assumed that operations would follow a controlled pattern, assured by a flow of intelligence. But the quality of intelligence was poor. Indeed, it was the MRLA which had the best intelligence, acquired by supporters among the subsistence farmers, and a network of agents in local government, in the public utilities, and even in the police force. Chin Peng's terrorist activity expanded to guerrilla raids involving up to 200 men.

Perversely, in such circumstances, police and military drew apart. The former, anxious to maintain their primacy in preserving order, tended to husband their information and act within their own organization. Hanging about for action, the military began to operate on their own initiative. Although a number of the army's enterprises during the first eighteen months involved small numbers—one or two platoons—acting as ferrets, the commanders from battalion level upwards favoured large-scale sweeps. In late 1949, for example, it was not unusual for a battalion or brigade operation lasting many weeks to end without a single engagement of a guerrilla band or the disruption of a base. At the end of his Command-in-Chief of the army in the Far East in that year, General Sir Neil Ritchie's conclusions included these revelatory remarks:

While it is true that without really good information such action does not produce spectacular results, its adoption is nonetheless necessary if the enemy is to be prevented from organising himself into relatively efficient large bodies which can be concentrated as, when, and where necessary, and so gain for him the initiative.

However true, this was not a basis for defeating the MLRA. Fortunately, General Ritchie together with his colleagues in the police and colonial government recognized that the key to progress lay in capitalizing their support among the other races in the Federation, Malays, Tamils, and Indians, and in winning over the mass of the Chinese. The police had arrested hundreds of suspects, principally from the villages of the landless Chinese squatters. Actual or potential supporters of Chin Peng, they had now to be won over. The squatters themselves needed to be resettled with tenure at a distance from the jungle-based guerrilla bands. First steps to this end were considerably hindered by the MLRA, however.

Lieutenant-General Sir Harold Briggs was appointed director of operations to produce an overall plan for future action. His ideas were sound but he lacked the authority to implement them. The police continued to work as much as possible apart from the army, forming a field force to minimize their need of troops. At the same time, a number of soldiers were required to undertake police duties in static posts. In October 1951, the High Commissioner was ambushed and murdered. He was replaced by General Sir Gerald Templer who accepted the appointment on the understanding that he had complete authority over the police and military as well as government. On this basis, he transformed the character of operations. Co-operation was thereafter required at every level of civil government, police, and military. State and district war executive committees, formed under the Briggs' Plan, were required to meet every day, 'if only for a whiskey and soda in the evening'.

As the resettlement of squatter farmers continued apace, the MLRA was denied food, while rehabilitation of prisoners and supporters, as part of the policy to capture the 'hearts and minds' of the populace, produced first the strands and then the substance of intelligence to permit precise as distinct from random counter-insurgency operations. Troops were withdrawn from police duties. Police field force operations were harmonized with those of the military. Both organizations were required to pool intelligence and the appropriate sum was passed to those requiring it for their daily work.

The army now found itself positively employed. Over the preceding years of the emergency, an excellent training process had been developed whereby units arriving from other theatres sent ahead selected cadres to a jungle warfare centre, and these officers and non-commissioned officers passed on their knowledge to their battalion or regiment before it was committed to operations. The focus of training was the individual soldier within the sub-unit, whether rifle section or platoon; all else was complementary. Thus, when the newcomers, mostly national servicemen, entered the 'green twilight' of the jungle to patrol, or to stalk a guerrilla group, they were familiar with the environment and the disciplines required for its exploitation. Royal Air Force transport support was integrated closely with the army command, where previously it had tended to respond on the basis of conferring favours. Special forces in a reorganized and reinvigorated unit, the Malay Scouts, under Lieutenant-Colonel George Lea, made a unique contribution to the ascendancy secured by a united effort.

Between January and July 1951 there were almost 600 guerrilla operations. In the same period of 1954, the figure was 100. In 1951, the MRLA numbered 8,000 active members. By 1955, their strength had declined to 3,000. As numbers dwindled, the hunting down of the hard core grew more difficult. Military operations continued with the police until 1960. By that date, locally recruited battalions of the Malay Regiment, commanded and partly led by seconded members of the British army, formed the greater part of the counter-insurgency forces. More than 100 British officers, warrant, and non-commissioned officers were also involved in dedicated intelligence work outside the duties of general staff intelligence. Many were holding appointments inside or directly associated with the police special branch. Their experience, and that of their predecessors, was to prove valuable elsewhere.

As operations in Malaya turned towards success, terrorism opened in Kenya. Educated Africans sought to overthrow colonial rule but were unable to capture widespread native support because national independence was too vague a notion for peoples rooted in tribalism. However, Europeans had settled in unoccupied land within the Kikuyu tribal area in the early part of the twentieth century and this provided a focus of grievance. Thus the Mau Mau movement began. Morning and evening prayers were made collectively for the recovery of the land as a handful of soil was held up before those attending. The Kenya Land and Freedom Army was formed, comprised of independently operating Kikuyu gangs. There was no land grievance among the other tribes.

On 20 October 1952, the Governor pre-empted a first attempt at the mass murder of settlers, police, government servants, and those marked as native collaborators. Some 8,000 Kikuyu were arrested. But the colonial government had neither the scale of local intelligence nor the forces to contain such a huge movement. Indeed, it is probable that had the Kikuyu possessed adequate firearms at that time, the scale of murder would have risen to a massacre.

The security forces tripled in number, partly by reinforcement of British troops but more widely by African recruitment. In late April 1954, 25,000 troops and police cordoned and screened Nairobi, in which 15,000 Africans, mostly Kikuyu, were arrested, while many more were sent back to their tribal reserved areas. Within the latter, the Malayan policy of 'villagization' was followed. The secret committees in the Kikuyu areas, through which political and military activity had been directed, were largely destroyed, and the armed gangs were forced to base themselves in the rain forests.

The military command did not, however, draw immediately on another important lesson learned in Malaya. The hunting of gangs was attempted by grand sweeps through the forests, and random ambushing on the fringes through which supplies were believed to flow. The Royal Air Force dropped huge numbers of bombs on targets chosen by guesswork. These failed. But the police and military intelligence network, which had evolved as an integrated body, infiltrated the gangs by joining them or by running pseudo-gangs, chiefly due to the initiative of a senior police officer, Ian Henderson, and a junior army officer, Frank Kitson. Accurate intelligence gained in this way led to the final defeat of the gangs and thus of the Mau Mau movement in October 1956.

Three commitments involving active service thus occupied the British army during the first half of the 1950s: Korea, Malaya, and Kenya. Others threatened. The arbitrary expropriation of British oil interests in Iran early in 1951 prompted the deployment of the 16th Parachute Brigade in case the Labour Government decided to intervene, if only to save the lives of British oil workers. Politically uncertain and stretched to the limit of military resources, Attlee capitulated. The parachute brigade was none the less retained in the Middle East. Egypt proposed to nationalize the Suez Canal and annex the Sudan, which the British government resisted. The parachute brigade strengthened the occupation forces along the canal as local terrorism developed. This commitment was eventually to require two divisions to hold the area during protracted negotiations, which lasted until the latter part of 1954.

Operation Musketeer: Port Said, 1956

The Anglo-Egyptian Agreement of 1954 guaranteed the international status of the Suez Canal and the operation rights of the Anglo-French Suez Canal Company. On this understanding, the British government agreed to withdraw its forces securing the canal zone. Evacuation was completed on 13 June 1956. Six weeks later, in his first month of office as President of Egypt, Colonel Nasser abrogated the agreement and nationalized the canal, ousting the Suez Canal Company.

Anthony Eden, the British Prime Minister, at once decided that this breach should be remedied by force of arms. Thus began Operation Musketeer.

The army was ordered to land at Alexandria, the Mediterranean port of the Nile. To deceive the Egyptians, Port Said was the indicated site, a decision regretted when the landing was actually switched to Port Said. The Middle East Commander-in-Chief, General Sir Charles Keightley, had put it to the War Office that a landing at Alexandria would be opposed by the weight of the Egyptian army, necessitating the deployment of an armoured division within the British force. This would have to come from the British Army of the Rhine and would involve withdrawal of a formation committed to NATO. Moreover, the Chiefs of Staff advised that preliminary bombardment of, and fighting in, a densely populated area would involve tens of thousands of civilian casualties.

The final land order of battle involved the Royal Marine Commando Brigade and the 16th Parachute Brigade, both involved in counter-terrorist operations in Cyprus, and the 3rd Infantry Division in the United Kingdom. All were warned for operations by 1 August. To bring these formations to war establishment, the regular army reserve and selected national service reservists were mobilized. Most of the latter were sent to units in home stations (Britain and Germany) to replace regulars posted to the Musketeer force. Lieutenant-General Sir Hugh Stockwell was appointed to command the landing force.

The airborne training of the parachute brigade had been necessarily neglected in Cyprus. It was flown home to undertake at least two parachute drops per man in combination with other skills such as day and night rallying on drop zones, preparation and dropping of weapons, equipment, and ammunition. There were then no platforms in service for parachuting vehicles and artillery but obsolescent systems for use with Hastings aircraft were resuscitated. The 3rd Division was hastily mobilized with much cross-posting amid training during August. Their vehicles, war equipment, and stocks were hur-

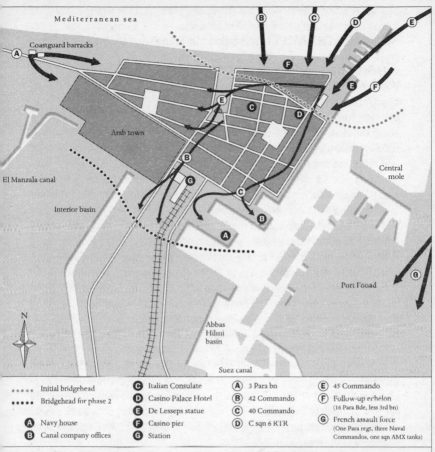

Phase 3 of Operation Musketeer, the Seaborne assault 5–6 November 1956

riedly embarked on sea transports at the end of the month, but the vessels remained at anchor while the destination came under question.

Meantime, France had become involved. A French parachute brigade joined 16th Parachute Brigade as it returned to Cyprus. The Commando Brigade completed refresher training in shore landings from helicopters, in association with the Mediterranean fleet, which was preparing to support the amphibious operation. During the summer, the Royal Air Force selected a range of targets whose loss would cripple Egyptian resistance.

Unknown to the military forces preparing, French and British political contacts had been made with the Israeli government, which was about to attack Egyptian forces in the Sinai desert. Details were revealed to the Chiefs of Staff in October. On 29 October, Israeli armour, preceded by parachute drops on two key passes, thrust south into the Sinai, opening an operation which routed local Egyptian forces in five days. Affecting to be alarmed by the threat of fighting along the Suez Canal, the British and French governments issued a twelve-hour ultimatum on 30 October to the Israelis and Egyptians to cease fighting, and when, as expected, there was no response, Operation Musketeer was launched. The air offensive began. The 3rd Division, less the Guards Brigade, embarked on 1 November. The 45th Commando and 16th Parachute Brigade landed by sea and air on 5 November.

The air offensive suppressed the Egyptian airfields not already attacked by the Israelis, but failed to destroy oil stocks, or cripple the Egyptian army. Cairo Radio continued to broadcast. One parachute battalion group—the 3rd—captured El Cap airfield by airborne assault; the remaining units, held back initially for deep airborne targets, travelled by sea to Port Said. The Commando Brigade captured all its objectives. The French parachutists took Port Fuad, opposite Port Said. Elements of the 16th Parachute Brigade under its commander, Brigadier M. A. H. Butler, and a contingent of the Royal Tank Regiment, set off south along the canal bank on 6 November to capture Ismailia.

Just before midnight, Brigadier Butler was ordered to stop on the hour, when a cease-fire would come into effect. This raised a difficulty. There were Egyptian forces ahead; the British column was in open desert with no defensible feature to hand. Brigadier Butler compromised, advancing until 00.15 a.m. to reach El Cap, where he sited the 2nd Battalion of the Parachute Regiment, with supporting detachments.

Political pressure from the United States obliged the British and French governments to accept the cease-fire terms drawn up by the United Nations. The 3rd Division landed to relieve the commandos and parachutists. While accepting a United Nations Emergency Force to replace the British presence, President Nasser none the less ensured that the canal could not be used by sinking or otherwise disabling forty-nine ships in the channel.

Launched without a clear aim other than revenge, with the abandonment of international diplomacy, Operation Musketeer was a failure in strategic terms. By mischance it covered the Soviet Union's military intervention in Hungary on 4 November. On this issue and, more generally, on the principle of premature military action against Egypt, the operation divided the British nation. It demonstrated the limitations of Britain's military capacity, and exposed errors in several staff functions, notably intelligence and movement control. Tactically successful, both in the sea and airborne assaults and the subsequent brief occupation, it was undertaken on the margin of capability. Thankfully, it was the last venture of its kind.

During this period, the British army's contribution to the NATO forces in Europe was gradually built up to the level of a corps of four divisions—the original offer of seven was never realized. The Commander-in-Chief of the British Army of the Rhine also assumed command of the NATO Northern Army Group. The Rhine Army base was adapted to function in war and similarly the line of communication forces which run through the Netherlands to British ports. United States funds made a substantial contribution to the progressive re-equipment of all these forces, including artillery with nuclear warheads, though a considerable portion of the cost fell thereafter to the British taxpayer. Important weaknesses remained, notably in radio communications at corps and higher levels.

For a brief time in the second half of the decade, the burdens of defence, particularly the demands on army manpower, appeared to be easing. A fresh plan was drawn up for reducing the size of the army. However, in April 1955, the Cyprus base, to which British forces had withdrawn in the Mediterranean from Egypt, was threatened by a Greek-Cypriot terrorist movement, EOKA, which sought the withdrawal of British colonial authority and the union of the island with Greece. Coincidentally, President Nasser of Egypt nationalized the Suez Canal Company contrary to the 1954 agreement with the British and French governments.

The seizure of Port Said was accomplished by Britain and France after much political deceit and Whitehall fumbling. It required the presence of the Royal Marine and 16th Parachute Brigades, and the 3rd Infantry Division, with a considerable administrative supplement to the base troops in Cyprus. United States intervention led to Anglo-French withdrawal in a matter of weeks at the end of 1956.

In Cyprus, EOKA terrorism swelled. The garrison was doubled, then tripled to exceed a division in numbers. Field Marshal Lord Harding was appointed as Governor with powers similar to those held by General Templer in Malaya. He was obliged to rebuild the special and criminal investigation branches of the demoralized police force; and to relieve the army

The Sandys Defence White Paper, 1957

On becoming Prime Minister in January 1957, Harold Macmillan made extensive changes in the government. Among these, Duncan Sandys was appointed Minister of Defence. Parliament was told that he would 'have authority to give decisions on all matters of policy affecting the size, shape, organisation, and disposition of the Armed Forces, their equipment and supply . . . and their pay and conditions of service'.

American dollar pressures on sterling had increased due to the Port Said operations. The new government looked to Sandys to cut defence spending substantially, and he arrived in office determined to challenge almost every function within the armed services. For example, given atomic weapons to confront the Soviet Union, the principal threat to Britain and her NATO allies, he asked why the army and Royal Air Force were organized to fight with conventional forces in Europe for an extended period? How did the Royal Navy justify its fleets and, particularly, aircraft carriers and cruisers? Why did the army require so many men to provide limited field forces?

Two answers were returned by General Sir Gerald Templer, Chief of the Imperial General Staff. The first was that the government's commitments were manifold. In the Far East there were security duties in Korea and Hong Kong, and counter-insurgency operations in Malaya. In the Middle East, Aden, the Trucial states, Muscat and Oman, and East and Central Africa required protection, Cyprus counter-terrorist forces. Four divisions were committed to NATO in Germany. Numerous small garrisons were required in colonial territories. Secondly, these were largely manned by national servicemen. At any given time, almost one-third of the army was being called up and put through basic and specialist training, on passage to a unit, or in the process of being released.

Duncan Sandys came to the view that the time had come to end national service, of which the army was preponderantly the client. It was clear that this would involve expenditure to make regular service more attractive, and that the battle-readiness of the Territorial Army would have to be enhanced, at some cost. A scheme was adopted which would permit the run-down of conscription from 1960. There would be compensatory savings in the training and movements organizations, and in accommodation.

The minister looked for more than this, however. He proposed that many of the overseas garrisons should be withdrawn. Aden, for example, could be policed by threat of air intervention in tribal areas turning to lawless behaviour, a return to the pre-war policy there and elsewhere in the Middle East. Neither the Foreign nor the Colonial Offices accepted this shift. The garrison providing protection to British Honduras against Guatamalan encroachment, as one among numerous examples, could not be replaced in this way.

The upshot was a new policy. As current overseas active commitments diminished in the Middle and Far East, small local garrisons and air facilities would be maintained to be reinforced from the United Kingdom if required. The transport command of the Royal Air Force would be strengthened and modernized to move troops to these advanced bases as necessary. Staging bases were to be developed, Gan in the Maldive islands being an important example.

An immediate beneficiary was the 16th Parachute Brigade, which had been due for reduction to a single parachute battalion group in 1956–7. Its mobility as a light force with the capability to land in undeveloped areas by parachute, or to capture airfields, as demonstrated at Port Said, would be retained as a whole. The Beverley, entering service, had the facility to drop vehicles, guns, and engineer plant on platforms. Though its range was relatively short, it could operate from unpaved air strips, making its superior cargo capacity valuable to move and supply other light troops operating forward from the overseas bases. Objections that soldiers would find it difficult to adapt rapidly to climatic changes were not supported within the army field forces, though it was conceded that, where jungle operations were required, a short training period would be necessary for reinforcement units arriving in this environment. This decision secured the retention of the jungle training school in Malaya.

These aspects of the new policy were accepted with enthusiasm by the army. Termination of conscription would permit concentration on professionalism. But inevitably it accentuated the split between those whose function required them to be in Germany, and those best fitted for other areas. Predominantly, the Royal Armoured Corps fell into the first category, though its reconnaissance units found some outlets in the second. The Royal Artillery, Royal Signals, and Royal Electrical and Mechanical Engineers also tended to become specialized for service in one or the other role. Those in Germany, or in units at home, dedicated to Germany on mobilization, regulars and Territorials, came to regard themselves as the notably professional body in the army. Those deployed to what was eventually entitled the Army Strategic Command regarded them as theorists forever engaged in exercise while the light forces undertook operations elsewhere. There was some truth in this.

In strengthening the authority of the Minister of Defence, that of the single-service ministers was diminished. The Prime Minister counted upon it; he was anxious to centralize many of the defence functions as a means to further economies. However, his hopes that the new policies would effect the necessary organizational changes were not realized. From the moment of Sandys's appointment, the service departments were determined to maintain their independence; the War Office and Air Ministry, for example, closed ranks with the Admiralty on 15 February 1957 to retain aircraft carriers in service. In these circumstances, the powers of the new minister were taxed to their limit simply to change the form of the forces over a given term, and to find compensatory savings in the process. Even so, though few of those in the government and the services' high command realized it, a profound shift had been accomplished towards centralization. There would be no turning back.

---

from the many police tasks it had necessarily assumed. However, detention, collective punishments, and resettlement were not appropriate to the circumstances. Fortunately, active EOKA numbers were small, less than 300, and although they were at first overwhelmingly backed by the Greek-Cypriot majority, their arrogance and ineptitude alienated many of their own people: informers were found; prisoners were turned. In the largely open, part-mountainous country, grand sweeps, using helicopters, paid a dividend. These, with night raids by 'snatch' squads, eroded EOKA strength and supplies. By 1960, Greek Cypriots had abandoned support for union with Greece, preferring an independent state of Cyprus. Britain was content to grant this, while retaining Sovereign Base Areas (SBAs) absolutely under British control.

While the counter-EOKA campaign continued, these bases were used for a second deployment of the 16th Parachute Brigade. President Nasser, in association with Ba'athist factions in the Middle East, aimed to overthrow the old order in the region. In July 1958, revolutionaries seized power in Iraq. Syria threatened the Lebanon. A pro-Egyptian movement prepared to murder the king in Jordan. While United States forces entered the Lebanon to demonstrate support for her sovereignty, the parachute brigade was flown to Amman with a similar task. Both were successful.

Even so, the political failure of the Suez Canal expedition, and the huge cost in mounting it, persuaded the British government that the old method of mounting operations outside Europe was wasteful. Garrisons overseas—Germany in this connection was considered to be a home station—would be reduced to as great an extent as possible, and new commitments would be met by reinforcements flown out from the United Kingdom. On this basis, the use of national servicemen was manifestly wasteful. The Defence White Paper of 1957 announced that, 'the government have concluded that it would be right to aim at stabilising the armed forces on an all-regular footing of about 375,000 by the end of 1962'.

The army was now alone in employing numbers of conscripts, but improved pay and conditions of service, combined with the challenge of recurrent overseas operations, aided regular recruitment. One last operation involved their use. In July 1961, Iraq threatened Kuwait. A British brigade and battalion of parachutists were sent to reinforce the common frontier in the height of summer. The Iraqis stood off. The greatest problem was maintaining sufficient water supplies to keep the British troops fit for operations in the intense heat. A parachute battalion group, including a tank squadron, was thereafter based on Bahrein island to deter Iraqi aggression.

This general area developed as the principal theatre of regular British army operations for the remainder of the decade. British troops and local forces led by seconded British officers and non-commissioned officers maintained internal security in Muscat and Oman, in the protectorate of Aden (later, the South Arabian Federation), and in the Trucial Oman. Internal security responsibility for East Africa also fell to the command headquarters in Aden.

To the east, in 1963, the garrisons in Malaya and Singapore, and in Hong Kong, each included a division, in which Gurkha forces were prominent. In that year, Indonesia began to threaten the former British Borneo territories, in which, inaccurately—perhaps forebodingly—a Foreign Office policy paper noted 'British troops are unlikely to be involved'.

Throughout the period 1945–63, the greatest threat and hence the greatest demand for the army appeared to successive British governments to be within the NATO central front. This important commitment absorbed the greater part of the Royal Armoured Corps and Royal Artillery, and funds for re-equipment. To a great extent, the army consisted of two discrete groups: those whose service lay between Britain and Germany; and those on the overseas round. The former became proficient, if somewhat entrenched, in high-intensity war preparations; sophisticated cooks who were never required to supply the banqueting table. The latter were plain cooks occupied continuously over a hot stove.

In both groups, the regulars provided the professionalism and continuity. Their success was enhanced by the presence of a mature core of commanders, staff officers, and specialists who had practised extensively in the Second World War. But for eighteen years after the end of the war, national servicemen formed the body of the army. They griped in it, they scoffed at it, they looked forward to leaving it, but most gave the best of themselves to it; and when they looked back on their service in the corps and regiments almost to a man they rated it the most rewarding period of their lives.

They were the 'battle dress' years of peace, one uniform for all purposes in temperate climates. Tunics and trousers for all ranks awaited their passing; the high-quality woollen pullovers and disruptive pattern field dress were trivial marks of a profound change in the character of a British army restored to a basis of long service and professional expertise.

16 THE THIRTY YEARS PEACE

JOHN STRAWSON

Between 1963 and 1992, the British army helped to keep the peace in Europe while waging numerous little wars elsewhere. Its strength declined from 170,000 to 153,000. Its capabilities were enhanced by excellent equipment which could be used as effectively in Europe as it could in the South Atlantic or Arabia. Although small the army led the world in experience. Its soldiers saw much active service as the campaign medals on their tunics showed. Composed entirely of volunteers, organized in regiments and corps with fiercely guarded tradition and spirit, it spread itself round the world and adapted itself to tasks as various as those in Cyprus, Belize, Borneo, the Falkland Islands, Arabia, Northern Ireland, and BAOR.

In 1963 Macmillan's Government argued that the Suez crisis had emphasized Britain's economic weakness. Military expenditure would have to be cut. This meant reducing overseas commitments. Moreover, it was decided to end national service. These measures were given effect by the Sandys White Paper of 1957, and determined the army's composition in the early 1960s. There was still much for the now all-regular army to do. In all 55,000 troops made up the British Army of the Rhine. In June 1961, 6,000 soldiers had been sent to Kuwait to meet a threat from Iraq. British forces were still committed in 1963 to support Aden's joining the Federation of South Arabia. There were bases in Kenya, Hong Kong, Malaya, and Singapore. The British army was soon to be heavily engaged in both the Middle East and Far East.

In Borneo the Brunei rebellion in December 1962 was quickly suppressed by dispatching soldiers there. But the threat remained. President Sukarno of Indonesia declared his confrontation of Malaysia, and in Sarawak the Chinese Clandestine Communist organization endangered internal security. At first there were very few British soldiers to guard the frontier with Indonesian Borneo and in April 1963 incursions by

Indonesian troops began. The British response was such that by the end of that year some 15,000 troops were deployed, and by a combination of intelligence, patrolling, and mobility, the army defeated every incursion. Gurkha soldiers again showed their excellence as jungle fighters; one, Lance-Corporal Rambahador Limbu, 10th Gurkha Rifles, won the Victoria Cross in a spirited display of courage and leadership at Serekin in 1965, when his platoon attacked a strong enemy position on a steep hill under intense automatic fire.

The British infantry quickly adapted to the need for jungle skills, stealth, and marksmanship. All were ably supported by the other arms. Logistic demands were heavy. General Walter Walker went further. He took the fight into Kalimantan itself, with so-called 'cross border operations' in which the Special Air Service (SAS) figured prominently. By September 1965 it was clear that Sukarno had failed.

The emergency in South Arabia was declared in December 1963. It ended with a British withdrawal four years later. There were two uprisings to deal with—the Radfan tribesmen in Aden Protectorate and the urban guerrillas in Aden itself. Without adequate power, neither campaign was winnable. Yet what the soldiers did, whether in the scorching arid mountains of the Radfan or the mean alleyways of Crater, showed their indomitable character; the SAS with their undercover work, Lieutenant-Colonel Colin Mitchell's Highlanders tightening their grip on Crater, British officers controlling a near-mutinous South Arabian army—the courage and example of these men are beyond praise. But it was all in vain.

While these operations in Borneo and Arabia were in progress, the government had changed. Harold Wilson formed his first administration in October 1964. New directions were both given and followed. Defence policy itself, guided by the dynamic Denis Healey, was transformed. By this time a new Ministry of Defence vested authority and responsibility in a single Secretary of State. Healey, with his mastery of both foreign affairs and weapon technology, was determined to bring Britain's defence expenditure into line with her resources. He was resolved also to scrap what he regarded as the outmoded remnants of Britain's imperial defence commitments. British troops deployed east of Suez were steadily reduced. Even the renowned Territorial Army was not immune. A major reorganization and reduction of reserve forces was carried out. One event, however, did much to remind the world of Britain's past imperial splendour and at the same time provide the army with an opportunity to display its genius for ordered ceremony—the funeral of Sir Winston Churchill in January 1965.

It was the first state funeral given to a subject since the Duke of Wellington's death, and was conducted with all the pageantry and precision at which the British army excelled. Under the faultless direction of the Household Division a solemn ceremony unfolded. The King's Troop fired mourning guns in Hyde Park. The procession was led by a Household Cavalry drum horse, drums funereal in black crêpe, while behind the coffin on its gun carriage officers of Churchill's regiment (formerly the 4th Hussars, now The Queen's Royal Irish Hussars) bore his Insignia and Standards. Innumerable military bands, as Churchill himself had wished, played fitting music including the Dead March from *Saul*, while soldiers lined the streets from Parliament Square to St Paul's heads bared, arms reversed. After the service at which a hundred nations were represented, six Grenadier Guardsmen carried the coffin to the River Thames. From Waterloo Station a Bearer Party of the QRIH took their Colonel on his last journey and laid him to rest at Bladon. It was not just the end of a great soldier. It was the end of an era.

Part of the price paid by Wilson after talks with President Johnson in June 1967 for United States' assistance with the British economy was his agreement to maintain a military presence east of Suez. British troop withdrawals were slow. British forces were to remain in Malaysia and Singapore until the mid-1970s, while no time was fixed for leaving either Hong Kong or the Persian Gulf. But some of these undertakings were reversed when, early in 1968, Wilson announced an end to Britain's imperial legacy east of Suez. The British withdrew from Aden in November 1967, fighting almost until the last. This was not the end of the army's involvement in south Arabia, however. Soon a different and successful campaign was to be fought in the Dhofar of Oman. Moreover, a British presence continued in the Gulf states with regiments in Bahrain and locally raised forces led by British officers in Abu Dhabi, the Trucial Oman, and Kuwait.

In the Far East, although there were substantial reductions of troops from Borneo and Malaya, regiments continued to be stationed in the peninsula and Singapore. Indeed, when Edward Heath formed his administration in June 1970, he instantly set about trying to change the policy in order to maintain an east of Suez military commitment.

By this time, however, another task had arisen much closer to home— one which was to continue for more than twenty years and still shows no sign of ending—that of countering a terrorist campaign mounted by the

SAS

Like the Parachute Regiment, the Special Air Service was born during the Second World War, the brainchild of an imaginative and determined young Scots Guards officer, David Stirling. Stirling had participated in a number of large-scale, but singularly unsuccessful Commando operations against targets on the Libyan coast. He became convinced that a radical rethink of sea-borne tactics was called for, and, in the summer of 1941, came up with the idea for the SAS while convalescing in a Cairo military hospital.

Stirling's idea was for the creation of a small unit of specialist saboteurs and raiders who, working in tiny teams, would be parachuted behind the enemy lines, where they would attack key targets such as aerodromes, vehicle convoys, ammunition dumps, and trains. Success would be dependent on tough selection and training standards, and, as crucially, on the use of surprise.

After bypassing the normal chain of command, Stirling obtained the resources and authority to create an experimental unit of about sixty men—L Detachment, Special Air Service. The SAS suffix was merely a ruse to deceive the enemy of L Detachment's true strength.

The first SAS mission against two Axis airfields was calamitous (half of L Detachment were killed or captured) but brought Stirling into contact with the Long Range Desert Group (LRDG). The LRDG were specialists at desert reconnaissance and travel, and had been given the task of picking up Stirling's men after their mission. Subsequent operations, some of which were spectacularly successful, involved both units, with LRDG providing wheeled transport to the target area.

The SAS grew rapidly, and extended its operations well beyond the desert. By late 1942 it had expanded to nearly 400 men, and was officially designated a regiment of the British army—1st Special Air Service. In 1943 a second regiment, 2nd SAS, was raised, and put under the command of David's brother, William. In 1944, an SAS Brigade was formed, consisting of two British SAS regiments, two French regiments, and a Belgian squadron.

Although its members served with the greatest distinction in the Middle East and Europe, the British SAS regiments were disbanded in late 1945. In 1947, a Territorial Army regiment, 21 SAS (Artists Rifles), was created, but the Malayan emergency ensured the return of the regular SAS. A special jungle warfare unit was raised by ex-SAS Second World War brigade commander and ex-Chindit Michael Calvert. At Calvert's suggestion, the new regular unit was officially designated as the Malayan Scouts (SAS).

Although not without problems for the reconstituted SAS, the Malayan campaign was successful. Calvert's men had the ability to operate deep in the jungle with minimal support, thus acting as a powerful psychological weapon against the Communist enemy. Moreover, the Malayan Scouts pursued a deliberate policy of winning over the 'hearts and minds' of the locals—a vital factor in many subsequent SAS operations. In 1952 the Malyan Scouts (SAS) evolved into 22 Special Air Service.

The growing problem of low intensity anti-guerrilla/anti-terrorist warfare in the post-colonial world ensured the regular regiment's survival and further emulation. Nevertheless the public in Britain were not always aware of what 22 SAS were getting up to in trouble spots like Oman, Borneo, and Aden and many in Britain had not heard of it until the 1970s. News coverage of the regiment's participation in Northern Ireland was partly responsible for a higher profile, as was the Mogadishu incident. But the event which really pushed the SAS into the headlines and legend was Operation Nimrod—the Iranian Embassy rescue in 1980.

The modern SAS is grouped into two Territorial (21 SAS and 23 SAS) and one regular regiment (22 SAS based at Hereford). At full strength, 22 SAS is over 700 strong and was involved in both the Falklands and Gulf campaigns in deep infiltration and reconnaissance work although it remains expert in counter-revolutionary warfare. It is known that SAS specialists based in London and Hereford are on twenty-four-hour alert in the United Kingdom, and it is probable that a squadron of SAS are currently based in Northern Ireland.

Soldiers in the regular SAS, who tend to be older than the army norm, have all served with other units (many as NCOs) before putting themselves forward for 'selection' as SAS troopers. Selection is a gruelling rite of passage, involving tests of physical and psychological stamina. The regiment seeks brighter than average men, athletically fit, who can cope with extreme deprivation and isolation. The high, or low, point of selection, depending on whether one passes it or not, is a rapid 40-mile hike across the Brecon Beacons with a 55 lb. rucksack and a rifle. After passing through this—some have died in the process—soldiers progress to continuation training where they learn basic SAS skills such as parachuting, marksmanship, and wilderness survival. After continuation training and formal recognition the SAS trooper will go on to acquire one or more specialist skills. It will take about eighteen months to two years for him to be fully trained, even though the basic SAS tour of duty is three years.

Recently, and most unusually, there has been significant criticism of SAS training and selection methods. It has been suggested that the SAS has become too obsessed with physical training, partly as a result of the number of ex-Parachute Regiment instructors in the regiment. There has also been some criticism of the modern SAS as being an NCO-dominated unit—what one military historian referred to in a different context as the rise of 'sergeant' power. However these issues are resolved, the SAS remains one of the most highly trained and operationally effective military formations in the world.

Michael Yardley

Provisional IRA. The 'troubles' began in 1968 when a civil rights movement created by the Roman Catholic minority flared into violent protest in Londonderry. It was in Londonderry in the summer of 1969 that Catholic reaction to the activity of the Orange Order and Protestant Apprentice Boys led to violence and loss of life. The British army thereupon deployed troops, in addition to the brigade already there, and gradually extended its operations throughout the Province. The IRA's campaign extended even to the mainland, where not only army establishments, but civilian targets too, were attacked with bombs.

From the early 1970s, the army's operations in Northern Ireland followed a familiar pattern. Special training was needed for regiments and battalions before they went off to try to contain terrorism while politicians floundered helplessly about in search of a political solution. Not only was the infantry involved; armoured, artillery, engineer regiments, and the other corps all took their share. Four months' emergency tours were often normal, while some regiments would spend a full eighteen months to two years in the Province with families and all their regimental accoutrements. Despite subsequent distractions like the Falkland Islands and the Gulf, we should not underestimate the profound influence of Ulster on soldiers' lives. This seemingly endless commitment calls much of the tune. It conditions deployment, training, movement, and logistics; it affects morale; it shapes the soldier's life. Powers of command, observation, alertness, stealth, cunning, tactical dexterity, versatility, endurance, anticipation, the need to act quickly and properly in a tight corner—all these things enhance a soldier's professionalism and pride in achievement. That the army has carried out these duties for so long so successfully says much for the quality of its people and its leadership, and of course this quality owes almost everything to regimental and corps spirit and tradition. In 1970 after the disbandment of the paramilitary B Specials, the Ulster Defence Regiment (UDR) was formed, a force of part-time soldiers, able to relieve the regular army of many security tasks, such as guarding installations and patrolling. The UDR eventually reached a strength of 9,000. One of the long remembered incidents of this long campaign was Bloody Sunday on 30 January 1972, a clash between Catholics taking part in a prohibited civil rights march in Londonderry and troops of the Parachute Regiment. Thirteen Catholics were killed and many others wounded. Heath suspended the Northern Ireland government at Stormont and imposed direct rule from Westminster with William Whitelaw as Secretary of State. Numerous political initiatives have failed to resolve the problem.

Before his imposition of direct rule in Ulster and despite his wish to retain a positive defence position overseas, particularly in the Persian Gulf and Malaysia/Singapore, Heath had been obliged to submit to the dictates of the economy and the extreme reluctance of both the Foreign Office and the Ministry of Defence to maintain a British military presence in the Middle and Far East. Withdrawal from east of Suez therefore went on. Yet in one particular area of southern Arabia, the Dhofar, the British army was able to demonstrate how to conduct a patient and eventually successful exercise in winning the hearts and minds of the tribesmen, so turning them away from armed Communist-led rebellion and back to allegiance to Oman's Sultan Qaboos. It was here that the SAS action was so important, raising and training the Dhofari irregulars, the *firqats*, to fight for the Sultan. It was essentially a war about people, about winning the support of the Djebel Dhofar tribesmen, with military action preceding proper civil development. The SAS devised a strategy by which the rebels would not be eradicated, but rather persuaded to change sides and join the government forces. It was done by establishing good intelligence cells, providing a proper information service, assisting the tribesmen with medical care for themselves and veterinary care for their animals; *and* by raising the *firqats* to fight for the Sultan. It took six years, from 1970 to 1976, yet once the government had shown that their authority held good on the *djebel* as well as in the coastal towns, it became a question of hunting down and eliminating the remaining rebels. There were some hard marches and bitter fights, and once again the SAS showed their unique skill, versatility, and courage.

There is always a temptation when examining military activity to concentrate on the scenes of action. So that to see the whole army in the mid-1970s we must look at it more broadly. In central America a battalion

The British Army in Northern Ireland

On 14 August 1969 British troops were called in to give 'Military Aid to the Civil Power' in Northern Ireland. Their initial task was to protect Catholics in Londonderry and on 15 August they deployed to the Catholic housing estates. Meanwhile the IRA—whose members had acted as stewards during the civil rights marches—considered how it should respond to the British army presence. The British troops might be protecting Catholic lives and homes but they were still representatives of the government which had helped to prevent a united Ireland. In December 1969 the organization split, a group of young hardliners setting up a Provisional IRA with a political wing called Sinn Fein ('ourselves alone' in Gaelic).

In 1970 the army had to contend with trouble from both Protestant and Catholic communities. However, it was not until 1971 that the first British soldier was killed—Gunner Curtis of the Royal Artillery. The same day, the army shot and killed a member of the Provisional IRA's staff, James Saunders. From this time on the situation began to deteriorate.

The Provisional IRA are reputed to have thought that if they could kill as many British soldiers as had died in Aden (38), the British government would be forced by public opinion to pull the troops out of Northern Ireland. Hence, the organization adopted tactics that were a mixture of terrorism and guerrilla warfare. In the eyes of some young Catholics, there was a certain glamour to these methods, and the Provisionals had no difficulty in recruiting volunteers. Indeed, they were so successful that the old official IRA—the 'Stickies'—decided to join the shooting and ambushed an army patrol on 22 May 1971.

In spite of its recent counter-insurgency experience in Kenya, Malaya, Cyprus, and Aden, the army was unsure how to respond. In 1971, a year in which 130 bombs exploded in the province—internment without trial was introduced. Intelligence was poor and the wrong people were interned, alienating most of the Catholic community. The army increased its visible presence and introduced more overt patrolling. Things went from bad to worse when members of the Parachute Regiment shot dead thirteen men and wounded thirteen others on what become known as 'Bloody Sunday'. Shortly afterwards the British Embassy in Dublin was burnt down and on 22 March 1972 the Parachute Regiment Mess at Aldershot was bombed by the Provisionals—their first mainland attack.

In the same month, the Ulster parliament at Stormont was dissolved and direct rule from Westminster was imposed. The army began a very serious consideration of both its intelligence-gathering system and its training methods. Special facilities were created where soldiers could practise marksmanship and patrolling in realistic conditions. Gifted officers like Frank Kitson rethought intelligence and tactics. In July Operation Motorman was launched to re-occupy Catholic 'no-go' areas in Belfast. Yet 1972 remains the worst year for the British army: 129 soldiers were killed; and there were 1,300 explosions and more than 10,000 shooting incidents.

After 1975 the troubles were more successfully contained; army and police tactics improved, and, crucially, intelligence operations became much more sophisticated. In 1976, a long-term political solution still no nearer, the process known as Ulsterization began. The Ulster Defence Regiment was expanded. In 1977 the British policy document, *The Way Ahead*, confirmed the primacy of the police. They would take over much of the army's high-profile role patrolling on the streets. The army meantime would be used to support police operations. In practice this meant an increase in undercover and surveillance operations. The SAS was formally deployed in the province in 1976, and at about the same time a new élite unit was created—14 Intelligence Company (known within the Army as 14 Int.). They would have a special responsibility for covert surveillance and many of their operations have subsequently been confused with those of the better known SAS.

The Provisional IRA's reaction to these developments was to reorganize itself. Heavily infiltrated, it adopted a cell structure of three- to five-man ASUs (Active Service Units). This new structure was not well suited to guerrilla warfare, but it was ideal for terrorist operations, and consequently the relative number of the latter increased.

The army in Ulster—whatever policy problems it may have suffered initially—has quietly and bravely got on with the job throughout the troubles. It has been said of the Northern Ireland conflict that it is 'a corporal's war' because of the great responsibility that is put onto young NCOs. It has certainly been a unique testing-ground for soldiers of all ranks, not to mention their families. For those who have not been there in uniform the strain of being 'a walking human target' can only be imagined. As a result of Northern Ireland, the British army has unique expertise in such skills as urban patrolling, bomb disposal, and covert surveillance. The army has developed much new equipment, better body armour, devices capable of jamming the radio transmitters of PIRA bombers, and, more controversially, sophisticated computer systems, capable of organizing huge quantities of intelligence data.

Northern Ireland District is organized in three brigade areas: 39 Brigade Lisburn, 3 Brigade Armagh, and 8 Brigade Londonderry.

The commitment to maintaining order in Northern Ireland occupied until

November 1995 about 18,500 servicemen and women, including 11,500 regular soldiers, 6,000 members of the Ulster Defence Regiment (merged with the Royal Irish Rangers in 1992 to become the Royal Irish Regiment), and 1,250 Royal Air Force and Royal Navy personnel. Some units would be on short tours and others on two-year tours.

After the Provisional IRA ceasefire was announced in August 1995 about three units, totalling 1,600 men, were withdrawn and Army patrolling in support of the RUC was radically scaled down. There was also a gradual dismantling of some of the more visible apparatus of counter-insurgency such as fortified observation posts. After the Docklands bombing in London in February 1996 which brought the ceasefire to an end, about 500 troops (a battalion of the Royal Irish Regiment) were redeployed to Ulster. However, at the time of writing the shooting war in Northern Ireland has not re-started.

During the twenty-seven years it has been involved in Northern Ireland's 'troubles', the Army has had over 600 of its members killed, and nearly 5,000 wounded as a result of the conflict.

Michael Yardley

---

group continued to guarantee Belize's security. It was an agreeable change of station. On the other side of the world, Gurkhas and other British soldiers did their internal security and frontier-watching tasks in Hong Kong. In Brunei the Sultan found it prudent to pay for a Gurkha battalion to be positioned there. In Cyprus there were both garrisons in our Sovereign Base Areas, and contributions to the UN peace-keeping force. In Gibraltar a battalion mounted guard at the Governor's Residence and kept an eye on the well-being of the apes. The Royal Engineers built bridges, roads, power plants, schools, and jetties in such far away places as Malawi, Bangladesh, Kenya, and Anguilla. To relieve the starving peoples of Sudan, Ethiopia, and Nepal, the air dispatch teams of the Royal Corps of Transport (RCT) dropped supplies from RAF Hercules aircraft. In Alberta battle groups conducted field firing exercises at the priceless Suffield ranges. Thus the army's activities were infinitely varied, its readiness a watchword.

Readiness has long been the keynote of the British Army of the Rhine (BAOR). In Germany some fifty thousand men, organized in four (later three) armoured and one artillery divisions, have been described as the best trained and equipped army that we have ever had in peacetime. It was no idle claim—as events in the Gulf were to show in 1990 and 1991. Before recent changes, I British Corps, supported by RAF Harriers and Chinooks, prided itself on its expertise in mobile warfare to meet, slow down, and stop any incursion across what was then the West German border. Soldiers could derive great satisfaction from mastering their excellent weapons—Chieftain and Challenger tanks, the Warrior, and the new Multi-Launch Rocket System with its devastating salvoes made even more so with rich information furnished by far-reaching surveillance and target acquisition devices. Helicopter regiments gave a new dimension to the basic elements of combat—fire-power and manoeuvre. Secure signalling enabled a third essential—command—to be properly exercised. The all-important question of assured supplies was facilitated by nimble, effective logistic teams. A hundred miles or so to the east of BAOR's border, moreover, was another garrison—the Berlin brigade, taking its part with comparable French and US forces in keeping West Berlin free and prosperous, and providing incidentally a popular station for British troops—good housing, excellent sporting facilities, culture galore, and a welcome change from other cantonments.

In 1975, Britain's best-known soldier, Montgomery, died. There has been no other recent field marshal to capture the nation's imagination in the same way, although Templer will be remembered not just as an outstanding soldier, but as the creator of the National Army Museum, and General Sir John Hackett has endeared himself to the nation by his lively TV appearances. What is the general public's idea of a British soldier? Wherever he may be stationed—in Germany, the Falkland Islands, Crossmaglen—we think of him in combat kit with a gun in his hand, or with his head visible from a tank turret, flying a helicopter, manning an artillery piece, bridge-building under shell fire—in short a fighting man. Yet to see the army in the round, we have to remember those soldiers whose activity and employment is not primarily concerned with the application of violence. Think of a soldier in the Royal Army Ordnance Corps and you may picture a man issuing stores, running a depot, sitting at a desk. This excellent corps, however, is also manned by those who, with their two o'clock in the morning courage, defuse deadly bombs, sometimes suffering mutilation or death and frequently being awarded a George Medal or MBE for gallantry.

All the army's supporting corps have done and still do their stuff. Butchers, bakers, electricians, plumbers, dentists, chaplains, medical men, cooks, pioneers and all make up the sum of it. The Army Catering Corps has transformed the quality, choice, and presentation of food in the dining-hall. Apprentice colleges turn out highly skilled young craftsmen and give them an adventurous sporting life into the bargain. The Redcaps still patrol and assert discipline, pay clerks see to it that soldiers' entitlements do not lag behind, computers are mastered, parachuting techniques perfected, recruits are trained, all the various Arms Schools teach officers, NCOs, and men their special skills, while Sandhurst shows officer cadets how to Serve in order to Lead. There is almost no trade or calling with which the army is not concerned. Yet many of these special tasks could be done by the soldiers of armoured, artillery, engineer, and infantry regiments, as they used to be. Of course they would have to be properly trained, but the savings in specialist corps overheads would be significant.

When it comes to ceremonial parades, what other army can bear comparison with the Household Division, or for that matter any corps in the army? Military music cheers, inspires, and entertains. And all this does not hold good only for the regulars, the Professionals. There is the Territorial Army too, about 60,000 to 70,000 strong, its volunteers giving up their time to train and serve, ready to reinforce or supplement the regular units in emergency. Nor must we forget the Women's Services. They are part of the British Army. An officer or other rank in the Women's Royal Army Corps (WRAC) or the Queen Alexandra's Royal Army Nursing Corps (QARANC), whether her job is Assistant Adjutant of an infantry battalion, on the staff of a Commander-in-Chief, driving a car, serving at table, or running a hospital ward, does it quickly and well, is articulate, elegant, and conscientious. Recruiting is good, morale high, their contribution to the army very great.

All the ups and downs of Defence Reviews have not changed the British army's incomparable achievements in keeping the peace, whether in Europe, Ulster, Belize, Cyprus, Hong Kong, or southern Arabia. In 1974, with another Labour Government in power, there was another Defence Review.

This review, like all such exercises, was designed to save money. It was dressed up under the guise of committing Britain's ground forces to the defence of Europe and shedding the remainder of our global responsibilities. In doing so 15,000 troops were to be saved. Britain's contribution to NATO was to be made more effective by a restructuring programme. The idea was that by eliminating one level of command—the brigade—the fighting strength of BAOR would be enhanced. Moreover certain functions, hitherto performed by a variety of combat regiments, such as flying helicopters, providing anti-tank weapons, and driving large supply vehicles, were to be carried out by single corps of the army. Far from enhancing the capability of the regular army, these measures reduced it. But one feature of the changes—that of integrating Territorial Army units into regular formations (temporarily called 'field forces' as the title brigade was taboo—a taboo soon lifted)—was good, in that it made far more effective use of the reserve army.

When this restructuring exercise was completed in 1978, the 1st British Corps contained four weak armoured divisions and a light infantry force. Earmarked to reinforce the corps from the United Kingdom Land Forces (UKLF) were the so-called 6 Field Force from Aldershot and 7 Field Force from Colchester. UKLF was also responsible for providing a substantial number of individual reinforcements for BAOR, together with logistic and rear area defence units, as well as being responsible for deploying home defence battalions. The government's continued desire to shed its overseas responsibilities was thwarted this time by the Turkish invasion of northern Cyprus in 1974, which ensured not only the continuance of the British Sovereign Base Areas, but also demanded the deployment of more British troops in a UN peace-keeping role.

Other features of the army's reorganization during the 1970s included the grouping of the infantry's 'large regiments' and individual battalions into Divisions. Thus we had The Guards Division, The Scottish Division, The Queen's Division, The King's Division, The Prince of Wales' Division, and The Light Division. In addition there were, and still are, the Brigade of Gurkhas, the Parachute Regiment, and the Special Air Service Regiment. Before this, however, the British army celebrated the Queen's Jubilee with a splendid mounted parade organized by the 4th Armoured Division at Sennelager in July 1977. Soon after this, in 1979, Mrs Margaret Thatcher became Prime Minister.

Even before the Falklands War, Mrs Thatcher had reason to be grateful to the SAS Regiment, for in May 1980 an Arab terrorist group took over the Iranian Embassy in Prince's Gate, and, in a glare of publicity, began negotiations with the police. The SAS had been instantly alerted and were deployed in London ready for a violent dénouement should this be necessary. It was. As soon as the terrorists had shot and killed a hostage, shoving his body out of the Embassy, the SAS, who had been planning and preparing their assault for several days, went into action. They killed all six terrorists, although not before one more hostage had been killed and others injured. But given the task facing them—to act with such speed and daring that they would stun the gunmen into inaction, to decide *who were* the gunmen, deal with them, and release the twenty hostages—it was an astonishing success, and gave a new expression to the anti-terrorist jargon; the gunmen had been 'negotiated'. Also in 1980 the army successfully assisted in establishing an independent Zimbabwe, both by keeping the peace before elections and by supervising the elections themselves. As usual the British soldiers' calm good nature and humour were most beneficial. Next came a far more complex and difficult operation in which the SAS again distinguished themselves. On Good Friday 1982, the Falkland Islands were seized by Argentina.

The Falklands campaign was short and victorious. It lasted from the beginning of April, when the first vessels of the Task Force sailed, until 14 June when General Menendez surrendered at Port Stanley. The first action on land was the retaking of South Georgia by the SAS and Royal Marines on 26 April. Nearly four weeks later units of the army and Royal Marines landed at San Carlos, and British troops quickly demonstrated their superiority over the poorly trained Argentinian conscripts. They could not have done it without the superb support of the Royal Navy and Royal Air Force. Many regiments distinguished themselves. The 2nd Battalion, Parachute Regiment, took Goose Green, with some 1,200 prisoners, losing their gallant Commanding officer, Lieutenant-Colonel H. Jones, killed in action and subsequently awarded a posthumous VC. The Royal Marines 'yomped' their way from one end of East Falkland to the other. The Welsh Guards suffered grievous casualties from an air assault on *Sir Galahad* at Bluff Cove. The Scots Guards took Tumbledown Mountain. The Gurkhas played their part. In all some 7,000 British troops were involved, with magnificent support from the Royal Artillery and helicopters, both RAF and Army Air Corps (AAC). 'As a military exercise, however,' wrote Kenneth O. Morgan in his *British History 1945–1989*, 'many gaps in British naval and air provision had been shown up; but it was a spectacular triumph.' Had John Nott, Defence Secretary at the time, had his way in reducing the Royal Navy, it may be doubted whether the operation could have taken place at all. For the army, it showed once more that 'the readiness is all'. And now, instead of a mere handful of Royal Marines, there is a substantial garrison stationed in the Falklands including a battalion group from the army.

As the 1980s advanced and Mrs Thatcher's administration was confirmed by the electorate both in 1983 and 1987, there were several changes in Defence Secretary, but few in defence policy. The flamboyant Mr

Heseltine lost his position in the Cabinet over the Westland affair in 1986, and although the subsequent row weakened the Prime Minister's position, it did not prevent her re-election the following year. By 1987 her position and that of the country had been greatly enhanced by her reputation as a world statesman. Military victory in the Falkland Islands and Britain's reviving economy gave an illusion of national strength. Yet Ulster smouldered on. The loyalist paramilitary organizations simply exacerbated the situation with many killings. Further initiatives leading to the Anglo-Irish agreement gave hope of better joint security action both sides of the border between the Irish Republic and Ulster, but the IRA campaign continues. It has still to be seen whether anything will come of the latest attempts to reconcile the seemingly irreconcilable. The British army maintains troops in Northern Ireland, its strength in 1992 being roughly 11,000 but the bill has been heavy—400 soldiers have been killed there since 1969.

In 1989 and 1990, to the great surprise and consternation of many, there began a thaw in the so-called Cold War. The weakness of the Soviet economy, combined with the effects of *perestroika* and *glasnost* encouraged Eastern European countries to cast off at last the chains of Marxist Leninism. Poland, Czechoslovakia, East Germany, Rumania, Bulgaria, even Albania opted for change. New disarmament agreements, both nuclear and conventional, hastened the process. The Berlin Wall came down. Germany was reunited. It was agreed that Soviet troops would eventually leave all these countries. The Warsaw Pact was no more. The Cold War was over. What then was the need for the deterrent strength of NATO? A peace dividend was called for, although on present form there looks like being little peace in the world. Yugoslavia exploded in 1991 and fighting broke out in various parts of the disintegrating Soviet Union. The Ministry of Defence at once began its studies for reducing the armed forces. It was said that we would need only thirty-two frigates and thirty-two infantry battalions. The Army of the Rhine could be withdrawn. Wholesale amalgamations or disbandments would be possible. And in the middle of all this conjecture and optimism, the dictator of Iraq, Saddam Husein, invaded Kuwait in August 1990. It would not be the first time that a foreign adventurer had come to the rescue of the British soldier, who, as Bernard Shaw pointed out, could stand up to anything but the British War Office. British sailors, soldiers, and airmen then played their splendid part in liberating Kuwait. The triumphant advance and success of the 1st Armoured Division with its 7th Armoured Brigade 'Desert Rats' and 4th Armoured Brigade, and certain features of their deployment, organization, and tactical use, provided important lessons for those charged with arranging the army's future.

In the first place it was plain at the very outset—when the decision to send troops to the Gulf was taken—that the peace establishments in both equipment and men of armoured regiments, infantry battalions, and other units were quite inadequate for war. Thus regiments not going to the Gulf were obliged to hand over numerous Chieftain tanks, Warriors, artillery pieces, vehicles, and substantial numbers of officers and men to bring up to operational strength those who were going. In other words previous planners, intent on saving money at the expense of efficiency, had as usual got it wrong. Moreover, large numbers of reservists were needed, particularly for the Royal Army Medical Corps (RAMC), yet the general system of calling on reservists to make up the numbers needed by fighting units did not appear to work at all.

To look, however, at the performance of the 1st Armoured Division and all the support it enjoyed—not least from the omnipresent and gallant Royal Navy and Royal Air Force—is to applaud commanders, logisticians, and fighting soldiers alike. The rapid acclimatization, tactical training, arms co-operation, and rehearsing of possible moves augured well for Operation Desert Storm when it was launched. It was pleasing to see that Mrs Thatcher brought General Peter de la Billière from near retirement to direct the British forces. Her confidence in him was wholly vindicated. When the land war started, having been preceded by the most devastating demonstration of what air supremacy can do, it was all quickly over bar the shouting. It was a striking example of the priceless value of deception, surprise, boldness, and speed; the paralysing power of manœuvre—and its dependence on assured supplies; the absolute indispensability in the land battle of all arms teams—tanks, infantry, sappers, artillery, and helicopters; the notable all-round contribution of helicopters; the killing power of artillery and especially of the Multi Launch Rocket System (MLRS); the way in which a night capability produced overwhelming advantages over those without it; the excellent satellite navigation aids; the way in which reliable surveillance, target acquisition, and precision strike transformed battle techniques; the enduring power of the SAS—above all, the unending need for clarity of purpose, concentration of force, and fire and movement, plus well-trained, well-led, well-equipped professional soldiers. The new weapon systems worked. It was blitzkrieg with a vengeance. Yet it took nearly half of the British Army of the Rhine to put one division in the field!

During the Gulf War John Major succeeded Mrs Thatcher as Prime Minister but Tom King remained Minister of Defence. King's Defence White Paper, *Options For Change*, appeared in July 1990. It proposed that the army's strength should be reduced from some 155,000 to about 116,000 (subsequently raised to 119,000 by Malcolm Rifkind), that is, by a quarter, but the fighting capability of the army should be cut disproportionately. It proposed that the infantry should lose seventeen of its fifty-five battalions (Rifkind later restored two battalions) and the Royal Armoured Corps (RAC) should lose eight of its nineteen regiments. These changes appear to be based on no strategic survey or calculation of what the army might be required to do and to have been imposed for budgetary reasons. The House of Commons Defence Committee severely criticized these proposals in its report of August 1991. What was needed was arguably a radical reorganization, with the aim of keeping enough battalions and regiments to meet the country's likely needs, and finding savings by despecializing the army and making all units and men more versatile, for example by combining the RAC and the AAC, whose roles—reconnaissance and strike—are so similar. A largely home-based army no longer needs specialist corps like the Royal Army Education Corps, the Royal Army Dental Corps, the Royal Army Veterinary Corps, and the Army Catering Corps, etc. while technical servicing could be largely civilianized.

As for deployment, *Options For Change* envisages that the three armoured divisions in Germany will be cut to one (and be part of a Rapid Reaction Corps), while another division, including two armoured brigades and an airborne brigade (plus 3 Commando Bde) will be based at home, as will also an airmobile brigade. The Territorial Army will be cut from roughly 70,000 to 55,000. The whole question of amalgamations and disbandments of regular regiments is still being worked out. A Gurkha Brigade of two battalions is to be retained. Apart from Germany and Britain, garrisons will be maintained in Hong Kong (until 1997), Brunei (paid for by the Sultan), Belize, Cyprus (plus UN peace-keeping), and the Falkland Islands. The regimental system is to be preserved; and all these reductions and reorganizations are to be completed by 1997. For those soldiers made redundant, generous compensation and help for re-employment will be wholly necessary.

What are these forces going to do? It is not enough to talk in an ano-
dyne fashion about the security of the realm. We must be more precise: the
integrity of Western Europe, a readiness to deploy forces for NATO (in
area or out of area) or whatever takes its place, defence of the United
Kingdom, garrisons for our lingering overseas territories, peace-keeping
for the United Nations, disaster relief in Africa, Asia, and the Middle East,
assistance to members of the Commonwealth, military aid to the community at home—what will we actually be required to do in the year 2000
and thereafter? Whatever it is, the need for certain capabilities will persevere: surveillance, secure communications, infinitely varied fire-power,
instantly deployable intelligence-gathering agents, detailed knowledge of
potential operational areas, readiness for combat, strategic mobility, a degree of capability for independent operations, tactical dexterity—all these
things will demand a properly balanced Royal Navy, a Royal Air Force
with a strategic transport fleet plus fighter/helicopter support—and for
the army as many armoured, infantry, artillery, and engineer regiments as
can be kept, for it is these units with proper logistic support that do the
work. It seems unlikely that there will be enough of these regiments for the
tasks facing them.

We have talked of the British army's new direction. What new directions have there been in the last thirty years? It has been largely a time of
peace. There has been no European war, although lately there have been
upheaval and conflict in the Balkans and in former republics of the Soviet
empire. There has been a decline from British imperial greatness, in which
a small, all-volunteer regular army has fought successfully a series of little
wars. The bulk of British citizens were not required to fight at all. These
little wars waged by the Professionals have been varied and widespread—
in Borneo to keep Malaysia intact, in the Dhofar to defeat Communist-
inspired rebellion, in the Falkland Islands to preserve their independence,
in the Gulf with allies to restore autonomy to an Arab sheikdom, and in
Northern Ireland. European peace was preserved by deploying a third of
the army in Germany and equipping it with expensive sophisticated
weapons. The army itself became relatively affluent, the soldiers able to
afford wives, cars, homes, holidays, and greatly adding thereby to the
expense of keeping a standing army. Britain's role in the world, a post-
imperial role, has been honourable, its armed forces' contribution to
peace-keeping and to resolving conflicts highly successful. This success
has been stimulated by the army's uniquely fortunate possession and retention of the regimental system—still the best way of raising, grouping,

training, and leading men in action devised by any army. The British soldier has continued to be a first-class example and ambassador all over the world.

As we move into the 1990s, we see a small, professional army of volunteers, taking infinite pride in their regiments' and corps' traditions and battle honours, and in action living up to them time after time. In the future we will see them still organized in these regiments and corps, perhaps with some more regroupings and amalgamations. It is to be hoped that as the regular content declines, the reserve element will increase. The imperial connection has gone. The European commitment is changing and will change more. In September 1991 the Soviet Union ceased to exist. What new defence arrangements will be required to meet these new circumstances? Some minor peace-keeping in Cyprus and Belize, in the Falkland Islands and Hong Kong, will continue for a time; there will be forces in Europe, more at home to go there or elsewhere. In Bosnia, British soldiers escort food supplies. Ulster may well smoulder on—to remind our soldiers of the unchanging condition of their lives—dealing with trouble. During these thirty years the British army, in spite of its being a thirty years peace, has been fighting some enemy somewhere. It has fought for the Regiment, the Queen, for comrades, for an exceptional leader, for honour. It has shown time after time that the performance of duty and the fulfilment of service are rewards more lasting than material matters. This splendid record will continue. The British army's perseverance will keep its honour bright.

17 THE ARMY OF BRITISH INDIA

T. A. HEATHCOTE

The ground forces of the British authorities in India consisted of two distinct elements. One was made up of troops belonging to the British army, sent to serve in India for a limited, albeit sometimes lengthy, period. Some went as individuals, to staff or singleton posts, but most went because their regiments had been ordered to India from another station, either in the United Kingdom or a colonial garrison, or a foreign campaign. In the days when soldiers enlisted, in effect, for life, or, after 1847, at least for ten years, some men served long enough to go to India with their regiments and in due course to return with them to the United Kingdom, or go on to some other location before doing so. With the change in 1870 to a system of short-service engagements, whereby most men served for a period of six years with the Colours before returning to civilian life as a reservist, regiments spent longer in India than the average soldier in their ranks. Thus men might go to India with their regiment or return with it, but in normal times would not do both. Usually, men would either be sent as members of replacement drafts to join units already there, or go back to the United Kingdom with drafts of men returning to take their discharge on the completion of their engagement. Those who wished to continue serving in India when their regiments went back to the United Kingdom were generally permitted to transfer to the regiments coming out to replace them. For officers and ordinary soldiers alike, service in India, where cheap labour was available to perform all menial tasks and most forms of relaxation were easily affordable, provided an easier life than could be found in a home station, despite the climate, the diseases, and the sense of exile from their homeland. Until well into the second half of the nineteenth century, officers who did not wish to go to India often exchanged into regiments that were staying at home, or that were coming home from India, and their places were taken by those who wished to go or to stay there. The latter were generally those to whom Indian service was attractive both because it offered greater opportunities for active service and promotion through wastage and because an officer without private means could live comfortably on his pay and allowances there.

The greater part of the British military forces in India, however, always consisted of troops recruited for permanent service in the subcontinent. Although eventually the overwhelming majority of these were Indian soldiers serving under British officers, there was always an element made up of European (i.e. British, at least in allegiance) soldiers, formed into their own regiments or corps. The first troops raised by the English East India Company, in the latter half of the seventeenth century, consisted of such men, sent out to serve as garrisons for the Company's forts and trading stations or 'factories' (so named because they were headed by 'factors' or agents). At the peak of their strength, in 1858, the Company's Europeans consisted of six regiments of light cavalry, nine battalions of infantry, seventeen troops of horse artillery, and thirteen companies of foot artillery, each able to man a battery of six guns. Most of these units were transferred to the British regular army in 1861, and the remainder were disbanded.

European civilians continued to serve in reserve units until the end of British rule in India. In so far as all Englishmen of military age had a liability under common law to serve in defence of the community when danger threatened, such units pre-dated the existence of the regulars in India as at home. In the wars of the seventeenth and eighteenth century, when the forces of local Indian rulers, or of rival European powers, menaced the English Company's settlements, all members of the trading community, including Armenians, were mustered into trained bands or town militias, which on occasions were involved in combat. During the crisis of the Indian Mutiny (1857–8), civilians were caught up in the fighting, and bore arms either as individuals or in volunteer corps raised for local defence. The successors of these corps formed the Indian Volunteer Force, recruited mostly from the middle-class ex-patriates who made up the British mercantile and commercial community in India. Men of mixed European and Indian descent could serve in this force, though not in the regulars. As members of a politically reliable group, many were employed on the Indian railways, when these were built, and provided most of the personnel of the railway battalions, intended for the protection of strategically important routes and installations. In 1917 all European British subjects in India were required to undergo compulsory part-time military training, just as they had in the militia in the early days of the East India Company's establishments. The Indian Defence Force, raised as the result of this legislation, absorbed the units of the Indian Volunteer Force; this was re-formed after the First World War as the Auxiliary Force (India) which was made up of ten regiments of light horse or mounted rifles, five brigades (later called regiments) of artillery, four companies of engineers, and thirty-four battalions of infantry, including ten railway units. Service was local and voluntary although the British professional engineers and su-perintendents who worked for the Indian railways were required to join as a condition of their employment.

During the Second World War members of the Auxiliary Force (India) continued to function as part-time soldiers, while contributing to the war effort by carrying on their normal occupation. Some became officers in the expanded Indian regiments, while the socially exclusive Calcutta Light Horse was involved in clandestine operations against German ship-ping in the neutral Portuguese port of Goa. After the war, the British Raj entered its twilight and, as widespread communal disorders broke out, units of this force were frequently called out for duties in support of the civil power. There was, however, no place for them in the armies of the two successor states of the British Indian Empire, and with the achievement of independence in 1947 they were disbanded.

The Indian Empire had grown from a number of coastal possessions, of which the most important were known as presidencies because the gover-nor or chief official held the title of president, just as factories were headed by factors. The three Indian presidencies, of Bengal, Madras, and Bom-bay, were until 1773 as independent of each other as were the Indian powers whose territories lay between them. Each had its own governor, its own administration, and its own army. After 1773 the head of the Bengal presidency held the title of Governor-General, and his government even-tually became the government of India. Nevertheless the governments of the two junior presidencies always retained a considerable degree of au-tonomy, including the right to correspond directly with the Court of Di-rectors of the East India Company and (after this post was created in 1858) the Secretary of State for India. Initially, each governor commanded his own presidency's army, but in 1748 the first Commander-in-Chief in the East Indies was appointed. Thereafter the 'Commander-in-Chief, India', directly commanded the Bengal army, and generally supervised the Madras and Bombay armies, although each of these remained a separate body until 1895, when they were combined into a single Indian Army. The Commander-in-Chief, India, and the Commanders-in-Chief, Madras and Bombay, took precedence immediately after the Governor-General and the governors of their presidencies respectively. They were answerable not to the British War Office but to the Company's Court of Directors or, after 1858, the India Office. Appointments to senior commands and to staff posts were made from both the British and the local Indian armies.

The strength of these armies lay in their Indian soldiers. For over a century the East India Company relied on European troops to provide such local ground forces as it required in time of war, and used Indian manpower as armed escorts or security guards rather than as soldiers. If the latter were required in larger numbers than could be provided from European sources, then reliance was placed on the existing armies of local Indian allies. During the War of the Austrian Succession, however, both the French and English East India Companies put European troops into the field in India in significant numbers. It became clear that European developments in musketry and field artillery, and the regimentation of drill and tactics needed to operate them effectively, enabled men, so equipped and so trained, to defeat much larger armies of men organized in the then conventional Indian manner, and consisting mostly of cavalry. With the Royal Navy making it difficult for them to bring reinforcements from Europe, the French tried the experiment of raising regiments of Indian soldiers organized on the Western model. They soon demonstrated their ability to master the necessary techniques, and both sides in the continuing Anglo-French conflict realized that such troops could be used as a cheaper, healthier, and more numerous substitute for European troops. They were given the name of sepoys (French *spahis*), from the Persian word *sipahi* which was applied to members of a permanent force as distinct from quasi-feudal levies. Major Stringer Lawrence, the first Commander-in-Chief, India, and generally known as the father of the Indian Army, began to raise companies of sepoys shortly after his arrival in 1748. Although the War of the Austrian Succession came to an end in that year, Frenchmen and Englishmen, in India as in North America, continued to fight each other as the allies of local protagonists. Robert Clive, once a civil servant but by then a colonel, became Commander-in-Chief, India, in December 1756, and in the following year began to group the Bengal sepoy companies into battalions. This system was adopted by the Madras army in 1759 and the Bombay army in 1767.

The victories won by the sepoys in their subsequent campaigns led to the emergence of the East India Company as an Indian power itself, and ultimately to the establishment of British hegemony over the whole subcontinent, with the army expanding to garrison each newly acquired possession. Its first and most famous victory in the field was at Plassey (1757), after which Mir Jafar, the grateful Nawab of Bengal, ceded to his British allies the *zamindari* (the right to collect the land revenue), of twenty-four *parganas* or tax districts covering 800 square miles, the first major British holding in the East. Forty years later the Bengal army numbered 24,000 sepoys, the Madras army 24,000, and the Bombay army 9,000. By 1805 these had increased to 57,000 in the army of Bengal, 53,000 in that of Madras, and 20,000 in Bombay, totalling 130,000 men. In 1824, with the British manifestly the paramount power in India, Bengal had a sepoy army of 13 regiments of cavalry and 68 battalions of infantry, Madras had 8 regiments of cavalry and 52 battalions of infantry, and Bombay had 5 regiments of cavalry and 24 battalions of infantry. In addition, sepoy units were raised for local service in the dominions of subsidiary princes, nominally for the defence of their territory, but actually to ensure that they were garrisoned by troops integrated into the British military system and controlled by the British government. Additional contingents were raised as British power spread, and, by 1857, the established total of Indian troops maintained by the East India Company amounted to 6 troops of horse artillery and 36 companies of foot artillery, 21 regiments of light cavalry and 33 of irregular cavalry, 115 battalions of regular infantry and 45 of irregular infantry. (Irregular units differed from the regulars only in having a smaller number of British officers and being armed and uniformed in the local Indian rather than European style of clothing.) All told, these amounted to some 200,000 men. By comparison, the European troops in India at this time totalled about 40,000, made up of 4 cavalry regiments and 22 infantry battalions from the British army, and 17 troops of horse artillery, 52 companies of foot artillery, and 9 battalions of infantry, from the Company's service. The British had conquered, and held, India by the use of Indian military manpower.

Not all, however, was well with this great army. In a land of many gods and spirits, the *Iqbal*, or Luck, of the East India Company had itself become an entity in the local pantheon. It was this luck, rather than the superiority of Western forms of military discipline and professionalism, that was believed to account for the victories of the sepoys in the hard-fought campaigns which, between 1774 and 1822, ended in the defeat of every local military power ranged between Nepal and Ceylon. Occasional defeats, such as those suffered at the hands of the Marathas at Wadgaon in 1779, or of Haydar Ali of Mysore in the Carnatic in 1780, did not affect the strength of the *Iqbal*. Numerically superior enemies were bound to secure occasional success, especially if a British general was outmanœuvred or surprised. What mattered was that the sepoys won the decisive battles, and that each series of campaigns ended with the extension of the Company's power and an improvement in the employment prospects of its civil and military servants. In the Afghan War of 1839–42, however, the outcome was different. The massacre of the brigade retreating from Kabul was, in military terms, insignificant, and a year later two British armies marched from opposite ends of Afghanistan, defeating all opposition, until they met in its capital. The campaign was nevertheless the Company's first long-term political defeat. The two Sikh Wars of the 1840s ended with the kingdom of Lahore, the last independent military power in India, becoming the British province of the Punjab, but only after battles in which, for the first time, the sepoys found themselves against a large army of men trained, drilled, and equipped like themselves, and found that such men could, in a fair field, come perilously near to defeating not only the sepoys themselves but also their British comrades-in-arms.

There were other considerations too. In the Sikh Wars, when the sepoys hung back, it was not entirely through fear of the enemy. Nationalism was in its infancy in India, and those who thought about such things at all perceived themselves as members of a particular community or subjects of a given ruler rather than as the inhabitants of a single country. Nevertheless, they had more in common with each other than with the British, and with the defeat of Lahore none would be left not under British domination. At a less philosophical level, the defeat of the Sikh army could be expected to be followed by a reduction in that of the Company, as a peace dividend now that there was no local power left to fight. The Punjab Frontier Force, raised to defend what had become the North-West frontier of British India, was levied from the disbanded sepoys of the defeated army of Lahore, and not from the victorious army of Bengal, except that the latter was increasingly drained of its officers, who volunteered for more rewarding civil and military posts in the Punjab and other newly annexed territories.

Among these was the kingdom of Awadh, annexed in 1856, from which 40,000 of the 120,000 sepoys in the Bengal army were drawn. While subjects of an independent monarch, they could count upon their families being given preferential treatment by his local officials in order, as they would suppose, to maintain good relations with their master's British allies. Now that those allies, on a legal technicality, had taken over the kingdom without a shot being fired, with a view to reforming its notoriously

Mutiny

Mutiny, in British military law, is a combination of two or more persons to resist or to induce others to resist lawful military authority. It is an offence for any officer or soldier to cause or join in a mutiny, or to fail to do his best to suppress it.

British forces in India, whose European officers and men were far from home, and whose Indian soldiers had no racial, religious, or national ties to the government which they served, were particularly prone to mutinous activities. The first incident occurred as early as 1683, when an officer of the Royal Navy, Captain Richard Keigwin, seized control of Bombay and governed it in defiance of the local authorities for eleven months. Keigwin and his fellow officers argued that they, although disobeying their immediate superiors, were acting in the best interests of the Crown (which in the event granted them full pardons, plus a bag of gold to Keigwin out of the revenues he had so successfully managed).

British officers of the East India Company's armies mutinied on several occasions. In 1754 an attempt by the government of Madras to court-martial some offenders among its officers resulted in them banding together to intimidate their fellows in order to avoid punishment. In 1766 and again in 1794 there were threats of mass resignation by officers of the Bengal army in protest at cuts in their allowances and the so-called 'White Mutiny' of 1809 resulted from a refusal by many officers of the Madras army to obey orders as a protest at the loss of field supply contracts. Punishment in these cases was mostly of a token nature, as many in authority sympathized with the officers concerned.

European soldiers also occasionally refused orders. In 1809 Madras infantrymen objected to being embarked as marines. In 1860 most of the Company's white soldiers objected to being transferred from local to imperial service without their consent. In 1919 reservists who had been embodied for service in the World War protested at the delays in their repatriation. In 1920 the Connaught Rangers mutinied in protest at British policy in Ireland. In 1946 wartime airmen of the Royal Air Force went on strike when it seemed that they would be retained in India.

Indian soldiers were not slow to follow their officers' example. In 1764 men of the Bengal Native Infantry mutinied with the intention of going over to the enemy for better pay. They were arrested and twenty-four of them were executed by being blown away from guns, four grenadiers claiming the position on

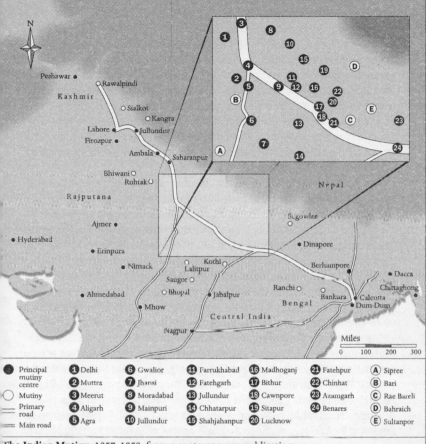

● Principal mutiny centre	① Delhi	⑥ Gwalior	⑪ Farrukhabad	⑯ Madhoganj	㉑ Fatehpur	Ⓐ Sipree
○ Mutiny	② Muttra	⑦ Jhansi	⑫ Fatehgarh	⑰ Bithur	㉒ Chinhat	Ⓑ Bari
— Primary road	③ Meerut	⑧ Moradabad	⑬ Jullundur	⑱ Cawnpore	㉓ Azamgarh	Ⓒ Rae Bareli
═ Main road	④ Aligarh	⑨ Mainpuri	⑭ Chhatarpur	⑲ Sitapur	㉔ Benares	Ⓓ Bahraich
	⑤ Agra	⑩ Jullundur	⑮ Shahjahanpur	⑳ Lucknow		Ⓔ Sultanpor

The Indian Mutiny 1857–1858, from a contemporary publication

the right of the line which was their place on parade. This method of execution was that used for mutineers by the Mughal emperors, from whom British authority in India descended.

At Vellore in 1805, sepoys of the Madras army mutinied over the issue of new orders intended to smarten their appearance but which were seen as a threat to their religion. Encouraged by the presence in exile nearby of the sons of the late Tipu Sultan, an old enemy of the British, the 1,500 sepoys in the Vellore fort attacked their British comrades and murdered every European they could find. When news of the outbreak reached Arcot, 16 miles away, the local commander, Colonel Rollo Gillespie, rode to the relief of the Europeans with a troop of 19th Light Dragoons, followed by the rest of his cavalry and horse artillery. Reaching Vellore ahead of his men, he climbed into the fort up a rope of buckled sword-belts, and, when his guns arrived, suppressed the revolt by swift and decisive action.

In 1824 at Berhampore the sepoys of the 24th Bengal Native Infantry, who had for religious reasons declined to go by sea to the Burma War, were ordered to march there overland. They refused to march, because no transport could be found, and eventually were dispersed by artillery fire. A few were hanged and others condemned to hard labour in chains. The remainder were dismissed, with the regiment being disbanded.

The mutiny of the Bengal army in 1857 took on the character of a servile revolt. The rapid spread of direct rule by the British over most of northern India, and a fear that their religion and culture were under threat, led regiment after regiment to throw off allegiance and make common cause with dispossessed local rulers who hoped to regain their lost independence. The murder of Europeans, including non-combatants, was matched by counter-terror from the British side, with captured mutineers blown from guns, and other fighters hanged for rebellion. After these troubles the whole civil and military system of British India was reorganized, and much more attention paid to the sensibilities of the communities from which the Indian Army drew its recruits.

The growth of the Indian nationalist movement had only a minimal impact on the Indian Army, which was carefully recruited from the most conservative elements. Nevertheless, the Mahratta Light Infantry mutinied in Singapore during the First World War, and the Royal Garhwal Rifles in Peshawar in 1930. Of the 60,000 Indian soldiers captured at Singapore in 1942, one man in three joined the Indian National Army formed under Japanese control. In 1946 seamen of the Royal Indian Navy mutinied and held control of Bombay harbour for five days before the Indian Army restored order, with hundreds of men dismissed their ships and sent to detention camps.

---

corrupt administration, the sepoy and his family were treated no differently from anyone else. The fact that most Bengal sepoys belonged to the yeoman class, and that new British administrators began enquiries into the titles by which members of that class held their land caused further ill-feeling. Respectable people throughout India, including the Muslims and high-caste Hindus who filled the ranks of the sepoy regiments, were alarmed by the spread of Western ideas, by the derogation of their own religious and social customs, and the replacement of their old rulers by foreigners who were, to the Muslims, infidels, or, to the Hindus, outcastes.

It was an attempt to improve efficiency that led to the mutiny of most of the Bengal army in 1857. A rearmament programme brought to India the new Enfield muzzle-loading rifle, to replace the smooth-bore percussion musket then in general service. The paper cartridge which carried the powder and ball was greased for lubrication so that, on being itself rammed into the bore, it acted as a tightly fitted wad. The cartridge end had to be bitten off to allow access to the powder and ball for loading. No special orders for the composition of the lubricant were given, and defence contractors, in their usual way, provided what would be the most profitable. These included pork fat and beef tallow, thus threatening pollution to Muslims and Hindus respectively. When men refused to handle the new cartridges they were punished. When they were punished, others took their part, until eventually every one of the ten regiments of the Bengal Light Cavalry, and sixty-one of the seventy-four battalions of the Bengal Native Infantry had risen in revolt, joined by many other units whose men came from the same communities. The mutineers, and the forces of local rulers who made common cause with them, were suppressed after a year and a half's desperate fighting. The Bombay army was scarcely affected, and the Madras army not at all. The Punjab Frontier Force also remained well affected to the British cause, some of its members having old scores to settle with the Bengal sepoys who had defeated the army of Lahore. Many Sikhs flocked to the British cause, especially when the mutineers declared they were fighting to restore the Mughal empire, which, under the zealous Aurangzeb, had persecuted Sikh holy men with the utmost cruelty.

As had happened so many times before in the history of India, the outcome was decided by the fighting around Delhi. It was from there that the early Muslim sultans had ruled all northern India, and from there that the Mughal emperors had extended that rule over virtually the entire subcontinent. After the outbreak of the mutiny on 11 May 1857 at Mirath, a day's journey away, it was to Delhi that the mutineers marched, announcing that they had come to restore the Mughal emperor, whose power the East India Company had usurped. That monarch, an aged and helpless figure, was merely the shadow of a great name, ruling as King of Delhi under British patronage, but, with his sons who saw an unexpected opportunity of restoring their dynasty's fortune, he was a potent political symbol.

Europeans in Delhi were massacred, but within a month British troops arrived from the Punjab and Mirath, to begin a siege which lasted until the
final assault, followed by several days of hand-to-hand street fighting, was
launched on 14 September 1857. The Mughal princes were taken prisoner
and then shot by a British officer in order to forestall their rescue. The king
was sent to exile as a state prisoner in British Burma. Serious fighting took
place in other areas, especially in Awadh and central India, where other
discontented local princes saw in the collapse of British authority a chance
to regain their own former state. Nevertheless, with the fall of Delhi, these
revolts were marginalized and eventually suppressed. What began as a
mutiny took on the nature of a servile war, fought with the cruelty characteristic of such, with men on both sides maddened by the murder of in-
nocent non-combatants, and tales of treachery and wanton slaughter.

On the restoration of British control, the civil and military systems by
which India was held were reorganized. With the rule of the Company
and the vestigial authority of the Mughal empire at an end, the British
Crown became supreme in India, and, in 1877, Queen Victoria formally
took the title Empress of India, sanctioned by the British parliament and
hailed by the princes of India. They for their part had been assured that no
more states would be annexed by the British. The annexations of Sind
(1844) and the Punjab (1849) brought the British Indian border up to the
mountains that divide south from central Asia. Separate frontier forces
were raised in each of these two provinces, to defend the local people and
caravans against marauders from the hill tribes. Later, these forces were
merged with the rest of the army, and their place taken by a variety of tribal
levies in British pay. The more heavily armed, and expensive, regular
troops were normally used only when local arrangements broke down, or
when a full-scale expedition into tribal territory was undertaken. The primary function of the regulars was to defend British India against an invasion by other regulars, Russians or Afghans with Russian support. Quetta,
at the top of the Bolan Pass, and Peshawar, at the foot of the Khyber, were
given strong garrisons to protect these two traditional gateways to India.

The whole local army was refashioned. The European units were transferred to the British army, nearly provoking a white mutiny when the men
were not granted the enlistment bounty that recruits were given. The Indian units were reduced in numbers, establishment, and armament. Except for a few batteries of mountain or light field guns, artillery, the most
potent arm of warfare, was henceforth kept in British Army hands. Indian
regiments were no longer regarded as alternatives to British, but as auxili-

aries. The number of British officers in a unit was reduced by two-thirds, giving Indian officers the command of companies and troops. This, based on the irregular system, was intended to improve the status and prospects of the latter, but as they continued to be promoted by seniority, from the ranks, without a proper military education, it left Indian regiments less able to match the performance of their British comrades. British regiments were now larger than Indian ones, and the proportion of British to Indian personnel under arms rose dramatically from one in ten to one in three. Moreover, the Indian troops were no longer to be equipped with the most modern weapons (it was just such a modernization programme that set in train the outbreak of the 1857 mutiny). Henceforth Indian troops were deliberately armed with weapons inferior to those of their British comrades, usually with those cast off by the British when they themselves rearmed with a better pattern of weapon. This combined the advantages of financial economy with those of military security. Nevertheless, it meant that Indian troops were less effective in combat. Even in appearance Indian soldiers from then on differed markedly from the British. Prior to the post-mutiny new modelling, the principle had been to assimilate the two as closely as local custom allowed. Henceforth the local clothing of the irregulars became the rule. To a certain extent this followed the evolution of military costume in Western armies in the mid-nineteenth century, which moved to a less restrictive type of clothing, partly in the interests of comfort and efficiency, partly following trends in civilian fashion. It also served, however, as visible evidence that the re-formed Indian army was intended to be as different from the apparently discredited pre-mutiny Indian army as it was now to be from the British army itself. It now actually looked more like an auxiliary to the latter rather than a substitute for it.

By 1865 the reorganization was virtually completed and, with further reductions, by 1887 the forces at the disposal of the government of India amounted to 73,000 British troops and 153,000 Indians. With such a limited establishment, the military authorities were concerned that every man raised from such a vast population was the best that could be had. India was perceived as a country of many different classes and communities. Such a view seemed reasonable enough at the time, in that the British Indian Empire had been built up in a series of conquests over separate states. Some British officers, indeed, deliberately urged the divide and rule principle, pointing out that the sepoys of the Madras and Bombay armies had remained at their duty when those of Bengal mutinied. Others, in the

The Afghan Wars

The modern Afghan state emerged in the mid-eighteenth century, when Ahmad Shah established a large kingdom which included not only the Afghan homeland, but parts of Iran, all the land between the Oxus and the Hindu Kush, and the whole of modern Pakistan with Kashmir. The Afghans were generally regarded by their plains-dwelling neighbours, with mingled condescension and alarm, as wild barbarians, whose fierce code of honour and sense of community made them difficult to govern, even by their own chiefs. Their internal feuds tempted outside powers to seek to control the country by supporting one or other of the conflicting parties. Ahmad Shah's grandson, Shah Shuja-ul-Mulk, ruled between 1803 and 1809, before being deposed by his brother Mahmud, and then made two attempts to return to power without success. All Ahmad Shah's conquests outside the Afghan heartland were lost, including the fertile province of Peshawar, at the foot of the famous Khyber Pass, the historic gateway to India. This, inhabited mostly by a population of ethnic Afghans, was taken in 1834 by Maharaja Ranjit Singh, the ruler of Lahore. The Amir Dost Muhammad, who became ruler of Afghanistan in 1834, sought the return of Peshawar, and when the British made it clear that, if pressed, they would rather have Ranjit Singh's friendship than his own, responded by receiving a Russian officer at his capital, Kabul. The British decided to restore Shah Shuja, hoping that, with the help of British money and troops, he would recover all Ahmad Shah's lost dominions and so establish a strong, pro-British state as a buffer against any further expansion in the direction of India by Russia or by Iran with Russian encouragement.

In the spring of 1839, therefore, a British army crossed into Sind, and marched up the Bolan Pass into southern Afghanistan. Kandahar fell without a fight. Ghazni was taken by a *coup de main*. Dost Muhammad fled from Kabul, and Shah Shuja re-entered his capital at the beginning of August. But for subsequent events, this would have gone down in history as one of the British Indian Army's most brilliant successes. A year later, the British government decided that it could no longer afford to keep troops in Afghanistan, and prepared to withdraw them. As the British position weakened, Afghan opposition to Shah Shuja increased. Finally, in January 1842, following a complete loss of control over the surrounding area, and the murder of British diplomats, the British garrison at Kabul marched out, with promises of safe conduct through the passes, for Peshawar. A combination of bitterly cold weather, lack of fuel

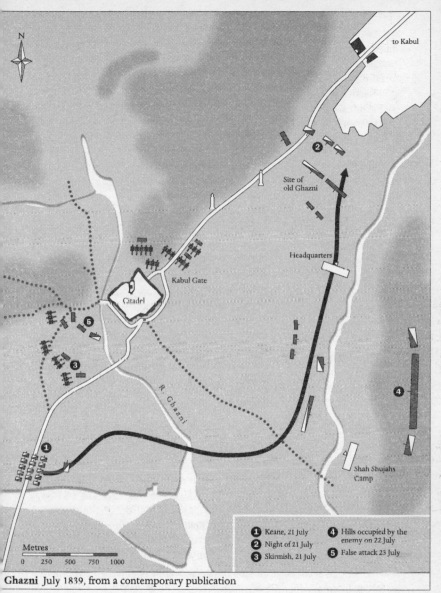

Site of
old Ghazni

Headquarters

Kabul Gate

Citadel

R. Ghazni

Shah Shujahs
Camp

Metres

0   250   500   750   1000

1 Keane, 21 July
2 Night of 21 July
3 Skirmish, 21 July
4 Hills occupied by the
enemy on 22 July
5 False attack 23 July

Ghazni July 1839, from a contemporary publication

and food, Afghan duplicity, and poor leadership by the British commanders, led to the destruction of the whole brigade, and a national uprising. The garrison at Jalalabad successfully withstood a six-weeks' siege. The troops at Ghazni surrendered in return for a promise of safe conduct which was promptly dishonoured. Kalat-i-Ghilzai held out until May 1842 when it was relieved by a column from Kandahar.

The British government had decided to abandon its Afghan policy (Shah Shuja himself was assassinated in April 1842), but the local commanders were given discretion to choose their own route home. Generals Pollock at Kandahar and Nott at Jalalabad marched their men back to India via Kabul, completely defeating Afghan forces opposed to them, rescuing the British officers and ladies given as hostages by the ill-fated Kabul brigade, and avenging the disaster of the previous year.

British troops did not return to Afghanistan until 1878. Sher Ali, the son and successor of the restored Dost Muhammad, was sandwiched between the Russian and British Empires, each of which had by this time expanded up to his own borders. The British used the visit of a Russian officer to Kabul to insist that Sher Ali accept a British envoy. When this was refused, British troops were sent into Afghanistan to force him to change his mind. Sher Ali fled and the British occupied Kabul in December 1878. Sher Ali's son Yakub Khan accepted a British envoy, but a mutiny by Afghan troops in September 1879 resulted in the murder of the envoy and his escort, and the return of a British army, under Sir Frederick Roberts, to Kabul. Yakub Khan abdicated, and Roberts himself was for a time besieged. In the spring of 1880 General Sir Donald Stewart marched with an army from Kandahar to take command of the Kabul garrison, arriving there after fighting off an attack at Ahmad Khel by large numbers of religious warriors. In July 1880 a brigade was sent out from the garrison left at Kandahar to intercept a force under Ayub Khan, a contender for the now vacant throne. This brigade encountered Ayub at Maiwand, but was overwhelmed and pursued back inside the walls of Kandahar. The consequent siege was lifted only by the arrival of Roberts at the head of a force which covered the 280 miles from Kabul in twenty days and fought a successful battle against Yakub on 1 September. The British once again decided to leave the Afghans to their own devices, subject only to Afghan foreign policy being conducted through the government of India.

The Third Afghan War (May–June 1919) broke out when a new king, Amanullah, declared his full independence and his sympathy for those affected by British internal security measures in India. The British, fearing this would encourage a revolt in Peshawar, dispatched three columns to break up Afghan troop concentrations and to keep the border tribes quiet. One column moved up the Khyber and defeated Afghan troops at Bagh, Landi Kotal, and Dakka. Another captured Spin Baldak. The third was pinned down at Thal until relieved by Brigadier-General Dyer from Peshawar. The British secured a military victory, helped by the use of motor transport, and strategic bombing by the Royal Air Force, but abandoned their claims to control Afghan foreign relations.

---

age of Darwinism, claimed that some communities produced men who through peculiarities of physique, culture, or other personal qualities, were naturally better fitted to the profession of arms than others. Tall fair men of the north-west, especially from the Punjab which by 1914 supplied the Indian Army with 80 per cent of its manpower, were preferred to small dark men of the south. Southerners, it was argued, like the men of Awadh, had once been potentially good soldiers but, after a generation or two of the peace which their arms had won, had lost their martial spirit. The countryman, brought up in the open air among simple rustic virtues, was preferred to the town dweller, especially if the latter had taken advantage of the urban facilities to obtain a Western-style education, and, with it, Western ideas of self-government.

The protagonists of the martial class theory, in seeking an explanation for the decline in the fighting efficiency of the Madras army in the second half of the nineteenth century, looked in the wrong place, and considered only the Indian men, not their British officers. Rather than believe the truism, so often taught in the British army itself, that there are no bad troops, only bad officers, these theorists argued that, in the space of a generation or two, the same communities whose sons had defeated the armies of the fearsome Tipu Sultan (or, indeed, had made up those very armies) had become so enervated and unwarlike through living in a peaceful countryside that they had lost the spirit to fight. But as the Madras army garrisoned regions of India where, through its own earlier victories, there were no longer any internal enemies, and where no external ones could arrive without first defeating the Royal Navy at sea or the other Indian armies on land, it was not the first choice of the most energetic or ambitious officers. The climate, which the theorists argued had enervated a population born and bred there, certainly had that effect on Europeans. This included the British officers of the Madras army who, often choosing the Indian service because they lacked the private income without which officers of the British army could not keep up the life-style expected of them, had generally failed to be selected by either the Bengal or Bombay armies. When the chance for active service did come, in the Burma Wars of 1852 and 1885, Madras regiments under such officers performed poorly enough for the theorists to claim their case proved.

By the end of the nineteenth century, it had become clear that the system of separate presidential armies, which had served well enough (during their first hundred years) for the conquest of India, and (during the next half-century) for the occupation of India, was not suited for the future defence of India. The separate armies themselves were abolished in 1895, and replaced by four Commands; the Punjab, including the Punjab Frontier Force; Bengal; Madras, including the Burma regiments; and Bombay, including the troops of the former Sind Frontier Force which also garrisoned Baluchistan and Aden. Each Command was under a Lieutenant-General who was directly responsible not, as the old presidential Commander-in-Chief had been, to the governors of their presidencies, but to the Commander-in-Chief, India. At regimental level however, no real change occurred. Regimental names and numbers remained the same as they had been in the old armies, and units continued to be localized for service, in time of peace, in the areas of the Commands just as they had been in the areas allotted to the presidential armies. Even within each new Command, units continued to be stationed in many small garrisons, ideally suited for holding the country against the threat of armed rebellion which no longer existed.

In 1902 the newly appointed Commander-in-Chief, India, was General Lord Kitchener, Britain's foremost soldier, then at the peak of his prestige after his conquest of the Sudan and his victories in the South African War. Contemptuous of the Indian military officers and men alike and regarding their service as the most expensive system of outdoor relief to be found anywhere in the British Empire, he determined on a fundamental reorganization that was intended to convert a collection of garrison and frontier forces into an army capable of the major operations of modern war. This reorganization was based on the principle that the government of India maintained its troops to defend British India rather than to occupy it. The threat, in his appreciation, was not an internal rising, but a foreign invasion, and as the Royal Navy's supremacy meant that no invasion could come by sea, an invader could only come by land, and the only army in Asia capable of mounting such an invasion was that of the Russian Tsar. Within two years Russian arms were to be defeated by those of a westernized Japan, which a generation later would, in a lightning campaign, drive the British Indian forces from Burma and reach the north-east frontier of India itself, but Kitchener's assumption suited the mood of the time. The historic gateways to India were the Khyber and Bolan Passes through the mountains of the North-West Frontier. This meant that Indian soldiers, in order to defend India, must be trained to operate in that theatre, and to fight against a European army, and that they should be organized, led, and equipped accordingly. All units were in future to be liable for service anywhere in India in peace as well as war, and in particular all were to take their turn on the Frontier.

To emphasize the homogeneity of the reformed army, the title 'Indian Army', which had previously been applied to all the forces at the disposal of the government of India, and which since 1895 had also been applied to the troops of the former Bengal, Madras, and Bombay armies, was henceforth to be used to denominate the force recruited and permanently based in India, together with its ex-patriate British officers. The term 'Army in India' was henceforth to be used to mean the whole of the land forces of the Indian Empire, including the 30 per cent provided by the British army at the Indian taxpayer's expense. The reorganized Army in India had a total establishment in 1903 of 218,965. The cavalry consisted of 6,056 British and 24,854 Indian Army personnel, the Royal Artillery of 17,140 British and 3,104 Indian, the sappers and miners of 4,877 Indian with 165 officers and men of the Royal Engineers, and the infantry of 77,075 British and 141,890 Indian, the latter including a number of pioneer regiments, unique, in the British service, to the Indian Army, capable of functioning either as infantry or field engineers. It was divided into a field army of nine infantry divisions (each of three brigades, each of one British and three Indian battalions), and eight cavalry brigades (each of one British and two Indian regiments); and the internal security troops, consisting of one British and fourteen Indian cavalry regiments, with twenty-five British and forty-five Indian battalions. In the entire army, however, there were only 480 field guns (including those of the horse artillery and mountain batteries) and 421 machine-guns.

Kitchener's reforms were intended to turn the Indian Army back from being the imperial gendarmerie into which it had been converted by the post-mutiny reorganizations, into a conventional regular army. Unfortunately, political and financial factors delayed the completion of his scheme, and his successors were not men of his own intense energy and ability. Although Kitchener had organized the Indian Army into permanent divisions and brigades, each with a common, fixed establishment (replacing the previous arrangements of *ad hoc* formation put together from whatever was the nearest available on the outbreak of war), accommodation problems had prevented many units from being physically regrouped. Little training, therefore, had been done at higher formation level prior to the outbreak of war in August 1914. Moreover, although the need for a continuing internal security role was accepted by Kitchener, his scheme did not provide for their command and administration after the field army formation headquarters, under whose authority they came in peace, moved elsewhere on mobilization. The logistic services, which lacked the prestige and influence of the more glamorous fighting arms were under establishment, while the continuing prejudice in favour of recruiting only from designated and predominantly rural so-called martial classes meant that there were too few of the artisans and technicians on whom any early twentieth-century army depended for effective and prolonged operations. The scale of casualties inflicted by machine-guns, quick-firing artillery, or even by well-trained magazine riflemen, meant that recruiters could no longer produce the carefully balanced, hand-picked numbers drawn from each small martial group. By the end of the war the traditional martial classes could, or in some cases would, no longer supply the number of recruits required for an army which had expanded to half a million strong. Classes which had hitherto been thought no longer to be (or even never to have been) martial were then allowed to furnish men, who proved that all, given proper training and leadership, could be both brave and efficient. Financial constraints resulted in only seven of the reformed Indian Army's nine divisions being ready for mobilization in 1914. Their artillery equipment was obsolete by European standards, their medical services primitive, and the industrial base of the country quite inadequate for a prolonged campaign.

In the event, the Army in India did not have to defend India's borders at all. Its troops were sent to fight those of the Ottoman empire in Palestine, Iraq, Salonika, and the Dardanelles, and those of the German empire on the Western Front as well as East Africa and other colonial sideshows. In November 1914 an Indian expedition captured the Turkish province of Basra, and secured the vital Gulf oil installations. A later advance on Baghdad failed, with the surrender in April 1916 of British-held Kut-al-Amara after a 146-day siege. With the collapse of Indian logistics, the War Office took over the campaign, and Mesopotamia (Iraq) was finally conquered in October 1918. This foreign service, though it allowed the officers and men of the Indian Army to display fortitude and courage, demonstrated a further weakness in the system by which units were maintained. The government's desire for cheapness, and the regiments' desire for exclusivity, had combined to encourage units to obtain much of their clothing and equipment from local contractors rather than the rudimentary ordnance organization. This was carried to its greatest extreme in the cavalry arm, whose troopers were paid at a higher rate than the infantry, in return for providing their own horse and saddlery, through a system administered by the regiments themselves. Not only did equipment so obtained often prove to be below the standard required on prolonged operations, but it was impossible to repair or replace when far away from the contractors who provided it. This method of organizing and maintaining troops, known as the *silladari* system, was revealed by the stress of major war to be a wasteful and inefficient anachronism.

In 1922 the Indian Army was reorganized again to take account, not only of the lessons of the First World War, but also of constitutional developments within India. Horsed cavalry which, as in all armies, until 1914 had been steadily increasing as a proportion of the order of battle, was reduced by 50 per cent in the Indian Army just as it was in the British. Even this reduction was smaller than it might otherwise have been because of the value placed on horse soldiers for duties in aid of the civil power, which were increasingly in demand as the Indian nationalist movement grew in intensity and inter-communal disorders became more frequent. The thirty-six pre-war cavalry regiments were reduced by amalgamation to twenty-one, and grouped into sets of three, each set with its own depot and recruited from the same areas. The *silladari* system and other irregular features were abolished. The Indian infantry was reorganized into a smaller number of regiments, each of a depot and several battalions, in place of the previous system of each regiment having only one combat battalion.

At the higher level, the army in India was divided into a field army of four divisions and five cavalry brigades, and a covering force of twelve brigades, intended to hold the North-West Frontier while the field army mobilized. The brief period of *entente* with Imperial Russia before and during the First World War had ended, and the rise of Soviet Communism had allowed the bogey of a Russian invasion of India through Afghanistan to be revived. The rest of the army was allotted to internal security duties. All told there were 76,000 British and 129,000 Indian combatant troops in the post-war army compared with 77,000 and 142,000 in the Kitchener system. Each brigade now consisted of one British and only two Indian units.

Indian politicians consistently pressed for further reductions, especially in the British element, seeing it, quite correctly, as being there to occupy at least as much as to protect India. Moreover, they were adamant that the Indian Army should be maintained for the defence of India rather than the defence of the British Empire in the East. British politicians tried to keep military expenditure as low as possible in order to divert expenditure into more constructive projects, hoping to placate moderate opinion if only by keeping taxes down.

As a result, the Indian Army during the period between the two World Wars was as starved of modern equipment as was the British army itself. The proportion of artillery to infantry was only one-third of what experience in the First World War had shown to be necessary, and the guns themselves became obsolescent. British cavalry when eventually mechanized were given armoured cars rather than tanks. Indian cavalry when mechanized were for the most part given lorries from which the troopers, like the dragoons of old, dismounted to fight on foot. By 1939 even the despised Afghan army had more tanks in its order of battle than the Indian Army which still looked to the Afghan frontier as its primary theatre of conventional operations.

A further issue during the inter-war period was that of the grant of full commissions to Indian officers. A special feature of the British military system in India was the existence of parallel military hierarchies at company or troop officer level. Indian officers held ranks with local titles, were appointed after having risen through the non-commissioned ranks, and had no powers of command over European soldiers. British officers were directly commissioned after formal education as cadets, had the same titles and duties as those in British regiments, but were fewer in number in each unit as most of the junior command appointments were held by Indians. The post-mutiny army reforms had reduced the number of British officers in an Indian unit to one-third of that in a British one. This was intended to enhance the prestige and job satisfaction of Indian officers and to reduce the cost of maintaining an Indian regiment (prior to 1857 half the annual cost of an Indian unit was taken up by the pay of its British officers). Indian officers, however, lacked the education and training required in field officers, so that a small number of British casualties could make an Indian unit ineffective. Proposals to make Indian officers more efficient were resisted by those who argued that such officers might then be able to lead their men against the British. Others claimed that Indians lacked the capacity for military leadership (contrary to all historical evidence) and that British officers were therefore essential for efficiency.

The Russo-Japanese War proved to Indian nationalists that Asians could defeat Europeans in modern conventional war, without foreign officers. The British then claimed that Indians able to master the necessary educational skills could only be found in the urban intelligentsia, a body which lacked the traditional military virtues of the politically inert and physically robust 'martial classes' of the countryside. When these classes too demanded a share of full commissions for their sons, in the same way as the western-educated classes had gained a large share of senior civil and judicial posts, the British had to make concessions. The first five Indian gentlemen cadets entered the Royal Military College, Sandhurst, in 1919 (one of them a future general and first president of Pakistan). Despite racial prejudice against them, and attempts to group them into special regiments with promotion prospects inferior to those of their British colleagues, the Indianization programme gathered pace. After the foundation of the Indian Military Academy in 1932, at Dehra Dun, Indian cadets no longer attended the R.M.C. With the outbreak of the Second World War, and the consequent demand for officers for the Indian Army's expansion to ten times its previous strength, all notions of segregation in the officer corps had to be abandoned.

The Indian Army was even less prepared for major war in 1939 than it had been in 1914. In India as in the United Kingdom, ministers had disregarded the advice of their defence departments in favour of that of their exchequers. With the loss of most of the British army's modern equipment in France in 1940, there was scarcely enough material to defend the shores of south-east England, and none at all for the borders of India. With the reluctant agreement of most Indian politicians, who felt that the achievement of independence from European rule would not be hastened by the victory of Fascism, Indian troops returned to the Middle East and shared in the early victories, later defeats, and final triumphs of Allied arms there in East and North Africa, and in southern Europe. But in 1942, while India's best-trained and best-equipped troops were committed to these campaigns, her eastern flank was left exposed to a Japanese onslaught. With the Royal Navy driven from the surrounding seas, and the Royal Air Force from the local skies, British and Indian forces, commanded by some of the worst generals in their history, were humiliated in Malaya,

Singapore, and Burma. Only at the very frontiers of India was a stand made, and a long slow counter-attack made by General Slim and his 14th Army, to turn defeat into victory.

During this, its last and greatest war, the Indian Army saw its greatest changes. Two million men, twenty lakhs of soldiers, a force larger than any army in India since medieval times, was mustered by voluntary recruitment. Officers and men were drawn from all sectors of society, despite the vested interests and class prejudices of the old establishment. Technical equipment, including armour and artillery, was placed in Indian hands. Units were trained in the central Indian jungles to fight in Burma, not on the north-west Indian mountains to fight in Afghanistan. By the end of the war there were ten infantry divisions and three tank brigades in the field, superior to anything that the armies of Germany or Japan could then muster. As the war went on, Indian soldiers, like British soldiers, became more politically aware, and thought of the future. In all 20,000 of the 60,000 Indians taken prisoner at Singapore, considering themselves betrayed by their British paymasters, joined the Indian National Army, which had been formed under Japanese encouragement with the intention of leading a march to Delhi that would drive the British from their Indian Empire. It was their tragedy, and their disgrace, that they broke their freely taken soldier's oath for the sake of five years. In 1947 the British left India to her own devices, and the British army set up a substitute imperial garrison on the north German plain where it remained for almost a further half-century. The Indian Army itself continues as an all-regular long-service professional volunteer force, maintaining the best traditions of its own history in protecting its country's borders and lawful constitution.

18 THE AMATEUR MILITARY TRADITION

IAN BECKETT

Traditionally, Britain has relied upon command of the sea as the main line of defence against invasion, itself a constant theme in English and British history. In consequence, the existence of a large standing regular army was distrusted on the grounds that it was both unnecessary and might promote military despotism, a lingering fear which actually pre-dated the creation of such a standing army. Thus, there was a distinct preference for amateur and temporary soldiers—the auxiliary forces—brought into existence as needs dictated for defence against invasion, as a means of maintaining domestic order in the event of any concomitant civil disturbances, and as a means of wider social control and assimilation through participation and example.

The military obligations imposed upon the English people from earliest times and the more systematic organization of local auxiliary forces from the mid-sixteenth century onwards therefore continuously reflected and transmitted traditional attitudes towards military participation in Britain. Indeed, in the absence of a standing army prior to 1660 (technically, prior to 1689) and in the absence of regular troops permanently visible to society as a whole thereafter, it was the ever-present auxiliaries who more often provided the essential point of contact between society and army in Britain. Auxiliaries frequently bore the brunt of popular antimilitarism and equally played an important part in projecting military values to an 'un-military' people. They were not only the subject of major national political controversy but their administration also constantly exercised local communities.

Sometimes referred to as the 'old constitutional force', the oldest of the auxiliary forces was the militia, which had its origins in the military obligations of the Anglo-Saxons. Generally, Victorian and Edwardian

The Militia Ballot

While militia service had always implied an element of compulsion, it was only in 1757 that England and Wales followed the lead of continental states in introducing a compulsory ballot. To create a force of 32,000 men serving a three-year term of service, each county was required to submit an annual return of eligible men aged between 18 and 50, the numerous exemptions including clergy, teachers, and those with large families. A county quota would then be apportioned so that each theoretically contributed the same proportion of its able-bodied manpower although, in reality, quotas fixed in 1757 remained unchanged until 1796 irrespective of intervening population change. A general Lieutenancy meeting would order chief constables to produce hundredal lists—a task effected in turn by parish constables—and then proportionally fix hundredal quotas. A series of subdivision meetings would hear appeals against inclusion and, having notified the results to a further general meeting, would fix parish quotas and ballot to fill them. After the ballot there was a further chance to claim exemption by substitution or payment of a £10 fine, any deficiencies then being made up.

It was a lengthy process though one presenting many opportunities to escape service. Apart from exemption, substitution, or fine, a man might also escape through the somewhat haphazard determination of what constituted physical disability. In some cases, a parish might find volunteers to serve for a bounty while, in addition, an individual might join an insurance club in which subscriptions were used to hire substitutes or were returned if none was required. Technically illegal unless confined to a single parish, such clubs nevertheless flourished on a wider scale and positively mushroomed once the prohibition lapsed altogether in 1786.

The proportion of men balloted who actually served in person was likely to be small. None the less, it was widely recognized that the burden of service would be thrown primarily upon the poorer elements of society as indeed proved the case. Consequently, widespread disturbances occurred as the Lieutenancies proceeded to implement the legislation in August and September 1757. Precisely the same thing happened in 1796 following legislation to raise a 'supplementary' militia of 60,000 men by ballot. There were familiar problems in finding those willing to serve in person despite the exemption fine being raised to £15. The extension of the ballot to those aged between 19 and 23 in Scotland in July 1797 provoked even more violent disturbances while the popularity of volunteers and yeomanry was also significantly increased by the exemption from the ballot first granted them in 1794 although their varying terms of service meant that not all were so exempted.

Contributing to the general unpopularity of the ballot was the cost to parishes of maintaining the families of militiamen during annual training and wartime embodied service, the latter also requiring the filling of casual vacancies and those caused by large-scale recruitment of militiamen into the regular army at differing periods. The renewal of war with France in May 1803 dramatically increased such burdens while ballots for militia and supplementary militia and, later, for the Army of Reserve and the Permanent Additional Force drove up the price of substitutes. Measures for even wider compulsory military training such as the Defence Acts in 1798 and 1803 and the Training Act in 1806 were averted by governments accepting voluntary offers in lieu of ballot and the militia ballot itself was suspended for varying periods between 1806 and 1813 although it was then applied to those aged between 18 and 30 to complete the local militia after 1808.

Ballots for both militia and local militia were then suspended with the conclusion of the Napoleonic Wars. While the ballot for the local militia was to be suspended annually until 1836—when the force was finally abolished—a new ballot for the militia was ordered in July 1816 although actual training was suspended annually until April 1820. Training was ordered in both 1821 and 1825 and another ballot was ordered in October 1828, but new legislation then authorized suspension for a year at a time. A ballot was once more announced in December 1830 in the wake of the domestic reform crisis and the fall of the French Bourbon monarchy but aroused considerable opposition, not least from the National Union of the Working Classes with the slogan, 'No Vote, No Musket', becoming increasingly familiar throughout the 1830s and 1840s. In deciding to suspend the ballot in July 1831, the political establishment concluded that support for compulsion appeared the equivalent of committing political suicide. When the militia was next revived in 1852, therefore, enlistment was on a voluntary basis. The right to compel service was reserved but no one seriously believed it possible to implement it, the one clear lesson of the militia ballot since 1757 being the British people's universal distaste for compulsion.

historians of the militia indulged in speculative excursions substituting regimental tradition for known fact, one even going so far as to claim its origin in the army gathered by Cassivelaunus to oppose Caesar's second invasion of Britain in 54 BC. Nevertheless, even if they misrepresented the Anglo-Saxon system, there was a certain continuity from those obligations requiring service in the fyrd transmitted through medieval legislation such as the Assize of Arms in 1181 and the Statute of Westminster in 1285 which was enshrined in the first militia statutes of 1558.

Thereafter, the militia had a formal statutory existence until 1604, from 1648 to 1735, from 1757 to 1831, and from 1852 until 1908. Even the absence of enabling legislation did not necessarily imply that the militia had ceased to function at other periods—Charles I claimed in 1642 that the 1558 statutes were still in full force even though repealed thirty-eight years previously—and technically at least the authority to raise the militia did not cease until 1953. The actual basis of service varied considerably from period to period as indicated by the addition of epithets such as 'exact', 'select', 'supplementary', or 'new' militia at various times. Essentially, however, the obligation was one imposed upon property until 1757 and then as a tax upon manpower with the force raised by compulsory ballot until 1831 although a voluntary system of enlistment was then applied from 1852 until 1908. The term 'trained bands' was used from 1573 to 1663 to describe a better-trained portion of the militia and continued to be used in respect of the militia of London until 1793. 'Militiamen' was also a term employed to describe those conscripted under the provisions of the Military Training Act of April 1939 but they had no connection with the original force.

In contrast to the militia as an institution of the State, supposedly self-sufficient volunteer forces existed under an often confusing variety of terms of service at other times or simultaneously with the militia such as during the 1650s, 1660s, 1715, 1745, and from 1778 to 1782 when the first specific volunteer legislation was enacted. Volunteers were principally created, however, in the French Revolutionary and Napoleonic Wars, being raised both as volunteer infantry and artillery but also as mounted yeomanry. Many infantry units transferred to the so-called local militia in 1808 but this was suspended in 1816 although the legislation remained on the statute-book until 1921. Other volunteers survived post-war reductions but had virtually all disappeared by the 1840s, only for the volunteer movement to be revived in 1859. Volunteers raised in 1859 primarily as rifle volunteers were initially governed by provisions dating from 1804 until new legislation in 1863, while the yeomanry, which had survived post-1815 reductions largely intact, continued to be governed by 1804 statute until 1901 when renamed Imperial Yeomanry, a term already utilized for those raised to serve in specially recruited mounted units during the South African War. An infantry unit, the City Imperial Volunteers, was also raised for service in South Africa whilst the volunteer force as a whole furnished service companies to be attached to regular battalions.

In fact, the title of Imperial Yeomanry was short lived for in 1908 a major consolidation of auxiliary forces resulted in the abolition of the militia—its units were incorporated into the new special reserve—and the merging of volunteers and imperial yeomanry in a Territorial Force. As it happened, the Territorial legislation did not remove that of 1863 from the statute-book and volunteer training corps, later renamed the Volunteer Force, were then raised during the First World War. Territorials were re-constituted in 1920 as the Territorial Army and have continued to the present time, the actual title of Territorial Army being revived in 1982 after being discontinued in 1967 when regular reservists and Territorials were combined in a Territorial Army and Volunteer Reserve. On occasions, Territorials have been encouraged to join *ad hoc* volunteer bodies such as the Defence Force in 1921 and the Civil Constabulary Reserve in 1926. In addition, volunteering was again revived during the Second World War when the Local Defence Volunteers, later the Home Guard, were raised under defence regulations drawn from older volunteer legislation. Indeed, some have claimed the right of a member of the Local Defence Volunteers and Home Guard to resign on fourteen-days notice until February 1942 as an example of the uniqueness of the force; in reality, the right had applied not only to the volunteer training corps of the First World War but also to Victorian and earlier volunteers since first enshrined in the Volunteer Consolidation Act of 1804. The Home Guard was briefly revived as a cadre force from 1951 to 1957.

Mention should also be made of other temporary wartime expedients during the French Revolutionary and Napoleonic Wars. In 1796 a so-called provisional cavalry reverted to the pre-1757 militia concept of an obligation upon property owners in a brief and unpopular attempt to levy one man and horse for every ten horses retained for riding or carriage-drawing. A wider *levée en masse*, contemplated in Dorset and some other counties in 1797–8 by utilizing the authority of the sheriff to call out the posse comitatus or civil power of the county, received government endorsement in the Defence of the Realm Act of April 1798 which required registration of inhabitants, livestock, and vehicles. The principle was then revived in both the Defence Act of June 1803 and the General Defence Act of July 1803. A Training Act in 1806, which was never effectively implemented but remained on the statute-book until 1875, suggested an even wider measure of national military training while two expedients to draft men into the army for home service, the army of reserve (also known as the additional army of England) of 1803, and the permanent additional force of 1804 to 1806 also imposed considerable burdens on local administration. In connection with home service, it should be noted that fencibles raised during the American War of Independence and the Revolutionary and Napoleonic Wars were not auxiliaries but regulars recruited for home service only.

It is also necessary to draw attention to the Lieutenancy which emerged during the troubled reign of Edward VI, the prefix 'Lord' Lieutenant originally deriving from the rank of those who filled the office and becoming a matter of custom. Indeed, technically there was no such office as Lord Lieutenant until the local government changes of April 1974, prior to which there was only His or Her Majesty's Lieutenant for a particular county. In fact, Henry VIII had issued commissions to some individual nobles to assume military command in more than one county but it was only in his son's reign that lieutenants were placed above the sheriffs and commissioners who had previously organized local military forces. In 1549 parliament recognized the appointment of Lords Lieutenant in times of crisis and they continued to make sporadic appearances with individuals being increasingly named for single counties until the system became generally applied to England and Wales by the end of the reign of Elizabeth. Ultimately, the Lieutenancy was extended to Scotland in 1794 and to Ireland in 1831, its direct role in the organization of auxiliary forces being maintained until 1871.

It will thus be apparent that there is indeed what can justifiably be termed an amateur military tradition with a remarkable continuity from the mid-sixteenth century if not before. Figures are not always reliable for earlier periods but, at any one time, a significant proportion of the country's male population was either serving in the auxiliary forces or had so served. In 1806, for example, perhaps 3.5 per cent of the population as a whole were serving in auxiliary forces. In 1877 some 6.36 per cent of the male population aged between 15 and 35 were serving in auxiliary forces, representing 3.6 per cent of the population as a whole and by 1898 it has been calculated that no less than 22.42 per cent of the entire male population of the United Kingdom between the ages of 17 and 40 had some cur-

rent or previous military or quasi-military experience, the majority in auxiliary forces rather than regular forces. If such figures appear superficially
small, they must be put into perspective. Thus, over 818,000 men passed
through the volunteers between 1859 and 1877 and the force rarely fell
below a quarter of a million after 1885. Similarly, a total of 935,000 men
passed through the militia between 1882 and 1904. The figures should also
be compared with the experience of mass mobilization during the First
World War when the 5.7 million men passing through the army, including the Territorial Force, still represented only 22.1 per cent of the male
population of the United Kingdom and only 10.73 per cent of the population as a whole.

Clearly, the constant threat of invasion, whether real or perceived, was
a major factor in the establishment and survival of auxiliary forces. The
introduction of the trained bands, for example, resulted directly from the
growing threat from Spain in the 1570s while the revival of the militia in
1852 and of volunteers in 1859 resulted from two of the so-called 'three
panics' in mid-Victorian Britain. However, auxiliaries were equally regarded as fulfilling a constabulary role. The Restoration militia safe-
guarded the monarchy against both internal dissent and the less frequent
attentions of the Dutch whilst most militia duty in the periodic invasion
scares of the late eighteenth and early nineteenth centuries took the form
of internal security. The yeomanry had a considerable role to play in aid of
the civil power after 1815, extending from the industrial disturbances of
the 1820s to the Swing riots in 1830–1, and the Chartist disturbances of the
1840s. The military role in aid of the civil power was, of course, an especially difficult one for troops whether regular or otherwise and the most
enduring image of the yeomanry is that of a class-bound instrument riding down the general population. Above all, perhaps, there is the issue of
the eleven dead and some 400 injured attributed to the forty members of
the Manchester and Salford Yeomanry Cavalry involved in dispersing a
crowd usually estimated at around 60,000 strong at 'Peterloo' on 16
August 1819. In fact, there can be few events so well documented as
Peterloo and yet so difficult to unravel from the tainted nature of the evidence presented by protagonists on both sides and some deaths were undoubtedly caused by regulars committed to extricate the yeomen who had
run into difficulties due to poor horsemanship. As it happens, it was not
the bloodiest confrontation between auxiliaries and rioters since at least
twelve individuals died when fencibles fired on anti-militia ballot
rioters at Tranent in east Lothian in August 1797. Probably the highest

death toll at the hands of regulars was the 285 killed during the Gordon riots in London in June 1780.

Magistrates preferred to rely on regulars but the problem was that so few were generally available. Eventually, the solution appeared to be organized policing in rural areas and those unchartered conurbations which had not enacted policing legislation. However, the Rural Constabulary Act of 1839 was merely permissive of county constabularies and even the mandatory provisions of the County and Borough Police Act of 1856 did not result in an immediate decline in the use of auxiliaries; it was only the alarming legal implications of the use of rifle volunteers as special constables during the Fenian outrages in 1867 that finally marked the last occasion on which any were employed in aid of the civil power. Territorials were specifically excluded from such a role after 1908 but, as already indicated, were still pressed into service in industrial disputes in the 1920s under the guise of *ad hoc* bodies such as the defence force.

Similarly, the emergence of organized policing did not remove the liability of regulars to be called to assist the civil power. Indeed, as late as 1888 the Stanhope memorandum, in listing the purposes for which an army existed, placed aid to the civil power in the United Kingdom as first priority ahead of Indian, imperial, and home defence. In September 1893 the death of two striking colliers at the hands of troops at Featherstone in the West Riding prompted an official inquiry and there was also to be a select committee in 1908 which, *inter alia*, determined that troops had been employed in aid of the civil power on twenty-four separate occasions since 1868. In fact, the last civilian to be killed by a soldier in aid of the civil power on the mainland of Britain was a looter mortally wounded during the Liverpool police strike in August 1919 although, technically, the five Arab terrorists killed by the SAS at the conclusion of the siege of the Iranian Embassy at Prince's Gate, London, in May 1980 should perhaps qualify for this honour.

Auxiliaries were also regarded as providing a measure of social control. It was the perennial desire of successive Councils in Elizabethan and Stuart England as well as of those who framed both the Restoration and mid-eighteenth-century militia legislation that men of wealth and position should serve personally. In the 1790s many entertained similar hopes for the volunteers and, although an older tradition stressing the baneful effects of military service persisted in radical and Nonconformist circles well into the nineteenth century, both Victorian militia and volunteers were increasingly characterized as generating social benefits such as habits of discipline and loyalty. Precisely the same benefits were being held out as inducements to employers to allow enlistment in the Territorials in the twentieth century.

In still another role, auxiliaries existed both as an alternative, and supplement, to the standing army, the perception of the militia in particular being that of a counterweight to the army, hence the title of 'old constitutional force'. This had less meaning after the seventeenth century but there were occasional echoes of the old arguments even in the nineteenth century. But, even as the militia's role as constitutional safeguard declined, there was increasingly the question of how far auxiliaries could genuinely supplement the army, regulars tending to interpret this as meaning that the militia in particular could be used simply as a manpower quarry. Such was the case in 1799, 1804–5, 1807, 1809, 1811, and during the Crimean War when the allegedly temporary expedient of directly recruiting regulars from the militia was instituted. Recruiting from the militia was temporarily suspended from 1860 to 1866 but thereafter the force became little more than a draft-finding body for the army and this was essentially the role to which it was converted by absorption into the special reserve in 1908. Indeed, from 1872 onwards, a militia commission became a recognized alternative route to passing through Sandhurst or Woolwich as a means of gaining a regular commission.

In most periods, regulars adopted a narrow professional view which gave scant encouragement to auxiliaries and it must be acknowledged that local patriotism frequently had a decidedly local flavour and that auxiliary forces were often poor substitutes for trained military manpower. Nevertheless, auxiliaries could be employed overseas although this invariably implied special enabling legislation and overcoming in-built resistance as when the Crown attempted to levy men from the trained bands for overseas service in the 1590s. Some militia did go overseas in 1813–14, 1854, and 1882 primarily for garrison service and, as indicated earlier, volunteers and yeomanry as well as militia served in South Africa. However, the so-called imperial service obligation had attracted few Territorials by 1914 and was one factor in Kitchener's decision to ignore the Territorials as a means of expanding the wartime army. In the event, twenty-three of the Territorials' twenty-eight infantry divisions and two of their five mounted divisions did serve overseas, Territorial units suffering over 577,000 casualties and winning seventy-one Victoria Crosses. In 1920 Territorials were made generally liable for overseas service but the liability was hedged with qualifications and not finally resolved until the creation of a single national army in 1939. While being fully integrated within the national wartime army, nine Territorial divisions fought in the 1940 campaign, one in Norway, four in North Africa, two in Sicily, one in Burma, one at Singapore, and eight in north-west Europe. Territorials won a further seventeen Victoria Crosses.

One of the ironies of a single national army being forged through the application of universal conscription was that the existence of auxiliaries had long effectively prevented its introduction. On the one hand, the fact that the militia itself had been subject to compulsion between 1757 and 1831, to sustained opposition, had increased the realization that compulsion for overseas service was not practical when that for home defence was so detested. In fact, a not inconsiderable factor in filling the ranks of the volunteers and yeomanry during the French Revolutionary and Napoleonic Wars was the exemption they enjoyed from the militia ballot. But the very existence of auxiliaries in such large numbers was also an additional argument against the necessity for conscription, those favouring compulsion recognizing the auxiliaries as an insurmountable barrier until the demands of mass modern warfare finally made it unavoidable.

But it was not just in preserving the voluntary system that the auxiliary forces performed a major role for the best part of four centuries. On occasions, auxiliary forces were a major issue in national politics as in the 1640s when the control of the militia proved a major factor in the outbreak of the Civil War. At other times, large numbers of auxiliaries sat as Members of Parliament where they often proved sufficiently powerful to frustrate government policy. Certainly, the relative independence of the auxiliary forces at different times was of frequent concern to the State and governments invariably employed financial means to assert control.

Inevitably, however, although their existence had consequences for the State and society as a whole, it was at the local level that the presence of auxiliaries was most felt. They were far more visible to British society than regulars, their administration alone proving a constant burden to the gentry and to local county and parochial officials. It was in their nature, too, to operate in the full glare of publicity. Vast crowds frequently attended auxiliary spectacles such as the 100,000 who witnessed the volunteer review in Hyde Park in 1800 or the 150,000 present at a similar review at Knowsley in 1860. It must be remembered that no regular body of troops greater than a battalion appeared in England between 1815 and the creation of the camp at Chobham in 1853 and that, while the metropolitan volunteers alone held a series of large-scale Easter reviews in all but two years between 1861 and 1877, the regular army's autumn manœuvres took place only from 1871 to 1873 and were not then revived until 1898. In all their activities, auxiliaries clearly projected military values which, in the late nineteenth and early twentieth centuries at least, contributed to the recognized growth of militarism. Moreover, the auxiliaries were projecting those values in a way that the regular army could not for the auxiliaries were far more representative of society as a whole even if they often fell short of a particular government's ideal of respectability.

The general impression is that it was a largely working-class pursuit, auxiliaries being unlikely to be those who would readily have joined the army or those who would otherwise have taken part in military affairs. They embraced a far broader cross-section of society either by choice or coercion than the army ever did. After 1757 militia service was largely a burden upon manual workers. Volunteers were supposedly more socially exclusive and both in the 1790s and 1860s operated such devices as entrance fees, proposing and seconding of members, annual subscriptions, and secret ballots. But, if they were initially composed of professional men and tradesmen, in the long term they tended to become dependent upon what might be termed artisans. Even the yeomanry tended to contain a significant proportion of tradesmen or manual workers for all that it was also a haven for the farming community and the county landed élite. Wartime voluntary bodies such as volunteer training corps and the Home Guard naturally tended to be men either above military age or those engaged in reserve occupations, which implied agriculture or industrial concerns crucial to the war effort.

In transmitting certain values to themselves and to those who merely watched them—values which would not have been transmitted but for their existence—the auxiliaries also bore the brunt of popular antimilitarism. This might either take the form of physical confrontation as in the frequent anti-militia riots or, more often, of popular ridicule which, in being reflected in popular literature, itself indicated the cultural impact of the amateur military tradition. Examples include Francis Beaumont and John Fletcher's play, *The Knight of the Burning Pestle*, satirizing the London trained bands in 1610, Dryden's 'rude militia' in his *Cymon and Iphigenia* in 1700, Gillray's cartoons attacking the pretensions of volunteers in the 1790s, *Punch* performing a similar function in the 1860s, and Robb Wilton's monologues concerning the local defence volunteers and Home Guard in the Second World War.

However, in certain circumstances, the prestige of a community could become linked to its local auxiliary forces and result in particular hostility to the disbanding or amalgamation of units. In reality, of course, there was a close interdependence between auxiliaries and society. Billeting did not cease as far as innkeepers were concerned in 1679 and auxiliaries were regularly billeted long after regulars could be accommodated in the barracks increasingly built from the 1790s onwards. Auxiliaries were also of significance because their presence generated trade. Uniforms and equipment were invariably provided by local tradesmen, which was often also an additional means by which political patronage might be extended through a community. On the other hand, auxiliaries themselves attempted to raise financial support from the public to supplement government grants although, on balance, they probably spent more than they took. Metropolitan rifle volunteers, for example, were given favourable terms by railway companies for their Easter reviews with the seaside towns favoured for such spectacles actually competing to attract the volunteers: in 1863 it was said volunteers and their families spent £50,000 when the review was held at Brighton.

Employment was an even more important link between the auxiliaries and society for they were civilians first and soldiers only second. In particular, their ability to fulfil military commitments depended upon the co-operation of employers who often opposed the military demands made upon their employees. In Elizabethan England the trained bands turned out on an average of ten days spread through the year. Restoration militiamen trained on perhaps twelve days per annum but, from 1762 onwards, the annual training period for militia was a continuous twenty-eight days in mid-summer. At times of emergency, too, the militia would be embodied for permanent service, as from 1759–62, 1778–83, 1793–1802, 1803–16, and 1854–6. Volunteer and yeomanry conditions of service varied enormously but, after 1815, yeomanry customarily attended a minimum of eight drills per annum and volunteers nine drills and an annual inspection. In practice most did far more and in 1901 compulsory annual camps of eight or fifteen days were introduced and these persisted into the Territorial Force.

The relationship between militia and agriculture was recognized at an early stage and, during wartime embodied service in the late eighteenth century, it was customary to allow furloughs in winter and at harvest time. Similarly, the yeomanry's activities were closely associated with the unchanging pattern of the agricultural year throughout its existence while tradesmen and artisans in volunteer or Territorial units equally had commitments be it in the 1790s, the 1860s, or the 1930s. There are examples of employers encouraging if not directly coercing their employees to join the auxiliaries but, much more frequently, employers put obstacles in the way of recruitment. Not unexpectedly, the Victorian volunteers supported the half-day holiday and early closing movements while employers have continued to be regularly courted by Territorials down to the present day.

It might well be wondered why men chose to serve in the auxiliary forces in such numbers in the face of frequent opposition and criticism. However, it is clear that service with the auxiliaries provided opportunity. This might be the opportunity of experiencing something different, or of enjoying recreational facilities, or of comradeship, which might not otherwise have been enjoyed. It might have been brought about by a conscious commitment to the status quo or a demonstration of loyalty to community, landlord, or employer. Victorian volunteering in particular has been characterized as confirming a rite of passage for upwardly aspiring working-class boys recruited to cadet corps and cadet battalions, for skilled members of the labour aristocracy, and for clerks. For officers, service in the auxiliaries was clearly a route to social assimilation although advancement was by no means assured if the rank and file had particular ideas as to the kind of officer they wanted and, of course, elections were hardly unknown. Tradesmen in particular often discovered themselves being barred from volunteer commissions as late as the 1870s. Equally, newcomers of wealth and property found a ready route into county society through service in the auxiliaries, notably the yeomanry. At the same time, however, auxiliaries often provided the traditional élite with an outlet for leadership as other avenues were increasingly closed to them during the nineteenth and twentieth centuries. The county Lieutenancies retained the right of nomination to first appointments even after the consolidation of 1871, from which point all auxiliary commissions emanated from the Crown. The County Territorial Associations—established in 1908 to administer the new force and which have survived to the present day in the form of larger regional groupings—only reluctantly surrendered nomination during the First World War. Indeed, the role of the auxiliaries in offering opportunities for local political or other patronage should not be ignored.

In short, the purpose fulfilled by the auxiliary forces was multifaceted and is a ready guide to the paradoxes of British attitudes towards the military. Indeed, auxiliary forces have been the real point of contact between army and society in Britain. None the less, it should never be overlooked that their most enduring *raison d'être* was the threat to stability posed by foreign invasion, internal disorder, or both. Effectively, for all that some served overseas (not least in two World Wars), the auxiliary forces were never tested against an invading army and this fact has perhaps obscured their wider significance for too long. Even in merely existing at times of crisis, auxiliaries were providing a focus and outlet for many who wished only to demonstrate their commitment to their country and, in doing so, to enjoy, in the words of a contemporary historian of the Home Guard, John Brophy, 'the incommunicable satisfaction of a job whose value lies beyond questioning'.

19 THE BRITISH WAY IN WARFARE

HEW STRACHAN

There has never been a British way in warfare. If this is too provocative a proposition with which to begin a chapter devoted to that very title, let it be clear that what is referred to is a precise proposition, not a loosely based collection of strategic ideas.

In 1932 Basil Liddell Hart declared that the purpose of his book, *The British Way in Warfare*, 'is to show that there has been a distinctively British practice of war, based on experience and proved by three centuries of success'. That practice was 'based, above all, on mobility and surprise— apt to Britain's natural conditions and aptly used to enhance her relative strength while exploiting her opponent's weakness'. Britain's 'natural condition' was maritime and 'her relative strength' was naval: the mobility and surprise to which Liddell Hart referred were therefore not the tactics of land warfare but the flexibility vouchsafed by dominance of the seas. 'This naval body', he went on, 'had two arms; one financial, which embraced the subsidizing and military provisioning of allies; the other military, which embraced sea-borne expeditions against the enemy's vulnerable extremities.'

But, for all its pretence to the contrary, Liddell Hart's book was not a history of British strategy. Indeed only one chapter was devoted to its declared purpose; the rest was a collection of largely unrelated essays on contemporary issues. Liddell Hart dressed up the past so that he could use it as evidence in support of his prescriptions for the future. Objectivity was never part of his repertoire. That is not a criticism in itself, for he made his intentions perfectly plain in the foreword to *The British Way in Warfare*.

Liddell Hart's contribution, therefore, lies in the realm of strategic ideas, not of military history. His use of the latter is to develop the former;

his purpose is didactic. And it is testimony to his fertility that his concepts should still provide the basis for debate and discussion. Used as theory, as a way of approaching problems, *The British Way in Warfare* remains a tool of analytical significance.

It is, therefore, the claim about Britain's historical practice that is misleading and wilful. Liddell Hart acknowledged that the British way in warfare had never become the basis of doctrine. But he did not go further and say that it had also never been a consistent basis for action. Britain's conduct of its major wars has been the product primarily of pragmatism and expedience, not theory. And, even when theory has played its part, it has lost its purity and even its direction in practice. On 3 August 1914 the Cabinet opted for a war which, it thought, would be waged through the 'two arms' of Liddell Hart's 'naval body': it could not have been more wrong.

It was of course the depth of the Cabinet's miscalculation in 1914 that prompted Liddell Hart to write *The British Way in Warfare* in the first place. And indeed it was thanks to the efforts of men like him, and also Maurice Hankey and Lloyd George, that in 1939 Britain could embark on another major war with so much faith still pinned on economic pressure and blockade rather than on major land operations on the Continent. The 'phoney' war was only phoney from a narrowly military perspective: Britain's long-haul strategy was to be exercised through sea power, and was implemented from the very outset.

Liddell Hart's argument relied for its vehemence on an antithesis. The opposite of a strategy that was maritime and British was one that was continental and European. Britain's failure in the First World War was to be sucked into a method of waging it that was alien to its culture and inappropriate to its geography. But the polarity is a false one—both in the context of the First World War specifically, and in relation to British experience more generally. Those who have replied to Liddell Hart have made two telling points.

First, Liddell Hart's theory relies excessively on examples drawn from the eighteenth century and before. This was an age when communication and trade were more effectively conducted by sea than by land. But from 1870 onwards the geopolitical shift made possible by the advent of the railway rendered the possession of large land empires no longer a liability but a potential asset. Germany and Russia, for example, were able to exploit their natural resources and apply them to domestic manufactures. They could move troops rapidly from one end of their domains to another.

Naval operations became more genuinely peripheral than they had ever been in previous centuries.

Secondly, even the apparently supreme historical example of the British way in warfare, derived from the eighteenth century and the era of maritime supremacy, did not necessarily endorse Liddell Hart's argument. Sir Julian Corbett, whose book, *Some Principles of Maritime Strategy* (1911), had in many ways anticipated Liddell Hart, made a particular study of the Seven Years War. In that war Britain's control of the sea allowed her to choose to fight in land theatres which could be sustained by the navy, campaigns limited in method and in geographical extent, but unlimited in their objectives. But Corbett acknowledged that to enable the application of such a strategy, Britain had had to be allied to a power for whom the war was unlimited. This was the role of Prussia in the Seven Years War, or of Spain, Austria, Prussia, and Russia in the war with Napoleon. For some allies, subsidies and a few token troops would not be enough. France in the First World War and Russia in the Second required major military contributions to operations on the mainland of Europe. In those circumstances the twin pressures of the naval arm would be insufficient.

These two criticisms, voiced especially by Paul Kennedy and Michael Howard, have underlined that Britain did not enjoy the freedom of choice implied by Liddell Hart in the 1930s. But in criticizing Liddell Hart, care must be taken not to over-correct, not to dismiss the maritime option as vehemently as he discounted the continental. In reality, the choice has been relative, the apparent options largely illusory. Just as Corbett and Liddell Hart neglected to stress the continental aspects of the evidence which they cited in favour of a maritime strategy, so continentalists have been in danger of neglecting the maritime element in continentalism. At the risk of stating the obvious, all British armies have relied on sea power even when deployed on the European Continent in the main theatre of the war. Naval dominance has been the unspoken assumption, the minimum without which nothing else has proved possible. The British Expeditionary Force of the First World War was reinforced and supplied entirely by sea. In June 1944, sea power was an essential prerequisite in enabling the D-Day landings. British strategic practice has therefore rested on the establishment of a balance along a spectrum of possibilities.

The danger, therefore, in rejecting the *British Way in Warfare* is that the baby will be thrown out with the bath water. It does not follow that, because Liddell Hart's history was sloppy and his arguments self-serving, all his ideas were unsound. Problems arose principally because his method of making his points could be so perverse. The dominance of the First World War in shaping his thoughts did not help. His examples, derived from that war and intended to establish the potential efficacy of the 'two arms' of his 'naval body', sea-borne expeditions and economic pressure, rested in the first case on counter-factual argument and in the second on tendentious assertion.

Liddell Hart maintained that, if the Gallipoli landings of 1915 had been properly supported, they would have opened the supply route to Russia, brought the Balkan states over to the *entente*, and established Serbia as a route into the Austro-Hungarian empire. In other words the war could have been won in short order for the commitment of 150,000 men. As it was, Gallipoli joined the long list of unsuccessful amphibious operations, ill planned and ill prepared, providing more evidence of a lack of harmony between army and navy than of fruitful co-operation. Bracketed with the Walcheren expedition of 1809, this argument serves not to support Liddell Hart's case but to undermine it. His critics go on to aver that, despite her maritime heritage, Britain has been perennially ill prepared for the conduct of amphibious warfare. But thus they begin to be as selective in their reading as he was in his. Paradoxically, the Crimean War, which Liddell Hart discussed not at all, was ultimately successful in its objectives and did prove his point. Nor are such illustrations confined, like the stunning success of Quebec in 1759, to a largely pre-industrial age. Britain's Mediterranean strategy in the Second World War was founded on the principles of sea-borne assault and maritime supply.

Similarly ill conducted was Liddell Hart's case for economic exhaustion. Liddell Hart's studies of the First World War are almost exclusively concerned with military operations. And yet he maintained that the blockade of Germany had won the war. At no stage did he provide evidence to prove his point. From the early 1920s there were available plenty of German statistics purporting to show the declining standards of German nutrition and their effects on public health. Liddell Hart used none of them. Moreover, he was wrong in his inference that the blockade as applied in the First World War was part of Britain's 'historic practice'. Blockade could be either naval, in other words designed to secure command of the seas from an enemy fleet, or commercial, and intended to cut off that enemy's trade. But in no previous war had economies been so advanced, and so import-reliant, as to make the commercial effects more important than the naval. In 1914, therefore, the Royal Navy planned a commercial blockade as a means of forcing the Germans out to engage in fleet action.

In the event commercial blockade became an end in itself. Furthermore, its implementation achieved a level of sophistication and complexity—legal, diplomatic, and financial—scarcely glimmered by Liddell Hart. But the imperfections in Liddell Hart's argument do not justify the conclusion that the blockade was marginal or even irrelevant to Germany's defeat. Germany was exhausted economically; her own conduct of the war played a large part in accomplishing that; but by the same token, blockade, at the very least, exacerbated an already worsening situation.

The substantive difficulty with the debate on the British way in warfare is much more to do with the issues it does not embrace rather than with those that it does. What concerned Liddell Hart in the 1930s, and continues to concern his critics, has been the question of British strategy in the event of European war. But Britain's military experience over the last two centuries has not been predominantly European. In only thirty-five of the 200 years since 1792 has Britain fought continental forces—in the Napoleonic Wars, in the Crimea, and in the two World Wars. And yet in almost none of the intervening periods have British soldiers not been engaged in operations and not suffered casualties. Britain's 'historic practice' has been colonial and imperial. The British way in warfare therefore creates a lop-sided view of the history of the British army. The main events have been left out. Continuity has been neglected in favour of change.

Liddell Hart was not alone in this distortion. Most professional theorists before and since have followed him. Men like E. B. Hamley, whose texts dominated Staff College thought for half a century, or Frederick Maurice, or G. F. R. Henderson, all wrote perceptively about European warfare, and held up continental models for imitation in the British army. However, their own service, under Wolseley and Roberts on the battlefields of Empire, found no reflection in their theories. The single significant exception to this generalization is Charles Callwell, a gunner officer, who fought the Afghans and the Boers, and whose book *Small Wars*, published in 1896, is the only major attempt to synthesize Britain's colonial military experience. Callwell also wrote about the relationship between sea power and the army long before Corbett or Liddell Hart. His *œuvre* embraced both arms of British strategy, and he can consequently lay claim to being the father of a much more genuine 'British way in warfare'.

In fairness to Corbett and Liddell Hart, if not to Hamley and Henderson, it must be conceded that in the eighteenth century colonial operations did not so obviously stand apart from European warfare. Britain's opponents outside Europe were not the indigenous populations but rival imperial powers. In 1739 the struggle with Spain for control of the West Indies led Britain into the War of Austrian Succession in Europe. In 1756 the ongoing competition with France for control of India and North America became fused with the Seven Years War. In 1776 Britain's break with the American colonists drew France into a renewal of the struggle for maritime supremacy in the Atlantic. As late as the 1790s the war with revolutionary France displayed the interrelationship and even integrity of the component parts of British strategy. Britain wrested from the French the islands of the West Indies. The growth of foreign trade, led by imports and re-exports of sugar and coffee from the Caribbean, provided revenue and credit for the government, and boosted the merchant marine, so underpinning the growth of the Royal Navy. Fighting in the colonies was therefore not peripheral to Britain's war effort in Europe, but vital to its maintenance.

In the nineteenth century the pattern changed. No serious European challenge to Britain's colonial hegemony emerged until the 1880s, and when it did so the competition was diplomatic and commercial not military. Imperial rivalries were settled at the conference table, and, even as late as 1911–14, could be a route to *détente* rather than to war. Britain's battles were now fought against the native populations of her African and Asian possessions. The army's task was to ensure the security, stability, and consolidation of the Empire.

The institutional implications for the army and navy were immense. During the 1830s, in the debates on the army estimates, the radical Member of Parliament, Joseph Hume, was wont to call for a return to the military establishments of 1792. This, after all, had been the eighteenth-century pattern. Armies, being manpower intensive, were expanded in time of war and reduced in time of peace. The navy, whose ships could not be so readily improvised, remained the fixed cost and the greater element in defence spending. But between 1815 and 1865 the Empire grew at the rate of 100,000 square miles a year. The guns of British battleships, designed to fight European opponents, became secondary not primary in Britain's defence priorities. Even at the height of Marlborough's campaigns in the War of Spanish Succession, the ratio of spending on the army and the navy had been 40 : 60; in the years 1816 to 1895, excluding the Crimean War, the ratio was reversed to 58 : 42. The 'long peace' and 'pax Britannica' were misleading titles, bought by dint of sustained campaigning on the part of the British army.

In the twentieth century also the Empire, not Europe, has been the more continuous element in soldiers' experiences. In the inter-war years, imperial policing, from Palestine through Iraq to the North-West Frontier of India, reinforced the notion that continental warfare was an aberration rather than the norm. And, since 1945, although the theory of war has been Eurocentric, the practice has not. Counter-insurgency in the 1950s and colonial withdrawal in the 1960s shaped the careers of senior officers still serving in the 1980s. Field Marshal Sir John Chapple, the Chief of the General Staff from 1988 to 1992, was a Gurkha officer in Malaya, Hong Kong, and Borneo. General Sir Peter de la Billière, British commander in the Gulf War in 1991, served also in Korea, Malaya, Jordan, Borneo, Egypt, Aden, Sudan, Oman, and the Falkland Islands. Admittedly by the 1990s such profiles were rare. But for neither officer were exercises on the north German plain the stuff of military life. Even as the twentieth century draws to its close Britain's recent military experience has more in common with its nineteenth-century colonial past than with the army's declared commitment to Europe. Sustained low-intensity warfare in Northern Ireland has been seen by some as the last stage of the withdrawal from the Empire. The Falklands War of 1982, with its use of sea power for force projection, although a clash between Britain and Argentina, remained limited both in geographical extent and in the means employed.

Since the late nineteenth century the persistence of Britain's colonial commitments has shaped the maritime–continental debate in a rather different way from that depicted by Liddell Hart. Liddell Hart's preoccupation was with the strategy most appropriate to Britain in time of war. But strategy has come to denote (however inaccurately) not only the actual use of force in war but also pre-war planning and peacetime defence policy. Britain's dilemma has been, apparently, whether to orientate her armed forces around a possible expedition to Europe or around the defence of the Empire. On 8 December 1888, Edward Stanhope, the Secretary of State for War, ranked 'the objects of our military organisation'. Aid to the civil power came first, India second, colonial garrisons third, home defence fourth. The dispatch of two complete corps to Europe was ranked fifth but was also stated to be improbable. By 1967, the assumptions of Stanhope's memorandum had been completely overthrown. Denis Healey, the Minister of Defence, announced Britain's withdrawal from east of Suez, and the army's concentration on its NATO role in Europe. Only the defence of the home base formed a continuity between the two statements.

Again, however, the consequence of polarity in argument is the distortion of actuality. The key determinant of Britain's policy has been geography. By lying athwart the main exits from the North Sea, Britain has commanded a vital position on Europe's trade routes to the rest of the world. But, by the same token, the occupation of the Low Countries by a dominant and hostile power has been able to threaten Britain's own access to world commerce. The independence but relative weakness of Belgium and Holland have therefore been strategic priorities for global and imperial reasons as much as for specifically European ones. The defence of the Empire began in Europe.

Technology has not undermined this relationship between geography and strategy as much as is sometimes imagined. The advent of the steamship in the 1830s and 1840s threatened, in the view of the Duke of Wellington, to make the Channel not a barrier but a bridge. The three French invasion panics of the nineteenth century, the German invasion scares before 1914—all were predicated on the assumption that fleets could now be concentrated and an army transported with a rapidity which would exploit any temporary absence or inferiority in the Royal Navy's home fleet. In the 1930s the development of the bomber, for which the Channel was no obstacle, brought a direct danger to British cities. Britain's defensive concerns in Europe moved inland from the Channel coast to encompass the operating radius of aircraft based on the Continent. But technology, although changing the profile of the threat, proved strategically neutral—in the sense that it could be used for defensive purposes as well as offensive. Steam power enabled defending fleets to assemble as efficiently as attacking ones; the fighter demonstrated in 1940 that the aircraft had the capacity to counter its own kind. In the missile age air attack remains the most significant danger. Sea-borne invasion has become no less problematic than in the past and—if attempted without adequate air cover—much more so.

Indeed, in the relationship between Europe and the defence of Empire, technological innovation has proved far more of an asset than a hindrance. Rapidity of deployment, through the use of steamships and latterly of aircraft, has allowed the progressive concentration of troops at home, within Britain. In 1869 Edward Cardwell, the Secretary of State for War, proposed to reduce the army abroad from 50,000 to 26,000 men, keeping seventy-one battalions in the colonies and seventy at home. His was the coping-stone to schemes adumbrated since the 1840s. In practice the plan proved unworkable: in 1879, with wars in Afghanistan and South Africa,

eighty-two battalions were abroad and fifty-nine at home. But the principle was fixed. And it was not, as the Stanhope memorandum makes
clear, evidence of creeping continentalism. The essence was flexibility.

The work of a later occupant of the War Office, Richard Burdon Haldane, illustrates a similar point. After the First World War, Haldane maintained that he had set about his programme of army reform in 1906, and
in particular the formation of the British Expeditionary Force, with a view
to its commitment to Europe. This was a selective interpretation of the
truth. Haldane's first task was to cut his department's estimates. The
British Expeditionary Force was created as a strategic reserve for deployment anywhere in the world. Until 1907, its most likely enemy was Russia
and its putative theatre of operations was India. Even after 1907 it required
special pleading to say that its six divisions could make any significant
difference against European armies possessed of almost 100 divisions each.
Not until 1910, and the appointment of the Francophile Henry
Wilson as director of military operations, was the British Expeditionary
Force prepared specifically for the European role with which it subsequently became associated.

Britain's commitments were therefore indivisible. For London, the
principal threats to the Empire lay, naturally enough, in Europe. For those
on the imperial periphery this could be a hard argument to swallow. What
made it particularly indigestible was the corollary to the Whitehall position, that the colonies, and particularly the self-governing Dominions,
should undertake the responsibilities of local self-defence. From the 1840s
onwards, this delegation of martial duties seemed to meet indifference
and even hostility. Memories of 1776, and the impact on America of drawing the cost of troops from local pockets, discouraged too strong a line
from Britain. Only the Indian Army took on a major imperial role beyond
its own frontiers, and even this is in danger of exaggeration. After 1857, the
memory of the mutiny was a powerful argument against over
reliance on Indian troops; it also served to underline that the principal role
of the Army of India was internal security not overseas expeditions. But it
would be wrong to conclude that the colonies were simply a drain on
Britain's defence budgets, bringing no return on a massive investment. In
the first half of the twentieth century the Dominions provided abundant
evidence that they took seriously enough the link between imperial defence and European security. In the First World War, and particularly in
its later stages, the Australians, New Zealanders, and Canadians provided

some of the crack troops in the British army in France and Flanders. In the Second World War, 73 per cent of the 8th Army's divisions in North Africa in October 1941 were imperial. The indivisibility stretched both ways.

The claim that the 1967 decision to withdraw from east of Suez resolved the tension between global and European responsibilities was true, but only up to a point, and only for a limited period. In the 1970s and 1980s, the British army developed, at least in its middle and junior ranks, a more continental ethos. However, colonial legacies still lingered. Even in 1991 ships and troops, albeit often in very small contingents, were distributed in twenty-five different locations around the world. The association of soldiering with exotic and exciting travel never entirely evaporated. Moreover, the end of the Cold War jeopardized the European scenario-building which had become the army's main rationale. Weapons costed and procured on the grounds of a fast-diminishing Soviet threat increasingly found their justification through reference to the uncertainties outside Europe as well as within it. NATO's formal response, the creation in 1991 of a Rapid Reaction Corps, bore testimony to a historically familiar pattern. Britain agreed to contribute two divisions, but their component parts were more likely to see service as individual air-mobile brigades outside Europe than within Europe as members of the full corps, with its complement of tanks and other heavy equipment. 'Double-hatting' was the jargon of the 1990s for the less ugly vocabulary of the Stanhope memorandum.

The reassertion of a global role, evident if guarded in the 1992 Defence White Paper, meant that the reduction in defence expenditure was low by comparison with other European powers. No major component of the armed forces was sacrificed. Therefore, the fact that the army took on board its commitment to Europe so belatedly and so reluctantly protected it from the traumatic restructuring that would have been essential for a conscript force built up almost exclusively of armoured divisions.

The institutions of the British army have been shaped far more by colonial continuities than by the intense but infrequent periods of continental warfare. Given the lack of attention to 'small war' theory, and given the tendency to judge the army by European yardsticks, such a conclusion may seem surprising. But it is a consequence of two features of Britain's experience which mark it out as different from the continental powers. First, the periods between major European wars have not been characterized by inactivity or genuine peace: the army's job in the 1840s, 1890s, or 1920s was not to prepare for the next war but to fight the current one. Secondly, the defence of the nation from invasion, although frequently stated as the army's prime role, has in practice been left to the navy. In the German army, for example, neither generalization has held good: its dominant experience has been struggles on its own frontiers for national survival.

Britain has therefore only once had recourse to national service in peacetime. The liberal justification for conscription rests on the argument that civic rights include civic obligations. But the obligation is to defend one's nation, not to support its aggrandizement. The efforts of the National Service League to call for the introduction of conscription in peacetime in the decade before the outbreak of the First World War pivoted on the possibility of the fleet failing to prevent a German landing in Britain. The League did not argue that conscripts should serve overseas. And this limitation on conscription had a practical as well as a theoretical bearing. Older men proved more resilient than younger to the vagaries and diseases of foreign climates; the sea journey and the period of acclimatization, when added to the time spent training, suggested that short service (say two to three years maximum) was impracticable. Furthermore, conscript armies could become dominated by the needs of basic training, undermining their readiness for service. Thus, by the late nineteenth century, the army's prime job stood at odds with the methods of procuring men prevailing elsewhere. Only when committed to Europe has the army's rejection of conscription seemed bizarre. A principal strength of conscription lies in the ability to recall discharged conscripts to the colours and so rapidly swell the army's cadres in times of crisis. Possessed of a long-service regular army rather than a short-service conscript one, Britain has never had an adequate reserve. The expansion of the army in the event of European war has been a matter of improvisation, productive of delay and initial defeats.

The lack of a reserve, and the clear distinction between the army's customary roles and its involvement in European war, have also militated against the development of higher formations. By 1914 European armies had divided their manpower into corps and their national territory into areas associated with those corps. The corps was simultaneously an administrative headquarters for a particular area in peace and a semi-independent command in time of war. On mobilization, it was the task of the corps to incorporate the reservists, and to establish depots to support the active corps in the field. Peacetime needs and wartime requirements therefore fused to encourage the creation of command structures appropriate to mass armies.

However, in Britain, even the division, approximately a third the size of a corps, was a rarity before 1914. The largest expeditionary force dispatched overseas between 1815 and 1899 was that sent to Egypt in 1882, and consisted of 35,000 men—little more than a single corps by continental standards. The force commanded by Wolseley in the Ashanti War of 1873–4 totalled 4,000 men and Roberts led 10,000 in his march from Kabul to Kandahar in 1880.

Command therefore remained personal and direct. In 1870, while Moltke was consolidating his reputation in France at the head of 462,000 men, Wolseley was establishing his in Canada with a force of 1,400. In mass armies, particularly before the advent of efficient radio communications, operational command had to be delegated forward. The role of the Commander-in-Chief was to co-ordinate and to manage. Wolseley required managerial skills, but principally to overcome the logistical problems of operating in territory that was inadequately mapped and underdeveloped. In battle he could do most jobs himself. The training of staff for operational roles could too easily seem redundant. Although the Staff College was established in 1856, attendance was not mandatory for the rising star. Sir John French, Commander-in-Chief of the British Expeditionary Force in 1914, was not a product of the Staff College. His successor, Douglas Haig, was. But he was still unprepared for the command of upwards of a million men. He therefore found himself without the skills or the structures to enable effective delegation or efficient consultation. By leaving subordinate formations to fight their own battles, he conformed to the norms of colonial warfare, but ran the risk that they would do so in their own way, without co-ordination with their neighbours, thus ensuring that the sum was less than the parts.

Nor, until 1906, did Britain have a general staff. For continental powers with conscripts and corps, and with clearly identifiable threats, planning was a major peacetime function. Therefore, a formal staff was essential. But for Britain, with flexibility as the priority, with the identity of the next enemy unclear, a general staff was in danger of preparing for the wrong war at the wrong time. There was also the fear that a general staff once formed would create its own sphere of responsibilities, and would pursue a strategy which would become the master of foreign policy and not its servant. Although the general staff did emerge as a significant political player between 1906 and 1914, to argue that it propelled Britain into continental war is to grant it an authority which it had yet to gain. This was particularly true within the army itself. In peacetime, the general staff was only one of three main divisions, alongside the adjutant-general's and quartermaster-general's departments. On the outbreak of war, rather than provide the structure for supreme command, it fragmented—its members split over different jobs—with its chief firmly subordinate both to the Secretary of State for War and the Commander-in-Chief in the field.

A principal casualty of the lack of a well-established general staff was doctrine. Uncertainty as to the army's principal role became the excuse for insufficient attention to theory. But, even when the army's task was clear-cut, it proved reluctant to theorize about its functions and the manner in which to execute them. The argument that armies that think about doctrine get caught in preparing to refight the last war became an excuse for not thinking at all rather than for thinking more rigorously. Not until the late 1980s and the full acceptance of the NATO commitment, was some change effected to this outlook. The external pressure, to align British operational thought with that of the other armies likely to operate in Germany, was a potent factor in remedying decades of neglect. In 1987 the higher command and staff course was established at the Staff College, and in 1989 a booklet, *Design for Military Operations: The British Military Doctrine*, was published. Much of this was predicated on corps operations in the European theatre. One implication, therefore, of the end of the Cold War was the removal of the foundations on which the edifice of British military doctrine was constructed. The existence of the Rapid Reaction Corps became vital as a focus for staff training and study, a case of the tail wagging the dog. Without it, the stress on the uncertainty of the army's future strategic role was in danger of undermining the development of a common doctrine.

The most potent symbol of all these themes, the counterpoint to a common doctrine and to a general staff tradition, has been the regimental system. That Britain possesses not an army but a collection of regiments is a truism which has long outlived the obvious rationales for the system itself. The debate, such as it was, generated in 1990–1 by the Ministry of Defence's post-Cold War review, *Options For Change*, illustrates this longevity. The army was left to decide which regiments should stay and which should amalgamate. Thus divided against itself, it failed to address the much broader questions of its collective role, shape, and size.

The justification for this extraordinary inversion of priorities was that the regiment, by virtue of the fierce loyalties which it generated, was the receptacle of the army's history and traditions, and was therefore the bedrock of the army's morale and fighting qualities. That an individual regiment elicits strong attachments is not in dispute; that it represents a genuine tradition is much more dubious.

Cavalry regiments and, until 1881, infantry regiments were numbered sequentially according to seniority. The regiments with the highest numbers were the most junior. Wartime expansion and peacetime reduction, until 1818, were accomplished by adding or subtracting these higher numbers. Infantry regiments numbered 71 to 124 appeared in the army list for the first time in the Seven Years War; they were disbanded again after 1763. The largest expansion of all occurred in the Napoleonic Wars, the battalions reaching number 135. In 1818, the most junior infantry regiment was the 93rd. Although a newly raised battalion might bear the same number as a previous battalion, it had no more in common with its predecessors than that.

In 1881, Hugh Childers, the Secretary of State for War, completed the process of linking the infantry battalions initiated by Cardwell. Most were paired, and given a new territorial title rather than a number. The regions to which the battalions were allocated frequently bore little relationship to the nominal county title previously borne. The 24th Foot became the South Wales Borderers, although its previous county title had been Warwickshire. The regiments established depots in their own county areas. But localization did not necessarily follow. Rural depopulation could make local enlistment difficult. Scottish regiments, even if they bore proud Highland titles, recruited disproportionately from Glasgow. London produced the largest number of recruits of any area, although it did not have infantry regiments in proportion. True localization, linking community and battalion in intimacy, was confined to the Pals battalions raised for Kitchener's New Armies in the First World War. Then not only specific towns but also specific trades formed units which became service battalions of existing county regiments. The devastating impact of heavy casualties on a circumscribed area suggested that this was not necessarily a sensible way to proceed.

There are of course genuinely ancient regiments, whose existence and title have been unbroken for 300 years or more. But for many the notion of continuity and of deep local roots has been assumed—an invented tradition. Such fabrications have been useful: they created a sense of belonging and an *esprit de corps*. But they have not had to possess historical claims of great antiquity to flourish: the Parachute Regiment is an example where function has created its own pride. A false historicism is none the less damaging when it becomes an end in itself.

In the twentieth century, the army has effected its reductions less by the earlier pattern of disbandment and more by amalgamation. The argument was that the newly formed regiment carried on the traditions of its parent units. In reality one partner has tended to dominate over the other. The Blues and Royals have become the Royal Horse Guards by any other name: the 1st or Royal Dragoons have effectively ceased to exist. The Royal Scots Dragoon Guards have reflected the traditions of the Royal Scots Greys (2nd Dragoons) not the 3rd Carbiniers. Both amalgamations show the illogicalities which the system has generated: the Royal Dragoons and the Royal Scots Greys were both dragoons, stood next to each other in the army list, and yet were not joined to each other. The tradition of function in battle was frequently lost to other considerations. The Royal Highland Fusiliers, an amalgamation of a fusilier regiment and a light infantry regiment, joined two ends of the infantry spectrum because both recruited from adjacent areas in south-west Scotland. And yet the endeavour to retain local links could produce titles, particularly for southern England, that struck few chords.

This creation of a bogus antiquity and an uncertain regionalization has had adverse tactical and operational repercussions. New technology creates new ways in warfare, and yet old regiments have carried associations with outdated methods. Between the two World Wars the cavalry regiments were mechanized. The Royal Tank Regiment, although its *raison d'être* was the armoured fighting vehicle, became simply the most junior of the armoured regiments. The tank was grafted on to the cavalry, rather than made the basis for fundamental reappraisal. In the 1980s and early 1990s a comparable situation arose with the helicopter, whose battlefield application in other armies has stretched far beyond a single formation. But in Britain the Army Air Corps was a junior regiment, lacking senior representation within the service, and posing a potential threat to existing interests. Britain was as a consequence far less dynamic in its adoption of the attack helicopter. Most striking of all was the status of the Royal Electrical and Mechanical Engineers, in 1990 the largest single corps in the army. Despite its pervasive importance to modern warfare, none of its officers could expect promotion beyond the senior ranks of the corps itself.

The historical background to the dominance of the regiment lies less in the traditions of individual units and more in the system itself. In the late nineteenth century, the operational emphasis in European warfare moved away from the infantry battalion of 800 men. The fire-swept battlefield fostered dispersion and delegation: the key single-arm tactical commands became the company, the platoon, and even the section. Administratively, the corps and then the division were the formations which combined the different arms in operational roles; as the twentieth century progressed that combination occurred at lower and lower levels. The role of the single-arm regiment or battalion was therefore squeezed from top and bottom. But in Britain the dominance of colonial garrisoning continued to give the infantry regiment a functional validity it was in the process of losing elsewhere. The battalion was a convenient size for a troopship, a sensible formation (neither too small nor too big) for an imperial outpost, and even a reasonable building-block in the comparatively smaller armies engaged in colonial wars. At the same time separation from home society through overseas service made the regiment more than just a military formation. It saw itself as an enlarged family, a self-contained community, with its own welfare arrangements, its own recreations and sports. The system therefore had a role.

The system's existence can also help explain the absence of militarism in Britain. Militarism is a vexed word, whose appropriateness to Britain many would dispute. Two definitions are helpful here. First, militarism can indicate the army's intervention in civilian politics. Secondly, it can describe the situation where the veneration of things military goes beyond that appropriate to the necessities of warfare. Britain has had a professional, regular army that by virtue of its overseas service has remained separate from the community as a whole. And yet the army has not carved out for itself an independent political tradition. The fact that loyalties are directed towards the regiment and not to the profession at large has contributed to that political quiescence. Furthermore, the regiment, with its attention to dress distinctions, to bands, to its own peculiar customs, has been the repository of that second form of militarism, which has thus been dispersed.

Britain's development as a liberal democracy has been both the cause and the consequence of its avoidance of the more overt forms of militarism. The small size of the army, its fragmentation geographically and regimentally, has enabled this to happen. And yet, by the same token, the army has not provided a sufficient guarantee against aggression from a continental power. The trade-off for a small army and for the rejection of

conscription has been the employment of advanced technology as a substitute. The Dreadnought at the beginning of the century, the bomber in
the 1930s, the nuclear missile since 1957—each has underpinned the ability of Britain to pursue maritime and colonial roles while retaining pretensions as a European power.

Such weapons specifically targeted the enemy's civilian population—
even if indirectly, through blockade, in the case of the pre-1914 battleship.
Their function has been as much one of deterrence as of battlefield application. The contributions of the Dreadnought to Britain's victory in the
First World War, and of the bomber to the Second World War, remain
controversial. Certainly they cannot claim to have achieved success independently of major land operations. Furthermore the procurement of
high technology in times of peace has meant that Britain, while relieving
the majority of its able-bodied males from military service, has instead had
to impose direct taxation earlier, at higher levels, and on lower rates of income, than its major European rivals.

The implications of Britain's military capability, for the nature of war
and for the growth of the State, have therefore been far more extensive
than the limited connotations of 'the British way in warfare'. David
Edgerton has preferred to label the British way in warfare 'liberal militarism'. In so doing he gives 'the British way in warfare' a universality
which robs Liddell Hart's formulation of any significance. He may equally
be twisting 'militarism' to denote any form of state activity with military
applications. But the basic point is well made. In focusing on the army
and the limitations in its role, military historians have been in danger of
minimizing the true nature and the broad extent of Britain's defence
policy.

20 TOWARDS THE FUTURE

MICHAEL YARDLEY

The future of the British army is currently more uncertain than at any time since the end of the Second World War. Under the *Options For Change* policy first announced by the British government in July 1990, and confirmed in the Defence White Paper of July 1992, the numbers of both the regular and Territorial Army are to be reduced considerably. The stated intention is to create a 'smaller but better' army more suited to the new international situation.

Today's army is made up of over 200,000 men and women; at the time of writing there are 145,000 in the regular army, and 70,000 in the Territorials. By the mid-1990s it is planned that the regular army should number 116,000 and the Territorial Army about 60,000. This target will be achieved largely by natural wastage but there will be some redundancies: most units will be affected, but the proposed cuts in the Teeth Arms are especially notable. By April 1995 the Household Cavalry and Royal Armoured Corps will have declined from twenty to twelve regiments, the Royal Artillery from fourteen to nine, the Royal Engineers from fifteen to ten, and the Royal Signals from fifteen to ten. By April 1998 the number of infantry battalions is also likely to have diminished from fifty-five to thirty-eight. Only the Army Air Corps will keep the same number of regiments (six). The Teeth Arms will retain the regimental system, but with the amalgamations of many units and with some being put into suspended animation. The cuts in the supporting services, however, are accompanied by a major reorganization which moves in a less traditional direction. To quote the 1992 defence White Paper: 'radical restructuring of the support organization and systems is well in hand. The logistical functions of service support and equipment support will be grouped into two larger corps'.

The first of the new large corps has already started life as the Adjutant-

General (A-G) Corps. It is an amalgam of the Royal Army Pay Corps, the Women's Royal Army Corps, the Royal Military Police, the Military Provost Staff, the Army Legal Corps, and the Royal Army Educational Corps. Women will not be confined to the new A-G Corps, as they were once confined to the WRAC. Representing about 5 per cent of the army's personnel many will now be able to serve in any unit other than infantry and armour.

The second new support corps is, from 1993, known as the Royal Logistical Corps. It includes what are now the Royal Ordnance Corps, the Royal Corps of Transport, the Royal Pioneer Corps, the Royal Army Catering Corps, and those members of the Royal Engineers responsible for postal services. However, the Royal Electrical and Mechanical Engineers, whose basic responsibility is servicing equipment, retain their individual identity as before.

Significant cost-cutting exercises concerning the training of recruits are also taking place at present. Basic induction training for adults, juniors, and apprentices will soon take place at a 'reduced number of larger and more efficient establishments'. All adult recruits will complete ten weeks of basic training at one of five new army training regiments to be formed at Glencorse, Lichfield, Bassingbourn, Pirbright, and Winchester. Similarly, army apprentices will in future undertake a standard one-year foundation course at a single Army Technical College, and then complete their training once posted to a unit.

There is also to be reorganization of administrative structures. The number of military districts in the United Kingdom is to be reduced from ten to six. The Western, North-Western, and Wales [sic] districts become the new Wales and Western district. A new Eastern District is created from the old Eastern and North-Eastern Districts, and a new Southern District is being created by merging the South-Eastern and South-Western districts. These changes will result in fewer commands for officers of general rank.

Perhaps the most significant of all the announced changes are those which affect what was the British Army of the Rhine (BAOR). Until very recently BAOR—the force which would have opposed an attack from the East in central Europe—has been the British army's prime commitment. In a build-up to war its 50,000 troops would have been reinforced by regulars and Territorials from the mainland to an intended fighting strength of about 150,000. Now, after the apparent collapse of Communism and the

Warsaw Pact, a new doctrine has been conceived. In future, the British army's main contribution to the defence of Europe will be as an element of the Allied Command Europe Rapid Reaction Corps (ARRC).

Some 23,000 troops will be permanently stationed in Germany, organized into three armoured brigades, while a more lightly equipped division will remain in the United Kingdom—the 3rd (UK) Division—and will also function as a strategic reserve. This formation includes 5 Airborne Brigade (the Paras), two mechanized brigades (armoured infantry plus support), and an air-mobile element. Under the new order of battle, there is also to be a multinational air-mobile division in which attack helicopters will feature significantly. The United Kingdom element of this will be 24 Airmobile Brigade; the other contributing countries will be Belgium, Holland, and Germany.

In all the literature, currently being produced about the British army by the Ministry of Defence much is made of the possibilities of multinational operations. In future, the British army might act as part of the United Nations, NATO, The European Community, the Western European Union (WEU), or the Committee for Security and Co-operation in Europe (CSCE). As yet, our multinational future is not clear, the politics still being worked out as organizations such as the WEU and CSCE take on new order.

From 1992, the defence of the United Kingdom home base will become predominantly a Territorial Army responsibility; but, like the regular army, the Territorial Army will be approaching all its tasks with considerably reduced manpower. Notably it will have to do without the Home Service Force (HSF). This 3,000-strong force was raised in the mid-1980s after considerable lobbying about the vulnerability of certain keypoints near Britain's coastline to attack by enemy special forces.

Although BAOR is being phased out, the army remains committed to heavy armoured formations. Two regiments of Challenger II Main Battle Tanks (MBTs) are being purchased. These will replace the Chieftain tanks that remain in service. Challenger I tanks that are currently in service will be updated with a new, more powerful gun. The army is also re-equipping itself with the Warrior fighting vehicle—a tracked armoured personnel carrier with an anti-tank capability—and the wheeled Saxon armoured infantry vehicle. Other significant purchases include: tracked Multiple Launched Rocket Systems (MLRs)—which have the capability to launch both 'bomblet' and mine-dispensing rockets; the AS90 self-propelled gun with a range of over 30 kilometres; and large numbers of the SA80 rifle (in spite of the many reported problems with this weapon in the Gulf and elsewhere). The army is also deploying an improved version of the well-proven Rapier anti-aircraft missile with a new capability for engaging multiple targets and defeating enemy counter-measures and is acquiring Starstreak, a high-tech. shoulder-launched anti-aircraft missile. A significant proposed purchase for the army is a dedicated attack helicopter: at the moment the British army has no dedicated weapon of this type (such as the Apache), and makes do with the Lynx helicopter equipped with TOW missiles instead.

The British army has been a world leader in the field of counter-terrorism. No major changes are planned, although the evolution of tactics and equipment continues, as does the policy of police primacy in Northern Ireland. Nevertheless, one important consequence, aggravated by the cuts in army numbers will be an increase in the frequency of Northern Ireland tours for most units. The shift of responsibilities in terroristic surveillance and intelligence from the police Special Branch to the security service (MI5) is also to be noted.

Conditions of service became a major issue in the late 1980s; soldiers, and, most especially, their wives, made it clear that they were no longer willing to accept the old status quo. One very sore subject was house purchase. Many soldiers found that the nature of their job, with frequent re-postings and relatively low pay compared with the civil sector, meant it was impractical to buy a house. The Ministry of Defence has taken action to make it easier for soldiers to buy houses in the future. Those who wish to will be able to open a special savings account to which their employers will make a contribution of £1 to every £3 saved.

Although the recently announced changes to Britain's land forces may appear quite radical in some respects, the primary structures of the British army and its operating philosophy will remain relatively unchanged in the 1990s (with one important exception—the army's capability for independent operations will be reduced). The British army of the immediate future will still be an army which sees its primary task as high-intensity conflict using heavy, highly complex, equipment systems. There may be much more talk of mobility and flexibility than a decade ago, but the army's present organization and equipment will not make the implementation of such ideas easy. The Teeth Arms are to retain the regimental system; the meagre land force commitment to the defence of the United Kingdom home base has, effectively, been reduced by the re-roling of the Territorial Army for the task; and, in spite of the trend towards a 'classless

Britain' in civil society and the rise of 'sergeant power' within the army, little has been done to reform the social structure of the army or to make the demands of service life less out of kilter with those of mainstream society.

As a number of critics have noted, the opportunity for a reorganization of defence from the ground up has not been taken. There has been no full-scale Defence Review. The maintenance of the status quo and the passive acceptance of multinationalism has been further supported by the result of the Gulf War in 1991. It means that senior soldiers, and the defence manufacturers may go on doing more or less what they have always done; but it may also mean the much-vaunted 'smaller and better' British army of the 1990s will be ill equipped to cope with future threats.

The biggest real change to the army will be the reduction in its numbers. Before considering anything else in detail, it is important to note that the reasoning behind the cuts (and those of other nations) may be empirically unsound—a symptom of the wish-dream for a safer world at a time of accelerating change and crisis. The first premiss upon which the cuts are based is the elimination of the old threat. There have certainly been enormous changes behind what was the Iron Curtain, and the nature of the threat has changed considerably; however, the future of the Commonwealth of Independent States (CIS) is far from certain. Anything might happen. Meanwhile, there remain very significant combat forces in what was the Soviet Union, not to mention a vast stockpile of chemical and nuclear weapons.

It has been said many times that it is imprudent to build defences on the perceived intent of potential enemies rather than their current capabilities. And, whatever the future of the CIS, the collapse of the old Soviet Union has led to potentially dangerous eruptions throughout Eastern Europe.

Democracy in the Western European sense is far from securely established: fanatical nationalism is on the increase. Genocide is once more a terrifying reality in Europe. The world economic system is far from secure. It may not be a comforting thought, but a re-run of something like the 1914 or 1939 scenarios is far from impossible under present conditions. Is this the moment to cut our defences?

BAOR was criticized with good reason for being inflexible and linked to a linear Maginot-like defence posture concentrated in one area of Germany. Its primary military function—it also had very significant political functions—was to buy a few days' negotiating time in the event of Warsaw Pact forces crossing or attempting to cross what soldiers used to call the inner German border (IGB). Even as it stood, 150,000 strong in time of war, BAOR was no match for the huge Red Army and its allies—a point to which most defence planners were happy to admit until very recently. To suggest that we might now cut the army because the threat has diminished or because 'warning times have increased' is to suggest that there were enough troops before. Many would argue there were not.

Much as we seem to be taking a very convenient view of what is happening in Eastern Europe and the CIS as far as accepting massive troop reductions is concerned, we also appear to be in danger of learning the wrong lessons from the Gulf War. Mutual back-patting concerning victory over a third-rate opponent should cause less comment than the fact that it took six months to get a viable Allied force in place. Assets in Germany and the United Kingdom had to be stripped to equip the 'Desert Rats' (to the point that BAOR ceased to exist as any sort of seriously operational force once the build-up to the Gulf War began). The Gulf War showed how very vulnerable the United Kingdom was to a double-theatre war. We are all the more vulnerable now that 3rd (UK) Division is roled both as an element of the ARRC and as a strategic reserve.

Apart from the effective defence of the home base itself, we still need the capability to conduct armoured warfare in central Europe—where a conflict is most likely to threaten the United Kingdom home base. We probably also need the capability to project heavy armoured resources out of Europe, and we certainly need a more effective capability to project lighter forces which combine tactical mobility with an effective tank and aircraft killing ability anywhere. Moreover, such highly portable but hard-hitting forces must be organized so that they could fight in conventional or low-intensity operations. What is actually happening? Senior officers and (for want of more precise expression) 'the accountants' appear to have come to an understanding: lip-service will be paid to mobility and flexibility, but the army will continue much as it always has, but smaller. The status quo within the army in general and the Teeth Arms in particular is maintained, bar some redundancies and a new focus on multinationalism (itself partly a result of the cuts and our consequent inability to undertake certain operations independently from now on).

The evidence that real change might have urgently been needed is not hard to find. For example, consider the delays in transporting men and material to the Gulf in 1990–1. They make one wonder what would have happened in Europe had the Warsaw Pact ever decided to attack to the north or south, rather than as we had always planned through central

British Army: Political Controls and Organization

The Secretary of State for Defence exercises political control for all three services as head of the Ministry of Defence. Standing above him constitutionally are: the Cabinet (within which is the Defence and Overseas Policy Committee), the Prime Minister, and, ultimately, parliament. In parliament, there is an annual army debate during which issues regarding land forces are discussed, and an annual debate on the defence estimates during which the expenditure for defence is sanctioned.

As well as being subject to political restraint, the army is also subject to a variety of laws. The modern version of the Mutiny Act, which establishes the legitimacy of a standing army, is known as the Army Act, 1955, and must be confirmed formally by parliament every five years. Common law also affects the army. Under it, the Crown has the prerogative to use armed force to defend the kingdom from attack, invasion, insurrection, or riot. There are also treaty obligations which affect the peace time and wartime deployment of the army (for example, NATO): and there are specific acts affecting the deployment of the army within the United Kingdom (notably the Emergency Powers Acts, 1920 and 1964). These acts govern the use of the armed forces in natural emergencies (Military Aid to the Civil Community—MACC), strikes (Military Aid to the Civil Ministries—MACM), and in cases such as Northern Ireland where public order is threatened (Military Aid to the Civil Power—MACP).

The Army Board of the Defence Council is the committee technically responsible for running the army. Its members include politicians—the Armed Forces Minister and the Minister of State for Defence Procurement—senior civil servants, and seven senior army officers: the Chief of the General Staff (CGS), the Assistant CGS, the Adjutant-General, the Quartermaster-General, the Master-General of Ordnance, the Commander-in-Chief of United Kingdom Land Forces, and the Commander-in-Chief of the British Army of the Rhine. There is a smaller executive committee made up of the senior army officers of the Board and one of its senior civil servants (2nd PUS) who handle the army's day-to-day management.

Outside the United Kingdom, the army's main commitment until recently has been the British Army of the Rhine (BAOR). This involved 50,000 troops permanently based in Germany who would have been reinforced by another 100,000 in the build-up to war. BAOR is now being phased out and a new multinational Allied Command Europe Rapid Reaction Force created. It will involve about 20,000 troops permanently stationed in Germany to be reinforced to about 80,000 in time of war.

Even in a post-imperial age, there are still significant deployments of troops outside the United Kingdom and Germany, most notably in Gibraltar, the Falkland Islands, Cyprus, Belize, and Hong Kong (a commitment which will cease in 1997). Northern Ireland, although technically part of the United Kingdom, is also a separate command.

Functionally, the army may be divided into arms and services. Modern war tends to lessen the distinction, but the idea is that there are Teeth Arms who may expect to be involved in combat directly; and supporting corps or services who provide back-up to those in the frontline. The Teeth Arms include the infantry, cavalry (tanks), artillery, signals, and engineers. The services (Royal Electrical and Mechanical Engineers apart) have recently been regrouped into two very large formations: the Royal Logistical Corps (which will include amongst others the Royal Corps of Transport, the Royal Army Ordnance Corps, and Army Catering Corps), and the Adjutant-General's Corps (which will subsume a variety of old corps concerned with administration, and the Royal Army Education Corps).

Within the regimental system, the infantry battalion and the armoured regiment are key army structures: they are an extended family to many soldiers. The infantry battalion numbers about 650 and is commanded by a lieutenant-colonel. Infantry battalions may be mechanized, partly mechanized, or non-mechanized (for example, airborne units). A mechanized battalion will have armoured personnel carriers and/or armoured fighting vehicles which allow troops to keep up with tanks. Armoured regiments, also commanded by a lieutenant-colonel, tend to be a bit smaller in manpower terms (400–500 men) than infantry battalions. There are two basic types of regiment, 'type 45' with forty-five tanks, and 'type 57' with fifty-seven tanks. As well as heavy armour regiments equipped with Main Battle Tanks (MBTs), there are armoured reconnaissance regiments equipped with small, high-speed, lightly armoured tank-like vehicles.

In times of war (or on exercise) mixed-arm battle groups will be created which might include formations or sub formations of any of the Teeth Arms, as well as supporting personnel from the supporting corps. It is also possible, indeed likely, that regular soldiers will be supported or reinforced by Territorial Army units.

Terms of service in the regular army vary. Officers may sign up for 'short-service' (three to eight years) or 'regular' (full-career) commissions end-ing in a pension at 55. Having passed an initial selection test (RCB) officers attend the Royal Military Academy, Sandhurst, after which they complete spe-cialist training appropriate to their selected branch of the service. Soldiers, who must also pass a selection test, may enlist as juniors or as adults. Adult sol-diers will choose to serve for three years or on open engagement with 'man-ning points' (options to extend service) at six, nine, and twelve years. After twelve years they sign on for a twenty-two-year total service contract. There are some possibilities for commissioning from the ranks, but the divide between enlisted men and officers is still wide.

Germany. Could we have mobilized sufficient forces at the right point in time? It seems most unlikely; such a surprise attack would have led to our defeat or the decision to use nuclear weapons immediately. There would have been little question of flexible response. Yet, this vital lesson from the Gulf, the need to be able to project significant strategic force quickly, has not really been learned.

Announcements concerning the purchase of Challenger II and the up-dating of Challenger I make it quite clear that the army remains commit-ted to the concept of the leviathan Main Battle Tank. No one denies the awesome power of such weapons, and their usefulness in major offensive operations but the problem with tanks is their long-range mobility and the amount of service support they require. Their prohibitive running costs mean that training is expensive and their bulk and related destruc-tive potential means that training areas for their use are very limited. It may make sense to retain such systems, most obviously for deployment in the flat lands of central Europe, but the army now has a clear gap between its heavy and light resources. Moreover, it may be the case that filling this gap is a better defence compromise in the current hard economic climate than continuing to support the purchase of heavy armour indefinitely.

The 24 Airmobile Brigade goes part of the way. It combines ground and helicopter components and was first unveiled in the 1980s as an opera-tional reserve for use within or on the flanks of NATO. Now it has been given the task of a counter-penetration force within the new multina-tional air-mobile division. A force of its type is much quicker to get on to the battlefield than combat groups based on tanks. But 24 Airmobile is, as nearly all expert opinion agrees, inadequate in numbers. It is particularly deficient in helicopters, most notably (as its own commander has stated) in its lack of an effective, dedicated tank-killing helicopter.

Currently, 24 Airmobile has thirty Lynx helicopters equipped with TOW missiles. The Lynx is not a good launch platform and those with the brigade, as yet, have no air-to-air capability. The brigade is not only ill equipped in respect of its helicopters, its infantry component has to rely on the good, but ageing, Milan anti-tank system (the intention is to phase in a new system TRIGAT in the mid-to late 1990s), and their physical arrival at the battlefield is dependent primarily on Royal Air Force Pumas and Chinooks. Moreover, 24 Airmobile has also been criticized within the army for its structural ratio of one helicopter regiment to three infantry battalions, a criticism which will shortly cause the ratio to change to 2:2. However, some authorities still think the balance is wrong and should favour helicopters more if the full mobility of this style of unit is to be achieved. One way to reduce the so-called 'drag' factor would be if 24 Airmobile's ground element were equipped with some sort of fast Light Strike Vehicle (LSV). Meantime 24 Airmobile, an interesting concept with lots of potential, remains a paper tiger.

The re-roling of the Territorial Army towards the defence of the United Kingdom home base and the axing of the Home Service Force are worrying in so far as our last-ditch defences are, effectively, reduced. If one accepts that economic reality forces us not to create forces to meet every possible eventuality, then one must, obviously, prioritize. By any analysis, however, the United Kingdom home base should head the list. Of course, it also makes sense to defend the United Kingdom off United Kingdom soil if possible. But, if all else fails, the 'hedgehog' approach—making ourselves hard to swallow by an enemy by means of in-depth mid-tech. defences—has much to recommend it. The major objection to it is that it would require a very differently structured army to achieve, probably one with a much greater emphasis on widespread part-time service. The Territorial Army is not up to the job at present as one senior Territorial Army NCO told me: 'The TA is full of good and committed people. But, the reality of the TA in the 1990s is that there are few resources for training. Recently we have not even been allocated sufficient petrol and blank ammunition for exercises. The fighting strength TA is much smaller than MOD statistics might suggest. It certainly isn't anything like 60 or 70 thousand. Many of the people on the books never turn up, moreover, our turn-over rate is enormous.'

What of the other changes recently announced? Those that affect the supporting corps are worthy of comment. Clearly, the danger is that a two-tier army will be created, or, perhaps, one should say reinforced. Whatever the arguments in terms of efficiency and cost, it seems that the reorganization of corps will result in a more homogeneous and less individualistic working environment for those servicemen and women not in the regimentalized Teeth Arms. Bearing in mind the fluidity of the modern battlefield and the mutual dependency of combat and support units it might seem more logical to start integrating combat and support units. One option might be for something like the American marine corps system, a formation which combines large-size, all-arms integration, and a very strong regimental-like family spirit.

However, integration is an idea very alien to the British army. Although on the modern battlefield tanks always fight with infantry, we still insist on separating tank and infantry units within the regimental system. In practical terms this means not only that soldiers develop a self-image as 'tankies' or 'footsloggers', but that their opportunities for working with colleagues with different fighting skills are reduced to training exercises and active service. The division between the Territorial Army and the regular army might be seen as part of the same tribalistic tradition. Nevertheless, it seems likely that the successful defence force of the future will find a way of combining the family feeling of regimentalism with an integrated approach which spans the traditional boundaries within and between services.

All of the above is not to say that there have not been positive developments recently, nor is it to deny that the British army remains one of the world's best. The army is really changing in some respects, not least in its attitude to female soldiers and its willingness to address real but previously hidden problems like bullying and racism. As far as female soldiers are concerned, it may be predicted that they will be seen in the infantry and armoured regiments in the not too distant future. Their participation in the Gulf War and the United Nations peace-keeping forces in Yugoslavia has shown that old arguments against their deployment on active service have lost much of their weight. In an army of increasing technical sophistication there are very few jobs of which it could be argued that women are incapable; there certainly seems little reason (even taking into consideration the current ban on female infantry and armoured personnel) why women should not account for more of the United Kingdom's land forces in the near future.

Before considering what the British army of the twenty-first century might look like, it is useful to consider what war may look like in the

future. The possibility of conflict leading to limited or all-out nuclear exchange remains. There may be a new spirit in Europe, but the weapons of
mass destruction still exist, and there is a growing instability in both Western and Eastern society. Militating against Armageddon are a new era of
co-operation between East and West and a growing realization, confirmed
by the Chenobyl incident, that nuclear wars cannot be won in any mean-
ingful sense: the weapons themselves are simply too destructive. Yet,
hopeful though the latter developments may be, an exchange between the
superpowers is far from the only conceivable nuclear scenario. As the old
nuclear threat appears to recede, a new nuclear threat emerges: one associated with the proliferation of nuclear weapons, and the possibility of them
falling into the hands of rogue states or fanatical groups.

Whatever happens, nuclear weapons themselves are likely to be around
for many years to come. Some strategists have pointed out their mere existence has fundamentally changed the nature of all war. It is certainly true
that nuclear weapons have changed the way we think about war, sometimes diverting our attention from very real but non-nuclear threats. It is
also true that nuclear weapons have changed the nature of armies: most
notably, they have allowed them to become smaller. Nuclear weapons provide 'more bang for the buck', and both West and East have became dependent on them for that reason. The nuclear-related shrinkage of
conventional forces was particularly apparent in Britain in the early 1960s,
when it allowed for the withdrawal of conscription. As conventional
forces decline further in the 1990s, we become even more dependent on
nuclear weapons *in extremis*.

The doctrines dictating the role of conventional forces in superpower
conflict have changed considerably in the last forty years. In the 1950s,
there was the trip-wire philosophy—the idea that conventional forces existed merely to act as an alarm when the enemy arrived, and before our
doomsday button was pushed. With constant sabre-rattling between the
superpowers, this became just too dangerous. Flexible response
emerged—the idea that we would respond to the enemy flexibly in the
event of attack and with due regard to the type of force being used by
them. Now, there is a new era. Nuclear war is possible, but unlikely,
nuclear stockpiles are to be cut by both sides, particularly with regard to
short-range nuclear weapons. The doctrine of flexible response based on
the idea of controllable or graduated nuclear war seems to have died. We
are back to something like the trip-wire concept of the 1950s, but without
the overt aggression between the superpowers.

Britain's land forces, meantime, are left in a state of some confusion.

BAOR has gone, but it is replaced with a force which looks much like it in some respects and which continues to prepare for the old style of suicide war (to be fought, we are told, in a new more mobile sort of way). Admittedly, the primary function of the British army does appear to be changing; its principal wartime role is no longer just to die in central Europe buying a few days' negotiating time for politicians.

A more internationalist and, in some respects, more practical idea is forming. Our army is to become something akin to a world policeman operating with forces from Europe, the United Nations, and NATO to protect 'wider security interests through the maintenance of international peace and security'. This *nouveau* imperialism, as it might be called, is subtly supported by the electronic news media who seem to have become obsessed with real-time footage from the globe's trouble-spots. However, all the publicity and drama surrounding international operations tend to take attention away from the home front, and the essential and most justifiable function of any post-imperialist army, the protection of the home base.

Meantime, military-orientated intellectuals and soldiers are conceiving new doctrines and theories which suit the new climate of opinion. In particular there seems to be a great deal of discussion about so-called 'LIC' (low-intensity conflict) at present. Many see it as the dominant threat of the future. Whether this is so (and it probably is), the pendulum has swung. There is a realization that in all the years that we have been planning for large-scale, probably nuclear, war, we have been fighting small ones, often less successfully than we might because of the orientation of our forces to superpower conflict.

As in the last half-century, Britain's army of the future will need to cope with any threat from total war to terrorism. It will probably meet these diverse threats with fewer, better-educated personnel. The army of tomorrow and beyond will have to operate increasingly complex equipment, and it will be under ever greater financial pressure, not least because of the cost of new equipment. Moreover, it will have a diminishing resource of young people from which to draw its recruits, which will lead amongst other things to it recruiting even more women, and may lead to radical changes in terms of service. The new army will have a more multinational orientation (to the point that it is a distinct possibility that the British army as we know it today could cease to exist), and it is likely to be under ever greater scrutiny from the media.

Changing standards of morality in the Western world, as reinforced by the media, will increase the pressures to fight war surgically, minimizing casualties to both friendly and enemy forces. The trend towards more mobile and flexible forces is likely to continue, and forces which may be used for both low- and high-intensity conflict are likely to become the most attractive to defence planners looking for cost-effective options. Our continuing commitment to heavy armour, therefore, seems unlikely to outlive the present generation of supertanks. Tanks are an excellent solution to a very specific problem—attack by armour under conditions when friendly forces cannot be certain of air superiority. Attack helicopters and light attack vehicles equipped with ground-to-ground and ground-to-air missiles are a most attractive alternative *if* air superiority is assured. They can fight a conventional armoured thrust, and they can do many other things too. LAVs in particular are cheap—one might buy thirty or more for the cost of one modern tank—and easily transportable.

Technology will profoundly affect our army at many levels. It will tend to break down the distinctions between combat and non-combat arms (not to mention the distinctions between services)—the service engineer and the computer operator are now just as relevant as the rifleman and the tank driver. Technology will change the psychological experience of war, as accuracy and the killing power of weapons increase, and it will change the way in which war is fought. One lesson of the Gulf conflict was that the widespread availability of night vision equipment meant fighting has become much more of a twenty-four hour activity than in the past. Meantime, the battlefield, day and night, has become much more dangerous. Achieving surprise is more difficult than ever, but more important too because the chance of surviving a fire-fight has diminished with the 'enhanced lethality' of modern weapons systems.

Advances in electronic intelligence-gathering and dissemination will continue, as will the development and use of electronic deception. Computer information systems to aid in command and control are likely to be used in the future at all levels. We may soon expect every soldier to have his or her own radio (or television) transceiver. The management of information will occupy far more time than in the past, and will change the focus of much training. Technology will also make training much more realistic.

Although, generally, technology will tend to increase the disparity between potential foes (assuming one is richer than the other), in some circumstances it may become a disadvantage to the side which appears to have the technological advantage. Technology is very difficult to control.

There are multiple dangers: the sheer cost, the acquisition or development of the wrong technology, the danger of becoming too dependent upon technology, and, perhaps the greatest danger of all, allowing one's army to be distorted by the need to support all the new systems. Potentially, and actually, technology aggravates the malaise of modern bureaucratic armies to become organizationally rather than functionally driven. This happened to the Americans in Vietnam. Their teeth to tail ratio was much smaller than that of the enemy who relied on simpler, but sufficiently effective, systems. Nevertheless, it may be assumed, for better and worse, that the British army, like many others, will become more technologically dependent, and, in some ways therefore, more vulnerable, in the twenty-first century.

Social change in society, in part caused by the microchip revolution, is also likely radically to change the army. For all the advantages of the British regimental system, it has several disadvantages. It is associated with a social order unacceptable to most young people; it is expensive because of its feudal/tribal idiosyncrasies; and it encourages artificial distinctions between the increasingly interdependent components of fighting formations. For these reasons, and especially because of its cost, it is unlikely to survive much past the end of the century.

In its social practice, the army of the future is likely to look considerably different. It may be that at some time in the next century the distinction between officers and other ranks will become meaningless. Already high technology is blurring many of the distinctions of the old world. Today's soldier expects more. In or outside the army, the old status quo is no longer acceptable: people demand greater social mobility and more information. It would be a most interesting experiment to create a unit now which operated on a less hierarchical rank system, a test bed for the future, the SAS has proved the fighting efficiency of less traditional structures.

The proportion of units like the SAS is likely to increase in the army of the future, although the problem of maintaining training standards will also grow, as more and more skill is demanded from all service personnel. However, it is possible that the sheer cost of military technology and training, not to mention military bureaucracy, will encourage the development both of intermediate-level defensive technology and a reawakening of interest in the non-professional citizen soldier. We might yet be forced into the position where all we can afford or justify in defence terms is a territorial defence of Britain based on a new scheme of part-time service with a handful of professional units like the SAS, Paras, and Royal Marine Commandos set aside for the unexpected.

One notable danger of the present, largely professional, system is that the public are less knowledgeable about defence than they might be. Admittedly the electronic and print media keep them informed to a degree, but their knowledge is second-hand and incomplete. In these circumstances two things are happening, one is that the army has become more and more of a caste apart, the second is that defence is losing its relevance to the bulk of the population. Few people understand that their exclusion from the defence process has shaped both the professional army and our nuclear posture. Politicians have encouraged apathy because it increases their own power, but the dangers are all too obvious if the trend continues.

Finally, it might be noted that our intellectual understanding of what war is has changed. War is not only politics by other means. Sometimes it is politics by other means, sometimes it is an irrational activity pursued for its own sake or for the gratification of the human ego, sometimes war just happens for no easily discernible reason. A defence policy built upon the supposedly predictable actions of potential enemies is dangerous folly. A sane system of defence must expect the unexpected. The British army of the future thus faces a great challenge. It must create structures and doctrines to cope with diverse threats in an unstable age which longs for peace but continues to fight wars. It must resist the temptation towards élitism, and find ways of maintaining interest in defence amongst a frequently apathetic population, and it must find a way of offering satisfaction to soldiers who, increasingly, will be asked to train for things they may never need to do. The lesson of history, meantime, is that the unexpected happens, both abroad and at home.

Note. This chapter was completed in 1992 for the first edition of this volume. Consequently, some predictions need revising. The army has now diminished in 1996 to some 112,000 men and women compared to 160,000 in 1991. Indeed, despite the 'Front Line First' initiative, it is currently some 4,000 men short of establishment. While the garrison in Northern Ireland has been reduced to 17,000 in the light of the recent easing of tensions, the commitment to NATO's IFOR, which replaced UNPROFOR in the former Yugoslavia in 1995, has risen from 3,000 to 13,000. Meanwhile, the TA is undergoing a substantial restructuring as a more general reserve, which will reduce it to some 59,000 in total. Outside of the former Yugoslavia, the army's main units remain committed to Allied Command Europe's Rapid Reaction Corps (ARRC) within NATO.

Chronology

1066	Battle of Hastings; Norman Conquest of England.
1070s	Introduction of feudal knight service to England.
1099–1135	Under Henry I, the royal household is capable of providing detachments of knights numbering 200 or 300.
1101	Henry I contracts with the Count of Flanders to receive mercenary troops.
1166	A survey of knightly military service is conducted, which shows a total due of over 5,000.
1181	The Assize of Arms sets out the obligation of free men to possess appropriate military equipment.
1190	Richard I institutes a code of military discipline.
1215	The expulsion of foreign mercenaries is demanded in Magna Carta.
1245	Lower quotas of military service are firmly established.
1277	A feudal muster yields a force of 228 knights and 294 sergeants.
1285	Statute of Westminster.
1294	Pardons offered to criminals in return for service in war.
1294–5	Forces of over 30,000 used to defeat Welsh rebellion. Recruitment is largely by means of commissions of array.
1297	Nearly all of the 700 cavalry on Edward I's campaign in Flanders provided by the royal household.
1314	English defeat at Bannockburn reveals weakness of heavily armed cavalry in face of well-organized infantry.
1322	A grant of infantry soldiers is made, with one soldier to come from every local community.
1327	Cavalry forces ordered to be prepared to fight on foot. Last effective summons of traditional knight service.
1330s	Development of the 'mounted archer', who rode to war, but fought on foot.
1337	The first use of contract as a method of recruiting an entire army.
1346–7	The English army reaches a total of about 32,000 on the campaign which saw the victory of Crécy and the successful siege of Calais.
1352	Edward III concedes in a statute that no one is obliged to provide soldiers unless a specific grant has been made in parliament.
1385	Last summons of feudal host.
1415	The battle of Agincourt reveals once again the superiority of English bowmen.
1453	English forces finally fail to retain the possessions in France.

1485	Victory of Henry VII at battle of Bosworth.
1509	Accession of Henry VIII.
1513	Battle of Flodden; death of James IV of Scotland.
1522–3	Invasion of Scotland and France by English forces.
1539–40	Dissolution of the monasteries and building of the coastal forts.
1542	Battle of Solway Moss; death of James V of Scotland.
1544	Henry VIII leads siege and capture of Boulogne.
1547	Death of Henry VIII; victory of English at Pinkie.
1549	Appointment of first Lords Lieutenant for groups of counties.
1550	Loss of Boulogne.
1558	Loss of Calais; death of Mary I; accession of Elizabeth I; first militia statutes.
1559–60	English intervention in Scotland.
1570s	English volunteers to Netherlands; trained bands and Lords Lieutenant emerge for single counties.
1585	Treaty of Nonsuch with the Dutch and Leicester's expedition to the Netherlands; war with Spain.
1588	Defeat of the Spanish Armada.
1589	Defence of Bergen-op-Zoom by English forces.
1596	Essex expedition to Cadiz.
1598	Tyrone's rebellion in Ulster.
1600	East India Company founded.
1601	Victory of Mountjoy over Tyrone and Spanish at Kinsale.
1603	Accession of James VI of Scotland, as James I of England.
1625	Dominance of Duke of Buckingham; accession of Charles I; war with Spain; expedition to Cadiz.
1627	War with France; expedition to the Isle of Ré.
1628	Assassination of Buckingham; Petition of Right.
1629	Peace concluded with Spain and France; parliament dissolved.
1639	First and Second Scots Wars (1640).
1640	Fort St George, Madras, founded.
1642	Outbreak of the Civil War; battle of Edgehill.
1643	Pym introduces war legislation; Solemn League and Covenant.
1644	Invasion of Scots, and defeat of Rupert and Newcastle at Marston Moor.
1645	Self-Denying Ordinance; creation of the New Model Army; its victory at Naseby.
1647	Army Council debates at Putney.
1649	Execution of Charles I; Cromwell in Ireland.
1650	Cromwell defeats Scots at Dunbar.
1651	Charles II, King of the Scots, leads invasion of England; defeated by Cromwell at Worcester.

1652–4	First Anglo-Dutch War.
1655	Alliance with France and war with Spain; capture of Jamaica.
1657	Battle of the Dunes; capture of Dunkirk.
1658	Death of Cromwell.
1659	Monck's army crosses border at Coldstream.
1660	Restoration of Charles II; New Model Army disbanded.
1661	'Guards and garrisons' formed.
1662	Tangier occupied; Bombay becomes an English possession.
1665–7	Second Anglo-Dutch War.
1666	Battle of Rullion Green, near Edinburgh.
1672–4	Third Anglo-Dutch War; British corps fights with French army in Germany and the Low Countries.
1678	England enters Franco-Dutch War.
1679	Battle of Bothwell Bridge.
1684	Tangier evacuated.
1685	Monmouth's rebellion and the battle of Sedgemoor.
1688	The Dutch invasion of England and the disbandment of James II's army.
1689	The re-formation of the army and England's entry into the Nine Years War (1688–97); siege of Londonderry; Schomberg at Dundalk Camp; battle of Walcourt in the Spanish Netherlands.
1690	Battle of the Boyne; battle of Fleurus in the Spanish Netherlands; Fort William, Calcutta, founded.
1691	Battle of Aughrim and the siege of Limerick.
1692	Siege of Namur and the battle of Steenkirke.
1693	Battle of Landen (Neerwinden).
1695	Siege of Namur.
1697	Peace of Rijswijk (Ryswick).
1697–9	Disbandment of the army to a cadre of 7,000 men.
1702	Accession of Queen Anne; second Grand Alliance declares war on France and Spain, Marlborough made Captain-General.
1703	Savoy and Portugal join Grand Alliance.
1704	The march to the Danube; storming of the Schellenberg and battle of Blenheim; Admiral Rooke captures Gibraltar; naval battle of Malaga.
1705	Passage of the Lines of Brabant; action of Elixhem; Peterborough takes Barcelona.
1706	*Annus mirabilis*: battle of Ramillies leads to conquest of the Spanish Netherlands; Eugene's victory and capture of Turin; establishment of Board of General Officers.
1707	Galway defeated at Almanza; Eugene fails to take Toulon.
1708	Battle of Oudenarde; siege of Lille; action of Wynendale; Capture of Minorca.

1709	Sieges of Tournai and Mons; battle of Malplaquet; Anglo-Dutch Treaty of Succession and Barrier.
1710	Sieges of Douai and Bethune; battles of Brihuega and Villaviciosa in Spain; capture of Port Royal in North America; Marlborough's influence waning.
1711	Passage of the lines of Non Plus Ultra; siege of Bouchain; Marlborough deprived of all offices.
1712	Ormonde made Captain-General; battle of Denain; Congress of Utrecht and preliminaries of peace between Great Britain and France.
1713	Second Anglo-Dutch Barrier Treaty; the Peace of Utrecht.
1714	The Peace of Rastadt; George I, Elector of Hanover and King of Great Britain, lands at Greenwich.
1715	Suppression of the 'Fifteen' Jacobite Rebellion; the battles of Sherrifmuir and Preston break the back of the 'Fifteen'.
1722	Death of John Churchill, 1st Duke of Marlborough
1727	Death of George I and accession of George II; publication of Lieutenant-Colonel Humphrey Bland's *Treatise of Military Discipline*.
1739	War of Jenkin's Ear; Porto Bello falls to Admiral Vernon.
1741	A joint attack on Cartagena in New Grenada is repulsed.
1742–8	Britain participates in the War of the Austrian Succession.
1743	Acting as an auxiliary of Maria Theresa, George II leads his army to victory at Dettingen.
1745	William Augustus, Duke of Cumberland, second son of George II, is appointed Captain-General, aged 23 years; an Allied army, commanded by Cumberland, is defeated at Fontenoy; Jacobite Rebellion in Scotland, led by Prince Charles Edward Stuart, the Young Pretender; government forces, under Lieutenant-General Sir John Cope, are defeated by the Jacobites at Prestonpans.
1746	The Jacobites are crushed at Culloden by Cumberland; Louisbourg is captured.
1747	The Maréchal de Saxe defeats an Allied army commanded by Cumberland at Laffeldt.
1748	The Treaty of Aix-la-Chapelle concludes the War of the Austrian Succession; Major Stringer Lawrence becomes first Commander-in-Chief, India.
1751	A Royal Warrant for regulating the colours, clothing, etc., continuing the policy of imposing uniformity of dress.
1754	The first royal regiment to serve in India, the 39th Foot, disembarks at Fort St David, Cuddalore.
1755	In the first major engagement of the French and Indian War in North America, Major-General Edward Braddock is defeated and killed by the French and Indians at the Monongahela river.

1756   Military activity in America merges into the Seven Years War; surrender to France of the Mediterranean fortress of Minorca, commanded by Lieutenant-General Edward Blakeney; loss of Fort Oswego.

1757   Bengal sepoy companies formed into battalions; royal and East India Company forces, under Lieutenant-Colonel Robert Clive, defeat the Nawab Siraj-ud-Daula at Plassey in Bengal; establishment of the new militia; the Duke of Cumberland, commanding a Hanoverian army, is defeated by the French at Hastenbeck. He is disgraced, and replaced on 24 October 1757 by General Sir John Ligonier with the lesser title of Commander-in-Chief. Cumberland's capitulation is repudiated, and British troops are sent to Germany to fight under the command of a Prussian general, Prince Ferdinand of Brunswick.

1758   Failure at Ticonderoga; capture of Fort Louis and Goree (West Africa); the French fortress of Louisbourg, Cape Breton, falls after a three-month siege by Major-General Jeffery Amherst; capture of Fort Duquesne.

1759   In India, a French siege of Madras is abandoned following the British victory at Masulipatam; 'His Britannic Majesty's Army in Germany', led by Ferdinand of Brunswick, defeats the French at Minden; capture of Fort Niagara, Ticonderoga, Crown Point, Guadaloupe, and Marie Galante; Quebec falls after a three-month siege when the British army, led by Major-General James Wolfe, defeats the French on the Plains of Abraham; Wolfe is killed in the fighting; publication of Molyneux's *Conjunct Expeditions*.

1760   Lieutenant-Colonel Eyre Coote defeats the French at Wandiwash, forcing them to retire to Pondicherry; Montreal, and with it the whole of French Canada, falls to Amherst's army; death of George II and accession of King George III.

1761   Capture of Dominica.

1762   The fall of the French West Indian island of Martinique opens the way to the seizure of Grenada, St Lucia, and St Vincent; Prince Ferdinand of Brunswick defeats the French at Wilhelmstal; the Spanish Caribbean fortress of Havana, Cuba, falls to Lieutenant-General George, Lord Albemarle, after a costly two-months' siege; the Spanish Philippines fortress of Manila falls to Colonel Sir William Draper.

1763   The Treaty of Paris concludes the Seven Years War.

1764   A mutiny of the East India Company's Bengal army, inspired by the Nawab of Bengal, is crushed at Buxar; issue of new drill book for British army.

1766–9   In the First Mysore War, Haidar Ali, Sultan of Mysore, wages successful campaigns against royal and East India Company forces.

1768   Royal Warrants for regulating military clothing for horse and foot mark a further stage in imposing uniformity.

1773   North's Regulating Act.

1775   An expedition launched by Lieutenant-General Thomas Gage to seize arms and ammunition stored by American colonists at Concord, Massachusetts, results in the first armed clashes of the American War of Independence; at the battle of Bunker Hill, General Gage reinforced, captures positions overlooking Boston, but at severe loss; an American assault on Quebec is repulsed by Major-General Guy Carleton.

1776   The British, commanded by General William Howe, concentrate a powerful expeditionary force off New York; the Americans escape destruction by Howe's army at the battle of Long Island.

1777   After surviving a long pursuit, George Washington successfully strikes back at the British at Trenton and Princeton; General Howe, having broken off his campaign in New Jersey, defeats Washington at the battle of the Brandywine in Pennsylvania, opening the way to Philadelphia being occupied on 26 September; a British invasion from Canada, led by Major-General John Burgoyne, ends in surrender at Saratoga.

1778   After evacuating Philadelphia on 18 June, the British, now commanded by Lieutenant-General Sir Henry Clinton, beat off a major attack at Monmouth and escape to New York; French intervention in North America.

1779   The Franco-Spanish siege of the fortress of Gibraltar begins.

1780   The beginning of the Second Mysore War, fought between royal and Company's troops and Haidar Ali, assisted by his son Tipu; the port of Charleston in the southern colonies falls to Clinton's army after a three-month siege; Lieutenant-General Charles, Lord Cornwallis, overwhelms an American army at Camden; in India, a small royal and Company army, 'Colonel Baillie's detachment', is destroyed at Pollilur by Haidar Ali and Tipu; British power is severely shaken; the Gordon riots take place.

1781   Cornwallis defeats an American army at Guildford Courthouse, but at great cost; he then marches into Virginia; Lieutenant-General Sir Eyre Coote saves Madras by defeating Haidar Ali at Porto Novo; in Virginia, Lord Cornwallis capitulates to a Franco-American army at Yorktown after a three-week siege. This proves the decisive battle in North America.

1782   Minorca, commanded by Lieutenant-General Sir James Murray, besieged since August 1781, falls to a Franco-Spanish invasion force; a major Franco-Spanish attack on Gibraltar is repulsed by Lieutenant-General Sir George Augustus Elliott; the first volunteer legislation is enacted.

1783   The Franco-Spanish siege of Gibraltar ends in failure; the war between Britain and the United States is brought to a conclusion by the Treaty of Paris; the last British troops leave New York.

1784   Pitt's India Act.

1793   Execution of Louis XVI; France subsequently declares war on Britain; siege of Toulon; battle of Hondschoote.

1794   Naval battle of 1 June; the yeomanry is created.

1795   Holland occupied by the French.

1796   East India Company's forces reorganized; establishment of supplementary militia.

1797   Naval battle of St Vincent; naval battle of Camperdown; the formation of the provisional cavalry.

1798   Napoleon occupies Egypt; naval battle of the Nile; Russo-British alliance; Defence of the Realm Act.

1799   Helder campaign.

1801   British land at Aboukir and liberate Egypt; first battle of Copenhagen.

1802   Treaty of Amiens between France and Britain.

1803   Resumption of hostilities; start of invasion scare; Army of Reserve created; Defence Act; General Defence Act.

1804   Napoleon becomes Emperor of France.

1805   War of Third Coalition: Austerlitz campaign and British invasion of Hanover; battle of Trafalgar.

1806   British raid Calabria; battle of Maida; Prussia defeated at Jena and Auerstadt; Training Act.

1807   Russia defeated at Friedland; Tilsit Treaty; second battle of Copenhagen; France invades Portugal.

1808   France invades Spain; battle of Vimiero; local militia created.

1809   Battle of Corunna; battle of Oporto; battle of Talavera; Walcheren expedition.

1810   France reinvades Portugal; battle of Bussaco; Wellington retires within the lines of Torres Vedras.

1811   Battle of Fuentes d'Onoro; battle of Albuera.

1812   Wellington storms Ciudad Rodrigo; Wellington storms Badajoz; battle of Salamanca.

1813   Battle of Vitoria; battle of Pyrenees.

1814	Battle of Orthez; Napoleon abdicates; battle of Toulouse.
1815	Battles of Ligny and Quatre Bras; battles of Waterloo and Wavre; Napoleon abdicates for second time; Second Peace of Paris concludes Napoleonic Wars.
1819	Peterloo disturbances in Manchester; Duke of Wellington becomes Master-General of the Ordnance.
1824	East India Company's forces reorganized again.
1828	Lord Hill becomes Commander-in-Chief.
1829	First regulation of corporal punishment (abolished 1881).
1830	Swing riots.
1831	End of militia ballot.
1832	Parliamentary Reform Act.
1833	Abolition of British colonial slavery.
1835	Lord Howick becomes Secretary at War.
1836	Report of the Royal Commission on Military Punishments.
1837–8	Rebellions in Lower and Upper Canada; publication of sanitary statistics compiled at the War Office.
1839	Rural Constabulary Act.
1840	Formation of the Royal Canadian Rifle Regiment.
1842	Duke of Wellington becomes Commander-in-Chief.
1846	Earl Grey becomes Colonial Secretary; Grey's cabinet paper on British military strategy; famine in Ireland.
1846–7, 1852–3, 1859	French invasion scares.
1847	Short term Enlistment Act.
1849	Annexation crisis in British North America.
1852	Death of the Duke of Wellington; Lord Hardinge becomes Commander-in-Chief; revival of the militia.
1854	Crimean War begins.
1856	Duke of Cambridge becomes Commander-in-Chief; County and Borough Police Act.
1857	Indian mutiny; report of the Royal Commission on the Sanitary Condition of the Army.
1858	East India Company's forces are transferred to the British Crown.
1859	Sidney Herbert becomes Secretary of State for War; Rifle Volunteer Movement established.
1860	Amalgamation of the Indian Army; reorganization of Bengal, Madras, and Bombay armies.
1861–5	American Civil War.
1863	Report of the Barracks and Hospital Improvement Commission; regimental management of canteens.
1864, 1866, 1869	Contagious Diseases Acts.

1867	Report of the Royal Commission on Recruiting for the Army.
1868–74	Edward Cardwell as Secretary of State for War.
1870	War Office Act and Army Enlistment Act.
1871	Abolition of Purchase.
1872	Localization Act.
1873	Ashanti War begins.
1879	Zulu War.
1880	First South African War begins.
1882	Egyptian War.
1884	Gordon Relief Expedition.
1888	Stanhope Memorandum.
1891	Hartington Report.
1893	Featherstone colliery riot.
1895	Resignation of the Duke of Cambridge as Commander-in-Chief; abolition of separate armies in India.
1896	Reconquest of the Sudan begins.
1899	Second South African War (to 1902).
1901	Establishment of Imperial Yeomanry.
1903	Report of the Royal Commission on the South African War; reorganization of British Indian forces into a single Indian Army (Indian troops), forming the major part of 'The Army in India' (including the British Army element).
1904	Abolition of the post of Commander-in-Chief.
1905	Richard Haldane becomes Secretary of State for War.
1906	Establishment of a General Staff.
1907	Territorial and Reserve Forces Act.
1908	Creation of Territorial Force.
1909	*Field Service Regulations Part II* issued.
1914	Curragh incident; Britain declares war on Germany; Field Marshal Lord Kitchener takes office as Secretary of State for War; Kitchener's first appeal for 100,000 volunteers is published; BEF lands in France; formation of First New Army authorized; battle of Mons; battle of Le Cateau; highest number of enlistments recorded in one day (33,204) during the whole of the First World War; battle of the Marne; Second New Army formally created; Third New Army created; first battle of Ypres.
1915	Battle of Neuve Chapelle; naval attack at Gallipoli; second battle of Ypres; Coalition Cabinet formed; first landing at Gallipoli; creation of Ministry of Munitions is announced; Munitions of War Act; second landing at Gallipoli; National Register is taken; battle of Loos; Allies disembark at Salonika; Derby Scheme in operation; siege of Kut (falls April 1916).

1916	First Military Service Act becomes law; battle of Verdun; final withdrawal from Gallipoli; Second Military Service Act; Kitchener drowns when HMS *Hampshire* is sunk by a mine off the Orkneys; Arab Hejaz revolt begins; Lloyd George takes office as Secretary of State for War; Asquith resigns as Prime Minister; Lloyd George succeeds Asquith as Prime Minister; Lord Derby appointed as Secretary of State for War; Neville Chamberlain appointed as Director-General of the Department of National Service; battle of the Somme.
1917	Kut retaken and Baghdad captured; Military Service (Review of Exceptions) Act, 1917; Lawrence and Arabs capture Aqaba; third battle of Ypres (Passchendaele); following Chamberlain's resignation, Brigadier-General Auckland Geddes is appointed Minister of National Service; battle of Caporetto; start of third battle of Gaza; control of recruiting transferred from War Office to Ministry of National Service; battle of Cambrai; Jerusalem captured.
1918	Military Service Act, 1918; start of German spring and summer offensives on Western Front; Military Service (No. 2) Act, 1918; Lord Milner succeeds Lord Derby as Secretary of State for War; battle of Hamel; battle of Amiens; start of general Allied offensives on Western Front; Allied offensive in Salonika; capture of Damascus, Beirut, and Aleppo; Armistice with Germany.
1919	Cabinet adopts the Ten Year Rule; the Geddes axe drastically reduces the services' budget.
1920	Reconstitution of Territorial Army.
1922	Indian Army reorganized.
1923	The Chiefs of Staff Committee created as a subcommittee of the Committee of Imperial Defence.
1927	Shanghai Defence Force; pioneering trials of mechanized forces on Salisbury Plain.
1932	Chiefs of Staff insist that the Ten Year Rule be abandoned.
1933	Hitler becomes Chancellor of Germany; Defence Requirements Committee appointed to report on worst deficiencies in the three services (first report in February 1934).
1935	Rearmament begins; Abyssinian crisis; army reinforcements sent to the Middle East.
1936	Germany reoccupies the Rhineland; Palestine crisis; army reinforcements sent to Palestine.
1937	Neville Chamberlain becomes Prime Minister and Hore-Belisha succeeds Duff Cooper at the War Office; purge of the Army Council; Gort succeeds Deverell as Chief of the Imperial General Staff; government Defence Review; continental commitment for the army given the lowest priority.

1938   German take-over *(Anschluss)* of Austria; Munich crisis, the army's weakness in anti-aircraft defences exposed.

1939   The Government accepts a continental commitment for the army's (regular) field force in event of German aggression in the West; Germany occupies the remainder of Czechoslovakia; the establishment of the Territorial Army is doubled; Chamberlain offers a guarantee to Poland; Military Training Act; conscription introduced in the form of militia service; political and military liaison with France begins; Britain declares war on Germany; Gort appointed commander of the field force and Ironside succeeds him as CIGS; the first four (regular) divisions of the field force dispatched to France; Germany (and the Soviet Union) overrun Poland, but in the West the Phoney War begins after Britain and France declare war.

1940   Royal Navy and an Anglo-French Expeditionary Force commence a two-month series of land and sea offensives in Norway that end in a mini-Dunkirk in mid-June; Germans launch blitzkrieg offensive against French and British forces on the Western Front; battle of France, BEF evacuates Dunkirk; formation of local defence volunteers (later Home Guard).

1941   Western Desert Force destroys the Italian 10th Army, which surrenders at Beda Fomm, Libya; Rommel and German expeditionary force arrive in Tripoli, Libya; British offensive in East Africa; British force is sent to Greece; first battles between Rommel and Western Desert force, including Operation Battleaxe; Wavell replaced by Auchinleck; Japanese attack Pearl Harbor; Japanese army invades Siam and Malaya; battle of Hong Kong; Anglo-Canadian defenders surrender Christmas evening.

1942   Japanese invade Burma; British 10th Army surrenders at Singapore; Rommel begins new offensive against Gazala Line; British surrender to Rommel at Tobruk; 8th Army retreats to El Alamein; first battle of El Alamein fought; Alexander relieves Auchinleck; Montgomery takes control of 8th Army; battle of Alam Halfa (second Alamein); third battle of El Alamein; Allies launch Operation Torch in French North Africa.

1943   Casablanca Conference; Germans attack US II Corps at Kasserine Pass and Sidi Bou Zid, Tunisia; battle of Medenine between 8th Army and Rommel's Afrika Korps; Tunisian campaign ends; Operation Husky, the Allied invasion of Sicily; British airborne operation at Primosole bridge, Sicily; Sicily campaign; Italian campaign opens; Operation Avalanche, the Salerno landings; Allied advance from Salerno to Cassino; Montgomery appointed to command 21st

Army Group for the cross-Channel invasion of France, Operation Overlord.

1944   Operation Shingle, the Allied invasion of Anzio; German counter-offensive at Anzio; third battle of Cassino; Japanese siege of Imphal and Kohima; Allies launch Operation Diadem; Allies commence break-out offensive from the Anzio beachhead; Allied forces liberate Rome; D-Day, the Allied invasion of France, Operation Overlord; Operation Epsom, the battle for the Odon river valley; Operation Goodwood, the British attempt to break the German stranglehold on Caen and seize the vital strategic plain of Falaise; Patton's 3rd Army breaks out at Avranches; Canadian and Polish forces attempt to block the Falaise Gap; Falaise Gap plugged, Normandy campaign ends except for mopping-up operations; British liberate Brussels; Operation Market-Garden fails; British offensive to drive the Japanese from Burma opens; The Battle of the Bulge (to mid-January 1945).

1945   Operation Plunder, Montgomery's offensive to breach the Rhine river; Germany surrenders, the Second World War in Europe ends; victory over Japan; conscription of women is terminated; British army in Palestine reinforced.

1946   Ceiling of 1.9 million set for armed forces, reducing to 1.1 million by end of year; last British forces withdraw from Dutch East Indies; India and Pakistan are formed as separate Dominions; reduction of forces is delayed; 91 regular infantry battalions to be maintained for foreseeable future.

1947   National Service Bill continues conscription; term of service is reduced to twelve months; principal garrison forces are withdrawn from Venezia-Giulia; British Indian Empire partitioned and Indian Army divided between the Republics of India and Pakistan; British army leaves India.

1948   First acts of Communist terrorism in Malaya; British troops complete withdrawal from Palestine; British occupation forces withdraw from Japan; state of emergency declared in Malaya; British forces hand over support role of Greek Military Forces to the United States; term of national service is increased to eighteen months.

1949   Final phase of reversion to peacetime accounting within the army is completed; first key plan for peacetime army accommodation is completed; NATO is established.

1950   North Korea invades South Korea; 27th British Commonwealth Brigade in operations in Korea; regular army reserve is recalled; national service is extended to two years; Chinese 'volunteers' enter the Korean War; 29th Independent Infantry Brigade Group enters operations in Korea.

1951   Battles of Imjin River and Kap'yong; 28th British Commonwealth Brigade relieves the 27th; Korean armistice talks begin; 1st British Commonwealth Division is formed in Korean operations; General Sir Gerald Templer is appointed High Commissioner in Malaya; Egypt abrogates Anglo-Egyptian Treaty of 1936.

1952   Iranian government nationalizes oilfields; 16th Parachute Brigade is deployed to Middle East to intervene; British government decides not to use force; Governor of Kenya declares a state of emergency.

1953   Korean War ends with signing of armistice.

1954   Operation ANVIL in Kenya; Nairobi is cordoned and screened; British troops withdraw from Suez Canal zone; Middle East base is re-established in Cyprus; EOKA movement becomes active in Cyprus.

1955   First EOKA terrorist operation; Field Marshal Sir John Harding is appointed High Commissioner in Cyprus; island garrison reinforced.

1956   Egypt nationalizes the Suez Canal contrary to the treaty of 1954; military operations end in Kenya; Operation Musketeer—British and French troops occupy Port Said and the northern end of the Suez Canal; British and French troops withdraw from Egypt.

1957   Government announces its intention to dispense with national service.

1958   16th Parachute Brigade is deployed to Jordan in response to request for assistance by King Hussein; British troops withdraw from Jordan.

1959   State of emergency is declared in Nyasaland; state of emergency ends in Cyprus.

1960   State of emergency formally ends in Kenya; state of emergency ends in Nyasaland; independent state of Cyprus is created; British Sovereign Base Areas are retained.

1961   Kuwait is threatened with occupation by Iraq; British parachute battalion group and infantry brigade from Kenya deployed to the territory at the request of the Ruler; British force withdraws from Kuwait; parachute battalion group is established in Bahrein with armoured element for support of Gulf emirates.

1962   Attempted coup in Brunei; British Gurkha forces intervene at the request of the Sultan.

1963   Macmillan's Government still in power; Indonesia declares support for Brunei coup; confrontation with Malaysia and United Kingdom in Borneo begins; recrudescence of dissidence in Muscat and Oman;

British army advisers survey requirement at request of the Sultan; last national servicemen are discharged from the army.

1964   Wilson becomes Prime Minister; Healey appointed Secretary of State for Defence.

1965   Funeral of Sir Winston Churchill.

1967   Healey's Defence White Paper announces withdrawal of British troops from South Arabia.

1968   Civil rights movement in Northern Ireland.

1969   Violence in Londonderry; British army deploys throughout Province.

1970   Heath forms administration; IRA campaign extends to the mainland; Ulster Defence Regiment formed.

1972   Bloody Sunday in Londonderry; direct rule from Westminster imposed on Northern Ireland; operations in the Oman continue.

1974   Wilson again Prime Minister; Defence Review changes army strength and structure; Turkish invasion of north Cyprus.

1977   The Queen's Jubilee parade, Sennelager; army restructuring completed.

1979   Mrs Thatcher becomes Prime Minister.

1980   SAS deal with Prince's Gate Iranian Embassy seizure; army helps to monitor Zimbabwe independence.

1982   Falkland Islands War; John Nott's proposed reduction abandoned.

1983   Mrs Thatcher wins election.

1984   IRA explode bomb in Grand Hotel, Brighton, during Tory Party conference.

1986   Mr Heseltine, Defence Minister, resigns over Westland affair.

1987   Mrs Thatcher again wins election.

1989   Thaw in Cold War begins; Ministry of Defence plans peace dividend.

1990–1   Gulf War; British army deploys a division which operates successfully.

1991   Yugoslavia disintegrates; Mr Major succeeds Mrs Thatcher as Prime Minister; Tom King at Ministry of Defence persists with *Options For Change*.

1992–3   British army deploys in Bosnia for UN peace-keeping (humanitarian) duties.

Bibliography

1. The English Medieval Army to 1485

ALLMAND, C. T., *The Hundred Years War: England and France at War, c.1300–c.1450* (Cambridge, 1988). A classic short analysis.

BEELER, J., *Warfare in England, 1066–1189* (Ithaca, NY, 1966). An adequate account.

BRADBURY, J., *The Medieval Archer* (Woodbridge, 1985). More wide ranging than the title suggests, this book makes some important suggestions.

CONTAMINE, P., *War in the Middle Ages* (Oxford, 1984). This book, translated from French, has become the classic exposition of the nature of medieval warfare.

HEWITT, H. J., *The Organisation of War under Edward III* (Manchester, 1966). A pioneering book, which did much to emphasize the importance of logistics in the medieval period.

HOLLISTER, C. W., *The Military Organisation of Norman England* (Oxford, 1965). An analysis of what is still a highly controversial topic.

MORRIS, J. E., *The Welsh Wars of Edward I* (Oxford, 1901). The classic account of the conquest of Wales, with much attention paid to the structure of English armies.

POWICKE, M. R., *Military Obligation in Medieval England* (Oxford, 1962). A useful introduction to a complex topic.

PRESTWICH, M. C., *War, Politics and Finance under Edward I* (London, 1972). Complements Morris on *The Welsh Wars of Edward I* with an analysis of English armies in the Edwardian period.

——*Armies and Warfare in the Middle Ages: the English Experience* (London, 1996).

SUMPTION, J., *The Hundred Years War: Trial by Battle, 1337–1347* (London, 1990). The first volume of a massive history of the war, largely written as a narrative.

2. Towards the Standing Army 1485–1660

ANDREWS, K., *Trade, Plunder and Settlement: Maritime Enterprise and the Genesis of the British Empire, 1480–1630* (Cambridge, 1984). Essential background to the military developments of the day.

BOYNTON, L., *The Elizabethan Militia, 1558–1638* (London, 1967). An admirably clear study of the part-time soldiery of the period, with a judgement on their effectiveness.

CRUICKSHANK, C., *Elizabeth's Army* (Oxford, 1966). The standard work on Elizabethan military organization, which includes accounts of three expeditions.

—— *Army Royal: Henry VIII's Invasion of France, 1513* (Oxford, 1969). A study of Henry VIII's first expedition.

—— *The English Occupation of Tournai, 1513–1519* (Oxford, 1971). The story of the costly acquisition Henry VIII gained as the result of his expedition.

DORAN, S., *England and Europe, 1485–1603* (London, 1986). A short guide to foreign relations in the period.

FALLS, C., *Elizabeth's Irish Wars* (London, 1950). An older work, still relevant, on a neglected subject.

FIRTH, C., *Cromwell's Army* (1902; new edn., with introd. by J. Adair, London, 1992). Classic study which still contains much of value.

FISSEL, MARK (ed.), *War and Government in Britain, 1598–1650* (Manchester, 1991).

GENTLES, I., *The New Model Army in England, Ireland and Scotland, 1645–1653* (Oxford, 1991). An authoritative study, not only of the campaigns but of the leadership, internal organization, and ideology of the first professional army in Britain.

HALE, Sir John, *Renaissance War Studies* (London, 1983). Several of the essays relate to England.

KENYON, J., *The Civil Wars of England* (London, 1988). A readable account of the British internal conflicts.

ROWSE, A. L., *The Expansion of Elizabethan England* (London, 1955). A pioneering study of, among other matters, the nation's military arrangements, set in the context of the growth of England's overseas commitments.

WEDGWOOD, C. V., *The King's War, 1642–1647* (London, 1958). Still deservedly popular.

WERNHAM, R., *Before the Armada: The Growth of English Foreign Policy, 1485–1588* (London, 1966). The standard work by an expert on the public records relating to the subject.

YOUNG, P., and HOLMES, R., *The English Civil Wars: A Military History of the Three Civil Wars, 1642–1651* (London, 1974). A survey of campaigns and battles.

3. The Restoration Army 1660–1702

CHILDS, John, *The Army of Charles II* (London, 1976).

—— *The Army, James II and the Glorious Revolution* (Manchester, 1980).

—— *The British Army of William III, 1689–1702* (Manchester, 1987). These three volumes give a political and social history.

—— *Nobles, Gentlemen and the Profession of Arms in Restoration Britain, 1660–1688: A Biographical Dictionary of British Army Officers on Foreign Service* (London, 1987). Contains biographies of professional army officers.

—— *The Nine Years' War and the British Army, 1688–97: The Operations in the Low Countries* (Manchester, 1991). The only modern account, in English, of the land campaigns in the Low Countries and Germany.

GUY, ALAN J., 'The Later Stuart Army: A Bibliographical Essay', *1688—*

Glorious Revolution? The Fall and Rise of the British Army, 1660–1714 (London, 1988). A critical modern bibliography.

HOPKINS, PAUL, *Glencoe and the End of the Highland War* (Edinburgh, 1986). Includes an account of the military aspects of the Jacobite war in Scotland.

JONES, D. W., *War and Economy in the Age of William III and Marlborough* (Oxford, 1988). Deals with the complexities of financing the Nine Years War and the War of the Spanish Succession.

ROUTH, E. M. G., *Tangier: England's Lost Atlantic Outpost, 1661–1684* (London, 1912). The best general account of Charles II's Portuguese inheritance.

SIMMS, J. G., *Jacobite Ireland, 1685–91* (London, 1969). Good account of the Williamite wars in Ireland.

WALTON, CLIFFORD, *A History of the British Standing Army, 1660–1700* (London, 1894). Contains a wealth of factual information.

4. The Great Captain-General 1702–1714

ASHLEY, M., *Marlborough* (London, 1939). Still the best short work.

ATKINSON, C. T., *Marlborough and the Rise of the British Army* (London, 1921). Ageing but useful.

BARNETT, C., *Marlborough* (London, 1974).

BURTON, I. F., *The Captain-General* (London, 1968). A valuable analysis of Marlborough's career, 1702–11.

CHANDLER, D. G., *Marlborough as Military Commander* (London, 1973).

—— *The Art of War in the Age of Marlborough* (London, 1975).

CHURCHILL, W. S., *Marlborough: His Life and Times* (London, 1933–8). To this day the standard biography—if in places partial.

DALTON, C., *English Army Lists and Commission Registers* (London, 1905).

FORTESCUE, Sir JOHN, *A History of the British Army*, i (London, 1910).

FRANCIS, D., *The First Peninsular War, 1702–13* (London, 1975).

GREEN, D., *Blenheim* (London, 1974).

HATTENDORF, J. B., *England in the War of the Spanish Succession* (New York, 1987). A full analysis of Grand Strategy.

HUGILL, J. A. C., *No Peace without Spain* (Headington, 1991).

ROGERS, H. C. B., *The British Army of the Eighteenth Century* (London, 1977).

SCOULLER, R. E., *The Armies of Queen Anne* (Oxford, 1966). An excellent analysis of the army as an institution.

TREVELYAN, G. M., *England under Queen Anne* (London, 1930–4). Very good for the overall background.

VAN CREVELD, M., *Supplying War* (Cambridge, 1977).

5. The Army of the Georges 1714–1783

BEATTIE, DANIEL J., 'The Adaption of the British Army to Wilderness Warfare,

1755–63', in Maarten Ultee (ed.), *Adapting to Conditions: War and Society in the Eighteenth Century* (Tuscaloosa, Ala., 1986). A case-study of British combat flexibility and tactical innovation in the New World.

BREWER, JOHN, *Sinews of Power: War, Money and the English State, 1688–1783* (New York, 1989). An essential account of the military/fiscal background to the operational history of King George's army.

COLLEY, LINDA, *Britons: Forging the Nation, 1707–1837*, (New Haven, Conn., 1992). A multifaceted study of the evolution of the British national character and institutions.

FREY, SYLVIA R., *The British Soldier in America: A Social History of Military Life in the Revolutionary Period* (Austin, Tex., 1981). A ground-breaking study of the rank and file of the Georgian army.

GUY, ALAN J., *Oeconomy and Discipline: Officership and Administration in the British Army, 1714–63* (Manchester, 1984). The administration of the army, as it was carried out at regimental level.

HARDING, RICHARD, *Amphibious Warfare in the Eighteenth Century: The British Expedition to the West Indies, 1740–1742* (London, 1991). An exemplary operational study.

HAYTER, TONY, *The Army and the Crowd in Mid-Georgian England* (London, 1978). A study of the army in its role as provider of aid to the civil power.

HOULDING, J. A., *Fit for Service: The Training of the British Army, 1715–1795* (Oxford, 1981). A truly indispensable survey of army life in the eighteenth century.

KOPPERMAN, PAUL E., 'The British High Command and Soldiers' Wives in America, 1755–1783', *Journal of the Society for Army Historical Research*, 60 (1982). A brief, but important, study of a neglected topic.

SAVORY, Sir REGINALD, *His Britannic Majesty's Army in Germany during the Seven Years' War* (Oxford, 1966). A traditional and excellent account of the army's most important European campaign between 1714 and 1793.

SHY, JOHN, *Toward Lexington: The Role of the British Army in the Coming of the American Revolution* (Princeton, NJ, 1965). An important study of the army's increasingly controversial role in imperial defence after the Seven Years War.

WILLCOX, WILLIAM B., *Portrait of a General: Sir Henry Clinton in the War of Independence* (New York, 1964). A biography of a controversial character, with many insights into the nature of British military planning and the clash of personalities which influenced the conduct of war.

6. The Army and the First British Empire 1714–1815

BLACK, J., *War for America: Struggle for American Independence, 1775–83* (Stroud, 1991).

CUNEO, J. R., *Robert Rogers* (New York, 1959).

FREY, S. R., *The British Soldier in America* (Austin, Tex., 1981).

HARDING, R., *Amphibious Warfare in the Eighteenth Century: The British Expedition to the West Indies, 1740–1742* (London, 1991). Good for medical factors.

HOULDING, J. A., *Fit for Service: The Training of the British Army, 1715–1795* (Oxford, 1981). Essential reading for the development of tactical forms.

MACKESY, P., *The War for America, 1775–1783* (London 1964). A good complete account.

MIDDLETON, R., *The Bells of Victory: The Pitt Newcastle Ministry and the Conduct of the Seven Years War, 1757–1762* (Cambridge, 1985).

PARES, R., *War and Trade in the West Indies, 1739–1763* (Oxford, 1936).

PARGELLIS, S. M., *Lord Loudoun in North America* (New Haven, Conn., 1933).

REILLY, R., *The Rest to Fortune: The Life of Major-General James Wolfe* (London, 1960).

STACEY, C. P., *Quebec, 1759: The Siege and the Battle* (Toronto, 1959).

SHY, JOHN, *A People Numerous and Armed* (New York, 1976).

SYRETT, DAVID, *The Siege and Capture of Havana, 1762* (London, 1970).

WICKWIRE, F., and WICKWIRE, M., *Cornwallis and the War of Independence* (London, 1971).

7. The Transformation of the Army 1783–1815

BURNE, A., *The Noble Duke of York* (New York, 1949).

FORTESCUE, Sir JOHN, *The British Army, 1783–1802* (London, 1905).

—— *History of the British Army*, 19 vols. (London, 1910–30).

GATES, D., *The Spanish Ulcer: A History of the Peninsular War* (London, 1986).

—— *The British Light Infantry Arm, c.1790–1815* (London, 1987).

GLOVER, R. G., *Britain at Bay: Defence Against Bonaparte, 1803–14* (London, 1973).

—— *Peninsular Preparation: The Reform of the British Army, 1795–1809* (Cambridge, 1963).

HALL, C., *British Strategy in the Napoleonic War, 1803–15* (Manchester, 1991).

HOULDING, J. A., *Fit for Service: The Training of the British Army, 1715–1795* (Oxford, 1981).

MACKESY, P., *British Victory in Egypt, 1801* (London, 1995).

RODGER, A. B., *The War of the Second Coalition, 1798–1801* (Oxford, 1964).

SHERWIG, J. M., *Guineas and Gunpowder: British Foreign Aid in the Wars with France, 1793–1815* (Cambridge, Mass., 1969).

WARD, S. G. P., *Wellington's Headquarters: A Study of the Administrative Problems in the Peninsula, 1809–14* (London, 1957).

8. An Unreformed Army? 1815–1868

ANDERSON, OLIVE, *A Liberal State at War: English Politics and Economics during the Crimean War* (London, 1967).

BAMFIELD, VERONICA, *On the Strength: The Story of the British Army Wife* (London, 1974).

BELICH, JAMES, *The New Zealand Wars and the Victorian Interpretation of Racial Conflict* (Auckland, NZ, 1986).

HARRIES-JENKINS, GWYN, *The Army in Victorian Society* (London, 1977).

SKELLEY, A. R., *The Victorian Army at Home: The Recruitment and Terms and Conditions of the British Regular, 1859–1899* (London, 1977).

SPIERS, E. M., *The Army and Society, 1815–1914* (London, 1980).

STRACHAN, HEW, *From Waterloo to Balaclava: Tactics, Technology, and the British Army, 1815–54* (Cambridge, 1985).

—— *Wellington's Legacy: The Reform of the British Army, 1830–54* (Manchester, 1984).

9. The Late Victorian Army 1868–1914

BECKETT, I. F. W. (ed.), *The Army and the Curragh Incident, 1914* (London, 1986). This work, which annotates over 200 relevant documents, supersedes all previous accounts of the Curragh incident.

—— and GOOCH, J. (eds.), *Politicians and Defence: Studies in the Formulation of British Defence Policy, 1845–1970* (Manchester, 1981). Three of these scholarly essays review the ministries of Cardwell, Arnold-Forster, and Haldane.

BOND, B., *The Victorian Army and the Staff College, 1854–1914* (London, 1972). An invaluable account of the origins of the Staff College which uses a wide array of primary sources.

—— (ed.), *Victorian Military Campaigns* (London, 1967). A useful collection of essays on various colonial campaigns.

CALLWELL, C. E., *Small Wars: Their Principles and Practice* (London, 1896). A definitive study of the theory of colonial warfare which has been reprinted by Greenhill Books, London, in 1990.

GOOCH, J., *The Plans of War* (London, 1974). The definitive work on the origins of the General Staff and of its influence on strategy.

HAMER, W. S., *The British Army: Civil–Military Relations, 1885–1905* (Oxford, 1970). A scholarly study of civil–military relations in this period.

LABARD, JOHN, *Kingdom in Crisis: The Zulu Response to the British Invasion of 1879* (Manchester, 1992). Incorporates the most modern research on the Zulu War.

MORRIS, D. R., *The Washing of the Spears* (London, 1986). The classic account of the Zulu War.

PAKENHAM, T., *The Boer War* (London, 1979). This work is based upon research in over eighty collections of manuscripts. It proffers a wide array of insights on the political and military aspects of the Second Boer War and includes a sympathetic reappraisal of Buller.

SKELLEY, A. R., *The Victorian Army at Home: The Recruitment and Terms and*

Conditions of the British Regular, 1859–1899 (London, 1977). An excellent work which supersedes all previous studies of the Victorian rank and file.

SPIERS, E. M., *The Army and Society, 1815–1914* (London, 1980). A study of the relationship between the army and society from the Napoleonic Wars to the First World War.

——— *Haldane: An Army Reformer* (Edinburgh, 1980). A revisionist account of Haldane's reforms.

——— *The Late Victorian Army 1868–1902* (Manchester, 1992). An overview of the late Victorian army at home and overseas.

10. The Army and the Challenge of War 1914–1918

BARKER, A. J., *The Bastard War: The Mesopotamian Campaign of 1914–1918* (New York, 1967).

BOND, BRIAN (ed.), *The First World War and British Military History* (Oxford, 1991).

DE GROOT, GERARD, *Douglas Haig, 1861–1928* (London, 1988).

FRENCH, DAVID, *British Strategy and War Aims, 1914–16* (London, 1986).

GARDNER, BRIAN, *Allenby of Arabia* (London, 1965).

GRIFFITH, PADDY, *Battle Tactics of the Western Front: The British Army's Art of Attack, 1916–18* (New Haven, 1994).

MOORHEAD, ALAN, *Gallipoli* (2nd edn., London, 1989).

PALMER, ALAN, *The Gardeners of Salonika* (New York, 1965).

PRIOR, ROBIN, and WILSON, TREVOR, *Command on the Western Front: The Military Career of Sir Henry Rawlinson, 1914–1918* (Oxford, 1992).

TRAVERS, TIM, *The Killing Ground: The British Army, the Western Front and the Emergence of Modern Warfare, 1900–1918* (London, 1987).

——— *How the War Was Won: Command and Technology in the British Army on the Western Front, 1917–1918* (London, 1992).

WILSON, TREVOR, *The Myriad Faces of War: Britain and the Great War, 1914–1918* (Oxford, 1986).

WINTER, DENIS, *Death's Men: Soldiers of the Great War* (London, 1978).

WINTER, J. M., *The Experience of World War One* (London, 1988).

WOODWARD, DAVID, *Lloyd George and the Generals* (Newark, NJ, 1983).

11. The Four Armies 1914–1918

ADAMS, R. J. Q., *Arms and the Wizard: Lloyd George and the Ministry of Munitions, 1915–1916* (London, 1978). Useful study of the expansion of Britain's munitions industry under Lloyd George.

BECKETT, IAN F. W., and SIMPSON, KEITH (eds.), *A Nation in Arms: A Social Study of the British Army in the First World War* (Manchester, 1985). Important collection of essays by various leading historians dealing with the impact of the war on the army as an institution and those who served in it.

CASSAR, GEORGE H., *Kitchener: Architect of Victory* (London, 1977). Scholarly biography with emphasis on Kitchener's term of office as Secretary of State for War.

GRIEVES, KEITH, *The Politics of Manpower, 1914–18* (Manchester, 1988). Excellent analysis of Britain's manpower problems in the First World War and of the gradual progress towards a more effective integration of military and industrial demands.

HAY, IAN (John Hay Beith), *The First Hundred Thousand* (London, 1916). Popular early account of life in the New Armies, written by a temporary officer.

History of the Ministry of Munitions, 12 vols. (London, 1920–2). Immense but invaluable reference work.

OSBORNE, J. M., *The Voluntary Recruiting Movement in Britain, 1914–1916* (New York, 1982). Perceptive analysis of recruiting in the early part of the First World War, with special reference to enlistment in Bristol.

RAE, JOHN, *Conscience and Politics: The British Government and the Conscientious Objector to Military Service, 1916–1919* (Oxford, 1970). A fine study of conscientious objectors and the working of the tribunal system.

SIMKINS, PETER, *Kitchener's Army: The Raising of the New Armies, 1914–16* (Manchester, 1988). Detailed examination of the expansion of the army in the first two years of the war.

WINTER, J. M., *The Great War and the British People* (London, 1986). Excellent social and demographic survey, including chapters on manpower and military service, and on the 'lost generation' and the social distribution of British casualties.

12. The Army between the Two World Wars 1918–1939

BOND, BRIAN, *British Military Policy Between the Two World Wars* (Oxford, 1980). The standard account of the inter-war army.

HARRIS, J. P., *Men, Ideas and Tanks* (Manchester, 1995). Re-examines the armoured enthusiasts in the army during the inter-war period.

JEFFERY, KEITH, *The British Army and the Crisis of Empire, 1918–22* (Manchester, 1984).

LIDDELL HART, Sir BASIL, *Memoirs*, 2 vols. (London, 1965). An unrivalled account of the inter-war army from the viewpoint of its arch critic and would-be reformer.

LUVAAS, JAY, *The Education of an Army* (London, 1965). Still worth reading for the essays on Wilkinson, Fuller, and Liddell Hart.

MACKSEY, KENNETH, *Armoured Crusader: Major-General Sir Percy Hobart* (London, 1967). A lively study of one of the leading tank pioneers.

MAYS, SPIKE, *Fall Out the Officers* (London, 1969). A rare and fascinating account of life in the ranks in Britain, Egypt, and India.

MINNEY, R. J., *The Private Papers of Hore-Belisha* (London, 1991). Still the only full account of Hore-Belisha's controversial tenure of the War Office (1937–40)—needs updating in the light of new documentary evidence.

TOWNSHEND, CHARLES, *The British Campaign in Ireland, 1919–21* (Oxford, 1975).

WINTON, HAROLD R., *To Change an Army: General Sir John Burnett-Stuart and British Armoured Doctrine, 1927–1938* (Lawrence, Kan., 1988). An interesting account of a moderately progressive officer, demonstrating how hard it was to 'change the Army'.

13. The Army and the Challenge of War 1939–1945

BIDWELL, SHELFORD, *The Chindit War* (London, 1979).

D'ESTE, CARLO, *Decision in Normandy* (London, 1983).

—— *Fatal Decision: Anzio and the Battle for Rome* (London, 1991).

ELLIS, JOHN, *Cassino: The Hollow Victory* (New York, 1984).

FRASER, DAVID, *And We Shall Shock Them* (London, 1983).

GRAHAM, DOMINICK, and BIDWELL, SHELFORD, *Tug of War: The Battle for Italy, 1943–45* (London, 1986).

HAMILTON, NIGEL, *Monty: The Making of a General, 1887–1942* (London, 1981).

—— *Montgomery: Master of the Battlefield, 1942–1944* (London, 1984).

HARMAN, NICHOLAS, *Dunkirk: The Patriotic Myth* (New York, 1980).

HASWELL, JOCK, *The British Army* (London, 1975).

JACKSON, W. G. F., *The North African Campaign, 1940–43* (London, 1975).

RYAN, CORNELIUS, *A Bridge Too Far* (London, 1974).

SHEPPARD, G. A., *The Italian Campaign, 1943–1945* (London, 1968).

SLIM, Viscount, *Defeat into Victory* (London, 1956).

SMITH, E. D., *Battle of Burma* (London, 1979).

WILMOT, CHESTER, *The Struggle for Europe* (London, 1952).

14. The Army and the Home Front, 1939–1945

BOND, BRIAN (ed.), *Fallen Stars* (London, 1992).

BOWEN, ELIZABETH, *The Heat of the Day* (London, 1949).

BRYANT, ARTHUR, *The Turn of the Tide* (London, 1957).

—— *Triumph in the West* (London, 1959).

CALDER, ANGUS, *The People's War* (London, 1969).

CHURCHILL, WINSTON, *The Second World War*, 6 vols. (London, 1948–54).

DANCHEV, ALEX, *Very Special Relationship* (London, 1986).

FERGUSSON, BERNARD (ed.), *The Business of War* (London, 1957).

FRASER, DAVID, *Alanbrooke* (London, 1982).

—— *And We Shall Shock Them* (London, 1983).

GILBERT, MARTIN, *Winston S. Churchill*, vi and vii (London, 1983 and 1986).

ISMAY, Lord, *The Memoirs of Lord Ismay* (London, 1960).

KEEGAN, JOHN (ed.), *Churchill's Generals* (London, 1991).

MACKENZIE, S. P., *Politics and Military Morale* (Oxford, 1992).

MACLAREN-ROSS, JULIAN, *Memoirs of the Forties* (London, 1984).

MACLEOD, RODERICK, and KELLY, DENIS (eds.), *The Ironside Diaries* (London, 1962).

MINNEY, R. J. (ed.), *The Private Papers of Hore-Belisha* (London, 1960).

ORWELL, GEORGE, *Collected Essays*, 4 vols. (London, 1968).

PERRY, F. W., *The Commonwealth Armies* (Manchester, 1988).

PRIESTLEY, J. B., *Postscripts* (London, 1940).

REYNOLDS, DAVID, *et al.* (eds.), *Allies at War* (New York, 1993).

SPIERS, Sir EDWARD, *Assignment of Catastrophe*, 2 vols. (London, 1954).

SWEETMAN, JOHN (ed.), *Sword and Mace* (London, 1986).

15. The Post-War Army 1945–1963

ALASTOS, DOROS, *Cyprus Guerrilla: Grivas, Makarios, and the British* (1960).

BARNETT, CORRELLI, *Britain and Her Army, 1509–1970: A Military, Political and Social Survey* (London, 1970).

BETHEL, NICHOLAS, *The Palestine Triangle: The Struggle for the Holy Land, 1935–48* (London, 1979).

CAMPBELL, ARTHUR, *Jungle Green* (London, 1953).

CHARTERS, DAVID, *The British Army and Jewish Insurgency in Palestine, 1945–47* (London, 1988).

CLAYTON, ANTHONY, *Counter-insurgency in Kenya* (Nairobi, 1976).

CLUTTERBUCK, RICHARD, *Riot and Revolution in Singapore and Malaya, 1945–63* (London, 1973).

Defence White Paper, Cmd. 8640 (London, 1957).

FARRAR-HOCKLEY, ANTHONY, *The British Part in the Korean War* (London, 1990).

GREY, JEFFREY, *The Commonwealth Armies and the Korean War* (Manchester, 1988).

KITSON, FRANK, *Gangs and Counter-Gangs* (London, 1960).

MADJDALANY, FRED, *State of Emergency: The Full Story of the Mau Mau* (London, 1963).

MOCKAITIS, THOMAS R., *British Counter-Insurgency, 1919–60* (New York, 1990).

STUBBS, RICHARD, *Hearts and Minds in Guerrilla Warfare: The Malayan Emergency, 1948–60* (Singapore, 1989).

16. The Thirty Years Peace

AKEHURST, JOHN, *We Won a War: The Campaign in Oman, 1965–75* (Salisbury, 1982).

BECKETT, IAN, and PIMLOTT, JOHN (eds.), *Armed Forces and Modern Counter-insurgency* (London, 1985).

BLAXLAND, GREGORY, *The Regiments Depart: The British Army, 1945–70* (London, 1971).

DEWAR, MICHAEL, *Brush Fire Wars* (London, 1984).

—— *The British Army in Northern Ireland* (London, 1985).

DOCKRILL, MICHAEL, *British Defence since 1945* (Oxford, 1989).

FREEDMAN, LAWRENCE, *Britain and the Falklands War* (Oxford, 1988).

—— *The Gulf Conflict, 1990–91: Diplomacy and War in the New World Order* (Princeton, NJ, 1992).

—— and GAMBA-STONEHOUSE, VIRGINIA, *Signals of War: The Falklands Conflict of 1982* (London, 1990).

JAMES, H. D., and SHEIL-SMALL, D., *The Undeclared War: The Story of the Indonesian Confrontation, 1962–66* (London, 1971).

JEAPES, TONY, *SAS: Operation Oman* (London, 1980).

KITSON, FRANK, *Low Intensity Operations* (London, 1971).

—— *Bunch of Five* (London, 1977).

MIDDLEBROOK, MARTIN, *Task Force: The Falklands War* (Harmondsworth, 1987).

MOCHAITIS, TOM, *British Counter-insurgency in the Post-Imperial Era* (Manchester, 1995).

PAGET, JULIAN, *Last Post: Aden, 1964–67* (London, 1969).

TOWNSHEND, CHARLES, *Britain's Civil Wars: Counterinsurgency in the Twentieth Century* (London, 1986).

17. The Army of British India

CADELL, P., *The History of the Bombay Army* (London, 1938). A definitive account of the Bombay army's development from 1660 to the eve of the Second World War.

CARDEW, F. G., *A Sketch of the Services of the Bengal Native Army to the Year 1895* (Calcutta, 1903). Official history, written to mark the amalgamation of the Bengal into the Indian Army.

COHEN, S. P., *The Indian Army: Its Contribution to the Development of a Nation* (Berkeley, Calif., 1972). A sociological study, by a distinguished American scholar, of the Indian military in the gradual approach to independence.

Government of India, *The Army in India and its Evolution* (Calcutta, 1924). Authorized history of the Indian Army, with full details of its organization at the date of publication.

HEATHCOTE, T. A., *The Indian Army: The Garrison of British Imperial India* (London, 1974). A social and organizational history.

—— *The Military in British India* (Manchester, 1995). A new overview.

LUNT, J. (ed.), *From Sepoy to Subahdar: The Memoirs of Sita Ram Pandy* (London, 1970; trans. J. N. Norgate, 1873). The narrative of an old Indian officer. This work, in the original Hindustani, was used as a set book for British officers in their compulsory study of this language.

MacMunn, G. F., *The Armies of India* (London, 1911). The British establishment view of the Indian Army, and a classical exposition of the martial caste theory.

Omissi, D., *The Sepoy and the Raj* (London, 1994).

Richards, F., *Old Soldier Sahib* (London, 1936). An account of life in the ranks of the British army in India in the early twentieth century.

Sen, S. N., *Eighteen Fifty Seven* (Delhi, 1957). A well-balanced, objective account of the mutiny and associated campaigns by a widely respected Indian historian.

18. The Amateur Military Tradition

Abels, R., *Lordship and Military Obligation in Anglo-Saxon England* (Berkeley, Calif., 1988). A revisionist study of the fyrd.

Beckett, Ian F. W., *The Amateur Military Tradition, 1558–1945* (Manchester, 1991). The only modern comprehensive study of the auxiliary forces.

—— *Riflemen Form: A Study of the Rifle Volunteer Movement, 1859–1908* (Aldershot, 1982). Examines the social, military, and political significance of the Victorian volunteers.

—— and Simpson, Keith (eds.), *A Nation in Arms: A Social Study of the British Army in the First World War* (Manchester, 1985). Includes essay on the Territorial Force.

Boynton, Lindsay, *The Elizabethan Militia, 1558–1638* (2nd edn., Newton Abbot, 1971). An excellent account of the militia under the Tudors and Stuarts.

Dennis, Peter, *The Territorial Army, 1907–1940* (Woodbridge, 1987). A fine study of the Territorials but one which gives too little attention to the Great War period.

Fortescue, John, *The County Lieutenancies and the Army, 1803–1814* (London, 1909). Still the only overall study of the auxiliary forces during the Napoleonic Wars.

Longmate, Norman, *The Real Dad's Army* (London, 1974). A popular account of the Home Guard.

Mackenzie, S. P., *The Home Guard* (Oxford, 1995). A new study of the Home Guard as a military and political institution.

Spiers, Edward M., *Haldane: An Army Reformer* (Edinburgh, 1980). Excellent study of the reform of the army including the auxiliaries.

Western, J. R., *The English Militia in the Eighteenth Century: The Story of a Political Issue, 1660–1802* (London, 1965). A fine account of the decline and revival of the militia.

19. The British Way in Warfare

Barnett, Correlli, *Britain and Her Army, 1509–1970: A Military, Political and So-*

cial Survey (London, 1970). The fullest history of the British army which discusses its themes in relation to the British way in warfare debate.

EDGERTON, DAVID, 'Liberal Militarism and the British State', *New Left Review*, 185 (1991), 138–69. Expands on the argument that recent literature carries a continentalist undertow and is influenced by contemporary debates.

FRENCH, DAVID, *The British Way in Warfare, 1688–2000* (London, 1990). Concerned with budgets rather than ideas.

GOOCH, JOHN, *The Prospect of War: Studies in British Defence Policy, 1847–1942* (London, 1981). Contains two important essays.

HOWARD, MICHAEL, *The Continental Commitment: The Dilemma of British Defence Policy in the Era of the Two World Wars* (London, 1972). A trenchant and succinct critique of the major issues in the British way in warfare debate.

—— *The British Way in Warfare: A Reappraisal* (London, 1975). Further penetrating thoughts.

JEFFERY, KEITH, 'The Eastern Arc of Empire: A Strategic View, 1850–1950', *Journal of Strategic Studies*, 5 (1982), 531–9. Provides some imperial correctives.

KENNEDY, PAUL, *The Rise and Fall of British Naval Mastery* (London, 1976; new edn., 1983). History of the British navy within the context of the British way in warfare debate.

PEDEN, G. C., 'The Burden of Imperial Defence and the Continental Commitment Reconsidered', *Historical Journal*, 27 (1984), 405–23. Contains more imperial correctives.

STRACHAN, HEW, 'The British Way in Warfare Revisited', *Historical Journal*, 26 (1983), 447–61. Discusses recent trends in the literature on this subject.

20. Towards the Future

BEEVOR, ANTONY, *Inside the British Army* (London, 1990). A wide-ranging, entertaining, and well-researched book about the modern British army.

Defence Statistics (London, 1992). Useful background information.

Defence White Paper, Cmd. 1981 (London, 1992). Essential reading for anyone interested in the changes taking place in the British army in the 1990s.

GALBRAITH, J. K., *The Culture of Contentment* (London, 1992). An account of the state, democracy, and the nature of the modern military establishment; especially interesting on the power of the military, military spending, and the delegation of military duty in modern society.

GOLITSYN, ANATOLIY, *New Lies for Old* (London, 1984). Various attempts have been made to discredit the Soviet defector but many of his predictions have proved extraordinarily accurate.

KITSON, FRANK, *Warfare as a Whole* (London, 1987). Worth reading to see how an academically inclined and fairly radical general thinks.

VAN CREVELD, MARTIN, *On Future War* (London, 1992). A well-written, thought-provoking book, which amongst much else reconsiders Clausewitz's philosophy, arguing that war should not be considered solely as politics by other means.

YARDLEY, MICHAEL, *Sandhurst: A Documentary* (London, 1987). An observational study which sheds light on the attitudes and aspirations of some of the students and staff of the RMAS.

——and SEWELL, DENNIS, *New Model Army* (London, 1989). A study of the British army as it was, as it is, and as it might be, written by two former army officers.

Index

This index includes major campaign areas and civil disturbances as well as battles, wars, and the names of people.

Page numbers in italics refer to the captions to maps. There are occasionally also textual references on the same pages. Sub-entries are arranged in chronological order.

OXFORD

MORE OXFORD PAPERBACKS

This book is just one of nearly 1000 Oxford Paperbacks currently in print. If you would like details of other Oxford Paperbacks, including titles in the World's Classics, Oxford Reference, Oxford Books, OPUS, Past Masters, Oxford Authors, and Oxford Shakespeare series, please write to:

UK and Europe: Oxford Paperbacks Publicity Manager, Arts and Reference Publicity Department, Oxford University Press, Walton Street, Oxford OX2 6DP.

Customers in UK and Europe will find Oxford Paperbacks available in all good bookshops. But in case of difficulty please send orders to the Cash-with-Order Department, Oxford University Press Distribution Services, Saxon Way West, Corby, Northants NN18 9ES. Tel: 01536 741519; Fax: 01536 746337. Please send a cheque for the total cost of the books, plus £1.75 postage and packing for orders under £20; £2.75 for orders over £20. Customers outside the UK should add 10% of the cost of the books for postage and packing.

USA: Oxford Paperbacks Marketing Manager, Oxford University Press, Inc., 200 Madison Avenue, New York, N.Y. 10016.

Canada: Trade Department, Oxford University Press, 70 Wynford Drive, Don Mills, Ontario M3C 1J9.

Australia: Trade Marketing Manager, Oxford University Press, G.P.O. Box 2784Y, Melbourne 3001, Victoria.

South Africa: Oxford University Press, P.O. Box 1141, Cape Town 8000.

HISTORY IN OXFORD PAPERBACKS
TUDOR ENGLAND
John Guy

Tudor England is a compelling account of political and religious developments from the advent of the Tudors in the 1460s to the death of Elizabeth I in 1603.

Following Henry VII's capture of the Crown at Bosworth in 1485, Tudor England witnessed far-reaching changes in government and the Reformation of the Church under Henry VIII, Edward VI, Mary, and Elizabeth; that story is enriched here with character studies of the monarchs and politicians that bring to life their personalities as well as their policies.

Authoritative, clearly argued, and crisply written, this comprehensive book will be indispensable to anyone interested in the Tudor Age.

'lucid, scholarly, remarkably accomplished . . . an excellent overview' *Sunday Times*

'the first comprehensive history of Tudor England for more than thirty years' Patrick Collinson, *Observer*

HISTORY IN OXFORD PAPERBACKS

THE STRUGGLE FOR
THE MASTERY OF EUROPE 1848–1918

A. J. P. Taylor

The fall of Metternich in the revolutions of 1848 heralded an era of unprecedented nationalism in Europe, culminating in the collapse of the Hapsburg, Romanov, and Hohenzollern dynasties at the end of the First World War. In the intervening seventy years the boundaries of Europe changed dramatically from those established at Vienna in 1815. Cavour championed the cause of *Risorgimento* in Italy; Bismarck's three wars brought about the unification of Germany; Serbia and Bulgaria gained their independence courtesy of the decline of Turkey—'the sick man of Europe'; while the great powers scrambled for places in the sun in Africa. However, with America's entry into the war and President Wilson's adherence to idealistic internationalist principles, Europe ceased to be the centre of the world, although its problems, still primarily revolving around nationalist aspirations, were to smash the Treaty of Versailles and plunge the world into war once more.

A. J. P. Taylor has drawn the material for his account of this turbulent period from the many volumes of diplomatic documents which have been published in the five major European languages. By using vivid language and forceful characterization, he has produced a book that is as much a work of literature as a contribution to scientific history.

'One of the glories of twentieth-century writing.' *Observer*

ILLUSTRATED HISTORIES IN
OXFORD PAPERBACKS

THE OXFORD ILLUSTRATED HISTORY
OF ENGLISH LITERATURE

Edited by Pat Rogers

Britain possesses a literary heritage which is almost unrivalled in the Western world. In this volume, the richness, diversity, and continuity of that tradition are explored by a group of Britain's foremost literary scholars.

Chapter by chapter the authors trace the history of English literature, from its first stirrings in Anglo-Saxon poetry to the present day. At its heart towers the figure of Shakespeare, who is accorded a special chapter to himself. Other major figures such as Chaucer, Milton, Donne, Wordsworth, Dickens, Eliot, and Auden are treated in depth, and the story is brought up to date with discussion of living authors such as Seamus Heaney and Edward Bond.

'[a] lovely volume . . . put in your thumb and pull out plums' Michael Foot

'scholarly and enthusiastic people have written inspiring essays that induce an eagerness in their readers to return to the writers they admire' *Economist*